CANADA
A NATION UNFOLDING

CANADA
A NATION UNFOLDING

DIANE EATON - GARFIELD NEWMAN

McGRAW-HILL RYERSON LIMITED

Toronto Montreal New York Auckland Bogotá Caracas
Lisbon London Madrid Mexico Milan New Delhi Paris
San Juan Singapore Sydney Tokyo

CANADA
A NATION UNFOLDING

Copyright © McGraw-Hill Ryerson Limited, 1994. All rights reserved. No part of this publication may be reproduced or transmitted in any form or by any means, or stored in a data base or retrieval system, without the prior written permission of McGraw-Hill Ryerson Limited.

ISBN 0-07-551425-7

1 2 3 4 5 6 7 8 9 10 ML 3 2 1 0 9 8 7 6 5 4

Printed and bound in Canada

Care has been taken to trace ownership of copyright material contained in this text. The publishers will gladly accept any information that will enable them to rectify any reference or credit in subsequent editions.

Canadian Cataloguing in Publication Data

Eaton, Diane F.
    Canada: a nation unfolding

Includes index.
ISBN 0-07-551425-7

1. Canada—History. I. Newman, Garfield.
II. Title.

FC170.E37 1994   971   C93-095006-2
F1026.E28 1994

Publisher: Janice Matthews
Associate Editor: Denise Shortt
Senior Supervising Editor: Carol Altilia
Permissions Editor: Jacqueline Donovan
Editorial Assistant/Permissions: Crystal Shortt
Copy Editor: John Eerkes
Cover and Interior Design: Brant Cowie/ArtPlus Limited

This book was manufactured in Canada using acid-free and recycled paper.

About the Authors...

Diane Eaton is a professional textbook writer and editor. She holds a Ph.D from the University of British Columbia and has almost fifteen years' teaching experience in secondary and university level English.

Garfield Newman is currently Department Head of History at Vaughan Secondary School in Thornhill, Ontario. He is senior author and editor of the recently published *Odyssey Through the Ages* (McGraw-Hill Ryerson, 1992).

CONTENTS

Guide to Skills and Career Focus Sections	ix
Acknowledgements	xi

Prologue: Twentieth-Century Canada — 1

Unit 1 Government and Law — 8

Chapter 1	How Is Canada Governed?	10
Chapter 2	Canadian Government in Action	30
Chapter 3	Canada's Judicial System	51

Skills Focus — 74

Unit 2 Laying the Foundations: From Confederation to 1911 — 76

Chapter 4	A Nation Emerges	78
Chapter 5	French–English Relations	100
Chapter 6	Canadian–American Relations	115

Skills Focus — 128

Unit 3 The War to End All Wars: Canada and World War I — 130

Chapter 7	War on the Western Front	132
Chapter 8	War on the Home Front	149
Chapter 9	Coming of Age	164

Skills Focus — 180

Unit 4 From Boom to Bust: Canada in the 1920s and 1930s — 182

Chapter 10	Prosperity and Depression	184
Chapter 11	Life in Canada in the 1920s and 1930s	208

Skills Focus — 226

Unit 5 War Returns: Canada and World War II — 228

Chapter 12	The Breakdown of Peace	230
Chapter 13	War on the Home Front	246
Chapter 14	Canada's Role in Ending the War	265

Skills Focus — 284

Unit 6   The Dawning of a New Era: The Cold War and Beyond — 286

- **Chapter 15**   Canada's Role on the International Stage — 288
- **Chapter 16**   French–English Relations — 314
- **Chapter 17**   Canadian–American Relations — 337

Skills Focus — 360

Unit 7   The Changing Face of Canada — 362

- **Chapter 18**   Life in Canada after World War II — 364
- **Chapter 19**   Canada from the 1960s to the 1980s — 382
- **Chapter 20**   Canada as a Multicultural Nation — 394

Skills Focus — 416

Epilogue: Entering the Twenty-first Century — 418

Photo and Illustration Credits — 424
Text Credits — 427
Index — 429

GUIDE TO SKILLS AND CAREER FOCUS SECTIONS

	Skills Focus	**Career Focus**	**Page**
Unit 1	Developing and Practising Thinking Skills	Entrepreneurship	74–75
Unit 2	Recognizing and Responding to Bias	Journalism	128–129
Unit 3	Research and Writing skills	Law	180–181
Unit 4	Self-Evaluation	Skilled Trades	226–227
Unit 5	Developing Presentation Skills	Sales	284–285
Unit 6	Formulating and Defending a Thesis	Travel and Tourism	360–361
Unit 7	Effective Problem Solving	Economics	416–417

ACKNOWLEDGEMENTS

To Allison Snelgrove for months of expert and unflagging effort as a researcher and for her ongoing enthusiasm and suggestions during the writing of the book.

To Curt, Brett, and Sarah Eaton, who gave their cheerful support through many long days and nights of writing over the past year and a half.

Diane Eaton

To Mathew and Geoffrey Newman, Dad extends the greatest love a parent can feel.

To Laura Gini, your support and caring throughout the past year have earned the deepest respect and admiration.

Garfield Newman

Of course, no book can become a reality without a strong team behind it. The staff at McGraw-Hill Ryerson have been superb.

To Janice Matthews for steering the book to completion with grace and generosity.

To Carol Altilia and John Eerkes for their contributions in the production and copyediting process. To Crystal Shortt and Jacqueline Donovan for their assistance in organizing the text.

And a heartfelt thanks to Denise Shortt, who worked so hard for so long bringing this textbook into being: it is as much hers as ours.

Diane Eaton
Garfield Newman

McGraw-Hill Ryerson and the authors would also like to thank our team of reviewers. We are deeply grateful to reviewers Larry Booi of Strathcona Composite High School, Alberta; Nick Brune of M.M. Robinson HS, Ontario; Marc Keirstead of Sacred Heart Catholic HS, Ontario; Mary McGuinness of Woodlands SS, Ontario; and Ian McKay of Queen's University, Ontario. We'd like to extend special recognition to Native issues expert Olive Dickason of the University of Alberta; to law expert John Zuber of Zuber & Kilaaji Barristers & Solicitors; and to the team of student reviewers from Vaughan SS, Ontario.

Others who deserve recognition are Gerry King and Carol Fraser, librarians at Vaughan Secondary School, who provided valuable research assistance; Daryl Wheeler, who scanned countless magazines and books, searching for photographs; and, especially, Sanish Samuel, who contributed the feature study on the Summit Series.

TWENTIETH-CENTURY CANADA

Nearly a century ago, Canada's prime minister, Wilfrid Laurier, proudly proclaimed, "As the nineteenth century belonged to the United States, so the twentieth century will belong to Canada" — a bold claim for the leader of a young nation. As the twentieth century draws to a close, we are left to reflect on his words. Has this indeed been "our century"? Would Laurier feel that his prophecy had been fulfilled, or would he be disappointed?

We often ask questions about our country in an attempt to understand who we are, where we have come from, and where we are going. Our answers depend on where we live, our cultural background, and our personal experiences. As you read about our history in this book, think about what it is that distinguishes Canada from other nations. To help you explore Canada's past, a number of important themes are addressed in the following pages. They include Canadian–American relations, French–English relations, Canada's international role, Canada's multicultural heritage, and Native culture in contemporary Canadian society. This book also examines the Canadian economy, government, and legal system. Studying these and other topics will enable you to appreciate Canada's past and present and will help you define what it means to be Canadian.

Canada's list of accomplishments and the respect it has earned internationally suggest that Laurier's claim has some validity. At the turn of the century, Canada was a colony in the British Empire. Now a fully independent country, it has distinguished itself on the battlefield, as a peacekeeper around the world, as a leader in science and technology, as a major supplier of food, and — perhaps most importantly — as one of the most livable countries in the world. The United Nations Human Development Report for 1992 ranked Canada as the best place in the world to live. This study is based on a long list of criteria, including health and life expectancy, education, income and employment, the treatment of women in society, and the environment. Internationally, Canada has earned a reputation for generosity and goodwill.

The vast expanse of this country and the diversity of the people who inhabit it make it difficult to clearly define what it means to be Canadian. Yet we are a distinct nation with a heritage of our own. Throughout this book, you will be introduced to the people, places, and events that have shaped our nation and created the country we proudly call home. But, before exploring our past, we need to clearly understand the themes and issues that underlie our study of Canada in the twentieth century.

WHO ARE WE?
Three Founding Nations

Until recently, most Canadians referred to the French and English colonists as the "two founding nations" of Canada. In fact, the Native peoples of North America had established complex civilizations long before the Europeans arrived. The arrival of both the French and the English in North America signalled the meeting of two "Old Worlds": Europe and Native North America. Present-day Canada is a rich tapestry woven from strands of Native, French, and British cultures as well as the numerous cultures that have become a part of Canada's mosaic. Look around you — what elements of different cultures do you detect?

The multicultural society that has evolved in Canada has not always been harmonious. Although most of us are immigrants to this country, certain groups have been discriminated against. Chinese railway workers in the nineteenth century, Japanese citizens during World War II, and black Canadians in Halifax have all had to deal with racism in Canada. Unfortunately, similar racial tensions remain today. The Canadian government has taken one step toward relieving racial tensions by creating the Canadian Charter of Rights and Freedoms, which helped to entrench fundamental rights of Canadians in the Constitution.

The rights guaranteed in the Constitution also help to protect the rights of women and minority groups such as people with disabilities and the gay community. Increasingly, Canadians have become aware of the need to protect the rights of all citizens regardless of their race, religion, age, or wealth. This awareness is helping to make Canada one of the most compassionate countries in the world, although we still have much work to do before all Canadians can be assured of a secure and equal future.

WHAT IS THIS COUNTRY CALLED CANADA?
Canada's Geography

Canada is a nation as diverse in its regions as in the people who populate it. Imagine flying over Canada in a small aircraft. Find a map of Canada and follow along as we begin our flight at Tuktoyaktuk, Northwest Territories. Here, in the High Arctic, winters are long and the summers are glorious and short-lived. Permafrost limits the vegetation in the North to small bushes, mosses, and lichens that produce beautiful flowers in summer. Discoveries of oil and gas have brought increased development to the North. This has helped to lessen the isolation and to bring new wealth to the Northwest Territories.

As we continue our flight south from Tuktoyaktuk, we pass over the Yukon, scene of the famous Klondike Gold Rush of 1898, and over the spectacular mountain ranges of British Columbia. The interior of British Columbia is one of the world's most scenic areas. Towering, snow-capped mountains, tall stands of trees, and the fertile Okanagan Valley are just a few of the province's attractions. British Columbia's largest city, Vancouver, located at the mouth of the Fraser River, has become a large, cosmopolitan city.

As we fly east, a dramatic change takes place. Shortly after crossing the British Columbia–Alberta border, the Rocky Mountains give way to the seemingly unending Prairies. Canada's Prairie provinces — Alberta, Saskatchewan, and Manitoba — are best known for their endless fields of wheat and grain elevators that dot the horizon. But a closer inspection of these provinces reveals a more varied resource base. Central to the economy of the Prairies are oil and wheat, as well as cattle ranching in Alberta, potash in Saskatchewan, and hydro-electric power in Manitoba.

Our flight eastward continues into northern Ontario, where another dramatic change occurs. As we leave the Prairies behind, we are greeted by extensive forests and thousands of small lakes that blanket the Canadian Shield. Rich in minerals such as lead, gold, copper, zinc, and uranium, the Canadian Shield covers more than half of Canada and stretches in a U-shape from the Northwest Territories down to the eastern part of Lake Ontario and up into northern Quebec and Labrador. The rich mineral deposits, extensive forests, and rugged beauty of the Canadian Shield have made mining, forestry, and tourism staples in the economy of northern Manitoba, Ontario, and Quebec.

Southern Ontario and southern Quebec are as distinct from northern Ontario as British Columbia is from Saskatchewan. This region has moderate temperatures and fertile soils. Many of the farms and small towns in southern Ontario date from the mid-1800s. The farms and towns in Quebec, along the St. Lawrence and in the Eastern Townships, are even older; some date from the mid-1600s. Southern Ontario and southern Quebec have traditionally been considered the industrial heartland of Canada, but this is changing. Despite the vastness of this country, about one-third of Canadians live in the area known as the Golden Horseshoe, which encompasses southern Ontario from Niagara Falls to Oshawa and includes Kitchener–Waterloo and London. Along the 1000-kilometre stretch from Windsor to Montreal are no fewer than ten of Canada's twenty-five largest cities. Many of these cities are important industrial centres producing everything from steel to textiles.

The last leg of our journey takes us into the Atlantic provinces — New Brunswick, Nova Scotia, Prince Edward Island, and Newfoundland. Our flight has now taken us from coast to coast and has touched on three oceans — the Arctic, the Pacific, and finally the Atlantic. It is the Atlantic Ocean that has most influenced the history and culture of eastern Canada. The common feature among all four of these provinces is the importance of the sea and of fishing. Forestry in New Brunswick, coal mining in Nova Scotia, dairy and potato farming in Prince Edward Island, and offshore oil in Newfoundland are other important sources of revenue.

Canadian–American Relations

Although Canada embraces cultures from around the world, few countries have had as great an impact on shaping this nation as the United States. We have not always welcomed the influence of the Americans; in fact, for much of our history, we have defined our Canadian nationalism in terms of anti-American sentiment. Even today, Canadians seem to admire American achievements but remain cautiously wary of emulating them.

Despite Canada's proximity to the United States, Canadians have often questioned American ideals. When thirteen American colonies rose up in revolt against England and created the United States of America, those loyal to the British crown and British traditions fled north to the colony of Nova Scotia and to what is today known as southern Ontario. These people, known as United Empire Loyalists, brought with them a strong belief in British values. In fact, for much of the nineteenth century, they tried to re-create British society in Canada. American-style government failed to influence Canada in either the War of 1812 or the Rebellions of 1837. Only since 1945 has Canada drifted from its strong British ties and become much more closely allied with the United States.

The American presence certainly cannot go unnoticed. Today the United States is our largest trading partner, our closest military ally, and the greatest influence on Canadian culture. As a result, a close examination of Canada's relationship with the United States will be an integral part of our study of Canada in the twentieth century. As you encounter issues and events related to Canadian–American relations, think about the kind of country you want to live in. What elements of American culture should we adopt? Should we be developing closer ties with the United States, or should we strive to take a more independent stance?

Canadian Culture and Society

Culture is an important element to consider when attempting to define who we are. Culture is everything that makes one group of people different from another. It includes political and economic systems, education, technology, religion, language, arts, dress, food, and values and attitudes. Canadian culture has evolved during the twentieth century as radio, motion pictures, and television transformed the entertainment industry. Along with the radical changes in technology, the influx of immigrants from around the world has greatly enriched the diversity of Canadian culture. From a largely European-based culture in the nineteenth century, Canada has developed a kaleidoscope made up of many different cultures.

Despite the richness and vitality of our national culture, we still often question who we are. Many Canadians wonder how to accurately define Canadian culture by asking questions such as: Is Canadian culture simply an amalgamation of transplanted cultures? What makes Canadian culture distinctive? When you listen to Canadian music or watch Canadian television, can you detect anything uniquely Canadian?

Canada and the World

To fully appreciate Canada's growth in this century, it is important to follow Canada's emergence on the world stage. Since the time of its colonial status at the turn of the century, Canada has come a long way in earning the respect of the world. During both world wars, Canadians distinguished themselves on the battlefield and have made achievements in science and technology, in sport, and in entertainment. Canadian inventions, from Pablum to the Canadarm, have helped to shape the world in which we live. Millions of people have been thrilled by the performance of Canadian athletes such as rower Silken Laumann and hockey superstar Mario Lemieux. Canada's contributions have earned the respect and admiration of people from around the world.

However, not all the events described in these pages are proud moments for Canada. This book is intended to present an honest look at Canadian history since Confederation. While there is much for us to be proud of in our past, we must also recognize that our history is not unblemished. The ill-treatment of Native peoples, racist immigration policies, and the failure to provide adequate assistance to those in need during the Great Depression are as much a part of our history as the heroic efforts of our soldiers or the triumphs of our scientists. But we have survived to emerge a wiser and stronger nation. Canada as a nation has met the challenges of the twentieth century to become one of the most exciting and livable countries in the world.

Studying the Past to Prepare for the Future

While it is untrue to say that history repeats itself, understanding our history is essential if we want to avoid repeating mistakes from our past. History is the study of change over time and is most concerned with the question *why*. By looking at the past, we can learn much about who we are and where we are headed. The study of Canadian history also allows us to see what is special or distinctive about Canada. Remember as you read the following chapters that the true relevance of history lies not in the past but in how it guides us in our future.

RESPONDING TO THE ISSUES

Now it is your turn to reflect on Canada and what it means to be a Canadian. The following questions and activities will allow you to express your opinions on several of the issues raised in this prologue.

1. A national anthem is much more than simply a song. It is a statement about values and represents the true character of the nation and its people. Research and examine the words of the national anthems of both Canada and the United States. What does each of the anthems tell you about the countries? Which anthem do you prefer? Explain why.

2. Reread the words of Wilfrid Laurier at the beginning of this prologue. Write a response to his claim. Has this been Canada's century? Base your response on the general knowledge you have of Canadian history. Put this response in a safe place in your binder; it will be interesting to compare what you write now with what you write after completing your study of Canada in the twentieth century.

3. On a blank map of Canada, write each of the following for each province:
   (a) the name of the province
   (b) its capital city
   (c) its current premier and governing party
   (d) its major source of revenue

4. Canada enjoys a rich multicultural heritage. What examples exist in your community of the diversity of cultures that make up Canada? What challenges does a multicultural nation face if it wishes to be fair and just to all people?

5. Write a one-page essay on what it means to be Canadian. Express your feelings honestly. You may want to discuss one or all of the following questions: Why are you proud to be Canadian? What problems does Canada need to address? Why do you agree or disagree with the findings of the United Nations? Should Canada be more or less like the United States?

Despite the pride we may feel for Canada, building this country was often achieved at a substantial cost. As you read the following poem, "History Lesson," by Jeannette Armstrong, make a list of the problems that she suggests have arisen from our past. How can we learn lessons from the past to ensure a better future?

History Lesson

Out of the belly of Christopher's ship
a mob bursts
Running in all directions
Pulling furs off animals
Shooting buffalo
Shooting each other
left and right

Father mean well
waves his makeshift wand
forgives saucer-eyed Indians

Red coated knights
gallop across the prairie
to get their men
and to build a new world

Pioneers and traders
bring gifts
Smallpox, Seagrams
and Rice Krispies
Civilization has reached
the promised land.

Between the snap crackle pop
of smoke stacks
and multi-coloured rivers
swelling with flower powered zee

are farmers sowing skulls and bones
and miners
pulling from gaping holes
green paper faces
of smiling English lady

The colossi
in which they trust
while burying
breathing forests and fields
beneath concrete and steel
stand shaking fists
waiting to mutilate
whole civilizations
ten generations at a blow.

Somewhere among the remains
of skinless animals
is the termination
to a long journey
and unholy search
for the power
glimpsed in a garden
forever closed
forever lost.

Source: By Okanagan author/artist Jeannette Armstrong. © Jeannette Armstrong. From *Seventh Generation*, published by Theytus Books.

UNIT 1

GOVERNMENT AND LAW

ALL ACROSS CANADA, young people are studying the Canadian government and legal system. Most people agree that it is important for Canadian students to be educated in civics and citizenship because active participation in politics requires an understanding of the political system. One of the great features of Canada is its democratic system of government, which is intended to respond to the needs and demands of the people. For Canada's democracy to work effectively, Canadians must be aware of important issues and participate in elections and referendums. By being involved in the political process, Canadians can help to safeguard their interests and ensure that politicians are accountable. Similarly, it is important for Canadians to be aware of their legal rights and to understand their legal system. Ignorance of the law could prove costly — not knowing your rights may prevent you from being treated fairly.

CHAPTER ONE
How Is Canada Governed?

CHAPTER TWO
Canadian Government in Action

CHAPTER THREE
Canada's Judicial System

This unit's three chapters lay the foundation for understanding how the government and legal systems work in Canada and will help you become an active participant in the decision-making process in your country. Chapter 1 introduces the concept of government and discusses why effective government is necessary for a society to function. Chapter 2 provides a detailed look at how the Canadian government works and focuses on a number of political issues. Chapter 3 provides an introduction to the Canadian legal system as well as a focus on the law as it applies to youth in Canada.

CHAPTER 1
HOW IS CANADA GOVERNED?

GLOSSARY TERMS

Parliament   The highest legislative body in Canada.
Union Jack   The national flag of Great Britain.
Legislature   A body of persons having the power to make, amend, and repeal laws for a nation or a unit of a nation, such as a state or province.
Amendment   A change made to a motion, a bill, or a Constitution.
Autonomy   The right of self-government, especially for a political community that is part of a larger political body such as the British Commonwealth.
Patriate   The act of bringing legislation back from a colonial government to the country where the legislation applies.
Amending Formula   An agreed-upon procedure for making amendments to the Canadian Constitution.

FOCUS ON:

- the role governments play in society
- comparing different kinds of government
- Canada's blend of democracy and monarchy
- Canada's changing Constitution
- how Canada's federal system works

Garbage bags pile up in back lanes during a municipal workers' strike. Newfoundlanders call for the Canadian navy to drive foreign fishing boats out of Canadian waters. Townspeople in British Columbia debate a proposal for putting fluoride in the local water supply. A neighbour hands around a petition protesting a long waiting list for open heart surgery in the province. No matter where you look, you see people and governments interacting. You cannot do the simplest things without being touched by **government** — whether you are watching television, going to school, playing a video game, buying a compact disc, riding a bus, or taking a job.

What is government, and why do we need it? Ideally, governments set and enforce the rules that allow people to live together in peace and security. Governments can protect the rights and freedoms of individual citizens. Governments can also protect people and property from criminals and foreign invaders. They can provide all kinds of important public goods and services — electricity, water, highways, schools, public housing, buses, medical care, and much more. And they can regulate the economy at home and establish trade and other relationships with nations around the world. These are all activities that individuals find difficult or impossible to carry out on their own. But governments can and do organize groups of individuals for important collective (group) actions.

In return for these benefits, citizens agree to certain limits on their actions. Canadians have to pay government taxes and fines, for example, whether they like it or not. Under certain circumstances, Canadians can be sent to jail or forced to serve in a war. Canadians' rights as citizens might even be taken away in a national emergency. People give up a certain amount of personal control over their lives in return for the benefits of government.

CANADA IS A DEMOCRACY

What kind of government does Canada have? It is usually described as a **democracy** — a "government of the many." The word "democracy" comes from two Greek words — *demos* (people) and *kratos* (power). A democracy is a system of government in which many people share political power: the citizens rule.

The ancient Greek city-state of Athens is a good example of a democracy. The population of Athens was small, and the number of citizens was even smaller because slaves, women, and men of foreign birth were not considered citizens. That meant that about 40 000 Athenian males were citizens and therefore had the right to vote. Because there were so few Athenian citizens, they could all meet together to discuss and then vote on important issues of the day. The majority vote won, but most Athenian citizens had the right to speak and participate equally. This is known as "direct democracy."

PARLIAMENTARY GOVERNMENT: REPRESENTATIVE DEMOCRACY IN CANADA

Unlike ancient Athens, however, most modern democratic nations have populations numbering in the millions. It is impossible for every citizen to vote directly on every public issue. Instead, citizens freely elect certain people to represent them in a government. Modern democracies are sometimes called "representative" democracies because the people's will is expressed through their representatives in a governing body.

Canada is a representative democracy, and its governing body is known as *Parliament*. In Canada, 17.5 million people elect their representatives in Parliament — about one representative for every 60 000 people. The elected members of Parliament (MPs) are placed in office by the voters in ridings (electoral districts) across the country. Holding power in the Parliament thus directly depends on the personal choices made by millions of Canadian voters. If MPs do

Our lives are affected on a daily basis by the actions of governments. Despite their efforts to govern effectively, governments are often harshly criticized by people such as these angry civil servants, who are protesting against Brian Mulroney's government.

TYPES OF GOVERNMENT

Throughout history, there have been many kinds of government. Five of the most common forms of government around the world are monarchy, dictatorship, oligarchy, aristocracy, and democracy. Read the following information outlining the different types of government and decide which you think would provide the best government.

Monarchy
Power is inherited and passed down the royal family line.
Advantage: This system allows traditions to be carried on.
Disadvantage: People have little or no say in government and no safeguard against unjust rulers.

Dictatorship
Power is in the hands of one individual, who usually has the support of the military.
Advantage: The leader can make decisions without having to be concerned about re-election.
Disadvantage: There is no guarantee that the needs of the people will be met.

Oligarchy
Power is in the hands of a few influential individuals.
Advantage: Leadership is provided by a group who can balance each other's interests.
Disadvantage: There is no guarantee that the needs of the people will be met.

Aristocracy
Power is in the hands of the elite or upper class.
Advantage: Power often lies with educated and influential people.
Disadvantage: There is no method to ensure that the needs of all social classes are met.

Democracy
Power lies in the hands of officials elected by the majority.
Advantage: All citizens have a say in government decisions and a choice of whether to re-elect officials.
Disadvantage: Decision-making is less effective when elected officials are trying to please all the citizens in order to stay in power.

VOTING RIGHTS IN CANADA

Voting rights are necessary to ensure that everyone is represented by the government. Today, almost all men and women have the right to vote in Canada, but this has not always been the case. By the beginning of the twentieth century almost all men could vote, yet this right was withheld from women, Asians, Native people, and people with mental disabilities until as late as 1988.

Today, young people are generally ignored in the political process. They are made to feel as though what they have to say really doesn't matter — because they are young. Should the government consider lowering the voting age further, from eighteen to sixteen years of age? It could be argued that students who are exposed to the political process through their classes may be better informed than many older voters about the issues confronting Canadians. Can you think of other reasons why the voting age should or should not be lowered to sixteen? If the voting age were lowered, what issues do you think would be important to teenagers?

Timeline of the Vote in Canada

1874	Secret ballot introduced.
1885	Property qualifications established to determine the right to vote: $300 for people in a city; $200 for people in a town; $150 for people in a rural area.
1918	Women receive the vote in federal elections.
1940	Women in Quebec receive the right to vote in provincial elections.
1948	Property qualifications for the right to vote are eliminated. Persons of Asian origin receive the right to vote.
1950	Most Inuit receive the right to vote.
1960	Native people living on reserves receive the right to vote.
1970	Voting age in federal elections reduced from twenty-one to eighteen years of age.
1988	People with mental disabilities given the right to vote.

Canadian women carried their demand for the right to vote outside Canada. This group joined in an American suffragette rally in Washington, D.C., at the turn of the century.

not satisfy most of the voters back home, they will not be returned to Parliament in the next election. As Canadian Senator Eugene Forsey once quipped, "Governments in democracies are elected by the passengers to steer the ship of the nation. They are expected to hold it on course, to arrange for a prosperous voyage, and to be prepared to be thrown overboard if they fail in either duty."

CANADA HAS A FEDERAL SYSTEM OF GOVERNMENT

Canada can also be called a federation because powers are divided between two levels of government: the federal (central) government in Ottawa and the provincial (regional) governments in provincial capital cities. Many other countries of the world, such as the United States, Germany, and Australia, also have federal systems of government. By contrast, Britain has a unitary system of government because all power is in the hands of a single, central government.

CANADA IS A MONARCHY

Canada can also be considered a monarchy. Historically, a state ruled by just one person — a king or queen — was called a "monarchy." Usually the title was inherited, and the position of power was permanent. Sometimes the king or queen was an all-powerful or "absolute" monarch. The monarch alone made law and saw it carried out. Whether people suffered or prospered under an all-powerful monarch completely depended on the good or bad government of their ruler.

Many of the old monarchies of Europe are still alive today, in countries such as Britain, Norway, Sweden, Denmark, Belgium, and the Netherlands. But these governments have changed over time and have become "constitutional monarchies." Modern-day European monarchs are still the legal heads of state, but their powers are limited by a set of laws called a **constitution**.

Canada as a Constitutional Monarchy

Canada is also considered a **constitutional monarchy**. British rulers have always headed the Canadian government, and Queen Elizabeth II still bears the title of Queen of Canada. The governor general is the queen's representative in Canada and acts on her behalf unless she happens to be in the country. Over the years, however, the power and importance of the monarchy in Canada has faded, and today the queen's powers are mostly symbolic and ceremonial. She has only the right to warn, the right to advise, and the right to be consulted. Her portrait still appears on Canadian stamps and money, but now Canadians sing "O Canada" instead of "God Save the Queen," and the Canadian maple leaf flag has replaced the British *Union Jack*. The monarchy is

Although her role is now primarily ceremonial, Queen Elizabeth II remains Canada's head of state. Prepare a list of arguments in favour of and opposed to Canada's remaining a constitutional monarchy.

COMPARING POLITICAL SYSTEMS

Canada

Type of Government: Constitutional monarchy — governed by a monarch (king or queen) whose powers are limited by the Constitution.
Head of State: Although the king or queen is the symbolic head of state, true power lies in the hands of the prime minister and the cabinet.
System of Government: Federal — a federal government looks after national issues, and provincial governments look after the needs of individual provinces.
Members of the Executive: Members of the executive, known as cabinet members, must be chosen from among elected members of Parliament. This is known as responsible government because the executive is held directly accountable by the electorate.
Upper House: Members of the Senate are appointed by the governor general on the recommendation of the prime minister. The role of the Senate is to review bills passed by the House of Commons.

United States

Type of Government: Republic — power lies in the hands of the people through their elected representative (the president).
Head of State: The president is the head of government and the commander-in-chief of the armed forces.
System of Government: Federal — a federal government in Washington, D.C., looks after national interests, and state governments look after the interests of individual states.
Members of the Executive: Members of the executive are non-elected officials chosen by the president on the basis of their expertise.
Upper House: The Senate is elected and is responsible to the voters. Each state, regardless of its size, is represented by two senators.

Britain

Type of Government: Constitutional monarchy — governed by a monarch (king or queen) whose power is limited by the Constitution.
Head of State: The active head of state is the prime minister and the cabinet. As the symbolic head of state, the monarch opens Parliament and attends ceremonial functions.
System of Government: Unitary — only one level of government looks after the needs of both the nation and the regions.
Members of the Executive: Cabinet ministers are selected from among elected members of Parliament.
Upper House: The House of Lords is similar to Canada's Senate. Members are appointed by the queen, and their role is to review bills passed by the House of Commons.

CANADA'S PARLIAMENT AND OUR BRITISH HERITAGE

Canada's parliamentary system of government is based on centuries of British tradition. Our present monarch, Queen Elizabeth II of the House of Windsor, traces her family tree back through the ages to such famous kings as England's Henry VIII. The roots of Canada's Parliament also lie in England, where the upper house is known as the House of Lords. Historically this house comprised members of the nobility and high church officials. The House of Commons was made up of "commoners" representing the various towns and counties of England.

Earlier in the history of the English Parliament, the king or queen was not required to govern according to the wishes of the members of either the House of Lords or House of Commons. In 1215, frustrated by King John's refusal to meet their demands, angry nobles rose in rebellion. King John was eventually forced to listen to their demands and agreed to sign the Magna Carta. The Magna Carta placed restrictions on the monarch's powers by requiring that the king govern in cooperation with Parliament.

When King Charles I attempted to ignore the wishes of Parliament in the 1640s, a civil war broke out. He was eventually captured and beheaded, and England was ruled as a republic from 1649 to 1660. By the time the monarchy was restored, more powers had been given to Parliament.

The powers of the British monarchy have continued to diminish. Today, the queen plays only a symbolic role in both Canada and Britain. The powers of Parliament, won through centuries of struggle, have been inherited by Canadians. In 1982, Canada cut its final ties with the British Parliament when the Canada Act gave Canadians the right to amend their own Constitution.

In 1215, England's King John was forced by an angry nobility to sign the Magna Carta. This document placed limitations on the powers of the monarchy. Nearly eight centuries later, the English monarchy remains intact, although its function is now merely ceremonial.

important today mostly as a symbolic link to Canada's British heritage.

CANADA'S CHANGING CONSTITUTION

All real political power lies in the hands of Parliament and each provincial *legislature*. The specific powers assigned to Canada's federal and provincial governments are set out in Canada's Constitution. A constitution is the set of rules that establishes the political and legal systems of a country. It contains the basic laws, customs, and principles used to govern a nation. A constitution is thus the supreme law of the land. Governments must exercise power according to its provisions, and courts must recognize constitutional laws as superior to all other laws in the country.

When Canada was a British colony, it was ruled under the Constitution of Great Britain. The British Constitution is largely an "unwritten constitution." No one document describes how the British system of government works. Instead, Britain's Constitution is the sum of unwritten rules, customs, and practices that grew up over hundreds of years of British history. By contrast, the United States Constitution is a "written constitution," a single document created by the founders of the American nation in 1789.

Making the Canadian Constitution: The BNA Act of 1867

The founders of the Dominion of Canada followed both British and American traditions. They created a constitution that was partly unwritten and partly written. In 1864, delegates from several British colonies in North America met in Charlottetown and later in Quebec City to discuss Confederation — the founding of a new nation in British North America. Three years later, the **British North America (BNA) Act** was finally ready. The BNA Act united Upper Canada (Ontario), Lower Canada (Quebec), New Brunswick, and Nova Scotia into a federation known as the Dominion of Canada. (Soon after, several more British colonies joined Confederation.) It also gave Canada its first constitutional rules and set out the division of powers between federal and provincial governments. The British Parliament passed the BNA Act into law in 1867.

The Unwritten Constitution

The BNA Act proclaimed that Canada's Constitution was to be "similar in principle to that of the United Kingdom." These words meant that — although few details were spelled out — Canada's new government would mirror Britain's parliamentary system of representative government. Like Britain, Canada was to be a constitutional monarchy with Queen

On May 24, 1868, hundreds of Canadians gathered on Parliament Hill to celebrate Queen Victoria's birthday. Despite a fire in the early twentieth century, the Parliament buildings look much the same today.

HOW IS CANADA GOVERNED?

CANADIAN SOVEREIGNTY: ESTABLISHING CANADA'S INDEPENDENCE

Sovereignty refers to a country's ability to control its own affairs without interference from other states. While sovereignty specifically refers to legal autonomy, in recent years it has come to be used in discussions relating to territorial, cultural, and economic issues. In 1867, the Dominion of Canada was created. Although Canada was a self-governing state, independence would not be attained until 1931, and it took until 1982, 115 years after Confederation, for Canadians to bring the Constitution home from Britain. Therefore, although Canada had control over domestic matters, issues related to foreign policy and to the amendment of the Constitution remained in part in the hands of the British. Today sovereignty remains an important concern for Canada in order to safeguard our culture and environment and to maintain an independent foreign policy.

TRADE

All nations have economic dealings — trade relationships — with other countries. In negotiating trade agreements with other countries, Canada must consider how these decisions will affect its economic well-being, as well as the environment, cultural institutions, and social programs such as medicare.

THE ARCTIC

For years Canada's claim to the Northwest Passage has been challenged. The United States argues that it has the right to send ships through the passage. Also, the former Soviet Union secretly sent nuclear-powered submarines into Canadian Arctic waters in the past. Both nuclear submarines and oil tankers pose serious threats to the environment and to the defence of the Canadian coastline. Consequently, Canada must consider how to best protect its sovereignty over Arctic waters.

FOREIGN POLICY

Governments usually develop a plan of action to deal with international relations. This plan is called "foreign policy." Foreign policy reflects the goals that are important to a country. For example, in 1985, the government of Canada published a list of foreign-policy goals that included unity, sovereignty and independence, justice and democracy, peace and security, economic prosperity, and the integrity of the environment.

Victoria and her descendants as its legal heads of state. Like Britain, Canada's Parliament was to be divided into two chambers. In both Britain and Canada, one chamber was known as the **House of Commons**. Its members were elected, and it held most of the powers in Parliament. In Britain, the second chamber was called the House of Lords; its members, who inherited their right to sit in the House of Lords, belonged to the titled aristocracy of Britain. In Canada, however, there was no titled aristocracy. Instead, the founders of Confederation created a Senate made up of "people with wealth," who were originally appointed as senators for life.

The BNA Act: The "Written Constitution" and Federalism

Despite clear similarities to the British Constitution, in some ways the BNA Act is closer to the American Constitution. Like the American Constitution, the BNA Act was partly a "written constitution" — a single document created at a specific time and place. And like the American Constitution, it created a federal system of government and listed the powers of the two levels of government.

Why did the founders of Confederation choose a federal system for Canada? First, British North America was a huge territory with a scattering of small independent colonies. Each British colony had its own special identity — its own history, culture, terrain, and natural resources. Several of the colonies were afraid of losing their independence in Confederation. They wanted to maintain control over local and regional concerns. Second, the new Dominion of Canada had historical roots in both Britain and France. French-speakers in British North America wanted to have special protections to guarantee the survival of their French language and culture in a largely English-speaking nation.

Because Canada was such a large and varied country, the founders of Confederation chose a federal system in which powers were shared between a central and regional governments. The central government in Ottawa oversaw matters of general interest such as trade, commerce, and national defence. The provincial governments kept control of local and regional affairs such as schools and property rights. Quebec, for example, was given special powers to preserve its language, its schools, and its civil law, which was based on French law.

PATRIATING THE CANADIAN CONSTITUTION

The BNA Act was a British law enacted by the British Parliament. Therefore, an *amendment* to the act could be passed into law by only the British Parliament. Britain also kept other powers over Canadian affairs, including ownership of crown (public) lands, trade relations, and foreign relations. The highest court in Canada was a British court — the Judicial Committee of the Privy Council.

Over the years, however, Canada moved toward *autonomy* — complete independence from British rule. In 1931, the British Parliament passed the **Statute of Westminster**, which gave legal recognition to full independence for Canada, including responsibility for foreign affairs. After 1931, Canada was almost fully autonomous. A few further steps nearly completed the process: in 1947, Canadian citizenship was defined as distinct from British citizenship; and in 1949, the Supreme Court of Canada replaced the Judicial Committee of the Privy Council as the highest court in Canada. In the same year, the Canadian Parliament was given the power to amend the BNA Act, provided the amendments did not alter provincial powers or affect constitutional guarantees of education or language rights.

The British government was also willing to let Canada "*patriate*" — or bring home to Canada — the BNA Act by "re-passing" it in the Canadian Parliament. But Canadians could not agree on a method for patriating the Canadian Constitution, partly because they could not agree on an *amending formula*. After ten unsuccessful rounds of negotiations between 1927 and 1980, the federal government and all the provinces except Quebec arrived at an acceptable amending formula in 1981. Most amendments could be made if approved by the federal government and by seven or more provinces that represented at least 50 percent of the Canadian population. They also agreed on important additions to the Constitution, including a new charter of rights. Quebec refused to accept the new constitutional package, partly because the amending formula did not give Quebec the right to veto (strike down) any proposed new amendment. Quebec felt it needed a veto to protect its French language and culture.

The Canada Act, 1982

Despite Quebec's opposition, the Canadian Constitution was patriated by an act of the British Parliament in 1982 called the Canada Act. The Canada Act included the BNA Act — renamed the Constitution Act, 1867 — as well as other important acts such as the Statute of Westminster, 1931. The Canada Act also contained a package of new additions entitled the Constitution Act, 1982. The new package included the new amending formula, the Canadian Charter of Rights and Freedoms, and a "notwithstanding" clause that allowed the provinces and Parliament to declare laws exempt from provisions in certain sections of the new charter.

The Canadian Charter of Rights and Freedoms

Perhaps the most important addition in the Canada Act was the **Canadian Charter of Rights and Freedoms**. The new charter was intended to protect individual Canadians from the state and to protect minorities from parliamentary majorities. It covers several areas, including fundamental rights, democratic rights, mobility rights, legal rights, equality rights, and language rights.

Before the Canadian Charter of Rights and Freedoms, Canadians' rights were spelled out in the Canadian Bill of Rights of 1960 and in various provincial bills of rights. But these laws had been created by the Canadian Parliament and by provincial legislatures, and they could be changed or taken away by legislative votes. Once personal rights and freedoms were guaranteed in the Constitution, however, they could not be taken away except by constitutional amendment. The courts of Canada were given the final word on whether other laws in Canada were in keeping with the Charter of Rights and Freedoms. Section 52 of the Canada Act states that "The Constitution of Canada is the supreme law of Canada, and any law that is inconsistent with the provisions of the Constitution is, to the extent of the inconsistency, of no force or effect." In other words, the charter is superior to any laws passed by any government in Canada. By the end of the 1980s, the Supreme Court of Canada had made judgments in more than twenty charter cases — many of them landmark legal decisions.

All Canadians have the right to freedom of expression and freedom of association guaranteed by the Canadian Charter of Rights and Freedoms. Why are these rights considered fundamental in Canadian society?

THE CANADIAN CHARTER OF RIGHTS AND FREEDOMS

GUARANTEE OF RIGHTS AND FREEDOMS
1. The Canadian Charter of Rights and Freedoms guarantees the rights and freedoms set out in it subject only to such reasonable limits prescribed by law as can be demonstrably justified in a free and democratic society.

FUNDAMENTAL FREEDOMS
2. Everyone has the following fundamental freedoms:
   (a) freedom of conscience and religion;
   (b) freedom of thought, belief, opinion and expression, including freedom of the press and other media of communication;
   (c) freedom of peaceful assembly; and
   (d) freedom of association.

DEMOCRATIC RIGHTS
3. Every citizen of Canada has the right to vote in an election of members of the House of Commons or of a legislative assembly and to be qualified for membership therein.

LEGAL RIGHTS
7. Everyone has the right to life, liberty and security of the person and the right not to be deprived thereof except in accordance with the principles of fundamental justice.
8. Everyone has the right to be secure against unreasonable search or seizure.
9. Everyone has the right not to be arbitrarily detained or imprisoned.
10. Everyone has the right on arrest or detention
    (a) to be informed promptly of the reasons therefor;
    (b) to retain and instruct counsel without delay and to be informed of that right; and
    (c) to have the validity of the detention determined by way of habeas corpus and to be released if the detention is not lawful.

EQUALITY RIGHTS
15. (1) Every individual is equal before and under the law and has the right to the equal protection and equal benefit of the law without discrimination and, in particular, without discrimination based on race, national or ethnic origin, colour, religion, sex, age or mental or physical disability.

OFFICIAL LANGUAGES OF CANADA
16. (1) English and French are the official languages of Canada and have equality of status and equal rights and privileges as to their use in all institutions of the Parliament and government of Canada.

GENERAL
...
28. Notwithstanding anything in this Charter, the rights and freedoms referred to in it are guaranteed equally to male and female persons.

ISSUES OF DISCRIMINATION AND THE CHARTER OF RIGHTS AND FREEDOMS

In 1982, Canada passed its new Constitution, which, for the first time in Canadian history, included a charter of rights and freedoms. This charter attempted to guarantee the basic rights of all Canadians by entrenching the rights in the Constitution. As a result of the new Canadian Charter of Rights and Freedoms, many people have brought to the courts issues of discrimination based on gender, religion, and lifestyle. Following are four sample cases and one actual case. How would you have ruled in each of these cases?

1. Mr. Singh, a Sikh, chose to be baptized at the age of 16 years and thereby committed himself to fulfilling the responsibilities of his faith and the five "Ks." The five "Ks" require that the Sikh wear long hair (Keshas); a comb (Khanga) as a general symbol for cleanliness of mind and body; a steel bangle (Kara) as a general symbol for purity of action; special underwear (Kachh) as a symbol for purity of character; and the sword (Kirpan) as an armour of protection and symbol for the primal power. Mr. Singh had an accident at work and was required to go for swimming treatment at a Workers' Compensation Rehabilitation Centre. He wore his Kirpan to the pool, but left it in the locker room prior to swimming. After swimming he put the Kirpan on again. Fellow patients complained that Mr. Singh was wearing a weapon and after much discussion Mr. Singh was told not to come to the rehabilitation centre while wearing the Kirpan. Mr. Singh complained to the Human Rights Commission, claiming that the rehabilitation procedure discriminated against him on the basis of religion (creed) and religious beliefs. What would your decision be? Give your reasons.

2. Klaus Triebsche, a 22-year-old single male, responded to a newspaper advertisement for a two-bedroom apartment. While viewing the apartment the rental agent asked Klaus his occupation and he replied that he was a university student. The agent stated that it was the management's policy not to rent to single students because they often have difficulty paying the rent and frequently disturb other tenants by having noisy parties. Klaus claims he is being discriminated against on the basis of age and marital status.

a. Do you think the owner of the apartment should be allowed to choose to rent to whomever he or she wishes? Under all circumstances? Give reasons for your answer.

b. Do you think Klaus has been discriminated against? Explain.

3. A visually impaired woman filed a complaint with the Human Rights Commission claiming that she was refused service by the owner of a cafe because she brought her guide dog. Should the woman be entitled to eat in the cafe, accompanied by her guide dog? Give reasons for your answer.

4. A married woman applied for a small loan from a finance company to purchase an item of household furniture. Her husband had an outstanding account with the company and his credit rating was not very good. Because of this, the woman was refused the loan. Her own credit

rating was very good. On what grounds, if any, do you feel this woman is being discriminated against? Explain your answer.

Read the following actual legal case and decide how you would have ruled.

Blainey and Ontario
Hockey Association et al.
(1986), 54 O.R. (2nd) 513

Justine Blainey, a 12-year-old girl, was an outstanding athlete having the ability to compete as a full member of a peewee hockey team, in the opinion of her coach. All the other members of the team were boys. Justine had been well-accepted as a full member of the team and had competed in four exhibition games. She was anxious to play for the team on a regular basis, but to do so, Justine had to be a member of the Ontario Hockey Association (OHA). This was not possible according to Regulation 250 of the OHA. Regulation 250 of the OHA states:

> Every male person *who is an amateur in accordance with the Association's definition thereof who is not under suspension by the C.A.H.A. or any of it branches, by any other member of the I.I.H.F., or any professional organizations, and is not a member of any club or team under the jurisdiction of any other member of the International Ice Hockey Federation shall be eligible for membership in a club in the Association. A player derives no benefit from any suspension.*

Mrs. Blainey registered a complaint with the Ontario Human Rights Commission on the grounds that her daughter was being discriminated against on the basis of her sex. The Ontario Human Rights Code provides in section 1 as follows:

> *1. Every person has a right to equal treatment with respect to service, goods, and facilities, without discrimination because of race, ancestry, place of origin, colour, ethnic origin, citizenship, creed, sex, age, marital status, family status or handicap.*

Furthermore, section 19(2) of the Act states:

> *19.(2) The right under section 1 to equal treatment with respect to services and facilities is not infringed where membership in an athletic organization or participation in an athletic activity is restricted to persons of the same sex.*

Justine claimed that section 19(2) was inconsistent with section 15 of the Charter. Therefore, the Ontario Human Rights Code should not allow the OHA to discriminate.

a. Disregarding the legal questions, do you think Justine should be allowed to play hockey for the team on a regular basis? Why?

b. Examine all the relevant sections of the different statutes and state whether you think section 19(2) is unconstitutional. Fully explain your answer.

Source: From *Applying the Law*, third edition, by Michael Liepner and Bryant Griffith. Reprinted by permission of McGraw-Hill Ryerson Limited.

The Meech Lake and Charlottetown Accords

When Queen Elizabeth II signed the Canada Act on April 17, 1982, Canada reached the last milestone on its road to autonomy. It was now a fully self-governing nation. But the patriation left Canada facing an unsettled future. In the 1980s and 1990s, fierce constitutional conflicts between French and English Canadians threatened to break up the nation. Under Prime Minister Brian Mulroney, a new constitutional agreement known as the Meech Lake Accord was hammered out in 1987. One of its aims was to try to reconcile Quebec to the 1982 Constitution, which it had refused to sign. The accord declared that Quebec was "a distinct society," and it gave provinces the right to nominate Supreme Court judges and the right to veto future constitutional changes in certain areas. The three major political parties and all ten provincial premiers supported the Meech Lake Accord. But the accord had to be ratified (passed) by all ten provinces within three years before it could become law. In the end, the accord failed to be ratified by every provincial legislature. By 1990, the Meech Lake Accord was dead.

Quebec was angered by what it saw as another rejection of Quebec's concerns. Quebec's premier, Robert Bourassa, announced that his government intended to hold a referendum (public vote) on Quebec independence. It looked as if the country might break apart. Soon after, a second round of constitutional talks began. The goal was to try once again to meet Quebec's needs and keep it in Confederation. Other special-interest groups — including women, Native peoples, and people concerned with social and economic justice — also

Former prime minister Brian Mulroney was applauded in the House of Commons by members of his government when he read his speech on proposed constitutional changes in September 1992. Why do you think party unity is important in Canadian politics?

THE VALUE OF CANADIAN CITIZENSHIP

Admission to Canada is governed by a set of complex rules and practices contained in the Immigration Act and the Regulations made under that Act. Major amendments dealing with refugees were made to the Act in 1988.

People arriving at a Canadian port of entry must pass through Canadian Immigration and demonstrate to an immigration officer their entitlement to enter Canada. The Immigration Act generally distinguishes between two classes of entrants: those who have the right to enter and those who might be permitted to enter. Canadian citizens and permanent residents have the legal right to enter Canada, whereas visitors and immigrants require permission to enter Canada.

Canadian Citizens

The Parliament of Canada has enacted legislation establishing the qualifications for Canadian citizenship. The Citizenship Act states that citizens are those persons who were born in Canada, or born outside Canada to a Canadian citizen, or who have been granted citizenship under the Act and have taken the oath of citizenship.

The criteria for acquiring Canadian citizenship if one is not born in Canada or of a Canadian parent are: citizenship shall be granted to a person who:

- is eighteen years of age or older
- was lawfully admitted to Canada as a permanent resident
- has resided in Canada for at least three of the last four years
- has an adequate knowledge of English or French
- has an adequate knowledge of Canada and the responsibilities and privileges of citizenship
- is not under a deportation order
- is not on probation, parole, or in a penal institution
- is not on trial for a serious criminal offence
- has not been convicted of an indictable offence within the past three years.

Citizenship must also be granted to children (under twenty-one years) of a citizen. It is clear under the Citizenship Act that all citizens have identical rights and duties regardless of how their citizenship was acquired.

Analyzing Legal Concepts

You and a classmate have just been appointed as members of the government panel that hears refugee claimants. Officially, one member of your team is the immigration adjudicator and the other is a member of the Immigration and Refugee Board. Each claimant must convince only one member of the panel that the claimant cannot risk returning to his or her homeland for political, religious, or other reasons.

Just one vote in favour means the claimant can apply for landed immigrant status, granted to those who pass security and health checks.

Case 1

- refugee claimant states that he is a member of a race that has been in conflict with a neighbouring race in his native country
- there is documentation indicating that these two races have been engaged in ongoing, violent clashes against each other for the past several years
- until about four years ago, claimant and his family lived in a farming village located on the border separating the opposing races
- about four years ago, claimant's village was attacked by a militant movement of the government
- as a result of the attack, the village was destroyed, and claimant and his family fled the area
- they lived in two different refugee camps for short periods of time
- a few years after this, claimant was arrested by the opposing forces, and then questioned and beaten by them
- following his release, he fled the country and came to Canada

Case 2

- refugee claimant testifies that she was imprisoned for three days in 1987 and that she received thirty lashes solely for her support of the pro-monarchy group (country of origin experienced a revolution about ten years ago in which the then monarch was overthrown in favour of a new regime)
- claimant was told by members of the government military forces that she would face execution if she was further involved in the pro-monarch group
- claimant's mother suffered imprisonment for three years, beginning about four years ago, for her involvement in hosting an anniversary party in honour of the former monarch and for showing a film that was critical of the new regime
- other members of her family were persecuted to varying degrees for their pro-monarchy views.

Source: From *Understanding the Law* by Steven Talos, Michael Liepner, and Gregory Dickinson. Reprinted by permission of McGraw-Hill Ryerson Limited.

CHANGING CANADA'S CONSTITUTION

The Canada Act of 1982 was considered a major accomplishment by many Canadians, yet others were dissatisfied with it. The province of Quebec refused to sign the Constitution without significant amendments (changes). Since 1982, there have been two attempts to alter the Constitution. The Meech Lake Accord in 1987 attempted to meet the needs of Quebec, but failed. In 1992, the Charlottetown Accord tried to balance the needs of Quebec with those of other unrepresented groups, including women and Native peoples. The following chart compares some of the major changes proposed in 1987 and 1992. Would you have supported either of these agreements?

Topics	Meech Lake Accord, 1987	Charlottetown Accord, 1992
Distinct Society Clause	Quebec's right to preserve and promote its distinct society would be guaranteed.	A new clause, known as the Canada Clause, and the Canadian Charter of Rights and Freedoms would recognize Quebec's responsibility to preserve its distinct society.
Canada Clause	No such clause.	Outlines the values and characteristics that define Canadians, including a commitment to the equality of men and women and to the well-being of all Canadians.
Senate Reform	The federal government would continue to appoint senators but from lists of candidates provided by the provinces.	Senate reform would become a priority, with the aim of designing an elected Senate that would provide better regional representation.
Native Rights	Not addressed.	Native groups would have been guaranteed self-government within ten years.

wanted to have their concerns met by constitutional changes.

After a series of public forums and commissions, the federal government proposed a sweeping new constitutional package called the Charlottetown Accord. It proposed major changes to the Canadian Constitution, including aboriginal self-government, Senate reform, and a new division of federal–provincial powers. It also proposed a statement of the principles of the Canadian nation, including the recognition of Quebec as a "distinct society." The proposal was put before the Canadian people in a nation-wide referendum in October 1992. But the tide of public opinion turned against the broad new constitutional accord in the last weeks before the referendum date. The Charlottetown Accord went down to defeat. Today, the constitutional debate remains unresolved. Canadians are still struggling to reshape the Canadian Constitution to meet the needs of today — and of tomorrow.

Former constitutional affairs minister Joe Clark shakes hands with Assembly of First Nations Chief Ovide Mercredi at a constitutional conference in Toronto in February 1992. Should Canada's Native people receive special status within the Constitution?

TEEN AND ADULT CONFIDENCE IN INSTITUTIONS

"How much confidence do you have in the people in charge of . . . "

% Indicating "A Great Deal" or "Quite a Bit"

	The Police	The Schools	TV	Court System	Relig. Orgs.	The Fed. Gov't.
Nationally						
1992	69	67	61	59	39	27
1984	77	69	—	67	62	40
Adults						
1990	70	55	55	43	36	13
1985	74	56	43	48	50	29

Source: Adapted from *Teen Trends: A Nation in Motion*, Reginald W. Bibby and Donald C. Posterski, Stoddart, 1992, p. 174.

KNOWING THE KEY PEOPLE, PLACES, AND EVENTS

In your notes, clearly identify and explain the historical significance of each of the following:

> Government
> Constitution
> British North America (BNA) Act
> Statute of Westminster
> Democracy
> Constitutional Monarchy
> House of Commons
> Canadian Charter of Rights and Freedoms

FOCUS YOUR KNOWLEDGE

1. Briefly describe at least four ways in which your life is directly affected by government actions.
2. Describe the role played by the monarchy in Canadian government.
3. How does the British North America Act reflect Canada's close ties to Britain?
4. What factors did the creators of the British North America Act have to take into account? Which of these remain relevant today?

APPLY YOUR KNOWLEDGE

1. What are the three most important reasons why a society needs a government?
2. Define representative democracy, and explain why it is better suited to Canada than direct democracy.
3. If you were to live under any system of government other than a democracy, what would be your preference? Explain your choice.
4. Why is a federal system of government best suited to meeting Canada's needs?
5. Why was the federal government given most of the powers under the British North America Act? Does a strong central government still best meet the needs of Canadians, or have changes made greater provincial powers a necessity?

EXTEND YOUR KNOWLEDGE

1. Most political philosophers share in the pursuit of an ideal form of government. Research the concept of Utopia and create your own perfect world. Describe the climate, geography, and style of government your Utopia would have. Also create a charter of rights and freedoms that outlines the rights of all the citizens of your new world. Finally, create a visual image of your Utopia using a map, drawing, or collage.

2. Create a time-line of constitutional change in Canada from 1867 to the present. Make it visually appealing by illustrating it and including brief bits of information so that it can be mounted on the classroom's walls.

3. Write a fictional story about Canada in the future. Assume that it is the year 2065 and that Canada's democratic system of government has been overthrown. In its place could be anarchy (no government), a dictatorship, or an oligarchy. Describe how Canada has changed as a result of this change in government. Be sure to explain how the new government works, what new laws exist, and what rights and freedoms Canadians have under the new system.

CHAPTER 2
CANADIAN GOVERNMENT IN ACTION

GLOSSARY TERMS

Medicare A government-run program of medical and hospital services.

Political Party An organization made up of people who share similar political beliefs and tend to take similar positions on major political issues. Its main objective is to gain political power by electing party members to government office.

Civil Servants Officials working in the administrative branch of a federal or provincial government.

Electoral District A constituency, or group of voters living in a designated area, who are represented by a member of a provincial legislature or by a member of the House of Commons.

Census An official count of a country's population.

Ambassadors The highest-ranking diplomatic representatives sent by one government or country to represent it in another.

Caucus A private meeting of members of the House of Commons who belong to the same political party.

FOCUS ON:

- the many ways in which Canadians are affected by government
- the different roles and powers of the three levels of government
- the role of the prime minister, cabinet ministers, and the opposition
- how Canadians elect government officials
- how laws are passed in Canada
- Canada's various political parties
- what individuals can do to influence governments

Brrring! It's 8 a.m. and the start of a new day. You flip on the light, and then you remember. Daylight saving time has just started, and you forgot to set your clock forward an hour. You're running late. You don't have time to shower, so you splash water on your face, give your hair and teeth a quick brushing, pull on your jeans, button on a shirt, slide into your shoes, and head for the kitchen. You gulp down some milk and cereal, and reach for your jacket. You almost trip over the dog as you head for the door, but you hear the jingle of the dog tag just in time. You're on your way!

Try replaying this imaginary scene over again to see how many laws are part of your life. Your alarm clock is set to government-regulated time zones that change by an hour twice a year — "spring forward and fall back." Your water is provided by government — water quality and treatment are regulated by law. Your toothpaste is affected by laws about food and drugs, and packaging and labelling. If you wear designer jeans, the trademark name is protected by law. Your shoes may be regulated under international trade law. The milk and wheat in your cereal bowl are subject to milk and wheat marketing board laws. The French and English labelling on the cereal box is also there by law. Even the family dog has to be licensed under a local by-law.

FEDERAL, PROVINCIAL, AND MUNICIPAL GOVERNMENTS

Whose job is it to make laws in Canada? The federal government and the provinces have shared law-making powers since Confederation. Under the British North America (BNA) Act of 1867, the federal government has the right to pass laws applying across Canada in a broad range of areas, including defence, taxation, and Native peoples and reserves. It is also responsible for the "peace, order and good government of Canada." This means that all powers not directly assigned to the provinces fall under federal control.

The provinces have responsibility for services that have to do with property, civil rights, transportation, and local government. They also run hospitals, provide many health and welfare services, and administer the justice system. In addition, they have important powers in labour relations and

DIVISION OF POWERS: FEDERAL, PROVINCIAL, AND MUNICIPAL

Federal Powers
- Defence
- Regulation of trade and commerce
- Citizenship
- Taxation
- Currency and coins
- Native peoples and Native reserves
- Postal service
- Patents and copyrights
- Marriage and divorce
- Navigation and shipping
- Fisheries
- Criminal law and federal penitentiaries

Provincial Powers
- Education
- Hospitals and charities
- Licences (e.g., driving and fishing)
- Private property and civil law
- Direct taxation (e.g., income tax and sales tax)
- Management of natural resources (e.g., forests and electrical energy)
- Local public works (e.g., roads and canals)
- Courts and the administration of justice
- Local (municipal) government

Municipal Powers
- Water and sewer service
- Public transit
- Fire and police protection and ambulance service
- Licensing and inspection (e.g., houses)
- Street lights, sidewalks, and local roads
- Public health services

URBAN MUNICIPAL GOVERNMENT

```
                          MAYOR & COUNCIL
        ┌──────────────────────┼──────────────────────┐
   Public Utilities        Library              Board of Police
     Commission             Board               Commissioners
        │                      │                      │
 ┌──────┬──────┬──────┬────────┼────────┬──────────┐
Community Parks & Public    Finance  Transportation Planning
Services  Recreation Works  Committee  Committee    Board
Committee Committee Committee
   │        │       │        │    │       │           │
 Clerk    Parks &  Public  Clerk- Treasurer Traffic & Planning &
 Fire    Recreation Works  Comp-  & Deputy- Streets   Urban
 Social                    troller Comp-    Industrial Renewal
 Services                          troller  Committee &
                                            Administration
                                            of Airport
```

RURAL MUNICIPAL GOVERNMENT

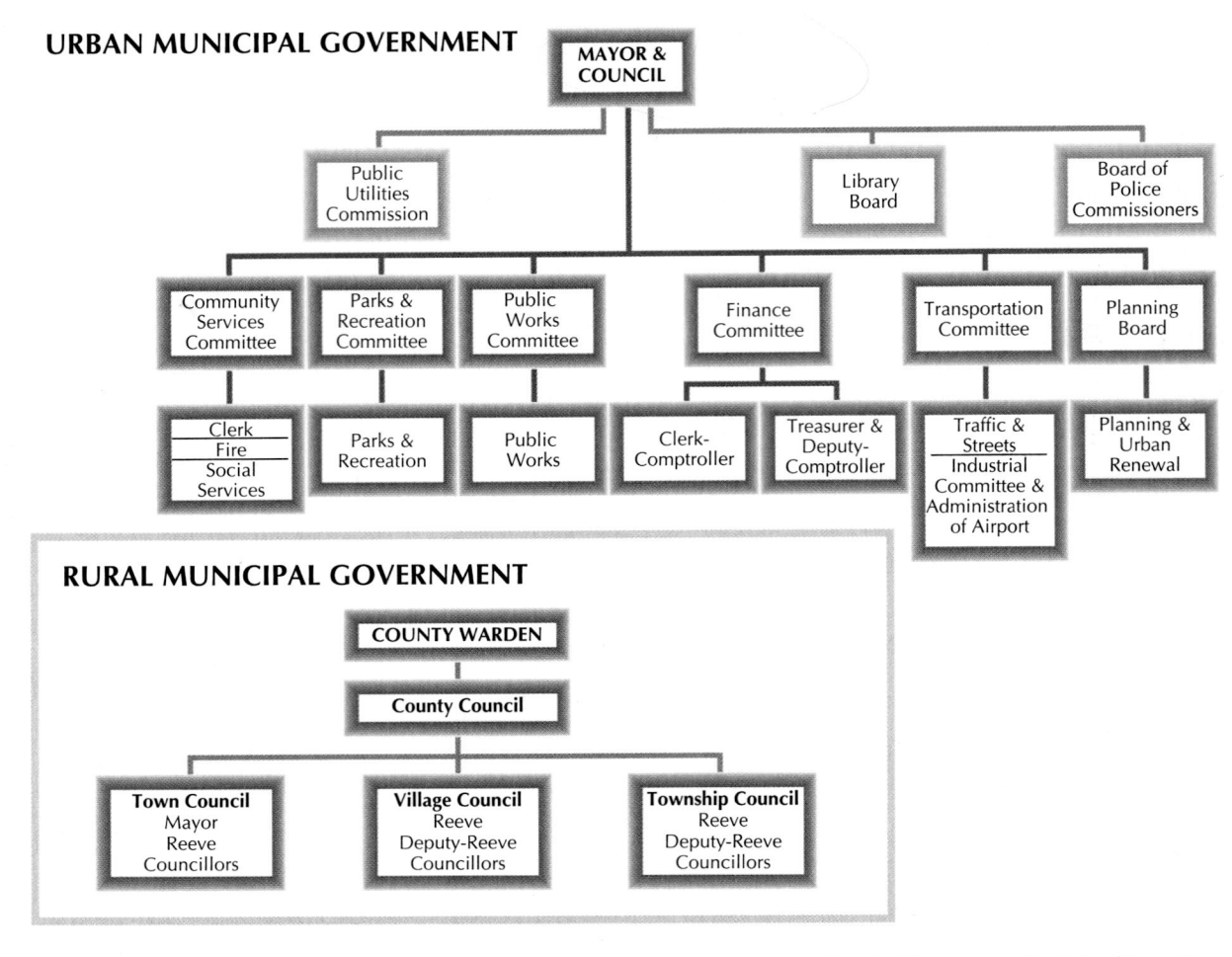

```
              COUNTY WARDEN
                    │
              County Council
        ┌───────────┼───────────┐
   Town Council  Village Council  Township Council
     Mayor          Reeve             Reeve
     Reeve       Deputy-Reeve       Deputy-Reeve
   Councillors   Councillors        Councillors
```

Source: Adapted from *Canada's Government and Law: Rights and Responsibilities,* Donald M. Santor, Prentice-Hall, 1992.

---

consumer protection, and they own and manage their natural resources. However, federal and provincial governments jointly share power over immigration and agriculture.

Canada is one of the few governments in the world to have three levels of government. The third level of government is local or municipal government. But local governments were not given separate powers under the BNA Act. Instead, it is up to the provinces to define the responsibilities of local governments and to set their boundaries. The provinces also have final authority over all municipal laws — called by-laws — passed by local governments.

Although local governments are structured differently from province to province, the basic unit of local government is the municipality. Municipalities range in size from villages to major cities. Municipal responsibilities also vary, depending on the size of the municipality and the specific

By the beginning of the twentieth century, Toronto was already a bustling industrial centre. Today, Toronto has developed into a major metropolitan centre. How would the growth of Canadian cities such as Toronto, Calgary, and Vancouver change the role of municipal governments in our lives?

responsibilities assigned to it by the province. There are also larger units of local government, including districts, counties, and regional governments. Big Canadian cities such as Toronto, Vancouver, Montreal, and Winnipeg have metropolitan governments that include the city and its surrounding municipalities. In Vancouver, for example, the metropolitan government is the Greater Vancouver Regional District (GVRD) and, in Toronto, it is Metropolitan Toronto (Metro).

FEDERAL AND PROVINCIAL GOVERNMENTS

The original division of powers under the BNA Act was intended to let the provinces pass laws for their own needs and to give the federal government control in matters concerning the country as a whole. However, Canada is no longer a nineteenth-century country of farms and forests but a highly industrialized nation of city skyscrapers and suburban shopping malls. It is also a part of a quickly changing global community. Canadian governments are now active in areas such as *medicare*, unemployment insurance, traffic regulations, environmental protection, bilingualism, and abortion. Governments at all levels now play a much bigger role in the lives of Canadians.

As Canada changed from a rural to an urban nation, the division of government powers also changed. Provincial powers have expanded as the demands for services under provincial control, such as education, transportation, welfare, and medical services, have grown. Federal and provincial governments now have joint responsibility in many areas. Medicare is just one example of many shared programs. The federal and provincial governments both foot part of the bill for medicare, and the provinces run the program. Local governments have also expanded areas of responsibility. In the 1790s, the first local governments in Canada only had power over fence heights and roaming animals. Now they have wide-ranging powers and provide many important community services.

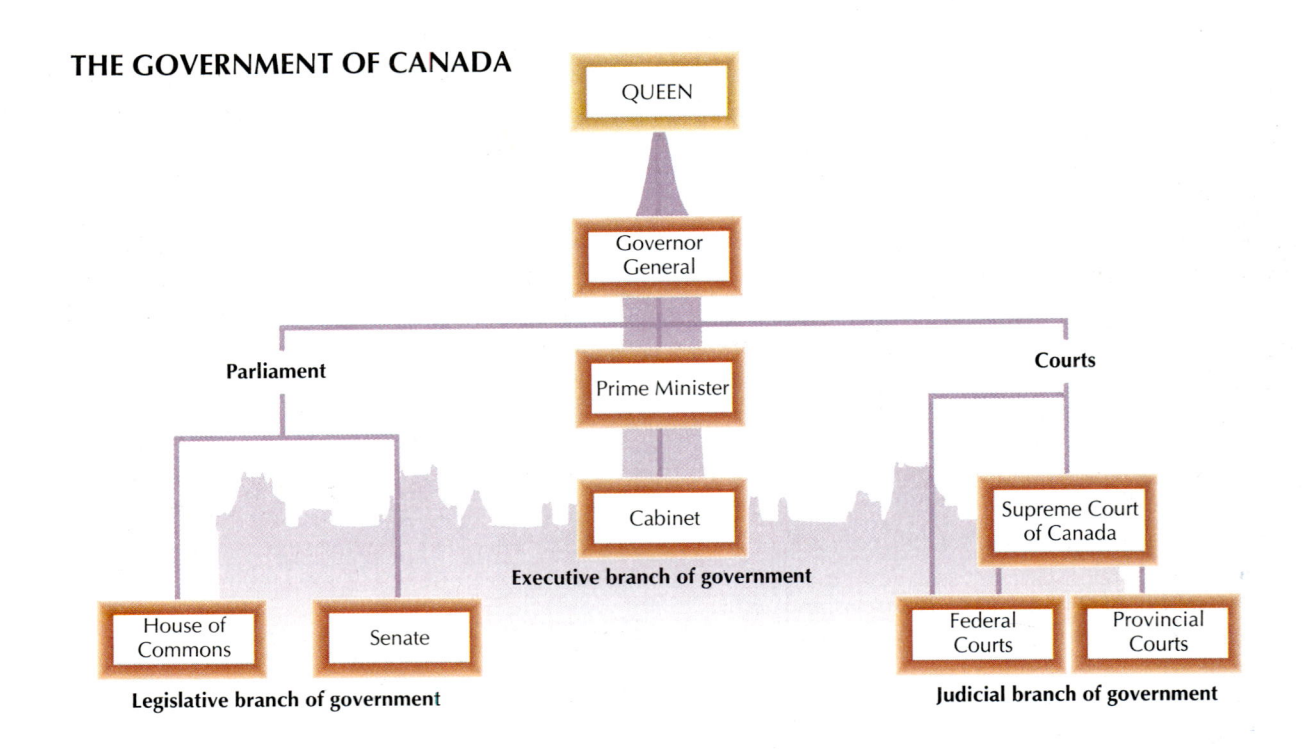

THE GOVERNMENT OF CANADA

```
                    QUEEN
                      |
                 Governor
                 General
                      |
       ┌──────────────┼──────────────┐
   Parliament         |            Courts
                 Prime Minister
                      |
                   Cabinet                  Supreme Court
                                              of Canada
       Executive branch of government           |
   ┌───────────┐                         ┌──────┴──────┐
   House of      Senate                  Federal    Provincial
   Commons                               Courts      Courts
   Legislative branch of government      Judicial branch of government
```

FUNCTIONS OF GOVERNMENT: EXECUTIVE, LEGISLATIVE, AND JUDICIAL

Government in Canada has three branches: executive, legislative, and judicial. The duty of the **executive branch** is to carry out and enforce laws. The executives of the federal and provincial governments are much alike. The federal executive is made up of the Queen of Canada (represented by the governor general), the prime minister, the federal cabinet, and the federal civil service. The provincial executive is made up of the Queen of Canada (represented by the lieutenant-governor), the premier, the provincial cabinet, and the provincial civil service.

The real executive power in Canada is wielded by the prime minister, the premiers, and their cabinets. The prime minister and the premiers are leaders chosen by the *political party* in power, and they are responsible to their party for their political decisions. **Cabinet members** are picked by the prime minister or the premiers from among the leading members of their party who hold seats in the legislature. Together, the prime minister or premier and the other cabinet members decide on the government's major policies. Most members of the cabinet are also placed in charge of a ministry or department such as

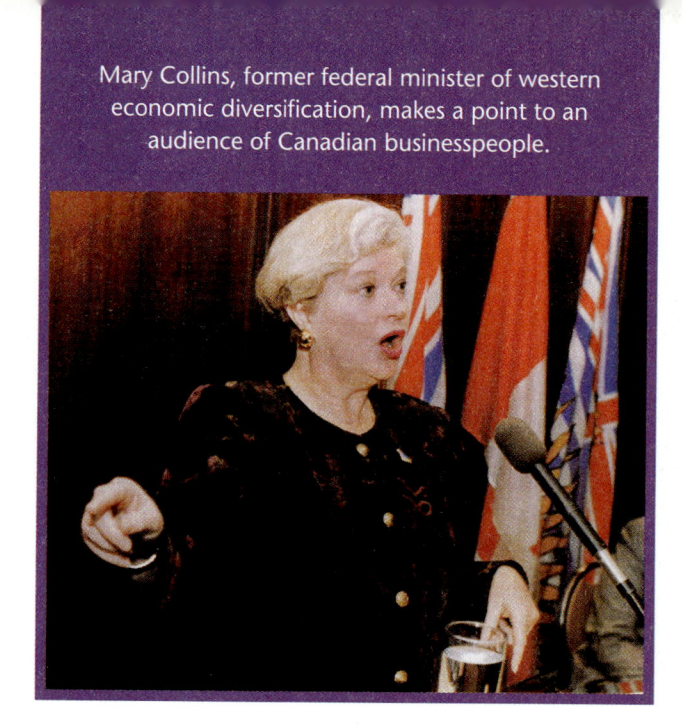

Mary Collins, former federal minister of western economic diversification, makes a point to an audience of Canadian businesspeople.

Agriculture, Justice, Environment, or Employment and Immigration. In turn, cabinet members depend on assistance and advice from *civil servants* (permanent employees of the executive) in their ministries as they make policy decisions. Led by the prime minister or premier, the cabinet team is so powerful that the words "cabinet" and "government" are often used as if they were the same.

The duty of the **legislative branch** is to enact (make), amend (change), and repeal (remove) laws. Here, too, federal and provincial governments are much alike. Parliament is the legislative body of the federal government. It is made up of the queen (governor general), the House of Commons, and the Senate. Members of the House of Commons are elected. Senators, however, are appointed. The legislative body at the provincial level is made up of the queen (lieutenant-governor) and an elected legislative body. All ten provincial legislatures are patterned on the House of Commons, and they function in almost the same way. However, there is no provincial legislative body that matches the federal Senate.

At the local level, executive and legislative bodies differ from place to place. The head of a municipal government might be called a chairperson, a mayor, a reeve, an overseer, or a warden. Members of local councils might be councillors, controllers, or alderpersons. Their powers and responsibilities also vary from place to place. The chart on page 32 shows a typical example of the organization of a municipal government.

The **judiciary** — the court system — performs the third function of government in Canada. The duty of the courts is to interpret and uphold Canadian laws. The court system is headed by the Supreme Court of Canada, which is the last court of appeal in Canada. Its decisions are always final. It also plays an important role in interpreting the Constitution, especially the Canadian Charter of Rights and Freedoms. All provinces have their own court systems. Provincial courts settle civil disputes and try people charged with lawbreaking. Two provinces — Nova Scotia and Quebec — also have municipal courts to hear matters concerning municipal by-laws.

THE CANADIAN PARLIAMENT

Every year the Canadian Parliament meets in Ottawa. During the months that Parliament is in session, members of Parliament are busy making new laws and repealing or amending old laws. For example, a new gun-control law banning automatic weapons recently passed in Parliament. Its purpose was to protect the public from dangerous weapons designed specifically to kill or maim people. The Young Offenders Act was recently amended to increase the maximum prison sentence for young offenders convicted of murder to five years. Old tax laws are sometimes repealed. The goods and services tax (GST) that you now pay whenever you buy many retail goods and services replaced an old tax that manufacturers used to pay on the products they made. The laws passed by Parliament — the Senate and the House of Commons — become the laws we live with every day.

THE NEED FOR SENATE REFORM

When Canada was created in 1867, the British North America Act established an Upper House (the Senate) and a Lower House (the House of Commons). At the time many people, including Canada's first prime minister, John A. Macdonald, had limited faith in democracy. To safeguard against bad laws being passed because of public pressure, the Senate was to be appointed and have the right to review and veto bills. Because senators are appointed to the Senate until the age of seventy-five, they are not subject to the same public scrutiny as elected members of Parliament.

To be a senator you must:

- be at least thirty years old;
- be a Canadian citizen;
- own $4000 worth of real property;
- be a resident of the province you represent.

Many Canadians now consider an appointed Senate outdated. For years, efforts to reform the Senate have been discussed, but no changes have occurred. A very popular idea for reform is known as the "Triple E Senate." A Triple E Senate would be:

- *Elected:* Senators would be directly elected by Canadians;
- *Equal:* Each province would have the same number of senators; and
- *Effective:* The Senate would have the power to pass or reject bills.

Do you think we should leave the Senate as it is, reform it, or abolish it altogether? What are the merits and/or problems of the Triple E Senate proposal? Can you think of other ways to effectively reform the Senate?

After studying this cartoon, explain the issue and the cartoonist's point of view. Do you agree with the statement being made?

The Senate

Senators are appointed on the recommendation of the prime minister. They remain in office until retirement at age seventy-five. Senate appointments are often seen as **patronage** appointments — as rewards for a new senator's past services to the political party in power. For example, Prime Minister Pierre Trudeau caused an uproar across Canada when he made a number of Liberal Senate appointments just before leaving office in 1984.

All bills (proposed new laws) approved in the House of Commons must also be approved in the Senate. The **Senate** was originally created to provide "sober second thought" about **bills** passed by the House of Commons. An appointed Senate was to serve as a check on what Sir John A. Macdonald described as "hasty or ill-considered legislation" in the elected House of Commons and to protect minority and regional interests. The Senate can review, amend, delay, and, in theory, defeat bills passed by the House of Commons. However, the real power to pass laws rests with the House of Commons.

The House of Commons

All members of Parliament (MPs) have been elected in a general vote from an *electoral district* called a constituency or riding. The system for electing MPs to the House of Commons is sometimes called representation by population. The number of MPs from each province roughly corresponds to that province's share of Canada's total population. Every ten years a Canada-wide *census* is taken, and the number of MPs representing each province in Parliament is changed to match shifts in Canada's population.

By law, an election must be called after a maximum of five years in office, but the prime minister may call an election any time within the five-year period. Most elections are called after a government has been in power for about four years. The prime minister usually waits for a time when public support looks strong and then asks the governor general to dissolve (put an end to) Parliament. Then the date for the election is set, and the election campaign goes into full swing.

A Nonconfidence Vote

In certain circumstances the government in power can be forced out of office. If a majority of members in the House of Commons vote against a budget or any other important measure presented to Parliament by the government, the prime minister and cabinet must resign or call an election. When this happens, the vote is called a vote of nonconfidence. For example, in 1979 Prime Minister Joe Clark's finance minister presented a budget to the House of Commons. The budget was unpopular among MPs, and a vote of nonconfidence was held. Clark's Progressive Conservative government was defeated, and his government resigned. It is an unwritten rule that a government stays in office only as long as it has the support of a majority in the House of Commons. This is an important principle of responsible government.

The Right Honourable Ramon John Hnatyshyn represents the queen in Canada. As Canada's head of state, the governor general greets foreign dignitaries and serves a ceremonial role. Here, he inspects the guards.

Getting Elected to Parliament

As soon as an election is called, the chief electoral officer sets the election machinery in motion. Returning officers make up voters' lists of all people eligible to vote in their ridings. In the seventh week before an election, an army of enumerators — 87 000 in the 1988 election — march out to knock on every door in the country. It is their business to register the names of eligible voters. Most Canadian citizens who are at least eighteen years old and who qualify as residents in a riding are eligible to vote. Returning officers also take the nominations of the candidates for office. Almost anyone who is eligible to vote can run for Parliament. Candidates do not have to be nominated by a political party or even live in the riding. It is very difficult, however, for a candidate to win an election without the backing of a political party.

Political Parties in Canada

For the past several decades, Canada has had three major federal political parties — the Progressive Conservative Party, the Liberal Party, and the New Democratic Party (NDP). That changed, however, in

For years, cameras were not allowed in the House of Commons. Today, television cameras are allowed to record and broadcast parliamentary debates. Do you think this change has made politicians more responsive to Canadians?

When the federal goods and services tax (GST) was introduced, thousands of Canadians took to the streets to protest. Do you think this is an effective way to let governments know how the public feels about an issue?

the 1993 federal election when the Progressive Conservatives and the NDP were nearly wiped out. They were replaced in Parliament by two new parties — the Bloc Québécois and the Reform Party.

Each party has a different platform, or package of ideas and policies, that it hopes will attract voter support. The "planks" of a party's platform are its stands on important public issues such as foreign policy, health care, unemployment, and the environment. Few voters agree with every plank in any party's platform. But they usually find that one party represents many of their own interests and opinions and support it.

Canada's political parties represent a range of political opinion from left to right. The Liberals and Progressive Conservatives, for example, have been known as moderate or "middle-of-the-road" parties. The Liberals are sometimes considered centre-left because of their historical support for social

FLOOR PLAN OF THE HOUSE OF COMMONS

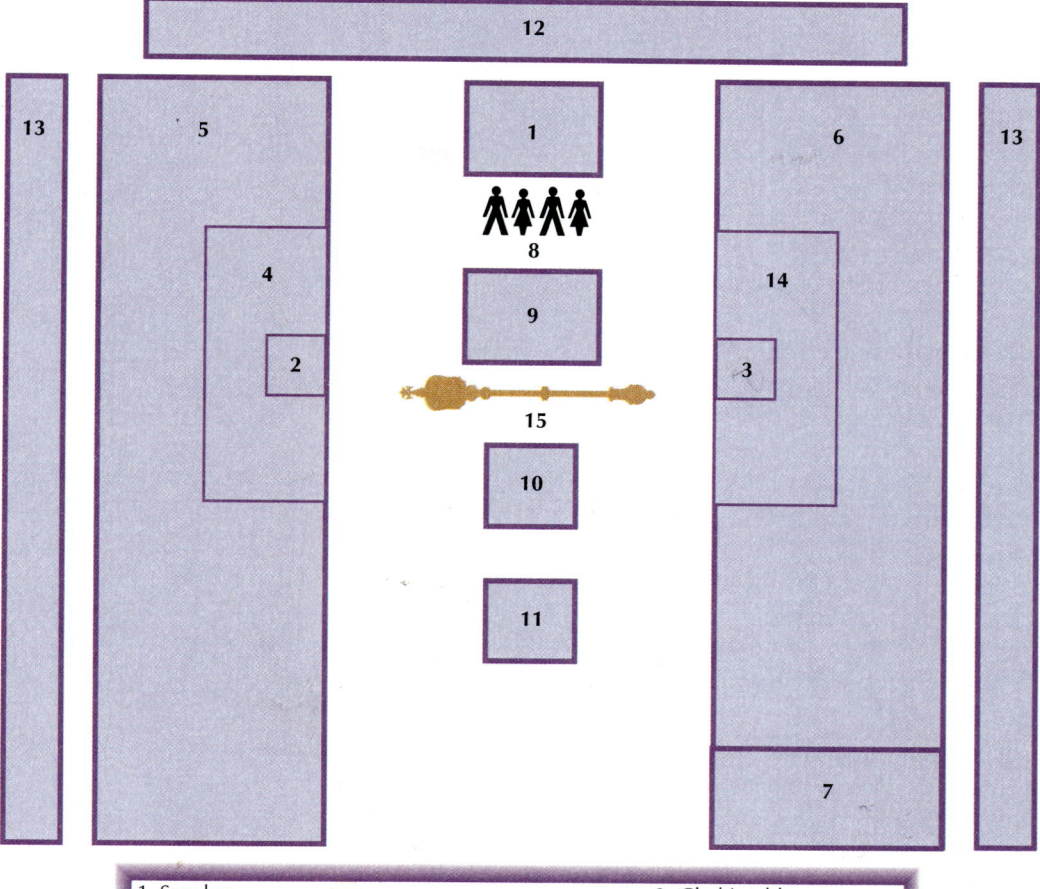

1 Speaker	9 Clerk's table
2 Prime Minister	10 Sergeant-at-arms
3 Leader of the Opposition	11 Hansard reporter
4 Cabinet	12 Press gallery
5 Backbenchers — Government party	13 Visitors' galleries
6 Backbenchers — Members of the Opposition party	14 Shadow Cabinet (Opposition)
7 Members of the other Opposition party	15 Mace
8 Page boys and page girls	

Speaker
- Oversees all business in the House of Commons.
- Announces the results of votes in the House of Commons.
- Controls and directs Question Period.
- Disciplines unruly members of Parliament.

Prime Minister
- Chooses cabinet ministers.
- Asks governor general to name new senators and judges.
- Works with provincial premiers on issues of national concern.
- Represents Canada on trips abroad.

Cabinet Ministers
- Advise prime minister.
- Help to form and defend government policy.
- Direct the affairs of their department.

Leader of the Opposition
- Leader of the second-largest party in the House of Commons.
- Role is to criticize and try to improve government legislation.

Shadow Cabinet
- Members of the Opposition appointed to scrutinize cabinet ministers and government policies.
- Helps to shape Opposition party policies.

CANADIAN GOVERNMENT IN ACTION

39

programs such as medicare and for government ownership of key industries such as transportation. The Progressive Conservatives have been considered centre-right because of their historical support for free enterprise — for limiting the role of government and keeping business and industry in private hands. However, both parties have been remarkably flexible on policy over the years. For example, free trade with the United States was historically a Liberal policy until Prime Minister Brian Mulroney's Progressive Conservatives took it up in 1985. Then the Liberals switched sides to oppose free trade in the 1988 election.

Sometimes new parties spring up on the political left or right to represent viewpoints outside the platforms of the major parties. For example, the NDP began as a socialist (leftist) party — the Co-operative Commonwealth Federation (CCF) — in 1933. It appealed to farmers and workers who believed that their voices were not being heard by the two major parties. The CCF came up with new ideas for social programs, including unemployment insurance and medicare. At first their ideas were considered by many people to be outlandish, but gradually many of these ideas became part of Liberal and Progressive Conservative policy. By the 1940s and 1950s, the CCF was losing support in federal elections. In 1961 it broadened and moderated its platform to attract voters in the middle of the political spectrum under its new name, the New Democratic Party.

More recently, two new parties have risen to political power. After the 1988 election, the Reform Party — already popular in Alberta for its focus on western concerns — gained wider support. Under leader Preston Manning, the Reform Party won 52 seats in the 1993 federal election — all but one in the four western provinces. In 1991, the Bloc Québécois was founded by former federal

In 1987 Frank McKenna's Liberals won every seat in the New Brunswick legislature. Do you think democracy can operate when all elected members of a government are from the same party?

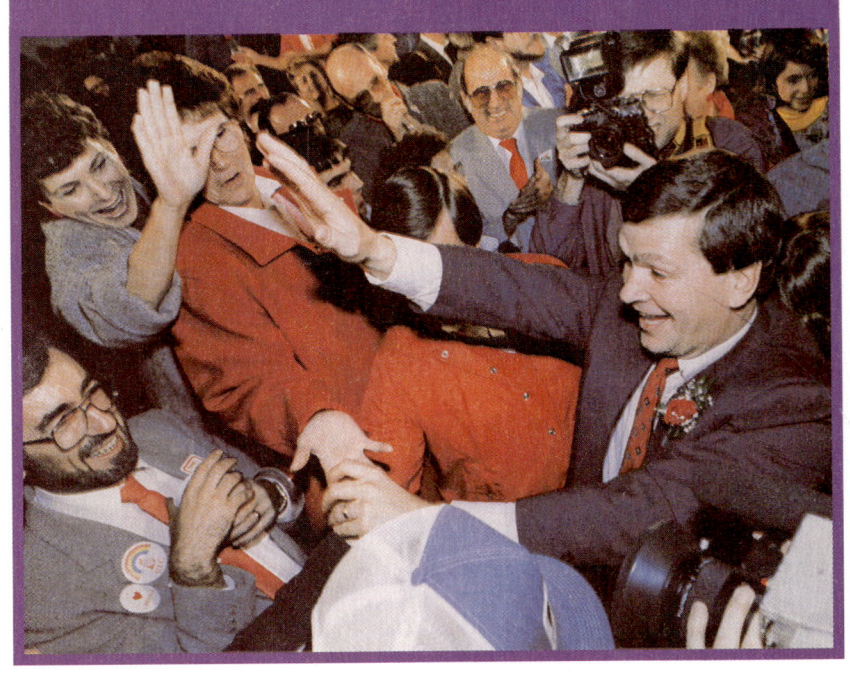

Elections in Canada occur over several intense, gruelling weeks. This photograph shows former prime minister Brian Mulroney on the campaign trail during the 1988 election.

POLITICAL FIRSTS FOR WOMEN

Kim Campbell became the first woman prime minister of Canada on June 25, 1993. Some other firsts for women in Canadian politics:

Get the vote — 1917 in federal elections for women with close relatives in the military; all women in federal elections, 1918.

First MP — Agnes MacPhail, 1921.

First senator — Liberal Cairine Wilson, 1930.

First federal cabinet minister — Ellen Fairclough, secretary of state, 1957.

First provincial party leader — Alexa McDonough, N.S., NDP, November 1980.

First premier — Rita Johnston, B.C., April 1991 (selected by party).

First elected premier — Catherine Callbeck, PEI, March 29, 1993.

First to run for national leadership — Rosemary Brown, NDP, 1975.

First leader of a national party — Audrey McLaughlin, NDP, December 1989.

Quote: "Thousands of (little girls) across Canada can actually say realistically: 'I would like to be prime minister of Canada.'" — political scientist Sylvia Bashevkin on the impact of Ms. Campbell's rise to the top.

Source: Adapted from The Canadian Press.

These four women were pioneers in the struggle to win the right to full political participation for Canadian women. Research the particular contributions made by each of these women.

PARTY PLATFORMS: 1993 ELECTION

	CONSERVATIVES	LIBERALS
DEFICIT REDUCTION	Progressive Conservative leader Kim Campbell has vowed to erase, over five years, the federal government's annual budget deficit.	The Liberals promise to reduce the deficit gradually to about 3 percent of gross domestic product, from 5.2 percent now. They also vow to eliminate the GST.
JOB CREATION	Increased trade and low inflation are the keys to creating jobs, the Tories say. The party says that it will not launch any major new job-creation programs because they would drive up the deficit and erode business confidence. In addition, the Tories have tightened eligibility rules for unemployment insurance.	The Liberals say that they will create jobs by: redirecting $100 million in existing spending over four years to a high-tech venture capital fund; encouraging banks to lend more money to small businesses; and launching a $5-million public works program to improve roads and other public facilities, with costs shared evenly by Ottawa and provincial and municipal governments.
SOCIAL PROGRAMS	Campbell has talked about eliminating medicare coverage for medically unnecessary services, but has not said what that would include. The Tories add that some social programs will have to be cut.	Liberal leader Jean Chrétien says that he is committed to maintaining medicare in its present form across Canada and will fight any move to introduce user fees. The party says that expanding the number of subsidized day-care spaces is a priority.
CRIME AND PUNISHMENT	The Tories recently passed amendments to the Young Offenders Act so that youths charged with murder can be tried in adult courts. Campbell has also called for tougher sentences for violent young offenders. Recently, the government passed laws to protect women from men who follow and threaten them, and to make possession of child pornography an offence punishable by five years in prison.	Among Chrétien's proposals: tighter gun-control laws; more funding for women's shelters; minimum five-year prison sentences for people convicted of living off child prostitution; and stricter controls on parole for high-risk offenders. The Liberals also say that they would double the maximum sentence for youths convicted of first-degree murder to ten years.
POLITICAL REFORM	Campbell says that she would prevent former MPs from collecting pensions until they turn fifty-five, allow more free votes in the House of Commons, and require lobbyists to disclose more information about their activities.	Along with more free votes for MPs, the Liberals say that they favour much tougher controls on lobbyists, including disclosure of both paid and voluntary work that lobbyists do for political parties.

NEW DEMOCRATS	REFORM	BLOC QUÉBÉCOIS
NDP leader Audrey McLaughlin says that the way to reduce the deficit is to ensure that more people are working and paying taxes. The party says that it would phase out the GST while imposing a minimum 14-percent corporate tax and raising taxes on those earning over $100 000.	One of the centrepieces of Reform leader Preston Manning's campaign is his promise to eliminate the deficit in three years. Among the cuts: eliminating all direct subsidies to business, reducing foreign aid, and targeting Old Age Security benefits toward low-income earners.	The Bloc advocates a reduction in federal spending of about $5 billion annually. Another $5 billion a year would be transferred from existing programs to job-creation programs. The Bloc maintains that at least $6 billion could be trimmed from government spending without touching social programs.
McLaughlin says that her party's promises — including vows to scrap the GST and create more day-care spaces — would generate 300 000 jobs over five years. The NDP pledges to tear up the Canada–U.S. Free Trade Agreement, which it says has cost Canada jobs.	The party maintains that high deficits and taxes are silent killers of jobs. Reduce those burdens, Manning says, and the private sector will create more employment. The party would not spend public money on job creation.	Bloc leader Lucien Bouchard says that he will continue to demand increased federal funding for job-creation programs in the province. The Bloc would also seek complete control of the unemployment insurance program in Quebec.
Like the Liberals, New Democrats pledge to maintain medicare in its present form. The NDP also promises to double the number of day-care spaces to 600 000 and create 47 000 child-care jobs.	Manning says that his party would let the provinces decide how to administer medicare—including the right to charge user fees. Reform would also cut about $5 billion over three years from the unemployment insurance program. They do not advocate additional funding for day-care.	The Bloc says that it opposes medicare user fees and supports universality—but says that provinces, not Ottawa, should control social programs. As well, the party wants Ottawa to hand over complete control of education, manpower, and training, while continuing to provide funding.
The NDP says that it would attack what it sees as the root causes of crime — including poverty, unemployment, and the physical and sexual abuse of children. It also advocates the publication of names of sexual offenders who are released on parole. It says that it would establish a crime-prevention council to work with provinces and municipalities.	Manning says that it is time to emphasize victims' rights rather than those of criminals. He wants to eliminate the automatic right to parole for repeat offenders, ensure that noncitizens, other than refugees, who are convicted of indictable offences face deportation, and ensure that fourteen- and fifteen-year-olds who are charged with repeated serious offences are tried in adult courts.	No policies announced yet.
McLaughlin was the first party leader to call for an impartial review of MPs' pensions. The NDP says that it would encourage civil servants to point out waste in their departments by passing legislation to protect so-called whistle-blowers. The party also favours abolishing the Senate.	The party supports more free votes for MPs, more referendums on major national issues, and the right to recall unpopular MPs. Reform says that MPs should not be allowed to collect pensions until age sixty. Manning is a longtime supporter of a Triple-E (elected, effective, and equal) Senate.	The Bloc's primary goal is Quebec independence. In the meantime, it favours abolishing the Senate.

Source: Adapted from *Maclean's Magazine*, Maclean Hunter Ltd. September 13, 1993, pp. 20–21.

CANADIAN GOVERNMENT IN ACTION

When the leader of a political party resigns, delegates from across Canada are brought together to select a new leader. In the 1993 Progressive Conservative leadership race, Kim Campbell won over her nearest rival, Jean Charest.

Progressive Conservative MP Lucien Bouchard and six other Quebec MPs. Dedicated to independence for Quebec, these MPs left their former parties to sit in the House of Commons as the Bloc Québécois. The Bloc won 54 seats in the 1993 election — all in Quebec — to become the official opposition party. The rise of regionally based federal parties marked a major change in Canadian politics.

On the Campaign Trail

Once candidates for political office are nominated, they hit the campaign trail. Campaign headquarters are the scene of a flurry of activity in the weeks before the election as paid staff and volunteers work to get their candidate into office. Candidates and their advisers consult communications specialists, pollsters, advertising people, and public relations firms for advice on running a successful campaign. They carefully tailor their messages about their party's platform to attract people in their own ridings. They look for a package of policies that will have something for everybody in their constituencies.

Then campaign workers issue news releases, hand out leaflets, campaign buttons, and bumper stickers, and make phone calls to people on the voters' list. Party headquarters from coast to coast spend millions of dollars to broadcast political announcements on radio and television and in newspapers. Volunteers knock on doors, trying to convince people to support their candidate.

Most people get their information about candidates from the media, especially from television. Candidates try very hard to make TV coverage work for them. Since paid television ads and free-time broadcasts are strictly limited by law, party strategists try to time political announcements so that they get free coverage in evening news broadcasts. They also create "photo opportunities" for the media by placing their candidates near eye-catching backdrops. Candidates learn how to deliver short, concise political messages that fit into the fifteen- to thirty-second time slots of most TV newscasts. Projecting the right image on TV can sometimes make the difference between winning and losing an election.

THE GOVERNMENT IN ACTION

By midnight on election day, the results in all but a few ridings are usually known. Newly elected MPs begin thinking about the job ahead, and the losers get ready to return to normal life. In most elections, one party wins more than half the seats in Parliament and forms the government. That party's leader becomes the new prime minister. This is known as a **majority government**. In this way, a vote for a local MP is also a vote for a political party and a prime minister. The party with the second-largest number of elected MPs forms the official opposition, and its leader becomes the leader of the opposition.

Sometimes the results are so close, however, that no party wins a majority of the seats in Parliament. In 1979, the Progressive Conservatives won 136 seats, but the three opposition parties — Liberals (114), New Democratic Party (26), and Social Credit (6) — won a combined total of 146 seats. This is known as a **minority government**. To stay in power, minority governments have to listen more carefully to opposition parties. Otherwise, the opposition might hold a vote of nonconfidence and force an election.

The Prime Minister

National party leaders are picked at a national leadership convention before an election campaign. During the campaign, these party leaders are the main symbol of their party and the major spokespersons for party policy. The party leaders also try to demonstrate the leadership qualities needed to become prime minister. These qualities include a solid education, personal charisma, political experience, fluency in French and English, a firm grasp of world affairs, and skill in public speaking.

The prime minister of Canada has wide-ranging powers. With recommendations from other government officials, the prime minister makes most of the important appointments in government, including cabinet ministers, senators, Supreme Court justices, *ambassadors*, and important civil servants. As the leader of the cabinet, the prime minister also plays a key role in making government policy. Together with other cabinet ministers, the prime minister decides what new laws to introduce as bills in Parliament. In addition, the prime minister and the cabinet must set the nation's course on foreign policy and negotiate international agreements. The prime minister also represents Canada in travels abroad and helps to create the image that other nations have of Canada and Canadians.

The Cabinet

Cabinet's main job is to draft policies for all Canadians. Acid rain and air pollution, youth unemployment and prison reform, and fisheries and farm subsidies are just a few of many policy areas under cabinet control. Cabinet decisions are influenced by the governing party's platform, by special-interest groups, by the press, and by demands from people in the ridings. But in the end, cabinet's policy decisions are made in secret discussions behind closed doors. In fact, cabinet ministers must swear an oath to keep "secret all such matters as shall be treated, debated and resolved on" in cabinet.

Ethel Blondin was the first Native woman elected to the House of Commons. She was first elected as a member of the Liberal Party in 1988 for the riding of Western Arctic. Do you think her election will help bring about change for the rights of Native women?

Every policy has to be approved by the whole cabinet before it is put into action. Cabinet members sometimes get into fierce disagreements over policy in cabinet meetings. Once a policy decision is reached in cabinet, however, everyone must support it in public. This principle is called cabinet solidarity. Occasionally, a cabinet member finds it impossible to publicly support a cabinet decision and resigns from cabinet.

HOW LAWS ARE MADE

A THE ROLE OF THE CABINET

- A policy proposal is presented to cabinet by a minister.
- Cabinet accepts or rejects the proposal.
- A Bill is drafted by the Department of Justice.

B THE ROLE OF THE HOUSE OF COMMONS

First Reading: Minister introduces title of bill to the House and asks for approval to print the bill.

Second Reading: Bill is debated in principle, each MP speaking only once. Bill is approved in principle.

Commitee Stage

- Standing Committee: Bill is referred to standing committee for clause-by-clause examination.

- Committee of the Whole: Recommendations of the standing committee are examined, amendments are made, and bill is debated.

Third Reading: Final reading is routine, vote taken.

C THE ROLE OF THE SENATE

First Reading
Second Reading } Process is similar to the House of Commons.
Committee Stage
Third Reading

If the bill is amended, it is returned to the House of Commons.

D THE ROLE OF THE CROWN

The bill is signed by the governor general (on behalf of the monarch) and it becomes law.

PARLIAMENTARY STANDING COMMITTEES, 1991
- Aboriginal Affairs
- Agriculture
- Communications and Culture
- Consumer and Corporate Affairs
- Energy, Mines and Resources
- Environment
- External Affairs and Trade
- Finance
- Forestry and Fisheries
- Health and Welfare, Women
- Human Rights
- Industry, Science and Technology
- Justice
- Labour, Employment, Immigration
- Management
- Multiculturalism and Citizenship
- National Defence, Veterans
- Official Languages
- Transport
- Public Accounts
- Privileges and Elections

Source: Adapted from *Canada's Government and Law: Rights and Responsibilities,* Donald M. Santor, Prentice-Hall, 1992.

Here, Liberal leader Jean Chrétien is applauded by caucus members during Question Period. After the Liberal victory in 1993, Chrétien moved from leader of the opposition to take up his seat as prime minister.

Backbenchers in the House of Commons

When the House of Commons is in session, cabinet members sit in the front row on their party's side of the floor. Behind them are the government **backbenchers** — all the MPs in the government's party who are not in cabinet. Although backbenchers do not have as much political muscle as cabinet ministers and play a smaller role in making policy decisions, they do meet almost weekly with the prime minister, the cabinet, and party members in the Senate in what is called a party *caucus*. No record of the meetings is kept so that MPs can talk freely among themselves. In caucus, backbenchers have a chance to play a role in making policy decisions.

Many policies approved in cabinet are written as bills — proposed new laws — and brought to Parliament for approval. The party in power naturally does everything possible to keep major bills from being voted down because the government must resign if defeated. Party discipline is very strong in Canada. An MP called the party whip makes sure that MPs show up when major bills come up for a vote in Parliament. The party whip also checks to see that every MP voted with the party.

The Opposition in the House of Commons

Across the floor of the House of Commons from the government benches are the benches of the **opposition** — all the MPs who do not belong to the party in power. Opposition parties serve as "watchdogs" to make sure that the party in power acts responsibly. The opposition examines and criticizes government policies, and it suggests changes in government bills. The House of Commons meets every afternoon when Parliament is in session. There is a daily question period, when the opposition grills the prime minister and other cabinet ministers on almost any topic. House debates — especially exchanges during the daily question period — are often broadcast on radio and TV and reported in the newspapers.

Passing a Bill

Making new law is the main task of the Canadian Parliament. A bill can be introduced in either the House of Commons or the Senate, but most are introduced in the House. A bill becomes a Canadian law, however, only after it has been approved by Parliament as a whole. All bills go through three readings, and they are discussed and debated at every step. At the first reading, a bill is presented to the House of Commons. At the second reading, the pros and cons of the bill are debated. During the second reading, the bill is carefully examined and sometimes amended. At the third reading, members of the House vote for or against the bill. If the bill is accepted, it goes to the Senate for approval. There, too, the bill goes through three readings. Once a bill is approved by both the House and the Senate, it is signed by the governor general and becomes Canadian law.

WHAT CAN YOU DO TO INFLUENCE YOUR GOVERNMENT?

Where do you stand on Senate reform? Youth violence? Pollution in the Great Lakes? Needle-replacement programs for drug users? The "right to die"? More powerful weapons for police officers? Gay rights? Abortion? You do not have to wait until you are eligible to vote to make your views known to your government. The member of Parliament who represents you has an office in your riding. Most MPs try to get back to their offices often in order to talk with their constituents. They also pay attention to letters and telephone calls from their constituents — after all, these are the people who put them into office and keep them there. Your provincial legislator also has an office in your riding and listens to the feelings and concerns of constituents, including you. You can also contact members of your local government. You have the right to make your views known to your representatives in government by phoning, writing letters, or talking with them in person. You can also join a political party and share your opinions at party meetings.

Joining a special-interest group is another way to have a say in politics. There are groups working for political change in all kinds of areas, including education, youth employment opportunities, poverty, AIDS, family violence, recycling, and racial equality. You might join Pollution Probe or Students Against Drunk Driving (SADD) or a dozen other groups. These pressure groups help make other Canadians — and Canadian politicians — aware of their aims and objectives. Politicians respond to the needs in their community, but it is up to individual Canadians to make their views known.

You can also take part in letter-writing campaigns or in peaceful political demonstrations. These actions increase the pressure on MPs and other government officials to listen and respond to the public's wishes. Recently, teens in British Columbia demonstrated against logging in local mountains after a city council voted to issue a logging permit.

Students at the University of Toronto staged a rally to protest government cutbacks in funding for Ontario universities. A group of high school students launched a recycling program for neighbourhood parks to show the local council they cared about neighbourhood recycling. One Canadian teenager sparked nation-wide attention when she started a campaign against violence on television. She hopes to get a federal law passed to set guidelines about violence on prime-time television.

You can do something about issues you care about. You can become informed by reading newspapers, following TV news, joining special-interest groups or political parties, going to public meetings, and talking with friends and family. Then you'll be ready to get involved in the action. The success of a democracy depends on the willingness of its citizens to take an active role in public life.

Canadians do not have to wait until election time to make their concerns known to the government. Peaceful protests such as this march on Parliament Hill allow Canadian concerns to be heard by the government. What are some of other ways you can get a government to listen to your concerns?

KNOWING THE KEY PEOPLE, PLACES, AND EVENTS

In your notes, clearly identify and explain the significance of each of the following:

> Executive Branch
> Legislative Branch
> Patronage
> Bills
> Minority Government
> Opposition
> Cabinet Members
> Judiciary
> Senate
> Majority Goverment
> Backbenchers

FOCUS YOUR KNOWLEDGE

1. Why has the role of municipal government undergone significant changes over the course of Canadian history?
2. List the three branches of government and explain the function of each branch.
3. In groups of six, role-play a session of government by having members of the group represent each of the following: the prime minister, cabinet members, backbenchers, the opposition, and senators. Choose an issue that can be debated while the government is in session.
4. Explain what is meant by "cabinet solidarity." Does cabinet solidarity enable governments to operate more effectively?
5. Explain why there is a push for Senate reform in Canada by outlining the Senate's original role and the reasons why many Canadians feel the Senate no longer serves a useful purpose.

APPLY YOUR KNOWLEDGE

1. By voting in a federal election, Canadians express their preference not only for the local member of Parliament, but also for the person they wish to become prime minister and the party they wish to govern Canada. As a voter, would you base your decision on the local candidates, the leaders of the federal political parties, or the policies of the parties? Explain your answer.
2. In selecting cabinet ministers, the prime minister must consider a variety of factors. List, in order of importance, three factors the prime minister considers when selecting cabinet ministers, and defend your ranking. How

important is it that cabinet ministers have experience in the areas for which they are responsible?

3. Explain how party discipline can prevent members of Parliament from voting according to their personal views. Do you think MPs should be forced out of a political party if they do not support a policy of the party?

4. Explain the role of the opposition in Parliament. Do you think their role is beneficial to the process of drafting laws and governing Canada? If you were a member of the opposition, how would you respond to (a) a bill that you supported in principle; (b) a bill that you opposed in principle; (c) a rumour of government error or corruption?

5. Do you think Question Period in the House of Commons should be open to the media? In answering this question, consider freedom of the press and Canadians' right to know what their government is doing, as well as the ways in which MPs take advantage of the media's presence to gain free publicity.

6. Explain the process by which a bill becomes a law and why it is necessary for the bill to go through three readings before being passed.

7. Using newspapers, research a current issue that concerns the federal government. Develop an organizer that compares the views of each of the major parties about this issue.

EXTEND YOUR KNOWLEDGE

1. Do some research on your local government. Try to find out (a) what the executive head and the members of the local legislature are called; (b) who represents your area; (c) who the reeve or mayor is in your community; and (d) a few of the important issues your local government is dealing with. Once you have gathered the information, present it to the class visually by using a bulletin board or charts.

2. After doing some newspaper research, prepare your own proposal for Senate reform. In preparing your proposal be sure to consider regional concerns, Native issues, and women's demand for equal representation. Also consider how senators should be selected; how many should come from each province; whether the principle of representation by population should be used; and what powers the Senate should have. Check your library's vertical files for newspaper articles on Senate reform.

3. Prepare a list of all the ways in which an individual can influence government. When your list is complete, select an issue of concern to you. Write a letter expressing your concern. Be sure to consider where the letter should be sent: the local newspaper, a politician, a company, or an individual.

CHAPTER 3
CANADA'S JUDICIAL SYSTEM

GLOSSARY TERMS

Parole Officers People who supervise a prisoner who has been released into the community before his or her prison sentence has been completed.
Rehabilitation Helping a criminal return to a useful and law-abiding life.
Disposition A sentence (punishment) in Youth Court.
Alternative Measures Program An alternative to a formal trial, usually for first-time offenders guilty of less serious offences.
Grievance A complaint of a wrongdoing or an unjust act done to someone by another person.

FOCUS ON:
- the difference between civil and criminal law
- the role of the police
- the role of the courts
- youth and criminal law
- the Young Offenders Act

Flip through a newspaper and you'll probably come across at least half a dozen stories about laws, lawmaking, and law-breaking. Laws are part of the fabric of everyday life in Canada. They define our responsibilities and give us ways to end disagreements peacefully. They protect the rights of individual Canadians and of minority groups in Canada. Laws also help make our lives safer and more predictable. Above all, they reflect our deepest values and most cherished beliefs as a society. As Canadian society changes over time, however, so do Canadian laws. "Laws should be like clothes," a lawyer once said. "They should be made to fit the people they serve."

The two most important kinds of law in Canada are **criminal law** and **civil law**. Criminal law concerns actions considered to be crimes against the community as a whole. When crimes are committed, the government — not private citizens — takes action. For example, victims of a gang attack are not expected to track down and punish their attackers; it is the government's job to find criminals and bring them to justice.

Civil law concerns property and civil rights. It covers all kinds of relationships between individual people or groups of people, including written and verbal contracts, separation and divorce, wills, relations between employers and workers, the buying and selling of goods, and the renting of an apartment or purchase of a home. In civil law, individual citizens or groups — not the government — bring cases to court. A civil law case might be about a dispute over personal injuries resulting from a car accident, the terms of a divorce, or an employer's treatment of an employee. Canada's civil law provides a fair and orderly way to settle private disagreements among its citizens.

CLOSE-UP ON CRIMINAL LAW

Let's take a closer look at criminal law. The Criminal Code of Canada specifies what acts are considered crimes and sets the maximum penalty for every criminal offence. Because the Criminal Code is federal law, it applies across Canada.

Parliament is always updating old provisions in the Criminal Code and passing new laws to deal with new criminal actions such as the pirating of computer software or the tape recording of private cellular-phone conversations. Some of the most important additions to Canadian criminal law are the Young Offenders Act, the Narcotic Control Act, and the Official Secrets Act.

Summary Conviction and Indictable Offences

In the Criminal Code, crimes are either **summary conviction offences** or **indictable offences**. Summary conviction offences — including making

PUBLIC AND PRIVATE LAW

In Canada, there are several types of law, which are divided into two main categories: public law and private law.

Public Law
Public law deals with issues related to matters between citizens and the government or between different levels of government. Included in public law are criminal law, administrative law, and constitutional law.

Criminal Law: Concerns acts that are committed by individuals against society in general and that are deemed to be unacceptable and deserving of punishment. It is with this type of law that people are most likely to come in contact with, either as victims, accused, witnesses, or jurors.

Administrative Law: Concerns issues between individuals and government agencies, such as legal cases involving immigration or workers' compensation.

Constitutional Law: Concerns the division of powers between the various levels of government — an often troubling issue in Canada. Courts often make rulings about which level of government has jurisdiction over a certain matter.

Private Law
Private law deals with those areas of law related to disputes between individuals. In almost all cases, private-law matters fall under provincial jurisdiction and therefore can vary from province to province. The emphasis in private law is to have victims of wrongdoing compensated in some way by the perpetrator of the act.

Contract Law: Spells out what constitutes legally binding agreements.

Tort Law: Concerns wrongs committed by one person against another ("torts"). The person who claims that a wrong has been committed against him or her may sue the wrongdoer for damages.

Family Law: Deals with relationships among members of a family. Included in this body of laws are marriage and divorce laws as well as laws related to child custody and support.

THE CANADIAN CHARTER OF RIGHTS AND FREEDOMS: LEGAL RIGHTS

7. Everyone has the right to life, liberty and security of the person and the right not to be deprived thereof except in accordance with the principles of fundamental justice.
8. Everyone has the right to be secure against unreasonable search or seizure.
9. Everyone has the right not to be arbitrarily detained or imprisoned.
10. Everyone has the right on arrest or detention
    (a) to be informed promptly of the reasons therefor;
    (b) to retain and instruct counsel without delay and to be informed of that right; and
    (c) to have the validity of the detention determined by way of habeas corpus and to be released if the detention is not lawful.
11. Any person charged with an offence has the right
    (a) to be informed without unreasonable delay of the specific offence;
    (b) to be tried within a reasonable time;
    (c) not to be compelled to be a witness in proceedings against that person in respect of the offence;
    (d) to be presumed innocent until proven guilty according to law in a fair and public hearing by an independent and impartial tribunal;
    (e) not to be denied reasonable bail without just cause;
    (f) ... to the benefit of trial by jury where the maximum punishment for the offence is imprisonment for five years or a more severe punishment;
    ...
    (h) if finally acquitted of the offence, not to be tried for it again and, if finally found guilty and punished for the offence, not to be tried or punished for it again; and
    (i) if found guilty of the offence and if the punishment for the offence has been varied between the time of commission and the time of sentencing, to the benefit of the lesser punishment.
12. Everyone has the right not to be subjected to any cruel and unusual treatment or punishment.
13. A witness who testifies in any proceedings has the right not to have any incriminating evidence so given used to incriminate that witness in any other proceedings, except in a prosecution for perjury or for the giving of contradictory evidence.

Police officers, whether as members of the Royal Canadian Mounted Police (RCMP) or a provincial or municipal force, help to ensure that Canadian society is safe and orderly. Have you personally had to deal with the police at any time?

indecent phone calls, setting off false fire alarms, and causing a disturbance — are generally less serious and carry a maximum penalty of six months in jail. However, indictable offences — including arson, break and enter, dangerous driving causing death, forgery, and possession of a dangerous weapon — are more serious. These crimes carry maximum sentences of over five years in jail. For the most serious indictable offences, such as murder, the maximum sentence is life imprisonment.

THE ROLE OF THE POLICE

What happens when a crime occurs in Canada? That's where the criminal justice system — the police, courts, and the prison system — comes into play. Criminal laws are just words on a page until police officers enforce them. Canada has a national police force called the Royal Canadian Mounted Police (RCMP), which enforces federal laws and polices federal property. Ontario and Quebec have their own provincial police forces — the Ontario Provincial Police and the Sûreté du Québec. In addition, about 750 municipalities in Canada have their own police forces. These municipal forces range from the very large police departments of Metropolitan Toronto and Montreal to single-person forces in small rural townships. The RCMP often provides policing services for provinces and municipalities that have not established their own police forces.

Police officers spend much of their time doing jobs such as directing traffic, controlling large crowds, making reports on car accidents, finding missing persons, testifying in court, and helping to settle family disputes. But they also investigate crimes and arrest criminals. To carry out investigations, police officers need the power to take people into custody, question them, search them and places, and seize evidence. The law tries to strike a balance between allowing police the powers needed to do their jobs and protecting the rights of individual Canadians. The Canadian Charter of Rights and Freedoms guarantees Canadians specific legal rights. Many of these rights place limits on the actions of police, courts, and prisons.

Police Questioning

Police can question anyone, including eyewitnesses and suspects, who may have information considered important in a criminal investigation. But this information must be freely and knowingly given to

When arrested for a crime, citizens are taken in for questioning by the police. Would you know your rights if you were detained for questioning?

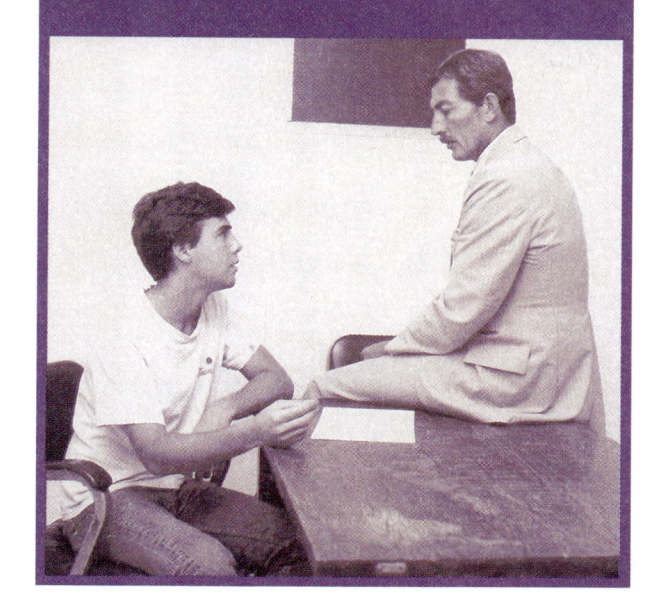

the police. Except in a few special circumstances, Canadians cannot be forced to answer questions against their will.

Arrest and Search

Police officers usually do not make arrests (take suspects into custody) for less serious offences. Instead, an officer might write out an "appearance notice," which states the nature of the offence and sets a date for a court appearance. Driving offences under the Highway Traffic Act are often handled this way. Or the officer might appear before a judge or justice of the peace and provide information about the offence. A summons or court order might then be issued, ordering the person named in the summons to appear in court on a certain date.

Police officers do make arrests, however, for serious crimes. But they must have "reasonable and probable" grounds before putting suspects under arrest. Mere suspicion or a hunch is not enough. In making an arrest, the officer must tell the suspect the nature of the offence and use only as much force as is "reasonable and necessary." Once under arrest, suspects are taken to the police station, where they may be fingerprinted, photographed, and searched. Depending on the crime, a number of federal and provincial laws also let police officers search a suspect's car and premises.

Suspects may also be questioned about events related to the crime. But they must be warned that they have the rights to remain silent and to seek legal counsel. A bail hearing and a court date must also be set as soon as possible. After all these steps are completed, suspects are either released or kept in jail until the trial.

THE ROLE OF THE COURTS

Once an arrest is made and charges have been laid against a suspect, the court system takes over. The courts are a shared federal–provincial responsibility. The federal government is responsible

These two police officers are arresting a suspected criminal. How much force should police be allowed to use in making an arrest?

CANADA'S JUDICIAL SYSTEM

55

FROM ARREST TO TRIAL: CRIMINAL PROCEDURE IN CANADA

Arrest: Once arrested, the accused must appear before a provincial judge or justice of the peace within twenty-four hours or be released. If the accused is not released, he or she is entitled to a bail hearing.

Bail Hearing: The decision whether or not to release someone on bail depends on the nature of the crime he or she is accused of, the circumstances of the charge, and the person's past record. If released on bail, the accused is told to appear in court at a later date.

Appearance Before a Provincial Court Judge: At this appearance, the charge is read and the accused enters a plea of guilty or not guilty. If a guilty plea is entered, the accused is sentenced. If a not guilty plea is entered, the case moves on to a trial by judge or trial by judge and jury. The accused can elect trial by judge and jury only for less serious indictable offences.

Preliminary Hearing: A preliminary hearing is designed to determine if there is enough evidence to put the accused on trial. If a judge concludes that there is insufficient evidence, the charges are dismissed. If there is sufficient evidence, the case proceeds to trial.

Trial: The following steps occur at the trial:

1. The charges are read.
2. The accused enters a plea.
3. The Crown attorney presents evidence against the accused.*
4. The defence attorney presents evidence in favour of the acccused.*
5. Both the Crown and the defence make their final arguments.
6. A verdict is handed down. If guilty, the accused is sentenced. If the accused is found not guilty, the Crown may appeal the decision. Any appeal from the accused or the Crown must take place within thirty days of the conclusion of the trial.

*Both the Crown and the defence are given the opportunity to cross-examine each other's cases. If the defence feels the Crown's case is weak, it can ask that the charge be dismissed.

DO POLICE HAVE TOO MANY OR TOO FEW POWERS?

Due to an increase in violent crime, many police officers are demanding more police powers. A few Canadian police forces have already switched to semi-automatic weapons, and other Canadian forces want to follow their lead. Other officers are unhappy about the many rules and regulations that they have to obey. They feel that such restrictions keep them from doing their proper job — catching criminals. They want more freedom to carry out investigations. Some officers are even asking for the right to break the law if lawbreaking leads to a successful investigation. One RCMP commissioner argued that undercover police officers in particular should be able to break the law from time to time — including travelling with false identification papers, registering under false names in motels, and breaking speed limits.

But many Canadians are concerned about the use and misuse of police power. In one well-publicized case in Nova Scotia, Donald Marshall, a Micmac Native, was accused of murder. Police in Nova Scotia suppressed evidence pointing to another man as the killer. As a result, Marshall served twelve years in jail for a crime he did not commit. In another incident in Calgary, police seized a family of five at gunpoint, looking for the killer of a cab driver. It was the fourth time in five months that Calgary police arrested the wrong person.

As a result of such incidents and the increase in crime in Canada, many questions related to police powers have arisen. Write short personal responses to each of the following questions:

1. How should society "police" the police?
2. Do police officers "serve and protect" all Canadians?
3. How much power do the police need to be able to do their jobs?
4. What can be done to ensure good relations between the police and the communities they serve?

These 6000 police officers and their supporters staged a protest march to show their support for increased police powers.

THE CANADIAN COURT SYSTEM

Supreme Court of Canada
- The final court of appeal in all civil and criminal cases.
- Decides constitutional issues such as the powers of federal and provincial governments.

Supreme or Superior Court of the Province

Trial Division
- Hears all civil cases involving amounts of more than $7500.
- Hears serious criminal cases such as murder, rape, and treason.

Appeal Division
- Hears appeals from both the trial division and lower courts in both civil and criminal cases.

District and County Courts
- Hear civil cases involving amounts of less than $7500 as well as appeals from provincial courts.
- A judge, with or without a jury, hears less serious indictable offences such as theft.

Provincial and Magistrate's Courts
- A judge, with no jury present, hears cases involving summary conviction offences such as common assault, disturbing the peace, and petty theft.

Family Court
- Usually a part of the provincial or magistrate's courts.
- Hears cases involving family matters such as custody, child support, and adoption.

Youth Court
- Usually a part of the provincial or magistrate's courts.
- Hears cases involving youths aged twelve to seventeen who have been charged under the Young Offenders Act.

for the Supreme Court of Canada and the Federal Court of Canada. The provinces are responsible for all other courts in the nation. Every province has created its own court system, and as a result court systems vary from province to province. In general, however, higher provincial courts look after more serious cases and lower provincial courts handle less serious cases. Provincial supreme courts consider appeals from lower provincial courts, and the Supreme Court of Canada considers appeals from provincial courts and from the Federal Court.

The way in which a case proceeds through the courts depends on what kind of offence it concerns. Summary conviction offences are always tried before a provincial court judge. Indictable offences may be tried in different ways, depending on the crime and the choice of the accused person. Some cases are tried by a judge; others are tried by judge and jury. However, a jury trial is required under the Canadian Charter of Rights and Freedoms for the most serious crimes, including murder.

Innocent Until Proven Guilty

Courts have two main decisions to make. Is the accused person guilty or not? If so, what should the sentence (punishment) be? Firmly embedded in English common law and guaranteed in section 11(d) of the Canadian Charter of Rights and Freedoms is the important legal principle sometimes called the "presumption of innocence": any person charged with an offence is presumed innocent until proven guilty. In a 1935 court case, a famous British judge gave an often-quoted explanation of the presumption of innocence: "The prosecution must prove the guilt of the prisoner; there is no such burden placed on the prisoner to prove his innocence and it is sufficient for him to raise a doubt as to his guilt: he is not bound to satisfy the jury of his innocence." In effect, the presumption of innocence assumes that it is better for some criminals to escape punishment than for an innocent person to be unjustly punished.

The Criminal Trial

The trial starts when an accused comes into court to plead guilty or not guilty to the charges. If the plea is guilty, the judge will decide on the sentence (penalty). If the plea is not guilty, the case goes on to trial. Trials in Canada are based on the adversarial system. In today's courtrooms, the battle is a verbal duel between the Crown and the defence. The Crown attorney presents the government's case against the accused person. The counsel for the defence acts for the accused. The judge lets the Crown attorney and the defence counsel present their cases as they see fit — as long as the proceedings are in keeping with principles of justice. The judge's role is to make sure that the accused person gets a fair trial.

In **jury** trials, twelve people are picked from a group of about a hundred citizens chosen from the community at random, often from voters' lists. Each person must be accepted by both the Crown attorney and the defence counsel before becoming a jury member.

Once the jury is chosen, the trial begins. First, the Crown makes its case against the accused person. The Crown attorney calls witnesses to testify about what they know or have

---

After studying this cartoon, explain the issue and the cartoonist's point of view. Do you agree with the statement being made?

Cartoon: COURTHOUSE — WEEKLY MOTIONS
- Actions in Bad Faith — 100
- Claims Designed to Embarrass — 113
- Dilatory Proceedings — 327
- Frivolous Claims — 208
- Nitpicking & Pettifogging — 120
- Motions to Impoverish the Parties — 101
- Ridiculous Arguments — 217
- Relief From Lawyers' Negligence — 311
- Security for Lawyers' Fees — 109
- ...us Proceedings — ...
- Examinations — ...

Bertha Wilson was the first woman to be appointed to the Supreme Court of Canada. Considering the role of the Supreme Court, can you think of reasons why many women saw this as a significant achievement?

seen. When the Crown attorney finishes questioning a witness, the defence attorney can cross-examine in an attempt to show how the Crown witness's testimony is mistaken, inaccurate, or not believable. The Crown can also bring into the courtroom physical evidence such as weapons, clothing, tape recordings, photographs, and financial records. These items are usually identified by Crown witnesses. For example, a police officer might state that a bag of cocaine was found in the accused's car, or a forensics expert might testify about blood samples found on a shirt.

Then the defence makes its case by calling its own witnesses. The defence counsel does not have to prove that the accused is innocent, but merely that the Crown has failed to prove guilt beyond a reasonable doubt. Every defence witness can also be cross-examined by the Crown attorney. When all the evidence has been presented, the Crown attorney and defence counsel make their closing addresses to the jury, in which they sum up their cases for and against a verdict of guilty. In jury trials, the jury members leave the courtroom to gather in a private room where they discuss the evidence and reach a verdict. The jury's decision must be unanimous.

Sentencing

If the accused person is found guilty, the judge hands down a sentence. Judges evaluate all sorts of information when deciding on a sentence. They ask themselves questions such as the following: How serious is the crime? What has the victim suffered as

SENTENCING

Deterrence: Deterrence is the use of a sentence to discourage convicted offenders from repeating their crime. It also involves showing other would-be criminals how seriously the crime is viewed. The aim of deterrence is to prevent, or deter, others from committing the same offence.

Punishment: Punishment involves ensuring that offenders are given what the public considers their "just deserts." It should reflect what society considers the proper degree of social condemnation of the offenders' actions — the punishment should fit the crime.

Protection of the Public: The public has the right to be protected from criminal acts. For example, when criminals are imprisoned, they cannot commit other offences against society, so putting criminals in jail may make the streets safer.

Rehabilitation: A main concern in sentencing is to rehabilitate, or reform, offenders — to help them "mend their ways." Since all but a few inmates will eventually be released back into society, it is important that penal institutions help them become better members of society. Educational and vocational training and psychological counselling are some of the ways used to help inmates prepare for their release.

a result of the crime? Has the accused committed other crimes? Is he or she likely to be a danger to society? Many of the answers are presented in pre-sentencing reports prepared for the court by *parole officers*. Recently, crime victims have also been asked to present information called **victim impact statements** — a record of the victim's suffering and loss as a result of a crime. The defence lawyer and the Crown attorney can also bring forward additional information in an attempt to sway the judge to pass a lighter or heavier sentence.

The judge weighs all the information and then imposes a sentence. Depending on the crime, a judge has a number of available choices. One choice is a suspended sentence: the convicted person is released without serving the sentence, because the crime is not serious and he or she seems unlikely to commit a further offence. In this case, the person is usually placed on probation. He or she must be law-abiding and report regularly to a probation officer or be returned to court for further sentencing. A fine — a sum of money imposed as a penalty — is another choice. Compensation or restitution is another. The court may require the convicted person to pay back a victim for losses resulting from the crime. Imprisonment is yet another choice: the convicted person must spend a specified time in jail. An "intermittent" prison sentence is served in local jails during weekends or nights. A term of under two years is served in a provincial prison, and a term of over two years is served in a federal prison. A prisoner can apply for parole, or early release, after serving one-third of a sentence. Members of a parole board then hear the evidence and decide if the prisoner should be granted parole.

YOUTH AND CRIMINAL LAW

A newspaper article entitled "A Walk on Vancouver's Wild Side" reads, "The story is all too familiar to Vancouver-area residents. Just after midnight outside the shuttered shops of trendy Robson Street, one young man lay dead, another gravely injured; a third would be charged with murder.... It was yet another instance of youths turning on each other."

Stories about youth crime often make the headlines. They might be about a twelve-year-old attacked in a quiet neighbourhood by a gang of girls who were after her fashionable jacket. Or they might be about youths who steal a car for a joyride and end up in a four-car crash on the freeway, or about a rise in drug-related crimes among "street kids."

When young people break the law, how should they be treated? How can laws help control and prevent youth crime? How old should lawbreakers be before they are considered fully responsible adults? Canadians around dinner tables and in courtrooms across the nation are talking about teenage crime and trying to decide what ought to be done about young offenders.

Sparsely furnished cells such as this one serve as home for inmates across Canada. Do you think the prospect of spending time in prison acts as an effective deterrent to crime?

THE TEEN CRIME EXAMPLE

On a typical weekend in the late summer of 1992, four youths between the ages of nine and 12 robbed a Toronto pizzeria, armed with a .22 calibre rifle. In another part of the city, a 17-year-old used a loaded rifle in the theft of a bicycle from a 13-year-old. One police official observed, "All over Toronto, younger and younger people are committing violent crimes." Considerable publicity has been given to the increase in crimes committed by teenagers. A Statistics Canada report released in late 1991 disclosed that, while charges against adults for all types of crimes had increased by about 40 percent since 1987, the increase was a whopping 70 percent for young people under the age of 18. Some 15 percent of the 60 000 juvenile court cases heard in 1990–91 involved violent offences, up by a third from 1987. The most common was assault, then possession or use of weapons, followed by robbery. Significantly, teenagers are also more likely than any other age group to be victims of violent crime. About one in four victims of violence in Canada are in their teens.

Some observers have noted "the new quality" of youth crimes — the random, mindless viciousness, complete with a penchant for weapons. Of particular concern is why this situation exists.

A recent examination of the issue by the Toronto Star cited a number of experts who point to a disturbing lack of ethical certainty in our culture. "Many young people seem to have no clear idea of what is good and bad," the story read. "And for that we have ourselves to blame." Dave Crowe, a Toronto probation officer who has worked with youthful offenders for 25 years, had this to say: "The breakdown of traditional institutions has left an ethical vacuum. Young people are looking for a set of fair rules, but we're not giving it to them." Catherine Challin, a psychologist with the University of Toronto's faculty of behavioural science, commented, "There is so much selfishness, so much dedication to Me. The Me-Generation is raising kids who show the consequences." In arresting an 18-year-old who had robbed eight people at gunpoint, veteran Toronto Detective Sergeant Frank Craddock heard the teen ask, "Do I have to go to jail for this?" Said Craddock, "They don't seem to realize how serious what they're doing really is." He maintains that highly publicized teen gangs are spontaneous, poorly organized groups that are quickly discovered by the police:

They're just a bunch of guys who get a sense of power from guns and money. They're macho jerks, guys who want to be big shots. But they aren't very bright, and they can't keep their mouths shut, so they get caught pretty quickly. Whoever shows the most force seems to get the most respect and gets to be the leader. It's as simple as that.

Most teenagers are not involved in crime. But those who are, in many instances, have seemingly thrown interpersonal norms to the wind. At such time, the message that everything's relative becomes irrelevant, annoying, absurd. We need more. So do young people.

Source: Reprinted with the permission of Stoddart Publishing Co. Limited, Don Mills, Ontario.

Violent actions, such as this youth's shooting spree, which wounded three students in Burlington, Ontario, have prompted some to call for revisions to the Young Offenders Act. Do you think tougher penalties would reduce crime committed by Canada's youth?

Changing Views About Young Offenders

In early-nineteenth-century Canada, youths were treated just like adult offenders. Young offenders were locked up with adult criminals in foul local jails or grim federal institutions such as the old Kingston Penitentiary in Ontario. Young inmates listed in the 1888 records of Dorchester Penitentiary in New Brunswick included twelve-year-old Herbert Smith, who was serving five years for breaking and entering; eleven-year-old Edward Chambers, serving two years for burglary; and fourteen-year-old Robert Welsh, serving seven years for manslaughter. Silence, hard labour, and strict prison rules were the cornerstones of penitentiary life. Even the smallest offences were swiftly punished, often by severe blows and beatings.

By the end of the century, Canadian social reformers were insisting that young offenders should not be treated like adult criminals. Instead, they wanted to rescue youths from lives of poverty, neglect, and crime and to protect them from the harsh world of adult prisons. The motto of these reformers — sometimes called the "child-savers" — was, "It is wiser and less expensive to save children than to punish them."

Canadian law was changed to reflect the new view of young offenders. Under the **Juvenile Delinquency Act of 1908**, a young offender was to be treated, not as a criminal, but as "a misdirected and misguided child, and one needing aid, encouragement, help, and assistance." The Juvenile Delinquency Act marked a turning point in Canadian law. Youths were seen in law as having special needs and requiring help and guidance rather than punishment.

By the 1960s, times had changed and the 1908 law was outdated. Citizens, parents, police, lawyers, and social workers were demanding a more modern law — a law that still took into account the special needs of young lawbreakers but also protected the community from crime and discouraged criminal activities.

THE YOUNG OFFENDERS ACT

In April 1984, the Canadian Parliament passed new legislation called the **Young Offenders Act**, which created a national system for dealing with young lawbreakers. It applied to all young people from twelve to eighteen years of age and dealt with all offences listed in the Criminal Code. The new law kept the principle that young people sometimes make mistakes and should not be given the same punishments as adults. It also retained the idea that people who are not fully adult need help and guidance in changing their lives for the better. The emphasis in the Young

When teenagers get involved with drugs and/or alcohol, they often end up in trouble with the law. What can be done to help teenagers avoid the dangers of drug or alcohol abuse?

APPLYING THE LAW

Canada is governed by many laws created by numerous statutes. In the following case, the court had to consider the rights of the young offender under both the Young Offenders Act and the Canadian Charter of Rights and Freedoms. The principal defended his position by referring to sections of the Education Act. What decision would you have made if you had been presiding over the case?

R. v. JMG
(1986), Dominion Law Reports (4th) 277

The accused was a 14-year-old student in Grade 7 at a school in Thunder Bay, Ontario. One morning the principal received information from a teacher that the accused had been seen by another student placing some drugs in his socks. The principal telephoned another school principal for advice in dealing with the situation and then called a police officer for additional advice. The principal went to the accused's classroom and requested that the boy accompany him to the principal's office. In the office, in the presence of the vice-principal and another teacher, the principal informed the student that he had reason to believe that he was in possession of drugs and proceeded to ask the student to remove his shoes and socks. There was some delay during which time the student swallowed a rolled cigarette that he took out of his pant cuff. The principal then took some tin foil from the accused's right sock; the foil was found to contain three butts of rolled marijuana cigarettes. The principal called the police again. The accused was arrested and charged with possession of a narcotic. The police officer cautioned the student and read him his rights, as required by the Charter.

The student was found guilty under the Young Offenders Act and fined twenty-five dollars. The accused is appealing the decision on the grounds that there was a breach of his constitutional rights, namely, sections 8 and 10(b) of the Charter. These sections are as follows:

"8. Everyone has the right to be secure against unreasonable search or seizure.

10. Everyone has the right on arrest or detention ...

(b) to retain and instruct counsel without delay and be informed of that right...."

On the other hand, the principal claimed that he had a duty to act the way he did, as outlined by section 236 of the Education Act. This section requires a principal to maintain proper order and discipline in school.

1. With a classmate, prepare an argument in favour of convicting the accused.
2. With a classmate, prepare an argument in favour of acquitting the accused.
3. What do you think the final decision of the court should be? Explain your answer.

Source: From *Applying the Law*, by M. Leipner and B. Griffith, 1990. Used by permission of McGraw-Hill Ryerson Limited.

Offenders Act was still on treatment and *rehabilitation* rather than strict punishment.

But the Young Offenders Act also tried to balance the special needs of young people with the right of other Canadians to be safe in their homes and on the streets. It placed a new emphasis on supervising, controlling, and disciplining young lawbreakers in order to safeguard other people. Under the Young Offenders Act, young people were viewed as having more responsibility for their wrongdoing than in the past.

Rights Under the Young Offenders Act

Before the Young Offenders Act was passed, the rights of young people had not been clearly defined by law. Under the act, youths were guaranteed the same legal rights as adult Canadians. In addition, they were granted special rights on account of their age, including a lawyer, free of charge, if the young person could not afford legal counsel.

Perhaps most important is the right to privacy. The Young Offenders Act protects the privacy of young offenders so that their future lives will not be blotted by a criminal record. The public and the media are allowed to attend the trial of a young offender, but it is against the law for the media to identify a youth charged with or convicted of a crime or to name young victims or witnesses at a trial. One exception — added in an amendment to the act in 1986 — is in the case of a young person who might be dangerous. In this case, the offender can be named to protect the community and to help police make an arrest. Court and police records about youth offences must also be kept confidential. Police records of convicted young offenders — including fingerprints and photographs — must be destroyed after a specified "crime-free" period.

Applying the Young Offenders Act

All young offenders are tried in Youth Court, a new court established under the Young Offenders Act.

Medieval justice assumed guilt and placed the burden of proof on the accused. Here, a man is tried without a jury and then paraded through the streets en route to his punishment. Public humiliation was considered a part of the judicial process.

All cases are heard by a judge. Once a case goes to trial and a young person is found guilty, the judge decides on a sentence — called a *disposition* in Youth Court. There is a wide range of available dispositions, including many sentences available in adult court. Youths who plead guilty can sometimes apply for an **alternative measures program**. Under most of these programs — primarily intended for less serious, first-time offences — young offenders do community service work or pay compensation to their victims. For example, a young offender might help coach a community sports team or work in a store for free to pay back the owner for a theft.

In general, youths can be tried as adults only after they turn eighteen years of age. However, a

CANADA'S JUDICIAL SYSTEM

65

YOUTH COURT DISPOSITIONS

Sentences in Youth Court are called dispositions. When a youth is found guilty of an offence, a judge may choose any of the following dispositions.

Absolute Discharge: If the judge feels it is in the best interests of the youth and not harmful to society, an absolute discharge may be granted — no conviction would be recorded, although the charge would remain on the record.

Fine: The judge may order that the youth be fined up to $1000.

Compensation: The judge may order a young offender to compensate the victim of the crime for damages to property, loss of income, or personal injury.

Restitution: A youth found guilty of a crime may be ordered to provide the victim with compensation for damages, either by paying an amount of money or by providing a service.

Community Work Order: As part of their punishment for a crime, young offenders may be required to do work in the community, such as cleaning up garbage in a park.

Medical or Psychological Treatment: If tests suggest that young offenders require medical or psychological treatment, the offenders may be detained in an appropriate institution. To do this, the court must have the consent of both the young offenders and their parents.

Probation: Young offenders may be placed on probation for up to two years.

Custody: Young offenders can be held in custody for up to three years. "Open custody" requires them to spend a specified amount of time in a group home, wilderness camp, or other youth-oriented institution. "Secure custody" requires them to spend a certain time in a special facility designed for young people, such as a training school.

Family court judges, such as Rosalie Abella, hear cases related to divorce and child custody. Some lawyers choose to practise family law exclusively. What are the advantages of having lawyers specialize in certain fields?

young offender charged with a serious crime such as rape, armed robbery, or murder can be transferred to adult court, where the youth is tried under the same rules as adults and faces the same penalties. For example, a young person charged with first-degree murder who is transferred to adult court will face a possible sentence of life imprisonment.

The Debate Over the Young Offenders Act

The Young Offenders Act has been under debate from the start. Some people defend its emphasis on providing help and guidance rather than punishment. They believe that young people who break laws should not face severe penalties. They argue that in the long run it is safer and better for everyone if young people are helped to put their crimes in the past and become law-abiding citizens. But many worry that there are just not enough treatment programs and community resources for helping young people in conflict with the law. They feel that more money should be put into helping young lawbreakers to make a fresh start than into punishing them for past mistakes.

Other Canadians feel that many young criminals are treated far too leniently by the criminal justice system. They want more active law enforcement and stricter sentencing to discourage other young people from committing the same kinds of crimes. Many also believe that the maximum age of young offenders should be lowered from eighteen years to sixteen or even fourteen years, and they are concerned that destroying criminal records and protecting the identities of young offenders puts the community at risk. They want a stronger emphasis on the idea of personal responsibility, and they want increased law enforcement and heavier sentences.

It is unlikely that Parliament will make a major overhaul of the Young Offenders Act or change its basic principles. But there have been a number of amendments to the act. In general, these amendments have toughened the law in cases of serious crime. In 1992, for example, the maximum prison sentence for a young offender convicted of murder was increased to five years.

CLOSE-UP ON CIVIL LAW

Under the Canadian Constitution, most civil matters are the responsibility of the provinces, and civil laws vary from province to province. Quebec's Civil Code — which is based on French

CANADA'S JUDICIAL SYSTEM

CONTRACTS AND YOUTH

Everyone in Canada is touched by civil law. The more independence you gain as you grow older, the more dealings you will have with civil law. Borrowing money to buy a new stereo, getting a driver's licence, taking out a student loan, or signing a lease for an apartment are all ordinary activities that are part of civil law. Knowing something about the civil law will help you to understand your legal rights and obligations.

Contracts are an important part of everyday life and a major part of civil law. A contract is a legally binding agreement between two or more people. It is often assumed that contracts are only legally binding when they are made between two adults. This, however, is not always true. The following two cases involve teenagers who have not reached the legal age of majority (eighteen years). Should the contracts be enforced in these situations?

Jane Gilligan, while a high school student, had a newspaper route. One of her customers was a Mr. Cheng, an elderly man who lived alone. Jane was always friendly and courteous towards Cheng, who became fond of her too. Cheng found out that it was unlikely that she would be able to go to university because of financial problems. When Jane Gilligan was in her last year of high school, Cheng gave her a letter promising to pay her $5000 per year for tuition and expenses while she was in university. As a result, she applied for admission to university and was accepted. Two months later, Cheng saw Gilligan smoking a cigarette and, because of his lifelong opposition to tobacco, he changed his opinion about her and refused to honour his promise.

Is Cheng legally obliged to pay Gilligan $5000 a year while Gilligan is in university? Why or why not?

Toronto Marlboros v. Tonelli
(1979), 23 Ontario Reports (2d) 193

Tonelli, a hockey player of exceptional ability, then aged 17, entered into a contract with the Toronto Marlboros which stipulated that the Marlboros would provide Tonelli with room and board, his school tuition, his expenses while on the road, and a small weekly sum. The Marlboros also agreed to provide coaching, instruction, and the opportunity for Tonelli to display his hockey skills. For his part, Tonelli agreed to play hockey exclusively for the Marlboros for three years and to pay them 20 percent of his first three years' earnings as a professional hockey player if he joined a professional team with which the Marlboros had no agreement respecting the draft of junior players. On turning 18 years of age, Tonelli repudiated the agreement with the Marlboros on the grounds that he was a minor when he signed it, and entered into a contract to play professional hockey with the Houston Aeros of the WHA. The Marlboros sued Tonelli for 20 percent of his first three years' earnings.

In the Ontario Court of Appeal, two judges held that the agreement between Tonelli and the Marlboros was not a contract of service for the infant's benefit. One judge dissented, holding that the agreement with the Marlboros provided for the training and experience necessary for professional hockey and, as a result, was a contract of service for the benefit of the infant. The Marlboros' claim was dismissed.

State whether you agree with the majority or the minority of the Ontario Court of Appeal, and why.

*Source: From Canadian Law by Zuber, Zuber and Jennings, 1991.
Used by permission of McGraw-Hill Ryerson Limited.*

civil law — is completely different from civil law in the rest of Canada. Civil law regulates relations between individuals in a society and provides a way to settle any disputes.

Court cases arise in civil law when someone claims to have been harmed or injured in some way by someone else. A civil suit might be a dispute about property or about a business or financial dealing. It might be about a personal injury or some other kind of personal *grievance* between one person and another. Or it might be about matters such as trespassing, defaming a person's character, selling faulty products, or wrongfully dismissing an employee from a job.

A Civil Lawsuit

Where there is a dispute in civil law, private citizens set the legal process in motion. A plaintiff — a person with a grievance against someone else — takes an action to court. The court action is called a civil suit. The point of a civil suit is usually to win compensation — a money award for damages — from the defendant. The defendant is the person accused of causing some kind of harm or loss.

If the amount of money at stake is less than a specific amount, the plaintiff can usually go to Small Claims Court. The amount varies from province to province; Ontario's limit, $3000, is the highest.

Until recently, women sentenced to a federal penitentiary were sent to Kingston's Prison for Women. Smaller, regional institutions have now replaced portions of the Kingston facility. What factors may have prompted the government to make such a decision?

DEMOCRACY AND ACTION: CITIZENS AND THE LAW

Laws are created to protect members of a society. To be responsive to the needs of the people for whom they are created, laws must result from the government's perception of what needs to be regulated. Consequently, citizens of a democracy have a central role in shaping the laws that govern their daily lives. Lobby groups often pressure governments to create new laws or amend existing laws to ensure that the group's concerns are met. They can be formed by any group of people who wish to voice their concerns and to have the laws changed. By writing letters to politicians, holding rallies or protests, and speaking with the media, lobby groups can make their concerns known and thereby influence government decisions. One example of a change in Canadian law resulting from the pressure exerted by lobby groups is the Criminal Harassment Bill. This bill, which is intended to prevent people from being followed or harassed by former partners, was drafted as a result of the pressure put on the federal government by women's organizations.

In 1993, the Progressive Conservative government proposed an anti-stalking bill designed to protect people who are harassed, badgered, or threatened. As a result of continual harassment by former husbands or boyfriends, many women in Canada feel like prisoners and fear to go out alone. A study carried out between 1974 and 1990 of 551 women killed in Ontario by their intimate partners found that many of the women had been harassed or stalked before being killed. As a result of women's groups and support groups for abused women working hard to bring the problem of stalking to the attention of the federal government, the anti-stalking bill was brought forward by then Minister of Justice Pierre Blais.

The anti-stalking bill has made harassment a criminal offence. Criminal harassment includes persistently following someone, spending large amounts of time watching someone's home or place of work, making harassing phone calls, contacting someone's co-workers or neighbours, and contacting and possibly threatening someone's current boyfriend or spouse. Those charged with criminal harassment could face up to five years in jail, although less serious offenders would face six months in jail or a fine of $2000.

Can you think of another area in which a law is needed to protect Canadians? How could you become involved in lobbying to have a new law passed to address your concern?

Small Claims Court is an inexpensive and informal court in which plaintiffs and defendants sometimes present their own cases instead of hiring lawyers. Claims of over $3000 are handled in higher provincial courts. The main purpose of awarding compensation is not to punish the defendant but to right the wrong done to the plaintiff.

WOMEN AND CHANGES IN CIVIL LAW

Civil law has changed over time to fit changing needs and values of Canadian society. In the nineteenth century, for example, wives were not treated as their husbands' equals under civil law. In fact, married women were considered to be the property of their husbands. In the 1850s, any wages earned by married women were legally controlled by their husbands. So was any property bought by married women. Wives could not make contracts or sue for damages on their own. If a woman's good name was defamed, for instance, she could not personally bring a lawsuit. Only her husband could sue for damages on her behalf. A wife could not even sue her husband for personal damages if he assaulted her. However, women in the nineteenth century fought hard to gain the legal right to sue, to make contracts, and to own property. And they began to gain ground in the battle for legal equality.

But the fight was far from over. In the early twentieth century, women still had trouble ending an unhappy marriage because the legal grounds for divorce were so limited. In fact, a married woman could not divorce a husband who had deserted her unless she could track him down. The federal Divorce Act was changed in 1968 to broaden the grounds for divorce and to allow divorce proceedings to begin after three years of separation. It was changed again in 1985 to provide for a no-fault divorce after a one-year waiting period. In Ontario during the late 1970s and 1980s, a series of family-law reforms also led to a greater recognition of women's contributions to marriage. Women began to be treated as equal partners in a marriage. Under Ontario's Family Law Act of 1986, all assets acquired in marriage were to be divided equally between the partners if they separated.

More changes will come in the future. There is already increasing pressure to reform laws about child custody and support payments after a divorce. Law concerning the legal rights of married women is just one area where Canadian laws are being refashioned to suit changing times. Retailoring old laws and creating new ones is the way that laws can "be made to fit the people they serve."

KNOWING THE KEY PEOPLE, PLACES, AND EVENTS

In your notes, clearly identify and explain the historical significance of each of the following:

> Criminal Law
> Summary Conviction Offences
> Jury
> Juvenile Delinquency Act of 1908
> Alternative Measures Program
> Civil Law
> Indictable Offences
> Victim Impact Statements
> Young Offenders Act
> Small Claims Court

FOCUS YOUR KNOWLEDGE

1. Clearly explain the differences between criminal and civil law.
2. Outline the stages in a criminal trial from arrest to sentencing.
3. Briefly outline the proceedings in a criminal trial, including the way in which the jury is selected.
4. What factors does a judge take into account when sentencing criminals? How might these considerations affect the sentences handed down?
5. How is the Small Claims Court different from other courts?
6. Outline the major changes that have taken place in Canadians' attitudes toward youth crime.
7. How did the Juvenile Delinquency Act of 1908 alter the way Canadians view and treat young offenders?

APPLYING YOUR KNOWLEDGE

1. When passing new laws, governments must be careful to protect the interests of society without violating the fundamental rights of citizens. Do you think that Canadian laws successfully balance these two aims? Can you think of any laws that should be repealed or strengthened?

2. In recent years, the controversy over police powers has led to a great deal of debate in Canada. Should police be granted more freedoms in carrying out investigations? Could police "serve and protect" society better if they had more powerful weapons and fewer restrictions on their use? Explain your answers.

3. Explain why you agree or disagree with the principle that it is better for some guilty people to escape punishment than for an innocent person to be unjustly punished.

4. What should the purpose of prisons be: to punish or to help rehabilitate criminals? If the purpose of prisons is rehabilitation, how should society deal with repeat offenders?

5. How have changes in Canada's civil law reflected the increasing recognition of women's full participation in society?

6. Does the Young Offenders Act effectively balance the needs of young offenders with their responsibility for their criminal actions? Why or why not?

7. Are the alternative measures programs a good idea for young offenders? Should they be considered for repeat offenders? Explain your answer.

EXTEND YOUR KNOWLEDGE

1. Over a two-week period, collect newspaper articles concerning the police. Once you have gathered your articles, create a mini-scrapbook about police issues. For each of the articles, write a forty-word summary of the story and a forty-word personal assessment that notes whether the news story is supportive or critical of the police. Also comment on whether or not each story shows a need for greater police powers or more restriction on the activities of police.

2. Watch a Canadian television program that involves a trial. As you watch the program, make notes on how the court proceedings are portrayed. Once you have watched the program and made some notes, write a short report on the accuracy of the program. Comment on the role of the judge, jury, Crown attorney, defence counsel, and trial proceedings. Alternatively, watch an American program and write a short report that compares and contrasts the Canadian and American legal systems.

3. Do some research on a typical Canadian courtroom. On the basis of your research, build a scale model of a courtroom. Label the places where various court officials, the jury, witnesses, the accused, and spectators sit.

4. Research the appointment and role of parole boards, and then hold a debate about the use of parole in Canada.

SKILLS FOCUS

UNIT REVIEW

1. Canada provides a clear example of the fact that governments and legal systems are constantly changing. How do the issues surrounding each of the following illustrate this?

    The Senate
    The Young Offenders Act
    Civil Law
    The Constitution

2. In general, a democratic system of government tries to provide all citizens with equal representation and should be responsive to the needs of the people. Select three features of our government that you think help to ensure fair and effective government.

3. Canadian law attempts to balance the needs of the individual with those of society. For each of the following, comment on how well the balance is met.

    The Young Offenders Act
    The Presumption of Innocence
    The Alternative Measures Program

DEVELOPING THINKING SKILLS

Being able to think effectively is an important skill, whether you are preparing for the world of work or for postsecondary education. Effective thinkers can interpret facts in new ways, present information creatively, and draw conclusions that may not occur to others. Two important steps in developing good thinking skills are learning to think divergently and learning to think critically.

One strategy that helps you to think divergently is called APC, or Alternative Possibilities and Choices. This strategy requires you to brainstorm with others to come up with as many ideas as possible. Form groups of two to three classmates to do an APC. In your groups, prepare a list of all the possible answers to the following question: "You let your cat out one evening and it failed to return. What happened?" Remember, all ideas are valid and should be written down. Do not prejudge the ideas given. The purpose of this exercise is to get you to think freely.

Being an effective thinker also requires you to learn to think critically. An effective strategy for developing critical thinking skills is called PMI — Plus, Minus, Interesting. Prepare a list of all the good and bad points of an idea as well as interesting possibilities that may result if the idea were to become a reality. Working with the same group with whom you did an APC, do a PMI on the following statement: "All students should be required to take a course in cooking." Record all of the group's responses under the headings Plus, Minus, or Interesting.

Now that you have had some fun with APCs and PMIs, try applying these strategies to the study of government and law. Use APCs and PMIs to explore the issues listed on the opposite page.

CAREER FOCUS

ENTREPRENEURSHIP

For many people, the possibility of being self-employed is appealing. However, buying an existing, profitable business can be expensive and is often out of reach, so some people put their own ideas to work for them by beginning their own business. These people are called entrepreneurs. Entrepreneurs are individuals who bring innovations and new ideas to the world. They may invent a new product, come up with a unique marketing strategy, or see the need for a new service.

At the turn of the century an enterprising young automobile maker, Henry Ford, reasoned that if cars were made more affordable by using an assembly line and if workers were paid more so that they could afford to buy the cars, the market for automobiles could be greatly expanded. Ford went on to become one of the biggest automobile manufacturers in the world. More recently, on a smaller scale, a creative landscaping firm north of Toronto found a way to increase business at a traditionally slow time of year by offering to put up people's Christmas lights for a fee. In both of these cases, the entrepreneurial spirit was alive: creative thinking was applied with successful results.

If you would like to be self-employed, there are few skills you will find more essential than thinking skills. Being able to think divergently, critically, and creatively will enable you to see potential markets, to avoid irrational decisions, and to plan effective and unique marketing strategies.

PRACTISING YOUR THINKING SKILLS

1. Do a PMI on the idea that the Canadian Senate should be reformed so that it is elected and includes equal representation from each province and territory.

2. Do a PMI on the idea that the voting age should be lowered to sixteen.

3. Do an APC on the following scenario. One hundred and thirty young people, all under the age of nineteen, are stranded on a deserted island. Although there is plenty of food and adequate shelter, there is little hope of being rescued in the near future. One of the first tasks facing the young people is to determine how decisions will be made and what laws will govern their actions. Given this situation, what form of government would be appropriate?

UNIT 2

LAYING THE FOUNDATIONS:
FROM CONFEDERATION TO 1911

THE LAST HALF OF THE NINETEENTH CENTURY was a period during which the nation of Canada was not only born but transformed. Between 1867 and 1911, Canada grew from four colonies to nine that stretched from the Atlantic to the Pacific oceans. It also emerged from its rural frontier roots to enter the twentieth century as a budding industrial and urban nation. The promise held out by a new country rich in natural resources attracted people from diverse backgrounds and laid the foundations for a multicultural nation. While this period of growth and change was accompanied by many problems, it was also a time of great optimism for many Canadians.

This unit portrays a nation undergoing significant changes as Canada emerges from its frontier period and prepares to step onto the international stage. Chapter 4 provides an overview of the period 1867–1911. It examines the changes that transformed Canada and explores the contributions of many kinds of people. These

CHAPTER FOUR
A Nation Emerges

CHAPTER FIVE
French–English Relations

CHAPTER SIX
Canadian–American Relations

contributions were as diverse as the individuals involved and ranged from art and literature to gold mining and railway building. Chapter 5 focuses on French–English relations. It examines the trials faced by two Canadian prime ministers — John A. Macdonald and Wilfrid Laurier — as they attempted to build a strong nation that recognized the differences between French and English Canadians. Chapter 6 surveys Canadian–American relations in the period from Confederation to the end of the Laurier era.

CHAPTER 4
A NATION EMERGES

GLOSSARY TERMS

Province of Canada The province formed in 1841 by the union of Upper Canada and Lower Canada, which then became the districts of Canada West and Canada East. In 1867, these districts became the provinces of Ontario and Quebec.

Maritimes The East Coast colonies (and, from 1867 onward, the provinces) of New Brunswick, Nova Scotia, and Prince Edward Island.

Provisional Government A temporary government, usually set up in response to a crisis and lasting until the crisis has been resolved.

Tariff A tax placed on goods imported from another country. Tariffs may protect a nation's manufacturers from foreign competition by raising the final selling price of foreign-made goods.

Cultural Mosaic A multicultural society in which immigrants and their descendants are encouraged to preserve their cultural heritage. The term is often contrasted with "melting pot," in which immigrants are encouraged to abandon their cultural distinctiveness in favour of the culture of their new country.

Tenement A building that has been divided into apartments or rooms for rent. The term is usually applied to run-down housing in very poor neighbourhoods.

Prohibition The banning of certain goods or activities, such as the drinking of liquor.

FOCUS ON:

- John A. Macdonald's role in creating Canada
- the building of a national railway
- the treatment of Native peoples and other minority groups during Canada's early years
- Canada's immigration policies during the Wilfrid Laurier era
- prosperity and poverty during Canada's first half-century
- the emergence of the women's movement in Canada

In 1864, two dozen men in top hats and swallow-tailed coats gathered on the front veranda of Prince Edward Island's Government House. They had come from the *Province of Canada* and the *Maritimes* as delegates to the Charlottetown Conference, and a photographer was about to record the historic event. **John A. Macdonald** eased himself down onto a lower step. His hat rested on his knee, and his face was turned squarely toward the camera. Several of the men around him gazed into the distance. One raised his top hat to shade his eyes from the late summer sun. Their casual attitude suggested that not much was happening.

But the Charlottetown Conference of 1864 became a turning point in Canadian history. These men came to be known as the Fathers of Confederation. From a handful of British colonies in the southeastern corner of British North America, they were about to create the nation called Canada.

FROM SEA TO DISTANT SEA

It seems fitting that John A. Macdonald is at the centre of the photograph. He and the other delegates from the Province of Canada encouraged Maritimers to consider the possibility of **Confederation** — a union of all the British North American colonies from sea to sea. The sheer size and imagination of the Canadians' proposals stirred excitement among the delegates. They met again in Quebec a month later. There they spent long, hard days mapping out a plan of union and pleasant evenings in a whirlwind of balls and parties. By the end of October 1864, the delegates had drawn up seventy-two proposals known as the Quebec Resolutions.

THE GROWTH OF THE NATION

The province of Canada eventually approved the Quebec Resolutions, but the Maritime colonies were uneasy. Maritimers had strong local loyalties and regional ties. They did not like giving up their independence as self-governing colonies to a faraway central government. On the West Coast, the colony of British Columbia also hesitated to join the new dominion. Only the promise of greater prosperity resulting from interprovincial trade finally drew them into Confederation.

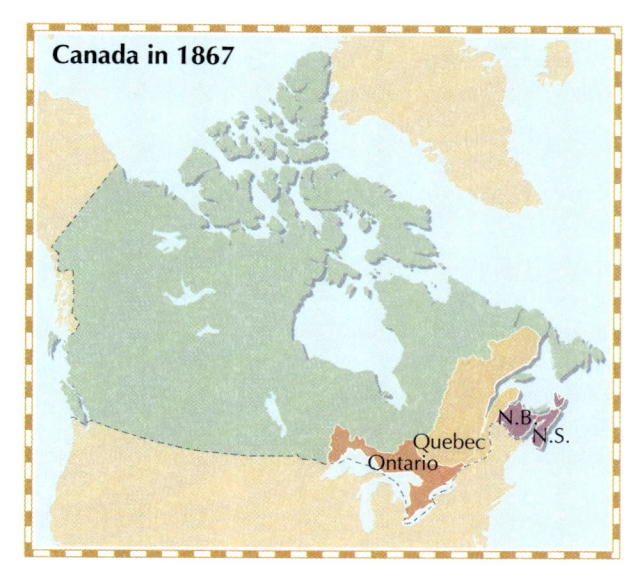

The Atlantic Colonies

New Brunswick and Nova Scotia agreed to Confederation on the condition that the new federal government pay off their provincial debts and build a railway from Quebec City to Halifax. Both

Canada in 1867

In 1864, politicians from the British North American colonies met in Charlottetown, Prince Edward Island, to discuss the idea of Confederation. This group, photographed on the veranda of Government House, included John A. Macdonald (seated, centre) who would become Canada's first prime minister.

colonies remained divided over the idea of Confederation. Some people felt that entering the union would force them to raise more money to meet the expenses of the new national government. Others were not convinced of the value of the promised railway. If the railway were built along the north shore of New Brunswick, southern cities such as Saint John would not benefit. Despite such opposition, there was enough support in both New Brunswick and Nova Scotia for the idea of a union of British North American colonies.

The **British North America Act** outlined the terms of Confederation. When it was signed on March 29, 1867, the Dominion of Canada was born as a union of four provinces: New Brunswick, Nova Scotia, Ontario, and Quebec. Its new capital was the little city of Ottawa. The Conservatives won the first federal election in 1867, and John A. Macdonald took his seat in the House of Commons as Canada's first prime minister.

The new nation continued to invite Prince Edward Island and Newfoundland to join Confederation. Prince Edward Islanders had discovered that they could not afford independence. Their colonial government had spent far too much money building a railway and was deeply in debt. Canada proposed a generous trade: if Prince Edward Island joined the union, the federal government would pay off the colony's debt and provide it with steamship and railway services. The islanders accepted Canada's terms with mixed feelings. When the Dominion flag was run up the flagpole at Government House on July 1, 1873, few islanders cheered. But Newfoundland had even fewer ties with the mainland. It remained independent for nearly eighty years, not joining Confederation until 1949.

This portrait of John A. Macdonald was taken around the time of Confederation.

British Columbia

When British Columbia joined Confederation in 1871, it also did so with some reluctance. Most non-Native British Columbians were British or American. They knew very little about Canada and cared less, but the colony, lying between the Rocky Mountains and the Pacific Ocean in the "West beyond the West," was isolated, underpopulated, and almost bankrupt.

British Columbians knew that if they were to prosper, they would have to join the United States or Canada. The Americans had just bought Alaska from the Russian government for $7.2 million and were keen to extend their territory up the Pacific coast. But the Canadian government offered British Columbia a railway linking the Pacific coast with the eastern provinces. The deal was too good to refuse. Soon school children in British Columbia were singing, "Our fair Dominion now extends from Cape Race to Nootka Sound."

The Prairies

Lying between Ontario and British Columbia was the vast territory then known as **Rupert's Land**. King Charles II of England had granted Rupert's Land to the Hudson's Bay Company two hundred years earlier, in 1670. Less than two years after Confederation, Macdonald sent delegates to England to try to buy Rupert's Land. The Hudson's Bay Company was not willing to sell, but the British government urged it on. The British were nervous about Americans who were eager to settle Rupert's Land. Macdonald agreed with the British government. "If we don't go there," he remarked, "the Yankees will." Six months later, the Canadian delegates sailed for home with the deal complete. Canada had agreed to pay the Hudson's Bay Company $1.5 million, or about one cent for every three hectares.

Native Lands and Western Settlement

When the Macdonald government gained control of the North-West Territories, as Rupert's Land came to be known, it encountered almost 26 000 Native peoples who were scattered across the Prairies. Before European settlers could take up farming in the West, the traditional inhabitants had to be displaced. Between 1871 and 1877, treaties were negotiated with the Cree, Ojibwa, and Blackfoot peoples. These treaties stripped Natives of title to most of the fertile land of the southern Prairies. In return for surrendering their traditional hunting grounds, Natives were given a one-time payment of $12 per person and an annual allowance of $5 for every man, woman, and child. As well, they were placed on scattered reserves where it was expected they would learn to farm.

Why did Natives agree to treaties that would have such a devastating effect on their traditional lifestyles? The answer to this question lies in the tremendous changes that had swept the Prairies in the mid-nineteenth century. The traditional prairie economy relied on the great herds of buffalo that roamed the grasslands of central North America. These herds had been declining for some years. By the 1870s, the slaughter brought about by a great demand for buffalo robes and the introduction of the repeater rifle had almost destroyed the buffalo herds. Sensing that their traditional economy was fast disappearing, Native leaders sought a new way to ensure the survival of their people. Those who at first refused to sign the treaties were eventually forced by hunger to surrender their lands to the government.

Manitoba's Stormy Entry into Confederation

At the time of Confederation, a community of several thousand Metis — people of part Native and part French Canadian ancestry — and white farmers and fur traders lived in the Red River settlement (now Winnipeg). When Canada purchased Rupert's Land in 1870, no one in Macdonald's government told the Red River settlers that Canada had bought the land under their feet. The Metis decided to stop the Canadian takeover, at least until the Canadian government talked with them about the terms of their inclusion in Canada. They wanted title to the lands they farmed and the rights to keep their Catholic schools, to speak French, and to form a provincial government.

Under the leadership of Louis Riel, the Metis stormed Upper Fort Garry in November 1869 and

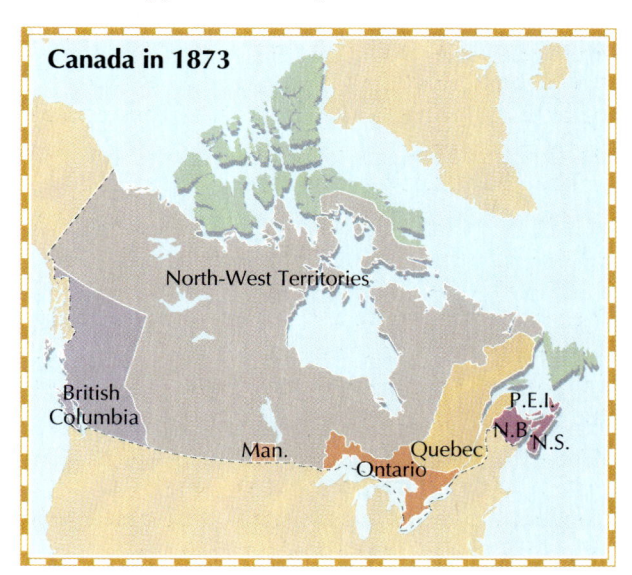

Canada in 1873

set up a *provisional government*. At first Macdonald ignored the Metis actions, but he was a shrewd politician and could see that a storm was brewing. On July 15, 1870, his government passed the Manitoba Act, which granted most of the Metis demands, and the new province of Manitoba entered Confederation.

Canada set such small borders for Manitoba that it was known as the "postage-stamp province." It took up only 1 percent of the North-West Territories. (Not until 1912 was the land around Hudson Bay divided among Manitoba, Ontario, and Quebec.) That left a huge territory still in the hands of Canada. As the Metis had feared, the Canadian government wanted the West settled by outsiders. By the turn of the century, waves of immigrants from the East had swept across the Prairies. Straggling little settlements at Regina, Saskatoon, Calgary, and Edmonton swelled into cities. By 1905, enough people lived in the Canadian West that Saskatchewan and Alberta entered Confederation as the eighth and ninth provinces. Canada now stretched from sea to distant sea.

Building a Railway to the Pacific

Macdonald believed that railways were the key to building the new nation and binding it together. Once British Columbia entered Confederation, he was ready to begin the promised railway. The new Pacific railway to British Columbia would be the longest ever built. It would cut across thousands of kilometres of unchartered wilderness, including some of the most difficult terrain in the world. The costs were sure to be astronomical. One judge spoke for many Canadians when he grumbled that Macdonald's plan was far too ambitious: "He's talking of running a railway from the Atlantic to the Pacific...next he will be talking about a railway to the moon."

The building of Canada's first transcontinental railway began soon after the federal election of 1872. Initially the contract to build the railway went to Sir Hugh Allan, who headed the Canadian Pacific Railway Company (CPR). Shortly after the contract was awarded, allegations of vote buying by the Conservatives and evidence that Macdonald had accepted large sums of money from Allan before awarding the contract forced a new election. In the election of 1873, the Conservatives were crushed at the polls and Canadians elected their first Liberal government, under the leadership of Alexander Mackenzie.

Despite being tainted by the scandal, Macdonald's career in politics was far from over. Mackenzie's Liberals had the misfortune of taking office just as the country was entering a long economic depression. As the depression deepened, Canadians began to criticize the Liberals for inaction. All Macdonald needed was a platform that would rally Canadians around him again. He found it in the "National Policy," which contained three proposals: a protective *tariff* (a tax added to the price of American-made goods), the completion of the railway, and large-scale immigration to the West.

Macdonald's National Policy caught the imagination of Canadians, and in 1878 the Conservatives were swept back into power. Immediately following his return to office, Macdonald concentrated on reviving the transcontinental railway. A new CPR venture, headed by George Stephen and Donald Smith, agreed to complete the railway to British Columbia by 1891.

After a slow start, the CPR brought in the young American, **William Cornelius Van Horne**, as general manager. He was responsible for keeping the construction of the railway moving at a breakneck pace. By the early spring of 1882, he had ordered the stockpiling of supplies in preparation for a summer assault on the Prairies. Soon hundreds of men were laying track under the hot summer sun. By autumn they had laid 800 kilometres of rails across the Prairies.

The next year, Van Horne set to work on the nearly impossible stretch of land north of Lake Superior. Workers had to blast their way through some of the hardest rock in the world. The muskeg swamps were so dangerous that, in one place, three locomotives and several kilometres of track were swallowed up. Despite these setbacks, the work moved ahead. When the Lake Superior section of track was well underway, Van Horne planned his strategy for the West. He shifted the proposed line of track farther south, closer to the U.S. border, to cut off any rival American lines.

Railway construction in the mountains was very dangerous. Workers dangled on ropes from cliff tops to set dynamite charges. Many died in the blasts. The roadbeds were narrow, and some men fell to their deaths. When it rained, mudslides swept down the mountains; when it was dry, forest fires raced through the woods. The CPR had trouble finding people to do such hard and dangerous work, so workers from China — almost 9000 of them — were brought to the Canadian West. They worked longer hours for lower wages than did Canadian workers, and they tolerated primitive living conditions in separate camps. Hundreds were killed in rock slides, explosions, and tunnel collapses, and hundreds more died of diseases resulting from filthy camps. Many nearly starved to death from trying to save as much of their meagre wages as possible for their families back home.

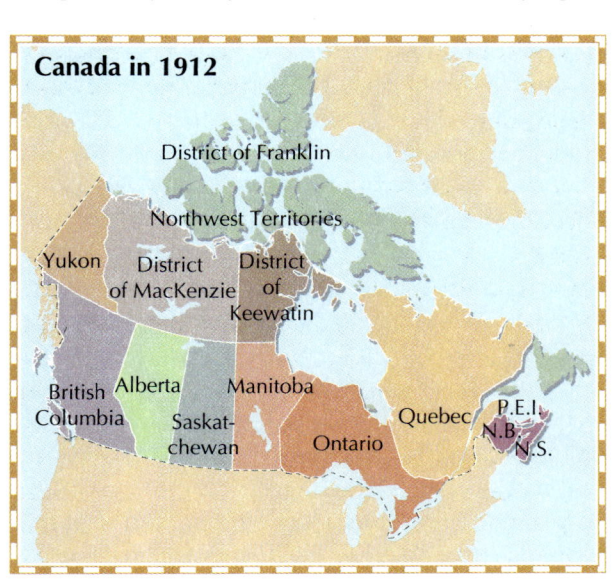

Chinese workers brought to Canada to help build the railway often retained their traditional dress and customs. Note the clothes and hair of these workers. Can you suggest reasons why they would choose not to assimilate?

Canada in 1912

By the spring of 1885, only a few short gaps remained in the railway. The CPR, however, had spent money recklessly and was almost bankrupt. Its directors begged the government for one last loan. In the meantime, a rebellion (again led by Louis Riel) had broken out in the Saskatchewan district of the North-West Territories. Troops from the East were dispatched to the rebellion on the new railway in a record-breaking seven days, and the CPR proved its worth to Macdonald's government. The company received its last loan. As a result, Canada's first transcontinental railway was soon completed when Donald Smith drove in the famous "last spike" near Revelstoke, British Columbia, on November 7, 1885.

The Early Years of Western Settlement

By the end of 1885, Macdonald's dream of a West under the plough and an East humming with industry seemed to be coming true. The CPR was completed, the Metis crisis was ended, and most of the Native peoples of the Prairies had been placed on reserves. The West was now open for settlers.

The Conservatives had passed the **Dominion Lands Act** in 1872 to make it easy for settlers to own their own farms. For just $10, an adult male could buy a "quarter section" (64 hectares) of prairie farmland. For another $10 he could purchase an option on an adjoining quarter section. All he had to do was break the sod, build a shelter, and live on the property at least six months a year for three years.

The Dominion Lands Act set off a land rush and wild speculation. By 1901, thousands of immigrants had made the long trip west and more than 85 000 Americans had taken up homesteads. But not all immigrants to the West chose to stay. Many moved on after a few years to live in cities or to farm in the United States. Thirty years after Confederation, the population of the Prairies stood at a disappointing 250 000.

The country itself discouraged settlers. Prairie winters were long and bitterly cold. Summers were hot and ferociously dry. Settlers' homes were mostly sod huts cut from hard prairie earth. The "soddies" stood alone on the high, wide grassland, far from neighbours and a day or more from the nearest town. Trees were scarce and wood was precious. The men and women of the Prairies worked hard to farm the harsh northern lands. But many were defeated by the country — driven out by drought, hail, cold winters, grasshoppers, wheat rust, bankruptcy, or despair.

Immigration at the Turn of the Century

John A. Macdonald died before the Canadian West was completely settled by outsiders. When the Liberal prime minister **Wilfrid Laurier** took office in 1896, he set out to complete Macdonald's dream. Laurier's ambitious young minister of the interior, **Clifford Sifton**, decided on an aggressive "open door" immigration policy.

Canada's "door" was not open to all, however. Sifton wanted to bring in very specific groups. First, he wanted only farmers — not urban workers — who could endure the hardships of the Prairies. Second, he wanted only immigrants from the United States and Britain and from northern, central, and eastern Europe. All other potential immigrants were discouraged.

Sifton pinpointed what he considered "desirable" countries and then flooded them with pamphlets, posters, and advertisements promising free land in the "Last, Best West." Soon immigrants were coming by the thousands — Germans, Americans, Swedes, British, Ukrainians, Dutch, Icelanders, Norwegians, Russians, and more. Canada's population swelled by two million in the first decade of the twentieth century.

Not all Canadians were happy about Sifton's open-door policy, and the Laurier government was struck by a backlash of feeling against non–English-speaking immigrants. Many English-speaking Canadians wanted only settlers of British background in order to keep Canada's ties with England strong. Many French-speaking Canadians were afraid that in a West of so many languages and cultures, their claims for French-language rights and separate Roman Catholic schools might be weakened.

Examine this photograph of a homestead in Saskatchewan carefully. Make a list of the hardships settlers faced on the Prairies.

CANADIAN SOVEREIGNTY: THE BUILDING OF A NATION

In the forty-five years between Confederation and the end of the Laurier era, Canada took great strides toward becoming an independent nation. Forged from a collection of British colonies, Canada soon spread from ocean to ocean, linked by a newly built transcontinental railway. Can you explain why each of the events listed below was significant in the development of an independent Canadian nation? You can find more details about each of these events in this chapter and by additional research. Spend a few minutes discussing with a partner how each of these issues affected Canadian sovereignty.

CONFEDERATION

- In 1867, Canada East (now Quebec) and Canada West (now Ontario) were joined by Nova Scotia and New Brunswick to create the Dominion of Canada. By 1905, Manitoba, British Columbia, Prince Edward Island, Alberta, and Saskatchewan had joined.
- Although still a British colony, the new Dominion of Canada was given far more powers to allow it to govern its own internal affairs.

BUILDING THE TRANSCONTINENTAL RAILWAY

- In order to bind together a nation stretching from the Atlantic to the Pacific oceans, the ambitious task of building a railway across Canada was begun.
- Completed in 1885, the transcontinental railway helped to ensure trade and travel between the distant ends of this vast country and was a vital factor in the settling of the West.

THE ALASKA BOUNDARY DISPUTE

- The Klondike Gold Rush resulted in a dispute between Canada and the United States over the ownership of the Alaska Panhandle. This area allowed the quickest and easiest access to the gold fields of the Yukon.
- The British sided with the Americans rather than the Canadians in the Alaska Panhandle dispute. The decision to award the Panhandle to the United States highlighted the need for Canadians to be in control of their own affairs.

Frank Oliver, a strong critic of Sifton's policy, became minister of the interior in 1905. In 1910, he changed the Immigration Act to slow the tide of non–English-speaking settlers into Canada. Oliver compared his Immigration Act with Sifton's open-door policy and proudly proclaimed that his approach was "restrictive, exclusive, and selective." This was "not an act to promote immigration," he said bluntly. For example, under section 37 of the 1910 act immigrants had to have a minimum sum of money, but the amount could "vary according to the race." Immigration officers could use such restrictions to turn away members of groups who were considered less desirable — especially Asians and American blacks, Jews, East Indians, and southern Europeans.

Other actions were taken during the Laurier years to restrict Chinese and Japanese immigration. In 1904, the entry tax on Chinese immigrants (the only group already subject to a "head tax") was raised to $500 — a staggering amount at the time. Anti-Asian riots in British Columbia also prompted restrictions on Japanese immigration. In Vancouver, 30 000 people gathered at a meeting of the Asiatic Exclusion League in Vancouver and then invaded Japanese neighbourhoods, breaking windows and looting. Japanese immigrants heard news of the approaching mob and banded together for protection.

Laurier apologized for the incident to Japan — an important military ally of Great Britain — but negotiated an unofficial agreement to restrict Japanese immigration to 400 people a year. Not until the 1950s were Canadians from Asia allowed to vote in federal elections or to work in certain professions, such as teaching and the civil service.

In spite of Oliver's policies, non-English-speaking immigrants from many countries continued to flow into Canada until the outbreak of war in 1914. The Laurier years marked the real beginning of the Canadian *cultural mosaic*. Many newcomers stayed in the industrial centres, and most major Canadian cities had an Italian district, a Polish quarter, or a Chinatown. Many more took up homesteads on the Prairies, and maps of the Canadian West are sprinkled with names brought from the "old countries," such as Strasbourg, Esterhazy, Verigin, and Stettler.

THE LAURIER YEARS: THE GOLDEN AGE OF PROSPERITY

Wilfrid Laurier's Liberal government was in power from 1896 until 1911. The Laurier years were a time of rapid economic growth. Canada left behind almost thirty desperate years of depression and looked toward a promising future.

By 1910, most of the Prairies had been settled by farmers, who soon prospered. Factories around the world were busy again, and Canada's wheat, minerals, and lumber were in demand to supply industries and their growing armies of factory workers.

The years from 1896 to 1911 have been called the Golden Years, the Spirited Years, and the Confident Years. An elegant Wilfrid Laurier, Canada's first French-speaking prime minister, appeared to be an ideal leader for the thriving young nation. He was fluent in both French and English and moved with ease in both cultures.

When Laurier came to power at the age of fifty-four, the task of nation-building

This candid photograph of Wilfrid Laurier was taken while he was on the campaign trail in 1911.

that had started with Confederation was not yet complete. The country was still divided by rivalries between French-speakers and English-speakers and by regional hostilities. But Laurier's sharp mind and skill at public speaking, his talent for compromise and fair play, and his practical understanding of politics marked him as the person to draw the various groups and regions of Canada together at last. At least in his first years as prime minister, Laurier seemed "made to order" for leading the new country to maturity as a nation.

The Klondike Gold Rush

The greatest gold rush in history began in the year that Laurier's Liberals came to power. The new-found wealth in the North seemed to symbolize Canada's golden prospects. In August 1896, George Washington Carmack and two Native partners, Skookum Jim and Tagish Charlie, discovered gold in a little creek near the Klondike River in the Yukon. The **Klondike Gold Rush** was on. Almost overnight, 40 000 people headed north to "strike it rich" or work in the raw frontier towns that sprang up near the gold fields.

The frontier town of Dawson was at the hub of the gold country, where the Yukon and Klondike rivers meet. In 1897, Dawson consisted of only a saloon and a sawmill. A year later, it boasted a dozen saloons, dance-halls, and theatres. Soon it grew to include 20 000 people and two banks, five churches, two newspapers, and a telegraph service.

Although the gold rush may have contributed to the general economic boom in Canada, Native peoples in British Columbia and the Yukon did not share in the prosperity. Few of the miners who flooded into the Yukon showed any concern about Native rights. They openly shot dogs and horses, interfered with Native traplines, and exploited the fish and game resources. Alarmed, Native leaders demanded and were successful at negotiating a treaty that gave them land rights to an area encompassing the northeastern corner of British Columbia and the southeastern corner of the Yukon.

Prairie Wheat Farming

On the Prairies, farmers were harvesting a different kind of gold. Europe and the United States were clamouring for wheat, and Canada's western "breadbasket" filled the demand. In the first two decades of the new century, Canadian wheat exports quadrupled — and so did wheat prices. Western wheat became the largest Canadian export.

The success of Canadian wheat farmers was made possible by new farming techniques and inventions. Farms became mechanized. New chilled-steel ploughs sliced through prairie sod with ease. The gasoline-driven tractors that slowly replaced horses enabled farmers to work much bigger parcels of land with less effort. In springtime improved harrows and seed-drills made planting more efficient, and in autumn better threshing machines helped farmers reap large harvests before the first snowfall.

Scientists developed hardier, high-yield grains that could mature within the short Canadian growing season. The new varieties included Red Fife, Red Calcutta, Garnet, Reward, and, above all, Marquis. It is estimated that, by 1918, Marquis wheat added $100 million every year to Canadian farmers'

Poundmaker, a powerful Cree chief, was arrested following the North-West Rebellion in 1885, even though he intervened to prevent his warriors from pursuing retreating soldiers.

COMPARING COSTS OF LIVING

Skimming a newspaper published in 1900 could lead a reader to believe that bargains abounded at the time.

However, to gain an understanding of the difference in the Canadian standard of living in 1900 as compared with the 1990s, it is important to consider both wages and prices. To understand how the standard of living has changed, answer the following questions.

1. Calculate the cost of a "basket of goods," assuming one of each of the items shown was purchased. What would have been its total cost?

2. Using a current newspaper or catalogue, calculate the cost of an identical basket of goods based on today's prices. What is the total current cost of these goods?

3. The Consumer Price Index (CPI) is a measurement of the average price of goods and services bought by a typical household. To calculate the CPI, divide the current cost of the sample basket of goods by the cost of an identical basket of goods in 1900 and multiply by 100. This calculation will give you the inflation rate from 1900 to the present. What is the inflation rate for these years?

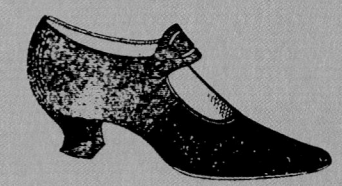

4. The average weekly wage earned by Canadian workers in 1900 was $7.78 for men and $3.65 for women. How many weeks' work would it have taken (a) men and (b) women to buy this basket of goods in 1900?

5. The current average weekly wage earned by Canadian workers in 1993 was $557.89. How many weeks' work would it take to buy the same basket of goods today?

6. To determine the difference in real wages between 1900 and the present day, the rate of inflation must be calculated. To calculate the real wage relative to the wage earned in 1900, divide the 1993 weekly wage by the CPI you calculated above. How much buying power do today's workers have in comparison with workers at the turn of the century?

Ladies' Suit
$15.00

Bicycle
$25.00

Solid Oak Table
$11.50

Men's Dress Pants
$1.25

Coal Stove
$42.75

Ladies' Dress Shoes
$2.00

incomes. The growth in wheat production was called the "Canadian miracle."

Farmers used the money from grain sales to buy food, clothing, and farm supplies. Towns sprang up to meet the new demand for these goods, and farm families joined townsfolk at fall fairs and seed fairs, or at travelling one-ring circuses and medicine shows. On the farm, comfortable frame houses replaced "soddies." Porches appeared, barns sported fresh paint, and pianos tinkled in front parlours. For many, life had never been so good.

Although the turn of the century was accompanied by a wave of prosperity for many Canadians, Natives had little to celebrate. Since being placed on reserves in the 1870s, their living conditions had continued to decline. The disappearance of the buffalo herds and the severe restrictions placed on Native peoples by the **Indian Act** of 1876 created desperate conditions on many reserves. This act combined many previous laws into one comprehensive body of regulations. Native peoples were already the most regulated people in Canada, and the Indian Act left no aspect of Native life free from government interference. Traditional Native ceremonies such as the potlatch were banned, an elective system of government was imposed, and laws prohibiting the purchase of alcohol and the playing of billiards were passed.

Life on the reserves was difficult for many Natives. Food shortages led some to take desperate actions such as eating the cattle that were intended to assist them in getting started as farmers. In 1883, three Cree chiefs attempted to draw John A. Macdonald's attention to the plight of their people by sending him a letter, in which they noted:

If no attention is paid to our case now we shall conclude that the treaty made with us six years ago was a meaningless matter of form and that the white man has doomed us to annihilation little by little. But the motto of the Indian is, "If we must die by violence, let us do it quickly."

While many saw the dawning of a new century as reason for optimism, Canada's Native peoples continued their struggle for economic and cultural survival.

Prosperity and optimism abounded in many Canadian cities by the turn of the century, and Halifax, Nova Scotia, was no exception. What can you see in this turn-of-the-century photograph that suggests prosperity and the dawning of a new age for Canada?

THE TITANIC: A SYMBOL OF ITS AGE

When the *Titanic* was launched in 1912, it generated a great deal of excitement as one of a trio of the world's largest steamers. The *Titanic*, along with its sister ships the *Olympic* and the *Britannic*, set new standards for size and opulence. Weighing 50 000 tonnes, these ships were 50 percent larger than any ships ever built. The *Titanic* could carry 2389 passengers and a crew of 860, a total of 3249 people.

Many believe the *Titanic* to be one of the most beautiful and graceful steamers ever built. This was evident on board, where the first-class quarter included a dining salon, a reading and writing room, a gymnasium, a squash court, Turkish and electric baths, a swimming pool, a barber shop, and a lending library. Individual rooms, decorated in a variety of styles ranging from Italian Renaissance to Old Dutch, were reported to be more than equal to those in Europe's finest hotels.

DISASTER STRIKES

The *Titanic*'s fame lay not only in its size and opulence, but also in the claim that it was unsinkable. It did not take long for the confidence of the ship's owners and builders to be shattered. On its maiden voyage, on April 14, 1912, the *Titanic* struck an iceberg off the coast of Newfoundland and sank. Of the 2227 people on board, only 705 survived. This incident became the world's worst maritime disaster as well as the most controversial, because the ship's crew had received numerous warnings about the threat of icebergs.

Could more lives have been saved if the warnings had been heeded? Were there enough lifeboats on board? Why were many lifeboats launched before they were filled to capacity? These and many other questions remain unanswered.

THE END OF AN ERA

In many ways, the *Titanic* and the disaster that befell it symbolize the age. The turn of the century was a time of prosperity and optimism. The numerous advancements made in science and technology in the previous half century had led many to believe that human achievements were potentially boundless and that progress was inevitable. Beliefs such as these led to the claim that the *Titanic* was unsinkable and later led to the conclusion that World War I was the "war to end all wars." In both cases the optimism of the age was shattered by these events. Thus the *Titanic* stands as a testimony to the grandeur and confidence of an age, while its fate signals the end of an era.

Painting by Ken Marshall from *The Discovery of the Titanic*, by Dr. Robert Ballard, published by Penguin/Madison Press Books, and protected by copyright as provided therein.

The Expansion of the Maritime Economy

Life for those in the Maritimes was much more prosperous. Traditionally the Maritime provinces had relied on shipbuilding and fish and timber exports. By the turn of the century, the boom in central Canada and the new market created by the settling of the West was having an impact on the economy of the East. Maritime entrepreneurs began to develop the coal and other mineral resources that were in great demand in central Canada. Fuelled by the coal and iron of Cape Breton, the Maritime provinces developed a wide range of steel products that won a large share of the expanding market in the Canadian West. By 1910, the Maritime economy had expanded to include pulp and paper, fish, timber, refined sugar, coal, and iron and steel products. The three eastern provinces shared in the prosperity sweeping the nation at the turn of the century.

The Growth of Cities

The profits from wheat exports energized the whole Canadian economy. Scientific advances transformed Canadian industry in the cities. The steam-driven engine, electricity, and hydro-electric power fuelled an industrial boom. So did a whole spectrum of new inventions, including the refrigerator car, the telephone, and the typewriter. The roar and clatter of heavy industry could sometimes be heard for kilometres. Young people left the farms for the cities. Men took jobs in factories and mills in the cities, and worked in construction and on the railways. Women worked in factories and offices, and as domestic servants for newly prosperous industrialists.

Canada in the nineteenth century had been a rural nation; four out of five of its people lived in the country. By 1920, however, half of them lived in towns and cities. Canada was fast becoming a modern industrialized nation. In the years between 1891 and 1911, the populations of Montreal and Toronto more than doubled. By 1921, Winnipeg was five times larger than it had been in 1891, and Vancouver had swelled to eight times its former size.

Civic pride swelled, too, as cities took up urban beautification schemes. From coast to coast they showed off new street lights, wide green boulevards, and tree-lined parks. Water and gas lines were laid, and sewage-treatment plants were built. Telephone

These newly arrived immigrants are studying to become Canadian citizens. Can you read the five duties of a good Canadian citizen?

and electrical wires leaped from corner to corner across the cities.

Canadians also had more ways to get where they wanted to go. Not one, but two more railroads were built in the West — the Canadian Northern and the Grand Trunk. The young (and not so young) took to bicycles, and a social revolution was born. The very rich bought themselves new contraptions called automobiles to show that they no longer lived in a horse-and-carriage world. Electric trams whirred through the downtown core and carried the first commuters to new suburbs. Fishing boats chugged out to sea, powered by gasoline engines. Everywhere Canadians were on the move, thanks to technology.

Wherever people turned, they took in the satisfying sight of yet another new convenience. Whether it was the telephone, the electric light, or a new threshing machine for harvesting wheat, waves of new inventions were transforming life in Canada. A belief in scientific progress took hold of Canadians as they confidently looked forward to even bigger and better things in the future. The phrase attributed to Laurier, "The twentieth century belongs to Canada," captures the optimistic spirit of the age. Two Canadians proudly boasted to a British audience,

> Fate holds in store for this young Dominion a golden future. In the vast forests, the coast and inland fisheries, the exhaustless coal deposits, the gold and silver mines, iron, copper, nickel, and nearly every other known variety of mineral, and, above all, in the tremendous possibilities of the grain fields, Canada holds the promise of such commercial prosperity as the world has seldom seen.

Poverty: The Underside of Prosperity

Not everyone shared in the optimism of the new industrial age. Behind the prosperity lay poverty, disease, and harsh working conditions. While many industrialists and businesspeople — the "tycoons" of the Golden Age — made huge fortunes, thousands of workers whose hard labour had made prosperity possible lived and worked in appalling conditions.

Many families could not afford decent housing. They crowded together in horrifying slum *tenements*. Reverend Charles Gordon, who wrote popular novels under the name of Ralph Connor, described Winnipeg's North End as "a howling chaos...an endless grey expanse of mouldering ruin." Dirty air and water, contaminated milk, and outdoor toilets meant that sickness and death were commonplace in the cities. One of every four babies born to poor parents died before its first birthday. For many people in Canada, the Golden Years were dark times.

Many workers in urban factories and in the western and northern mining, logging, and railway camps were non–English-speaking immigrants. Penniless, frightened, and confused by the new culture and strange language, these newcomers were a source of cheap labour. Employers believed these immigrants would accept without complaint pitiful wages for long, hard days in cramped, dirty, and dangerous working conditions. Wages were so low that many families could not survive on one income, and women and children had to take jobs outside the home just to make ends meet. In many urban centres, women and children accounted for as much as a third of all workers. Forced to take whatever jobs came their way, they often did the same work as men but for half the wages.

Employers tried hard to keep trade unionists out, and most workplaces were not unionized. But wages were so low and conditions so bad that strikes flared up in almost every industry, from the coal mines of Cape Breton and Vancouver Island to the cotton factories of Quebec and the switchboards of Bell Telephone. Strike breakers and the militia were often used to force workers back onto the job. The labour unrest that began in the Laurier years was to swell over the next few

NELLIE McCLUNG'S STRUGGLE TO WIN THE VOTE

The turn of the century was a time of tremendous change in Canada. The rapid increase in industrialization, the growth of cities, and the numerous inventions that changed the way people lived gave many reasons for optimism. Unfortunately, many Canadian women were unable to participate fully in society because they had neither political nor legal equality. Before 1917, an eligible voter in Canada was defined as "a male person, including an Indian and excluding a person of Mongolian or Chinese race…. No woman, idiot, lunatic, or criminal shall vote."

Besides lacking political rights, women also had very little economic security. They were paid less than men, and the money married women earned was legally the property of their husbands. Husbands also had control of their children and were legally entitled to physically abuse their wives.

By the time of the Laurier era, several women had become active in the struggle for women's rights. Central to the struggle was winning the right to vote, for with the vote would come the opportunity to influence political decision-making. One of the leading supporters of women's right to vote was Nellie McClung, who began her campaign for women's suffrage in Manitoba in 1911. In 1912, she helped to form the Political Equality League.

One of the barriers McClung had to face was the attitude of the government of Manitoba at the time. Premier Rodmond Roblin once commented, "I don't want a hyena in petticoats talking politics at me. I want a nice gentle creature to bring me my slippers." When a delegation led by McClung presented its case for the right of women to vote to the Manitoba legislature, Roblin responded:

Let it be known that it is the opinion of the Roblin government that women's suffrage is illogical and absurd as far as Manitoba is concerned. Placing women on a political equality with men would cause domestic strife…it will break up the home; it will throw the children into the arms of servant girls…. The majority of women are emotional and very often guided by misdirected enthusiasms, and if possessed of the franchise would be a menace rather than an aid.

McClung seized upon Roblin's remarks as an opportunity to make a mockery of the arguments against female suffrage. The day following Roblin's remarks, the Political Equality League held a "mock parliament," during which Nellie McClung turned the male arguments inside out:

The trouble is that if men start to vote, they will vote too much. Politics unsettles men, and unsettled men means unsettled bills, broken furniture, broken vows, and — divorce…. If men were to get into the habit of voting — who knows what might happen — it's hard enough to keep them home now. History is full of unhappy examples of men in politic life — Nero — Herod — King John….

By making the most of her opportunities to speak out publicly, Nellie McClung was able to build a solid base of support for women's suffrage. Success finally came for the women of Manitoba on January 27, 1916, when the Enfranchisement of Women Act was passed, giving women the right to vote. Over the next few years the work of Nellie McClung and several other suffragettes proved fruitful; eventually all Canadian women won full political rights.

The English suffragist Emmeline Pankhurst (left) and Canada's Nellie McClung were leaders in the struggle to win political and legal equality for women. Although they were successful, the struggle for social and economic equality continues. What changes need to be made in our society to further guarantee the equality of men and women?

decades as the union movement took hold across the nation.

The Reform Movement in Canada

Many Canadians were distressed by the growing poverty of the new industrial poor. Some reform-minded city councils and provincial governments tried to improve working and living conditions, but the amounts they spent on social reform were still woefully small. Laurier was committed to laissez-faire principles — "Let things be" — and the federal government did little to remedy the growing urban problems of worker exploitation, poverty, crime, and disease. Private charities were left to help the poor and sick.

As a result, newspapers began to publish sensational accounts of urban horrors. They aroused a public outcry, and social reformers swept into action. In 1911, J.S. Woodsworth, a social worker in Winnipeg's North End, published *My Neighbour,* in which he made an emotional appeal to Canadians to take action on the tragedy of the urban poor. Herbert Ames, who had written an exposé of the Montreal slums, became head of the city's board of health and worked hard to implement badly needed health reforms. In Ontario, J.J. Kelso founded children's aid societies to deal with homeless street children.

Church groups such as the Women's Christian Temperance Union (WCTU), the Young Men's Christian Association (YMCA), and the Salvation Army played an important role in the reform movement. Many Protestant reformers preached a "social gospel," teaching that it was everyone's duty to help improve the lot of less fortunate people. Women were often leading lights in the Christian reform movements. They pressed for better wages and safety standards in the workplace. They lobbied for the *prohibition* of child labour, prostitution, and alcohol. They demanded changes in education and health regulations and advocated many other social reforms.

The Women's Movement in Canada

Many female reformers were especially concerned with women's issues. Women's groups sprang up and made headlines in their fight for women's rights. Many prominent Canadian women became active in the growing **women's movement**. Lady Ishbel Aberdeen, the wife of the governor general, launched the National Council of Women in Toronto in 1893. Nellie McClung championed the fight for women's right to vote, as well as prohibition and urban reform. Marie Gérin-Lajoie rallied French Canadian women to push for higher education, fairer rights under the law, and legal protection for women and children. Dr. Emily Stowe, who was forced to seek her medical training outside Canada, and her daughter Dr. Augusta Stowe-Gullen lobbied hard for women's access to higher education and the professions.

The lives of women from all walks of life were changing rapidly at the turn of the century. More and more women entered the workforce. By 1901, over 13 percent of Canadian workers outside the home were women. Most worked as domestic servants or in the factories, mills, and sweatshops of the clothing industry. During the first decade of the twentieth century, a wide variety of white-collar jobs began opening up for women. These included teaching, sales and clerical positions, and telephone-operator jobs. Although more women worked in white-collar jobs, they continued to be paid less than men for doing the same work.

Art and Literature

Despite the country's economic and social problems, Canadian artists shared in the new spirit of national pride. They were keen to paint Canadian subjects, but many of them felt uncomfortable with the changes brought about by industrialization. With few exceptions, artists turned away from the cities to celebrate the Canadian landscape. Horatio

Walker, Homer Watson, and Ozias Leduc painted peaceful scenes of life in rural Ontario and Quebec. James Wilson Morrice and his friend Maurice Cullen used the techniques of the French Impressionist painters — short, quick brushstrokes and a palette of light, bright colours — to paint outdoor scenes around the St. Lawrence, especially in wintertime. Morrice was the first Canadian painter to win an international reputation. Cullen liberated Canadian landscape painting from the more formal Victorian tradition, and was highly regarded by the young artists who later became famous as the Group of Seven.

Writers were also keen to bring Canada into their writing and to help define the new nation. As the Canadian West opened up, dozens of short stories and novels recounted tales of western settlers, trappers, and prospectors, and of Metis, Mounties, and outlaws from the Prairies to the Pacific coast.

Many of the best-known writers of the time were poets, such as Charles G.D. Roberts, Isabella Valancy Crawford, Archibald Lampman, Pauline Johnson, Bliss Carman, and Duncan Campbell Scott. Some of their very best poems were tributes to Canadian nature. In "Winter Uplands,"

Maurice Cullen travelled to Paris, where he received much of his early training. Paintings such as *Logging in Winter, Beaupré* introduced impressionism to Canadian landscape painting.

Maurice Cullen, *Logging in Winter, Beaupre*, 1896. Art Gallery of Hamilton

While many young artists rushed off to Paris, Homer Watson drew his inspiration from the rich rural culture that flourished near his home in Doon, now a suburb of Kitchener, Ontario. Paintings such as *The Stone Road* established Watson as a prominent Canadian painter.

Homer Watson, *The Stone Road*, 1881. National Gallery of Canada

Lampman captured the wintery delights of the Canadian countryside at sunset:

> *The rippled sheet of snow where the wind blew*
> *Across the open fields for miles ahead;*
> *The far-off city towered and roofed in blue*
> *A tender line upon the western red;*
> *…The crunching snowshoes and the stinging air,*
> *And silence, frost and beauty everywhere.*

The End of the Laurier Era

In his early years as prime minister, Wilfrid Laurier had been successful in working out acceptable compromises. As time went on, however, the country was transformed and Laurier's policies became less effective. Canada had grown from a primarily rural country to an urban and industrialized nation. The peoples of Canada — especially western Canada — were now from many different cultures, and ethnic tensions were increasing across the country. The prosperity of the new industrial age had brought with it poverty and labour strife. Pressure was mounting on the federal government to take more decisive action on social and political reforms.

As the world teetered on the brink of World War I, smouldering hostilities between French-speaking and English-speaking Canadians were fanned into flame as Canada tried to decide how much it would support Britain in the upcoming conflict. The deep divisions within the country were finally too much for Laurier to mend. Nevertheless, during his fifteen years in office, Canada had been transformed into a modern, industrialized, and confident nation.

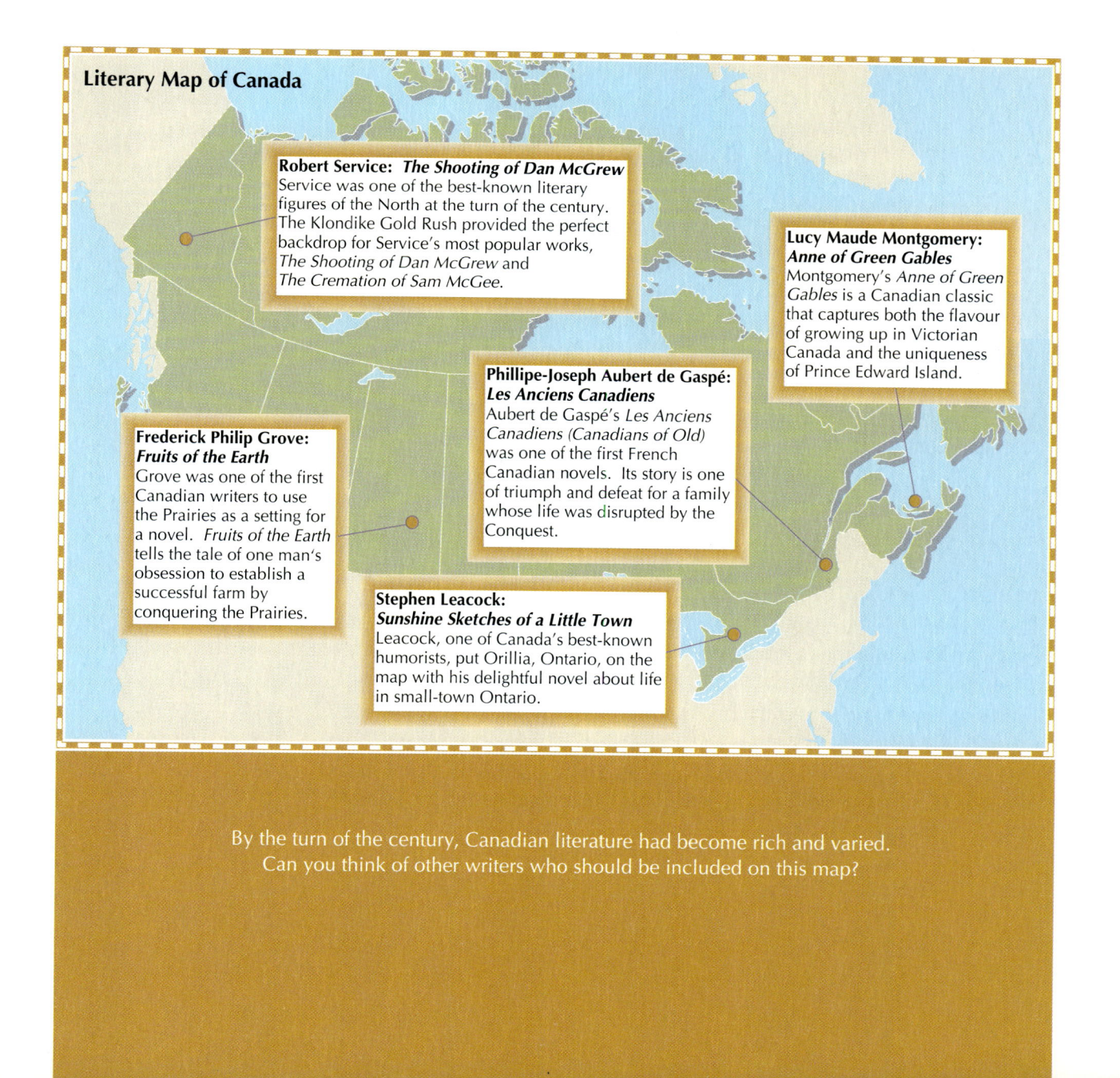

Literary Map of Canada

Robert Service: *The Shooting of Dan McGrew*
Service was one of the best-known literary figures of the North at the turn of the century. The Klondike Gold Rush provided the perfect backdrop for Service's most popular works, *The Shooting of Dan McGrew* and *The Cremation of Sam McGee*.

Lucy Maude Montgomery: *Anne of Green Gables*
Montgomery's *Anne of Green Gables* is a Canadian classic that captures both the flavour of growing up in Victorian Canada and the uniqueness of Prince Edward Island.

Phillipe-Joseph Aubert de Gaspé: *Les Anciens Canadiens*
Aubert de Gaspé's *Les Anciens Canadiens (Canadians of Old)* was one of the first French Canadian novels. Its story is one of triumph and defeat for a family whose life was disrupted by the Conquest.

Frederick Philip Grove: *Fruits of the Earth*
Grove was one of the first Canadian writers to use the Prairies as a setting for a novel. *Fruits of the Earth* tells the tale of one man's obsession to establish a successful farm by conquering the Prairies.

Stephen Leacock: *Sunshine Sketches of a Little Town*
Leacock, one of Canada's best-known humorists, put Orillia, Ontario, on the map with his delightful novel about life in small-town Ontario.

By the turn of the century, Canadian literature had become rich and varied. Can you think of other writers who should be included on this map?

KNOWING THE KEY PEOPLE, PLACES, AND EVENTS

In your notes, clearly identify and explain the historical significance of each of the following:

John A. Macdonald	Confederation
British North America Act	Rupert's Land
William Cornelius Van Horne	Dominion Lands Act
Wilfrid Laurier	Clifford Sifton
Frank Oliver	Klondike Gold Rush
Indian Act	Women's Movement

FOCUS YOUR KNOWLEDGE

1. Construct a time-line to show when each province entered Confederation and the circumstances under which it entered.
2. What role did Chinese workers play in the building of the CPR?
3. Give three examples of racism in Canadian immigration policy during the Laurier era.
4. What conditions had to be met in order for someone to purchase a quarter-section (64 hectares) of land under the Homestead Act?
5. Describe life on the Prairies for early settlers. Discuss the climate, settlers' homes, and the hardships they faced.
6. What government actions were forced on the Native peoples of the Prairies before the West was opened up for white settlement? Why did Native peoples accept such actions?
7. Describe how life changed in the cities at the turn of the century. Discuss the living and working conditions of urban labourers and the poor. Use specific examples to illustrate both the poverty and prosperity of the age.
8. Describe how women's roles in Canada changed during the Laurier era.
9. What did groups such as the Women's Christian Temperance Union, the Young Men's Christian Association, and the Salvation Army and individuals such as J.J. Kelso do to try to ease the social problems that existed during the Laurier era? Give specific examples.

APPLY YOUR KNOWLEDGE

1. While some historians portray John A. Macdonald as a nation-builder, others see him as a politician whose primary aim was to benefit Ontario and Quebec. Reflecting on Confederation, the building of the CPR, and the National Policy, which view do you think is the most accurate?

2. Despite Canada's efforts to attract settlers, the West experienced little if any real growth in population during the Macdonald era. What factors account for the greater success of the Liberals under Laurier?

3. "Canadian prosperity at the turn of the century was to some degree achieved at the expense of Native peoples." How would you respond to this statement? Should the actions of the Macdonald government be taken into account by today's federal government in its negotiations with Canada's Native peoples? If so, how?

4. The women's movement at the turn of the century focused its efforts on winning political and economic equality and on preserving traditional family values. What evidence can you find in this chapter to support this argument?

5. How are the Klondike Gold Rush and the *Titanic* symbolic of their age?

6. The Laurier era is generally perceived as an age of prosperity and optimism. While this may have been true for some, it was certainly not the case for all Canadians. Which groups of Canadians would have disagreed with this description, and why would they disagree?

EXTEND YOUR KNOWLEDGE

1. Research your community or area to find out what it was like at the turn of the century. How has it changed in the past century? Present your findings to the class by using a bulletin-board display that contrasts life in your community then and now. Consider in your research the population, industry, architecture, ethnic make-up, and other relevant factors.

2. Working in groups of four, try to renegotiate the land treaties between the Government of Canada and the Native peoples of the West. Two students should role-play government officials, while the other two role-play the Native chiefs. Do some background research before sitting down to negotiate. Both sides should approach the discussion with a clear set of objectives and a strategy.

3. Select one of the writers or works of literature that appears in the Literary Map of Canada on page 97. Research the writer or work of literature and share your findings with the class in a short presentation. Provide a brief biographical sketch, and explain to the class how this writer reflects the Laurier era or the changes occurring at this time.

CHAPTER 5

FRENCH–ENGLISH RELATIONS

GLOSSARY TERMS

Habitation The French word for "residence," associated with the dwelling Samuel de Champlain built at Quebec in 1608.

Seigneurial A French system of land ownership established in New France.

Habitants The farmers of New France.

Protestant Any of the Christian churches that separated from the Roman Catholic Church during the Reformation (in the sixteenth century) or afterward, including the Anglican, Baptist, Lutheran, Methodist, Presbyterian, and Reformed churches; also refers to a member of one of these churches.

Nationalists People who are devoted to the interests of their own nation.

Conscription The forced enlistment of recruits for the Canadian armed forces in World Wars I and II.

FOCUS ON:

- the nature of traditional French Canadian society
- how industrialization threatened French Canadian culture
- the divisions between the French and the English in Quebec
- the roots of Quebec nationalism and separatism
- Wilfrid Laurier's attempts to build a nation by compromise

In 1534, Jacques Cartier made his first voyage up the St. Lawrence River. He returned to the St. Lawrence area again in 1535 and 1541, before becoming disappointed in the region's resources. The French did not come to stay until seventy years later, when Samuel de Champlain sailed up the St. Lawrence River to Cape Diamond. In the chilly days of autumn 1608, he and a few followers began cutting the timber for their *habitation*. It was the beginning of the first permanent settlement in New France. This time, the French would leave their mark deep in the soil of North America.

France's claims to Canada were challenged by the British during the Seven Years War, a conflict between France and England from 1756 to 1763 that eventually spilled over into North America. When Quebec City fell to the British in September 1759, French rule in North America was nearing an end. After the surrender of Montreal the following spring, New France was handed over to the British. The first British governor of the conquered colony assumed that all its French roots had been cut and that New France would soon blossom as a British colony.

FRENCH CANADA BEFORE CONFEDERATION

By 1850, the two districts of the Province of Canada, Canada East (Quebec) and Canada West (Ontario), shared a British-style parliamentary government. But Canada East remained French to the core. Its system of land holdings was still rooted in the French *seigneurial* system, and its laws were was based on the French Civil Code. Life revolved around the family, the parish, and the Roman Catholic Church. Two centuries of history in North America had only strengthened a society rich in French customs, traditions, memories, and language.

French Canada in the 1850s

The pattern of life in Canada East in the 1850s had its roots in the earliest days of New France. The first *habitants* had settled side by side on narrow strips of land along the riverbanks. They cut back the forest and made clearings for fields, a small meadow, a barn, a stable, and a farmhouse with a patch of maple wood at the back for a sugary.

Over the years, the children and grandchildren of the original French settlers cleared their own land nearby. By 1850, settlements had spread inland along dirt roads that threaded across the countryside. The younger generations settled along the roads, often within shouting distance of relatives and neighbours. They still built their farmhouses in the French style. Although factory-made cloth — especially cotton — had appeared by the mid-nineteenth century, many French Canadians still wore clothing made of rough homespun wool or hand-woven linen.

In the mid-nineteenth century, men still sported the clay pipes and pony-tails that had been a common sight among habitants for generations. Many French Canadian farmers sold commercial farm products such as wheat, dairy goods, and meat for export. But many others still practised the farming methods of their French ancestors on subsistence farms, where families grew only what they needed.

Everyone in the large habitant families worked hard on the farm every day of the week, except Sunday. This was a day of rest, when families went to Mass and then gathered on the church steps to socialize with friends and neighbours. Sunday was also a time for visiting. Guests sometimes stayed till late at night, talking and laughing, singing and dancing, playing cards and telling favourite old tales. When families and friends gathered for special ceremonies — a wedding, a baby's christening, or a religious holiday — the celebration might last four or five days.

FRENCH CANADA AFTER CONFEDERATION

By the late nineteenth century, the pace of change had quickened in Quebec. In 1913, Louis Hémon published his beautiful and moving tribute to habitant life, **Maria Chapdelaine**. But the life it celebrated was fast slipping away. Only half of

The popular French Canadian novel Maria Chapdelaine was made into a successful film. Why do novels from the turn of the century still appeal to Canadians?

Cornelius Krieghoff, The Habitant Farm, 1856. National Gallery of Canada

KRIEGHOFF: ARTIST OF FRENCH CANADIAN LIFE

The special rhythms of habitant life in mid-nineteenth-century Quebec were captured in an astonishing number of paintings by **Cornelius Krieghoff**. Krieghoff, who grew up in Europe, was a fun-loving and sociable man who enjoyed the simple pleasures of ordinary experience. The close-knit society of rural Quebec suited him. His paintings are filled with intimate details of everyday habitant life.

In *The Habitant Farm*, a horse-drawn sleigh has come to a stop at the doorway of a farmhouse. The tired horse has its head in a feed bucket, munching oats. A large dog lifts its nose and wags its long, silky tail to welcome the family home. A woman has stepped out of the warmth of the house into a cold winter afternoon to listen to a child's tale of recent adventures. A young boy cracks a horsewhip in the air, and a man in a bright red tuque bends to lift a basket from a sleigh. In the distance, a traveller trudges up the snowy road with his walking stick in hand. Just beyond the traveller is the neighbour's barn, its steeply pitched roof gently lit by a pale afternoon sun.

The habitant farm and its inhabitants were Krieghoff's favourite subjects, and he painted them over and over again.

French Canadians still lived in the countryside; many had been forced to leave their childhood villages to make a living in larger communities. Habitant families were large, and existing farms were inherited by the oldest son.

In earlier times younger children had been able to clear lots in nearby forests, but by 1850 most of the good farmland in the St. Lawrence Valley had been settled. The only untouched land was in the back country of the Canadian Shield. It was a beautiful place of birch and white pine forests studded with lakes, but it was not suitable for farming. Those who tried to take up farming there often had to double as lumberjacks in the logging camps just to earn enough to live on.

Migration to the United States

In the 1830s, French Canadians sometimes went south to bale hay in Vermont or cut wood in Maine, but they almost always came home again. After 1860, however, many moved to the United States permanently. New England had become a centre for the textile and shoemaking industries, and factories were hiring men, women, and children. Between 1870 and 1900, thousands of French Canadians emigrated to the United States. By 1901, so many were living south of the border that some New England towns had their own French Canadian parishes, schools, and churches.

The massive loss of population to the United States alarmed many French Canadians. They were afraid that their language and culture might not survive in Quebec. The parish priest of St. Jerome worried that migration would be "the graveyard of the [French] race." One twentieth-century geographer has described the migration as a great "hemorrhage" draining the lifeblood of Quebec — its people. The flow of French Canadians to the United States did not stop until the U.S. government stopped most immigration during the Great Depression of the 1930s.

Rapid urbanization and industrialization brought with it deplorable living conditions for many who were not fortunate enough to share in the boom of the Laurier era.

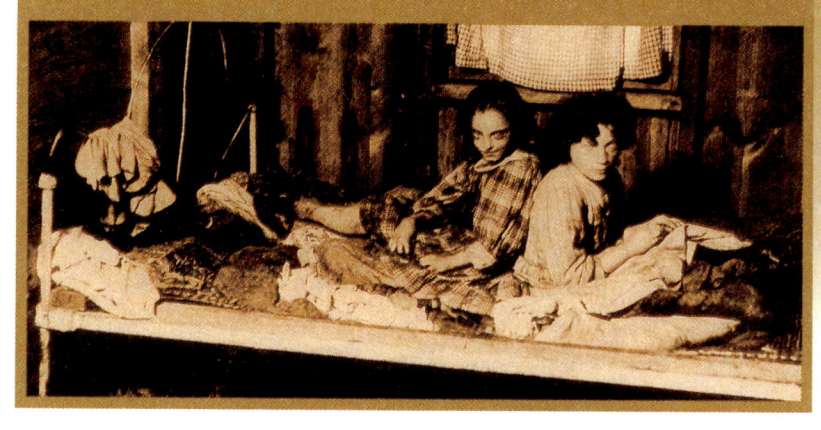

Migration to the Urban Centres of Quebec

Not all French Canadians who left the countryside headed for the United States. Many drifted into the cities of Quebec, especially Montreal. In the 1850s and 1860s, Montreal had undergone an industrial boom. It changed from the commercial centre of a thriving import–export trade to a major North American manufacturing centre. Its major industries were flour milling, sugar refining, wood processing, ironmaking, and shoemaking. By the time of Confederation, Montreal was the largest city in Canada. In the 1880s, it experienced a second manufacturing boom, and more new industries — including meat curing, tobacco, textiles, and clothing — sprang up along the Lachine Canal and the St. Lawrence River.

The factories of Quebec needed more workers, and many French Canadians left their villages to take low-paying jobs as unskilled workers in the newly industrialized centres. Almost half of them settled in Montreal. Between 1851 and 1891, Montreal's population grew from 57 715 to 219 616 — an astounding 280 percent growth rate. The new arrivals often crowded together into poor working-class neighbourhoods close to the factories.

FRENCH–ENGLISH RELATIONS

103

They lived in row houses thrown up quickly by speculators who paid little attention to planning, building codes, or sanitation. The houses were badly lit and badly ventilated. Many had only outdoor toilets. At first, water was sold door-to-door. When piped water was introduced in 1850, it was not filtered and caused outbreaks of typhoid. Most Montreal streets were unpaved dirt roads, dusty in the heat and muddy in the rain. Pigs, chickens, goats, and cows foraged in backyards and roamed city streets in spite of by-laws forbidding animals. Removing rotting animal carcasses was a constant concern for municipal health authorities. Poverty, lack of sanitation, and disease meant that death rates in working-class neighbourhoods — especially for infants — were high.

Working-class neighbourhoods were new to Montreal. Before industrialization, workers and merchants had tended to live together near the harbour. But in the 1860s, rich businesspeople and industrialists began moving to higher ground. They often settled on the slopes of Mount Royal in palatial stone homes surrounded by wide, green gardens. The area was so luxurious that it was soon nicknamed the "Golden Square Mile."

Most of the wealthy Montrealers were English-speaking, since *les Anglais* (the British) controlled business life in the cities. Many had come from towns and cities in Scotland and England. They were used to urban life and were familiar with commerce and industry. They became capitalists and canal builders, merchants and industrialists. In fact, so many British immigrants came to Montreal that for almost thirty-five years English-speakers were in the majority. By the mid-nineteenth century, Montreal was culturally and politically a British city.

Once French Canadians began taking jobs in the factories and the immigration from Britain slowed, the trend reversed. After 1865, French speakers were once again in the majority in Montreal. For the most part, French Canadians formed the working class and laboured in shops and factories for *les Anglais*. However, some French Canadians did become millionaires in the industrial boom of the late nineteenth century. Jean-Baptiste Rolland was one of them. A penniless farmer's son who moved to Montreal in 1832, he apprenticed as a typesetter and printer. Ten years later, he began peddling books and paper in the Quebec countryside. His business interests widened to include publishing and bookbinding, real estate and construction, and paper manufacturing. When Rolland died in 1888, he left a sizable fortune to his four sons.

But Rolland's career was an exception; French Canadians did not often enter the highest circles of commercial or social life. Montreal was at heart a divided city. Its social and economic divisions were so visible that it was sometimes called the "city of wealth and death."

Tensions between the English and the French communities grew. Struggles between town and country and between the wealthy and the poor joined the age-old conflicts over cultural and religious issues. The industrialization of Quebec and the dominance of the English upper classes upset many French Canadians. Their culture had been carefully preserved for two centuries, but they feared that the rural Catholic values on which their culture had been founded would not survive in such a different world.

Quebec: Homeland of French Culture

One of the reasons for the creation of the Dominion of Canada was to end the war between the two "nations" inside the Province of Canada. Quebec was to be the homeland of French culture and the Roman Catholic Church. The new Constitution would guarantee that the distinctive culture of French Canadians would be protected inside Quebec; it was to be a state within a state. Ontario would be British and *Protestant,* with some protections extended to its French Catholic minority.

THE WOODCARVERS OF SAINT-JEAN-PORT-JOLI

As home to some of the oldest European settlements in North America, Quebec is a province rich in traditions spanning several centuries. The picturesque town of Saint-Jean-Port-Joli is one Quebec village in which the past is preserved in cultural traditions. It is renowned for its woodcarvers, miniature boat builders, and weavers. In fact, this small town boasts the largest concentration of woodcarvers in North America.

The long tradition of woodcarving can best be seen in the Church of Saint-Jean-Port-Joli, which was built in 1779. Inside are exquisite woodcarvings spanning the years 1740 to the present. The oldest piece, which predates the church, is the tabernacle, carved in 1740 and later covered in gold leaf. In 1937 one of the church's most famous pieces, the pulpit, with carved figures of saints, was completed by two of Saint-Jean-Port-Joli's best-known woodcarvers, Médard and Jean-Julien Bourgault.

Credit for the tremendous revival and growth of woodcarving in Saint-Jean-Port-Joli falls to the three Bourgault brothers, Médard, André, and Jean-Julien. These three men not only established Saint-Jean-Port-Joli as a major woodcarving centre but also established the first school of woodcarving in Quebec, thereby ensuring that the tradition of woodcarving would continue to thrive.

Like the society of Quebec, which has evolved and changed over the century, the woodcarvers of Saint-Jean-Port-Joli too have undergone significant change in their art. Religious themes, which initially dominated, gave way in the 1930s to habitant themes that reflected the traditional lifestyle of rural French Canada. While habitant scenes remain popular, the current generation of artists in Saint-Jean-Port-Joli are experimenting with interpretative ways to capture youthful personalities.

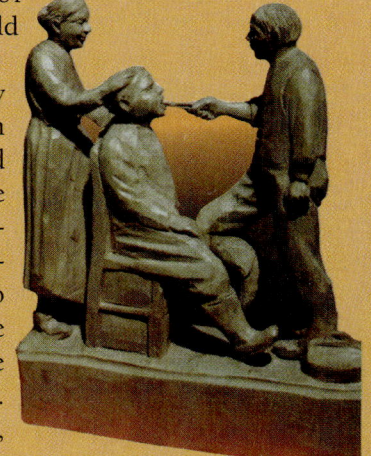

These three photos reflect very distinct phases in woodcarving in Saint-Jean-Port-Joli. The first is a modern piece, called *Près de l'étang*, by Pier Clautier. The second is a typical paysan or peasant scene, carved by André Bourgault, while the third is of the church, showing the influence of religion in early French Canadian society.

Confederation was to bring peace to the French-speaking and English-speaking communities by setting each on its separate but cooperative way.

French Canadians wanted to be sure that Confederation would be good for them. A French Canadian newspaper of the time said, "If the plan seems to safeguard Lower Canada's special interests, its religion and its nationality, we'll give it our support; if not, we'll fight it with all our strength." The federal government offered Quebec constitutional protections for its distinctive French culture. Quebec could make its own decisions about language, law, and religion; this promise was included in the British North America Act. In addition, French was also made an official language of the federal parliament and federal courts.

But many French Canadians were worried that the federal government might not keep the promises guaranteed in the Constitution and give in to majority English Protestant feeling. In the sixty years after Confederation, French and English Canadians clashed repeatedly over questions of French minority rights. French Canadians often wondered whether they were being treated fairly in Confederation or being exploited by the English majority.

SHOWDOWN IN THE WEST

Although Quebec emerged from Confederation as the "national" homeland in which French language and culture were free to flourish, there were pockets of French culture outside Quebec. Two such groups were the Acadians in the Maritimes and the Metis on the Prairies. One of the first threats to the fragile new peace between French and English occurred in the Red River settlement, then part of the North-Western Territory.

The Creation of Manitoba

In 1869, the Metis leader **Louis Riel** led most of the residents of Red River in establishing a provisional government. The Metis demanded recognition as a provisional government because no official government was in place at the time. Canada was just about to buy the lands of the North-Western Territory from the Hudson's Bay Company. Riel and his followers wanted to negotiate the terms under which their territory would become part of Canada. In part, they wanted their own provincial government and guaranteed protections for their language and religion. The Metis were successful in pressuring the Macdonald government into meeting their demands. In 1870 the Canadian government passed the Manitoba Act, which created a new provincial government, made French an official language of the new province, and provided for separate Catholic schools and for instruction in French.

Before the crisis, French Canadians had known very little about the French-speaking Metis or their wide-open country in the West. One French Canadian commented that most Quebeckers thought of the North-Western Territory as "a savage land, situated 'at the end of the world,' from which one only returns with the prestige of a great traveller." Once French Canadians learned more about their Catholic cousins in Manitoba, however, they were glad to have the Metis as allies in Confederation.

Renewed Conflict in Central Canada

But the Manitoba confrontation opened old wounds between the French and English communities of central Canada. During the crisis, a Protestant troublemaker called Thomas Scott was executed for treason by Riel's men. Protestants in Ontario were outraged and howled for his "murderers" to be brought to trial. Later, English-speaking recruits from Ontario were sent to act as voluntary soldiers at Red River. An Ontario volunteer was responsible for the death of a French-speaking Catholic named Elzéar Goulet. Now it was the Quebeckers' turn to be outraged. The hostilities over Red River sparked a new round of bitter accusations between French

METIS CULTURE AND SOCIETY

The Metis people represent the earliest blending of cultures in Canada. The Metis, who are the offspring of Native and European unions, drew from both cultures to create a new and distinctive culture.

Metis culture today reflects its European and Native origins. For example, the Metis have combined the leather skills of their Native ancestors and the glass beads introduced by Europeans to produce beaded moccasins, coats, belts, and mittens of superb artistry. Typical of the Metis work is the dog blanket shown here. Intricate bead work and vibrant colours combine to create a pleasing and enlivening effect.

Also, dance, a popular form of entertainment among the Metis, combines the intricate footwork of the traditional Native dances with elements of Scottish jigs. A popular instrument with the Metis is the fiddle, which they inherited from their Scottish ancestors. Often handmade from maple and birch, the fiddles were said to be tuned to "the cry of the loon and the bellow of a rutting moose."

Metis ingenuity is often credited with playing a critical role in the settling of the West.

By adapting carts common in Quebec to suit the needs of the Prairies, the Metis were able to fulfil the essential role of freight carriers in the late nineteenth century. Metis with their carts became such a common sight that a way was developed to describe them in a universal sign language among the Native peoples of the Prairies. Literally translated, the sign said the Metis were half wagon and half human.

Source: Dog blanket, Indian, Subarctic, Athapaskan. Fibre, bead, metal, skin. 45.0 x 42.0.
Collection: McCord Museum of Canadian History, Montreal.

These Metis traders from Saskatchewan are shown with their half-wagons. The unique wagons were used for moving to different locations.

and English in central Canada. In the midst of the turmoil Louis Riel fled to the United States, where he spent the next fifteen years.

The North-West Rebellion

By 1885, trouble in the West was brewing once again. Many of the Metis had left the Red River settlement. When the railway reached the eastern Prairies, it brought a human cargo of settlers to Manitoba. The settlement was swamped by the new arrivals. Many of them were English-speaking Protestants from Ontario who had no fondness for the French language or the Catholic Church. The Metis were unable to live in the old way, and they looked for another place where they could hunt and farm in peace.

They headed for the far western plains, but once again they began to sink under an advancing tide of settlers. Fearing for their lands and way of life, the Metis and white farmers looked to the Canadian government for help. Ottawa bureaucrats received long, worried reports from missionaries, police officers, and ordinary tradespeople about a rebellion brewing on the western Prairies. Macdonald's government did almost nothing. Finally, the Metis called on Louis Riel to help them once more. After being invited back to Canada to lead the Metis, Riel headed an armed rebellion on the plains of western Saskatchewan. This time, his actions ended in defeat.

Riel was captured, tried for treason, and condemned to death. However, the jury recommended mercy; Riel had suffered from bouts of insanity, and he may not have been sane at the time of the uprising. His fate was in Prime Minister Macdonald's hands. Macdonald, however, was not just weighing one man's fate; he was also thinking about reactions in Ontario and Quebec. His minister of the interior put the matter to Macdonald this way: "If he is not hanged — unless the evidence of insanity be clear — Ontario will be furious and if his sentence be commuted to imprisonment in a lunatic asylum, Quebec will be unceasingly clamouring for his discharge." Mercy lost out. Macdonald declared that Riel "shall hang, though every dog in Quebec bark in his favour." Louis Riel died on the gallows at Regina in November 1885.

At his trial, Louis Riel spoke in his own defence. Although some questioned his sanity, Riel spoke passionately and eloquently at his trial. He was hanged for treason on November 6, 1885.

The Legacy of Louis Riel

To many Ontarians, Riel was a treasonous rebel and the murderer of Thomas Scott. To many Quebeckers, he was a brave if misguided defender of a French Catholic minority, and at his death a storm of protest broke out in Quebec. When the young **Wilfrid Laurier** addressed a giant rally in Montreal after Riel's execution, he said, "Had I been born on the banks of the Saskatchewan I would myself have shouldered a musket."

Riel's death jolted French Canadians into thinking that the English majority might be able to control the federal government. The Quebec leader Honoré Mercier saw Riel's death as "a declaration of war on the influence of French Canada in Confederation, a violation of right and justice." He called on French Canadians to form a "national" front within the borders of Quebec.

But Confederation was not broken, and the three French Canadians in Macdonald's cabinet stayed in the government. Eleven years later, Wilfrid Laurier was ready to make a fresh start. When he became prime minister, he called for English and French to remember the spirit of Confederation and "live in peace and harmony."

Laurier and the Art of Compromise

As Canada changed from a rural to an industrialized nation during the Laurier years, Canadians were often divided about what was best for the nation. Laurier had to find a delicate balance among different interests and rival groups. It was no easy task; his success depended on drawing conflicting groups together in a spirit of tolerance and fair play.

Laurier turned compromise — finding an answer that would satisfy all sides — into a political art. His first challenge came during the disagreement between French-speaking and English-speaking Manitobans over funding for Roman Catholic schools. Laurier gave a speech in which he retold Aesop's fable about the competition between the sun and the wind, in which the sun succeeded in making a traveller take off his coat by shining down sunny warmth while all the fierce blowing of the cold north wind had failed.

Laurier's "sunny way" was the heart of his strategy as prime minister. He used discussion and persuasion rather than direct federal action to settle disputes. He tried to steer a middle course between the strongly Protestant elements in English-speaking Canada and the French Catholics of Quebec and Manitoba for the rest of his political career.

The Manitoba Schools Act

Laurier's skill at bringing French and English together was first tested in Manitoba. Bad feeling over Riel was still in the air when new trouble broke out in the West. French-speaking Catholics had been guaranteed official bilingualism and separate Catholic schools when the province entered Confederation. However, in 1890 Manitoba passed the **Manitoba Schools Act**, which cut off money for Roman Catholic schools in the province and made English the only language of instruction. What Riel and his followers had won for the Metis in Manitoba was now being taken away. Manitoba's Catholics appealed to the federal government for help. In the Manitoba Act, Ottawa had made constitutional promises to take action if the rights of the French Catholic minority in the province were threatened. The only question was whether Macdonald's government had the political will to enforce the law.

Macdonald decided to wait, and when he died in 1891 the problem was still not settled. Five years later, Wilfrid Laurier came to power and the Manitoba schools issue was still simmering. Laurier was a French Canadian and a Roman Catholic. His deepest sympathies lay with the French Catholics of Manitoba, but when it came to possibly explosive French–English conflicts, Laurier was very wary.

> As leader of the opposition Liberal Party in Quebec, Honoré Mercier often stated that Quebec would be better off as an American state than as a Canadian province. How would you respond to this statement today?

He looked for a way to give something to both groups. Eventually he struck a compromise: Manitoba would not have to support Catholic separate schools, but the public system would provide a half hour at the end of each school day for religious instruction. Also, a French-speaking teacher would be provided wherever ten or more students spoke French. The compromise was accepted, but it did not satisfy anyone completely. It was less than Catholics had demanded and not all that the Manitoba government and Protestants had hoped for. Laurier's compromise did not work for long. In 1916 the Manitoba government withdrew all the concessions won by Laurier, and English became the only language used in Manitoba schools.

The pattern was set for schools in the West. When Saskatchewan and Alberta were preparing to enter Confederation, a new quarrel erupted over Roman Catholic education and French-language rights and these provinces' French-speaking minorities were left with few protections. The story of the West seemed to be the slow whittling away of French minority rights.

RISING NATIONALISM IN QUEBEC

The events on the Prairies caused a bitterness among French Canadians at being treated like foreigners in the western provinces of their own country. The bitterness lasted long after the political crisis had ended. Many French Canadians came to believe they could only be comfortable in Quebec. The Quebec leader **Henri Bourassa** was in many ways a barometer of changing hopes and fears in Quebec's French-speaking communities. He commented on Quebeckers' growing sense of isolation from the rest of the nation — their feeling that Canada was not "Canada for all Canadians." The people of Quebec, Bourassa added, "are bound to come to the conclusion that Quebec is our only country because we have no liberty elsewhere."

Bourassa was the grandson of Louis-Joseph Papineau, the leader of a rebellion in Lower Canada in 1837. Like his grandfather, Bourassa led the fight for the rights of the French Canadian minority. French Canadians were intent on *la survivance* — the preservation of French Canadian society. Bourassa and many other Quebeckers became even more strongly committed to protecting and promoting the French heritage inside Quebec.

Nationalism in French and English Canada

Although both French and English Canadians had faith and pride in their country, they had very different ideas about Canada. Most French Canadians were deeply patriotic, but it was a patriotism rooted in Quebec and the French language. As a young man in 1834, **George-Étienne Cartier**, one of the founders of Confederation, wrote a song called "O Canada! My Land! My Loves!" The first verse (translated from French) reads,

The stranger sees with the envious eye
The St. Lawrence's majestic course;
At the sight the Québécois cries out,
"O Canada, my land, my loves!"

It is the French Canadian homeland along the St. Lawrence River that Cartier celebrated in the song.

The Boer War and French–English Conflict

Many English Canadians also were deeply patriotic, but they thought of Canada as a self-governing

British colony. Their love for Canada was expressed as loyalty to Queen Victoria and the British Empire. They shared in Britain's dreams of empire-building, of flying the Union Jack over British colonies all around the globe.

In the fall of 1899, Canadian imperialists were urging Canadians to help Britain in its battle for two small South African republics, the Transvaal and the Orange Free State. The Boers (Dutch settlers) who lived there had clashed with Uitlanders (mostly British immigrants) over the Uitlanders' migration to newly discovered gold fields and the question of Uitlander civil rights under Boer rule. Tensions mounted between the Boers and the British. In 1899, under the leadership of the Transvaal president, the Boers declared war on Britain. Britain asked Canada to send troops to South Africa to help defeat the Boers.

When the **Boer War** broke out on October 11, 1899, English and French Canadians were divided over Canada's role. Many English Canadians — especially in Ontario — were proud to be part of the British Empire. They felt that Canada should take an active role in British imperial affairs. French Canadians, led by Bourassa and his newly formed nationalist group, La Ligue Nationaliste Canadienne, were against Canada's participation. They were joined by some farm groups who shared Bourassa's view that Canada should not have to fight a British war in a far-off continent. Canada had enough troubles at home without entering into Britain's imperial adventuring abroad. Canadians who opposed sending troops to South Africa were also worried that the action would set a precedent. In future, they believed, Canada would be obliged to take part in every new British conflict around the world.

Laurier was determined to steer a cautious middle course and find a compromise acceptable to both French and English Canada. He feared that otherwise the country would rupture along French and English lines. "A greater calamity could never take place in Canada," he warned. Convinced that the English Canadian majority would not be satisfied without at least token Canadian support in South Africa, Laurier decided to outfit a voluntary force of 1000 infantry and send them to South Africa. Once Canadian troops reached Cape Town, however, it was up to Britain to pay for their keep.

In all, about 7000 Canadian soldiers and nurses took part in the Boer War. Laurier's compromise had been grudgingly accepted, but it satisfied few Canadians. Bourassa nicknamed the prime minister "Waffley Wilfy" because Laurier refused to take a clear stand on Canada's role within the British Empire. Some English Canadians called him "Sir Won'tfrid" because he refused to provide more than token support to Britain.

The Naval Bill

Tensions between English and French Canadians flared up again only a few years later. Britain and Germany were flexing their military muscles and preparing for a fight. Britain knew that naval power was the key to victory, but the German fleet was among the best in the world. British spies had discovered that Germany was building four more "dreadnoughts" — large, heavily armed battleships. The cry for more British battleships — "We want eight and we won't wait" — rang out across the British Isles, and Britain turned to Canada for help.

Henri Bourassa, the founding editor of *Le Devoir*, became a chief spokesperson for French Canada against Canadian entanglements in British imperial wars such as the Boer War. Was Bourassa right to warn French Canadians of the dangers of British imperialism?

The 2nd battalion of the Canadian Mounted Rifles leaving for home in 1902, at the end of the Boer War. Considering Canada's connection to the British Empire, do you think Canadian troops should have fought in this war?

Again Laurier offered a compromise — this time, the **Naval Service Bill**. Canada would not contribute to the British navy, but it would build a small navy of its own that could be placed under British control with the consent of Canada's Parliament. Pro-British Canadians were still waiting for a chance to show the unity and strength of the British Empire. They sneered at what they saw as another instance of token Canadian support. They called the proposed five cruisers and six destroyers a "tin pot" navy and accused Laurier of giving Britain too little, too late.

French Canadian *nationalists* were outraged that Canada was prepared to help Britain at all. They still felt that the rest of the British Empire should look after itself. "Let Canada first be looked after," Bourassa declared, and he founded the daily newspaper *Le Devoir* in 1910 partly to defeat Laurier's naval plans. He and his followers believed that Canada would now be drawn automatically into every fight Britain became involved in around the world. They argued that *conscription* — involuntary military service in wartime — would soon follow.

In a by-election just before the national election of 1911, French Canadian nationalists dressed up as recruiting officers and knocked on doors across Quebec to get out the vote against the Liberals. Many French Canadians believed that only they were being asked to compromise. English Canadians, they claimed, had had it all their own way since Confederation.

Laurier had dedicated himself to easing tensions between Canadians through reason and fair play, but he found himself scorned by English and French alike. In a campaign speech in 1911 he said, "I am branded in Quebec as a traitor to the French, and in Ontario as a traitor to the English.... In Quebec I am attacked as an Imperialist, and in Ontario as an anti-Imperialist. I am neither. I am a Canadian." On September 21, 1911, Laurier's government went down to defeat. The Laurier years had come to an end.

KNOWING THE KEY PEOPLE, PLACES, AND EVENTS

In your notes, clearly identify and explain the historical significance of each of the following:

- *Maria Chapdelaine*
- *Les Anglais*
- Wilfrid Laurier
- Henri Bourassa
- George-Etienne Cartier
- Naval Service Bill
- Cornelius Krieghoff
- Louis Riel
- Manitoba Schools Act
- *La Survivance*
- Boer War

FOCUS YOUR KNOWLEDGE

1. How was life changing for French Canadians in the late nineteenth century?
2. How was Confederation supposed to help ensure the preservation of French Canadian culture?
3. Did the patriotism of French Canadians differ from English Canadian patriotism? If so, how?
4. Explain why French Canadians were reluctant to become involved in the Boer War and the compromise worked out by Laurier.
5. Why were neither French Canadians nor pro-British Canadians pleased with the Naval Service Bill?

APPLY YOUR KNOWLEDGE

1. The industrialization of Quebec not only challenged the traditional lifestyle of French Canadians but also served to heighten tensions between the French and English. What evidence in this chapter supports this statement?
2. Although Confederation included guarantees to Quebec, French-speaking Canadians living outside of Quebec, such as the Metis and the Acadians, had no such guarantees. Provide evidence of this by referring to issues such as the Riel rebellions and the Manitoba Schools Act.
3. What evidence in this chapter suggests that the separatist movement in Quebec today had its roots in the rising nationalist movement of the late nineteenth century?

EXTEND YOUR KNOWLEDGE

1. Do further research to prepare for a discussion of the issues surrounding Confederation. Some students should represent French Canadian concerns, and others should role-play the part of John A. Macdonald and other English Canadian politicians. All students should prepare a brief outlining either their demands or the compromises they are willing to make to ensure that Quebec enters Confederation.

2. After carefully reading current newspapers and magazines, try to discover what the major concerns of French Canadians are today. Groups of three or four should then prepare charts for display that list (a) French Canadian concerns during the past century; (b) French Canadian concerns today; (c) English Canada's response during the past century; and (d) English Canada's response today.

3. Hold a festival to capture some of the flavour of the traditional French Canadian lifestyle. This will require selecting a particular holiday, such as St. Jean Baptiste Day, as well as researching and preparing traditional foods, clothes, music, and games.

CHAPTER 6
CANADIAN–AMERICAN RELATIONS

GLOSSARY TERMS

American Civil War The armed struggle in the United States, from 1861 to 1865, between the Union of northern states and the Confederacy of southern states. It was won by the North after the loss of more than 600 000 lives.

Confederacy In the United States, the union of eleven southern states from 1861 to 1865.

Annexation The result when a country or territory is taken over and made part of another nation.

Expansionism The policy of extending influence over other lands or countries, either by taking territory by force or by increasing economic control.

Reciprocity A Canada–United States trade agreement allowing a large number of goods to cross the border without a tariff.

Nationalism Support for the interests and advancement of one's own nation, even at the expense of other nations.

Continentalism The policy of establishing strong economic and/or political ties between the United States and Canada.

Imperialism The policy of extending authority or control by one country or empire over other lands by using political, economic, or military means.

FOCUS ON:

- how the American Civil War helped push Canada toward Confederation
- why Canadians were fearful of American expansionism
- the many troubles facing the young nation of Canada in the years following Confederation
- the debate between continentalists, imperialists, and nationalists
- why Wilfrid Laurier's government was unable to sell the idea of free trade to Canadians

On July 1, 1867, Canada celebrated its first day as a nation. In Ottawa, the largest party in the city's history began with parades, speeches, and picnics. **John A. Macdonald** and the other founders of **Confederation** had succeeded in creating a new nation, but what kind of nation was it? What would hold it together once the celebration was over? Would the new nation be worth all the effort?

The Dominion of Canada faced many challenges. Accommodating regional and cultural differences was one of the obstacles that had to be overcome. Even Canada's political identity was doubtful. Canada was not yet a complete and free nation, but part independent country and part British colony. Its flag was the British Union Jack, its monarch was Britain's Queen Victoria, it had adopted English systems of law and government, and all Canadians were considered British subjects. In fact, creating Canada was as much a British as a Canadian idea. In the years before Confederation, Britain had wanted to lighten the financial burden of supporting its colonies across the Atlantic. It had urged its North American colonies to take up nationhood.

By contrast, the colonies that became the United States had come together of their own accord and in defiance of Britain. They had proclaimed a new nation in the Declaration of Independence and then had thrown off British rule in the **American Revolution** of 1776. Having won their liberty, the Americans cut all their ties to England and set up an independent republic.

TROUBLED RELATIONS

If Canadians could not say exactly what they were, many knew what they did not want to be — Americans. Although Canada had chosen a model similar to the American system of a federation, it was a federation with a difference. Instead of having an elected House of Representatives and Senate along the lines of the American Congress, Canada followed the British lead by creating an elected House of Commons but a nonelected Senate. Although Canada had no titled aristocracy who inherited the right to sit in a House of Lords, it did have a small, privileged, and wealthy upper class whose members could be appointed to the Senate. Under the British North America (BNA) Act, anyone appointed to the Senate had to have at least $4000 — a large amount in 1867 — to qualify for the appointment. Senators were to hold in check the elected members of the House of Commons and, in Macdonald's words, make sure that no "hasty or ill-considered legislation" was passed.

Many Canadians thought of American democracy as the nearest thing to mob rule. The United States had an elected president instead of a monarch, and the final power rested with the people through their votes. "**Mobocracy**," in which the votes of the poor and undereducated counted just as much as those of the propertied and educated elite, was sure to result in a society that was rough, crude, disorderly, unpredictable, and violent. It was even suggested that the beginning of that nation in a bloody revolt against the British king had set America on the road to lawlessness. The editor of *University Magazine* wrote, "The United States began with an act of lawlessness and their conduct ever since has been moved by that spirit."

By contrast, many Canadians felt that the British system of constitutional monarchy was based on a proper sense of order and respect for authority. Holding fast to British government and the British monarch, they thought, would keep British North America free of American ideas.

Confederation and the American Civil War

Especially frightening to Canadians at the time of Confederation was the violent spectacle of the *American Civil War* — one of the bloodiest wars

"WE IN CANADA SEEM TO HAVE LOST ALL IDEA OF JUSTICE, HONOR AND INTEGRITY."—THE MAIL, 26TH SEPTEMBER.

J.W. Bengough was one of the best political cartoonists of the late nineteenth century. What Canadian scandal is this cartoon referring to?

The American Civil War was one of the first in history to be photographed. How would pictures such as this one of the Gettysburg battlefield affect people's attitudes toward war? What impact might these images of the Civil War have on Canadians?

ever fought in North America. The United States was a union of separate states under the umbrella of a federal government. But under the U.S. Constitution, the states were strong and the federal government was weak. Unhappy in the Union for a number of reasons, eleven southern states claimed "states' rights" and began to raise their own armies. The U.S. government had been powerless to stop them. The country divided when the southern states left the Union to form the *Confederacy*, and the northern states joined battle to keep them in the Union.

To Macdonald the grim spectacle of the Civil War was proof enough that a federal system of government would surely disintegrate unless the central government was the supreme power. He insisted that the Canadian government should have a tight hold on the reins of power. This was achieved above all by the sweeping constitutional powers granted to the federal government under the BNA Act to maintain "peace, order, and good government."

Some British North Americans gloated at the sight of the American republic being brought to its knees by civil war. But there was a real threat that the northerners might attack Canada in revenge for British support of the South during the war. For example, Britain had let southerners build and outfit the so-called "merchant marine ship" *Alabama* in a Liverpool drydock, but it was really a deadly battleship. For two years the *Alabama* plagued the northern U.S. seaboard. American newspapers later claimed that the *Alabama* had kept the war going for two extra years at a cost of $4 billion and countless lives. Northerners were furious about damage from the *Alabama*'s attacks. In revenge they threatened to invade Britain's territory in North America once they had defeated their enemies in the South. Meanwhile, they would fight one war at a time.

The threat of forced *annexation* with the United States sent shock waves of fear through the British North American colonies. It seemed that there

Ships such as the Confederate ship *Alabama*, built in British shipyards, angered the United States government, which sought to retaliate by striking at Canada. How might American threats help to hasten Confederation?

might be safety in numbers; at least, that was the view Britain urged on its colonies. Several colonies decided to take cover in Confederation to save themselves from American invasion. One Quebecker spoke for many worried colonists in saying, "Unless we hurry up and head with all sails into Confederation, the currents will carry us rapidly toward annexation." Another Quebecker put it even more simply: "Separate from each other, we'd be sure to be invaded and crushed one after the other."

The Threat of American Expansionism

It is not surprising that British North Americans feared their next-door neighbours. The United States had never hidden its strong leaning toward *expansionism*; its aim had always been to stretch across the face of North America. American expansionists talked about America's **Manifest Destiny** to form a continental nation that included Mexico and Canada. The United States had already acquired sizable pieces of the North American continent. As one angry Canadian nationalist of the time, G.T. Denison, put it, the Americans "wanted Florida, and they took it; Louisiana and Alaska they annexed; California and Mexico they conquered; Texas they stole." He claimed that the Americans had also "swindled" Canada out of half the state of Maine and had tried a dozen ways to conquer British North America. Denison believed that "the Yankees are our greatest, if not only, enemies…we should never trust them." Not everyone was as hostile toward the United States, but suspicion of American expansionism was shared by many Canadians.

In the years after Confederation, the United States seemed more interested in taking Canadian territory through politicking and diplomacy than through open warfare. But Canadians remembered the War of 1812 and did not rule out the possibility of yet another American invasion. Even after the four horrifying years of the Civil War and half a million dead, American military strength continued to increase. Canada knew that if the United States decided to make war, it was powerless to stop them. Nor could Britain be counted on for help. The British did not have the military might or the political will to fight the United States. American threats of annexation, real and imagined, continued to haunt Canadians for decades after Confederation.

Canada–U.S. Conflicts on Other Fronts

Relations between the two countries on other fronts were also strained for many years. In 1866, the Americans ended a *reciprocity* (free trade) agreement and began imposing tariffs on imports of Canadian natural-resource products. Many Canadians saw this as a move to weaken the Canadian economy and force annexation with the United States. Fisheries agreements with the United States on the Atlantic and Pacific coasts also proved to be painful and costly. One Canadian politician protested, "Canada gets the shells and the United States gets the oysters." Although Canadian sealing boats in the Bering Strait were seized by U.S. warships, as the Americans explained, to save dwindling seal herds, American sealers were allowed to hunt undisturbed. One of the worst economic blows came near the end of the century with the McKinley Tariff, which imposed a new tax on Canadian wheat and endangered Canada's important U.S. grain trade. Western farmers were angry; when Macdonald toured the West in 1890, he found they could talk of almost nothing but the "dirty dealing" by the Americans.

A STRUGGLING YOUNG NATION

The young country had its own problems, and by the late 1880s predictions of Canada's collapse were common. The execution of Louis Riel and conflicts over French-language rights had split French and English Canadians into warring camps. The

118

THE REAL McCOY

As the twentieth century dawned, the world was undergoing significant technological change. New inventions such as the telephone, the automobile, and the radio abounded in Canada and the United States. Many Canadian inventors spent countless hours developing their ideas in an attempt to achieve fame and fortune.

Among the Canadians who made significant contributions to the world of technology was Elijah J. McCoy, a black Canadian from Colchester, Ontario, who revolutionized machinery operation and maintenance with the invention of a self-lubricating device. So great was the demand for the "lubricator cup" that people who had the device began to boast about having "the Real McCoy," a phrase that is still popular today. McCoy's lubricator cup continues to be widely used in the industrial world.

Quebec nationalist leader Honoré Mercier swept to power in the province on a wave of separatist feeling. A lingering economic depression was driving farmers and working people to the edge of despair. Western farmers were reeling under a cycle of drought, poor crops, and low world prices. They complained bitterly about tariffs and freight rates that seemed to favour the manufacturers of central Canada. Workers suffered under low wages and sometimes appalling working conditions.

As a result, thousands of young Canadians headed south to seek a better future in the United States. The 1890 census estimated that 1.5 million Canadians — equal to nearly a third of Canada's population — lived in the United States. The troubles faced by Canada led Wilfrid Laurier to worry out loud that the young nation was ready to break apart: "We have come to a period in the history of this country when premature dissolution seems to be at hand." The only question seemed to be which fragments would fall into American hands.

CANADIAN NATIONALISM AND THE NATIONAL POLICY

The combination of American hostility and Canada's domestic troubles made Canada's future look bleak. By 1890, Canadians were asking Prime Minister Macdonald how he intended to save the young nation. His answer was to repeat the plan he had followed since the election of 1878 — the **National Policy** — including a proposal for a new tariff, or tax, on the price of American-made goods. The tariff policy was strongly linked to two other policies: completing the transcontinental railway and encouraging immigration to the West.

What was the connection between tariffs, railways, and immigration? A protective tariff was meant to keep less expensive American goods out of Canada and help struggling new industries in central Canada. The idea behind this policy was that once a thriving population of new immigrants settled the Canadian West, they would buy Canadian products and in return supply eastern Canada with wheat and natural resources. Once the east–west trade was under way, Macdonald predicted, the Canadian economy would boom. As all Canadians grew wealthier, tensions between rich and poor and between the nation's regions would ease. Above all, Canada would be saved from the threat of American economic domination. It was to be "Canada for Canadians."

The National Policy: For Better or Worse?

The word "national" in National Policy was no accident. Macdonald believed that if Canada entered into an economic union with the United States, it would be just a matter of time before it would enter a political union with the United States. He saw the National Policy as a way to protect an independent Canadian nation in North America.

What were the results of Macdonald's National Policy? Historians do not agree on the answer. High tariffs did benefit certain groups and regions; in fact, Macdonald's finance minister was mobbed by people wanting tariff protection. He complained that everyone "who had ever raised a pig or caught a smelt wants protection for his industry." Under tariff protection some Canadian industries, especially those in Ontario and Quebec, began to prosper. But the tariffs on American goods were high. In 1879, tariffs as high as 30 percent were added to the cost of a wide range of goods, including refined sugar, woollen and cotton cloth, nails, engines, and farm equipment. That meant that Canadians faced price increases on all kinds of ordinary goods.

Not all regions shared in the growing prosperity of central Canada. In the Maritimes and the West, people felt the pinch of tariff protection. Angry fishers, shipbuilders, farmers, and others complained about paying too much for tariff-protected equipment at work and for clothing and food at home. Western grain farmers were the angriest of all. They complained about the high cost of shipping their wheat by Canadian railways and about the high tariff slapped on American farm tools that were cheaper and often better made.

Some historians think that the struggling new industries of central Canada needed protection from an expanding American economy. They say that tariffs, railways, and western settlement all helped to create a strong and close-knit Canadian economy. Others are not so sure about the benefits of the National Policy. Was it really "national"? Or did it help certain classes or regions at the expense of others? Did Canada survive as a nation because of the National Policy, or in spite of it?

Life on prairie farms at the end of the nineteenth century was difficult at the best of times. How would you have gone about attracting settlers to the West and getting them to stay?

CONTINENTALISM AND IMPERIALISM

Not everyone a century ago agreed with Macdonald that *nationalism* was the answer to Canada's troubles. Even though the National Policy had been official policy since 1878, by the last decade of the nineteenth century Canada was still sliding toward disaster. Some Canadians thought that *continentalism* would heal the young nation's wounds, while others felt that *imperialism* was the only cure. The debate among Canadian nationalists, continentalists, and imperialists raged on.

Canadian Continentalism

Continentalism is the belief that the economic geography of North America is naturally oriented north and south. Continentalists pointed to rivers that flowed north and south and to the Great Plains extending from both sides of the Canada–U.S. border as proof that the continent was meant for north–south traffic. Therefore there ought to be free trade between Canada and the United States. To force commerce in an east–west direction was against the natural order, they argued, and would impair Canada's ability to develop its economy successfully. Canadians and Americans would each find national strength in a closer north–south economic union.

Some continentalists also argued that tariffs against American goods had actually created the regional and class conflicts that threatened to destroy the young country. Tariffs set Maritimers and western Canadians against central Canadians and pitted manufacturers against farmers and workers, rich against poor. Only tearing down the trade barriers could save the troubled young nation, economically and politically. A common market would create a healthy trade between Canada and the United States. It would also bring peace to Canada, they said, by reducing regional hostilities and class conflict.

But not all continentalists cared about the survival of Canada. Some were happy with the idea of a political union with the United States. **Goldwin Smith**, a leading Canadian historian and journalist, was a committed continentalist. He argued that Canadians shared with Americans the same traditions, language, social customs, and political values. Together, he said, the two nations should create a single English-speaking nation of North America. Smith argued that Canadians' traditional suspicion of the Yankees was foolish. The Americans, he said, had "no craving for more territory"; there was nothing to fear in political union. Other Canadians agreed with him that Americans were no longer enemies. At the New Brunswick centennial celebrations in 1887, the Stars and Stripes snapped in the breeze next to the Union Jack. The lieutenant-governor proclaimed that "no feeling of hostility new exists between ourselves and our American cousins."

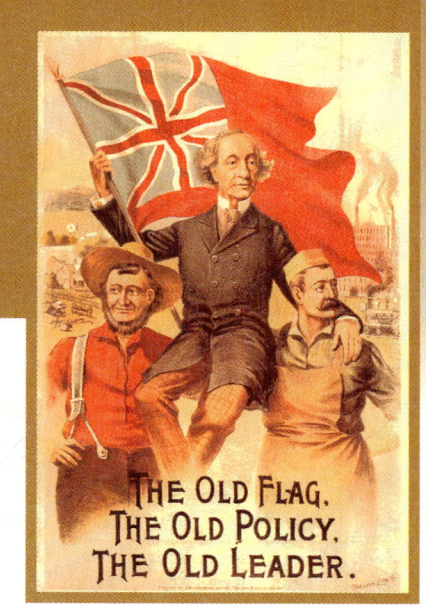

This poster from the 1891 election campaign hailed the virtues of the National Policy. Why does the poster include a happy farmer, a factory worker, a prosperous-looking prairie farm, and a new locomotive in front of a factory?

THE OLD FLAG.
THE OLD POLICY.
THE OLD LEADER.

Canadian Imperialism

To Canadian imperialists, however, no fate could be worse than closer ties with the Americans. Canada's rightful place was where it had always been, within the British Empire. Canada's salvation, they said, lay in closer economic and military associations with England. An **Imperial Federation League** sprang up in Canada in reaction to talk about closer economic links with the United States, which they called "political suicide." They appealed instead to sentiments of loyalty and duty toward the British Empire. The pro-British feeling was often centred on the aging English queen who reigned over an empire covering a quarter of the globe. On the sixtieth anniversary of her coronation, the Ontario poet William Wilfred Campbell wrote an ode to Queen Victoria:

> And we, thy loyal subjects far away
> ...Across the thunder of the western foam,
> O good, grey Queen, our hearts go home, go home,
> To thine and thee!

By the early decades of the twentieth century British imperialism had taken hold in Canada, especially in the long-settled areas of Ontario and the Maritimes. By 1910, school children in Ontario were memorizing speeches, poems, and songs about the splendours of the British Empire. Wilfrid Laurier was a clever politician. He knew that Canadian imperialism was growing stronger, and he felt that he had to provide Canadian support for British military adventures in Africa and Europe. Laurier forged the close imperial links between Canada and Britain that remained well into the twentieth century.

Canada's close imperial ties made the sixtieth anniversary of the reign of Queen Victoria a reason for the Diamond Jubilee Procession pictured here. In 1992, Queen Elizabeth II marked the fortieth anniversary of her reign. What does Canadians' limited response to this event suggest about Canada's relationship with Britain?

IMPROVING RELATIONS WITH THE UNITED STATES

Relations between Canada and the United States also began to improve. During the Laurier years, Canada began to prosper. Factories in Quebec and Ontario multiplied, and western wheat exports fuelled an economic surge. The gloom and uncertainty of the past were replaced by a sense of security and confidence in Canada's future. Growing Canadian prosperity and confidence set the stage for friendlier relations with the United States. At the same time, many smaller disputes that had sharpened Canadian–American hostilities were settled.

The Alaska Boundary Dispute

Clashes continued to occur, however, and fear and distrust of the Americans remained for years to come. The **Alaska Boundary Dispute** was a case in point. Both Canada and the United States claimed ownership of the so-called Alaska Panhandle, which stretched almost 1000 kilometres down the coast of the Yukon and British Columbia. During the Klondike Gold Rush, Canadian and American merchants became rivals in selling supplies to the miners. The Americans claimed that they owned the Panhandle, including all coastal inlets — especially the Lynn Canal. If the United States claim was accepted, Canada's convenient water access to the Yukon through the Lynn Canal would be cut off and the American traders would benefit.

Who actually owned the territory was an open question. In 1903, the dispute was referred to an international joint commission of six officials — three from the United States, two from Canada, and one from Great Britain. Canada had stood by Britain during the Boer War; surely, Laurier thought, the British Foreign Office, which still handled Canada's foreign affairs, could be counted on to support Canada in the boundary dispute. But the American

This stamp, issued on December 7, 1898, clearly shows the pride felt by many Canadians in being part of the vast British Empire. How important do you think Canadians felt their role was in the Empire, judging by this stamp?

president, Theodore Roosevelt, was known for his bullying "big stick" diplomacy. He put pressure on Britain to settle in the United States' favour. American goodwill was important to Britain, so the British appointee on the tribunal voted with the Americans and the Alaska Panhandle was awarded to the United States.

Many Canadians were left fuming at both the Americans and the British. One newspaper claimed that Britain had led Canada "like a lamb to slaughter," and a theatre crowd in Vancouver booed when "God Save the King" was played. The incident confirmed Canadian suspicions, both about American aggression and about Britain's willingness to put its diplomatic interests before Canada's. Many Canadians became determined to hold their nation's destiny in their own hands.

Reciprocity and the 1911 Election

By 1911, despite setbacks such as the Alaska Boundary Dispute, Canada's relations with the United States were generally peaceful. Laurier decided to risk accepting a trade agreement offered by the United States. **Reciprocity** — the broad new trade agreement — provided for free trade in the natural products supplied by Canadian farms, fisheries, and forests, but left most of the protective tariffs on manufactured goods untouched. The wisdom of Laurier's decision to pursue a free-trade agreement seemed to be confirmed during his tour of the West. He was surprised at the depth of farmers' resentment toward the big-business interests of central Canada, including banks, railways, grain elevator companies, manufacturers, and milling companies. Reciprocity was meant to make peace with western farmers by giving them easier access to the vital United States grain market — and, of course, to secure their votes for the Liberals in the upcoming election.

Laurier was convinced that Reciprocity would be welcomed in the West and easily accepted in other regions of the country. The Conservatives thought so, too, and were in despair. The Conservative leader, Robert Borden, considered resigning. Canadians had once enjoyed free trade in natural products, during the years of the 1854–66 Reciprocity Treaty. Any Canadian government, Liberal or Conservative, would have welcomed a return to free trade in natural products, but this was the first time that the Americans had offered to renew the treaty. It looked as if Laurier and his Liberals were destined to win the 1911 election.

But the Conservatives were not about to give up. They soon began to attack. They raised the fear that other tariffs on manufactured goods would soon be stripped away. Canadian industries needed tariff protection to remain prosperous, they argued. Otherwise, shops and factories would shut their doors forever, and Canadians all over the country would find themselves out of work. The Conservative newspaper *The Toronto News* plastered its windows with anti-Reciprocity banners. One said, *"Protection Progress and Prosperity, Not Reciprocity Retrogression and Ruin."* Another banner shouted, *"Steady Work, High Wages and Good Food, Not Unemployment, Starvation Wages and Soup Kitchens."*

The Conservatives were led by a group of unhappy central Canadian manufacturers, bankers, and businesspeople, including Laurier's former cabinet minister, Clifford Sifton. Other important Canadian businesspeople included J.C. Eaton, president of T. Eaton Co., R.J. Christie of the milling and biscuit company Christie and Co., and William Van Horne of the CPR. Van Horne was afraid that new north–south trade relations might ruin his east–west railway. He came out of retirement, he said, just to "bust" the Reciprocity agreement.

Reciprocity had many defenders, however, especially farmers and many working people who were paying the price for high tariffs in more expensive food, clothing, and household items. They soon counterattacked. Under the slogan "Laurier and larger markets," they argued that Canadian industries needed access to the huge American market to survive and prosper. They also said that the trade deal would mean cheaper goods for ordinary people. The rival Liberal newspaper, *The Toronto Daily Star*, mounted a banner over its offices that read, *"A Vote for Reciprocity Is a Vote to Take the Taxes Off Your Food."* In its window display were food items bought in Toronto and Buffalo, accompanied by their price tags. It was intended to convince people passing in the street that Reciprocity would result in lower prices for Canadian consumer goods.

Although the debate began on economic issues, it was soon muddied by emotional appeals to Canadian patriotism and national survival. Canadian nationalists argued that, sooner or later, a trade deal would lead to a political takeover by the United States: Canada would be swallowed up.

Canadian continentalists counterattacked. They said that the only way to save the young country was to vote for Reciprocity. They believed that the trade deal would make Canada's economic future brighter without endangering its political independence. Once Canada's economy was strong, they said, the Canadian nation would be better able to keep Americans at bay.

Comments by American politicians did not help the defenders of Reciprocity, however. An American member of Congress, Champ Clark, remarked that he was for the Reciprocity bill because he hoped "to see the day when the American flag will fly over every square foot of the British North American possessions clear to the North Pole." U.S. Senator McCumber proclaimed, "Canadian annexation is the logical conclusion of reciprocity with Canada." That was enough to convince many nervous Canadians that although America might seem to smile on Canada and offer economic favours, its real aim was to draw Canada into an economic union and then annex it.

Through all the high emotion and heated debate, Laurier tried to remind Canadians that the Reciprocity Treaty was actually a very limited agreement and that strong tariff protections on most manufactured goods remained in place. The nation's regions were divided in their response. On election day, Laurier's Liberals won in Alberta, Saskatchewan, and the Maritimes, and they squeaked by in Quebec. But his party crumbled under a landslide Conservative vote in Ontario, and Robert Borden's Conservatives came to power in 1911.

It seems that in the early years of the twentieth century, Canada was not ready for freer trade with the United States. Many questions raised in 1911 about Canada–U.S. trade relations are still being asked today. Does Canada have a strong, independent national economy? Does it need tariffs to protect its economy from American influence or domination? Does tariff protection favour some regions at the expense of others? Does Canada–U.S. trade strengthen or weaken Canada's chances of survival as a nation?

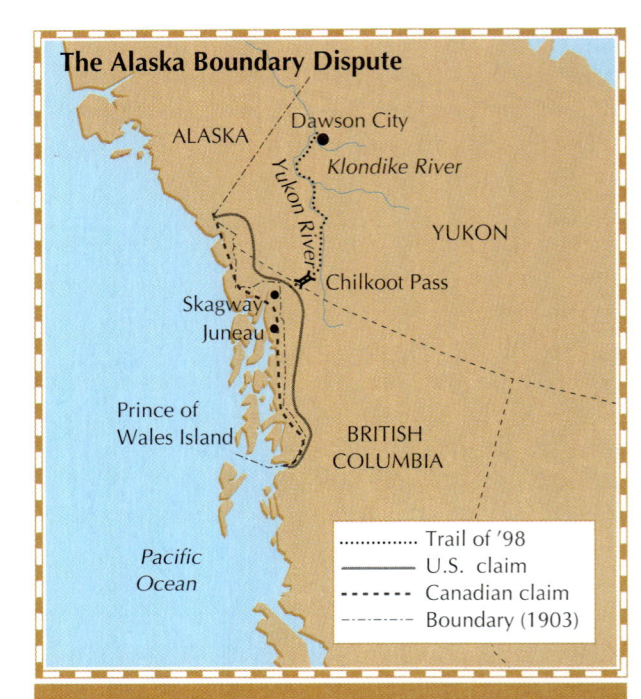

The Alaska Boundary Dispute

- .... Trail of '98
- ─── U.S. claim
- ------ Canadian claim
- —·—·— Boundary (1903)

The dispute over the Alaska Panhandle led many Canadians to fear American aggression and to question Britain's support.

REGINALD FESSENDEN: CANADA'S FORGOTTEN INVENTOR

The late nineteenth century was a time of tremendous change in North America. Many innovative ideas that radically altered life in North America flowed back and forth between Canada and the United States. Alexander Graham Bell, Thomas Edison, and Guglielmo Marconi are all familiar names in the history of invention. But what about Reginald Fessenden? Despite his more than 500 inventions and his profound contributions to the development of radio, sonar, and television, Fessenden remains an obscure character in Canadian history.

Reginald Fessenden was born in East Bolton, Quebec, on October 6, 1866, and was educated at Trinity College School in Port Hope, Ontario, and Bishop's College School in Quebec. His lifelong fascination with mathematics and science and his incredible inventiveness led to numerous achievements. He once stated, "An inventor is one who can see the applicability of the means to supplying demand five years before it is obvious to those skilled in the art."

Persistence was one of Fessenden's greatest attributes. At the age of twenty, having found teaching to be unstimulating, Fessenden moved to New York City, where he made numerous efforts to be hired by Thomas Edison, considered the leading inventor of the day. He was hired by Edison only after repeatedly knocking on his door. Impressed by Fessenden's ideas and abilities, Edison quickly promoted him to chief chemist after only three months. Following Edison's bankruptcy, Fessenden went on to work for Westinghouse, the United States Weather Service, and two American universities.

Fessenden's greatest efforts and achievements lie in the field of telegraphy, particularly in sending intelligible speech through air rather than wires. But he was a prolific inventor in many fields. For example, he invented a lamp that could be rolled up and down the inside of industrial chimney stacks so that workers could see the chimneys while repairing them. Following the sinking of the *Titanic*, Fessenden developed a system using electrical impulses to determine the location of icebergs. During World War I, he created a submarine-to-shore radio and the forerunner of today's sophisticated sonar.

Despite his numerous inventions and the respect he earned from his colleagues, Fessenden was snubbed by his own country. When McGill University established a department of electrical engineering, he was turned down for the position of chair of the department in favour of an American. Later, in 1909, when Fessenden and a group of Montreal businesspeople founded the Fessenden Wireless Telegraph Company of Canada to ensure that transatlantic communication remained in Canadian hands, the Laurier government granted sole wireless rights to the Marconi Wireless Telegraph Company of Canada.

Although Fessenden undoubtedly earned the respect of his colleagues and a reputation as a great inventor, his achievements are little-known by Canadians. He remains one of our obscure heroes.

A tireless worker, Reginald Fessenden spent many hours working on his inventions.

KNOWING THE KEY PEOPLE, PLACES, AND EVENTS

In your notes, clearly identify and explain the historical significance of each of the following:

> John A. Macdonald
> American Revolution
> American Civil War
> Manifest Destiny
> Continentalism
> Imperial Federation League
> Reciprocity
> Confederation
> Mobocracy
> *Alabama*
> National Policy
> Goldwin Smith
> Alaska Boundary Dispute

FOCUS YOUR KNOWLEDGE

1. In the years 1867–1911, what features of Canada and Canadians set them apart from the United States?

2. Why did Canada feel threatened by the outcome of the American Civil War?

3. What actions prior to the Civil War led Canada to feel threatened by American expansionism? In light of these events, was the fear justified?

4. Aside from threats of American expansion into Canada, other actions on the part of the Americans caused relations between Canada and the United States to deteriorate. List and describe at least three of these.

5. The young nation of Canada faced challenges not only from its neighbour to the south, but also from within its own borders. List and describe three of these challenges. Place them in order of importance, and justify your ranking.

6. According to John A. Macdonald's vision of Canada as shown in the National Policy, the East and West were to play separate and distinct roles. What were these roles? Why would the railway be instrumental in enabling each region to fulfil its role?

7. Under the headings Continentalist, Imperialist, and Nationalist, provide a brief description of each viewpoint, focusing on how its vision of Canada differed from the others' visions.

8. List the arguments for and against the Reciprocity agreement. Which side had the stronger argument? Why?

APPLY YOUR KNOWLEDGE

1. "In the first half century of Canada's existence, the United States played a critical role. Out of fear and intimidation by the Americans, Canada was born and spread from coast to coast." From what you have read in this chapter, assess the degree to which this statement is true.

2. For decades, many Americans have assumed that Canadians and Americans are essentially the same. What evidence shows that Canadians were distinct from Americans in the period 1867–1911? Have Canadians remained distinct? Explain.

3. In the decades immediately following Confederation, several conflicts led to talk of separation in some regions. To this day, the issue of "de-Confederation" or the splitting up of the country remains an issue. Have Canadians failed to solve the problems that plagued this country a century ago, or have new problems replaced the old? To answer this question, reflect on what you have learned in this chapter as well as on the major issues facing Canada today. Perhaps your parents or your school librarian can help you review today's challenges.

EXTEND YOUR KNOWLEDGE

1. Write an editorial for a turn-of-the-century newspaper in which you adopt and defend either a continentalist, imperialist, or nationalist stance.

2. Working with two to three other students, prepare a bulletin board that uses charts, photos, drawings, and maps with brief captions to capture some of the issues related to Canadian–American relations in the period 1867–1911.

3. Do further research to script and record, on video or audio tape, an interview with either John A. Macdonald or Wilfrid Laurier. In the interview, ask questions related to Canadian–American relations both during the time period being studied and today. An interesting twist to this activity would be to also involve a current politician in the interview. This would allow you to ask similar questions of characters from both the past and the present.

SKILLS FOCUS

UNIT REVIEW

1. The years between 1867 and 1911 were formative years for Canada. Using the following headings, record the significant changes Canada underwent and the accomplishments of Canadians during this period.

   Geography
   Industrialization
   Urbanization
   Culture
   Economy
   Politics

2. Although the years between 1867 and 1911 are generally considered years of growth and prosperity, not all groups in Canada shared in the good times. In chart form, clearly explain the position of the following groups in Canadian society between 1867 and 1911.

   Women
   Natives
   French
   Non-European Immigrants
   Metis

3. Despite the steps toward nationhood it made at the turn of the century, Canada remained a country closely tied to its British roots. What evidence can you find in this unit's chapters to support this statement?

4. The period 1867–1911 was a time when regional differences became increasingly apparent. In a chart distinguishing the following regions, list and briefly explain the issues and events that were significant and that set each region apart from the others.

   British Columbia
   The West
   The North
   Ontario
   Quebec
   The Maritimes

RECOGNIZING AND RESPONDING TO BIAS

Among the many skills learned through the study of history are analytical skills, which enable students to identify and respond to biases in the writing or statements of others. Bias refers to a slanted or prejudiced attitude that can prevent people from understanding the truth. Although people's perspectives on an issue may differ, they need not be biased if their opinions are not derived from prejudice.

Recognizing and responding to biases is an important skill for all well-informed citizens because it safeguards them from personal opinions that are presented as fact and allows them to assess the media critically rather than to blindly accept the word of the media as the truth. Everyone's views are shaped by their personal circumstances, such as where they live, their cultural and religious background, and their socio-economic situation. It is perfectly reasonable for French Canadians and English Canadians to have different views about the federal government's reluctance to grant special constitutional rights to Quebec. Thus any book, including this text, can contain some biases, and it is important for students to be trained to recognize and respond to this bias. Recognizing biases in writing can shed light not only on the past but on the writer and on the period in which he or she is writing.

In recognizing and responding to bias, use the following questions as a guide.

1. Who is the author, and what is his or her background?

2. What was the author's intent in writing the piece? Did this influence his or her point of view?

3. Who is the intended audience? How might this have biased the writing?

4. How might the period in which the author was writing have coloured his or her view of the events discussed?

CAREER FOCUS

JOURNALISM

Several careers require an ability to deal with bias. One such career is journalism. Journalists must not only gather newsworthy information and present it to the public in an interesting way, but they must also be careful to present a balanced view. This is not to suggest that journalists are without their own biases. Many well-known journalists have earned their reputation for the point of view they present. To remain credible, however, journalists must ensure that their opinions are based on solid evidence and that important facts are not overlooked. In gathering the information to report, journalists face an unending parade of biased views and slanted opinions. To present a reasonably coherent and accurate picture requires journalists to be able to recognize the bias of their sources and to temper their reporting with these biases in mind. Those who fail to take into account the biases of their sources and who fail to support their own positions with tangible evidence may never gain reputations as top-notch reporters.

Being a Journalist at the Turn of the Century

1. Working in groups of three or four, use the knowledge and thinking skills you have learned in this unit to produce a turn-of-the-century newspaper that features articles on issues from the time. Carefully select the city in which you want to base your newspaper, and be sure that the stories reflect the regional perspective of this city. Compare your newspaper with those produced by other groups in the class who have dealt with similar issues from different regional perspectives.

2. Prepare a documentary, either on video or cassette tape, that deals with selected issues from the period 1867–1911. In preparing your documentary, interview different interest groups from various regions on each of the issues. Prepare a list of interest groups to interview before beginning this exercise. Here are some possible issues to explore.

   Confederation
   The National Policy
   The Hanging of Louis Riel
   The Manitoba Schools Question
   Immigration Policies
   The Boer War
   Reciprocity

3. Select ten newspaper articles from current newspapers that reflect themes similar to those studied in this unit, such as French–English relations, Canadian–American relations, Native issues, regional concerns, and international relations. For each of the articles, write a forty-word summary and explain what bias, if any, you can detect.

5. What key words are used to distinguish fact from opinion — for example, "I feel" or "In my opinion"?
6. Are the writer's statements based on solid factual evidence or speculation?
7. Do other sources on the same topic support or challenge the view presented?
8. Are sufficient facts presented to provide a firm basis for the argument?

Once you have carefully reviewed the piece of writing in question, compared it with other sources, and reflected on the background of both the writer and the audience, you will be better able to draw conclusions about why different groups view similar events in different ways and about which views reflect a bias.

UNIT 3

THE WAR TO END ALL WARS:
CANADA AND WORLD WAR I

THE TURN OF THE CENTURY swept in on a wave of prosperity and optimism, but the tide shifted in 1914, when war broke out in Europe. Because of its close ties with Great Britain, Canada quickly stepped into the war on Britain's side. Its participation in World War I profoundly altered Canada. Although it suffered heavy casualties, Canada emerged from the war a proud nation that had earned the respect of both its allies and its foes.

This unit examines the impact of the war both at home and abroad. Chapter 7 focuses on the underlying causes of World War I and Canada's response to the call to arms. Chapter 8 explores the implications of war on the home front, including the role women played in the war effort and the debate over conscription that raged

CHAPTER SEVEN
War on the Western Front

CHAPTER EIGHT
War on the Home Front

CHAPTER NINE
Coming of Age

between French and English Canadians. Chapter 9 traces the final stages of the war and examines Canada's role in peacemaking and the creation of the League of Nations. Overall, this unit provides an appreciation of the sacrifices made by Canadians in the war that was thought to be "The War to End all Wars." It will assist you in understanding the issues that united and divided Canadians during the war years and the ways in which Canada experienced growth as a nation.

CHAPTER 7
WAR ON THE WESTERN FRONT

GLOSSARY TERMS

Shrapnel Sharp-edged metal fragments released from an exploding shell.
Alliances Agreements or treaties between two or more nations to cooperate for specific purposes.
Militarism The policy of continually building up armaments and armed forces or of threatening armed aggression against enemies.
Turrets Tower-like, heavily armoured, revolving coverings for guns mounted on a ship's deck.
Imperialism One nation's extension of its authority over other lands by political, economic, or military means.
Nationalism Devotion to the interests of a nation, sometimes leading to putting the interests of the nation above everything else.
No-Man's Land A belt of unoccupied land lying between enemy trenches.
Ross Rifle A Canadian-made gun used by Canadian troops in the early years of World War I.
Trench Foot A condition of the feet caused by standing for a long time in cold, wet conditions, common among World War I soldiers in the trenches. Its symptoms are sharp pain and swelling, sometimes leading to gangrene.
Parapets Defensive walls or barriers of earth or stone built in front of a trench.
Going Over the Top Climbing out of the trenches to cross no-man's land and make an attack on enemy trenches.
Artillery Barrage A heavy firing of mounted guns and cannons, intended to slow enemy action or to allow troops to operate with fewer casualties.

FOCUS ON:

- the events that led to the outbreak of World War I
- Canadians' response to the call of war
- the new weapons that soldiers had to face
- the critical role played by Canadians at battles such as Ypres and the Somme
- the horrors of living in the trenches

When **Robert Borden** came to power on September 21, 1911, Canada was riding a wave of prosperity and optimism. Borden and thousands of other Canadians expected that together they would fulfil Laurier's dream that the twentieth century would be Canada's century. Yet, all too soon, a shadow fell over Europe and darkened the Canadian prime minister's future — and his country's. Borden was destined to lead Canada into World War I.

Most Canadians knew that Britain and Germany were locked in a bitter power struggle. They had heard reports that Europe was crackling with tension, and rumours of war were in the air. Yet few people were prepared for the almost unthinkable events of the summer of 1914 that led Europe into a devastating war.

Britain declared war on Germany on August 4, 1914. News of the declaration reached Ottawa that evening. As a part of the British Empire, Canada was automatically at war with Germany; only the level of participation was to be determined by the Canadian government. Cheering Canadians poured out into the night, jubilantly waving their handkerchiefs and hats.

Military experts planned on a quick victory in which the loser — Germany — would pay the costs. Almost everyone expected a short war, in which the troops would be home by Christmas. Some soldiers would be killed, they knew, and others would suffer severe wounds. But most would have a glorious adventure to talk about for the rest of their lives. Eager young men stood for hours in the heat of an unexpectedly hot August, waiting for their chance to sign up. Some of them worried that the war would be over before they reached the front. But not until Christmas 1918 — four brutal and bloody years later — did Canadian troops finally come home again. More than 60 000 Canadians never returned from battle at all; another 250 000 soldiers returned home battle-scarred.

During the Laurier years, technology had brought economic growth and new prosperity. In World War I, however, technology was used to create new weapons of mass destruction. Because of the terrible efficiency of modern weaponry, the number of casualties on the battlefields of Europe was beyond imagination. Heavy artillery dropped hundreds of kilograms of explosives on troops, blasting the ground out from under them. Machine guns brought down a dozen soldiers in the blink of an eye. Fast-firing field artillery guns spat out shells that burst into showers of deadly *shrapnel*. Mustard and chlorine gas rolled over the battlefield, inflicting slow, agonizing death on thousands of men at a time. Later in the war, tanks, airplanes, and submarines added to the reign of terror. Only a few military technicians had fully anticipated the destructive powers of twentieth-century weapons of war.

Massive Canadian casualties were just part of the terrible price that Canada paid in the "Great War," a war unlike any the country had seen before. Canadians were asked to dedicate everything, including their lives, to the war effort.

By the end of the war, Canada was bleeding badly on both the battlefield and the home front. But the young nation had also taken great strides toward maturity. In 1914, Canada entered the war as a part of the British Empire. By 1918, it emerged as a nation in its own right.

Europe and the Alliance Systems, 1914
(Prior to World War I)

- The Triple Entente
- The Triple Alliance
- Neutral States

WHAT CAUSED WORLD WAR I?

In the last few decades of the nineteenth century, European nations were often involved in conflicts with each other. The French had suffered a humiliating defeat at the hands of German armies in 1871. Afterward, France and Germany raced to see who could build the bigger army. They began stockpiling cannons, explosives, and other artillery to fuel their rival war machines. By 1914, the European powers had squared off against each other in two hostile camps. France, Russia, and Britain stood together on one side; Germany, Austria-Hungary, and Italy stood against them on the other side.

The Alliance System

Britain and its allies — "the Allies" — were known as the **Triple Entente**. Germany and its allies — "the Central Powers" — were called the **Triple Alliance**. These systems of *alliances*, or treaties between governments, were intended to keep peace in Europe. War with any allied nation meant war with the whole alliance, a threat that was intended to tame warlike nations. But the alliances were dangerous. If war did break out anywhere in the "powderkeg of Europe," as the region was called, it was sure to flame right across the continent.

Militarism

Militarism is the policy of building up military forces and weaponry and threatening armed aggression. In Britain and Germany, it began when these two nations spent millions of dollars to build up their armies and navies and to equip them with the latest weapons of war. At the turn of the century, Germany had the most powerful army in Europe, but Britain "ruled the waves." Britain pushed hard to keep its naval advantage over Germany. In 1906, British shipyards began building a new class of sophisticated warship known as the **dreadnought**. It was a big, fast ship with devastating firepower concentrated in ten giant guns mounted in heavy *turrets*. The dreadnought could outrun and outgun any ship in the German navy.

Germany challenged Britain's supremacy at sea in 1908 by launching its own huge naval expansion. Britain replied to the German challenge by building four more dreadnoughts. By 1914, Germany had amassed a navy of seventeen warships and seven dreadnoughts, and the British navy boasted twenty-nine battle-ready dreadnoughts.

Imperialism

The naval race between Britain and Germany was driven largely by economics. At the turn of the century, European nations were arguing over their possession of faraway colonies. Colonies were of vital economic importance as places where European countries could secure raw materials for their industries and sell their manufactured goods. Britain's Queen Victoria ruled over the largest empire: the Union Jack flew over Canada, New Zealand, Australia, Burma, Malaya, India, the East and West

The size and power of the dreadnoughts elevated naval warfare to a new level. Why was a powerful navy essential to maintaining an empire at the turn of the century?

Indies, South Africa, and various colonies in Africa and the Pacific Ocean. Britain's navy gave the nation an important advantage in retaining its existing colonies and seizing new ones.

Imperialism is the extension of one nation's authority or control over other lands by economic, political, or military means. By acquiring colonies, nations were able to build empires that spanned the globe. France occupied parts of northwest Africa and the Far East. Russia held a vast stretch of land across northern Europe and Asia. The United States pushed across the Pacific Ocean to claim the Hawaiian Islands and the Philippines. But Germany, a relative newcomer as a European power, had only a few colonies. If it was to be a world player, it needed an empire of its own.

Germany looked to the Balkans and the Middle East to feed its growing appetite for raw materials and new markets. It built a railway from its capital city of Berlin to Baghdad and planned lines deep into Egypt and other parts of Africa. Britain, however, was dead set against the German plans because it felt threatened by Germany's aggressiveness. Russia feared that a German railway through the Balkans might prevent its access to the Mediterranean Sea. These and many other quarrels over access to distant resources and markets pitted nation against nation.

Nationalism

Nationalism and imperialism often went hand in hand. *Nationalism*, or deep patriotism and loyalty to the home country, was on the rise in Europe. The great European powers raced to have the largest armies and navies. Extreme nationalism also fuelled the drive for overseas colonies. Each time a European nation seized new lands, it stepped up the ladder toward economic domination. Ruling over a vast overseas empire was also a symbol of national pride; the European powers were always eager for new territory on their continent and beyond to enhance the glory of the homeland.

When war was declared in 1914, anxious volunteers lined up in towns and cities throughout Canada. Why did the rush of volunteers slow to a trickle by 1917?

THE EVENTS THAT TRIGGERED WORLD WAR I

In the imperialist chess game, small nations were often the pawns captured by their more powerful neighbours. The Austro-Hungarian Empire was not a nation of one people, but an empire of many nationalities, mainly Austrians, Hungarians, and Slavs. Austria and Hungary had agreed to form two separate kingdoms under one crown in 1867. Then, Austria-Hungary annexed the provinces of Bosnia and Herzegovina in 1908. However, many Slavs in the two provinces resented their Austro-Hungarian masters. They wanted to join the small new state of Serbia, an idea that Serbia welcomed. It encouraged Serbian nationalists, one of whom, Gavrillo Princip, fired the shots that started World War I.

Assassination at Sarajevo

It happened on a bright Sunday morning, June 28, 1914. On that day, the archduke of Austria, Francis Ferdinand, was to be officially welcomed to

Sarajevo, capital city of the province of Bosnia. Francis Ferdinand stepped into the open car to sit beside his wife, Sophia. The motorcade set off, with the royal couple nodding and waving to the well-wishers massed along the parade route. Seven Serbian terrorists from a group called the Black Hand took up positions among the cheering crowds. Their target was the heir to the throne of the Austro-Hungarian Empire — Archduke Francis Ferdinand.

The visitors' open car rolled toward the nineteen-year-old Serbian terrorist, Gavrillo Princip. He stepped forward, aimed a pistol at the archduke, and fired twice. Later that day, a coded message from the Black Hand flashed across the border to the Serbian capital: "Excellent sale of both horses." Archduke Francis Ferdinand and his wife Sophia were dead.

War Spreads to Western Europe

The two shots fired in a remote corner of Europe brought down an avalanche. Austria blamed Serbia for the assassination of the archduke and declared war on the little Slavic kingdom. Russia mobilized its army to defend Serbia. Germany declared war on Russia; France declared war on Germany. Germany then declared war on France, and moved to attack France by way of Belgium. When Germany invaded Belgium — a nation that Britain had promised to protect in a half-forgotten treaty signed almost a century before — Britain declared war on Germany. Canada was not a fully independent country but part of the British Empire, so once Britain was at war, Canada was automatically at war, too. Within hours, Canada added its voice to Britain's declaration of war. World War I had begun.

Germany's first target was France. The German general Alfred von Schlieffen had planned an attack on France nine years earlier, and he knew that Germany would have to fight both France and Russia. The Russian army was large, but it was badly trained, poorly equipped, and scattered across a huge country. It would take time for Russia to mobilize. Schlieffen's plan was to defeat France while Russia was struggling to get its army in order. Then Germany could turn its full firepower on Russia.

France had heavily fortified its border with Germany. Schlieffen realized that a direct frontal attack across the French–German border would take too long, so he planned an attack on France through the "back door" of Belgium. According to Schlieffen's plan, a small force would be sent straight across the French–German border to attract French troops. The German force would then retreat, pulling the French army after it into the mountains of Lorraine. Meanwhile, a much larger German force would march across neutral Belgium and into France. Once on French soil, they would swing wide to the west and then circle back toward Paris to catch the French army in a giant trap.

Schlieffen realized that invading Belgium would bring other nations, especially Britain, into the war. But he believed that invading Belgium was worth the risk if Germany was able to score a quick

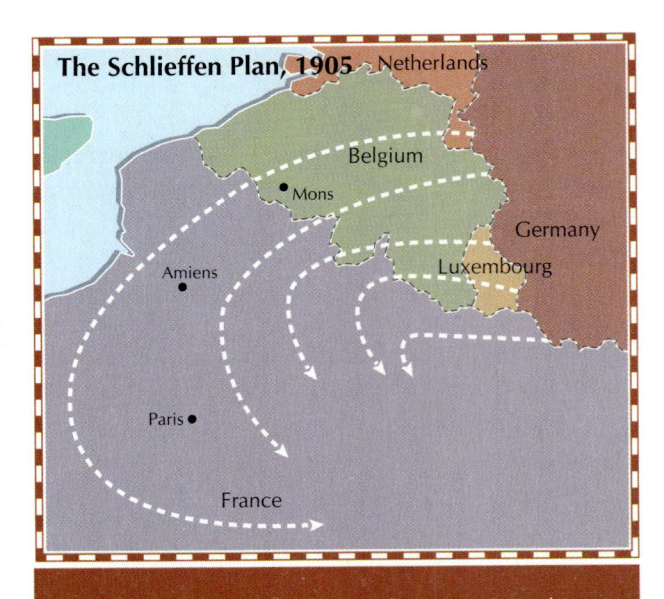

According to Schlieffen's plan, conceived in 1905, Germany would strike France by sweeping south through neutral Belgium. The key to the plan's success would be the speed by which it was carried out. Why was this a risky plan?

victory over France. But his plan failed; the French troops rallied and stopped the German army on the River Marne. Although the Germans had captured France's rich industrial region and had almost reached the gates of Paris before they were halted, they failed to score a decisive victory. The chance for a short, decisive war was gone.

After the Battle of Marne, the armies bogged down. Both sides began to dig in for the winter. Soon, two thick systems of trenches twisted across Europe from the English Channel through a corner of Belgium and across France to Switzerland. Enemy troops stood in the trenches and faced each other across a wasteland of mud and tangled wire called *"no-man's land."* By Christmas 1914, the Germans were locked in combat against the Allied forces all along the trenchworks of the Western Front. The conflict was a stalemate. It was also the beginning of a new kind of warfare — **trench warfare**.

CANADA PREPARES FOR WAR

On the other side of the Atlantic, Canadians from coast to coast were gearing up for war. Although, as a part of the British Empire, Canada had no choice but to stand by Britain and declare war on Germany, it could decide how far to support Britain's war effort. In the early days of the war, Canada's support was more than whole-hearted; it was overwhelming. When the call went out for volunteers to fight in Europe, recruiting stations across the country were mobbed with people wanting to enlist for duty. By September 1914, more than 30 000 men had signed up.

Canada was better prepared for war than many Canadians had expected. Defence spending was already six times higher than it had been at the turn of the century. Since 1909, most provinces had made military training a requirement for high

Aptly termed "no-man's land," the area between enemy trenches was every soldier's nightmare. How did the new weapons of war contribute to the horrific conditions faced by soldiers on the battlefield?

LIFE AT THE FRONT: A SOLDIER'S VIEW

It is difficult to imagine the horror of the conditions faced by the soldiers who served on the Western Front during World War I. Although photographs and paintings give us visual images, they cannot convey the thoughts and feelings of the individuals who endured countless shellings in muddy trenches. Fortunately, many of the letters sent home by soldiers during World War I have been preserved. These letters, although censored by the army, provide invaluable insights into what it was like to serve on the front lines during the war.

The following letters were written by Roy Macfie to members of his family. Macfie was from a farm near Parry Sound, Ontario. He served with the 1st Canadian Infantry Battalion, 1st Brigade, and saw action in virtually all of the battles in which Canadians participated, including Ypres, the Somme, Vimy Ridge, and Passchendaele.

Roy to Muriel　　　　　Camblain l'Abbe, France
　　　　　　　　　　　　　April 14, 1917

Another little short letter tonight[.] I know you will be geting tired of these short notes of mine, but it can't be helped now. You people at home are the only ones that I have time to write to at all, you will likely have seen a good spiel in the papers by this time, and you know why we are so busy. We are glad to sleep any time we are not on the go, and the weather is still beyond discription, it has rained or snowed every day this month I think and we wade in mud here the same as you do in snow[.] My clothes are yellow and stiff with mud from head to foot[.]

Arthur was certianly lucky to get away as he did, but its funny he does'nt drop me a line, and tell me where he is, and John he never writes at all. And I never write to him because I dont know where he is[.] I dont know how the other fellows made out this time, I havnt had a chance to see them for a long time, Henry Payette was wounded the same time as Arthur.

No we havn't even a barn to sleep in now. A good barn would be a treat I'll tell you, we have a dug out with a leaky old canvass over the top, the only way to get dried at night is to sleep with all your clothes on, but it does'nt seem to do us any harm. If the horses were feeling as fit as we are I'd be contented but they are all playing out at once, and we have a big job to keep things moving....

I have none of my old pals now at all, Sgt Murphy is L[i]eut. Murphy now, and that cuts me out as long as the war lasts and I don't feel as contented as I used to when the old bunch was here. This is where a good chum or two counts too I'll tell you[.] Well I'd better stop or you will think I am getting melancholy; I'll pull through alright don't you fret, when they havnt killed me so far surely they wont do it now, Good Night Molly[.]

Roy to Muriel　　　　　　　　　　　France
　　　　　　　　　　　　　　Jan. 8, 1918

... So I have a sister a munition worker eh? That sounds fine, (in a way) but I wish every body in the world would stop making munitions altogether. If I thought you had a hand in making the noise that we had to go through in the last place we were in, I would give you a talking to when I get home. ...

Roy to Muriel　　　　　　　　　　　Buxton
　　　　　　　　　　　　　　Feb. 15, 1918

... I have been expecting for over two weeks that every days as it came would be my last here. And still I am sticking around. My name isnt on the orders tonight either so thats another day. ...

So the censor was taking liberties with one of my letters, eh? I guess I'll have to be carefull or I'll find myself in a bad fix. I can't remember what it could be that offended him so I guess you'll never know what that part of it was.

Well I must close, I can't write letters any more. I'll soon have to get home I guess. There is a possibility of us getting leave this spring too, but don't count on it till you see me.

Source: From *Letters Home* by John Macfie © 1990.

Sam Hughes created a mini-tent city at Valcartier to train raw recruits before they were sent overseas.

school students. Military plans for keeping bridges, canals, and ports safe from "sneak attack" were in place. So was a detailed plan for mobilizing 25 000 volunteers as a Canadian expeditionary force.

But the controversial minister of militia, **Sam Hughes**, was suspicious of professional soldiers and their plans. He thought that amateur soldiers could out-think and outfight professionals. He scrapped the military's mobilization plans and ordered a huge new training camp to be built at Valcartier, Quebec. An army of workers was assembled on the sandy plain outside Quebec City. They began laying out roadways, mess halls, latrines, drill fields, and the biggest rifle range in the world. Thirty days later, the huge tent city — complete with a power plant, a chlorinated water supply, and a rail link to Quebec City — was ready.

By early September, more than 30 000 soldiers and 8000 horses had poured into **Valcartier Camp**. The volunteers were issued equipment, and training began. But their equipment was often badly designed and poorly made. On one occasion a load of boots arrived, all for the right foot. Hughes insisted on using the *Ross rifle*, which was excellent for sharpshooting but useless in trench warfare. It was long and heavy and easily jammed by dirt. When it was fired rapidly, the firing mechanism overheated and seized up.

But the Ross rifle was Hughes's favourite rifle, and he would not accept any criticism of it. On the battlefield, Canadian troops unofficially re-equipped themselves with Lee-Enfield rifles stripped from dead British soldiers or stolen in raids on British arms depots, even at risk of possible court martial. But an official British War Office investigation had to be undertaken before Canadian forces were officially outfitted with Lee-Enfields in 1916. The Ross rifle was just one example of Canadian equipment that failed the test of warfare.

Training was also hit-and-miss, and discipline was slack. Many recruits had only two hours of target practice a day — not nearly enough to prepare them for battle. One day, Hughes made a surprise tour of inspection. He found just twenty-one officers in camp. The remainder of the 1500 officers had gone fishing or into the nearby town.

Emotional goodbyes were a common scene in many Canadian cities as young recruits left to do their part for the war effort.

Winter was coming on, and the Valcartier Camp was not equipped for the Canadian cold. Hughes wanted to get the training over and have the men packed off to war. Prime Minister Borden, like most other Canadians, was impressed with Hughes's efforts. He gave permission for all 32 000 volunteers to ship out. On September 23, the soldiers were ready to board their ships for England. But the disorder in loading men, horses, and equipment on thirty ships was beyond description. As the convoy was about to leave, Hughes handed out leaflets that read, "Men, the world regards you as a marvel." Many of the men crumpled the leaflets up and threw them to the ground.

The Canadian forces spent the winter of 1914 in tents on the windswept Salisbury Plain in southern England. It was the wettest winter in memory, and the plain was a sea of mud. Every morning, soldiers hung their blankets up in the rain to wash out the caked mud. They were always wet, cold, and hungry. Rations were short, and the soldiers were lucky to get porridge and tea for breakfast, and leftover porridge and a bit of meat stew for supper. However, a few things changed for the better. Some of the Canadian equipment was scrapped and replaced by stouter British-made issue. One Canadian soldier wrote, "We have been given new black boots, magnificent things, huge, heavy 'ammunition' boots, and the wonderful thing is they don't let water in. They are very big, and they look like punts, but it's dry feet now."

The Canadian troops were placed under the command of the British general, Sir Edwin Alderson. At this point in the war, Canadian officers were not yet ready to take command of a full division. Alderson weeded out the worst of Hughes's recruits. Now the real training began. The Canadian troops drilled and marched, fired rifles, dug trenches, and practised with bayonets in the hard winter rains of England. But the reality of battle they would learn only in the trenches of France. By February 1915, the Canadian Division was ready for the **Western Front**. It took up its position close to the small Belgian town of Ypres. There, Canadians learned first-hand the horror of trench warfare.

IN THE TRENCHES

The armies' defence systems were a maze of trenches zigzagging across mud, shell craters, minefields, and barbed wire. The front-line trenches closest to enemy guns were the firing lines. Machine guns were placed at key positions to rake enemy lines with bullets. Three or more lines of support trenches at the rear served as command and supply posts. Running at right angles between them were communication trenches. Sometimes, small trenches called "saps" snaked out to lookout posts or machine-gun nests in no-man's land. There were also blind alleys to confuse the enemy if the trenches were captured.

Duty on the front-line trenches usually lasted six days. Soldiers then fell back to the support trenches for six more days, where their job was to ferry ammunition and food rations up to the front. Then they were taken out of the trenches altogether for

This photograph of Canadian soldiers in the trenches gives us a good sense of living conditions at the Western Front. Can you imagine what this trench would look like after a heavy rain?

The Trenches

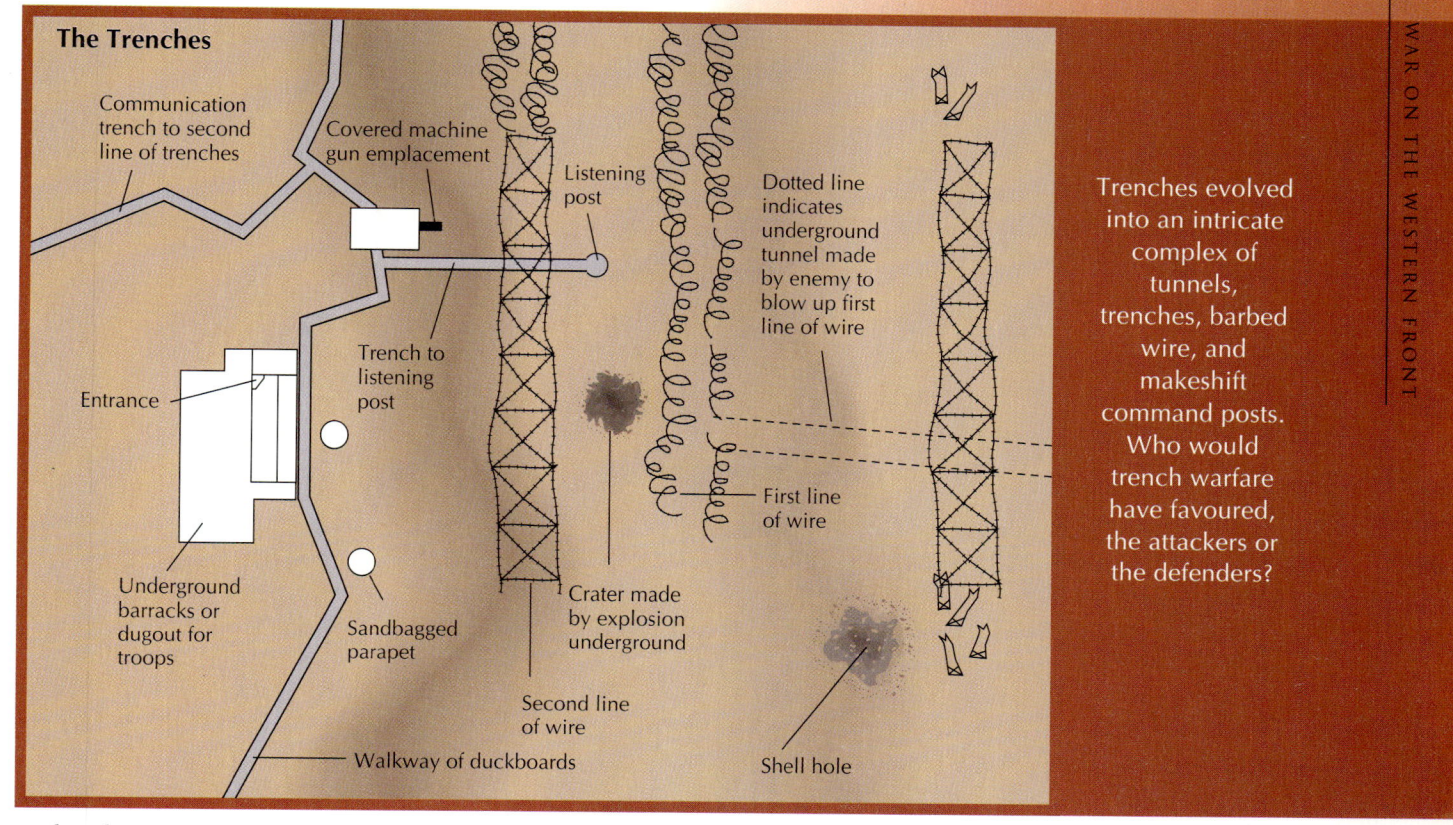

- Communication trench to second line of trenches
- Covered machine gun emplacement
- Listening post
- Dotted line indicates underground tunnel made by enemy to blow up first line of wire
- Trench to listening post
- Entrance
- First line of wire
- Underground barracks or dugout for troops
- Sandbagged parapet
- Crater made by explosion underground
- Second line of wire
- Walkway of duckboards
- Shell hole

Trenches evolved into an intricate complex of tunnels, trenches, barbed wire, and makeshift command posts. Who would trench warfare have favoured, the attackers or the defenders?

twelve days to rest in tar-paper barracks, barns, or abandoned villages to the rear of the battlefield.

On their tours of duty, soldiers ate, fought, and slept in the trenches. In the front line, days were spent standing sentry duty and repairing collapsing trench walls. The front-line trenches were usually about two metres deep by two metres wide and were dug down until water began to seep in. In wet weather, the men on patrol often stumbled through thick mud and slimy water up to their knees. One trooper with the Royal Canadian Dragoons described his first trip through a communications trench to the front line: "The trench was about three feet deep and wound across a swamp and every step squelched as one stepped on one of the bodies that floored the trench. The walls were part sandbags and part more bodies — some stiff with rigor mortis and others far gone with decay."

The trenches were also full of rats and lice. A British officer wrote of the rats, "There are millions! Some are huge fellows, nearly as big as cats. Several of our men were awakened to find a rat snuggling down under the blanket alongside them." The soldiers often went for weeks without washing or changing clothes, and most were infested with body lice. Others got *trench foot* from days spent knee-deep in water. Their feet swelled up to two or three times their normal size and went numb. "You could stick a bayonet into them," one soldier wrote, "and not feel a thing." But when the swelling went down, the pain was agonizing. If gangrene set in, the soldiers' feet and legs were amputated. Conditions were so wet and filthy that even small sores became badly infected.

Miserable conditions were only one part of the horror of trench warfare. Daytime at the front was

NATIVE INVOLVEMENT IN WORLD WAR I

Canadian Native peoples were involved in all aspects of the war, including active duty at the front on land and in the air, as well as serving as railway troops and in forestry units.

Initially the minister of the militia, Sam Hughes, decided not to accept Native recruits, claiming: "While British troops would be proud to be associated with their fellow subjects, yet Germans might refuse to extend to them the privileges of civilized warfare." However, many Natives had already enlisted and were being readied for active duty overseas. In 1915, as the need for more recruits increased, Hughes reversed his decision. By the end of war, over 3500 Natives from all of Canada's provinces had enlisted.

Private David Kisek, a member of the Shoal Lake Band in Ontario, was awarded the Distinguished Conduct Medal for his bravery. The citation that accompanied the medal read:

He displayed marked courage and intelligence during the attack on enemy positions at Tilloy on 1st October 1918. When his company was held up by heavy fire, he on his own initiative ran into the open, and, with his Lewis gun at the hip, fired four pans into the enemy machine guns. His fire was so effective that a party of the company on the right were able to advance and capture four machine guns together with about 70 prisoners….

Two other Natives who distinguished themselves on the battlefield were Henry Norwest and Francis Pegahmagabow. Norwest, a Cree from Alberta, has been described as one of the most successful snipers on the Western Front. At the time of his death on August 18, 1918, Norwest was officially credited with 115 hits. Pegahmagabow, an Ojibwa from the Parry Island Band in Ontario, was also an excellent sniper, whose bravery earned him the Military Medal three times: at Mount Sorrel in 1916, at Passchendaele in 1917, and at Amiens in 1918. Pegahmagabow, Norwest, and Kisek were only three of the many Native soldiers who made valuable contributions to Canada's war effort.

Private David Kisek.

dangerous. Front-line trenches were sometimes within 25 to 100 metres of enemy lines, and soldiers moved carefully with their heads down. A head above the trench line was an easy target for German sharpshooters. During five "quiet" months, one Canadian battalion lost a quarter of its men — nearly 200 were killed or wounded.

Night-time was worse. Men had to climb out of the trenches for patrols in no-man's land and to repair the *parapets* and string barbed wire. Night was also the time for surprise attacks. Raiding parties would creep across no-man's land, using wire cutters to cut their way through the barbed wire. Then they would descend on enemy troops with grenades and bayonets.

Dawn was the worst time of all. It was the favoured hour for major attacks and *"going over the top"* — climbing out of the trenches and charging across no-man's land in an attempt to capture enemy trenches. The attacking troops were cut down by machine guns and artillery shells or tangled in barbed wire. Only a few made it to enemy lines. Men who lay wounded in no-man's land could not be rescued. Sometimes it took days before they died, and their companions could hear them crying out for help.

The miseries and danger of trench warfare were too much for some soldiers, and they suffered nervous breakdowns. Victims of "shell shock," or battle fatigue, they were unfit for fighting and sent away to asylums in England and Canada. Many never recovered. Some soldiers hoped for a "blighty" — a wound serious enough to cause the injured soldier to be sent back to England. At some time almost every soldier must have wondered what he was doing at the front. A popular song in the trenches, sung to the tune of "Auld Lang Syne," made a grimly humorous reply:

We're here because we're here because
We're here because we're here
We're here because we're here because...

CANADIANS UNDER FIRE: THE BATTLE OF YPRES

The Canadian Division reached the Western Front in February 1915. Two months later, the Germans decided to unleash a new and terrible weapon — **chlorine gas**. They chose Ypres as the site for the first gas attack in history. The new Canadian troops had just joined French-Algerian troops in the trenches at Ypres. It was considered an honour to defend the last scrap of Belgian soil under Allied control.

Their trenches were surrounded on three sides by German trenches. The Germans quietly carried 5730 cylinders of chlorine gas to the front line and set them in place. In the early evening of April 22, they let off the chlorine gas. Allied High Command had been warned about a possible gas attack, but they failed to tell their soldiers on the front lines about it or to provide any instructions or means of defence. When the French-Algerian troops saw the cloud of strange, green gas rolling toward them, they panicked and ran. The Germans then smashed through the gap left by the panicking troops.

Soon a wall of deadly gas about three metres high began to drift over Canadian positions. Soldiers all over the battlefield gasped and cried as they breathed in the chlorine gas and began to suffocate. Word spread that soaking a handkerchief in urine and holding it up to one's mouth would give some protection against the gas. Canadian troops held their position for three more days under repeated artillery and gas attacks until they were relieved by British reinforcements. A British soldier described what he witnessed when he reached the front: "There were about 200 to 300 men lying in a ditch. Some were clawing their throats. Their brass buttons were green. Their bodies were swelled. Some of them were still alive. Some were still writhing on the ground, their tongues hanging out."

When the Canadian troops withdrew from the battlefield four days later, fewer than half the

NEWFOUNDLANDERS AT THE BATTLE OF THE SOMME

The morning of July 1, 1916, is one Newfoundlanders remember with pride and sadness. On this morning, the Newfoundland Regiment was sent across no-man's land to face the deadly fire of German machine gunners. At the end of the day, 710 of the 800 Newfoundlanders who participated in the Battle of the Somme lay dead or wounded. They were only a few of the over 57 000 who fell during the battle many have described as the greatest military disaster in the history of the British army.

Before launching the attack, the British unleashed a heavy artillery barrage intended to knock out the German machine gunners and destroy the barbed wire. Unfortunately, neither of these objectives was achieved. When the first wave of English, Welsh, and Scottish soldiers were sent across no-man's land, it was broad daylight. It took only a few minutes for the German machine gunners to eliminate the entire first wave of soldiers from the battlefield.

Upon hearing of the failure of the first wave to capture enemy territory, General Douglas Haig ordered the second wave, the Newfoundland Regiment, to go over the top. The soldiers, burdened with packs weighing from 30 to 75 kilograms, were instructed to walk across no-man's land. The failure of the pre-attack bombardment to destroy the German barbed wire was to prove fatal. The Newfoundlanders, marching into a steady stream of machine-gun fire, were forced to funnel through a single gap in the barbed wire. This allowed the German machine gunners to train their sights on a single spot. In twenty-two minutes it was over; the Newfoundland Regiment was destroyed. One witness described the actions of the Newfoundlanders as "a splendid example of disciplined valour which failed because dead men can advance no further."

The memory of the brave soldiers who died on the battlefield of the Somme on that day has not been forgotten. To ensure that their memory would live on and that their bravery would be remembered, after the war the women of Newfoundland took up a collection and bought the land where their husbands, fathers, sons, and brothers fell. To this day the land, still etched by the bomb craters and trenches of World War I, preserves the memory of those Newfoundlanders who fell during one of the bloodiest disasters of the war.

soldiers had survived. Although Canadian casualties totalled 6037, the Canadian "raw necks," as inexperienced troops were called, had stood fast. The Canadians won high praise as courageous fighters. Their first major battle was a harsh lesson in the heroism and hardship of days to come.

THE BATTLE OF THE SOMME

In 1916, the German army began pressing the French hard at Verdun. The British commander in chief, **Douglas Haig**, decided to go on the offensive and smash through the German lines in what came to be known as the **Battle of the Somme**. Haig was slow to adjust to the new demands of trench warfare. By the time he had adjusted, countless Allied lives were lost in a series of badly planned and poorly executed battles along the Somme.

For five days before the Allied attack, the British and French bombarded the German lines with 1.5 million rounds of ammunition. Haig hoped that the shelling would wipe out the German front lines and break up the barbed-wire defences. But the Germans withdrew into trenches protected by massive concrete walls and nine-metre-wide rolls of barbed wire until the bombardment ended. As a result, the German casualties were much lower than Haig had expected and the Germans' barbed wire remained in place. Massive craters from the shelling made it hard for Allied infantry and cavalry units to charge the German line, however. The craters also were ideal as machine-gun nests for German gunners.

When the Allied shelling stopped, the Germans knew that an attack was coming. One hundred German machine guns were waiting to sweep the Allied attackers with a hail of bullets. The first battle in the Somme campaign began under a cloudless blue sky on July 1, 1916. A British officer scrambled out of the trenches and waved his troops forward. The men went over the top that day to meet the most ferocious *artillery barrage* they had ever faced. One German soldier described the fighting from a machine-gunner's point of view: "When we started firing we just had to load and re-load. They went down in the hundreds. You didn't have to aim, we just fired into them."

That dreadful first day on the Somme did nothing to stop the Allied pursuit of victory. Haig insisted that the Somme campaign go forward, despite alarming casualty rates. During the next three months of fighting, the French and British lost more than 600 000 dead and wounded soldiers. The Canadians were spared until the attack on Flers-Courcelette on September 15, 1916. Two Canadian

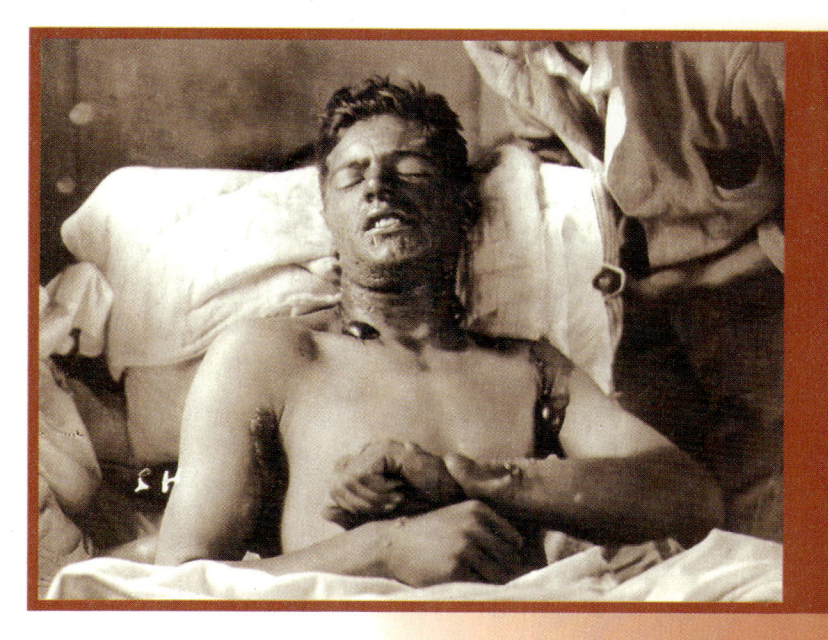

This soldier's wounds show the effect of chlorine gas. In a war that used a variety of efficient killing machines, ranging from the machine gun to the tank, was chlorine gas a less acceptable weapon of war?

battalions — the French Canadians of the 25th — captured the town of Courcelette and held it under repeated and savage German attack. "If hell is as bad as what I have seen at Courcelette," a French Canadian colonel wrote in his diary, "I would not wish my worst enemy to go there."

Canadian troops fought battle after battle in the Somme campaign, including Flers-Courcelette, the Sugar Factory, Pozieres Ridge, Fabeck Graben, and Regina Trench. They gained most of their objectives but lost nearly 24 000 men. After 141 days, heavy winter rains forced Haig to call a halt. The Allied troops were utterly exhausted, as were the Germans. A total of 1.25 million men had been killed or wounded during the five-month Battle of the Somme. But after it was all over, the British army had advanced less than a dozen kilometres and the stalemate continued. By the end of 1916, the mood of Canadians both on the battlefield and on the home front had swung from hope to despair. It seemed as though the war might go on forever.

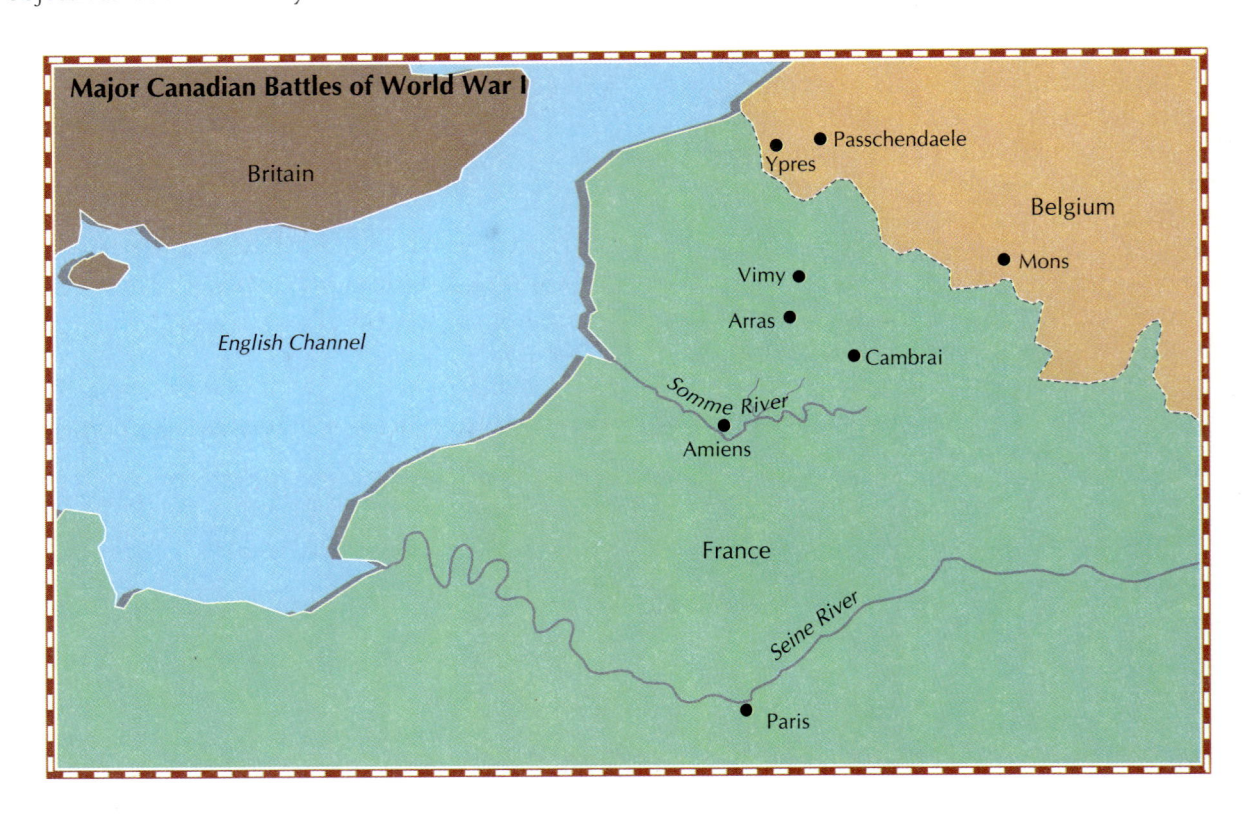

Major Canadian Battles of World War I

KNOWING THE KEY PEOPLE, PLACES, AND EVENTS

In your notes, clearly identify and explain the historical significance of each of the following:

- Robert Borden
- Triple Alliance
- Trench Warfare
- Valcartier Camp
- Chlorine Gas
- Battle of the Somme
- Triple Entente
- Dreadnought
- Sam Hughes
- Western Front
- Douglas Haig

FOCUS YOUR KNOWLEDGE

1. What was Canadians' reaction to the outbreak of war? Would Canadians react in a similar way if Canada were involved in a major conflict today?

2. What was the purpose of alliances in the pre-war years? What was the unintended result of the emergence of opposing alliances?

3. Why did an arms race develop in Europe at the beginning of the twentieth century? If an arms race were to develop in the future, would it likely lead to a major conflict?

4. Why did many European nations consider it important to acquire vast empires?

5. Why did the assassination of Archduke Francis Ferdinand occur? How did the resulting actions lead to the outbreak of World War I?

6. What was Alfred von Schlieffen's plan for the invasion of France? Why did Germany consider France to be its primary objective? Why were the Germans willing to risk the wrath of other nations by invading a neutral country?

7. Why was the night a particularly dangerous time for soldiers in the trenches? What often took place at dawn?

8. Describe the events that happened at Ypres, and explain why Canadians earned such high praise at this battle.

APPLY YOUR KNOWLEDGE

1. Four main causes for the outbreak of war in 1914 have been discussed: alliances, imperialism, nationalism, and militarism. Reflecting on each of these causes, prepare a written argument of not less than 150 words that explains why you think that World War I was or was not avoidable.

2. Was the assassination of Archduke Francis Ferdinand a trigger to a tragic chain of events or a convenient excuse for a war that many wanted and expected? Explain your answer.

3. Reflect on the new weapons used in World War I. Select three of the new weapons and explain how each altered the nature of warfare.

4. Reflect on what you know about the British officer Douglas Haig. Why was he a controversial figure? Should Haig have been promoted to field marshal following the Battle of the Somme? Why or why not?

EXTEND YOUR KNOWLEDGE

1. Using the information in the feature study "Life at the Front: A Soldier's View" and the information contained in this chapter, write a series of letters to a member of your family, or a friend, from the perspective of a soldier during the war. You may wish to do additional research if time permits.
   Letter One, March 1915: Explain your experiences from the time you left the Valcartier Camp to February 1915, when you were sent to the Western Front.
   Letter Two, April 1915: Express your feelings about what took place at Ypres.
   Letter Three, July 1916: Explain what life was like in the trenches, including daily routines and living conditions.

2. Record on a cassette a medley of songs that deal with the issue of war. These songs can be from any period and include any style of music. For each of the songs, write at least fifty words explaining why you included that song in your medley.

3. Working with a partner, prepare a bulletin-board display on one of the following topics. Be sure to include written explanations for each part of the display.

   New weapons of war   Life in the trenches
   Valcartier: Preparing for war

4. Do further research into the construction of trench systems in World War I. Using the medium of your choice (sand, papier mâché, clay, Plasticine, etc.), build a model of a trench system. Be sure to label the important elements of your model.

5. Do further research on one of the people listed below, and then conduct an imaginary interview with the selected character. The interview could be done live in front of the class or recorded on video or audio tape. Be sure to ask questions that force the character to explain or defend his actions.

   Sam Hughes   Douglas Haig   Robert Borden   Alfred von Schlieffen

CHAPTER 8
WAR ON THE HOME FRONT

GLOSSARY TERMS

Pacifists People who believe that violence and war are wrong and that disputes should be settled by negotiation.

Militia A reserve group of civilian soldiers who are called out periodically for drill and exercise but who perform military duties only in times of emergency.

Private Enterprise Economic activity in an economic system in which business and industry are largely privately owned and directed.

Profiteering Making unfairly large profits, especially in times of scarcity.

Suffragists People who advocate women's right to vote.

Enfranchise To give political rights, especially the right to vote, to individuals or a group.

FOCUS ON:

- how Canadians of all ages contributed to the war effort
- how Canadians of German and Austrian descent were treated during the war
- the booming munitions industry that flourished in Canada
- the critical role played by women during the war
- the sacrifices and profits of war
- the crisis over conscription and how it divided the nation

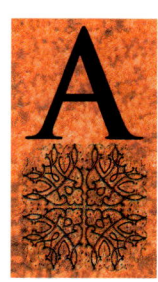

At the outset of the war, Canadians knew little about the horrors that their relatives and neighbours were facing in the trenches. A government press censor banned all news stories considered harmful to the war effort. The Canadian press was ready to prove its patriotism by cooperating fully with the censor, so information about the war was carefully controlled. Government propaganda posters appeared on street corners all over the country, and some artists were commissioned to paint pictures glorifying the "Great War."

Before 1914, many Canadians had been against war on principle. Once Britain declared war, however, many former *pacifists* became staunch war supporters. The few Canadian pacifists who continued to speak out against war, such as the well-known social reformer Rev. J.S. Woodsworth, often lost their jobs. Pacifist religious sects that had been welcomed to Canada before the war — the Doukhobors, the Mennonites, and the Hutterites — were now treated with suspicion and hostility. Many Canadians believed that defeating the Germans was Canada's moral duty. Some even believed that Canadians who opposed the war were as dangerous as the enemy across the Atlantic.

GEARING UP FOR WAR

In 1914, Canadians from coast to coast rallied for the war effort. Hundreds of church groups, women's organizations, and charities sprang into action. *Militia* organizations around the country recruited and outfitted thousands of soldiers at private expense. A **Canadian Patriotic Fund** began to collect money for soldiers' families struggling to survive on a private's pay of $1.10 a day, and within three months it had raised $6 million in donations. A military hospitals commission set up hospitals and health-care units in Canada to care for sick and wounded soldiers. Another organization founded and equipped a Red Cross hospital in London, England. Women's voluntary societies provided food, clothing, medical supplies, and ambulances for returning troops. The Young Men's Christian Association (YMCA) and other groups set up clubs and canteens for soldiers on leave in England and Canada. Everywhere, patriotic Canadians were busy "doing their bit" for the war effort.

Food and fuel were harder to come by in wartime. Families voluntarily changed their eating habits so that more butter, meat, sugar, wheat, and other foods could be sent to troops overseas. Women and children were left to harvest vital farm crops. Almost 12 000 boys became "**Soldiers of the Soil**" to help out on Canadian farms. Even young children pitched in; they went without their favourite foods at home and bought 25¢ "thrift stamps" to help the government pay for the war. When they had pasted $4 worth of stamps into their stamp books, they received a government war savings stamp worth about $5 after the war. School rallies and variety shows were held to raise money for the personal items Canadian soldiers appreciated, such as candy, cigarettes, and soap, as well as army equipment. Children even scavenged along the railway for coal to burn in furnaces at home when the fuel shortage hit. Almost everyone contributed to the war effort and made do with less at home.

Canada's "Enemy Aliens"

Canadian patriotism did have its dark side, however. Some Canadians came to hate anything German. They pressured the government to fire German and Austrian immigrants who held government jobs. They put a stop to the teaching of German in Canadian schools and universities and objected to symphony orchestras playing the music of Beethoven and other German composers. They even forced the Ontario city of Berlin to be renamed Kitchener in honour of the British secretary of war.

At the time of the war, there were approximately 500 000 immigrants from Germany and Austria in Canada. Many Canadians feared that these immigrants were still loyal to their homelands and might secretly work for the enemy. These "**enemy aliens**," as they were sometimes called, were often treated with open hostility in their communities. Many were fired from their jobs and found their churches and clubs forcibly closed and their homes and businesses vandalized. Anti-German gatherings stormed through the streets in several Canadian cities. In Calgary, a mob of soldiers and

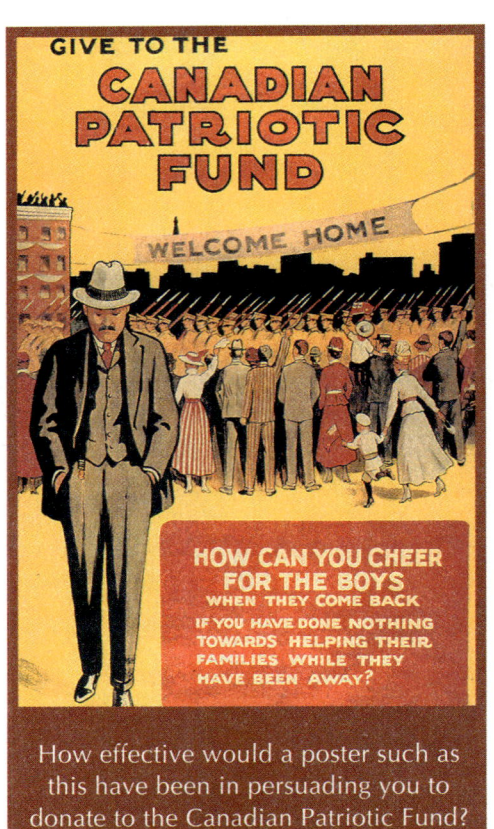

How effective would a poster such as this have been in persuading you to donate to the Canadian Patriotic Fund?

civilians rampaged through the city's large German-speaking community, smashing windows and looting stores, while frightened families barricaded themselves inside their homes.

By April 1915, feelings against "enemy aliens" were running so high that the federal government was forced into action. It ordered more than 8000 people — most of them harmless immigrants — to be rounded up and taken to four remote internment camps. By mid-1916, however, workers were badly needed for farms and factories, and most of the internees were released to take jobs for the war effort.

CANADA'S CONTRIBUTION TO THE WAR EFFORT

Canada's main contributions to the war — aside from thousands of soldiers — were food and munitions. When war broke out, Russian wheat exports to Europe abruptly stopped. Soon after, the German army rolled across France, and much of France's rich farmland fell into German hands. The Allies were desperate for food for soldiers and citizens alike. They needed all the food that Canadian farmers could produce.

Food for the War Effort

Fortunately, 1915 had a perfect growing season for prairie wheat, and western farmers that year harvested the biggest cash crop in their history. Wheat prices shot up, and thousands of people who had never farmed in their lives rushed to buy or rent prairie farmland and reap the profits from wheat. Between 1914 and 1918, more than 16 million hectares of soil were brought into wheat production. Included in this land were the "greater production farms" established on Native reserves by W.M. Graham. Although Native funds and land were used to produce food for the war effort, the Native peoples were not consulted.

By 1917, the effect of war in Europe was being felt at home in Canada. Judging from this poster, how did the Canadian government attempt to deal with increasing food shortages and growing debt? Why do you think the government refused to use rations to control food consumption?

During the war years, Canadian farmers supplied millions of tonnes of food to Britain and France. Foodstuffs, including meat and dairy products, were one of the nation's most important contributions to the war effort. Even when crop yields dropped by half in 1917, skyrocketing wheat prices meant that the smaller crop earned farmers even more than the bumper crop of 1915 had. But intensive wheat farming was ruining the prairie soil. Farmers in the West were beginning to create the disastrous conditions of the 1930s "dustbowl," in which badly eroded topsoil blew away in dry weather.

Canada's Munitions Industry

Munitions — military weapons and ammunition — were another of Canada's significant contributions to the war effort. By 1917, Canada had shipped millions of dollars' worth of shells and explosives from over 600 munitions factories. More than 250 000 Canadians worked in the thriving munitions industry. At the outbreak of war, however, Canada had just one small government factory outside Quebec City that cranked out only seventy-five shells a day. Assembling the machinery and labour required for munitions production was not easy; making munitions required precision tools and highly trained workers. A faulty shell could blow a gun apart and kill the soldier firing it. But in 1914 there were few precision instruments in Canada and very few skilled workers.

Britain was desperate for munitions and was willing to pay well for them. Canadian industrialists quickly realized that they could make large profits in the war munitions business. Friends of the minister of the militia, Sam Hughes, soon got his support to form a "shell committee." Its job was to bid for British artillery-shell contracts and find Canadian manufacturers to fill the orders. Hughes's Shell Committee won $170 million in British contracts, and Canadian manufacturers with experience in metal work, such as bedspring makers, farm machinery factories, railway shops, and structural iron works, switched their operations to munitions making.

But the Shell Committee was dogged by problems. By 1915, evidence revealed that Hughes's friends on the committee were making huge profits from dishonest contract deals. At the same time, the committee was able to deliver on only $5.5 million of the $170 million worth of British contracts, and most of those deliveries were late. Britain's new minister of munitions, David Lloyd George, told Canadian Prime Minister Robert Borden that Canada would not receive another British order until the munitions industry was completely overhauled.

Borden agreed to scrap the Shell Committee and set up the **Imperial Munitions Board** (IMB), which answered directly to the British government. A self-made millionaire in the bacon-exporting business, Joseph Flavelle, was picked to head the new board. He put together a team of experienced business managers who had risen to the top during the Laurier boom years.

Flavelle and his new team completely overhauled the Canadian shell-producing industry. Some greedy war contractors were charging far too much, and Flavelle forced them to roll back their prices. Others were making inferior products; a few even faked inspection stamps and filled holes in metal shell casings with paint. Flavelle and the IMB worked hard to make sure that Canadian-made munitions were up to standard. Once, the IMB rejected 10 000 shells made by a British Columbia contractor because there was too much lead in their varnish.

By 1917, the Canadian munitions industry was setting records for both the quantity and the variety of its products. When the United States entered the war and needed to buy a whole range of new weapons, the Canadian munitions industry

With thousands of young men away at war, women were called upon to fill the labour shortages, especially in munitions factories, as shown here. Once the war ended, should the women have been expected to return home and leave the jobs to the returning soldiers?

POSTERS, PATRIOTISM, AND GOVERNMENT PROPAGANDA

During World War I the federal government worked very hard to enlist the support of all Canadians in the war effort. Whether at home or in active duty on the Western Front, Canadians were urged to do their part to help ensure victory. In an age before television or the widespread use of radio, posters and full-page advertisements in newspapers were among the most effective means for the government to elicit support for its cause.

Most posters produced by the government in World War I served one of four purposes: (i) to encourage young men to enlist; (ii) to convince Canadians to buy Victory Bonds to help finance the war; (iii) to encourage Canadians to be thrifty and conserve food; and (iv) to urge Canadians to contribute to the Patriotic Fund, which provided assistance to the families of men fighting overseas.

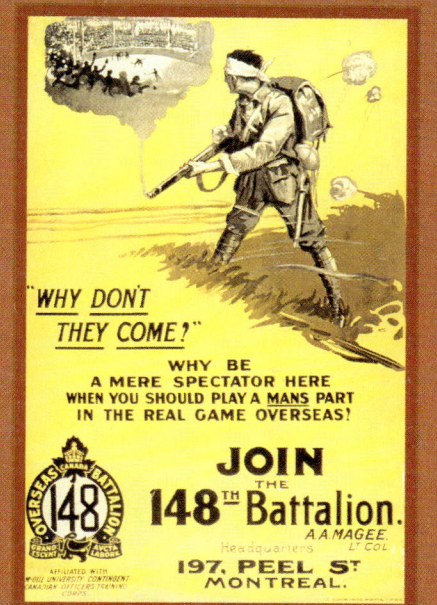

Carefully study each of the accompanying posters from World War I before reflecting on the following questions:

1. What is the purpose of each of the posters?

2. How are Germans portrayed in the posters? How did this portrayal help the government gather support for the war effort? What are the dangers of using such propaganda?

3. Identify the recruiting posters aimed at French Canadians and at English Canadians. How are the posters different? Speculate about why the government used a different approach for each group.

4. One of the posters suggests that men should not be at home playing sports while others are fighting overseas. How does it use emotion?

blossomed. By 1918, Canada was manufacturing airplanes and airplane engines, guns, cargo ships, chemicals, and many other weapons of war. Fifteen hundred factories in ninety Canadian cities employed more than a third of a million people.

Profiteering and Scandal in the War

When World War I began, the Canadian economy was turned upside down because many peacetime industries suddenly had to change over to war production. Although the government relied on *private enterprise* to direct the wartime economy, industrial scandals and charges of *profiteering* made the headlines time and again during the war years. Hughes's friends on the Shell Committee were not the only ones accused of profiting from shady deals in the war industry. Others were accused of hoarding food and fuel to drive prices up. The federal government seized about 400 000 tonnes of wheat when speculators tried to manipulate its price and reap big profits. There were also charges of profiteering in drugs, bandages, and optical instruments.

Many Canadians had made substantial personal sacrifices for the war. As food and fuel became scarcer, they had tightened their belts and shivered through the winter. So they were stunned to see some millionaire industrialists growing richer from dishonest dealings in war contracts. Angry voices across the nation called for the government to do something about "food pirates and price manipulators." There was a public outcry to "conscript wealth" for the war. Some people even wanted the government to nationalize (take over) the nation's banks and industries until the war's end.

But Borden had promised not to interfere with business in 1914 and was reluctant to change his policy. In 1916, the Borden government appointed a fuel controller with the power to imprison dealers who hoarded coal and a food controller to oversee rising food prices. But instead of rolling back food price increases, as many Canadians had expected, the food controller asked citizens to stop eating so much and to change their tastes. Thus, no serious attempt was made to curb the corrupt practices of private enterprise during World War I.

WOMEN DURING THE WAR YEARS

Women's lives were dramatically changed by the war. Many watched in fear as their husbands, brothers, and sons trooped off to fight. They stayed behind to shoulder the responsibilities of family life alone. Many also suffered the anguish of the death of loved ones in battle. These were years of hardship and sacrifice, but the war years also brought women new successes.

Women played a key role in Canada's industrial achievements. They had worked in textile factories and other industries as far back as 1880, but they had been kept out of jobs in heavy industry. By late 1915, however, so many men had gone to war that Canadian industries were crying out for workers. About 30 000 women stepped in to take up jobs in machine shops, metal foundries, munitions plants, aircraft factories, and shipyards across Canada. They

Early in the war a small number of women joined quasi-military organizations, in which they participated in shooting drills. Should women have been prepared for combat roles, or should they have restricted their activities to other types of patriotic work?

also worked on trams and buses, in the police forces and the civil service, for banks and insurance companies, and on the farms.

Many Canadian women also crossed the Atlantic to make important contributions overseas. In all, 2400 Canadian women took jobs as nurses in military hospitals to care for Allied soldiers. Some nurses lost their lives, and some were decorated for valour and awarded Red Cross medals. Other Canadian women signed up to drive ambulances and to run clubs and canteens for soldiers on leave. Yet others staffed armed forces offices.

Women in Canada and abroad shouldered their fair share of war work, but working in wartime was not a simple matter. At first, labour unions fought hard against hiring women. In the factories, women often worked side by side with men but were paid half the wages. Working conditions were sometimes dangerous and unhealthy. In munitions plants, for example, the acid fumes from high explosives damaged workers' lungs and turned their skins bright yellow, and accidental explosions were always a risk. Little effort was made to ease the change from the home to the workplace. Few employers thought to provide child care for working mothers or even to set aside toilets for female workers. The message was clear: once the men were back from Europe, women were expected to return home to their traditional roles as wives, mothers, and domestic workers.

WOMEN, SOCIAL REFORM, AND THE VOTE

Still, women were taking on a stronger role in public life. They were increasingly active in fields such as social work, journalism, teaching, and public health. They were pushing open the doors into medicine and law and continued working for political and social reforms. In the cities, women campaigned for better working conditions, improved housing, and health inspection. The Halifax Local Council of Women created a women's employment bureau to give women better career training and opportunities for job advancement.

On the Prairies, women worked for new laws about women's ownership of property. Reformers like Emily Murphy persuaded Alberta legislators to pass the Married Women's Relief Act, which entitled widows to a portion of their husband's estate. Other prairie women worked to change laws that kept unmarried women and some wives from getting free legal title to lands under the Homestead Act.

In British Columbia, reformers tackled the plight of female workers who suffered from low wages, long hours, and miserable working conditions. Labour activist Helena Rose Gutteridge helped organize unions for city laundry and garment workers. A law passed in 1918 restricting hours of work for women was, in part, a result of Gutteridge's efforts.

During World War I, women entered many occupations that had been dominated by men. How important was the war in advancing women's role in Canadian society?

With the passing of the Wartime Elections Act in 1917, many women received the right to vote. These Canadian nuns are voting for their first time while stationed at a hospital in France in 1917.

women if he were re-elected. He kept his word; when the war ended, women over the age of twenty-one had the right to vote in federal elections. But this long-overdue victory was a limited one because most of the Native peoples of Canada and Canadians of Asian descent still did not have the vote.

Reformers in other provinces also demanded protection for female workers, and by 1920 laws had been passed in the Maritimes, Ontario, Quebec, and the Prairies.

In 1914, however, women were still denied the vote. Many *suffragists* continued to campaign hard for women's right to vote in provincial and federal elections. The first big breakthrough in Canada occurred in the West on January 26, 1916. A group of women journalists, including Nellie McClung, Cora Hind, and Francis Beynon, won for Manitoba women the right to vote in provincial elections. Within months, Saskatchewan and Alberta followed Manitoba's lead, and by 1917, women in British Columbia and Ontario could also vote in their provinces. By 1925, women were able to vote in New Brunswick, Nova Scotia, and Prince Edward Island. Only Quebec stubbornly resisted; not until April 1940 could the women of Quebec cast ballots in provincial elections.

Borden's government decided during the war that it was time to give women the right to vote in federal elections. At first, only certain women were *enfranchised*. The **Wartime Elections Act of 1917** gave Canadian nurses with the armed forces and the wives, sisters, and mothers of Canadian soldiers a vote in the upcoming federal election. During the campaign, Borden pledged to extend the vote to all

PAYING FOR WAR

Toward the end of World War I, the cost of the war skyrocketed. By 1918, it had reached a staggering $1 million a day. Borden's government hurried to find new ways to pay for the war. In peacetime, Canadian government spending had always been sharply limited. When times were hard and government revenues were down, the government just reduced spending. That policy did not work in wartime, however; no matter what the cost, the government had to keep supplying soldiers, food, and munitions. At first, Canadians believed the war would be short and that Germany would be made to pay. But as the war dragged on, huge sums of money were spent. In 1914, the federal government spent about $72 million on defence. Four years later, government spending had shot up to $439 million.

How could the government raise so much money? One idea was to create new taxes. Borden's government reluctantly introduced two new income taxes, intended only as temporary measures in a time of desperation. The tax on business income was announced in 1916, and the tax on personal income was introduced in 1917. But together these taxes brought in just over $50 million, so more

THE EXPENSES OF WAR

When the war ended on November 11, 1918, much of Europe lay in ruins. Nearly 15 million soldiers and civilians were dead, and millions more had been wounded. In financial terms, the war had cost the nations involved a total of $280 137 000. Canada's share of this enormous cost, while considerably less than that of the major European powers, was significant, especially considering its relatively small population of 7.5 million people.

The following charts illustrate the human and financial cost of war for Canada. As you examine these charts, keep in mind that at the outset of war, most military experts believed that a nation the size of Canada should be able to contribute 50 000 troops. Do these figures reflect an extreme effort on the part of Canadians? Did Canada try to do too much?

THE HUMAN COST

Volunteer enlistments	477 048
Conscripted enlistments	142 588
Total Enlisted	**619 636**
Killed in action	34 925
Missing, presumed dead	4 430
Died of wounds	12 260
Died at sea	133
Died of disease or injury	7 796
Total Deaths	**59 544**
Wounded in action	126 594
Gassed	11 572
Injured	34 784
Total Non-Fatal Casualties	**172 950**

THE FINANCIAL BURDEN

Budget Expenses ($million)

Year	Defence Budget	Veterans Budget	National Budget
1911	10	—	463
1914	72	1	750
1915	173	1	974
1916	311	3	1410
1917	344	8	1871
1918	439	30	2638
1919	347	75	2978

money had to be found. Another idea was to borrow money and let future generations of Canadians help repay the loan. The finance minister, Thomas White, explained that coming generations should pay part of the cost of World War I since the war was waged "in the interests of human freedom and [for] their benefit."

For the first time in history, Ottawa offered government bonds called **Victory Bonds** for sale, at a 5 percent interest rate. Canadians responded enthusiastically. Although the finance minister hoped to raise $50 million from Victory Bonds in 1915, more than $100 million worth were sold. In 1917, a special issue of Victory Bonds was offered. This time, the government hoped to sell $150 million worth. Instead it sold almost $500 million worth. As a result, although bonds and income taxes were brought in as temporary measures at a time of crisis, these new sources of government revenue became a permanent part of Canadian life.

FRENCH–ENGLISH CONFLICT AND THE CONSCRIPTION CRISIS

Conflict between French and English Canada was also beginning to look like a permanent problem. Canada entered the war united, but it was soon torn by the worst French–English crisis since the hanging of Louis Riel. In 1913, the Ontario Department of Education brought in **Regulation 17**, which limited the use of the French language in schools — even in regions with large French-speaking populations. One supporter of Regulation 17 described it as a step toward the use of only one language in Canada — English. Howard Ferguson, a future Ontario premier, declared that the "experience of the United States, where their national school system recognizes but one language, simply proves the wisdom of the system." French Canadians in Ontario and Quebec were furious at what they saw as an attack on the French-language rights guaranteed by Confederation.

When World War I began, the leading Quebec nationalist, Henri Bourassa, hoped that Ontario might repeal Regulation 17 as a gesture of national unity. Instead, the war seemed to make many English Canadians less accepting of differences: by 1916, the Prairie provinces had rejected the old compromises that allowed the use of French in schools. The federal government refused to be drawn into the fight over Regulation 17. Tempers flared on both sides of the school debate, and an angry Henri Bourassa declared that the real war was being fought not in Europe but in Ontario, where the English majority was hacking away at French minority rights. Many French Canadians agreed with him that Quebec's worst enemies were not across the trenches of Europe, but across the Ottawa River. This growing bitterness toward English Canada weakened support for the war in Quebec.

The Decline in Voluntary Enlistments

Regulation 17 alone was not enough to divide the country into two hostile camps. It was the battle over conscription, or compulsory military service, that finally split the nation. In 1914, Canadian volunteers had flooded into recruiting offices. Borden declared that conscription would never be necessary in Canada, but by 1916 the flood of volunteers had slowed to a trickle. From July 1916 to October 1917, only 2810 men volunteered for the Canadian infantry.

There were good reasons for the drop in volunteers. Already, one-sixth of Canadian men between fifteen and forty-four years of age had joined the infantry. Thousands more had joined other branches, such as the artillery, forestry, and railway units, engineers or medical corps, and the Royal Flying Corps. Many Canadians felt that enough Canadian soldiers had been sent to Europe. Canada had already given more soldiers in proportion to its population than either Britain or France had. A further loss of men, they argued, would only undercut Canada's ability to supply vital foods and war materials.

On a visit to England, however, Borden became convinced that more Canadian soldiers were needed. There he spent as much time as possible in military hospitals, walking the long rows of beds and talking with the wounded soldiers. Borden learned that many of them might be returned to the trenches if replacements were not found. He was deeply moved by their plight. In his New Year's message of 1916, Borden pledged 500 000 soldiers for the war — despite the fact that the population of Canada totalled only about 7.5 million people.

Where could the new recruits be found? Voluntary enlistments in Quebec (and the Maritimes) were lower than elsewhere in the country. Charges were common in English Canada that Quebec had not pulled its weight in the war effort. Many English Canadians pointed to Quebec as the place to find able-bodied Canadians who had not yet volunteered for war.

There were a number of reasons for Quebec's lagging enlistments. Many Quebec (and Maritime) couples married young, and it was harder for married men to volunteer. Also, Quebec was an agricultural province, and farm workers were needed at home. Enlistments in the rural areas of Ontario and the Maritimes as well as Quebec lagged behind those in urban areas.

Historians sometimes blame Sam Hughes for failing to give French Canadians a stake in the war; while most other provinces had their own fighting units in the First Contingent, Quebec did not. Instead, French-speaking volunteers were distributed among English-speaking units. French Canadians felt that they were being treated as second-class citizens. An attempt was made to repair the damage by creating the French Canadian 22nd Battalion in the Second Contingent. Known as the Van Doos (after the French *vingt-deux*, or twenty-two), the 22nd Battalion was one of the most distinguished units in the war and won over 150 medals.

Conscription: The Military Service Act

To many English Canadians, anything less than complete commitment to the war was unthinkable and unacceptable. The call went out for **conscription**. If able-bodied Canadian men did not volunteer for service, they argued, then they should be forced to serve. Borden knew that bringing in conscription would touch off an outcry in Quebec. If many Quebeckers had refused to volunteer, what would they do if they were forced to join? He was convinced, however, of the need for more Canadian soldiers.

On May 18, 1917, Borden stood up in the House of Commons to announce a new policy of conscription. "All citizens are liable for the defence of their country," he said, "and I conceive that the battle for Canadian liberty and autonomy is being fought on the plains of France and Belgium." The **Military Service Act** was introduced a month later in the House of Commons. It made military service compulsory for all men between twenty and forty-five years of age.

Almost half of all Canadians were against Borden's conscription bill. Farmers were irate that their remaining sons and hired hands might now be taken away. Labour leaders considered calling a national general strike to protest conscription. But the reaction in French Canada was angriest of all;

THE CONSCRIPTION CRISIS OF 1917

Month	Enlistments	Casualties
January	9 194	4 396
February	6 809	1 250
March	6 640	6 161
April	5 530	13 477
May	6 407	13 457
June	6 348	7 931
July	3 882	7 906
August	3 117	13 232
September	3 588	10 990
October	4 884	5 929
November	4 019	30 741
December	3 921	7 476

the day after the bill was introduced, riots broke out in Montreal. Peace was restored, but bitter opposition to conscription remained.

Henri Bourassa spoke out against the Military Service Bill. The Liberal leader, Wilfrid Laurier, joined Bourassa in opposing conscription. "If this military service bill is passed," he warned, "we will face a cleavage which may rend and tear this Canada of ours down to the roots." After a summer of debate, the bill was passed in late August 1917. Borden formed a new **Union government** — a coalition of Conservatives and Liberals outside Quebec — and fought the election of 1917 on the conscription issue.

It was the most explosive election campaign in Canadian history. As Laurier predicted, Canada was torn apart by the bitter debate over conscription. On December 6, 1917, just eleven days before the election, the war came to Canadian shores. A French ship loaded with explosives caught fire and exploded in Halifax harbour. It devastated the city, killed approximately 2000 people, and injured thousands more. The terrible **Halifax Explosion** seemed to symbolize the tragic forces that the European war had touched off in Canada. The new Union government won the election, but Borden was now the leader of a deeply divided nation.

The Military Service Act was enforced after the election. When the first group of 404 395 conscripts was called, 380 510 appealed for an exemption. Many who did not win exemptions simply disappeared, and ultimately only 20 000 men reported for training. On the Easter weekend of 1918, military police in Quebec City grabbed a young man who had no exemption papers. Soon a mob gathered and attacked a military service registry office. They hurled office records out of windows and then turned to smashing and looting businesses owned by English Canadians. When local police took no action, Ottawa sent in 700 Ontario soldiers to restore order. On Easter Monday, an angry crowd surrounded soldiers in a city square and began pelting them with bricks and snowballs. The soldiers opened fire. Before the rioting ended, four people were killed and many more were injured. In the end, only 24 000 conscripts saw action in Europe. Some Canadians wondered if conscription had been worth the price of national discord.

When the soldiers finally came home, they returned to a Canada deeply divided over conscription. The bitterness was to last long after the war ended, but Canada was also a more confident and independent nation. Although the war on the home front had been marred by profiteering scandals, many Canadians had worked hard in the war effort. Canada's extraordinary successes in agriculture and industry were a source of national pride. Women had also taken a step forward on the road toward equality. They made important contributions to the war effort in the home and took on new roles in the workplace. They were active in social reforms, and they were winning the battle for the vote.

The issue of conscription made the 1917 federal election among the most controversial in Canadian history. Do you think men such as these, voting at the Western Front, voted for or against Borden's pro-conscription government?

DISASTER STRIKES HALIFAX: THE EXPLOSION OF 1917

The morning of December 6, 1917, began like any other in the bustling port city of Halifax, Nova Scotia. Soldiers in the garrison had begun their duties for the day, labourers were going about their work, businesspeople were heading to their offices, and children were preparing to begin classes for the day.

The war had brought prosperity to Halifax because it had become the chief Canadian port of the Royal Navy. From here, vital war supplies were shipped to Europe, guarded from German submarines by convoys. As a major wartime port, Halifax played host to ships from numerous countries carrying a wide range of cargoes. Two of these ships were the *Imo* from Norway and the *Mont Blanc* from France.

The *Mont Blanc* was a cargo steamer that had been loaded with about 2400 tonnes of high explosives. As the *Mont Blanc* was steaming toward the Narrows, the *Imo* was heading out of the harbour, beginning its journey across the Atlantic. What happened next is not entirely clear, but the two ships lightly collided.

Many who witnessed the events in the harbour that morning knew immediately of the danger of a burning munitions ship. Vincent Coleman, the train dispatcher in the Richmond Station, hurriedly sent this message to the station at Truro: "Munition ship on fire, making for Pier 6, Goodbye." It was the last message he would ever send. At 8:55 a.m. on the morning of December 6, the *Mont Blanc* blew up. The explosion was reported to have been heard more than 300 kilometres away and destroyed a large part of the city of Halifax. In its wake the explosion left 2000 dead, 9000 injured, and thousands homeless.

Following is a brief extract from a witness's account of the horror and destruction.

Glass wounds of all degrees seemed to constitute the larger number of casualties, and the face and especially the eye injuries were beyond anything known in frequency and severity…. While working on the floor with a poor woman covered with glass wounds, I was hastily summoned by a nurse…to the other end of the ward to see the urgent cases just brought in on one mattress…. When we reached the mattress on the floor with its two occupants, the one to whom I was summoned was lying peaceful and still in death…with scarcely a mark upon her, probably dead from shock or internal injury, and the other possibly a sister or stranger, with one eye gone…her face terribly cut and torn, blinded and disfigured for life, and yet with a good pulse, plenty of vitality, and would probably live…. When one observed the destructive effects of the explosion on the glass all over the city and Dartmouth, their number is not surprising, as there must have been a lightning-like hail of millions of particles of flying glass, much of it travelling with terrific velocity.

The Halifax Explosion brought the horrors of war to Canada's doorstep. It served as a reminder of the death and destruction that had plagued Europe for three years and that would continue unabated for nearly another full year.

KNOWING THE KEY PEOPLE, PLACES, AND EVENTS

In your notes, clearly identify and explain the historical significance of each of the following:

- Canadian Patriotic Fund
- Enemy Aliens
- Wartime Elections Act of 1917
- Regulation 17
- Military Service Act
- Halifax Explosion
- Soldiers of the Soil
- Imperial Munitions Board
- Victory Bonds
- Conscription
- Union Government

FOCUS YOUR KNOWLEDGE

1. What major contributions did Canada make to the war effort, aside from providing thousands of soldiers? What challenges faced Canadians in producing large amounts of munitions?
2. List and describe the various roles that women filled during the war years. What kinds of political and social reforms did women achieve during the war?
3. Prepare a short time line that indicates when women in each of the provinces received the right to vote provincially and at the federal level.
4. What groups of people remained without the vote after World War I?
5. What did it mean to "conscript wealth for the war"? Why did many Canadians insist that this happen?
6. How did Borden's government raise funds to pay for the war effort?
7. Why were men from Quebec less eager than those in other provinces to enlist in the army? Give at least three reasons.

APPLY YOUR KNOWLEDGE

1. Considering that Canada was at war with Germany and its allies, were Canadians justified in questioning the loyalty of recent German and Austrian immigrants in Canada? Explain your answer.

2. Is it moral for people and industries to profit from war? Why or why not?

3. Despite the shortage of labour in Canadian industry during the war, Canadian women still encountered roadblocks when they tried to enter the workforce. Why were men reluctant to allow women in the workplace? What evidence suggests that women were not seen as a permanent part of the workforce but only as temporary wartime help?

4. Was the Wartime Elections Act of 1917 a fair and just move on the part of the Borden government, or was it enacted for other reasons?

5. Prepare a chart outlining the arguments for and against the use of conscription in World War I. When your list is complete, give each argument a score from 1 to 10: the arguments that you believe to be very important will score high, while the less significant arguments will score lower. Tally the total scores for and against. Would you have been a supporter of Borden's Union government, or would you have supported Laurier in his opposition to conscription?

EXTEND YOUR KNOWLEDGE

1. In Chapter 7, you were asked to write a series of letters from a soldier to his family. Now, rather than writing as a soldier, write a letter from the perspective of a mother, girlfriend, father, brother, or sister at home, to a soldier in Europe. In this letter, be sure to comment on how the war has affected daily life in Canada.

2. Working with a partner, prepare a visual display that depicts activities related to the war on the home front. Select a particular theme; for example, "Women and War," "Feeding the Troops," or "Government Propaganda and the War Effort."

3. Closely study the posters featured in this chapter. Prepare your own poster to help with the war effort, using one of the following topics:
   - Recruiting soldiers
   - Donating to the Patriotic Fund
   - Selling Victory Bonds
   - Limiting Home Consumption

4. Write a newspaper editorial in which you explain your reasons for supporting or opposing conscription. Clearly explain who you are and why you have taken the stand you have.

CHAPTER 9
COMING OF AGE

GLOSSARY TERMS

Reconnaissance A survey of enemy territory to gather military information about such things as the enemy's strength and position.
Mockup A built-to-scale model of an object.
Mortars Short cannons used to fire shells at high angles.
Armistice An agreement to stop fighting while a peace settlement is negotiated.
Automata Mechanical devices that are relatively self-operating; robots.

FOCUS ON:

- the exploits of Billy Bishop, one of Canada's heroes
- the war in the air and at sea
- how the sinking of the *Lusitania* brought the United States into the war
- the importance of Vimy Ridge to the outcome of the war and to Canada's national pride
- the horrors of the Battle of Passchendaele
- Canada's role as an independent nation in the signing of the Treaty of Versailles and the forming of the League of Nations

During the summer of 1915, the horses and riders of the Canadian cavalry troops were deep in the mud of southern England, struggling to train for the war raging across the English Channel. By night the Canadians could see brilliant flashes of artillery fire flaming across the sky over France, but by day all they knew was an endless sea of mud.

One day in early July, a young Canadian cavalry officer, **Billy Bishop**, slogged across the parade ground, knee-deep in muck, on an inspection tour. Suddenly, a tiny airplane flitted out of the storm clouds to settle for a moment in a nearby field, "as if scorning to brush its wings against so sordid a landscape." It was the mud, he said, that made the legendary Billy Bishop — perhaps Canada's most celebrated pilot — take to the air.

THE WAR IN THE AIR

Pilots did not suffer the mud and filth of the trenches. They had clean beds, good food, and brandy and champagne. They did not die the impersonal deaths of foot soldiers or cavalry troops, who were killed by faceless enemies in poison gas attacks or artillery barrages. Instead, they fought in single combat, high in the sky. Their names and exploits were known and individually recorded.

German and Allied air "aces" became the new knights of battle on the Western Front. The feats of Bishop and other famous Canadian pilots such as Billy Barker, Raymond Collishaw, "Wop" May, and Roy Brown were a source of consolation and national pride. Their names appeared in newspapers around the world, and their stories were told by a whole generation of Canadians.

But flying was perhaps the most dangerous job of all. Most pilots were dead within three weeks of joining their squadrons. In fact, over a span of just two weeks, thirteen Allied pilots were shot down by German flying squadrons under the command of **Manfred von Richthofen**, the famous "Red Baron." A month after Bishop set foot in France, so many pilots had gone down that he had become one of the squadron's veteran flyers. During his flying career, Bishop took part in more than 170 air battles and shot down a record-breaking 72 enemy aircraft. But Billy Bishop was one of the few lucky ones who lived to enjoy his celebrity.

Despite their high casualty rate, airplanes held great appeal for soldiers who had experienced the horrors of the trenches. Would photographs like this one spark your interest in joining the air force?

Canada's most famous flying ace in World War I was Billy Bishop, of Owen Sound, Ontario. With skill and luck, he beat the odds and survived the war.

Airplanes as Weapons of War

In the beginning, the new flying machines were used to scout enemy territory. On August 19, 1914, both sides made their first *reconnaissance* flights across enemy lines. When the first two reconnaissance planes passed within a few metres of each other, the pilots only looked at each other and flew on without incident. Neither plane carried any weapons. But the value of air reconnaissance struck home when British and French flyers reported in September 1914 that the German army had overextended itself. This information enabled the Allies to stop the German advance in the Battle of the Marne. From then on, airplanes were a serious part of the war strategy.

Pilots began smuggling aboard pistols, rifles, light machine guns, and even bricks to attack enemy aircraft. But soon more sophisticated weapons were developed for the war in the air. New German Fokker airplanes were mounted with a synchronizing device that let machine guns fire straight ahead without hitting the propeller blades. Soon the new device was copied by the Allies, and Allied pilots were firing at German Fokkers with their own synchronized machine guns.

THE WAR AT SEA

Canada also helped Great Britain wage war at sea. Perhaps Canada's greatest contribution came from its shipyards; it produced more than 60 steel antisubmarine ships and more than 500 antisubmarine motor launches. But Canada's navy was also transformed. In 1914, Canada's "tin pot" navy consisted of two ships and 350 personnel. By 1918, it had 112 war vessels and 5500 officers and enlisted men under the command of a British Royal Navy officer.

Ruling the Seas: German U-Boats

At the beginning of World War I, Britain still had the world's largest navy and continued to rule the waves. But Germany's new ships were big and efficient, and, unlike most British ships, had steel hulls. Despite their smaller fleet, the Germans felt ready to challenge the British at sea. They also had a revolutionary new weapon of war — a fleet of deadly submarines called **U-boats** (short for *Unterseebooten*, "undersea boats"). German U-boats carried twelve torpedoes that could be unleashed without warning. By the end of 1914, the U-boats had sent 200 British supply ships to the ocean floor.

The Germans knew that controlling the seas was the key to defeating Britain. Britain was an island nation and depended for its survival on supplies brought from abroad by merchant ships. Germany wanted to starve England into submission by cutting off all war materials and personnel, raw and manufactured goods, and foodstuffs. The U-boats went after British merchant ships with a vengeance.

The Nieuport was a popular airplane in World War I. Would you have felt safe flying over enemy territory in this plane?

The luxury liner Lusitania, *suspected by Germany of carrying arms, was sunk near Ireland and prompted the United States to enter the war. Should vessels carrying civilians and weapons be considered fair targets in wartime? How accountable for shipping disasters are those who use civilian vessels to transport arms?*

Even civilian passenger ships were at risk from U-boat attacks. The German government had announced that passenger ships would be sunk on sight. Despite the warning, passengers boarded the splendid British ocean liner, the **Lusitania**, in New York City on May 2, 1915, and set sail for Liverpool, England. As the ocean liner was nearing Ireland five days later, it received warning that U-boats were prowling off the headlands of the coast.

The commander of the German submarine U-20, Walter Schweiger, tracked the *Lusitania*'s changing course through his periscope. At 2:15 p.m., he fired two torpedoes through the water toward the ocean liner. Eighteen minutes after the first torpedo hit, the *Lusitania* lay on the bottom of the ocean. The ship's 1198 passengers went with it to a watery grave.

Among the dead were 128 Americans, mostly women and children. Americans seethed with rage at the attack on U.S. civilians. The U.S. government had been officially neutral in the war, and until the attack many American citizens had been actively pro-German. Germany insisted that it had sunk the *Lusitania* because the ship was armed and carrying explosives, although the ship apparently had only a small amount of rifle ammunition on board. American sentiment shifted sharply, and everything German was despised. The sinking of the *Lusitania* prepared the way for the American declaration of war on Germany in 1917.

The Battle of Jutland

Both sides in the war knew how important it was to rule the seas, and they were reluctant to risk their fleets in open sea battles. In fact, the two fleets met in just one major sea battle, on May 31, 1916, at **Jutland**, off the coast of Denmark. When the battle was over, the British had lost yet more ships and more lives. Six thousand British sailors died in the icy northern waters of Jutland — more than double the German losses. But the British fleet was still large enough to maintain its defence of the British Isles against the Germans. The German navy returned to port and never sailed out again. Thereafter, the Germans concentrated on fielding ever-larger numbers of U-boats.

The British Naval Blockade of Germany

Britain countered Germany's blockade of shipping with its own naval blockade of Germany, which was so successful that by the winter of 1916–17 Germany had been almost drained of resources by its war effort. What little meat and dairy products were still available were sent to German soldiers at the front. Old men, women, and children behind the German lines had nothing to eat but the turnips grown as fodder for animals. As a result, that winter became known as the "turnip winter."

The outlook in Germany was so bleak by February 1917 that Kaiser Wilhelm II, the German monarch, was desperate for a quick victory. The Germans could still win the war if they cut off all supplies to Allied countries. The U-boats were

German submarines like this one were a menace to Allied shipping efforts and led to the need for convoys to protect valuable cargoes.

COMING OF AGE

unleashed again with orders to attack ships of any nationality in British waters, a policy called "unrestricted submarine warfare." By the end of 1917, 6 billion tonnes of cargo bound for Britain had been destroyed by German U-boats.

The United States Declares War on Germany

Ironically, the very success of German U-boat attacks helped bring about Germany's defeat. The U.S. president, Woodrow Wilson, was so angry at Germany's policy of unrestricted submarine warfare that he broke off diplomatic relations with Germany. Then the American ships *City of Memphis* and *Illinois* were torpedoed. On April 6, 1917, the U.S. Congress declared war against Germany. The declaration marked a turning point in the war. Just when nations on both sides of the battlefield had almost exhausted their personnel and resources, the entry of the United States changed the balance of power.

The Americans, however, were not yet ready to join the fighting. The U.S. army had fewer than 200 000 soldiers, and most of its weapons were badly outdated. It would take months for the Americans to gear up for war. The Germans began a race against time. They hoped to win a decisive victory before the Americans were ready to fight. Germany's chance for a quick success suddenly looked promising: its war with Russia on the Eastern Front was coming to an end, and Russia was ready to make peace with Germany.

Russia Makes Peace with Germany

On the same day in March 1917 that U-boats torpedoed two American ships, a revolutionary government toppled the Russian monarchy and came to power. Soon the new Russian government was overthrown by communist revolutionaries led by Vladimir Lenin. Only days after taking power, Lenin announced that Russia wanted to discuss terms of peace with Germany. The country was exhausted by the war, its people were starving, and the new government was intent on building a communist state. Russia was ready to accept defeat. With the

In preparation for their attack on Vimy Ridge, Canadians built light railways as a central part of the "creeping barrage."

Russians out of the war, Germany could now concentrate its full attention — and firepower — on the Western Front.

THE WESTERN FRONT, 1917–1918

The year 1917 was pivotal in World War I. Russia's withdrawal from and the United States' entry into the war altered the balance of power on the Western Front. Everyone believed that the bloody stalemate would come to an end at last. But no one could predict whether Germany or the Allies would emerge triumphant. In 1917, victory still hung in the balance. Two long, desperate years of fighting lay ahead.

The Battle of Vimy Ridge

In the brutal trench warfare of the Western Front, Canadian troops were steadily gaining a reputation as tough, effective, and courageous fighters. The Battle of Vimy Ridge, a major turning point in the war, was the high point of Canadian military achievement in World War I.

Vimy Ridge was a long, whale-shaped hump of land that rose 60 metres out of the Douai Plain. The ridge gave the Germans a commanding view of the British army. It also protected a vital area of occupied France where mines and factories churned out supplies for Germany. Vimy Ridge was strategically important and had been strongly fortified. The Germans had dug a maze of deep trenches and dugouts and carved out huge underground chambers. Some of them were large enough to shelter whole German battalions from Allied barrages. The Germans had also built machine-gun positions that were footed in thick concrete and wrapped in hedges of thick barbed wire. Although French and British troops had made several attempts to capture the heavily defended ridge, they had been stopped and turned back by German artillery. The German army was confident that nobody could force it off Vimy Ridge.

The taking of Vimy Ridge now fell to the Canadian Corps under the command of the British general, Julian Byng. Under Byng's command was Major-General **Arthur Currie**, the Canadian-born commander of the First Canadian Division. Currie once said, "Thorough preparation must lead to

Afro-Canadians played a significant role in World War I. The men pictured here were part of the No. 2 Construction Battalion.

success. Neglect nothing." Unlike earlier Allied attempts on Vimy Ridge, the Canadian assault left nothing to chance. Every stage of the attack was rehearsed to the last detail.

Using aerial photographs taken by the Royal Flying Corps and information from intelligence raids across enemy lines, the Canadians pinpointed the locations of every trench, machine gun, and battery. A full-scale *mockup* of Vimy Ridge was built, and key positions were marked with flags and coloured tape. Canadian troops practised every step they would take on the day of attack. High in the air above the troops, Canadian pilots repelled German reconnaissance planes.

Currie and Byng agreed that the strategy at the Somme had failed. When the artillery fire had stopped just before the assault, German troops had known what to expect. The advantage of a surprise attack had been lost. The new strategy was to keep up a "**creeping barrage**" during the assault that would lay a curtain of gunfire just in front of the advancing troops. The assault plan worked because of detailed planning and the courage and discipline of Canadian soldiers. By noon, the Canadians were looking down from Vimy Ridge at the grey backs of thousand of German soldiers in full retreat.

The Vimy victory cost Canadians dearly. More than 3500 lives were lost. The German lines had been broken, however, and an important strategic position was now in Allied hands. Vimy showed the world that Canadians were capable of devising and carrying out a well-planned and successful attack. Currie was promoted to commander of the Canadian Corps in June 1917. It was no longer necessary for British officers to command Canadian soldiers. For the first time, Canada had its own officers in command of the Canadian Corps.

The Battle of Passchendaele

Unfortunately, Vimy was not the last battle of the war. Against all advice the British general, Douglas Haig, was determined to break through the German front. He launched a disastrous drive across Belgium in 1917, and in early October the Canadian Corps was ordered to prepare for the capture of Passchendaele.

It was the same front that Canada had defended in the Battle of Ypres. Four million shells had destroyed dams and drainage systems, and as a result the battlefield was a nightmare of marshes and swamps. The Germans were on high ground above the battlefield. From their commanding position, they had the advancing Allied forces at their mercy. Currie reckoned that it would cost 16 000 Canadian lives to

It was common for Canadians to label shells before firing them at the Germans.

take Passchendaele. He could not believe the military objective was worth the waste of lives, but Haig insisted on the offensive.

Beginning in late October, the Canadians made a series of attacks. They crawled forward, often waist-deep in mud and under a deadly hail of German shells. At last they reached the outskirts of the ruined village of Passchendaele and held on grimly for five days. By the time reinforcements finally came, the Canadians had been torn apart; only one-fifth of the attack force was still alive. When the fighting stopped on November 15, the British had gained just 6 kilometres and Canadian casualties stood at 15 654. Despite the casualties, Canadian soldiers performed admirably. Nine Canadian soldiers at Passchendaele were awarded the Victoria Cross, the British Commonwealth's highest military honour.

The mud was so deep at Passchendaele that Canadian troops had to lay trenchmats, also known as "duckboards," to advance across the battlefield. Why do you think the trenchmats earned the nickname "duckboards"?

The Last Battles

In the spring of 1918, Germany decided to strike hard before the United States could enter the war. On March 21, German forces began a massive assault on the Western Front. Using new tactics based on mobility and surprise, the German army smashed through Allied defences and began to advance rapidly toward Paris.

The German offensive nearly succeeded. The German army overran Allied forward positions and cut off Allied supply and communications lines. Using airplanes, trucks, and mobile machine guns, they advanced within 70 kilometres of Paris. Although exhausted Allied troops reeled back and retreated under the massive assault, the Allied front did not collapse. Germany's last desperate bid for victory had failed.

Even though both sides had suffered heavy losses in the German offensive, Germany suffered more. The success of the British naval blockade had cut off food supplies, and German morale both at home and at the front was slipping badly. Germany was finding it almost impossible to replace the thousands of soldiers it had lost in the war. At the same time, American troops had arrived in force to fill out the Allied ranks. Now the Allied army had the superior forces. The tables were turned; it was time to mount a final Allied offensive.

Canada's Hundred Days

Using all the new techniques of mobile warfare, the Allied troops rolled forward to recapture French and Belgian territory taken by Germany in the first months of the war. By now, the Canadian Corps were regarded as outstanding soldiers and were used as storm troops. They spearheaded the thrust through the German defences. August 8 to November 11, 1918, came to be known as **Canada's Hundred Days**. The Canadians advanced

CANADIAN WAR ART

William Roberts, The First German Gas Attack at Ypres, National Gallery of Canada

A unique contribution was made by many of Canada's artists during World War I. Their paintings and sculptures captured both the valour and the horror of war. The Canadian War Memorial Fund, set up in November 1916, offered an officer's rank and pay to Canadian artists to capture images of the war. By the war's end, artists, including members of the famous Group of Seven, had risked their lives to record the events of the war. The result was some of Canada's best and most haunting images and a collection of war art now valued at over $500 million.

Unlike some earlier war artists, who tended to glorify war, the Canadian war artists worked from on-the-spot sketches they made while at the front. Their paintings ceased to be concerned only with battles. They captured the many ways in which human lives were affected by the war — soldiers in battle or at rest, women ploughing on farms at home, or members of the Imperial War Cabinet planning strategies. The result was often disturbingly honest portrayals of the horrors of war and the trials faced by those caught in the struggle.

The two paintings shown here depict the effects of war on two different groups. The first, by William Roberts, is titled *The First German Gas Attack at Ypres*. It shows the anguish of Canadian soldiers caught unprepared for a chlorine gas attack. The second painting, by George Clausen, is titled *Returning to the Reconquered Land*. It shows women, children, and elderly people returning to the bombed-out shell of what had been their village. The sign at the left now reads, "This *was* Ablains Nazaire."

Sir George Clausen, Returning to the Reconquered Land. Canadian War Museum

Why do you think that Prime Minister Borden felt it was important to visit Canadian troops overseas?

130 kilometres and captured 31 537 prisoners, 623 guns, 2842 machine guns, and 336 *mortars*.

The German armies were on the edge of collapse. Kaiser Wilhelm II was forced to give up the throne and flee to the Netherlands, and a republican government took power in Germany. As Allied armies approached the borders of Germany, the new government asked for an *armistice*. The Germans were exhausted and ready to talk terms of peace. On the same day that the armistice ended World War I, Canadian troops entered the Belgian city of Mons. Mons had been the scene of the first battle between British and German troops in 1914. Now it was the end of the road; the men could come home.

CANADA MATURES: FROM WAR TO PEACE

In 1914, Canada had responded to Britain's call to war with a spirited and innocent "Ready, aye, ready." When Britain was at war, Canada was at war. It was not a choice, but a matter of course. As part of the British Empire, Canada's duty was to stand by Britain — even though Canada had no voice in making the decisions that had led to war.

By 1918, however, Canada would never again automatically say "Ready, aye, ready" in answer to a British call to arms. At the end of the war, Canada was no longer a minor partner in the British Empire but a nation in its own right. Canada's wartime prime minister, Robert Borden, had seen to that. A British official once said, "When Borden gets his toes in, he usually shoves hard." Borden "got his toes" into the principle of equal nationhood for Canada, and he kept pressuring Britain until Canada had it.

Once Canada was at war, its soldiers were placed under British officers and British control. Canada had no say in the choice of commanders for Canadian troops; the British Admiralty even took command of Canadian ships without asking Canada's permission. The Canadian government was told little about Britain's war policy, so Borden

THE TREATY OF VERSAILLES

When World War I ended on November 11, 1918, Germany was not only defeated but utterly exhausted. Germany had marshalled all of its resources in an attempt to win a decisive victory before the Americans became a factor in the war. Failing to win such a victory had left Germany with little bargaining power when it finally sued for peace. The Treaty of Versailles, signed in 1919, reflects the balance of power that existed at the end of World War I.

Following are a few of the highlights of the Treaty of Versailles. As you read these, reflect on the four main causes of the war: alliances, militarism, imperialism, and nationalism. Considering the events surrounding the outbreak of war, was the treaty fair? Which of the clauses were justified? Which were vindictive and unfair?

- Germany and its allies were required to accept full responsibility for the outbreak of the war.
- All German overseas investment was confiscated and given to the Allied powers.
- Germany was not allowed to build any military fortifications along the French–German border.
- Germany was required to give up control of the coal mines in the Saar Basin to France.
- Germany was ordered to return the areas it had taken from France and Denmark.
- Germany was required to acknowledge the independence of Austria and Czechoslovakia and not to join in any union.
- Germany was ordered to greatly reduce its military forces and was not to rearm in any way. It was not to have any naval or air forces.
- Germany had to agree to pay heavy war reparations (compensation) to France, Britain, and Russia, as well as to other nations affected by the war.

had to piece together information from newspapers and from rumours and speculations by unofficial observers. He complained about the lack of consultation between London and Ottawa, and insisted that Canada should have some say in the war effort. But his complaints were politely ignored. In a rage, Borden wrote to a friend, "It can hardly be expected that we shall put 400 000 or 500 000 men in the field and willingly accept the position of having no more voice and receiving no more consideration than if we were toy *automata*."

On the morning of December 9, 1916, Borden's demands were finally met. The newly elected British prime minister, David Lloyd George, decided to ask the prime ministers of the British dominions to join in a new **Imperial War Cabinet**. Lloyd George invited Canada and the other dominions "to discuss how best they could cooperate in the direction of the war." After all, he said to his aide, "they were fighting not for us but with us."

The implied promise of "autonomy within the Empire" — Borden's cherished dream — was not enough. Borden wanted to see that promise in writing, and he got it in the War Cabinet's Resolution IX. South Africa's General Jan Smuts was generally credited for the resolution, but it was really the handiwork of Robert Borden, even its phrasing. In the words of Resolution IX, Canada and the other dominions were given "full recognition…as autonomous nations." The details remained to be worked out after the war, but in principle Britain recognized Canada as a full partner in the British Empire.

The Paris Peace Conference

As the war was ending, Lloyd George called Borden to Paris, where the Allied leaders were gathering for the armistice. There the Allies would set the terms of peace. They would dispose of their enemies and shape the new Europe. Lloyd George assumed that Borden would be pleased to represent Canada, Australia, and the other British dominions as one of Britain's five delegates at the Paris Peace Conference. Borden flatly refused. Canada, he insisted, would sit at the peace conference in its own right. Sacrifice in war was the bloody price Canada had paid for equal nationhood, and Borden meant to have it.

The Treaty of Versailles and the New Face of Europe

After strong resistance, especially from the United States, Canada was given two seats at the Paris Peace Conference. The Canadian delegates had no votes, and the peace treaties were written by the major powers. But Canada had won a symbolic victory. It signed the **Treaty of Versailles**, which applied to Germany, and the four other treaties applying to the other losing nations, in its own right as an independent country. "The nation is clothed," Borden said, "with new dignity." Participation in the peace conference also guaranteed Canada a seat — and this time a vote, too — in the new League of

By 1917, disabled soldiers were a common sight on Canadian city streets. This painting, entitled A War Record, by Stanley F. Turner, shows a scene on a street corner near Toronto's main military hospital.

CANADIAN SOVEREIGNTY: A NATION FORGED IN FIRE

When the British declared war on Germany in August 1914, there was no doubt that Canada, too, was at war. Since Canada was a self-governing colony of Britain, its foreign-policy decisions were still made by the British. Only the degree of participation could be determined by Canadians. By the end of the war, Canadians had so distinguished themselves on and off the battlefield that a true sense of nationhood was felt by many. The capture of Vimy Ridge in 1917 led Brigadier General Alex Ross to exclaim:

At zero hour the barren earth erupted humanity. From dugouts, shell holes and trenches men sprang into action, fell into artillery formations, and advanced to the ridge, every division of the Corps moved forward together. It was Canada from the Atlantic to the Pacific on parade. I thought then, and I think today, that in those few minutes I witnessed the birth of a nation.

By the time the war finally ended in 1918, Canadians had won for themselves a place at the peace talks. Although Britain, France, and the United States dominated the talks, Canada was able to send an independent delegation, headed by Robert Borden. Never again would Canada be drawn into a war without the consent of the Canadian Parliament. Despite the enormous cost in human lives, Canada gained greater sovereignty during World War I.

Nations. In 1918, Canada stepped onto the world stage as a mature nation both in its own eyes and in the eyes of the world.

The **League of Nations** had been created by the Treaty of Versailles. Its role was to guarantee the peace and punish aggressive nations. The Treaty of Versailles was meant to ensure that World War I was indeed the "war to end all wars" and that Europe would enjoy a lasting peace.

A new Europe emerged out of the ashes of World War I. The old Russian, German, and Austrian empires disappeared. Britain, France, and the United States — "the Big Three" — took their pencils to the map of Europe and redrew its borders. They left Germany a crippled nation, stripped of its wealth and most of its armed forces. And they made sure that Germany was humbled. In signing the Treaty of Versailles, Germany was forced to accept all blame for the war.

The War Guilt Clause and Reparations

Article 231 of the Treaty of Versailles was perhaps the bitterest pill of all for Germans to swallow. Germany was forced to accept sole blame for World War I, even though many Germans believed that they had fought to protect themselves from the military aggression of Britain and France. On the basis of the so-called "war guilt" clause, Germany was also forced to pay reparations for damage done during the war. German payments for war damages poisoned the atmosphere in Europe for years to come.

The exact amount of German reparations was not spelled out in the peace treaty, but France and Britain were determined that Germany should be forced to pay for the devastation it had caused. The harshness of the Treaty of Versailles created an unstable peace in Europe because Germans w[ere] not content with the settlement.

What did the future hold for this new Europe? On Armistice Day, Borden wrote in his diary, "The world has drifted from its old anchorage and [no one] can with certainty prophesy what the outcome will be." In 1918, no one realized that the Treaty of Versailles had sowed the bitter seeds of World War II. Twenty years later, the world would reap a harvest of destruction.

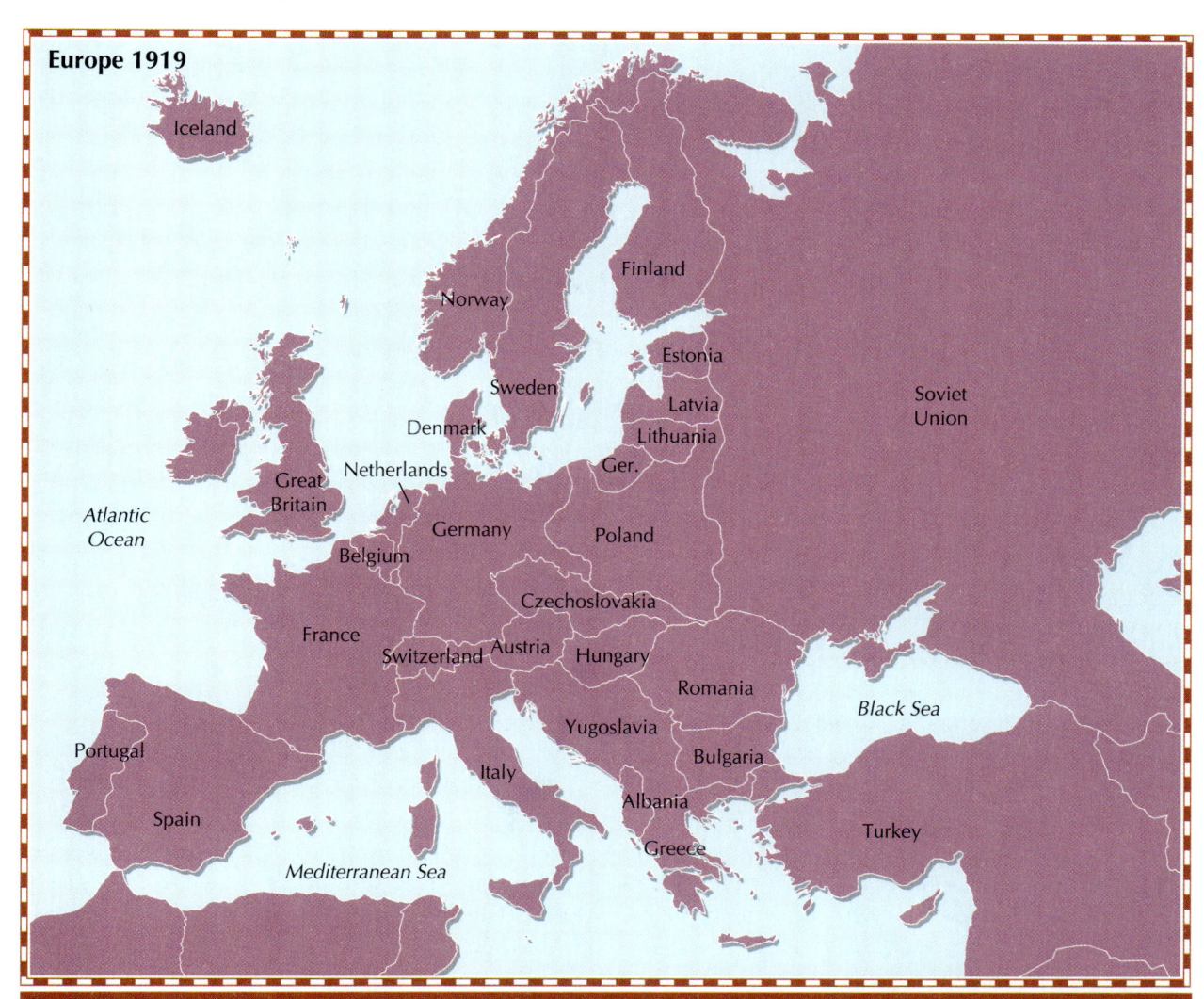

Europe 1919

Compare this map with the one on page 133, of Europe in 1914. What are the major boundary changes resulting from the Treaty of Versailles? Which countries appear to be the big losers? Judging by the territorial changes, does the treaty appear to have been fair?

177

...ING THE KEY PEOPLE, ... AND EVENTS

...rly identify and explain the historical significance of each of

U-boats
Jutland
Creeping Barrage
Imperial War Cabinet
League of Nations

Manfred von Richthofen
Lusitania
Arthur Currie
Canada's Hundred Days
Treaty of Versailles

FOCUS YOUR KNOWLEDGE

1. What were the attractions and the dangers of being an airplane pilot in World War I?
2. Describe the evolution of both the purpose and design of the airplane in World War I.
3. How did Canada's navy change during the course of World War I?
4. Explain the events that led the United States to enter World War I.
5. Describe the measures taken by the Canadians in their preparation for the assault on Vimy Ridge.
6. Describe the conditions faced by the soldiers at Passchendaele.

APPLY YOUR KNOWLEDGE

1. For four years, the war's combatants were trapped in trench warfare because both sides failed to win decisive victories. What events eventually tipped the balance in favour of the Allies? How important was the entry of the United States into the war? Explain your answers.
2. Vimy Ridge is considered by many to be Canada's greatest military achievement. Explain this battle's importance in several paragraphs by responding to the following questions: How did Arthur Currie's planning and leadership differ from that of Douglas Haig? What new strategies were employed by the Canadians? How do you think the victory at Vimy Ridge made the soldiers feel?

3. It could be argued that, for Canada, the most important victories were won at the diplomatic table rather than on the battlefield. Explain both this statement and why you agree or disagree with it.

EXTEND YOUR KNOWLEDGE

1. In Chapter 7, you were asked to write a series of letters that ended in July 1916. Continue writing letters in the same format, but describe the following events:

   Letter One, April 1917: Explain what happened at Vimy Ridge and your reaction as a participating soldier.

   Letter Two, October 1917: Explain what it was like to take part in the Battle of Passchendaele.

   Letter Three, November 11, 1918: Explain your reactions to the signing of the armistice and the end of war.

2. Working with a partner, prepare a visual display that depicts the evolution of the fighter plane in World War I. Use brief but informative captions to describe the changes.

3. Using the statistics from Chapter 8's feature study "The Expenses of War," prepare a display that uses various graphs to show:

   (a) the number of soldiers as a percentage of the total population of the major countries involved;
   (b) the percentage of Canadian soldiers killed and wounded in the war;
   (c) the rate of enlistment from 1914 to 1918 as compared with the casualty rate for the same period;
   (d) the financial cost of the war for the major nations involved.

   You may wish to present your graphs, as well as any conclusions you have drawn from them, to the rest of the class.

4. Using the feature study "The Treaty of Versailles," rewrite the treaty to reflect what you feel would have made it fair and just. Compare your revised treaty with one written by another student to see whether you both agree on the changes that should have been made. Can you negotiate an agreement that incorporates points from both revisions? Present your revised treaty to the class and ask for their response.

5. Select one of the battles or significant events in the war and relate it to a painting from World War I. Use the feature study "Canadian War Art" as a guide for ideas.

SKILLS FOCUS

UNIT REVIEW

1. Since the end of World War I, historians have debated the impact of the war on Canada. While no one doubts that participation in the war drastically changed Canada, there is less of a consensus about whether the changes were good or bad. Prepare a chart that lists both the ways in which World War I strengthened Canada as a nation and the ways in which it was detrimental. When your chart is complete, write a brief personal statement that assesses the impact of the war on Canada.

2. It has been said that the world entered the twentieth century during World War I. What aspects of change during the period 1914–1918 both at home and abroad support this statement? Considering the nature of the changes occurring during the war years, should "entering the twentieth century" be perceived as a good or a bad thing? Why?

3. Considering the treatment of Canadian soldiers during World War I, do you think their war experiences, despite the inevitable horrors, could have been made more bearable? If so how? If not, why not?

DEVELOPING RESEARCH SKILLS

To be successful in the study of history, you must be able to carry out research. This skill can yield substantial results both in your academic pursuits and in future careers. To develop an in-depth understanding of a topic, you must dig into the past by using a variety of resources, including books and magazines, CD-ROMs, microfiche, and computers. All of these sources are important tools in carrying out research. Once you begin to unearth the mysteries of the past, you will discover the delights and challenges that history holds. When you have acquired good research skills, you will be ready to explore the past without relying on this textbook or the classroom.

STEPS IN CARRYING OUT EFFECTIVE RESEARCH

1. Select a broad topic that can be narrowed down as your research progresses.

2. Once you have selected a topic, do some background reading in textbooks and encyclopedias.

3. After you have done enough background reading to be familiar with your topic and are certain that the issues related to this topic still interest you, prepare a list of sources that might be useful in your research. In preparing this list, be sure to:
   (a) consult the card catalogue and microfiche;
   (b) check the periodical index;
   (c) consider doing an interview, if possible;
   (d) review newspapers from relevant dates, using CD-ROMs if they are available;
   (e) look through bibliographies in other books to see if they can suggest useful books;
   (f) ask teachers, parents, friends, and others to suggest other sources for your topic.

4. When you are ready to begin using the sources you have listed, check the short, readable sources first. Use long, detailed sources as references only; do not attempt to read the whole book unless you have a good deal of time.

5. Make use of books' tables of contents and indexes to help you find the relevant information quickly.

6. When making research notes, use cue cards. Make point-form notes on the cards. Place only one main point on each card, and note the source and page reference for the point on each card. Use abbreviations to save time and space.

CAREER FOCUS

LAW

Being able to locate and use relevant information is an important skill for people in many careers. Lawyers, for example, must carefully research and document each case they handle. The arguments they present to the court must be based on sound factual evidence if they are to carry weight in the eyes of a judge or jury. If lawyers fail to research and prepare a case carefully, they run the risk of losing the case.

To carry out the necessary research, lawyers must know where and how to go about their search. The skills they use are very similar to those of a historian. In both cases, careful searches through a variety of sources are necessary to unearth information that may shed light on the issue being studied. Another similarity between historians and lawyers is that both use the information they find to support the argument they are trying to build.

There are many reasons why the study of history is valuable, especially to those pursuing a career in law. One of these is that the study of history develops the ability to carry out research — a skill essential to all good lawyers. Also, by understanding the history of Canada, lawyers are better able to comprehend the evolution of Canadian law.

Use historical research to obtain information that you can use in one of the following assignments.

1. There is a great deal of controversy over General Haig's leadership during the war. Put General Haig on trial for incompetence. Playing the role of either the Crown attorney or the defence attorney, prepare the arguments you would use in court.

2. During World War I, shell shock was not a recognized psychological ailment resulting from battle experience. Soldiers who could not return to the front lines due to shell shock were often court-martialed and sometimes executed for desertion. Several Canadians faced this fate. Re-create one of the court-martial trials that led to the execution of Canadians for desertion in World War I. Prepare arguments either for or against using shell shock as a reason for refusing to return to the front.

3. Write a brief attack on or defence of the Treaty of Versailles. Take into account the causes of the war as well as any relevant events during the war in defending your position.

---

7. Organize your research notes under broad subheadings.

WRITING REPORTS

Once you have completed your research, you can make use of it in a number of ways — in presentations, essays, and reports. Reports differ from essays in not having a central thesis or argument around which they are built. Instead, reports summarize the information gathered, usually by providing an introduction to the topic at the beginning and an assessment of the information at the end. Also, reports are organized under subheadings. Select one of the broad topics from the list below and prepare a written report of 400–750 words. The report should be based on research from a minimum of three sources besides your textbook and should offer a personal assessment at the end.

1. New Weapons of War
2. War on the Home Front
3. Canadian Heroes of World War I
4. Life on the Western Front

UNIT 4

FROM BOOM TO BUST:
CANADA IN THE 1920s AND 1930s

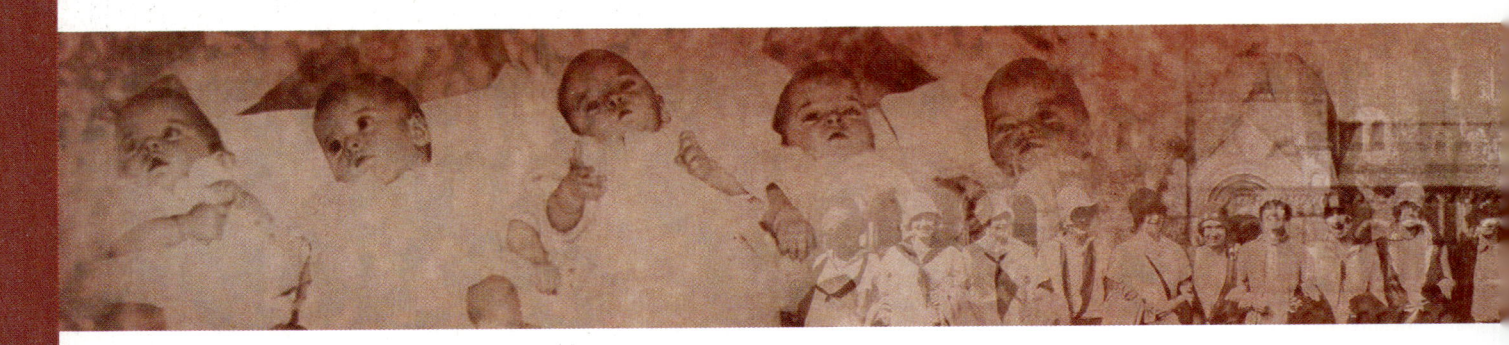

IN THE TWENTY YEARS between the end of World War I and the beginning of World War II, Canadians experienced both unprecedented wealth in the Roaring Twenties and dreadful poverty during the Great Depression. As a result of these wide swings in the economy, the Canadian government came to play a far more active role in society. New political parties such as the Co-operative Commonwealth Federation and the Social Credit Party also emerged to broaden the Canadian political spectrum. In many ways, the two decades between the wars were formative years for Canada. Women came to play a more active role in society, Canada made enormous strides toward establishing complete independence, and the world of entertainment was revolutionized by the development of the radio and film industry.

Chapter 10 focuses on the major political and economic events of the 1920s and 1930s. This chapter examines Prime Minister Mackenzie King's efforts to establish Canadian autonomy and various political efforts to end the Depression of the 1930s. As

CHAPTER TEN
Prosperity and Depression

CHAPTER ELEVEN
Life in Canada in the 1920s and 1930s

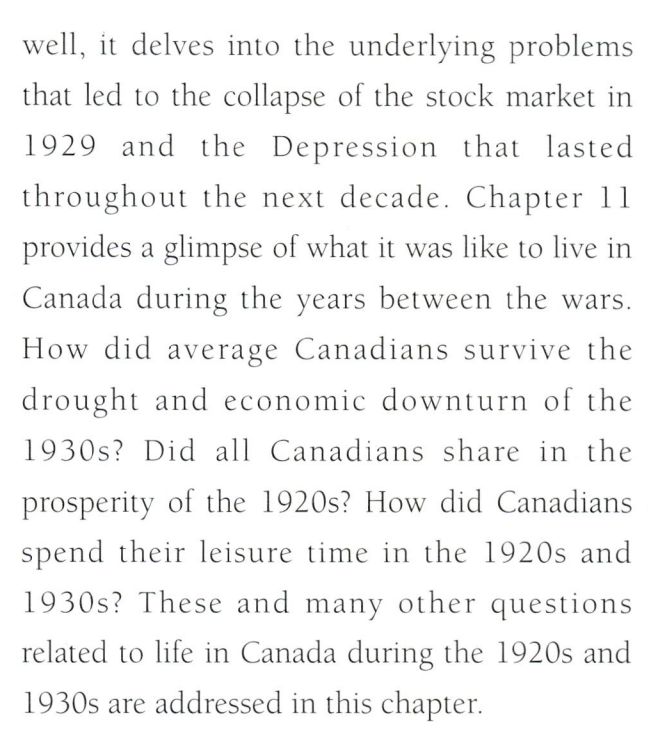

well, it delves into the underlying problems that led to the collapse of the stock market in 1929 and the Depression that lasted throughout the next decade. Chapter 11 provides a glimpse of what it was like to live in Canada during the years between the wars. How did average Canadians survive the drought and economic downturn of the 1930s? Did all Canadians share in the prosperity of the 1920s? How did Canadians spend their leisure time in the 1920s and 1930s? These and many other questions related to life in Canada during the 1920s and 1930s are addressed in this chapter.

CHAPTER 10: PROSPERITY AND DEPRESSION

GLOSSARY TERMS

Panhandlers People who stop others on the street and ask for money.
Great Depression The period of economic depression, marked by a severe decline of business activity, that began in 1929 and lasted through most of the 1930s.
Civil Servant An official working in the public service branch of government.
Foreign Policy A nation's plan of action in its relationships with other nations.
Privy Council In the United Kingdom, a body of advisers appointed by or serving the Crown on state matters.
Stock Market A place where bonds and stocks, or shares of corporate capital, are bought and sold.
Secondary Manufacturing Making products from processed, or secondary, materials rather than from primary, or raw, materials.
Drought A long period of dry weather.
Malnutrition Poor nourishment resulting from eating the wrong kinds of food or from lack of food.
Laissez-faire A French term ("let it be") for the policy of strictly limiting government control and direction of trade, business, or industry.

FOCUS ON:

- how Mackenzie King stayed in power for more than twenty-two years
- Canada's increasing independence from Britain
- the wave of prosperity that swept over many parts of Canada in the 1920s
- the causes and major effects of the Great Depression of the 1930s
- solutions to the economic crisis that were proposed by the various political parties
- measures taken by governments and individuals to cope with the Depression

The long horror of the European war was over at last. A few years later, the "Roaring Twenties" were in full swing. The 1920s were a decade remembered for easy money and high living, short skirts and raccoon coats, jazz music and the Charleston, American gangsters and Canadian rum-runners, fast cars and bathtub gin. But the bubble of economic prosperity in the Roaring Twenties burst in 1929, and the good times gave way to hard times. The 1930s were sometimes called the "Dirty Thirties" or the "Hungry Thirties." For many Canadians it was a time of soup kitchens and *panhandlers*, hobo camps and drifters, drought and duststorms, gunnysacks for overshoes and newspapers for blankets. Two generations of Canadians were deeply scarred by the poverty and despair of the *Great Depression*. The Depression lifted only with the start of a bloody new European war in 1939.

Mayfair, a magazine of fashion and taste for the wealthy, illustrates the extravagance and luxury of the 1920s.

THE AGE OF MACKENZIE KING

The leader of the federal Liberal Party, Wilfrid Laurier, died not long after the end of World War I. The young Mackenzie King became the new Liberal leader in 1919. King was proud of being the grandson of William Lyon Mackenzie, the fiery reformer who sparked the 1837 Rebellion in Upper Canada. But William Lyon Mackenzie King was a very different sort of man. Cautious and moderate, King was a successful *civil servant* and expert labour negotiator. Like Laurier, he was skilled at using compromise to hold the nation together. And, like Laurier, King put Canadian unity ahead of every other political goal.

Mackenzie King would become Canada's longest-serving prime minister. First elected as prime minister in 1921, King went on to win elections in 1925, 1926, 1935, 1940, and 1945. He was out of power only briefly in the summer of 1926 and for the five years from 1930 to 1935. For almost thirty years, he stood at the very centre of Canadian political life.

CANADA'S GROWING AUTONOMY FROM BRITAIN

After the war, both Canada and its new prime minister had had enough of European conflicts. In the early 1920s, Mackenzie King was bent on keeping Canada out of any future wars on the other side of the Atlantic. He wanted Canada to free itself from British *foreign policy* and to determine its own relations with other nations. In 1923, Prime Minister King attended an Imperial Conference — a meeting of all the member countries of the British Empire. Britain was trying to persuade delegates to stay united in support of British foreign policy. But King reminded Britain that Canada was a self-governing country. He insisted that "the decision of Canada on any important issue, domestic or foreign, we believe should be made by the people of Canada."

Campaigning 1920s style, Mackenzie King addresses a large crowd from the back seat of his car during the 1926 election.

PROSPERITY AND DEPRESSION

The British foreign secretary was deeply unhappy with the Canadian prime minister's insistence on Canadian independence, but King won out. Canada was to be autonomous in its foreign (external) policy as well as its domestic (internal) policy. The formal details of autonomy were spelled out at another Imperial Conference in 1926. It was declared that member countries were all self-governing nations, "equal in status" to each other and "freely associated" with the British Commonwealth. This declaration marked the end of old-style British imperialism. The British Empire had become a "Commonwealth of Nations." It was now an association of equal nations bound together by common interests and loyalty to the British monarch.

In 1931 the British Parliament passed the **Statute of Westminster**, which gave Canada (and other British Commonwealth countries) complete control over their relations with other nations. Now Canada was almost fully independent. Some direct political links remained between the Canadian and British governments. For example, the British Parliament still had to formally amend the Canadian Constitution (the BNA Act), and Britain's Judicial Committee of the *Privy Council* was still the highest court in Canada. Canada and Britain remained close both politically and culturally. Nevertheless, Canada had passed a major milestone on the road to sovereignty.

THE POSTWAR YEARS

The two decades after World War I were marked by economic upswings and downturns. Just after the war, prices soared and the cost of living shot up in Canada. At the same time, munitions plants closed down and few new factories opened up. Jobs were hard to come by. When thousands of veterans returned home and began looking for jobs, unemployment rose even higher. Women were often forced out of work so that returning men could take their jobs. But there were still not enough jobs for the returning soldiers.

In 1917, Robert Borden's government had promised soldiers "full re-establishment" after their "holocaust of blood." Veterans looked to the government to keep its promise. Disabled veterans were given small government pensions. So were dependants of the war dead. A few new veterans' hospitals were built, and some homesteads were offered to returning soldiers. But veterans' demands for a cash bonus of $2000 for war service were turned down flat. Many veterans were angry and desperate.

Canadian war workers were also angry with government and business. During the war, the Borden government had passed legislation denying workers the right to strike for better pay and working conditions. But Borden had only gently prodded employers to pay fair wages and negotiate with their employees. Most employers had simply ignored the government's directions. Bitter workers who had given their all in the war effort resented their treatment.

Worker unrest did not end with the war. Rising prices for food and clothing meant that paycheques bought less. Some workers began to join unions in order to bargain for more pay. Whole new groups of workers joined the union movement, including police, municipal employees, West Coast loggers, and workers in meat-packing houses and garment shops in Toronto and Montreal. Most factory owners and city councils had never faced unions before and strongly opposed the new unions. But in the postwar labour turmoil, nothing could stop the union movement. By 1919, there were more than 420 strikes in Canada, and many working people outside the unions marched in support of worker demands.

The Winnipeg General Strike

Labour unrest came to a head in the **Winnipeg General Strike** of May 1919. Metal-trades workers, supported by more than 30 000 working people, tied up the city for six weeks. The Winnipeg strike

Chaos swept Winnipeg in June 1919. Do you think the police responded appropriately or with excessive force?

sparked dozens of sympathetic strikes from Vancouver Island to Nova Scotia. Many government and business leaders panicked at the worker revolt sweeping across Canada. They feared a "red (communist) menace." A communist revolution of Russian workers had toppled the government of the Russian czar in 1917, and some Canadians were afraid that a communist-style revolution was about to be repeated in Canada.

The Winnipeg General Strike came to a climax on "Bloody Saturday" — June 21, 1919. A crowd of demonstrators had gathered on Winnipeg's Main Street to protest the pre-dawn arrest of ten strike leaders. They were also angry about strike-breaking Winnipeg streetcar drivers returning to work. Some of the demonstrators stopped a streetcar near City Hall and set it on fire. Winnipeg's mayor called out the troops. Royal North-West Mounted Police charged the crowd on horseback while the crowd hurled bricks and bottles. Eventually the police began to fire revolvers. By the end of the day, two people were dead, dozens more were injured, and scores were arrested.

The general strike had been broken, and the labour movement was left in tatters. Soon after, Canadian business began a strong anti-labour campaign with the support of government troops and police. Labour organizers were blacklisted and fired, and strikes were put down by armies of strike-breakers. During the 1920s, union membership dropped off sharply, but the Winnipeg General Strike did mark the beginning of a new working-class awareness and a new political involvement. Over the next few years, labour leaders were elected to all levels of government. In the 1920 Manitoba provincial election, for example, eleven labour representatives were elected — including three people who were serving jail terms

During the Winnipeg General Strike some people, like these two women volunteers, tried to keep the city functioning. Would you have supported the strikers or volunteered your time to limit the effects of the strike?

PROSPERITY AND DEPRESSION

187

after the Winnipeg General Strike. And in the 1921 federal election, another activist in the Winnipeg General Strike — social reformer J.S. Woodsworth — became a member of Parliament.

THE BUBBLE OF PROSPERITY

People often look back on the Roaring Twenties as a time of unbroken prosperity and optimism. But in the early 1920s, Canada was hit by a recession. Between 1921 and 1923, many small businesses failed and many workers found themselves without jobs. Some Canadian banks were teetering on the brink of bankruptcy. One bank — the Home Bank — collapsed, and all of its seventy-one branches shut their doors. The grain-growing regions of Europe had been devastated by war, and Canadian wheat was in big demand. As a result, wheat prices soared in 1919. But by 1921 European grain farmers were back in business. Australia and Argentina were also producing bumper crops of wheat. As the supply of wheat grew, the price of wheat dropped. Canadian wheat prices slid from $2.45 a bushel in 1918 to 80¢ a bushel in 1921. Many farmers were badly hurt by the price drop.

The mid-1920s saw the return of a shaky prosperity. There was a new global economic recovery, and the world began wanting more Canadian goods. Canadian wheat was in demand again, and wheat prices rebounded. Wheat exports climbed from $45.5 million in 1911 to $352.1 million in 1928. Markets also returned for Canadian resources like lumber, newsprint, and metals. Investment money began pouring into Canada. American money was behind many of Canada's new businesses, factories, mines, smelters, and hydro-electric projects, but no one really noticed. It was returning prosperity that was in Canadians' minds. Whole new industries sprang up. Hydro-electric plants hummed into action, and the output of electricity quadrupled between 1921 and 1930. There was a huge U.S. demand for newsprint as the American newspaper trade went into high gear, producing newspapers twice as big as in 1920. Pulp-and-paper mills were soon built in British Columbia, Quebec, New Brunswick, Nova Scotia, Manitoba, and Ontario to meet the new demand.

The Canadian Shield was full of mineral wealth, and Canadian mineral resources were also in great demand. Small airplanes called bush planes flew over the northern landscape, carrying prospectors, geologists, and stock promoters in search of new wealth. Mines opened in northern

Jazz took the 1920s by storm. Originating in New Orleans, jazz music's innovative use of bass, piano, drum, and brass instruments made it popular in nightclubs throughout North America and Europe. Bands like the Elks Jazz Band, seen in this photograph, brought the sound of jazz to Canadian cities in the 1920s.

ARTISTS OF THE 1920s AND 1930s

Emily Carr

Born in Victoria, British Columbia, in 1871, Emily Carr became one of Canada's best-known painters. After studying art in San Francisco and making trips to England and France, Carr returned to Victoria, where her style began to take shape. By the late 1920s, Carr's paintings were becoming very popular. Influenced by the Group of Seven, Carr captured the wilderness and the way of life of Native people in the Queen Charlotte Islands.

Source: Emily Carr, *Big Raven*, 1931. Canvas 87.3 x 114.4 cm. Collecrtion Vancouver Art Gallery, Emily Carr Trust

Paraskeva Clark

Like Emily Carr, Paraskeva Clark was a Canadian woman who became well-known for her paintings; but here the similarities end. Clark, born in St. Petersburg, Russia, in 1898, moved to Canada with her Canadian-born husband in 1931. Clark's painting reflected the influence of Cubism, learned in Soviet studies, and contrasted sharply with the style of the Group of Seven. In her work, she focused on Toronto during the 1930s and 1940s, often reflecting the social distress of the Depression.

Source: Paraskeva Clark, *Petroushka*, 1937. Collecrtion of the National Gallery of Canada. Reproduced with permission of the Estate of Paraskeva Clark.

Canada, and millions of dollars worth of copper, zinc, iron, and nickel began flowing out to markets around the globe. Mining communities like Sudbury, Kirkland Lake, Flin Flon, and Trail began to flourish. Natural resources were Canada's main source of economic growth, but manufacturing industries were also on the upswing. Canadian growth industries included railroad equipment, automobiles, and farm machines as well as electrical, rubber, petro-chemical, cement, and leather products.

Canadians were ready to enjoy their new prosperity. After years of sacrifice, it was time to be carefree and enjoy life. Money was "easy come, easy go." People began buying cars, radios, telephones, and electric appliances — often on credit (borrowed money). They went to nightclubs to listen to American jazz and dance the Charleston. They flocked to fancy new motion-picture theatres and swooned over the stars of the silent screen. Many played the *stock market* for the thrill of the risk, and some came away with millions of dollars. Easy money and the glitter of good times were the hallmarks of the Roaring Twenties.

THE NOT-SO-GOOD TIMES

But the good times were not spread evenly across Canada. Prosperity came to central Canada and to city dwellers, but even Canadian cities were populated by both the rich and the poor. Although middle- and upper-class Canadians were enjoying the payoff from economic growth, one historian has noted that the 1920s "hardly roared" at all for Canadian workers. First, rising prices meant a lower standard of living. Then, the recession cost many people their jobs. Even after prosperity returned, new jobs could be hard to get. Many jobs in Canada still paid poorly. Women and new immigrants suffered most of all from low wages and often deplorable working conditions.

Canadian Farmers

Prosperity was also hit-and-miss on the Prairies. The price of wheat determined whether times were good or bad. Between 1920 and 1924, the incomes of wheat farmers dropped by 40 percent. But after 1924, the price of wheat and world demand began edging steadily upward. By 1927, the incomes of Alberta farmers totalled almost $170 million, a figure that would not be topped until the end of World War II. Some farmers splurged and built themselves big new farmhouses. They also bought up-to-date farm equipment to work their larger and more mechanized farms. Cars and trucks began to replace horses in farm yards, and more tractors and threshers lumbered across the prairie landscape.

But buying larger farms and more farm equipment often meant going heavily into debt. Later on, many farm families would find themselves burdened with debts they could not repay. The motto of "Buy now, pay later" would return to haunt them. Even in the good years of the mid-1920s, many other Canadian farmers lived drab and uncertain lives. Every week, people left their farms to seek a better life in the cities. They wanted a stake in the good life that they had heard so much about but had never seen for themselves.

The Maritimes

Most people in the Maritimes had had a taste of economic prosperity during World War I, when the region had prospered. But almost as soon as the war ended, hundreds of soldiers and sailors vanished from Halifax streets, and a thousand civilians who had provided services for the armed forces found themselves out of jobs. At about the same time, the demand for Nova Scotia coal dropped off. The coal industry was hit hard by the recession in the early 1920s and by a switch from coal to oil and electricity. Miners were laid off for months or years. Some never returned to the coal mines. The heavy-steel industry was also hit hard. There were repeated strikes and lockouts in the troubled mining and steel industries of Cape Breton between 1922 and 1925. So many militia were sent to end outbreaks of violence that, at one point, half of Canada's army was on duty in Cape Breton.

Between 1920 and 1926, *secondary manufacturing* industries nearly collapsed, and almost 42 percent of the manufacturing jobs in the Maritimes disappeared. In the early 1920s, the United States raised tariffs on fish and farm goods. Maritimers who made their livings from fishing and farming suffered under the economic blow. The limping Maritime economy was weakened even further by government decisions about tariffs and railway freight rates. For example, between 1917 and 1923, freight rates in the Maritimes went up between 140 and 216 percent. The added shipping costs made Maritime goods more expensive to buy in central Canada and gave central Canada's producers an advantage over Maritime producers. While the new policies helped central Canada prosper, they badly hurt the Maritimes. Hard times in the 1920s forced many Maritimers to leave home and look for work elsewhere in Canada.

THE DEPRESSION BEGINS

Public confidence was generally high in Canada in the last years of the 1920s, and many Canadians were optimistic. However, the uncertain prosperity of the Roaring Twenties was coming to an end. A dramatic signal of the approaching end took place in October 1929. On October 24, thousands of speculators lost money in a sudden stock-market tumble on the Winnipeg Grain Exchange. Five days later, the New York stock market crashed. Too many people had bought stocks using borrowed money. As long as stock prices were rising, speculators could sell their stocks, pay off their debts, and still make a profit. But when stock prices began to fall, they could not cover their debts by selling off stocks. A drop in stock-market prices set off a panic wave of selling. It was "sell, sell, sell" as thousands

Without unemployment insurance or a welfare system for assistance, people such as this unemployed blacksmith and his family found the 1930s very difficult to live through.

of speculators rushed to get rid of their stock shares before prices dropped even lower. But there were fewer buyers, and prices continued to plunge. Thousands of people saw their stocks become worthless almost overnight. It was an early warning sign of the beginning of the **Great Depression** — the worst economic downturn in Canada's history.

CAUSES OF THE DEPRESSION

Canada was not the only nation to suffer during the Great Depression. The Depression was a worldwide economic disaster that affected countries as far away as Germany, Norway, Chile, Japan, and the United States. Not surprisingly, an event as devastating and complicated as the Great Depression had many causes. Economists disagree about the role of the American stock-market crash in October 1929 in deepening the economic trouble already "in the air." However, most recent economic studies of the Great Depression suggest that the stock-market crash frightened American consumers and businesspeople, creating what one economist described as "uncertainty about future income."

American consumers, worried about having less money to spend in the future, stopped buying expensive items called "durable goods," such as cars, stoves, and washing machines. For example, U.S. automobile sales dropped sharply in November and December 1929. Because of the drop in consumer demand, American manufacturers began cutting back on the production of consumer goods. As American industrial production declined, workers were laid off and unemployment grew. Then, the mistaken monetary policies of the American government and a series of U.S. bank failures turned uncertainty into pessimism, and American consumer spending and business investment dropped even further. As a result, the Great Depression in the United States deepened in the early 1930s.

At the same time, other countries also experienced economic problems, which worsened as the effects of staggering economies in large countries like the United States and Great Britain spread around the world. Canada was hit especially hard because 33 percent of its gross national income came from selling goods to other countries. The United States had overtaken Great Britain as the largest foreign market for Canadian exports. When the American economy slumped badly, so did Canada's economy.

A key factor in the Great Depression was "deflation," a worldwide drop in the prices of a wide range of goods as a result of falling demand and overproduction. For example, there was more wheat on

During the difficult times of the Depression, when many people were out of work, scenes like this one, of a Montreal family being evicted from their home, were common. What should the government have done to help those who lost their homes during the Depression?

STATISTICS OF THE GREAT DEPRESSION

The hardships endured by the Canadian people during the Great Depression are reflected in the accompanying statistics. By examining these statistics, you can clearly see how badly affected the Canadian economy was during the 1930s.

Activities

1. Using the statistics in Chart #1 create bar graphs for the years 1928–29 and 1933 for each province. When you have completed your graphs, calculate the percentage decrease in per capita incomes for each province.

2. Study the bar graphs and the statistics in Chart #1 carefully. Can you explain why the most drastic decline in incomes took place in the West? Does the fact that the decline was the least dramatic in the Maritime provinces suggest that these provinces were better off than the rest of Canada in the 1930s? Why or why not?

3. Create a functional graph using the statistics in Chart #2 and another using the statistics in Chart #3. After studying these graphs, answer the following questions:

    (a) In what year was unemployment at its worst?

    (b) Gross national product (GNP) represents the total dollar value of all the goods and services produced by a country in a year. What relationship do you see between the trends in GNP and the unemployment levels? Why might such a relationship exist?

Chart #1

DECLINE IN PER CAPITA INCOMES BY PROVINCE, FROM 1928–29 TO 1933

	1928–29 Average ($ per capita)	1933 Average ($ per capita)
Saskatchewan	478	135
Alberta	548	212
Manitoba	466	240
British Columbia	594	314
Prince Edward Island	278	154
Ontario	549	310
Quebec	391	220
New Brunswick	292	180
Nova Scotia	322	207
Canada	471	247

Source: Rowell-Sirois Report, Book I: Canada: 1867-1939, 150.

Chart #2

ESTIMATED UNEMPLOYMENT RATE, 1926–1939

Year	Percent
1926	4.7
1927	2.9
1928	2.6
1929	4.2
1930	12.9
1931	17.4
1932	26.0
1933	26.6
1934	20.6
1935	19.1
1936	16.7
1937	12.5
1938	15.1
1939	14.1

Source: National Bureau of Economic Research, *The Measurement and Behavior of Unemployment* (Princeton, 1957), 455.

Chart #3

GROSS NATIONAL PRODUCT, 1926–1939

Year	GNP (billions of dollars)
1926	5.1
1927	5.6
1928	6.1
1929	6.1
1930	5.7
1931	4.7
1932	3.8
1933	3.5
1934	4.0
1935	4.3
1936	4.6
1937	5.2
1938	5.3
1939	5.6

Source: Statistics Canada, 13-531, 13-201.

the world market than there were buyers for it. Because of the worldwide glut of wheat, prices for Canadian wheat fell sharply.

Between 1929 and 1933, farm-product prices dropped by half. Prices for other manufactured goods did not fall quite as fast, but trouble in one major industry meant trouble for all. For example, one-third of all Canadians worked in farming. When farm incomes took a plunge, farming families all over the nation stopped buying things like tractors, cars, appliances, factory-made clothing, books, and life insurance. With the drop in demand, some businesses feared that they could not find markets for all their goods. They began cutting back production. Manufacturing production fell by one-third between 1929 and 1932.

Banks became nervous at the industrial slowdown and became less eager to extend credit to businesses. "Tighter money" meant that business slowed down even more. As industries cut back production and struggled with tight money and sometimes large debts, some workers lost their jobs. Others had to make do with wage cuts. These workers bought less, and as a result the demand for products fell even lower. The economy continued spiralling downward.

At the same time, nations around the world began to place high tariffs on foreign-made goods. Using high tariffs to keep out foreign goods is called protectionism. Protectionism amounted to international economic warfare. Every country attempted to save its own industries by trying to ensure that they did not face tough competition from foreign industries. As a result, industries in other countries suddenly found their usual markets closed off. Protectionism strangled world trade as country after country shut its doors to goods from abroad.

Canada was a trading (exporting) nation. Eighty percent of the products from Canada's farms, forests, and mines were sold abroad. When the foreign demand for Canada's wheat, pulp and paper, and minerals decreased, many large Canadian businesses began to collapse. Industries that had grown up alongside them also began to crumble. For example, when wheat exports to Europe began to decline, the railways that carried wheat to market made less money. Railway companies began to cut jobs and stopped buying goods like boxcars and rails. As a result, production and employment in the railway-car and steel industries of Ontario and Cape Breton dropped, too. Canada was badly hurt by the collapse of international markets and worldwide protectionism.

FIRST REACTIONS TO THE DEPRESSION

When the stock market crashed, very few people expected a depression to follow. Mackenzie King told Canadians that "business was

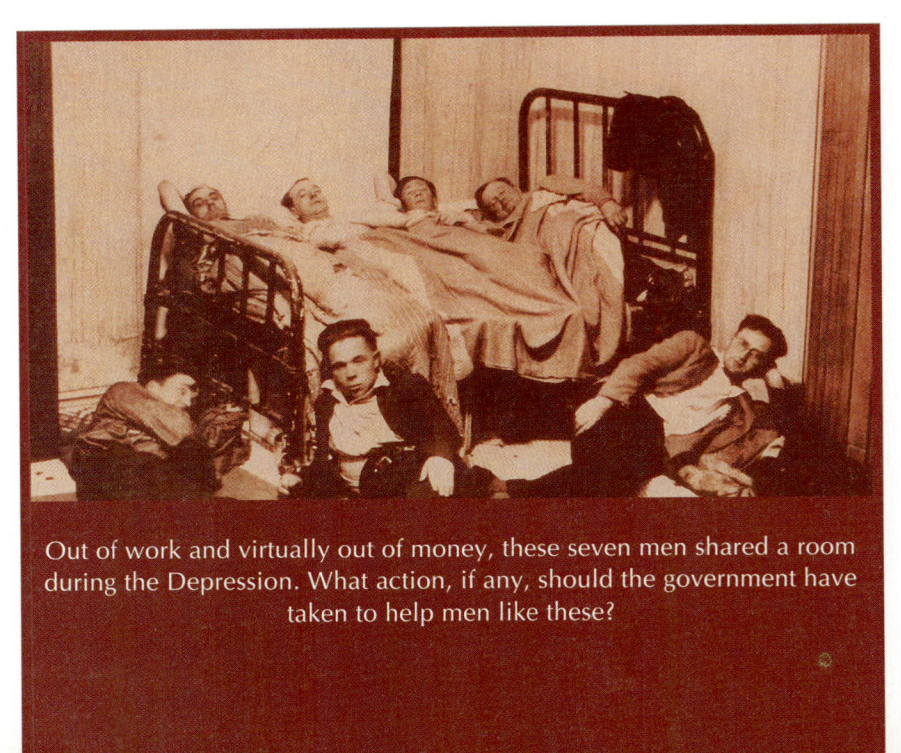

Out of work and virtually out of money, these seven men shared a room during the Depression. What action, if any, should the government have taken to help men like these?

never better, nor faith in Canada's future more justified." The prime minister was not alone in thinking that the crash was just temporary. It was normal for an upswing of economic prosperity to be followed by a downturn toward recession and then a rebound toward economic prosperity again. It was all a part of what is sometimes called the business cycle of alternating economic upswings and downturns. As the well-known Canadian historian J.L. Granatstein put it, "King was blind, but so was everyone. No one conceived of an end to prosperity; no one had thought that world trade would collapse; no one realized that Canada, as an exporter of primary products, would be hurt as much as or more than any country in the world by the crash."

As the recession deepened, poverty and hardship spread across the nation. Cash-strapped provinces called for federal grants to help the growing army of unemployed people. However, Prime Minister King viewed unemployment as a provincial responsibility. King felt that if provincial governments wanted money for the unemployed, they should raise their own taxes for it. He was especially unhappy about giving money to the five Conservative provincial governments. In April 1930, he told Parliament that "I would not give a single cent to any Tory (Conservative) government." The Conservative opposition erupted into a chorus of "Shame! Shame!" At that, King shot back, "What is there to be ashamed of?... I would not give them a five-cent piece." King's remarks became known as his "five-cent speech."

That night, King confessed in his diary that perhaps he had gone too far: his words made him seem "indifferent to the conditions of the unemployed." He was right. The opposition leader, R.B. Bennett, made the most of King's remarks and of the widespread unhappiness about the deepening economic slump. He accused King of being unwilling and unable to deal with the Depression. Canadians listened. In the 1930 election, the Conservatives defeated King's Liberals.

R.B. Bennett became the new prime minister. On election night, King cheered himself with thoughts of future success. "It looks as tho' it means Bennett for a while then a Liberal party with a long lease of power later on," he wrote in his diary. "I believe it is all for the best." Mackenzie King's prediction of a return to a long Liberal reign came true five years later.

It fell to Bennett to lead Canada through the very worst years of the Great Depression, from 1930 to 1935. But Bennett did not understand just how severe Canada's economic problems were. He told Canadians to be patient and wait for the economy to correct itself. But this time there was no recovery in sight. The downturn hit both Canadian farming and Canadian manufacturing at once. The double blow to the economy was just too much. Canada was in for a full-blown depression — a deep and long period of economic failure.

R.B. Bennett was a self-made millionaire who believed governments should not interfere in the economy. Why do you think he changed his mind before the 1935 election?

Disaster on the Prairies

The worst-hit region was the Prairies. Wheat prices dropped to an all-time low. A bushel of No. 1 Northern wheat that had earned a farmer $1.63 in 1928 was worth 35¢ in 1932. The land had been overfarmed, and as a result the prairie topsoil was easily eroded. When *drought* struck the plains of southern Alberta and Saskatchewan year after year, the topsoil turned to fine dust and blew away. Fierce windstorms whirled the dust up into fence corners and drove it under windows and doors. Almost nothing could grow under the onslaughts of nature. Grasshoppers and cutworms destroyed whatever crops did manage to struggle into life. On some farms, not a stalk of wheat was left standing.

In 1928, the average Saskatchewan farmer had a net income of $1614. Families could afford to buy sugar and coffee, clothes, school books, and gasoline, and even to put aside some savings. But by 1933, the same farmer earned only $66. Prairie farmers were facing terrible times. "We were all poverty stricken," recalled a farmer in Camrose, Alberta. "I had neighbours who were living on skimmed milk and potatoes. The telephones were taken from one farm home after another, until we were finally the only farm with a telephone." Doing without a telephone on a farm 20 kilometres from town and 2 kilometres or more from the closest neighbour was not just an inconvenience. It meant real isolation and even danger in times of trouble.

Duststorms like this one blew the topsoil off many prairie farms in the 1930s. Drought and depression made the 1930s a decade of despair in the West.

BENNETT'S RESPONSE TO THE DEPRESSION

The Great Depression was a terrible time for many other Canadians, too. Mines, sawmills, and paper mills shut down. Construction dropped off. So did Canadian manufacturing. People across the country were laid off. By 1933, almost one-third of all Canadian workers were out of a job. A legion of young men began "riding the rods." They hitched rides on railway boxcars to travel the country, looking for jobs that were not there. Except for a very small old-age-pension scheme, there was no social-welfare system. There was no unemployment insurance, no health care for the sick, no welfare for the poverty-stricken. By 1933, 800 000 Canadians — men, women, and children — were forced to ask private charities or governments for help. Although the Bennett government made grants and loans to provinces for farm aid and unemployment relief, the $255 million in aid between 1930 and 1935 was not nearly enough to relieve the distress of Canadians.

"Living on the Pogey"

The slang term for getting government vouchers for food, boots, clothing, coal, and shelter was "living on the **pogey**." It was a terrible experience for many hardworking people to ask for relief. Some men broke down and cried when they finally had to walk into a relief office. "In the thirties, Canadians had their pride," remarked one city relief officer.

"Relief was a disgrace. Men would say that never in the history of their family — and they'd usually mention something about the British Empire Loyalists, or coming West with the first CPR trains — never had they had to go on relief."

But governments insisted that no one had the right to free handouts. "The individual cannot...forever turn to the state to correct every misadventure which may befall him," said the cabinet minister in charge of relief grants. Relief payments were purposely kept lower than the lowest-paying job to discourage people from applying for relief. It took at least $7 a week to feed a family of five in Ontario in 1932. In Toronto the weekly food allowance was $6.93, and Toronto was generous, compared with most other places. The food allowance in Quebec was $3.25, and in Newfoundland it was about 6¢ a day for each family member. In fact, Newfoundland — still an independent dominion — was deeply in debt and could not get credit to borrow more money. It gave up self-government and allowed itself to be governed by a British commission to try to cope with its credit problems. But most Canadian provinces were also short of money, and relief payments were never enough anywhere. Like Newfoundlanders, many Canadian families lived close to starvation. *Malnutrition* and disease, especially among children, were common.

Many desperate Canadians wrote to Prime Minister Bennett, telling him of their troubles. A young man from New Brunswick wrote Bennett this letter in 1933:

I am a married man age 26 with one child and have been working for the last three months for little more than my board and have had to break my home up.... I am willing to do any kind of work and any length of time. I sincerely hope that you might have some kind of job that you could offer me so that I may get back with my wife and child.

I am sleeping and eating just wherever I can and I have nearly frozen in this last week looking for a job with the few clothes I have. I have no underwear and I don't care to ask for relief as I think something might turn up and there is poorer people than I who need it....

A young mother from Alberta wrote this letter to the prime minister in 1935 and received $5:

Please don't think I'm crazy for writing you this letter, but I've got three little children, and they are all in need of shoes as well as underwear but shoe's are the most neaded as two of them go to school and its cold, my husband has not had a crop for 8 years only enough for seed and some food, and I don't know what to do. I hate to ask for help. I never have before and we are staying

PROSPERITY AND DEPRESSION

This photograph captures the frustration of many Canadians who desperately sought work but could not find jobs.

WHY SHOOT THE TEACHER?

Despite the economic despair and the drought that ravaged crops on the Prairies, Canadians living in the West managed to survive the 1930s by relying on their own resourcefulness and the support of their neighbours. Max Braithwaite, one of Canada's best-known writers of humour, tells a story of life on the Prairies that is sometimes grim and sometimes hilarious, but always honest. The story is that of a young school teacher who accepts an ill-paid teaching assignment in an isolated school in Saskatchewan during the Great Depression.

In the following excerpts, the young teacher describes his first day on the Prairies and his experience at a community dance. As you read these excerpts, try to imagine how you would have reacted under similar circumstances. Continue the story by adding one or two paragraphs to either of the excerpts.

A Home Where the Buffalo Ought to Roam

I didn't sleep well that first night in Willowgreen School District. The McDougall house was small and cold. There was no insulation in walls or ceiling and the house was heated, as were many prairie homes, by the kitchen range and a round ornate heater in the living room. Neither was kept burning all night. It just wasn't practical. McDougall had no coal to burn, and he couldn't be expected to stay up all night to shove wood into a stove.

Besides, who needs a fire at night? McDougall and his wife could certainly keep each other warm. The children slept together in their long, fleece-lined underwear and cuddled spoon style, generating enough heat for them. No provision was made for a visiting schoolteacher. Why should there be? He was something foreign in the body of this culture.

When I awoke in the morning it was pitch dark. I heard somebody in the kitchen clanging stove lids. Then I heard the kitchen door open and the sound of stamping feet. I knew it must be time to get up.

I slid my feet out from under the covers and onto the floor. Then I quickly slid them back again. The floor was like a block of ice. By fishing around on the floor I found my socks, wiggled into them, and made another try at the floor. This time I made it.

I found my pants, got a match from a pocket, and lit the coal-oil lamp. In the pale yellow light I could see frost clinging to the inside of the wall. Hurriedly I scrambled into my underwear and pants and picked up the big white pitcher to pour out some water. None came. A quarter of an inch of ice covered the surface. It was the first, but not the last, wash and shave I ever had in ice water.

The Dance

Over the course of the years I've attended dances in posh wardrooms, army messes, and ballrooms twenty times as big as Willowgreen School. I've waltzed, rhumba'd and cha cha'd to small combos and big bands whose members are world-renowned musicians. But the dance that sticks in my mind for all time is the one in Willowgreen School when Orville Jackson played the fiddle and Grandma Wilson chorded on the organ.

I first got wind of it after school on Friday when, instead of slouching down the aisles making desultory passes at dust, Charlie McDougall and his band of helpers began by energetically pushing all the desks to the sides, back and front of the room.

"What's the idea?" I asked.

"Dance tonight."

"Here?"

"Yep."

"Who's coming?"

"Just about everybody in the district, I guess."

"Nobody said anything to me about it."

He merely shrugged at this and then, as an afterthought, "Oh yeah. Dad said to tell you they'll need your bed for the babies."...

So they came, the old and the young, each with their bundles, many with babies. Some had come from as far as twelve miles, a three-hour journey over a winding snow trail. In the bottoms of their sleigh boxes they'd put stones, heated in the stove and wrapped in newspaper, for footwarmers. Some of the sleigh boxes were half filled with straw so that the children could snuggle down out of the wind like mice in a stack.

Why did they come? It was a break in the dreary drag of the winter months. They were sick to death of playing rummy and cribbage and of the sound of each other's voices. They'd had a bellyful of togetherness, babies, grandmothers, old-maid aunts, grown-up sons with no place to go, huddled in a few draughty rooms like foxes in a den, satiated with the sight and sound and smell of each other. This was their chance to break out for a few hours, see different faces, hear some gossip. Find out about that cow of Mark Brownlee's that was due to calf, the vicissitudes of fate, the shortage of feed, the uselessness of the Bennett nickel — a five-cent bonus on every bushel of wheat paid through the good offices of a prime minister who, like everyone else, was rendered confused and inept by the magnitude of the depression.

Excerpted from Max Braithwaite, *Why Shoot the Teacher?* (Toronto: McClelland and Stewart, 1979), pp.12–13, 51–52, 54–55.

---

off relief if possible. What I wanted was $3.00 if I could possible get it or even some old cloths to make over but if you don't want to do this please don't mention it over radios as every one knows me around here and I'm well liked, so I beg of you not to mention my name. I've never asked anyone around here for help or cloths as I know them to well.

The Not-So-Badly-Off

R.B. Bennett was a personally charitable man. He saw to it that every letter was answered. Many letter-writers found $5 from Bennett's own pocket tucked into an envelope along with the prime minister's reply. But Bennett was a self-made millionaire. He had made a middle-sized fortune in business and law in Calgary. By 1926, he controlled the E.B. Eddy Paper Company, and his fortune had grown even larger. During his years as prime minister, Bennett never earned less than $150 000 a year, at a time when a unionized factory worker was lucky to make $1000. The prime minister looked every inch the millionaire in his top hat, expensive gloves, freshly pressed coat and pants, and shiny patent-leather shoes. He believed that people should help themselves and disliked spending government money on relief payments. He did not think that unemployment was a major problem. He told a group of students that one of the "greatest assets" a person could have "on entering life's struggle is poverty."

It was a view shared by many people who were not hurt by the Depression. Even when about one-third of the population was out of work, two-thirds of Canadian workers still had jobs. These were the lucky ones. "With bread at 5 cents a loaf, hamburger at 10 cents a pound, and

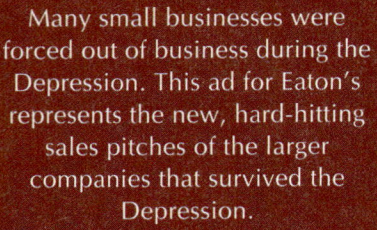

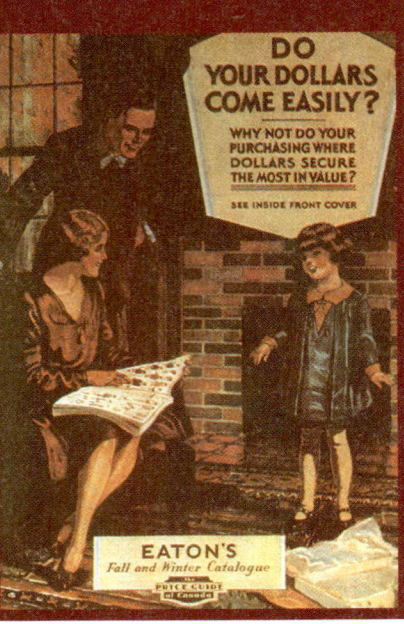

Many small businesses were forced out of business during the Depression. This ad for Eaton's represents the new, hard-hitting sales pitches of the larger companies that survived the Depression.

a good brick house valued at $4000," said one Canadian historian, "a family with a wage earner employed at wages of $20–$30 a week got along quite nicely." John David Eaton, heir to the T. Eaton Company fortune, later described the Depression as a time of fun and good times. "You could take your girl to a supper dance at the hotel for $10," he recalled. "I'm glad I grew up then. It was a good time for everybody." Many people with money and jobs had little sympathy for the poor and unemployed.

Prime Minister Bennett did provide some money for relief and public works — more than ten times the amount spent in the 1920s. It was still a small amount, however, in terms of the need. He also carried out an election promise to raise tariffs on certain goods. Higher tariffs did help manufacturers in Ontario and Quebec, but they did nothing for the harder-hit rural regions or the Canadian Prairies.

Relief Camps

Bennett also created relief camps for the army of single, homeless men who roamed the country in search of work. These drifters were widely feared as a danger to the peace and safety of many communities. To move them away from towns and cities, the federal government built relief camps deep in the bush. The camps were run on a shoestring budget by the Department of National Defence. Men in the camps were given food, shelter, army-style clothing, and 20¢ a day. In return, they built bridges or roads, cut trees or dug ditches, or worked at other public-works projects. But many young men rebelled against life in relief camps, which gave them no hope for the future. How could they ever have families or homes of their own on 20¢ a day?

In the summer of 1935, they organized the **On to Ottawa Trek** to demand "work with wages." Thousands of young men poured out of relief camps, climbed onto railway boxcars, and headed east. But the protesters were stopped in Saskatchewan and warned to go no farther. Bennett had no sympathy for the marchers and ordered the Royal Canadian Mounted Police to turn them back. The On to Ottawa Trek ended in riots and bloodshed in Regina. Bennett's decision to make use of the police in Regina turned many Canadians against his government.

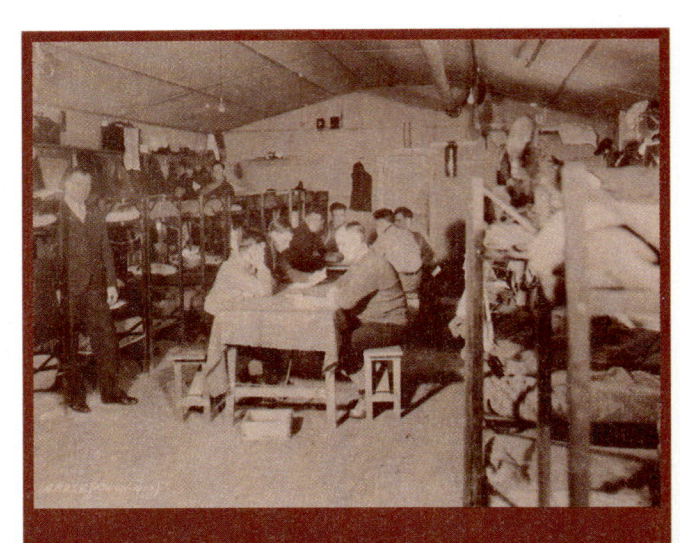

These sparsely furnished barracks served as home for many unemployed young men who worked in relief camps. Judging from this photograph, what kinds of entertainment did these men have in their barracks?

About 1800 unemployed workers "rode the rails" en route to Ottawa to protest government inaction. Here, the march has stopped in Regina in June 1935.

THE RISE OF NEW PARTIES

The two major political parties seemed to be giving Canadians the same old answer: "Wait and see." Both the Liberal and Conservative parties supported "hands-off" or *laissez-faire* ("let it be") economic policies, and neither wanted to tamper with the economic system in any major way. Meanwhile, tens of thousands of Canadians were in desperate economic circumstances. A sign of growing Canadian frustration was the practice of naming many make-do measures after Prime Minister Bennett. People with no money for gasoline and oil lifted the engines out of their automobiles and hitched horses to the bumpers. They called their horse-drawn cars **Bennett buggies**. There were also Bennett blankets (newspapers), Bennett barnyards (abandoned Prairie farms), Bennett coffee (roasted wheat, brewed like coffee), and Bennettburghs ("hobo jungles," where homeless drifters camped out).

The nation was restless for different answers than the mainline parties seemed to be offering. Disgust with "the system" caused many people to turn away from these two parties. As a result, Canada saw the rise of new political parties, especially in regions that had suffered the most.

The small but active Communist Party of Canada, under the leadership of Tim Buck, was busy staging rallies and organizing both workers and the unemployed. It wanted to begin a revolution that would completely change Canada's economic system. The "red menace" was widely feared and severely repressed by the Canadian government. The Communist Party of Canada was outlawed, and Buck was jailed from 1932 until 1934. However, there was no real danger of a revolution to overthrow the Canadian government. In Quebec, a new Union Nationale Party under Maurice Duplessis took power. It began as a protest movement with a program of new social reforms, but talk of reform stopped soon after Duplessis took power in 1936. The Reconstruction Party was created by Bennett's former minister of trade and commerce, Harry H. Stevens. Stevens uncovered corrupt business practices by large Canadian corporations. Big businesses were surviving the Depression by squeezing out smaller businesses. Stevens broke with the Conservatives to become the protector of small business. He managed to win away hundreds of thousands of votes from the Conservatives in the 1935 election.

The most significant movements arose in western Canada. In the summer of 1932, members of socialist farm and labour groups and others met to create a single, nationwide socialist party, the **Co-operative Commonwealth Federation (CCF)**. They met again in Regina a year later to hammer out a political platform, the Regina Manifesto, which set out the aim of the CCF's program — to replace Canada's free-enterprise system with a new social order. Among other things, the Regina Manifesto called for government ownership of banks, transportation, and other large enterprises; help for farmers; publicly organized medical services; a system of unemployment insurance and old-age pensions; and a foreign policy to promote international peace and cooperation. The CCF's first leader was the Labour M.P. from North Winnipeg, J.S. Woodsworth. (The Labour Party had emerged as an alternative political party in Canada in the late nineteenth century.)

Another new party also had its roots in the West. Canada's **Social Credit Party** was the brainchild of a Calgary high school principal and radio preacher named William Aberhart. Aberhart's popular Sunday afternoon radio sermons had a quarter of a million Alberta listeners. At first, Aberhart preached only Christianity, but then he read a book on Social Credit and began preaching the economic doctrine of Social Credit as well. The idea behind Social Credit was that there were plenty of goods for sale in Canada but not enough money or credit in people's pockets to buy them. It was "poverty in the midst of plenty."

Aberhart proposed that the government give out "social credits" — dividends of $25 a month for every Albertan — so that people could afford to buy. "Where does all the money come from?" he asked his radio listeners. "We don't use money. Then where does all the credit come from? Why, out of the end of a fountain pen." Although most economists attacked Aberhart's economics, his message had appeal for many people frightened by poverty and debt. Aberhart swept into power in Alberta in 1935. No social dividends were ever paid. Once in office, Aberhart gave Albertans a conservative government not too much different from that of the federal Conservatives. Social Credit governments governed

With money scarce, many families found creative ways to make ends meet. "Bennett buggies," automobiles with their engines removed and drawn by horses or oxen, were one way people managed to survive on little money.

in Alberta until 1971 and in British Columbia almost continuously from 1952 until 1992.

BENNETT'S "NEW DEAL" AND THE 1935 ELECTION

Prime Minister Bennett realized that he was in serious trouble in the upcoming 1935 election. He also began to doubt the wisdom of laissez-faire economic policies. On January 3, 1935, he made a coast-to-coast radio speech that shocked many Canadians. It even caught members of his own cabinet off guard. "I am for reform," he told his listeners, "and, to my mind, reform means government intervention, it means government control and regulation, it means the end of laissez-faire." In several radio addresses, Bennett made a series of promises, including an unemployment-insurance program, a minimum wage, a limit on work hours, insurance against sickness and industrial accidents, fair treatment for employees, marketing boards for farm products, a new credit program for farmers, and a trade commission to stop price-fixing by businesses.

The promises were known as "**Bennett's New Deal.**" They were patterned on the new economic program of U.S. President Franklin Roosevelt, who promised "a new deal for the American people." Many of Bennett's proposals were passed by Parliament, but they were later struck down by the courts. Social welfare legislation, the courts decided, was an area under exclusive provincial control. The Bennett government showed that it was willing to take action in the economic arena, but Bennett's last-minute reforms did not save his party in the 1935 election. More than 300 000 Conservative voters were ready to pick another political party.

Mackenzie King's Liberals had been fairly quiet in Parliament during the Bennett years, and they did not make many campaign promises during the 1935 election campaign. King offered Canadians a slogan — "It's King or Chaos" — but few new policies to deal with the Great Depression. Despite years of hardship, however, most Canadians were not ready for more radical politics: the Liberals took 173 seats, the CCF won 7 seats, Social Credit took 17 seats, and the Reconstruction Party captured one seat with the election of H.H. Stevens. A handful of other candidates — including the United Farmers of Ontario–Labour candidate, Agnes Macphail — also won seats. That left the Conservatives with just 40 seats. The Conservative defeat marked the beginning of twenty-two unbroken years of Liberal government under Mackenzie King and Louis St. Laurent.

MACKENZIE KING AGAIN

Mackenzie King led Canada through the last years of the Great Depression. The return of the Liberals also marked a return to "hands-off" economic policies. "What is needed more than a change of economic structure is a change of heart," King declared. He introduced lower tariffs and

J.S. Woodsworth was a church minister, social reformer, and labour leader. He was one of the leaders arrested in the Winnipeg General Strike of May 1919, and his socialist ideals were the foundation of the CCF in the West.

CANADIAN SOVEREIGNTY: MACKENZIE KING AND CANADIAN AUTONOMY

Throughout his long term in office, Prime Minister William Lyon Mackenzie King strove to establish full Canadian independence from Britain. On several issues, King took a firm stand against Britain in defence of Canadian sovereignty. Following are accounts of two important events that occurred in the 1920s and 1930s.

THE CHANAK AFFAIR

In 1922, British troops stationed near Chanak, on the Dardanelles, were threatened with attack by the Turks. The British government issued a request for military support from the colonies. Unlike the case eight years earlier, when World War I broke out, Canada did not automatically consider itself active in the conflict. Instead, Prime Minister King insisted that the Canadian Parliament decide on the course of action Canada would follow. By the time the issue had been debated in the House of Commons, the threat at Chanak had passed. Nonetheless, King made his point: Parliament would decide the role that Canada would play in external affairs.

THE KING-BYNG AFFAIR

Following the 1925 election, King and the Liberals clung to power — despite having fewer seats than the Conservatives — by forming a coalition with the Progressive Party. In 1926, charges of corruption in the Canadian Customs Department forced King to ask the governor general, Lord Byng, to call an election because he had lost the support of the Progressives. Byng, who had been appointed by the British government, refused to grant the election. Instead, he opted to give Arthur Meighen's Conservatives the opportunity to form the government. Shortly thereafter, the Conservatives also lost the support of the Progressives and were forced to request an election. This time the request was granted. King was infuriated because an appointed British official was determining when Canadian elections would be held. In the end, King won back his majority government, and Canada made another step toward independence.

signed a new trade agreement with the United States. But King's main goal was to slash government spending and balance the federal budget. He closed down the relief camps as an economy measure. He also opposed giving more federal aid to the provinces, even though several provinces were desperately short of money.

King had studied economics, however, and he did begin to think about new economic ideas. One new idea was that governments should spend money to get a stalled economy moving again. King's 1938 budget leaned toward greater government spending. King also moved toward creating a federal unemployment-insurance scheme, and he appointed a royal commission to look into federal–provincial relations. But overall the Liberal prime minister was "waiting out" the Depression.

The Great Depression in Canada ended only with the beginning of another bloody world war in 1939. New ideas were in the air, however, and people were beginning to talk about the need for government management of the economy. Many Canadians were also thinking about the need for broad new social welfare programs. After World War II, government would be ready to take a strong hand in Canadian economic life.

KNOWING THE KEY PEOPLE, PLACES, AND EVENTS

In your notes, clearly identify and explain the historical significance of each of the following:

- Statute of Westminster
- Great Depression
- On to Ottawa Trek
- Co-operative Commonwealth Federation (CCF)
- Winnipeg General Strike
- Pogey
- Bennett Buggies
- Social Credit
- Bennett's New Deal

FOCUS YOUR KNOWLEDGE

1. What was Mackenzie King's primary aim regarding Canadian foreign policy?
2. Outline the problems that led up to the Winnipeg General Strike.
3. Describe and organize into a chart the economic conditions in Canada for each of the following periods: 1919–21, 1921–29, and 1929–39.
4. Why were the 1920s often referred to as the "Roaring Twenties"?
5. List and explain three causes of the Great Depression.
6. How did the Liberal government under Mackenzie King react to the Depression before the 1930 election?
7. What catastrophe hit the Prairies in the 1930s, increasing the problems faced by western farmers?
8. How did R.B. Bennett react to poor Canadians: (a) as the head of the federal government and (b) on a personal basis?

APPLY YOUR KNOWLEDGE

1. Mackenzie King enjoyed tremendous success with Canadian voters. What factors were important to his electoral success? Would you have voted for King? Explain your answer.
2. Considering the size of the Winnipeg General Strike, do you think it was handled effectively? What advice would you have given the mayor of Winnipeg on how to deal with the strikers?
3. How appropriate was the term "Roaring Twenties" for the Canadian Prairies and the Maritimes? How could the federal government have acted to better ensure economic prosperity for all regions of Canada?

4. Explain the role that the American stock-market crash of 1929 played in bringing on the Depression in Canada.

5. Why was Mackenzie King's "five-cent speech" so controversial? Would a speech like this have influenced you if you were voting in the 1930 election? Explain your answer.

6. Why did many people find living on "pogey" a difficult experience? Do you think the government should have been more generous in the aid it gave out and more lenient in granting assistance to the poor? Defend your answer.

7. Considering the severity of the Great Depression, do you think the government should have done more to help generate jobs? Were relief camps a fair and sensible way to keep young, unemployed males occupied during the Depression?

8. During the 1930s several new political parties arose, each proposing a different solution to the economic crisis. Of the parties mentioned in this chapter, which do you think had the most appealing policies? Which party would you have been most opposed to? Defend your answers.

EXTEND YOUR KNOWLEDGE

1. Write a news editorial on the Winnipeg General Strike from one of the following perspectives: a striker, a government official, or a factory owner. Before beginning to write, reflect on how your perspective of the events would have been shaped by your position in society. When you have finished your editorial, compare it with one written by another student who has taken a different perspective. Discuss how your editorials differ.

2. Select one region of Canada and create a pair of collages comparing the 1920s and 1930s. Each collage should include aspects of daily life in the selected region. Be sure to portray a cross-section of rural and urban life as well as the various cultures of the region you have chosen.

3. Do some extra research and prepare a series of graphs that illustrate the changes in Canadian exports from the early 1920s to the late 1930s. In preparing your graphs, compare the exports in wheat, pulp and paper, and minerals. The graphs should be large enough to be displayed to the class and should be accompanied with brief descriptions.

4. Do some research to find out what life was like in the relief camps. Imagine that you are one of the young men working in the camps. Write a letter to a friend, describing your experiences in the camp and your hopes for the future.

5. Select one of the political parties that ran in the 1935 election (Liberal, Conservative, Communist, CCF, Social Credit, or Reconstruction) and create an election poster that attempts to attract voters by highlighting some of the party's major policies. Make your poster colourful and visually appealing.

CHAPTER 11: LIFE IN CANADA IN THE 1920s AND 1930s

GLOSSARY TERMS

Canadian Shield An ancient rock formation, formerly called the Laurentian Plateau. Caused by glaciation, it is centred on Hudson Bay and extends over about half of Canada.

Status Symbol An object or possession intended by its owner to convey social importance or prestige.

Barnstorming Exhibitions of stunt flying in an airplane.

Royal Commission A person or persons commissioned by the Crown to investigate an issue on behalf of the federal or provincial government, and to report on the issue and recommend appropriate action.

Jazz Age A popular term for the decade of the 1920s, when jazz dance music, which originated with southern black American musicians, became widely popular.

Crime Syndicate An organization of criminals for the purpose of coordinating and controlling illegal activities.

Bootlegging Making, transporting, or selling illegal alcoholic liquor.

Indian Affairs Branch The department in the federal government responsible for administering Native affairs.

Sun Dance An important ceremonial dance of the Native peoples of the Prairies.

Potlatch A ceremonial festival of certain Northwest Coast tribes during which guests were given gifts by the host and property was destroyed as a display of wealth.

Residential Schools Government-supported boarding schools for Native students, usually run by missionary groups.

FOCUS ON:

- how new technology changed the lives of Canadians in the 1920s
- the increasing Americanization of Canada and the efforts of the Canadian government to ensure the preservation of a distinct Canadian culture
- the continuing struggle of women to achieve full equality in Canadian society
- the determination of Canadian Native peoples to preserve their culture

Canadians came out of World War I with growing self-confidence. The nation's record of wartime bravery and its march toward political maturity brought new pride in Canada. National feeling blossomed in the 1920s, and Canadian artists and writers deliberately began to explore Canadian themes in their work. The 1920s were the heyday of the famous painters known as the **Group of Seven**. They were determined to create a new kind of art for Canada — one that captured the Canadian experience. The Toronto-based group, including A.Y. Jackson, Lawren Harris, and Arthur Lismer, filled their canvases with brilliant, heavily layered colour and strong, sweeping forms. They fashioned a bold new style of painting to celebrate the Canadian landscape.

Most Group of Seven members turned their backs on the city scenes and took sketching trips into the untamed wilderness of northern Canada. Some of them travelled east to Quebec and Nova Scotia for Canadian subjects. Others painted in the Prairies, the Rocky Mountains, and the Arctic. But the rugged landscapes of the *Canadian Shield* in Ontario — especially Algonquin Park, Algoma, and Georgian Bay — were their earliest and best-known subjects.

Tom Thomson drowned while on a canoe trip in Algonquin Park in 1917. But Thomson's early paintings, like this one, called *Afternoon, Algonquin Park*, helped to inspire the bold new style and spirit of Canadian painting.

NEW INVENTIONS AND THE FIRST MODERN DECADE

The 1920s also saw the strengthening of ties among Canada's various regions. This period has been called the first modern decade. In the 1920s, automobiles, airplanes, telephones, motion pictures, radios, and many other modern conveniences became part of everyday life. The spread of new technologies and inventions in the 1920s and 1930s helped draw together a sprawling and sparsely populated country. The barriers of time and distance that had separated Canadians began to crumble, and rural regions were drawn into the Canadian mainstream.

Automobiles

The automobile had been a *status symbol* for the rich before the war, but in the 1920s many more Canadians could afford cars. An American, **Henry Ford**, had pioneered the use of mass production in automobile manufacturing. By applying the method of mass production — which used standardized parts, an assembly line, and specialized workers doing very specific jobs to produce any number of identical products — Ford was able to produce cars at a price that middle-class people could afford. In 1924, the famous Ford Model-T cost just under $400 in Canada. By the late 1920s, cars and trucks were competing with horse-drawn wagons for the right-of-way on Canadian roads. By 1930, over a million automobiles were registered in Canada.

Owning an automobile meant a whole new type of freedom. Farm families could travel to town more

Almost every Canadian was buying a motor car in the 1920s. Closed cars and better roads paved the way for luxury motoring.

LIFE IN CANADA IN THE 1920s AND 1930s

209

often. Friends and relatives could visit each other more easily. Travelling salespeople used automobiles to sell door-to-door over much bigger territories. Young people could drive to new American-style nightclubs outside of town called roadhouses, where they could dance to the latest music out of sight of watchful parents. City dwellers could escape the summer heat by driving to nearby country cottages or taking road trips to vacation spots farther away. By the end of the 1920s, 130 000 kilometres of hard-surfaced roads had been built in Canada. Tourist cabins and hotels sprang up along the roads to serve Canada's first generation of automobile vacationers.

Automobiles in the 1920s, however, were anything but reliable. Headlights, clutches, and brakes were apt to fail, and a tow rope was standard equipment for most drivers. Motorists never knew when they might be stranded by the roadside with engine trouble or sunk up to the axles in mire after a rainstorm turned dirt roads into mud. Taking a long trip was a major challenge. A Toronto man described driving up to Georgian Bay for a summer holiday as "a kind of adventure, each time." There were only a few service stations, so drivers had to take along extra cans of gasoline. Cars often stalled going up long grades, and passengers had to climb out and push the car until it started again. "And tires…" the Toronto man recalled. "Hate to think how many inner tubes I patched in those days." It was not unusual to have ten flat tires in a 200-kilometre trip. By the end of the 1930s, however, the boxy-looking black Model Ts had given way to sleek, colourful, and elegant designs. Car interiors were spacious and comfortable, and the automatic transmission was revolutionizing driving. The automobile age had arrived.

Airplanes

Travel in the 1920s and 1930s was still mostly by automobile, railway, and ship — not by airplane. There was only one scheduled air-passenger service in Canada until 1927, when a few more city-to-city links were started. Still, Canadians were getting used to the sight of an airplane silhouetted against the sky. Many ex–World War I pilots who found civilian life too tame for them took to the air by "*barnstorming*" across Canada. They landed on farmers' fields and offered adventurous locals the thrill of flight for $2 a ride. They amazed and terrified spectators at country fairs with daring air stunts, doing barrel rolls and loop-the-loops and even hanging from the wings of their planes.

A Canadian air service was created in 1920 and renamed the **Royal Canadian Air Force (RCAF)** in April 1924. RCAF pilots often did civilian duties by patrolling for forest fires, taking aerial survey photographs, checking on commercial fishing, and watching for signs of smuggling along the coasts.

Small bush planes also became the workhorses of the North. These fragile craft opened up the vast Canadian Shield to mineral exploration where no roads or rails had yet cut through the bush. Bush pilots had few navigational aids; they "flew by the seats of their pants," mostly in tattered war-surplus planes held together by baling wire and ingenuity. By 1929, there were twenty-nine companies flying into the North, carrying freight and passengers.

The Canadian Post Office Department also began contracting for scheduled air mail service to remote settlements in 1927. Sometimes the weather was so bad that pilots had to tie mail bags onto parachutes and toss them out the window to the people waiting below. Canada's pilots sometimes risked their lives flying in stormy weather across distant terrain, but they forged an important link between remote regions and the rest of the country. Canada did not have a national airline system, however, until the federal government established Trans-Canada Air Lines in 1937.

Radio

Radio was another great new invention in the Roaring Twenties. For the first time the human voice could travel through the air by radio waves and be picked up at home on primitive radios called "crystal sets." In 1901, Canadian inventor Reginald Fessenden had become the first person to make a wireless transmission of the human voice when the joking message, "Is it snowing where you are, Mr. Thiessen?" crackled out to an assistant stationed 1600 metres away. The Italian physicist **Guglielmo Marconi**, however, is usually credited with inventing the radio. Marconi also set up the first commercial radio station in the world — station XWA in Montreal. It hit the airwaves in 1919 with a medley of news, weather, and recorded music, and it still operates in Montreal today as the English-language station CFCF.

Radio technology improved quickly, and the crystal sets with their earphones were soon replaced by more elaborate radios with speakers. By the 1930s, many Canadian families gathered in the evenings around ornately carved walnut radio cabinets for broadcasts of programs like "Major Bowes' Amateur Hour," "The Singing Lumberjacks," "True Detective Mysteries," or "Buck Rogers in the 25th Century." Canadians were crazy about radio, and owning a radio set became a new status symbol. There were fewer than 10 000 radios in Canada in 1923, but just six years later there were an astounding 297 000 radios.

A number of small radio stations emerged to supply the demand for radio programming. Under a 1913 law, a licence was required to broadcast, but some Canadians ignored the law and set up stations without a licence. These stations often operated on shoestring budgets because there was little on-air advertising in the early days. As a result, radio production was mostly an amateur affair. Broadcasts were irregular, technical production was hit-and-miss, and programs often featured untrained announcers, local musical talent, and even spelling bees and high school debates broadcast from nearby schools.

Meanwhile, American stations had been making money by advertising from the very start, and broadcasting stations quickly grouped together into broadcasting networks to sell advertising air time to large companies. Ads for products like Eveready batteries, Kellogg's Corn Flakes, and Maxwell House coffee — often with catchy jingles — helped pay for top American performers. The Americans were also making headway in building transmitting stations. By 1924, there were 51 radio stations in Canada, compared with more than 200 in the United States. American stations provided hours of regular programming every day of the week. There was something for everybody: live and recorded music, soap operas, comedy shows, detective and western dramas, children's stories, and religious programs, as well as news, weather, and sports broadcasts.

Many of the American stations were close to the Canadian border, and Canadian radios were often

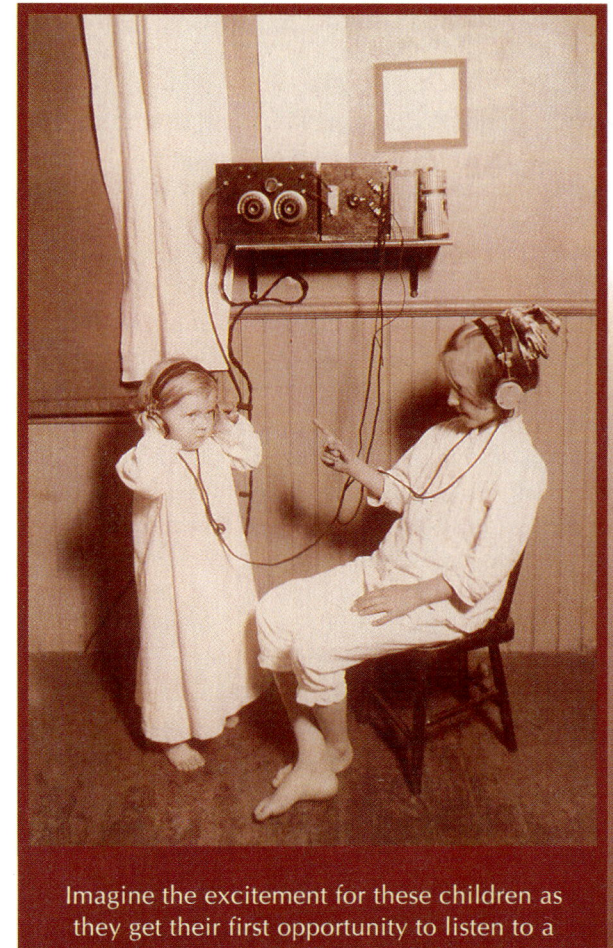

Imagine the excitement for these children as they get their first opportunity to listen to a new "crystal set" radio!

To many people during the Depression, the CBC represented a Canada that wasn't all bleak and desperate. *The Happy Gang* was a popular CBC program begun in 1937.

tuned to programs from the south. One exception was the new Canadian sports show called "Hockey Night in Canada." In March 1923, Toronto broadcaster **Foster Hewitt** gave the first play-by-play account of a hockey game from a small soundproof booth in Toronto's Mutual Street Arena. A Canadian national institution was born. By the early 1930s, Hewitt, with his famous line, "He shoots. He scores!" was known as the voice of hockey.

Some Canadians began to worry about what R.B. Bennett called the "insidious American influence" of U.S. radio programs. Should the Canadian government take steps to control American broadcasts and promote Canadian radio programming? In 1928, a *royal commission* headed by Sir John Aird was established to investigate radio broadcasting. The Aird Commission studied broadcasting systems in half a dozen countries. Then it recommended that the federal government establish a government-owned broadcasting corporation much like the British Broadcasting Corporation (BBC). The Canadian Radio Broadcasting Commission (CRBC) was created in 1932 and then reorganized in 1936 under the new name of the Canadian Broadcasting Corporation (CBC). Its job was to regulate both public and private broadcasting. It also offered quality Canadian programs as alternatives to American radio shows and provided radio service for remote areas in Canada. By 1940, almost 90 percent of Canadians were within reach of CBC broadcasts.

CBC radio helped to end regional isolation and to foster a sense of Canadian national unity. Radio was immediate. Canadian politicians could now address the whole nation at one time. Canadian performers could touch the lives of thousands of listeners with a single performance. Canadian listeners from coast to coast could share moments of grief during a mining disaster in the town of Moose River, Nova Scotia, in 1936 or of joy during the six-week royal tour of Canada by King George VI and Queen Elizabeth in 1939. CBC radio helped draw Canadians together in a way that newspapers, books, or magazines never could.

Motion Pictures

In creating the state-owned CBC, Canada had made a clear choice, in R.B. Bennett's words, between "the state or the States." Even though Canadian airwaves were still filled with American programs, the CBC provided Canadians with a satisfying alternative. Motion pictures were also gaining enormous popularity during the 1920s and 1930s. In an effort to encourage a Canadian film industry, the federal government funded agencies to make Canadian films, but most of the resulting movies were expensive failures like the film called *Fishing Just for Fun*. Major success in the Canadian film industry did not come until the National Film Board (NFB) was founded in 1939.

Canadians loved Hollywood movies and idolized American film stars like Charlie Chaplin, Rudolph Valentino, and Greta Garbo. Many talented Canadians headed for Hollywood, seeking — and sometimes finding — fame and fortune. **Mary Pickford**, known and loved across North America as "America's Sweetheart," was born Gladys May Smith in Toronto in 1893. She started working on the Toronto stage at age five, but by 1907 she was in Hollywood, where she became the most popular film actress of the 1920s. With her husband, Douglas Fairbanks, and Charlie Chaplin, Mary Pickford founded the motion-picture studio United Artists in 1919.

United Artists and other major American studios produced hundreds of movies, and Canadians were delighted to spend their Saturdays caught up in the magic of Hollywood films. Tired of the miseries of World War I, Canadians were ready for sheer entertainment. Hollywood movies offered an exciting mixture of comedy, glamour, romance, sophistication, and adventure. They exactly matched the high-stepping spirit of the *Jazz Age*, as the 1920s were sometimes called, and they attracted ever-increasing audiences.

Canada and the United States were already closely linked by geography and politics. Radio and motion pictures forged whole new cultural ties between the two nations. The growing domination of Canadian culture by American culture meant that — for better or worse — Canada was becoming part of a North American culture rather than remaining a distinctly Canadian culture. Canadian response to the changes was mixed. Many Canadians shared in the new national pride represented by the Group of Seven, and some resented the growing Americanization of Canada. When it came to entertainment, however, most Canadians delighted in American-made radio and films, and, as a result, Canadian society became more like that of its neighbour to the south.

PROHIBITION

On both sides of the border, the Jazz Age was a sophisticated, fast-paced, anything-for-a-laugh time. But it was also a lawless time of widespread crime and public corruption. The notorious Chicago gangster Al Capone symbolized the dark side of American life in the 1920s. He headed a huge *crime syndicate* and was thought to have been responsible for some 400 gangland killings. He and his mobsters also bribed scores of public officials, judges, and law-enforcement agents — in effect, Capone ruled Chicago. Canada had its own smaller version of the American mobster — **Rocco Perri** of Hamilton, Ontario, known as the "Canadian Al Capone." Perri once told a reporter that he was against the use of violence, but he headed a brutal gang of criminals in the Niagara Peninsula. Seventeen murders were attributed to the Perri gang, and Perri's wife, Bessie, was shot to death in the garage of the couple's palatial Hamilton

Canadian-born Mary Pickford became a major film star in the United States, where she earned the nickname "America's Sweetheart."

FADS, FASHIONS, AND ENTERTAINMENT OF THE TWENTIES AND THIRTIES

Slang of the Era

all wet	wrong, mistaken
bee's knees	wonderful person
big cheese	important person, big shot
bunk	nonsense
baloney	nonsense
cat's meow	superb, very sharp
hep	cool, up-to-date
ritzy, swanky	elegant
real McCoy	genuine article
spiffy	fashionable
blind pig	secret distillery
horse feathers	nonsense
heebie jeebies	the jitters
hooch	bootleg liquor
kiddo	friendly form of address
scram	leave quickly
swell	marvellous
speakeasy	a bar selling illegal liquor
sheik	a young man with sex appeal
Sheba	a young woman with sex appeal
gyp	cheat
gate crasher	uninvited guest
flat tire	boring person
drugstore cowboy	a young man who hangs around public places trying to pick up girls
kisser	lips
high hat	snobbish

keen	attractive
smeller	nose
giggle water	alcohol
ossified	drunk
dogs	human feet
a line	insincere flattery
flapper	typical girl of the 1920s with bobbed hair, short skirt, and rolled-down stockings
lamps	eyes
cheaters	eyeglasses
applesauce	nonsense
upchuck	to throw up

Dances of the 1920s

Shimmy
Waltz
Black Bottom
Bunny Hop
Charleston
Fox-Trot
Tango
Strut
Cheek to Cheek
Butterfly
Turkey Trot

Radio Programs of the 1930s

Amos 'n' Andy
True Detective Mysteries
NHL Hockey
   with Foster Hewitt
Buck Rogers
   in the 25th Century
The Happy Gang
Jack Benny
Gangbusters
The Singing Lumberjacks
King Edward Hotel
   Dinner Music
The Kate Aitken Show
Major Bowes' Amateur Hour
Stella Dallas
Fleischmann Sunshine Hour
   with Rudy Vallee

home in 1930. Perri disappeared without a trace in 1944 — perhaps a murder victim himself.

Much of the criminal activity in the 1920s and early 1930s resulted from American prohibition. **Prohibition** — a law that banned the making, selling, or drinking of liquor — was in effect in the United States from 1919 to 1933. By law, the United States was a "dry" country. But many "dry" Americans were thirsty and willing to pay for illegal alcohol. Profits from *bootlegging* (selling illegal alcohol) were enormous. A case of twelve bottles of liquor bought in Saskatchewan for about $50 could be sold south of the border for as much as $300. Smuggling Canadian bootleg liquor into the United States — sometimes called rum-running — became big business. Some of Canada's wealthiest families got their start in the trade in illegal alcohol during American prohibition.

Many Canadians looked on Canadian rum-runners with amused tolerance. To many, they were modern-day Robin Hoods, cleverly outsmarting and outrunning American law-enforcement agents. But in the United States, bootlegging was a deadly serious underworld business. The attraction of huge profits from the illegal trade quickly drew machine-gun-toting American mobsters, and they brought with them gang warfare, murder, and the wholesale corruption of police, judges, and government officials. The lawlessness spilled across the Canadian border and gave some Canadian supporters of prohibition second thoughts. In 1923, a Manitoba supporter lamented that the world had been "turned upside down by bootleggers, bandits, and bank robbers. The cure is ten times worse than the disease." Prohibition began to look like as much of a social evil as the drunkenness it tried to stop.

Canadian Prohibition

Canada had tried its own version of prohibition during World War I. By the time the war ended in 1918, every province but Quebec had brought in prohibition laws. Ottawa had also taken steps in 1917 and 1918 to place strict limits on importing, manufacturing, and transporting liquor. Canadian prohibition brought benefits at first; once saloons and bars shut down, there was less public drunkenness and domestic violence.

But prohibition was unpopular with many Canadians and with many Canadian governments. Government officials realized that they were losing money to bootleggers, money that could be a source of government revenue. Moderation leagues — often funded by breweries and distilleries — sprang up, arguing that the control of liquor was better than an outright ban. Federal prohibition laws lapsed in 1919. During the 1920s, one province after another repealed prohibition and set up government outlets to regulate liquor sales and make money for the government without raising taxes. By 1930, all provinces but Prince Edward Island — which remained "dry" until 1940 — had become officially "wet" again.

Even when some provinces were officially dry, Canadian liquor laws often allowed the manufacture and transport of alcohol. On the Prairies, distilleries were allowed to make liquor for "non-drinking" purposes such as industrial, scientific, or medicinal uses. It was also legal to import alcohol for export to countries where drinking was not against the law.

Many "rum-runners" looked for creative ways to smuggle liquor into the United States. How many bottles of liquor do you think this man could smuggle while wearing a large overcoat?

THE *I'M ALONE* AFFAIR

With prohibition in effect in the United States throughout the 1920s, Canadian bootleggers found a thirsty and insatiable market for their liquor. Each month, millions of dollars' worth of liquor was illegally smuggled into the United States. Much of the illegal alcohol was smuggled either through "Rum Alley," in the Detroit–Windsor area, or to the Gulf of Mexico, where American speedboats picked up the illicit cargo from Canadian schooners. Seldom did these schooners return to Canada empty. They often smuggled back into Canada thousands of dollars' worth of textiles and tobacco products that undercut Canadian manufacturers.

The American government did not take Canadian smuggling lightly. Special agents attempted to seize illegal alcohol entering the United States through Rum Alley, while the American Coast Guard fought a full-scale war with rum-runners. In 1929 the Nova Scotia schooner *I'm Alone* attempted to smuggle liquor into the United States. As long as the schooner remained outside the territorial waters of the United States, it could not be arrested by the U.S. Coast Guard. But the Americans were serious about stopping the smuggling. After pursuing the *I'm Alone* for two days, American cutters managed to close in on the Canadian schooner. Despite being 390 kilometres out at sea, well into international waters, the *I'm Alone* was captured and sunk by cannon fire. Despite the controversy created by this incident, Canadians continued to smuggle alcohol into the United States until prohibition ended in 1933.

Much of the alcohol made and shipped in Canada went to the United States. It is estimated that about 22 million to 45 million litres of Canadian liquor entered the United States illegally each year during American prohibition.

During most of the 1920s and early 1930s, rum-running was common along the largely undefended North American border and down both coasts. The biggest bootlegging traffic occurred between Windsor, Ontario, and nearby Detroit, Michigan. In warm weather, a fleet of more than 800 rum-running speedboats plied the 2-kilometre stretch of water between Windsor and Detroit. In winter, dozens of old cars and trucks swarmed across the frozen river with bootleg liquor. Prohibition was a

Not all smugglers were successful. When this "blind pig," or secret distillery, was raided at Elk Lake, Ontario, 160 kegs of liquor were seized and destroyed.

major disappointment for its supporters. It was meant to end drunkenness and raise standards of behaviour, but it seems to have had the opposite effect. It turned liquor into gold, and the resulting illegal liquor trade sullied everyone who had a hand in it.

Women in the 1920s and 1930s

Many women who had fought for prohibition had also worked for women's right to vote. They believed that getting the vote would bring greater equality for women and allow them a more active role in public life. After initial success, however, they too were disappointed. By 1920, women had won the right to vote in federal elections and in provincial elections in all provinces except Quebec. The 1921 federal election was the first one in which women over 21 could vote and run for political office. But of the five women who ran for Parliament, only one — **Agnes Macphail**, of Ontario — was elected. Re-elected four times thereafter, Macphail was the only woman to sit in the House of Commons until 1935. Nellie McClung was elected as a member of the legislative assembly (MLA) in Alberta in 1921 and became the third woman to sit in the Alberta legislature. But the number of women elected to provincial governments across Canada also remained disappointingly small.

Agnes Macphail was Canada's first woman MP. She was also an advocate for civil rights, social reform, and health services.

Women in Sport

There were some successes for women on other fronts. The 1920s and early 1930s have been called the "Golden Age of Sports" for women. Many youth groups, especially the Young Women's Christian Association (YWCA), encouraged organized physical activities and games for young women. The biggest change was in the growth of women's amateur sports and athletic clubs. Inter-school women's sports leagues mushroomed across Canada. Basketball and baseball were among the popular sports. The famous women's basketball team, the **Edmonton Grads**, was the most successful team anywhere in competitive basketball. Over its twenty-year history, the Edmonton Grads won an astounding 502 out of 522 games and four Olympic gold medals.

Women also made their mark in other sports. In the 1928

The Edmonton Grads were the most successful basketball team in history. Why do you think interest in women's sports such as basketball declined during the 1930s?

THE MANY FACES OF WOMEN IN THE 1920S

During the 1920s women in Canada enjoyed greater participation in society than ever before. They were involved in sports, politics, and new careers, and enjoyed many leisure activities including dancing, swimming, and snowshoeing.

Amsterdam Olympics, high-jumper Ethel Catherwood — known as "the Saskatoon Lily" — won a gold medal in the high jump and sprinter **Fanny ("Bobbie") Rosenfeld** won silver and gold medals. A magnificent athlete, Rosenfeld also set records in discus throwing and long-jumping and was a star tennis and hockey player. She was named to Canada's Sports Hall of Fame as an all-round athlete. In 1934, swimmer Phyllis Dewar of Moose Jaw, Saskatchewan, won four gold medals at the British Empire Games.

But women's triumphs were few and far between. By the mid-1930s, doctors and educators were arguing that women were too delicate for competitive sports like baseball, and "girls' rules" were introduced to restrict physical contact, limit exertion, and keep women's sports "feminine." After that, women's sports went into an eclipse until the 1960s.

The Persons Case

The decline of women's sports was just one sign that the struggle for equality was far from over. Canada was still dominated by men, as women discovered during the long-drawn-out "**Persons Case**." Section 24 of the BNA Act declared that "qualified persons" could become senators, and other laws for appointing government officials contained similar declarations. But did women qualify as "persons" under the law? For years government officials argued that women did not qualify, while women's groups argued that women were "persons," in a see-saw legal battle spanning more than a decade.

Judge Emily Murphy led the fight. She had become the first female judge in the British Empire when she was appointed a police magistrate in Edmonton in 1916. Lawyers appearing in Judge Murphy's court repeatedly objected that she was not a judge because she was not a "person" under the law for appointing judges. Day after day, Judge Murphy noted the lawyers' objections, overruled them, and went on with the cases. Finally, in 1920 a lawyer tried to use the "persons" argument to get his bootlegger client — found guilty in Judge Murphy's court — freed on the grounds of improper procedures. He appealed the case to the Supreme Court of Alberta. The Alberta court ruled in Judge Murphy's favour: she was a "person" and therefore qualified to sit as a judge.

One of the graduates of this University of Toronto class of '28, Elsie Gregory MacGill, was the first woman to graduate with a degree in electrical and aeronautical engineering.

Judge Murphy decided, however, that the provincial decision was not enough. She wanted to set a national precedent by testing whether women qualified as "persons" to be named to the Senate of Canada. Murphy and her supporters carried the battle all the way to the British Privy Council, the highest appeal court in Canada at the time. The Privy Council ruled in favour of their claim, declaring that the "exclusion of women from all public offices is a relic of days more barbarous than ours." The court decision was a triumph for Canadian women. After the "Persons Case," however, the women's movement lost momentum. It would not regain that momentum until the 1960s.

CANADA'S NATIVE PEOPLES

Canada's Native peoples continued to suffer discrimination and poverty in the years after World War I. By the early twentieth century, most of the Natives in Canada's southern regions had signed treaties and had selected their reserves. They were officially viewed as wards (dependants) of the *Indian Affairs Branch* of the Canadian government. It was official government policy to try to assimilate Native peoples — to make them part of white culture — in whatever way it could. As the Canadian poet and deputy superintendent of the Department of Indian Affairs, Duncan Campbell Scott, put it in 1921, the department's policy was "to continue until there is not a single Indian in Canada that has not been absorbed into the body politic and there is no Indian question, and no Indian Department...." Natives were expected to give up their cultural heritage and become part of white society.

Efforts were made to take away every sign of tribal life. Bans on traditional ceremonies like the *Sun Dance* of some prairie tribes and the *potlatch* of the Northwest Coast were enforced in the early 1920s. Native children were taken away from their families to *residential schools* run by missionary groups. Anything that connected students to their Native heritage was ruthlessly excluded from school life. Traditional religious practices were forbidden. Native children who spoke in their own language were severely punished. They were dressed in European clothes and groomed to become English-speaking Christians. Even their games and sports were to be "thoroughly, distinctly white."

Native students who moved into Canadian towns and cities rarely found acceptance, however. Hostility and prejudice remained strong in white communities. Some Natives did become part of mainstream Canadian life, but many found themselves pushed to the margins of white society. Most Native students returned to their reserves, only to find that they no longer felt at home. As one former residential school student explained,

> *When an Indian comes out of these [schools] it is like being put between two walls in a room and left hanging in the middle. On one side are all the things he learned from his people and their way of life that was being wiped out, and on the other are the white man's way which he could never fully understand since he never had the right amount of education and could not be part of it. There he is, hanging in the middle of the two cultures and he is not a white man and he is not an Indian.*

Many Natives felt cut adrift from both worlds and sank into despair. Poverty, disease, and alcohol abuse were all too familiar to Natives both on and off the reserves.

Yet, in the 1920s, some Native leaders emerged to lead the struggle for economic and cultural survival. The Ontario Mohawk chief F.O. Loft had fought in World War I. On returning to Canada after the war, he tried to draw public attention to the plight of his people. Frustrated by the lack of concern both in Ottawa and in London, England, Loft organized a national group called the **League of Indians**. He wanted Natives to have the right to vote without having to give up special status. He also wanted greater Native control over band property and funds.

Native leaders elsewhere also organized for social change and to protest white intrusions into Native lands. In British Columbia, miners, loggers, and white settlers were taking over the ancestral lands of Native bands in the region. Reverend Peter Kelly, a Haida, and Andrew Paull, a Squamish, led a new organization called the Allied Tribes of British Columbia. The organization disbanded in 1927, but the Native Brotherhood of British Columbia took up the struggle to defend Native peoples' lands and fishing and hunting rights in 1931. The new organizations marked the beginning of a Native activism that would blossom in the 1960s.

SURVIVING IN THE 1930s

The 1930s were dark times for many other Canadians. Some people found it hard to say anything good about these years, which were sometimes called "the Years of Despair." Said one survivor who was asked to talk about the Great Depression: "The Dirty Thirties! Just put in your book that you met Harry Jacobsen and he's 78 years old. Might say I never took a backward step in my life until that Depression whipped me, took away my wife, my home, a section of good land back in Saskatchewan. Left me with nothing. Write that down." Other Canadians turned tragedy into black comedy and swapped Depression jokes like this one about a farmer in the notorious "Dust Bowl" of Saskatchewan: "In a high wind, a farmer went to the bank to get a loan on his property. The banker said, 'I'd kinda like to see your land.' Just then, a big gust hit the side of the bank, and the farmer answered, 'Well open up your window, cuz here she comes.'"

Some Canadians remember the 1930s with surprising fondness. The novelist Hugh Garner, who spent much of the decade "riding the rails" as a hobo, later wrote:

The Depression was tough, but it wasn't all hunger and sadness. There were picnics, corn roasts, and cheap dances.... Young people fell in love and married. After all, a married relief cheque was better than two single people getting

Both marriages and birthrates declined during the 1930s, and birth control became a national controversy. It's not surprising, therefore, that Canadians were fascinated by the birth of the Dionne quintuplets in 1934.

This colourful poster attracted thousands of Canadians to the Canadian National Exhibition, held yearly in Toronto since 1879. The CNE was especially important in the 1930s because it offered an escape from the hardship of the Depression.

nothing at all.... Babies were born, whether their fathers were unemployed or not, and their young mothers made do with handmade or hand-me-down layettes. A wicker laundry basket is just as good a bassinet as a store-bought one. Do you want to know something? I don't think I'd have wanted to miss the Great Depression for the world.

Many other Canadians looked for ways to escape the worries of the Depression years — at least for a while. Many made do with homemade entertainment. They played sandlot baseball in the summer and football in the fall. Curling became a favourite winter pastime. Every town had its curling rink, and everyone, male and female, from teenagers to old folks, joined in the fun. At school, children played games of curling with jam tins filled with frozen mud and looped with wire handles. There were old-fashioned pleasures like horse races, picnics, swimming, and berry-picking, as well as sleigh-rides, school plays, and church socials to keep people entertained. And there were new fads like roller skating, miniature golf, card games like bridge, and board games like Monopoly to take people's minds off their troubles.

Above all there were the "talkies" — motion pictures complete with sound. The 1930s were the first full decade of the "talkies," and Canadians who could find the 25¢ to 50¢ for a ticket could escape into a completely different world of comedy, romance, or adventure. They could see Alberta-born actress Fay Wray swinging in the hairy grasp of King Kong or a young Judy Garland skipping down the yellow brick road in *The Wizard of Oz*. *Gone With the Wind*, released in late 1939 and starring Clark Gable and Vivien Leigh, became the world's most-watched movie. Going to the movies let Canadians escape from the bleak realities of soup kitchens, relief vouchers, and gaunt young men in hobo jungles. After all, the Great Depression could not last forever.

KNOWING THE KEY PEOPLE, PLACES, AND EVENTS

In your notes, clearly identify and explain the historical significance of each of the following:

Group of Seven	Henry Ford
Royal Canadian Air Force (RCAF)	Guglielmo Marconi
Foster Hewitt	Mary Pickford
Rocco Perri	Prohibition
Agnes Macphail	Edmonton Grads
Fanny ("Bobbie") Rosenfeld	Persons Case
League of Indians	

FOCUS YOUR KNOWLEDGE

1. Why have the 1920s been called Canada's first modern decade?
2. Describe the ways in which the automobile changed the lives of many Canadians.
3. Why are the 1920s and early 1930s considered the "Golden Age of Sports" for Canadian women?
4. Describe the treatment of Canada's Native peoples during the 1920s and 1930s by discussing their lives both on and off the reserves.
5. What evidence of an emerging Native activism can be found in the 1920s and 1930s?
6. Describe the various leisure activities enjoyed by Canadians during the 1930s. Which of these remain popular today?
7. Why were movies of comedy, romance, and adventure so popular during the 1930s?

APPLY YOUR KNOWLEDGE

1. How did airplanes help Canadians to overcome the barriers of time and distance that had separated the regions of Canada before the 1920s?
2. Why was the Canadian Broadcasting Corporation created? Is there still a need today for a government-funded radio and television corporation to ensure quality Canadian programs?

3. How did American radio programs differ from Canadian programs in the 1920s? To what degree was on-air advertising essential for quality programming in the early days of radio?

4. During the 1920s and 1930s, Canada was flooded with American movies and radio programs. At the same time, a new sense of national unity and pride could be seen in the art of the Group of Seven and as a result of the work done by the CBC and the NFB. Do you think the 1920s and 1930s were decades of growth for Canadian culture, or were they a period when Canada began to lose its unique identity to Americanization? Explain your answer.

5. Why were Canadians and Americans concerned with the need to restrict the consumption of alcohol in the 1920s? Compare and contrast the methods used by the Canadian and American governments to control the sale and consumption of alcohol. Which method is a more effective way to deal with the problems brought on by excessive drinking: regulating alcohol or imposing an outright ban?

6. Explain the significance of the "Persons Case" to women's struggle for equality in Canada.

7. Why did Canada's Native peoples feel out of place in their traditional culture and in mainstream Canadian society during the 1920s and 1930s? What changes would Canadians and the Canadian government have to make in order for Natives to feel comfortable in Canada?

EXTEND YOUR KNOWLEDGE

1. Select and research a major movie star or a popular movie of the 1930s. (The 1930s were the decade when Walt Disney began releasing animated feature films such as *Fantasia* and *Pinocchio*, so you may want focus on an animated film.)

2. Write a short story describing one or several of the leisure activities that young Canadians enjoyed during the 1920s or 1930s. Do some research before writing your story.

3. Write a poem or song that captures both the despair felt by the Native peoples in the 1920s and 1930s and the determination for cultural survival that would lead to Native activism. You may want to illustrate the poem or song and put your work on display for others to see.

4. Do some research on rum-running. Prepare a bulletin-board display that shows the creative methods used by rum-runners to smuggle alcohol into the United States and Canada.

5. Prepare a collage that captures the many images of women in the 1920s and 1930s. Your collage could include sports, entertainment, fashion, and careers, as well as other leisure activities and daily routines.

SKILLS FOCUS

UNIT REVIEW

1. The 1920s and 1930s were in many ways formative decades for Canada and Canadians. What evidence can you find in this unit's chapters to support this statement? Consider the role that women played in society, Canada's role on the international stage, changes in entertainment, and changes in Canada's political spectrum.

2. The boom of the 1920s and the Depression of the 1930s heightened regional differences in Canada. Create an organizer that allows you to compare and contrast the following regions or groups during these two decades: the Maritimes; Quebec and Ontario; the Prairies; Natives.

3. Throughout the 1920s, William Lyon Mackenzie King strove to establish Canadian autonomy. While he was quite successful at gaining greater independence from Britain, the Americans came to have an increasingly greater influence on Canada. Discuss this issue by referring to entertainment, investments, and politics.

SELF-EVALUATION: AN IMPORTANT SKILL IN THE STUDY OF HISTORY

Historians are the recorders and interpreters of past events. They offer a mirror that reflects people and their society. It is important, therefore, for historians to strive for accuracy, clear expression, and logical analysis. They must constantly evaluate and revise their work to make it as precise as possible.

Historians also challenge themselves to deal with issues such as bias by asking themselves questions about their work: "Am I being fair?" "Are there facts or interpretations that I should include or leave out?" "Are there other sources of information that I should look at?" These questions are part of the self-evaluation process that trains historians to evaluate their work and effort.

All successful professionals and entrepreneurs are particular about their work and are seldom satisfied until they have done the best job possible. They have learned how to evaluate their work honestly. No matter what you are studying or what kind of work you are doing, self-evaluation is an important skill. Whether you enter the business world, practise a trade, or pursue academic studies, you will earn the most respect when you put forward your best effort. And only you can determine when you're working as well as you can.

Using the following questions as your guide, self-evaluate one of the Unit Review questions from above. As you evaluate your work, be as honest as you can; try to be neither too harsh on nor too lenient with yourself. Remember, you can benefit a great deal from becoming an effective self-evaluator. Take the time to pause and reflect on your effort, on the quality of your work, and on how you can continue to improve.

1. How completely have I answered the question?

1	2	3	4	5
Poor		Adequate		Excellent

2. How clearly have I expressed my ideas?

1	2	3	4	5
Poor		Adequate		Excellent

3. How successful was I in locating the information necessary to answer the question?

1	2	3	4	5
Poor		Adequate		Excellent

CAREER FOCUS
SKILLED TRADES

Canada is a nation built by many skilled people. Most often we read about the politicians, bankers, and educators who contributed to the building of this country. Unfortunately, the many skilled hands that helped to build the roads, railways, and buildings have been overlooked. Take a look around you and you will see many examples of Canadian skill and ingenuity.

Numerous careers are available in the skilled trades, such as plumber, electrician, tool and die maker, and carpenter. These trades offer young Canadians a chance to earn good salaries in fields in which there is often a high demand for skilled workers.

Success in most skilled trades requires self-motivation and the ability to self-evaluate. Knowing where your strengths lie and what areas need to be improved is essential for you to experience growth in any career. Especially important is being able to judge when you have produced the best work possible. Many people in the skilled trades have no one overseeing their work. Instead, they must be critical of their own work and be able to see their own mistakes.

Canada's future still depends on highly skilled tradespeople. As we head toward the twenty-first century, the traditional trades, such as plumbing, electricity, carpentry, and tool and die making, will be joined by high-tech trades in computer technology and telecommunications. These trades will continue to serve as the foundation of our future.

With the assistance of a guidance teacher, select a skilled trade that interests you. Do some research into this trade by visiting the library, appropriate teachers, and local tradespeople in your community. Try to find the following information on the trade you selected:

- the qualifications necessary for a career in this trade;
- possible apprenticeship programs;
- approximate salary range;
- work conditions and possibilities for advancement.

Once you have completed your research into the skilled trade you have selected, find out what role this trade has played in building Canada. Prepare a report that includes a discussion of the importance of this trade to Canada's past and future. Your report should be presented to the class or displayed on a bulletin board in the classroom.

UNIT 5

WAR RETURNS:
CANADA AND WORLD WAR II

AS TENSION MOUNTED IN EUROPE IN THE 1930s, Canada — like Britain and the United States — hoped to avoid being drawn into another major conflict. Despite Canada's reluctance at becoming entangled in another European war, Adolf Hitler's march across Europe soon drew Canada into the fray. By the war's end, Canada had again given a great deal in the struggle against oppression and had, in the process, faced some radical changes.

In Chapter 12, the rise of Fascism in Italy and Germany and the growing militarism in Japan are examined, as is Canadian foreign policy in the 1930s. The central figure in World War II is Adolf Hitler. This chapter introduces his ideas and the means he used to secure enough power to launch a nearly successful war against most of Europe. Chapter 13 focuses on Canada's efforts on the home front. This chapter explains the

CHAPTER TWELVE
The Breakdown of Peace

CHAPTER THIRTEEN
War on the Home Front

CHAPTER FOURTEEN
Canada's Role in Ending the War

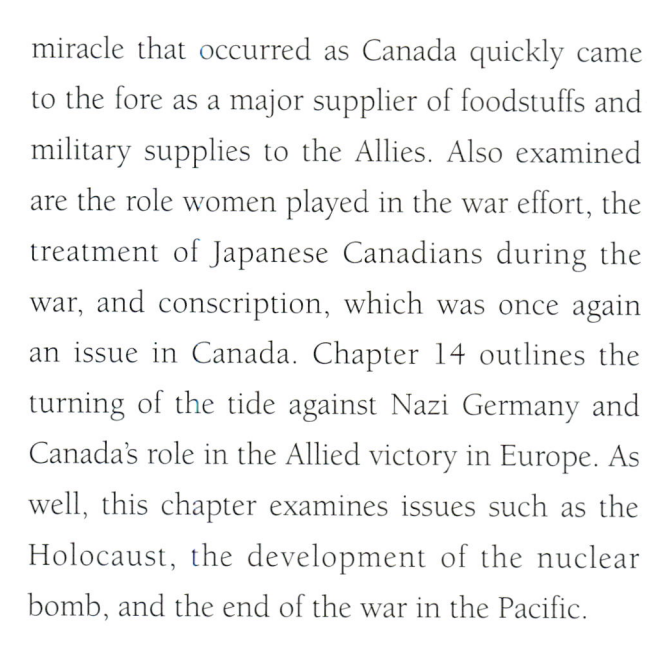

miracle that occurred as Canada quickly came to the fore as a major supplier of foodstuffs and military supplies to the Allies. Also examined are the role women played in the war effort, the treatment of Japanese Canadians during the war, and conscription, which was once again an issue in Canada. Chapter 14 outlines the turning of the tide against Nazi Germany and Canada's role in the Allied victory in Europe. As well, this chapter examines issues such as the Holocaust, the development of the nuclear bomb, and the end of the war in the Pacific.

CHAPTER 12: THE BREAKDOWN OF PEACE

GLOSSARY TERMS

Reparations Money paid by a defeated nation as compensation for damages to civilians and property during war.
Putsch An attempt to overthrow a government by violent means.
Reichstag The lower chamber of the German parliament.
Chancellor The chief minister of state in Germany.
Fascism A system of government that is based on strongly centralized powers and that permits no opposition or criticism.
Isolationism The policy of avoiding participation in international affairs or alliances with other nations.
Demilitarized Free from military control.

FOCUS ON:

- how Adolf Hitler was able to capture the imagination of the German people
- Fascism and anti-Semitism in Canada during the 1930s
- Neville Chamberlain's policy of appeasement and failed attempt to preserve peace
- Hitler's annexation of Austria and Czechoslovakia
- blitzkrieg and early German successes in World War II

On September 1, 1939, the German army invaded Poland. Within two days, Britain and France declared war on Germany, and Europe was once again engulfed in war. Would Canada step to Britain's side in the coming conflict? The answer was delayed but never in doubt. On September 10, 1939, a popular 1930s tune was playing on the airwaves when the Canadian Broadcasting Corporation interrupted its programming for a special announcement: Canada had formally declared war on Germany.

There was none of the wild enthusiasm that had swept Canadians into the streets at the declaration of war back in 1914. This time, Canadians sat quietly at home and braced for the bloody ordeal ahead. It was the second time in twenty years that war had come to their doorsteps. Almost every family had a neighbour or loved one buried in French or Belgian fields. Every Canadian town and city had its share of war survivors maimed in body or mind as daily reminders of the horrors of war.

WAR RETURNS TO EUROPE

World War II was, in some ways, a rematch of World War I, but some of the players had changed. Italy switched sides and joined Germany in 1940. Japan also joined the war on the German side after attacking the United States at Pearl Harbor in late 1941, and the United States stayed out of the conflict until Japan's surprise attack on Pearl Harbor dragged it into war. The Soviet Union remained neutral until it was invaded by Germany in 1941. But the hostilities of World War II had their roots in unresolved conflicts of World War I.

When Canada's Parliament met to consider declaring war on Germany, only a scattering of members of Parliament — one or two members from Quebec and the pacifist leader of the Co-operative Commonwealth Federation (CCF), J.S. Woodsworth — raised their voices in protest. Most Canadians reluctantly agreed that Canada should go to war. By the end of the first month of war, 70 000 people had signed up for armed service. By the end of the war, more than 1 million Canadian men and women had served with the armed services. Before it was over, 42 042 Canadians lost their lives.

Soldiers who survived the slaughter of World War I had come home in the belief that they had won the "war to end war." Their children, they swore, would never know first-hand the horrors of battle. It was with deep regret that Canadians watched their children march off to the battlefields of Europe once again.

In Smiths Falls, Ontario, one veteran boarded the troop train carrying his son to Europe, in order to go with him as far as Montreal. "They were a fine lot of men," he said of the Canadian troops, "and I felt pretty sad seeing them going overseas to finish the job we thought was finished twenty years ago."

POST-WW I GERMANY: INFLATION, DEPRESSION, AND POLITICAL UNREST

The Treaty of Versailles had imposed harsh conditions on Germany that were designed to keep the German nation from rising up again. The result of the treaty was that by the early 1920s the German economy was in tatters. Overwhelmed by war debt, the shrunken and crippled German nation was in no shape after the war to pay huge *reparations*. The German government began printing

Britain's declaration of war on Germany on September 3, 1939, created much concern in Canada, as can be seen by the crowd gathered around this newsstand.

This poster, which carries the slogan "Hitler, Our Last Hope," reflects the frustration of the German people and their trust in Adolf Hitler's leadership.

ADOLF HITLER AND THE RISE OF NAZI GERMANY

The person who profited most from Germany's desperate search for solutions was **Adolf Hitler**. A master at public speaking, Hitler said out loud what many Germans secretly thought and wanted. He promised to tear up the hated Treaty of Versailles and restore Germany to greatness. A mighty German army would rise from the ashes of World War I. German lands and peoples inside the borders of nations created by the peace treaty — Austria, Czechoslovakia, and Poland — would be returned to German rule. The victors of World War I would feel the weight of a new German empire.

Hitler's Rise to Power

Adolf Hitler was born in Austria in 1889. He left school early and drifted from job to job until the outbreak of World War I. After Germany's defeat, he dedicated himself to restoring the German nation to

paper money to pay its debt. But the newly minted money set off a spiralling inflation that destroyed the wealth of the German middle classes. A loaf of bread, which cost 2 marks (Germany's currency) in 1918, cost about 6 million marks in 1924.

Soon it took a shopping bag full of money to buy a cabbage or a streetcar token. Some workers carried their wages home in wheelbarrows. They began demanding a paycheque every day because they knew that the next day their money would buy even less. Others, instead of taking cash, which dropped in value every day, began bartering, or trading goods and services. By 1932, almost half of Germany's workers, 6 million people, were without jobs. Desperate families fled to the countryside to try to scrounge enough to eat from forests and fields, while anxious farmers took up rifles to force them away. The cities turned savage as starving people roamed the streets, looking for work or a target for their frustration. What could be done to lift Germany from ruin?

The rapid rise in prices in Germany during the 1920s left German money virtually worthless. Here, German workers sit beside boxes of money that had little real value.

military glory. Hitler went to Munich, where he took control of a small right-wing political group, built up its membership, and changed its name to the National Socialist German Workers Party — later known to the world as the Nazis.

In November 1923, Hitler tried to seize control of the Bavarian government as the first step in taking over the German democratic republic. The so-called **Beer Hall Putsch** failed and Hitler was jailed, but the *Putsch* (armed revolt) won him nationwide attention. To make the most of his new fame, Hitler wrote **Mein Kampf** ("My Struggle") in prison. The book was a rambling mixture of personal stories, threats against "enemies" of the German peoples, and mostly secondhand political ideas. It was not widely read until Hitler became a national figure. Even then, it was dismissed by many readers as the ravings of a lunatic.

But in *Mein Kampf*, Hitler set out the goals that rallied the German nation. He claimed that "Aryans" (Germans) were a master race destined to rule over "inferior races," such as the Jews and Slavs of eastern Europe, especially Poles, Czechs, and Russians. Hitler also called for more *Lebensraum* ("living space") for the German people, to support a growing German population, and demanded **Anschluss**, the unification of Austria and Germany. He planned to extend German rule over the lands held by the Poles, Czechs, and Russians. The conquest of eastern Europe was to be achieved by unleashing a new and all-powerful German army. Hitler claimed he would lead the German nation to greatness.

The September 1930 election was an alarming indication of Hitler's growing power. Hitler's Nazi Party won a million votes, more than seven times the number it had received in 1928. With 107 *Reichstag* (German parliament) seats, it became the nation's second-largest political party. In 1933, Hitler became the *chancellor* of Germany and took for himself the title of "der Führer" ("the leader"). This marked the end of the German democratic republic and the start of the Nazi "Reich." Soon Hitler would bring the Reichstag down in ruins and set himself up as an absolute dictator.

By 1933, the persecution of German Jews had begun. At first, Jewish citizens were removed from jobs in government, teaching, and the media. They were banned from many shops and public sports grounds. They were forced into separate Jewish schools, placed under a nightly curfew, and forbidden to marry non-Jews. They were attacked on the

By the 1930s Adolf Hitler had amassed widespread support and was staging impressive marches. Why do you think he used symbols such as the swastika and military parades to build support among the German people?

This classic portrait of Adolf Hitler would have been common throughout Germany following his rise to power in the 1930s.

THE BREAKDOWN OF PEACE

233

streets by Nazi supporters, and their homes and businesses were vandalized. Later, many Jews were systematically rounded up and herded off to concentration camps. Germans who spoke up for their Jewish friends and neighbours were brutally silenced. Hitler would stop at nothing to destroy his "enemies," and Hitler's will was law — the only law.

FASCIST ITALY

Hitler had patterned his Nazism on **Fascism**, a new political movement founded in Italy under the leadership of Benito Mussolini. Mussolini's rise to power was fast and bloody. By 1922, his black-shirted Fascists were strong enough to march on Rome and destroyed Italy's stumbling democratic government. Mussolini took for himself the name of "Il Duce" ("the leader"). The Fascists banned opposing political parties and workers' unions. They censored newspapers to stop freedom of expression and spread propaganda glorifying the Fascist Party, the Italian state, and Il Duce. A secret police force was set up to terrorize people into obeying Mussolini and his Fascist followers.

The Rome–Berlin Axis

Mussolini's aim was to build a new Italian empire that would circle the Mediterranean Sea. In newspapers and radio broadcasts, on movie screens and street posters, Italians were bombarded with Fascist war slogans, such as "A minute on the battlefield is worth a lifetime of peace!" and "Believe! Obey! Fight!" In 1936, the Italian army marched into Africa and seized Ethiopia. Italy also formed close ties with Hitler's Germany that were formalized in an agreement in 1936 known as the Rome–Berlin Axis. At that time, Hitler was preparing to invade Austria, and Mussolini promised not to interfere with Hitler's plans for attack. In return, Hitler promised to limit future German empire-building to northern and central Europe. Il Duce was free to build an Italian empire in southern Europe.

FASCISM, NAZISM, AND ANTI-SEMITISM IN CANADA

Fascist movements soon arrived on Canadian shores. Italian consulates in Montreal and Toronto planted Fascists in the cities' Italian communities to win support for Fascist aggression in the Mediterranean. Some Italian Canadians were convinced that Mussolini's conquest of Ethiopia was a heroic deed. Although the Royal Canadian Mounted Police (RCMP) had claimed that there were "no Nazi activities nor any Nazi movement in Canada," the German consulate began to sow Nazi ideas among some German people in Canada. The movement was most active in Saskatchewan, with its large German-speaking population, and in Manitoba, especially Winnipeg.

Canada also had its own Fascist organizations. As Fascism took hold across Europe, Canadian-born Nazi groups in Winnipeg, Toronto, and Quebec grew bolder and stepped into public view. The Nazi leader in Quebec, Adrien Arcand, was even given financial support by R.B. Bennett's federal Progressive Conservative Party. The Winnipeg-based Canadian Nationalist Party took to wearing badges showing a swastika surrounded by maple leaves and topped with a beaver. Canadian Nazis published newspapers full of Nazi slogans. They dressed up in matching shirts and paraded the streets, shouting slogans against "foreigners" and Jews. Occasionally, riots broke out in Toronto, Winnipeg, and Montreal as Fascist and anti-Fascist marchers clashed.

Some Canadians were attracted to Fascism because it seemed to offer a way out of the Great Depression. Hitler appeared to be turning the

German economy around and putting people back to work. Some Canadian Nazis hoped for the same economic transformation in Canada. But sympathy with Hitler's anti-Semitism — his deep-seated hatred of Jews — was the bedrock of most of the Fascist groups in Canada.

Many Canadians who were not Fascists shared their prejudice against Jews. There were hiring quotas for Jews in businesses, the civil service, and the professions. In many places, Jews were forbidden to buy property or to join certain clubs and organizations. Occasionally, in Winnipeg, Toronto, and Montreal, violence broke out between Jews and anti-Semites. Despite an increase in European Nazi violence toward Jews — which caused thousands of Jews from Germany, Austria, and Czechoslovakia to emigrate as refugees by the summer of 1938 — few Canadians were willing to let them come to Canada.

Like many Americans, some Canadians leaned heavily toward *isolationism* and believed that North America was one of the safest places in the world. Canada was separated from world "hot spots" by the Atlantic and Pacific oceans. An isolationist Canadian diplomat called Canada "a fireproof house far from inflammable materials." Many Canadians believed that Canada could safely turn its back on the world and worry about setting its own house in order. A deepening economic depression at home was more than enough trouble for many Canadians.

GERMAN REARMAMENT AND THE MILITARIZATION OF THE RHINELAND

In March 1935, Hitler began to show his contempt for the treaty terms that limited German military strength. He revealed the existence of a German air force and announced plans for military conscription and a thirty-six-division army. Publicly, Hitler claimed that Germany was building up its armed forces to gain military "equality" with the strongest European nations. Secretly, he was aiming for armed superiority. Once Germany had enough troops and weapons to tip the balance in Europe in its favour, Hitler could ignore the Treaty of Versailles completely. For the next few years, he told his cabinet, it must be "everything for the armed forces."

By March 1936, Hitler was ready for the next step. He marched his troops into the *demilitarized* Rhineland. He was careful to tell his soldiers to make the occupation seem as peaceful as possible because he did not want to stir up European fears about an immediate invasion. Anti-aircraft guns and Luftwaffe fighter squadrons were moved in, but no tanks and no bombers were visible; they would come later. For now, Hitler wanted it to look as if peacetime soldiers were simply taking up defensive posts in their own country. On the day that Nazi troops marched into

To some Canadians, Adolf Hitler's style of politics was appealing. These young men, known as "Blueshirts," are giving the Nazi salute at a rally in Montreal in the 1930s.

THE *ST. LOUIS*

On May 15, 1939, 907 Jews sailed from Hamburg, Germany, aboard the ship *St. Louis*, hoping to find a safe haven in Cuba. When they arrived in Havana, their entrance visas were rejected by the Cuban government and the refugees were turned away. After all the Latin American countries had turned down requests to accept the Jews aboard the *St. Louis*, Canada and the United States became the last hope for refugees.

The United States ignored an appeal, and it was made clear that Canada did not consider the *St. Louis* its problem. Frederick Blair, director of the Canadian Immigration Branch, claimed that no country could "open its doors wide enough to take in the hundreds of thousands of Jewish people who want to leave Europe: the line must be drawn somewhere." As a result of several countries' refusal to accept the Jewish refugees, the passengers aboard the *St. Louis* were forced to return to Europe. Many died there in the Nazi death camps.

Canada did not have a good record of providing a safe haven for European Jews. In the end, Canada accepted fewer than 4000 Jewish immigrants, while Britain had taken in 85 000, the United States 240 000, and even small, poor Colombia 20 000.

This Jewish refugee ship is leaving Canada en route to Israel after the war. Can you read the banner on the side of the ship?

the Rhineland, Hitler declared to the world, "We have no territorial demands to make in Europe. Germany will never break the peace."

THE POLICY OF APPEASEMENT

The new British prime minister, **Neville Chamberlain**, came to power in 1937 under the thunderclouds of approaching war. Memories of World War I were still fresh, and Chamberlain was unwilling to oppose Hitler for fear of another "Great War." He hoped that diplomacy could save the fragile peace. Chamberlain favoured a policy of **appeasement**. Hitler was a reasonable leader, Chamberlain believed, and some German demands were just. The British prime minister wanted Hitler to tell the world exactly what Germany wanted. Then, through diplomatic negotiations, Germany's needs could be satisfied (or "appeased") and the Wehrmacht (army) could be kept safely inside German borders. Chamberlain was convinced that Hitler was a man who kept his promises. Once his demands had been met, he would not ask for more.

Today Chamberlain is often criticized for his policy of appeasement, but in 1937 few people in Britain and Canada argued that Chamberlain was wrong in failing to take bold action against the Nazi dictator. Canada's prime minister, Mackenzie King, also supported appeasement. In 1937, King travelled to London, Paris, and Berlin to seek a peaceful settlement of the European conflict. In Berlin, he met and talked with the Führer himself. Hitler made a "very favourable" impression on King as a "man of deep sincerity." King was convinced that Hitler was not about to "permit any resort to war." He agreed with Chamberlain that the Nazi dictator could soon be appeased.

Mackenzie King had what he believed were good reasons for supporting appeasement. The Canadian prime minister felt that Germany had been treated too harshly in the past and that adjustments had to be made. Many Canadians backed King's views. The *Winnipeg Tribune* argued that "a Germany with her self-respect restored...may be the means of dispelling the war clouds hanging so ominously over Europe." Furthermore, King might not like Hitler's heavy-handed tactics, but the Führer was not the only bully in Europe. In the new Soviet Union, the communist leader Joseph Stalin was killing hundreds of thousands of Russian generals, intellectuals, politicians, and ordinary citizens who opposed him. Nazis and communists were deadly enemies, and Nazi Germany might keep the dark menace of the Soviet Union from spreading across Europe. Above all, King was also unwilling to push for a strong stand against Germany for fear that Canada might be drawn into another world war. "No sacrifice can be too great," King wrote in his diary, "which can save war."

Nazi propaganda often portrayed Hitler as a father figure. The inscription on this photograph reads, "Frequently in pictures one sees the Führer surrounded by kids." Do you think photographs like this would be effective propaganda?

FIRST IMPRESSIONS: MACKENZIE KING'S MEETING WITH ADOLF HITLER

Adolf Hitler was aided in his rise to power by his tremendous diplomatic skills and ability to convey sincerity. From 1933, when he became chancellor of Germany, until the outbreak of war in 1939, Hitler was able to convince world leaders of Germany's right to rearm and to expand its national boundaries. Canada's own prime minister, William Lyon Mackenzie King, was particularly impressed with the German dictator when they met for two hours in Berlin, Germany, on June 29, 1937.

Following are extracts from Mackenzie King's diary for the day of the meeting. As you read these extracts, remember that the atrocities of World War II had not yet happened. Consider the following questions:

1. What is Mackenzie King's assessment of Hitler?
2. What is it about Hitler that seems to have impressed Mackenzie King?
3. Is King conveniently ignoring aspects of the Nazi regime? Explain your answer.

When I was formally shown into the room in which Herr Hitler received me, he was facing the door as I went in; was wearing evening dress; came forward and shook hands; quietly and pleasantly said he was pleased to see me in Germany....

I told him I had been anxious to visit Germany...because I was most anxious to see the friendliest of relations existing between the peoples of the different countries.... I spoke then of what I had seen of the constructive work of his regime, and said that I hoped that that work might continue. That nothing would be permitted to destroy that work. That it was bound to be followed in other countries to the great advantage of mankind. Hitler spoke very modestly in reference to it, saying that Germany did not claim any proprietorship in what had been undertaken. They had accepted ideas regardless of the source from which they came, and sought to apply them if they were right.... I said to him that I hoped it would be possible to get rid of the fear which was making nations suspicious of each other, and responsible for increases of armaments. That could only do harm in the end. That I was a man who hated expenditures for military purposes; that the Liberal Government in Canada all shared my views in that particular; that I had the largest majority a Prime Minister had had in Canada.... Hitler nodded his head as much as to say that he understood. He then went on to say that in Germany, they had had to do some things which they, themselves, did not like.... All our difficulties grew out of the enmity of the Treaty of Versailles, being held to the terms of that Treaty indefinitely made it necessary for us to do what we had done. He spoke of the advance into the Rhur [sic] as being a part of that assertion of Germany's position to save perpetual subjugation.

He went on to say, however, that now most of the Treaty of Versailles was out of the way, moves of the kind would not be necessary any further. He went on to say so far as war is concerned, you need have no fear of war, at the instance of Germany. We have no desire for war: our people don't want war, and we don't want war....

In speaking about the Conference in England, I told him that I had been at the Conferences of 1923, and 1926, and this one, and had never seen the time when the feeling towards Germany was more favourable and friendly than it was at this last Conference. That there were things that many of the

English could not understand, and did not like, but as for any desire to dislike Germany rather than to like her, to be on friendly terms, I could not discover that in conversation with the people or with the Government....

As I got up to go, Hitler reached over and took in his hands a red square box with a gold eagle on its cover, and taking it in his two hands, offered it to me, asked me to accept it in appreciation of my visit to Germany. At the same time, he said he had much enjoyed the talk we had had together, and thanked me for the visit. When I opened the cover of the box, I saw it was a beautifully silver mounted picture of himself, personally inscribed. I let him see that I was most appreciative of it, shook him by the hand, and thanked him warmly for it, saying that I greatly appreciated all that it expressed of his friendship, and would always deeply value this gift....

To understand Hitler, one had to remember his limited opportunities in his early life, his imprisonment, et cetera.... His face is much more pre-possessing than his pictures would give the impression of. It is not that of a fiery, over-strained nature, but of a calm, passive man, deeply and thoughtfully in earnest. His skin was smooth; his face did not represent lines of fatigue or weariness; his eyes impressed me most of all. There was a liquid quality about them which indicate keen perception and profound sympathy. He looked most direct at me in our talks together at the time save when he was speaking at length on any one subject; he then sat quite composed, and spoke straight ahead, not hesitating for a word, perfectly frankly, looking down occasionally toward the translator and occasionally toward myself.

Source: Adapted from Williasm Lyon Mackenzie King Diary of 29 June 1937. Courtesy of National Archives of Canada.

The Invasion of Austria

The first sacrifice made for the sake of peace was Austria. It was a new democratic state that had been carved out of the old Austro-Hungarian empire by the Treaty of Versailles. Its people were German-speaking, a fact that gave Hitler all the excuse he needed for Anschluss, or the "union" of the German peoples of Austria and Germany in a "Greater Germany." No European nation was willing to risk war to stop Hitler from moving into Austria.

Austria's chancellor was left with no choice; his country was too small to fight the Nazis alone. When Germany invaded Austria on March 12, 1938, it met no resistance. Without losing a single soldier, the German army rolled into Vienna and seized control of the government. The next day a beaming Hitler proclaimed the Anschluss. He was triumphant; a quiet Austrian surrender meant that the Nazi invasion could be described as the reunion of peoples unhappily kept apart by the Treaty of Versailles.

Czechoslovakia and the Munich Agreement

Hitler's next target was Czechoslovakia, another nation created by the peace treaty of 1919. The new "Greater Germany" now surrounded Czechoslovakia on three sides. Since the twelfth century, Germans had been migrating to the Sudetenland, now a region of Czechoslovakia. Although the Sudetenland had never belonged to Germany, Hitler saw that he could use the excuse of "liberating" the German-speaking Sudetenlanders to seize Czechoslovakia. He told Nazi leaders in the Sudetenland to stir up protest against Czechoslovakia's treatment of its German-speaking minority. "The misery of the Sudeten Germans in indescribable," Hitler shouted. "The depriving of these people of their rights must come to an end!" Then he demanded a reunion of the "suffering" Sudetenlanders with Germany.

Once again, Britain and France were unwilling to risk all-out war with Nazi Germany over troubles in a small central European nation. In a radio broadcast on September 27, 1938, Neville Chamberlain spoke to the British nation: "How horrible, fantastic, incredible it is that we should be digging trenches and trying on gas masks here because of a quarrel in a far-away country between people of whom we know nothing.... If we have to fight, it must be on larger issues than that." Czechoslovakia was forced to accept Hitler's demands to give up territory to the Nazis or fight it out alone. Another small democracy was cast away to appease Hitler.

The Munich Agreement

The leaders of Italy, France, and England met with Hitler in Munich in September 1938 to decide Czechoslovakia's fate. Neither the Soviet Union nor the Czechs were asked to attend. The four men struck a bargain: Hitler could have the Sudetenland — one-third of Czechoslovakia — but he must promise to stop all demands for more territory. Hitler solemnly agreed to the terms, and, delighted, Chamberlain returned to London to announce the agreement reached in Munich. "I believe it is peace for our time," he declared to cheering crowds. Chamberlain genuinely believed that the crisis had passed. In Canada, the **Munich Agreement** was greeted with relief. Only the *Winnipeg Free Press* asked, "What's the Cheering For?"

Hitler never intended to stop short of an all-out conquest of Czechoslovakia, however. Six months later, he attacked Czechoslovakia, and by March 15, 1939, he stood in the president's palace in Prague, proclaiming the end of Czech independence. Even Chamberlain now realized that Hitler was bent on world conquest and that nothing short of war would stop him. Britain was determined to draw the line at Poland, but Hitler was just as determined to take it. As Germany prepared for the invasion, its Nazi propaganda machine began pouring out demands for "justice": the return of the "Polish Corridor," which gave Poland access to the sea and split Germany in half. But first Hitler had to make sure that the Soviet Union would not side with the Poles when the Wehrmacht started to roll into Poland.

The Nazi–Soviet Pact

Hitler hated communism, and Stalin hated Nazism just as fiercely, so it seemed unlikely that Nazi Germany and the Soviet Union could come to an agreement on Poland. But in 1939 the two nations shocked the world by signing the **Nazi–Soviet Pact**, in which they promised not to go to war against each other and secretly agreed to divide Poland between them.

Stalin probably knew that the pact would fall apart one day, but he believed that Hitler would first attack western Europe. Nothing suited him better than a war between his enemies, the democratic and Fascist countries of Europe. While both sides exhausted themselves in long, hard trench warfare, the Soviet Union would have plenty of time to build up its army and prepare for an inevitable war with Germany.

Hitler also knew the pact was only temporary, but he did not want to fight a war on two fronts at once. First he would conquer western Europe, and then turn his guns on the Soviet Union. For Hitler, the Nazi–Soviet Pact kept the Soviet Union quiet while he used his armies elsewhere. Once the pact was signed, Hitler was free to take Poland. At the crack of dawn on September 1, 1939, the German Wehrmacht rolled across the German–Polish border. There was no official declaration of war. The uneasy peace was ended with a barrage of German gunfire.

BLITZKRIEG AND THE ATTACK ON POLAND

In the attack against Poland, the world had its first chilling encounter with the German **blitzkrieg**, a revolutionary style of hard, fast warfare based on a surprise attack. The key to its success was close cooperation between German panzer (tank) divisions and dive-bombing aircraft of the Luftwaffe (air force). First a wave of panzers crashed without warning through weak spots in the enemy line and pushed forward as fast and far as possible. Overhead, German warplanes knifed out of the air, their sirens shrieking, to dive-bomb enemy units. The effect of the sudden and massive attack was to spread confusion and panic among enemy troops.

Meanwhile, selected sabotage troops, using parachutes or gliders, dropped behind enemy lines to destroy key transport and communication sites. Then the main body of infantry, in motorized transport, skirted around pockets of heavy resistance to swoop deep into lightly defended areas at the rear of enemy lines. In the lead were motorcycle troops

By 1936, the Nazi army was being proudly displayed for the world to see, despite the fact that the Treaty of Versailles had placed severe restrictions on the size of Germany's armed forces. Should other countries have enforced the treaty, even at the risk of war?

armed with machine guns in sidecars, scouting the country ahead to report on enemy positions.

The effect of the blitzkrieg was shattering. The Germans struck at Poland from three directions at once — north, west, and south — and moved with astonishing speed toward the Polish capital of Warsaw. The Polish defenders were stunned by the pace of the attack and the sheer weight of the German aircraft, tanks, and guns levelled against them. A bewildered Polish High Command lost contact with its armies and could not rally a defence. The Poles bravely tried to fight back, but the Polish army relied on cavalry troops and heavy, outdated equipment, while the German soldiers had the very latest and best equipment. In less than a month, the Germans had defeated an army of over 700 000 Poles and lost only 14 000 soldiers.

The "Phoney War"

While the bulk of the German army was thrown against Poland, a much smaller German force sat tight along the French border. On the other side of the border, British and French troops stood glaring at them. But not a shot was fired. Meanwhile, the British air force dropped propaganda leaflets on Germany, and the first Canadian troops stepped ashore in Britain. Still nothing happened. The "sitzkrieg," or "phoney war" as it was sometimes called, held western Europe in a strange calm for seven months.

BLITZKRIEG ACROSS WESTERN EUROPE

The calm in western Europe was shattered in April 1940, when the blitzkrieg hit Denmark and Norway. Canadian troops were immediately ordered to Scotland to board a ship for Norway. The next day, however, the order was changed and British troops took their place. The Canadians were spared the sting of a quick and overwhelming defeat. By May, Norway and Denmark had fallen to the Nazis, and by May 20, the German Wehrmacht had punched through France as far as Amiens. The following day, the panzers reached the English Channel. Retreating British forces were trapped in the French coastal town of Dunkirk. Hitler ordered the Wehrmacht to pull back and give the Luftwaffe the honour of striking the final blow. Fortunately, a dense fog pinned the German aircraft to the ground and gave British forces time to plan an escape. The delay would prove to be Hitler's first major mistake. In the meantime, however, the new British prime minister, Winston Churchill, warned the British House of Commons to prepare for disaster.

The Miracle of Dunkirk

Some historians believe that only the **Miracle of Dunkirk** prevented Hitler from winning the war before the end of May 1940. A call went out for boats to help the British troops escape Dunkirk.

Europe in 1939–1942

- Nazi-occupied Europe 1942
- Soviet-occupied Europe 1942
- Fascist Italy

Almost 900 boats of all sizes — sightseeing boats, river ferries, fishing smacks, and pleasure boats — joined up with heavy British destroyers. The makeshift flotilla sailed across the English Channel to ferry soldiers back to Britain. It was expected that only 10 000 men could be saved, but the rescue effort succeeded beyond all hopes. When it ended, 340 000 soldiers had been rescued from certain destruction by the German Wehrmacht.

The evacuation of Dunkirk was called a miracle, but France faced disaster. The French army, once considered the most powerful in the world, had collapsed. On June 14, the Nazis marched into an undefended Paris, and three days later France surrendered. In revenge for World War I, Hitler forced France to sign the surrender in the same railcar at Compiègne in which Germany had accepted defeat in 1918. Hitler was now master of Europe from Poland to the Atlantic.

Now only Britain and its Commonwealth allies were left to prevent a complete Nazi takeover of Europe. No one doubted that Hitler would let loose a savage attack against Britain; when France fell to the Nazis, a French general predicted that Britain would fall in three weeks. Britain had only the Royal Navy, the small but effective Royal Air Force, and a few infantry divisions, including the well-equipped Canadian division, to fight off the German attack.

Canadians and the European War

Canadians felt the hot flames of war licking across the Atlantic. If Britain fell, Canada faced disaster because the well-being of the Canadian economy depended on selling goods to Britain. Even more frightening was the threat of a Nazi invasion of North America. Canada had counted on the British navy to protect its vulnerable eastern coast. Canada's only remaining hope was for American protection. Both Mackenzie King and the American president, Franklin Delano Roosevelt, were concerned about protecting North America from Hitler.

The time had come for Canada to mobilize all its resources for the war against Hitler. Canadians pinned on lapel buttons that said, "Chin up, there'll always be an England" and got ready to "do their bit." Meanwhile, the Canadian government stepped up its war contributions for the defence of Britain and prepared for an all-out war effort on the home front.

Posters like this one reflect Canada's confidence that Adolf Hitler would eventually be defeated. What does this poster tell you about the role the air force had come to play by World War II?

WHEN? *It's up to you!*

KNOWING THE KEY PEOPLE, PLACES, AND EVENTS

In your notes, clearly identify and explain the historical significance of each of the following:

> Adolf Hitler
> *Mein Kampf*
> Fascism
> Appeasement
> Nazi–Soviet Pact
> Miracle of Dunkirk
> Beer Hall Putsch
> Anschluss
> Neville Chamberlain
> Munich Agreement
> Blitzkrieg

FOCUS YOUR KNOWLEDGE

1. Describe the treatment faced by German Jews under the Nazi regime.
2. Describe the nature of the Fascist movement in Canada and the activities it carried out here.
3. Outline the major events between March 1938 and September 1939 that led to the eventual outbreak of war.
4. Why did Stalin and Hitler agree to sign a pact despite their mutual hatred of each other?
5. How did the blitzkrieg revolutionize warfare, and why was it so successful?
6. What factors led to the successful evacuation of British soldiers at Dunkirk? Why are the events at Dunkirk regarded as Hitler's first major mistake?
7. Why did Canadians greet the outbreak of World War II with far less enthusiasm than they had greeted World War I? How did Canada prepare for war?

APPLY YOUR KNOWLEDGE

1. Some historians have described the two world wars as a ten-year European civil war with a twenty-year lull in the middle. Considering the issues and events surrounding the outbreak of World War II, would you agree or disagree that this war was the product of unresolved issues from World War I?
2. Why was Hitler so popular in Germany? Is it possible for someone like Hitler to gain power in a troubled nation today?

3. Canada, like many other nations, chose not to act when Hitler gathered strength in the 1930s. Considering Hitler's actions prior to the invasion of Poland, should Canada have taken an earlier and firmer stand against Nazi Germany?

4. Hitler has been described as perhaps the greatest gambler in history for the risks he took and his ability to bluff his opponents. Is this an accurate title? Defend your answer by using concrete examples.

EXTEND YOUR KNOWLEDGE

1. Create an illustrated time-line of Hitler's rise to power from the end of World War I to the invasion of Poland. Use your own caricatures or find photographs to illustrate the key people, places, and events.

2. Write a series of editorials to a Canadian newspaper in which you express your opinion about Canada's foreign policy in the years leading up to the outbreak of World War II. Base your letters on the following events.

    (a) Canada's reaction to the Jews aboard the *St. Louis*

    (b) The Anschluss

    (c) The Munich Agreement

3. Conduct a poll among your family, friends, and classmates to determine whether they feel it would be possible for a person like Adolf Hitler to seize power today. Your poll should include questions such as:

    (a) Could a dictator like Hitler gain power today?

    (b) In which country would a fanatical dictator be most likely to gain power?

    (c) Which present world leader is the greatest threat to world security?

    Use bar graphs to illustrate the responses you receive, and display them in your classroom.

CHAPTER 13 WAR ON THE HOME FRONT

GLOSSARY TERMS

Convoy Ships Merchant ships that travel in a group and are protected from enemy attack by naval escort ships or air force planes.

Navy "Plotters" Naval personnel who keep track of ship movements in a specified area.

Blackout A turning out of lights or preventing of the lights of a city from being seen at night, as a protective measure against an air raid in wartime.

Treason The crime of working for the enemies of a nation or of trying to overthrow a nation's government by illegal means.

War Measures Act A law passed in 1914 giving the federal government sweeping emergency powers in times of war, invasion, or rebellion. It severely limits the freedoms of Canadians.

Defence of Canada Regulations Rules proclaimed in 1939 under the War Measures Act, giving the government wide-ranging powers to control dissent and to protect Canada against its enemies.

Unemployment Insurance A federal program introduced in Canada in 1940 to provide financial support for unemployed workers.

FOCUS ON:

- how Halifax played a key role as a navy seaport
- the perceived threat of a Japanese invasion of the West Coast
- why the Canadian government interned Japanese Canadians
- the "economic miracle" that occurred in Canada during World War II
- how the government came to play a central role in regulating and managing the Canadian economy
- the central role played by Canadian women in the war effort, both at home and abroad
- the conscription debate in Canada

On May 17, 1939, King George VI and Queen Elizabeth landed at Quebec City for a whirlwind tour of the Canadian provinces. It was the first time that a British monarch had set foot in Canada. Everywhere the royal couple appeared, crowds gathered to cheer, Mounties in red tunics and carefully polished boots stood at attention, and young girls stepped forward to hand the visiting British queen a bouquet while the king looked on. But the royal visit had a special — and disturbing — significance. The king had come to rally support from his loyal British subjects. Hitler was on the move, and Britain might soon need every bit of help it could get from Canada.

In 1939, more than half of all Canadians were of British (English, Scottish, or Irish) origin, while another third were French Canadians. A growing number of English Canadians were starting to call themselves simply "Canadians," but ties to Britain remained strong. Still, Prime Minister Mackenzie King, like many Canadians, was unhappy about Canada going to war. Canadians had enough problems at home. "The idea that every twenty years this country should automatically and as a matter of course take part in a war overseas," the prime minister had grumbled, "seems to many a

The visit of King George VI and Queen Elizabeth to Canada in 1939 drew large crowds wherever they appeared. Here the royal couple are shown visiting Medicine Hat, Alberta.

nightmare and sheer madness." Mackenzie King never questioned that Canada would step to Britain's side. However, he was determined to keep Canada's commitment as moderate as possible.

WAR COMES TO CANADIAN SHORES

Soon after the outbreak of war, Mackenzie King's hopes for a limited Canadian role began to fade. The horrifying series of victories by Germany and its allies (the Axis) across Europe and Africa frightened Canadians. Soon the shadow of the European war had fallen across Canada's eastern seacoast. One historian commented that Halifax had to face conditions that were "in some ways like those of a beleaguered and refugee-crowded city in Europe." Ships arriving from Europe were crammed with European refugees, evacuated British children, German prisoners of war, returning air crew, and survivors of torpedoed boats. The city bulged with newcomers.

Halifax was also the centre for Canadian naval operations in the North Atlantic and a base for British and Allied shipping. One British commander called it the most important Allied port in the world. Accents from all over the British Commonwealth could be heard in Halifax streets as soldiers, sailors, and merchant marines from Wales, northern England, and Scotland mingled with New Zealanders, South Africans, and Australians. Day after day, convoys of ships formed in Halifax Harbour and then slipped out to make a run across the North Atlantic with troops, guns, tanks, shells, foodstuffs, and tonnes of other vital war materials for Europe.

The Germans did everything in their power to interrupt supply lines. Sometimes *convoy ships* were mined or torpedoed within hearing distance of Halifax. Most deadly of all were the German U-boat (submarine) teams called "wolf packs," which broke through convoy escort ships to pick off merchant ships one after the other. U-boats sent hundreds of merchant and military escort ships to the ocean bottom and destroyed millions of tonnes of cargo.

This propaganda poster suggested the possibility of Canada being invaded if the Nazis were not stopped in Europe. How real was this threat? Do you think this poster would have been effective in mobilizing support for the war effort?

The federal government went to great lengths to warn Canadians about the danger of gossip and careless talk. Canadians were reminded that the presence of spies was a constant threat and they should not talk about things such as defence plans, munitions factories, or supply stores. This poster shows how careless talk led to a train being sabotaged.

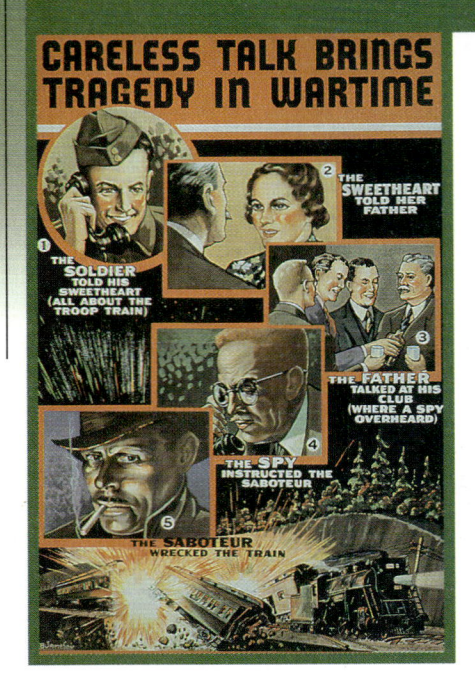

In and around Halifax, navy "plotters" tracked ship movements, including those of the silent and dangerous U-boats, in the North Atlantic. Many of the plotters were women of the Women's Royal Canadian Naval Service (WRCNS). One WRCNS plotter later said, "Most Canadians had no idea just how close those German U-boats got — way up the St. Lawrence."

Newfoundland's Role in the War

The island of Newfoundland was still independent in 1939, but for the first time the cooperation between Canada and Newfoundland was close. Newfoundland was key to the defence of North America, but it did not have the money or personnel to ward off a German attack. (The Newfoundland government had gone bankrupt in the 1930s. At its own request, Newfoundland was being run by a "commission government" of British civil servants.)

With Newfoundland's consent, Canadian troops were stationed on the island, and Royal Canadian Air Force (RCAF) aircraft flew out of airports at Gander and at Goose Bay, Labrador. Canadian forces were joined by Newfoundland troops, including two infantry battalions, two anti-aircraft regiments, three coastal batteries, and a number of administrative and service units. The people of Newfoundland began to enjoy a new prosperity from war and defence spending. Some Newfoundlanders began to think that union with Canada might not be such a bad idea. But first, North America had to survive the war.

The War in the Pacific and on Canada's West Coast

Times were also tense along Canada's West Coast. In the Far East, Japan had invaded large parts of China and was moving south toward Indonesia and Australia. The U.S. and British naval fleets in the Pacific had been crippled by Japanese surprise attacks in 1941. Three months later, the Japanese had swept across the Philippines, Malaya, Burma, and Singapore, and they were marching toward Australia.

Concerned about a possible Japanese invasion, the Canadian government built coastal-defence gun installations like this one at Alert Head, British Columbia.

The opening of a new war zone in the Pacific frightened Canadians on the West Coast. The suddenness of the Japanese attacks, the number of their targets, and the ease of their victories made western Canadians fear that the next Japanese target might be British Columbia. For days after the attacks on Pearl Harbor and Hong Kong, Vancouver enforced a *blackout* at night. School children were drilled to respond to a gas attack, and nervous adults tried to prepare for an invasion. As it turned out, the only direct Japanese attack on Canada was a submarine shelling of a Vancouver Island lighthouse in June 1942. However, the Japanese did occupy the Aleutian Islands off Alaska in mid-1942; they were later pushed off by a combined Canadian and American force. Fear of the enemy in the Pacific quickly turned white British Columbians against their Japanese neighbours at home.

THE INTERNMENT OF JAPANESE CANADIANS

In the early 1940s, about 22 000 people of Japanese descent lived in British Columbia. The first Japanese immigrants had come to work on the railways and in mines and lumber camps. Later, many settled on the coast, where they bought fishing boats or plots of land. Most earned their living from fishing, market gardening, and small business. Their hard work was paying off, and some Japanese Canadians were beginning to prosper. However, their success was resented by many white British Columbians.

Even before the war, Japanese Canadians had been targets of anti-Asian rioting and treated as second-class citizens. They were denied the right to vote, teach, or take jobs in the civil service

Thousands of Japanese Canadians were sent to internment camps in northern British Columbia and northern Ontario. How can we safeguard against such injustices in the future?

and other professions. Japan's attacks on Pearl Harbor and Hong Kong opened the floodgates of long-standing racial hostility. Japanese Canadians were suddenly seen by many as spies and enemy aliens bent on helping Japan to destroy Canada. In a radio speech on the evening of the attack on Pearl Harbor, Mackenzie King assured Canadians that the authorities were "confident of the correct and loyal behaviour of Canadian residents of Japanese origin."

In Vancouver, the RCMP had been keeping a close eye on Japanese Canadian residents since 1938. It concluded that the Japanese community was loyal to Canada. Japanese Canadians had been patriotic boosters of Red Cross work and Victory Bond drives, and many were eager to fight for Canada. No sign of *treason* or treachery was uncovered at that time — or at any time later.

On its own, Mackenzie King's government would not have taken harsh measures against Japanese Canadians on the West Coast. But anti-Japanese feeling was running high in British Columbia. Rumours sprang up about a Japanese invasion, and the stories grew wilder as they were passed on from one person to the next. Newspapers, patriotic societies, service clubs, and town and city councils cried out against people of Japanese descent.

Ottawa eventually gave in to the mounting public pressure. At first, only male Japanese nationals — men without Canadian citizenship — were rounded up and taken to internment camps well away from the coast. Soon, however, the Japanese conquest of British-held Singapore hit the headlines. The news fuelled racist feelings, and white British Columbians pressed Ottawa even harder. Under the *War Measures Act* and the *Defence of Canada Regulations*, the internment order was extended to everyone of Japanese descent — Canadian citizen or not.

Soon, Japanese Canadians were herded onto eastbound trains. Most were sent to internment camps in the interior mountains of British Columbia. Others were sent east of the Rocky Mountains, to sugar-beet farms in Alberta, or farther east to Manitoba and Ontario. The government also placed about 70 Japanese Canadians it considered dangerous behind barbed wire in northern Ontario.

The Japanese Canadians interned in British Columbia lived in shacks or makeshift houses measuring about 4 x 8 metres. Some shacks had no running water or electricity, and none were built for the bitter mountain winters. Often families were broken up, and the father was sent to one camp while the mother and children went to a different one. The men were put to work building roads and cutting trees. Frank Moritsugu, a Canadian-born nineteen-year-old from Vancouver, was sent to the Yard Creek Camp, near Revelstoke, B.C., to work on what would become the Trans-Canada Highway. "There was no barbed wire," he said, "but we had sentries guarding us from a pillbox. With its beautiful scenery, Yard Creek in other circumstances would have been a delightful place; to us it was a symbol of shame."

When the Japanese Canadians were interned, they had to leave most of their belongings behind in the "safekeeping" of a government agent called the Custodian of Enemy Property. But the authorities auctioned off all their property, including fishing boats, cars, houses, shops, and personal belongings, to others.

The shameful treatment did not stop at the war's end. After the war, Ottawa passed a law to deport Japanese Canadians, and almost 4000 were sent to Japan before the law was repealed in 1947. Many had never been to Japan before. For several years after the war, Japanese Canadians had to report to the RCMP if they travelled more than 80 kilometres from home. By 1949, however, Japanese Canadians had gained the right to vote in federal and provincial elections. The Canadian government did not formally apologize for the injustices until 1988, when Brian Mulroney's government offered $20 000 to every survivor of the **Japanese internment**.

REFLECTIONS ON AN INJUSTICE

David Suzuki was a young child when his family was interned by the Canadian government during World War II. The memories of this injustice have remained with him to this day. In the essay below, Suzuki reflects on the lessons Canadians can learn from history. As you read this essay, consider the following questions:

1. What protections exist in the Canadian Constitution to help ensure that future injustices like the internment of Japanese Canadians do not occur again?
2. How can the study of history help us to avoid the mistakes of the past?

Our Fragile Democracy

The tacit assumptions about race and behaviour often become evident at the time of a racial "incident." I experienced the results of such assumptions when Japanese Canadians were incarcerated during the Second World War. On April 8, 1968, the Monday after Martin Luther King was assassinated, faculty and students at the University of British Columbia held a memorial service in front of the library.

As one of the speakers, I talked about the lesson King had given us, namely, that even in a democracy you have to fight for freedom and equality. But, I said, Canadians should not feel smug or superior to the Americans, for we too have a sorry history of racism and oppression. I talked about the sad state of Canadian native peoples and went on to remind them about the Japanese-Canadian evacuation and incarceration in British Columbia in 1942. Later, a newspaper editorial chastised me and said that I should not stir up old memories that were best forgotten, lest they revive the antagonism of those who had suffered at the hands of the Japanese.

History provides us with the only real lessons about the fragility of human rights, and today, as the Keegstra trial (for teaching that the Holocaust did not occur and that there is a Jewish conspiracy to control the world) and the Zundel conviction (for spreading anti-Semitic hate literature) remind us, they are so easily distorted or forgotten. Japanese Canadians were insistent that their incarceration, loss of property and forced dispersion should be acknowledged as wrongs and their losses redressed with financial settlements. On April 12, 1985, we had another compelling reason to keep the Japanese-Canadian experience in the public view. On that day, the Ontario Command of the Royal Canadian Legion formally asked the federal government not to make any financial settlement with Japanese Canadians. James Forbes, assistant provincial secretary of the Ontario Command, stated that if Japanese Canadians "are awarded money, then the Japanese government should be pressed to compensate Canadian veterans who were held in concentration camps" (The Globe & Mail). But what on earth has the treatment of Canadian citizens by the government of Canada got to do with the treatment of Canadian citizens by an enemy government?

I can't think of a better example of the fragility of democratic ideals. What a tragedy that war veterans, as the one group of people who have put their bodies on the line to preserve our high principles, should be the ones to deny them. When it comes to Asians, Canada has had a tough time living up to its stated civil rights. History informs us of race riots against Asians, racial quotas in university professional schools, denial of the vote to Asians, native born or not, until 1948, restrictive covenants on property — these were just some of the injustices. But we have learned from past experience and now work to eliminate our inequities. The notion that there is only one class of citizen, guaranteed all the full rights of citizenship whether native born or naturalized, must be the goal of this young nation.

The Royal Canadian Legion, at least the Ontario branch, succumbed to the commonly held notion that any rights of citizenship can be abrogated for target groups in times of perceived stress. Yet it is in times of stress that those rights and guarantees matter most. Furthermore, some people appear to believe that guarantees of freedom and equality are for the Caucasian majority. A few years ago, CTV's flagship current affairs show, "W5," demonstrated how seductive this notion is when they reported that foreign students from Asia were taking advantage of the Canadian taxpayer by enrolling in our universities. To illustrate their thesis, they showed pictures of Asian students on campus without regard to whether they were Canadians or not! The assumption seems to have been that if they're Asian they're not Canadians — exactly the sentiment underlying the Ontario Command's submission to the government.

By the reasoning of the Legionnaires, we should press B.C.'s Doukhobors for compensation for the Soviet Union's destruction of the Korean Air flight. Do we blame third-generation Irish Canadians for the atrocities in Belfast? Is every Afro-Canadian responsible for the excesses of Idi Amin? I hope even the Legionnaires would not make such absurd claims.

Then what do we make of their contention that the Japanese-Canadian evacuation is justified on the basis of the terrible treatment of Canadian soldiers in concentration camps in the Pacific theatre? Do they not know that the Japanese were also the enemy of Japanese Canadians? How ironic that Japanese Canadians, denied freedom and equality by their country, nevertheless struggled for the right to join its army. They fought and died for Canada in the Second World War but not for the bigoted nation embodied by the Ontario Command of the Royal Canadian Legion. The Legion's position can only be understood as racism. It assumes that loyalty and commitment are genetically determined rather than acquired socially.

In the interests of democracy in Canada, this bigotry must be exposed at every opportunity. Every time I speak out on the issue of injustice to Japanese Canadians and receive letters or phone calls from bigots who castigate me for daring to raise the issue "after what the Japs did to us," I feel it benefits Canadians to see how fragile our democracy is.

That is why the Japanese-Canadian push for redress had to be pursued vigorously, as an act of commitment to principles for which so many died in battle. It is to the Brian Mulroney's government's credit that in October 1988 it formally apologized to Japanese Canadians for their incarceration and announced a $20 000 compensation for every surviving internee.

Japanese Canadian internment camp.

CANADA'S WARTIME ECONOMY

In 1939, Canadians across the nation were gearing up for war. Mackenzie King was hopeful that Canada's major contribution would be the **British Commonwealth Air Training Plan** (BCATP), which was announced on December 17, 1939. By the end of the war, Canada had paid $1.6 billion toward the BCATP, three-quarters of the plan's total cost. Under the plan, air crews were to be brought to Canada from all over the Commonwealth for training as pilots, navigators, air gunners, bombardiers, and wireless operators. Canada provided airfields, aircraft, and basic services, far out of range of the German Luftwaffe, while Britain supplied instructors. The program turned out more than 130 000 graduates, including 50 000 pilots. Almost 73 000 of the graduates were Canadians.

Many factories, such as this Inglis plant in Toronto, were converted to munitions or weapons factories. These workers played a critical role supplying the Allied forces with weapons.

"Total War" and Canada's Economic Miracle

Despite Mackenzie King's hopes for a limited war effort, the BCATP was just the beginning of Canada's commitment. Once Hitler had occupied most of Europe and the Japanese were driving swiftly across the Far East, Canadians began to talk about "total war" — using everything possible for the war effort. By the end of 1941, industries across the nation were working overtime to produce war materials. Unemployment vanished. In fact, competition for workers had become so stiff that the government created a **National Selective Service** (NSS) to tell Canadian workers about the industries in which their labour was most needed. If workers took jobs without NSS approval, they could be fined $500 and jailed for a year. Canada's economy, crippled by the Great Depression, was up and running again.

The weather cooperated, and the Prairies had turned green at last. Farmers began harvesting bumper crops and selling them at satisfying prices. In 1942, high school and university students from the East and Native people from the North headed into Saskatchewan to help harvest a record-breaking crop of wheat. Hungry Britons were desperate for food, and Canadian farmers began to produce a wider range of products to meet the new demand, including pork, beef, dairy products, flax, and oil seeds. Lumber from British Columbia's forests, mineral ores from mines on the Canadian Shield, and fish from the Maritimes were all welcomed.

The biggest change occurred in Canadian manufacturing. Vancouver shipyards, Hamilton steel mills, Toronto munitions plants, and Montreal aircraft factories began to run shifts around the clock, seven days a week. Canadians also started making many items at home that they used to buy abroad. For the first time, Canadians produced diesel engines, synthetic rubber, roller bearings, electronic equipment, and high-octane gasoline and other products. The cabinet minister in charge of industrial production, **C.D. Howe**, predicted, "Never again will there be any doubt that Canada can manufacture anything that can be manufactured elsewhere." He was right. Many new industries survived into peacetime and became a permanent part of the Canadian economy.

Canadian farms and factories produced more and more to meet the war's needs. In 1939, war orders stood at $60 million; by 1942, they had climbed to $2.5 billion. By the end of the war, Canada's per capita production was the highest of all the Allied countries. In all, Canada gave Britain $3.5 billion in aid. "Canada could help others," one Canadian journalist remarked, "because above all, it had worked its own economic miracle: a threadbare nation had become a vast arsenal and farm."

The Wartime Economy and Government Controls

Prime Minister Mackenzie King was determined to manage the war effort so that it was an efficient, orderly, and honest affair. He put a group of cabinet ministers in charge of the shift to a wartime economy and the minister of munitions and supplies, C.D. Howe, in charge of the war production effort. Britain desperately needed all kinds of supplies. Howe obtained contract after contract for guns, tanks, trucks, uniforms, ships, and much more.

But many of Howe's contracts were for products that Canada had never made before. He turned to top businesspeople across Canada for help in meeting wartime production demands. He asked them to take a "holiday" from work and to become civil servants until the war ended. They became known as **"dollar-a-year men"** for the token salary paid by the government. (Many companies continued to pay their salaries while they worked for Howe's department.) Canadian factories that had been making refrigerators were switched over to producing tank tracks or Bren guns. Railway shops started making tanks. Automobile makers stopped making cars and began producing army trucks.

Soon Canada was geared up for war production. By 1944, Canadians were building 4000 trucks and 450 armoured vehicles a week. "When you consider that prewar Canadian industry had never made a tank, a combat airplane or a modern high-caliber rapid-fire gun," the American magazine *Fortune* marvelled, "the speed with which industry was organized and production started ranks as an industrial miracle."

Widening Government Controls Over Industry

C.D. Howe's **Department of Munitions and Supplies** had been given new powers over private enterprise. It could tell businesses what to produce, where to sell their products, and even when to deliver them. If a business refused to cooperate, the department could take over the plant and schedule production itself.

New crown corporations were created by Howe's department whenever private enterprise could not supply a specific demand. By the end of the war, there were twenty-eight crown corporations, producing everything from wood (Veneer Log Supply Limited) to synthetic rubber (Polymer Corporation). One crown corporation, Eldorado Mining and Refining, even secretly processed uranium for the U.S. atomic bombs that were dropped on Japan in 1945. Never before had a Canadian government taken such wide-ranging control over private enterprise.

The Hyde Park Declaration

One of the most important crown corporations was War Supplies Limited. This corporation sprang from a meeting between Prime Minister Mackenzie King and his friend, U.S. President Franklin Delano Roosevelt, at Roosevelt's family estate in Hyde Park, New York. King explained to the U.S. president that

Canada, in trying to help Britain, would soon be in financial difficulty if it did not earn more American dollars. However, if the United States bought products from Canadian industries worth roughly as much as the products that Canada was buying in the United States, Mackenzie King said, Canada's foreign-exchange problem would disappear. Roosevelt did not know much about foreign exchange, but he liked Mackenzie King's proposal and the two leaders signed an agreement known as the **Hyde Park Declaration**. More than $1 billion worth of Canadian goods were eventually sold to the United States. The declaration marked the beginning of a new era of close economic ties between the two nations.

To rally support for the war effort, posters like this one portrayed the ruthlessness of the Nazis.

Wage and Price Freezes and Rationing

The booming wartime economy brought Canadians new prosperity. More people were working, and they had more money in their pockets than ever before. But most of Canada's resources were going into wartime production, with the result that fewer consumer goods were on store shelves. Mackenzie King's financial advisers were worried that with "so many dollars chasing so few goods," prices would rise quickly. The result would be a crippling inflation. It had happened in World War I, and Mackenzie King was determined that it would not happen again.

Managing the Wartime Economy: The Problem of Inflation

A Nova Scotia lawyer, **James Ilsley**, was put in charge of Canada's financial affairs. Ilsley used large tax increases, forced savings, and the sale of Victory Bonds to keep prices down. In 1938 Ottawa had collected just $42 million from personal income taxes, but by 1943 it took in $815 million. Ilsley also mounted nine huge publicity campaigns for War Loans and Victory Loans. Celebrities — including child movie star Shirley Temple and the five-year-old Dionne quintuplets — were used to make public appeals for Victory Bonds. Posters and magazine advertisements with slogans like "The Men Are Ready... Only YOU Can Give Them Wings" popped up everywhere. Some advertisements even used scare tactics to keep the money rolling in; one shows a mother and baby menaced by two silhouetted black hands, one with a Nazi swastika and the other with the symbol of Japan. It reads, "Keep These Hands Off! Buy the New Victory Bonds." The publicity effort was a stunning success, producing $8.8 billion for the war effort.

Wage and Price Controls and Rationing

Despite Ilsley's efforts, prices were going up by 1941. Mackenzie King's government worried that explosive inflation lay ahead. In November 1941, the **Wartime Prices and Trade Board** (WPTB) took the revolutionary step of freezing all prices and wages to prevent inflation. The WPTB also decided who could buy scarce goods. Consumers who wanted to buy items such as electric stoves, typewriters, or rubber tires first had to get a permit from the WPTB. The permits went to people who showed that their use of an item contributed most to the war effort.

Food rationing was also introduced in 1942, and quotas were placed on a number of everyday commodities. Canadians were limited to 250 grams of

Posters like this encouraged the conservation of materials that could be used in making war supplies. What stereotypical assumption does this poster make? How would you update this poster for the 1990s?

sugar, 250 grams of butter, 30 grams of tea, 115 grams of coffee, and 1 kilogram of meat per person per week. More than 11 million ration books were handed out, and ration coupons became a part of Canadian life. But rationing was more of a nuisance than a real hardship. In European eyes, Canadians still lived in a land of plenty. Even Americans faced tighter rationing than Canadians did.

Government Intervention at the End of the War

Massive government intervention in the wartime Canadian economy seemed to have paid off. Canada had managed to keep inflation in check without slowing down the economy. In fact, the country's record on keeping inflation under control was the best in the world. The expanding web of government regulations, including National Selective Service rules, rationing, and wage-and-price controls, had severely limited Canadians' freedom of action. But scarce goods had been shared out fairly equally among Canadians, and many workers enjoyed a higher standard of living.

As the war came to an end, however, Canadians feared a return to the Great Depression. Many began to think that the federal government should continue to direct the economy. Mackenzie King's government had already provided for *Unemployment Insurance* in 1940 and Children's Allowance, or "baby bonus" — a monthly payment for food and clothing for children — in 1944.

After the war, Mackenzie King added a package of veterans' benefits. There was a severe housing shortage, and the federal government took steps to promote home building. It also brought in programs to help industries shift to peacetime production and to secure export sales, and it increased federal aid to health care. Mackenzie King's new programs were popular, and his government was re-elected in 1945. These programs were the beginning of a whole new involvement of the federal government in social and economic affairs.

WOMEN'S CONTRIBUTION TO THE WAR EFFORT

The war effort also opened new doors for women, at least while the war was on. Men going overseas left job vacancies behind, so there were jobs for everyone willing to work. In fact, the federal government began actively recruiting women into the labour force. "Women! Back Them

Displays like this encouraged Canadians to support the war effort by saving fat and bones, which would then be used to produce high-powered explosives and glue. Who are the "Three Droops" referred to in this display?

Up — To Bring Them Back" said one government campaign poster urging women to take jobs in munitions work. "Roll Up Your Sleeves for Victory!" shouted another poster.

At first, the government campaign targeted single women, but by September 1942, labour shortages were so acute that all women between the ages of twenty and twenty-four were required to sign up with the National Selective Service. Later, the government campaigned for married women to take jobs, and near the end of the war, women with children were targeted for the labour force. With federal help, Ontario and Quebec set up a few day-care centres to free mothers for war work. By 1944, almost 1 million women had taken jobs across Canada.

Women in Industry

At the peak of wartime production, 30 percent of the people working in aircraft plants — 25 000 workers — were women. More than 260 000 women had jobs in munitions plants. There were 4000 female workers in shipbuilding and 4000 in construction. Women drove taxis, buses, and streetcars in major cities from coast to coast. They assembled radio tubes and Bren guns, and worked at spot welding, auto assembly, riveting, and meat packing. The female war worker, wearing trousers and a bandana wrapped around her head to keep long hair out of machinery, became a kind of national heroine. Sometimes nicknamed "**the Bren Girl**," the female war worker appeared on billboards almost as often as the Canadian soldier did.

Women were still being paid less than men for doing the same jobs, although the differences between men's and women's wages were smaller than before, and they almost always had male bosses. Many still worked in traditionally female jobs, but a sizable number took on jobs usually done by men. The divisions between "women's work" and "men's work" were beginning to blur.

Women in Agriculture

Many young men and women left the farms for service overseas or better-paying jobs in war industries. As a result, the burden of agricultural production often fell to the more than 800 000 women who stayed on the farms. Women had always done their share of farm work, but in the war years they often had to work double-time to compensate for missing husbands and farm workers. One farm wife managed to do the heavy farm work, service the equipment, run the house, look after the children, and still have time for hunting and curling. When her husband came back from the war, she handed him the bank book. "There is more money in there," she proudly told him, "than we ever had in our lives."

Women in the Services

Nurses had been a part of Canadian military tradition since the Boer War. About 2800 Canadian women had served as nurses in World War I, and many served again as nurses in World War II. The armed forces resisted recruiting women into any other jobs, however, so many Canadian women decided to prepare themselves for a more active part in the war. At first they joined unofficial women's service groups, where they learned how to drill, drive and fix trucks, read maps, operate wireless equipment, and give first aid. One group, the Canadian Auxiliary Territorial Service (CATS), was started by a columnist with the *Toronto Daily Star*. Soon more than 3000 women were singing the CATS theme song:

We will fight for the might that we know is right, And even Mussolini knows that CATS can fight…

Many women in voluntary organizations lobbied to be accepted into official military service. Their request was ignored until military personnel shortages became critical in 1941. The air force was the first to realize that women had a place in uniform. The army and navy followed its lead. By 1945, more than 17 400 women had served with the Canadian Women's Auxiliary Air Force (CWAAF), more than 21 500 had joined the Canadian Women's Army Corps (CWAC), and 7100 had signed up with the Women's Royal Canadian Naval Service (WRCNS).

Women's roles in the armed forces expanded during the war years. For example, the number of trades for women in the air force grew from eleven to fifty by February 1943, including jobs as armourers, mechanics, fitters, and welders. And, by May 1944, selected groups of CWACs were being sent to combat areas in Europe.

Women as Volunteers

Women without paid war work also made key contributions as unpaid labourers at home and as volunteers. At home, they coped with food shortages and remade old clothes to prevent waste. They faithfully practised the conservation that the WPTB preached: "Use It Up, Wear It Out, Make It Do, and Do Without." Women's groups taught classes on how to cook nourishing home meals with few supplies. They also ran huge salvage campaigns under the motto, "Dig In and Dig Out the Scrap." They salvaged paper, rags, iron, aluminum, edible fats, bottles, and even meat bones for aircraft glue and milkweed for life preservers. The contributions of women at home and overseas were vital to Allied success in the war.

Women After the War

Once the war ended, however, women were expected to return to more traditional roles such as homemaking, teaching, nursing, and secretarial work. They had been told that taking a job was their patriotic duty during wartime, but it was made clear that paid work was not their right in peacetime. All government-supported day-care centres were closed despite efforts to keep them open. The three women's service corps were disbanded. Government and private industry let women workers go in order to provide jobs for returning veterans.

After the war, women hung up their uniforms and took off their slacks and bandanas. Fashions for women changed to underline their return to more traditional and "feminine" roles. Flared skirts, worn tightly

Women carried on the vital task of caring for the wounded, a tradition started by Florence Nightingale a century earlier. These Nursing Sisters cared for the wounded at a Canadian General Hospital in France after the landing at Normandy.

CANADIAN WOMEN AT WAR

Although the two world wars were separated by only two decades, the change in women's roles was enormous. During World War I, women were limited to conventional wartime contributions, such as nursing or volunteering. As labour shortages developed, more and more women worked in munitions factories, but when the war ended, women's roles remained nonmilitary.

World War II proved to be a watershed for Canadian women. For the first time, they played a military role: 45 000 Canadian women signed up for military service. However, not everyone was ready for such a change. A former member of the WRCNS recalled the reaction to her enlisting: "My parents lived in a small town — very much removed from the war — and I got the impression when I'd be home on leave that some people thought that it was wrong for me to be in uniform. They hardly seemed to realize there was a war on, some of them."

Women and men overseas also shared the frustrations of the secrecy and security measures that are a part of war. The following poem was saved by a former member of the WRCNS who had been serving overseas:

These five women were among the first CWACs to arrive in Normandy, France, following the D-Day invasion in 1944.

On Duty

Woe is me
You asked me to write
Now what will it be?
I can't write a thing
'Cause it's censored, you see.

Can't mention the weather
Whether raining or shine.
'Bout all I can say is
That I'm feeling fine.

Can't say that we're drafted.
Can't say where we'll go
One reason for that is
We usually don't know.

Can't mention the work
That we're doing each day
And it's hardly worth mentioning
The wages they pay.

Can't take any snaps
Within miles of shore
There's really not much
We can do any more.

Can't keep a diary
About what we do.
Just hello and goodbye
If I telephone you.

If we tell any secrets
We're sure in a spot.
We're C.B.d for two weeks
If perchance we get caught.

Please write and remember
In spite of the wars
Write all that you know
'Cause they don't censor yours!

Former member, WRCNS

cinched at the waist, replaced casual trousers. Comfortable low-heeled shoes gave way to high platform shoes or high-heeled pumps. Women's magazines ignored the career woman and published glowing articles on the pleasures of the homemaker. The proportion of women in the workforce dropped from 31.4 percent in 1945 to 22.7 percent in 1946. The equality barrier between men and women in the workplace had cracked, but it had not broken. Still, Canadian women could take pride in the vital contributions they had made at home and overseas.

THE FIGHT OVER CONSCRIPTION

Canada had been torn apart in World War I by the bitter fight between French and English Canadians over conscription. Mackenzie King was determined to avoid another disastrous conscription battle. He took Canada into World War II with the solemn pledge that no Canadians would be conscripted and forced to fight against their will. French Canadians accepted Canada's declaration of war on the understanding that they would never be conscripted to fight in Europe.

But Hitler's victories in Europe soon had many English Canadians thinking about conscription. Pressure mounted, and King reacted with the **National Resources Mobilization Act** (NRMA). In King's words, it let the government "call out every man in Canada for military training for the defence of Canada." Under the NRMA, men could be conscripted and trained as soldiers, but only for home defence within the borders of Canada. The NRMA conscripts could not be sent overseas to fight.

A growing number of English Canadians came to see the men conscripted for home duty in the NRMA as less than patriotic because they refused to fight in Europe, and these conscripts were soon nicknamed "Zombies." English Canadians mistakenly believed that most of the "Zombies" were French Canadians and grumbled that they should not be allowed to "sit comfortably" in Canada while the battle raged in Europe. The army tried all kinds of threats and promises to get the NRMA men to "go active." Its tactics were sometimes harsh, and many "Zombies" finally agreed to active service. But a tough core of NRMA conscripts, fully trained for service, steadily refused to go to war.

The conscription issue was becoming a political "hot potato" for King, who was locked into his pledge against conscription. Public support began to swing to the Progressive Conservative Party. The architect of conscription in World War I, Arthur Meighen, was asked to come back as the Conservative Party leader. He agreed, and it began to look as if the Liberal Party might be beaten on the conscription issue just as it had been in World War I.

Then King had an idea. He would hold a plebiscite, a federal referendum open to all Canadian voters. He would ask Canadians whether or not they favoured releasing his government from its earlier pledge against conscription. On April 27, 1942, almost 4 million Canadians went to the polls to vote. The plebiscite passed, and King was freed from his promise. Once again Canada was divided into warring camps over conscription, and so was King's government. Quebeckers were outraged at what they saw as his betrayal.

King was now free to bring in conscription, but he was in no hurry to do it. He feared that conscription might trigger massive civil disorder in Quebec. He had once told a Liberal caucus that if conscription were brought in, "we would have to enlarge our jails and use our tanks and rifles against our own people." King summed up his position in the famous motto: "Not necessarily conscription, but conscription if necessary."

For a while, voluntary enlistments kept pace with the demand for new recruits. But after a time the flow of volunteers slowed, and the invasions of

CANADA'S WAR BRIDES

When World War II finally ended in the summer of 1945, Canadian soldiers were finally able to return home to civilian life. Many of them brought with them new wives and children, primarily from the United Kingdom. In total, 48 000 women came to Canada after World War II as brides of Canadian soldiers. These marriages, the product of chance meetings in the midst of war, drew together men and women of diverse backgrounds and personalities.

Often, women who had grown up in bustling cities such as London, England, found themselves wedded to a Canadian farmer from the Prairies or a coal miner from rural Nova Scotia. The experiences of Canada's war brides in adjusting to life in their new homes were sometimes sad and sometimes humorous. Following are a few of the stories told by the war brides.

Eunice Partington found a lot of happiness on her prairie farm. She tells us what being a war bride has meant to her:

As I look back on the past forty-six years, I thank Canada for what she has given me and I have no regrets as to the life I chose. Of course, I still glance back with fond memories of my days in England's green and pleasant land and hope that I will have the chance to return one more time in the near future, before I am laid to rest in the land I learned to love.

Many Canadian regiments were stationed near Shoreham by Sea, Sussex, during the war. Phyllis Clements met her husband, Joe, when he was on guard at a place called Buckingham Park, which was just a few minutes from her home. Her mother had taken their dog, Flash, for a walk and returned with the news that there was a very nice, shy soldier she had been speaking to at the park gates.

I immediately decided Flash needed another walk. I met Joe and started seeing him often. I was fifteen years old and, like many girls, just loved the uniform and accent. We became engaged in 1944. Joe had borrowed money from my mother until his payday to buy the ring in Brighton. I borrowed two bridesmaids' dresses from a girl I met in the hospital where I had my tonsils out. My poor mother had been very busy saving rations and scrimping to manage a lovely luncheon for our reception, which was held in our back garden.

Since most of these women had lived in large towns, it is easy to understand the shock they must have felt when they arrived in rural areas of Canada. "Tiny Red Head" Campbell describes what greeted her at her new home in Arthurette, New Brunswick:

No inside plumbing, no electricity, no gas, no facilities of any kind, and a little hand pump outside the house. The outhouse was by the barn, 300 feet away. My sister-in-law had an ugly rooster, Jimmy Duke. I guess he didn't like or trust an English accent, as every time I went out the door he came trotting. Therefore, I had to have someone escort me to the toilet and wait for me. It just stayed around and waited for me.

Source: From *Promise You'll Take Care of My Daughter*, by Ben Wicks. Reprinted with the permission of Stoddart Publishing Company Limited, Don Mills, Ontario.

Before leaving for Canada, a mother and daughter share an evening with grandparents, learning about the country that would become their new home.

Italy and France began taking their toll of Canadian soldiers. The Canadian forces lost 23 000 soldiers in Italy and France, most of them in the infantry. By 1944, the infantry replacement pools were drained.

Seeing that the last hope for volunteers had disappeared, King did an about-face on conscription. He agreed to conscript 16 000 for active duty, and about 12 000 NRMA conscripts were sent overseas. By the time they arrived in Europe, however, the war was winding down. Fewer than 2500 conscripts reached the front, where 69 were killed in action. King faced some political hostility for his switch to conscription. There were brief riots in Montreal, and a brigade of NRMA men in British Columbia commandeered their training camp and refused to move out. But King had secured the support of his young justice minister, Louis St. Laurent, before announcing conscription, and St. Laurent's presence helped soften public opinion in Quebec. In fact, King credited St. Laurent with saving both his government and Confederation.

The conscription crisis had once again divided the nation, and a bitter Quebec would not forget its treatment at the hands of English Canada. But in the election of 1945, Mackenzie King's Liberal Party still looked better to Quebec than the other parties did. The Liberal government was returned to power. Quebec was quiet, if not happy. The transition to peacetime went smoothly, and a more prosperous Canada looked forward to a new era of peace and security.

KNOWING THE KEY PEOPLE, PLACES, AND EVENTS

In your notes, clearly identify and explain the historical significance of each of the following:

- Japanese Internment
- National Selective Service
- "Dollar-a-Year Men"
- Hyde Park Declaration
- Wartime Prices and Trade Board
- National Resources Mobilization Act
- British Commonwealth Air Training Plan
- C.D. Howe
- Department of Munitions and Supplies
- James Ilsley
- "The Bren Girl"

FOCUS YOUR KNOWLEDGE

1. How did the naval activity in Halifax reflect the significance of Canada's role in the war effort?
2. Explain why the British Commonwealth Air Training Plan was critical to the Allied war effort.
3. How did the government's role in World War II differ from its role in World War I?
4. List three specific areas in which women's roles changed during World War II.
5. Who were the "Zombies"? Why did some refuse to fight overseas?
6. Explain what the phrase "Not necessarily conscription, but conscription if necessary" meant. Was this Mackenzie King's way of avoiding the issue, or was it a wise move to meet most people's demands?

APPLY YOUR KNOWLEDGE

1. After carefully studying a map of Canada, explain why Newfoundland would be vital to the defence of Canada if a serious invasion attempt were made. How did World War II help to hasten Newfoundland's entry in Confederation?
2. Was the internment of Japanese Canadians the product of paranoia or of racist attitudes in Canada? What can we do in the future to ensure the security of Canada without violating people's basic human rights?
3. Carefully examine the propaganda posters that appear in this chapter. Select the most effective poster and explain its appeal. How did the government use emotion to gain Canadians' support for the war effort?

4. How much power did the government have over industry during World War II? In which situation would you support such control by government over private enterprise: (a) only in wartime; (b) anytime; or (c) never? Defend your answer.

5. Why did the threat of rampant inflation exist during World War II? Prepare an organizer that lists the various boards and organizations set up by the government, indicates the role each played, and shows how effective each was in achieving its objectives.

6. As you can see from the organizer you prepared in response to question 5, World War II led to an increase in government involvement in social and economic affairs. Has this involvement led to a better Canada, or has it been bad for Canada? Defend your answer.

7. Prepare an organizer that shows the various ways in which women contributed to the war effort and the importance of each contribution to the war. How did postwar events reflect the limited change in society's perceptions of women's roles?

EXTEND YOUR KNOWLEDGE

1. Working in groups, research and create a large-scale map that shows the potential threats to Canada that existed during World War II. This map should show Japanese expansion in Asia and the South Pacific as well as marine and military activity on Canada's east and west coasts. Present your map to the class, and lead a discussion about the measures the government took or should have taken to ensure Canada's security.

2. Do some research into economic statistics for two periods: the 1930s and 1939–1945. Use your library to find figures relating to unemployment, gross national product, value of exports, and average incomes for these two periods. Using these statistics, construct bar and line graphs to illustrate the drastic changes in the Canadian economy. Consult your math teacher if you need further assistance.

3. Use one of the following themes to create a wartime poster designed to enlist Canadians' support in the war effort. Your poster should target a specific audience.

    (a) Recruitment

    (b) Saving material for the war effort

    (c) Buying Victory Bonds

    (d) Wartime secrecy

4. Write a diary entry from the perspective of a Japanese Canadian teenager who has been interned during World War II. Discuss your feelings about being Canadian yet unjustly imprisoned, the hardships you face, and your feelings toward Canada after your release.

CHAPTER 14 CANADA'S ROLE IN ENDING THE WAR

GLOSSARY TERMS

Flak Anti-aircraft fire from guns directed at enemy combat planes.
Squadrons The basic tactical units of the air force.
Ruhr An important mining and industrial region in Germany, centred on the Ruhr River Valley.
Incendiary Bombs Specially adapted bombs used for setting property on fire.
Sampans Flat-bottomed boats used to navigate the rivers and harbours of China.
Sherman Tank A U.S.-made tank commonly used in World War II.
Brigades Large bodies of troops, usually consisting of several regiments, battalions, or squadrons.

FOCUS ON:

- air warfare over Britain
- how Hitler's nearly successful invasion of the Soviet Union led to Germany's defeat
- why the Japanese launched a surprise attack on Pearl Harbor
- Canadians at the Battle of Hong Kong
- the controversy surrounding the Battle of Dieppe
- Canada's role in the recapturing of Italy
- victory on the Western Front and the Normandy campaign
- the persecution of the Jews and Nazi death camps
- the development and use of the atomic bomb

In June 1940, only 35 kilometres of cold, grey water stood between the victorious German Wehrmacht and the British coast. Adolf Hitler had conquered almost all of Europe. All that remained outside his grasp were the British Isles to the west and the Soviet Union to the east. Without the watery barrier of the English Channel, Britain would have fallen to the Nazis as quickly as France had. Hitler had already drawn up a plan for the invasion of Britain under the code name **Operation Sea Lion**. It called for the landing of twenty-five divisions along the south coast of England and a quick thrust forward to take London. But the panzer (tank) divisions that were the key to the German invasion forces, as well as the infantry troops and motorized equipment that rolled in behind them, could only reach Britain by ship. To control the ocean route to Britain, however, Germany first had to seize control of the air.

THE BATTLE OF BRITAIN

The bombing of civilian targets such as London became a horrifying aspect of World War II. Why were these bombings referred to as "terror bombings"? Can they be justified as a necessary part of war?

On July 10, 1940, Hitler let loose a savage air attack on British ships in the English Channel. The **Battle of Britain** had begun. By mid-August, nearly 2000 German aircraft were swarming the skies over Britain. The British air force was small by comparison, only about half the size of the German Luftwaffe. The future of the British people, and perhaps of North Americans as well, depended on the success of just a few fighter pilots.

At first the Luftwaffe was devastatingly successful, knocking out airfields and supply factories with ruthless efficiency. The Royal Air Force (RAF) could do little to counter the German attack. Then, a blunder by two night-flying Luftwaffe pilots gave Britain the opening it needed. On August 24, two airplanes that were bombing aircraft factories and oil storage tanks along the Thames River strayed off course. When they ran into *flak*, the pilots realized that they were lost. They released their bombs to lighten their aircraft and turned for home.

What the pilots did did not know was that they were flying over London, a city that Hitler had declared off-limits for German bomb attacks. Churchill ordered bombing raids on Berlin in reprisal. Hitler was outraged, and at a mass rally in Berlin he promised Germans that the British would suffer for the raids: "We will raze their cities to the ground."

The bombing raids on Berlin goaded Hitler into changing his successful tactics against the British. The Luftwaffe stopped concentrating on airfields and factories and turned to attack British cities, especially London. But now the RAF knew where the Germans would attack, and they were ready and waiting. The German attacks peaked on September 15, when more than 1000 Luftwaffe bombers and nearly 700 fighters flew over London in a daring all-out daylight raid. RAF Spitfires and Hurricanes climbed high to meet them, and the sky over London was streaked with vapour trails from aerial combat. The Luftwaffe's losses that day were heavy enough to convince the Germans that their tactics were not working. Germany had failed to seize air supremacy over the English Channel, and Operation Sea Lion was abandoned.

CANADA'S CONTRIBUTIONS TO THE WAR IN THE AIR

Canadians were often in the thick of the air war, both in the Battle of Britain and afterward in Europe, Africa, and the Pacific. A quarter of a million Canadians served in the RAF and the Royal Canadian Air Force (RCAF) as air crews, ground crews, transport crews, and flight instructors. By the end of the war, 17 101 members of the RCAF had died in battle. The RCAF fatalities were equal to the number of infantry deaths in Europe. The casualty figures show how important war in the air had become.

Canadians flew all kinds of airplanes during the war, and the fighting was often vicious. Some flyers provided air cover for infantry or armoured divisions in North Africa. When the Luftwaffe's daylight raids over England had almost stopped, RAF and RCAF fighter and bomber *squadrons* began to make raids on German-occupied France. Canadian bomber units attacked German air bases, gun positions, rail and road traffic, and military headquarters in France.

Although Canadian bomber crews were not in the centre of public attention, their work was dangerous and their casualty rates terrifyingly high. Canadian bomber units became experts at night-bombing techniques against targets. On their night missions, their job was to fly "blind" in the darkness to bomb targets deep inside Germany.

By mid-1943, Canadian crews flying Lancaster and Halifax bombers were dropping huge loads of high explosives on German factories and steel mills in the *Ruhr*. They also rained destruction on German civilians in the cities of Hamburg, Frankfurt, and Berlin. On July 24, 1943, 800 bombers destroyed the port of Hamburg. Three days later, they returned to drop *incendiary bombs* into the smoking ruins of the city. The bombs touched off a terrible firestorm that killed almost 50 000 men, women, and children. A week later, the bombers hit the ruins of Hamburg for a third time.

Hitler denounced the attacks on Hamburg and other German cities as "terror bombing." Although Germany had begun the bombing of civilian targets in raids on Warsaw, Rotterdam, London, and Coventry, the Allies perfected the strategy. Hitler was forced to pull the Luftwaffe back to protect German cities and industrial sites from Allied bombing raids. By mid-1944, the Allies ruled the skies over Europe. The Luftwaffe was in full retreat.

GERMANY'S INVASION OF THE SOVIET UNION

After being thwarted in the Battle of Britain, Germany turned to confront its enemy to the east. On June 22, 1941, Hitler took the biggest gamble of the war by launching a massive attack on the Soviet Union. Code-named **Operation Barbarossa**, the blitzkrieg ended the Nazi–Soviet Pact, and the Soviet Union suddenly found itself in the Allied camp. Hitler was sure that the blitzkrieg would bring the Soviet Union to its knees within months, but he badly miscalculated. He underestimated the Soviets' will to resist and

Canadian World War II flying ace George Beurling is shown here recording another of his hits on the side of his plane.

counted on capturing Moscow and most of the Soviet army before winter set in. However, the sheer size of the Soviet Union and the harsh Russian winter would finally beat Hitler.

In Operation Barbarossa, the Nazis used the blitzkrieg on a much larger scale than ever before. At first the Soviets were unable to stop the German forces and suffered more than 1 million casualties — more than double the German casualty toll. But, even though the tactics of blitzkrieg were as successful as ever, Russia was so huge that a quick victory was almost impossible. The Soviet army could keep retreating into an almost unlimited country.

By late fall 1941, the Wehrmacht had reached the outskirts of Moscow. They had, however, expected to reach Moscow well before winter and were unprepared for temperatures as low as −50°C. It was so cold that German soldiers sometimes found their soup frozen solid before they had time to eat it. They had no warm winter clothing and no antifreeze or oils suitable for the cold-weather operation of their tanks and transport vehicles. As a result, they suffered terribly in the bitter Russian winter. Meanwhile, tough, warmly clad Siberian troops had been brought in to defend Moscow. They were ready for winter fighting and stopped the Wehrmacht just over 50 kilometres from the city.

Hitler's gamble had failed. The Soviet army, though bloodied, fought back. A quick, decisive victory had escaped the German troops. They were locked into a long hard war against a Soviet army with huge reserves of soldiers at its call.

THE WAR IN THE PACIFIC

About the same time that Operation Barbarossa ground to a halt in the Russian winter, U.S. naval ships were swinging at anchor in the Hawaiian waters of **Pearl Harbor**. Relations between Japan and the western nations had reached the breaking point, and the United States had stationed its naval fleet in Hawaii in case war broke out in the Pacific Ocean. Britain had also decided to strengthen its forces in the region, but few troops could be spared from the defence of the British Isles. Britain asked Canada to help by sending Canadian soldiers to the British colony of Hong Kong, on the south coast of China. By early December 1941, two Canadian brigades had settled into the British garrison at Hong Kong.

The Attack on Pearl Harbor

Meanwhile, the United States tried to hammer out a peace treaty with Japan. What no one in the West knew was that the Japanese had decide to make war on the United States and Britain three months earlier. The peace talks were meant to keep the Allies off guard while Japan prepared for the attack. Japan aimed to conquer the West's resource-rich colonies in East Asia and the Pacific.

The only major barrier to a Japanese victory in the East was the U.S. fleet at Pearl Harbor, which was out of reach of a Japanese land-based attack. Japanese Admiral Isoroku Yamamoto planned a surprise attack using fighter planes launched from Japanese aircraft carriers. Attacks on the U.S. base

The spectacular Japanese attack on Pearl Harbor jolted the Americans out of their neutrality and brought them into the war against Japan and Germany. How important do you think their entry into the war was in the eventual defeat of fascism?

in the Philippines and the British possessions of Malaya and Hong Kong were also planned for the same date — December 7, 1941.

At 8 a.m., the first wave of Japanese war planes appeared in the sky over Pearl Harbor and began bombing their targets. Japan had not declared war on the United States, and no one in Hawaii expected an attack. When the surprise attack ended less than two hours later, almost nothing was left of the American Pacific fleet. Eighteen warships and 349 aircraft were lost or damaged, and 3581 American combatants and 103 civilians were killed or injured.

The United States Enters the War

Now the United States was in the war, and victory seemed almost certain. In 1941, the United States was the richest nation in the world. With the world's largest steel industry and a population ten times larger than Canada's, the United States could invest enormous amounts of money, arms, and personnel into the war effort. It would take time for the Americans to mobilize for war, but once they did, the Allies could begin planning to liberate Europe. Meanwhile, Canada and the other Allied nations still faced a bloody struggle in Europe and the Far East.

The Canadians at Hong Kong

Just a few hours after the attack on Pearl Harbor, Japan began its invasion of Hong Kong. When the invasion ended, every Canadian soldier in Hong Kong had either been killed or captured by the Japanese. Why were two battalions, the Royal Rifles of Canada and the Winnipeg Grenadiers, sent into a deathtrap? This question has haunted many Canadians. One bitter veteran said about Hong Kong, "They sent us into a position where we'd either be killed in action or be taken prisoner. There was no escape. Only Mackenzie King knows why were were sent there.… The lost years. The pain. The lost lives."

What the Canadians in Hong Kong did not know was that before the attack on Pearl Harbor, more than 50 000 Japanese soldiers had been massed within 50 kilometres of Hong Kong for an invasion. They were well equipped and hardened by four years of fighting in China. The Japanese plans for conquering Hong Kong had been laid out more than a year before under the code-name Hana-Saku — "flowers in bloom, flowers in bloom."

The Canadian soldiers, by comparison, were unready for battle. The troops were classified as C Force: "in need of refresher training or insufficiently trained and not recommended for operations." Almost 30 percent of the Canadian soldiers had never fired a shot in rifle practice. The raw Canadian troops joined a small Commonwealth defence force that totalled no more than 14 000 people, including nurses and civilian volunteers. Although the Canadians were garrisoned on the Chinese mainland, their job was to defend positions on the nearby island of Hong Kong.

On December 8, 1941 (December 7 across the international dateline in Canada), Japan launched its attack on Hong Kong. Less than two weeks later, Canadian troops heard the first wailing of air raid sirens. The Japanese air force destroyed docks, military barracks, gun emplacements, and the five old RAF airplanes on the British airfield. Now the defenders had no protection in the air. They also had no help from the sea: the U.S. fleet had been crippled at Pearl Harbor, and the two great British warships, *Prince of Wales* and *Repulse*, were sunk by the Japanese off Malaya.

The defence forces on the mainland were far too small and had too few guns to withstand the Japanese attack. The troops were ordered to retreat across the water to Hong Kong Island, and many Canadian soldiers believed that Hong Kong would never be captured. But, as darkness closed in on December 18, 1941, thousands of Japanese troops began crossing the strait to Hong Kong Island in collapsible boats and *sampans*.

CANADIAN PRISONERS OF WAR IN JAPAN

World War II is remembered for the brutality inflicted on humans in all aspects of war, and Canadian soldiers stationed in Hong Kong faced some of the most barbaric treatment. From the fall of Hong Kong in 1941 until the end of the war, Canadians were brutalized and starved in Japanese prisoner-of-war camps.

In December 1941, the Japanese launched an invasion of the British colony of Hong Kong. In the key Battle for Wong Nei Chong Gap, 100 British and Canadian soldiers managed to hold off two Japanese regiments for some time. But they were greatly outnumbered, and with surrender came horror for those Canadians taken as prisoners. The wounded Canadian and British soldiers were murdered where they lay, and their bodies were burned.

When the Japanese troops entered Hong Kong, further atrocities were committed. A private school had temporarily been converted to a field hospital and was crowded with wounded Canadian, British, and Indian soldiers. On the morning of December 25, 1941, Japanese soldiers stormed the hospital. When doctors and nurses tried to surrender, they were brutally killed.

Many expected that the suffering would end with the official surrender of the British to Japan. But the prisoners did not receive humane treatment in the prisoner-of-war camps. For the next three and a half years, Canadians were crowded into barracks and used as slave labour. Some were put to work building landing strips; others worked in shipyards near Tokyo; and yet others worked in coal mines in northern Japan.

The prisoners were given only a single serving of plain rice three times a day. Those who fell ill from exhaustion, malnutrition, or diseases such as pneumonia, diphtheria, or cholera had little chance of survival. Red Cross packages destined for the camps were seized and sold on the black market. Medicines were also withheld, leaving camp doctors powerless to help the sick. As a result of the appalling conditions, the death rate in Japanese prisoner-of-war camps was six times higher than in German camps.

During the summer of 1945, all surviving Canadian prisoners of war were sent to work in coal mines, and the order was given that if Japan were invaded, all prisoners were to be executed. Following the dropping of the atomic bombs on Hiroshima and Nagasaki, this order was voided and the emperor announced the surrender of Japan. The agony of the Canadian soldiers was finally over.

These Canadian soldiers survived the harsh conditions of the Japanese prisoner-of-war camps. Here they intently listen to Japanese Emperor Hirohito announcing the unconditional surrender of Japan. Their ordeal is finally over.

On December 19, the Winnipeg Grenadiers, looking down into a place called Happy Valley, were startled to see hundreds of bushes advancing up the hill toward them. Japanese soldiers, using bushes as camouflage, were on the attack. The Canadians were outnumbered by ten to one, and on Christmas Day 1941 Hong Kong officially surrendered. The battle had lasted only seventeen days. In all, 286 Canadians died in action or were killed afterward by Japanese soldiers. But the worst was yet to come for Canadians taken prisoner. Another 266 Canadians would die in Japanese prisoner-of-war camps.

THE WAR IN EUROPE, 1942–1945

In Europe, the tide of war was about to turn in favour of the Allies. But before it did, Canada suffered another tragedy on the battlefield — the **Battle of Dieppe**.

The Battle of Dieppe

In August 1942, 5000 Canadian troops stationed in England were picked for a raid on the French port of Dieppe. They had been trained in England for almost three years. Along with another thousand British commandos and American Rangers, the Canadians were to attack the strongly defended port. The raid on Dieppe was launched to find out what was needed to make a full-scale Allied invasion across the English Channel a success. It was also intended to draw German forces away from the Russian front.

The defeat of Canadian soldiers came almost before the attack began. Well-placed German defence forces fired down on the landing craft from high cliffs above the beaches. Many Canadians were killed as they charged down the ramps of the landing crafts. The few who made it onto the beaches were killed as they raced for cover. Only a few soldiers made it into the town of Dieppe, where they took on the German defenders in close combat.

The casualty toll in those few bleak hours at Dieppe recalled the mass deaths of World War I. The Canadian magazine *Saturday Night* called Dieppe "another Passchendaele." Of the 5000 Canadians who sailed for Dieppe, almost 1000 died and more than 500 were wounded. Almost 2000 Canadians were captured and became prisoners of war.

Despite the tragedy at Dieppe, the war began to shift in favour of the Allies. Big American armies were taking the field against the Axis powers, and the Soviet army was holding off the German Wehrmacht. After six months of fierce fighting at Stalingrad, the Soviets managed to encircle the German forces, cut off their supply lines, and reduce them to starvation. Now the tables were turned. By April 1945, the Soviet troops were marching into the German capital of Berlin. In North Africa, the British general, Bernard Montgomery, had scored a major victory at El Alamein. His troops defeated the Afrika Korps of the famous German general, Erwin Rommel, known

This painting by Canadian war artist Charles Comfort depicts the ill-fated Dieppe raid of August 1942. Here the Canadian assault is moving up the pebbled shingle beach in front of Dieppe's Casino.

as "the Desert Fox." At the same time, the Allies made landings at Algeria and Morocco and began moving east across North Africa. These events marked important successes for the Allies.

Canadians in Sicily and the Italian Campaign

By the summer of 1943, Canadian soldiers had been in Britain for almost three and a half years, waiting for a chance to fight. On June 26, the word came at last: they were told to pack up their bedrolls and get ready to move out.

The Canadians were headed for Sicily, the island just off the toe of the Italian "boot." There they would join the British Eighth Army under the hero of El Alamein, General Montgomery. The battle plan was to invade Sicily and trap German and Italian soldiers between the British Eighth Army and the U.S. Seventh Army before they could escape to Italy. From Sicily, it was a short jump onto the Italian mainland. The next step was to attack Italy, the weakest of the Axis powers.

When the first Canadian troops were preparing to wade ashore onto Sicily on July 10, 1943, they could hear assault troops blazing away with rifles and automatics. One soldier said, "Dieppe was in our minds. We wondered how many of us would live through the day." But the invasion took the Italians by surprise, and the Canadian force made its landing without casualties.

Sicily fell fairly quickly, and many Italians were captured. The Allied "trap" had closed too slowly, however, and tens of thousands of German troops escaped to Italy. The Allies were now ready to invade the Italian mainland. Canadians were part of the Allied forces that moved from Sicily to the toe of the Italian boot. They landed on September 3, 1943, and began moving up the Italian peninsula. Fresh Canadian troops from Britain joined in the attack.

The mountainous Italian countryside was a nightmare for Allied troops. Although Italy surrendered in September 1943, little changed for the Allies because German soldiers took over the country. The German defenders had built a line of fortified hilltops and mountain peaks that ran the length of Italy. The soldiers of the Wehrmacht were also experienced fighters. As a result, it cost the Allies far more in men and equipment to capture German positions than it cost the Germans to defend them. But the Allies were slowly gaining ground; by the late autumn of 1943, the Canadians had moved 650 kilometres up the central mountains of Italy. The Allies were on their way to Rome. The Germans, however, ensured that there was no safe way to get there.

The Canadians at Ortona

As Christmas approached, the Allies found that their route toward Rome was blocked at **Ortona**, an ancient town situated on cliffs above the Adriatic Sea. The Canadian forces were ordered to capture Ortona. The Germans had blown up all bridges in the area, and the steep countryside gave them the advantage. The German defenders were the first-rate 90th Light Panzer Grenadier Division, famed for their tough fighting in North Africa.

Two days after Christmas, the Canadians captured Ortona. The town fell to a

After landing in Sicily, Italy, in the summer of 1943, these tanks of the Three Rivers Regiment rumbled through the devastated town of Regalbuto in support of the 1st Canadian Division.

regiment from Edmonton, and for weeks afterward, a sign stood in Ortona that read, "A West Canadian Town." But the Canadian losses were high; since crossing the Moro River, the 1st Canadian Division had lost 2339 soldiers. Sixteen thousand more had to be evacuated because of sickness or battle fatigue.

In the spring and summer of 1944, the Canadian forces were assigned to fight in the centre of the Italian peninsula. They played an important role in breaking the line of German defences. By June 1944, the Allies had succeeded in capturing Rome. Canadian forces continued to fight in Italy until February 1945, when all Canadian troops were reunited in northwestern Europe as the 1st Canadian Army.

D-Day and the Normandy Invasion

Two days after capturing Rome, the Allied forces invaded France. The lessons of Dieppe were taken to heart in planning the invasion. Massive air and naval firepower and better communications from ship to shore were put in place. New versions of the *Sherman tank*, called "Funnies," were built. They could wade through water, bulldoze obstacles, explode mines, and throw bursts of flame. Allied soldiers worked hard to prepare for action. By early June, more than 30 000 Canadians were ready to do their part on "**D-Day**," the day scheduled for the Allied invasion of Europe.

The invasion plan called for five divisions to land along an 80-kilometre front. American forces were to attack at the western end of Normandy Beach, and British and Canadian troops were to land farther to the east. The 3rd Canadian Division was to land with the first wave of attackers in an area called Juno Beach. The sky above Juno Beach was to be protected by RAF bombers, many of which were flown by Canadian bomber crews. The invasion force also included 171 air squadrons to knock out the German Luftwaffe and destroy enemy tanks. More than 7000 Allied ships of all descriptions — navy landing craft, destroyers, cruisers, corvettes, frigates, torpedo boats, and minesweepers — were also scheduled for the invasion.

D-Day Begins

It took enormous care and great good luck to keep the massive invasion plans secret, but the Allies had done it. As dawn broke on June 6, 1944, surprised German defenders looked out to see a huge flotilla of ships sweeping toward the French coast. "As far as

In June 1944, Canadians joined the Americans and the British in launching the Normandy invasion. This photo shows soldiers struggling ashore in an attempt to establish a beachhead.

FARLEY MOWAT'S WORLD WAR II EXPERIENCE

Like many young men in 1939, Farley Mowat envisioned war as a great romantic adventure. When he sailed for England in July 1942, Mowat was eager to see action. The horrors he encountered on the battlefield quickly shattered any illusions he held. As part of the Canadian force that landed at Sicily and drove north through Italy, Mowat was engaged in bloody, fierce fighting.

Since returning to Canada, Farley Mowat has become one of Canada's best-known authors and has written classics such as *Lost In the Barrens* and *Never Cry Wolf*. The excerpts below are taken from his book *And No Birds Sang*, which has been described as his finest work. In this gripping war story, Mowat tells of his own experiences and the reality of war. As you read these excerpts, reflect on Mowat's message to the reader. Do you think Mowat would support another war? If so, under what circumstances? If not, why not?

[A note to his parents before leaving Canada]
Thank heavens, this is it! It's worth two years of waiting. A couple of months' battle training with the Regiment and then, praise be, we'll get a show to try our talents on…. Apart from you two, I don't in the least regret leaving Canada even though there is the chance I may not see it again. If we get a damn good lick in at the Hun, it'll be worth it….

[Recollections of a battle]
One…dash took me close to a hut whose partly collapsed stone walls still seemed capable of providing some protection, and the banshee screech of Moaning Minnie rockets sent me scuttling frantically toward this ruin. I reached it just as the bombs exploded a few score yards away. The blast flung me through the empty doorway with such violence that I sprawled full-length on top of a prone human figure who emitted a horrid gurgling belch. It was an unconscious protest, for he and two of his three companions — gray-clad paratroopers — were dead, their bodies mired in the muck and goat manure on the floor. The fourth man—dimly seen in that dim place — was sitting upright in a corner of the little unroofed room and his eyes met mine as I struggled to my hands and knees.

In that instant I was so convinced I had had it—that he would shoot me where I knelt—that I did not even try to reach for the carbine slung across my back. I remained transfixed for what seemed an interminable time, then in an unconscious reflex effort to cheat death, I flung myself sideways and rolled to my feet. I was lurching through the doorway when his thin voice reached me.
"Vasser…haff…you…vasser?"

I checked my rush and swung up against the outer wall, knowing then that I was safe, that he posed no threat. And I felt an inexplicable sense of recognition, almost as if I had heard his voice before. Cautiously I peered back through the doorway.

His left hand was clasping the shattered stump where his right arm had been severed just below the elbow. Dark gore was still gouting between his fingers and spreading in a black pool about his outthrust legs. Most dreadful was a great gash in his side from which protruded a glistening dark mass which must have been his liver. Above this wreckage, his eyes were large and luminous in a young man's face, pallid to the point of translucency.
"Vasser…please giff…vasser."

Reluctantly I shook my head. "Sorry, chum, I've got none. Nein vasser. Only rum, and that's no good for you."

The eyes, so vividly alive in the dying body, pleaded with me. Oh, hell, I thought, he's going anyway. What harm!

I held the water bottle to his lips and he swallowed in deep, spasmodic gulps until I took it back and drank from it myself. And so…and so the two of us got drunk together. And in a little while he died….

The blanket that screened the shattered cellar door was thrust aside and a party of stretcher-bearers pushed in among us. Al Park lay on one of the stretchers. He was alive, though barely so…unconscious, with a bullet in his head.

As I looked down at his faded, empty face under its crown of crimson bandages, I began to weep.

I wonder now…were my tears for Alex and Al and all the others who had gone and who were yet to go? Or was I weeping for myself…and those who would remain?

Source: Reprinted with permission of Farley Mowat Limited.

your eye could see, there were ships," said one sailor aboard the Canadian minesweeper *Canso*. "I always said that if you could jump a hundred yards at a clip you could get back to England without even wetting your feet. That's how many ships were involved."

The invasion did not go perfectly because some of the German positions had not been knocked out by the massive Allied air and sea bombardments. Many soldiers had to scramble for cover across exposed beaches raked with artillery fire. The landing of the 3rd Canadian Division was delayed by reefs and choppy seas for an hour and a half. By the time the Canadian forces touched down on Juno Beach, the enemy was ready for them. The worst trouble, however, occurred in the American sector at Omaha Beach. American forces were at the mercy of German defenders who fired down at them from high ground. Casualties were heavy, and the Americans lost 7500 soldiers.

Despite the heavy setbacks, the invasion was considered a success. By the end of D-Day, more than 155 000 soldiers, 6000 vehicles, and 3600 tonnes of supplies had been landed in France. The fighting on the beaches had destroyed the defending German division, and Allied forces moved inland.

The Canadians had pushed to within 5 kilometres of the city of Caen, farther inland than any other Allied troops. Canadian losses were also lower than had been feared. Still, almost a thousand Canadian soldiers were killed, wounded, or captured that day.

Germany was now fighting the land war on three fronts: the Soviet Union, Italy, and France. On the Eastern Front, the Soviet Union continued to drive Germany back. In Italy, the Allies were pressing north. A new invasion through France would almost certainly mean the defeat of Germany.

The Drive into Germany

As the Allies drove toward the Rhine River, Hitler made a last attempt to hold off the inevitable defeat. He extended the age limits for armed service to take in all German males between 16 and 50 years of age. As a result, he managed to muster 750 000 soldiers and 3000 tanks to push back the advancing Allied forces. But this last desperate German gamble failed, and the remains of the Wehrmacht were forced to retreat. Although the last German assault made no difference to Germany's fate, it probably changed the map of postwar Europe. The attack delayed the western Allies' advance for six or eight weeks and gave the Soviet Union vital time to sprint across eastern Europe and seize territory during its drive toward Berlin.

By the end of March 1945, the Allies had crossed the Rhine River from the west and invaded Germany. By April 30, the first Soviet troops were picking their way through the rubble of Berlin. Some troops were already within blocks of the bomb-proof bunker, deep under the chancellery building, where Hitler had gone into hiding. Hitler and his companion, Eva Braun, carried out a suicide pact. Their bodies were carried out of the bunker, doused with gasoline, and set ablaze. Meanwhile, in Italy, the Fascist dictator Benito Mussolini had been captured and killed as he tried to escape to Switzerland.

Movement of Allied Forces 1944–1945

As the end of war in Europe neared, the German army was pushed out of eastern Europe by the Soviet Union and out of western Europe by a coalition of nations, including Britain, Canada, and the United States.

THE NAZI CONCENTRATION CAMPS AND GERMAN ANTI-SEMITISM

The aftermath of war revealed a fresh legacy of Nazi horror. Canadians had heard rumours of Nazi concentration camps, but many had believed that the rumours were only war propaganda. What the Allies found when they arrived at the concentration camps was indescribable: piles of corpses, mass graves, camp survivors so starved they looked like walking skeletons. Millions of people had been murdered and had died of disease or starvation in Nazi concentration camps. They included political prisoners, communists, certain religious groups such as Jehovah's Witnesses, homosexuals, prisoners of war, resistance fighters, and ethnic groups such as Gypsies and Poles. But the single largest group was European Jews. Six million Jews were murdered by the Nazis in mass murders that came to be called the **Holocaust**, the attempted extermination of the Jews.

German Persecution of the Jews

Anti-Semitism — hatred of Jews — was a key element in Nazism. Hitler blamed the Jews for Germany's failures, and Nazis persecuted Jewish Germans mercilessly throughout the 1930s, despite the fact that Jews had lived in Germany for centuries and had become part of the life of the community.

When World War II began, the persecution of Jews moved into a new and terrible phase. When Germany invaded Poland in 1939, almost 3 million Jews fell into Nazi hands. When it conquered Denmark, Norway, the Netherlands, and France, hundreds of thousands more fell under Nazi control. Jews were forced to leave their homes and were crowded into slums called ghettos. Often, several families shared a single room. The Nazis also forced the Jews to wear the yellow Star of David and to work as labourers for the Nazi regime. Food was in such short supply and living conditions so brutal in the ghettos that thousands of Jews died of starvation and disease.

As the Nazis were driven out of western and eastern Europe, the full extent of the atrocities committed in death camps and concentration camps came to light. This man, standing in the mud at Auschwitz, shows the effects of the deprivation that victims of the Holocaust suffered. Millions died in these camps. They were executed, gassed, starved, or simply worked to death.

The Holocaust: The "Final Solution"

When the Wehrmacht marched into the Soviet Union in 1941, the Nazis began to work on another solution to the "Jewish problem." The Wehrmacht was followed by special SS (Schutzstaffel) "action squads." These Nazi death squads began the mass execution of Jews during the winter of 1941–42, when half a million people were shot to death. The Russian holocaust sealed the fate of European Jews and began one of the most frightful episodes in history. In January 1942, top SS officials met in the Berlin suburb of Wannsee to work out the details of the Endlosung, "the final solution of the Jewish problem." They prepared a plan for secretly murdering 11 million Jews in Europe.

After the **Wannsee Conference**, the Nazis began to step up the construction of huge gas chambers at specially constructed death camps. The ghettos of Europe served as holding places until enough concentration camps were ready. Then "consignments of Jews" were rounded up by ghetto police and delivered to the SS for shipment to Nazi concentration camps at Auschwitz, Treblinka, Bergen-Belsen, and elsewhere.

The death camps were run by the SS units known as "Death's Head *Brigades*." When the deported Jews arrived at the camps they were separated into two groups. Those who could work were kept alive as slave labour. One prisoner describes what he saw on his first day in a work camp: "We're at a gravel-pit, prisoners in striped clothing are shovelling gravel. Emaciated. Covered with wounds from blows. A Capo (supervisor) shouts and beats the prisoners with the handle of a shovel. Actually they're walking skeletons. Will we one day look like this, too?" The hard labour under conditions of great cruelty was intended to result in death. Slave labour was called "productive annihilation."

Those who were unable to work — mostly the elderly, mothers, and children — were immediately killed in the gas chambers. To prevent resistance, prisoners were tricked into believing that they were getting ready for deportation. Treblinka, for example, had a fake front that resembled a large railway station. Signs directed new arrivals to onward trains, and the station even featured a painted clock. In some camps, the gas chambers were disguised as shower rooms. Some prisoners, after being told that they were being sent to Canada, were ordered to place all their belongings in a "Canada Room." Then they were herded into the deadly "shower rooms." In Auschwitz, about 2000 people at a time could be gassed. When the gas chamber was full of adults, small children were shoved in over their heads. Then, deadly Zyklon-B gas was released into the sealed chamber.

Word of the secret slaughter began to filter out of the death camps. Jews in Warsaw and other European ghettos bravely fought back, even though they were far outnumbered and mostly unarmed. It took the Nazis months of fighting to put down the resistance in Warsaw. They finally destroyed the Warsaw ghetto by systematically blowing up houses.

It is estimated that by the end of the war, almost two-thirds of the Jews of Europe had lost their lives. Only about 1 million people survived the Nazi death camps. When the first photographs of death-camp survivors were published, the world was horrified. How could a thing like this happen? Today the horror of the Holocaust remains. For us the question is, How can we keep anything like this from ever happening again?

THE ATOMIC BOMB AND VICTORY IN THE PACIFIC

By 1944, the United States had retaken New Guinea, the Solomon Islands, and the Philippines from Japan. By early 1945, the British Commonwealth forces, with the support of China, had retaken Burma. The Japanese fleet was almost destroyed, and a circle was slowly closing around the Japanese army. But the Japanese were digging in and fighting a tough defensive war from tunnels and prepared positions. When American forces invaded Okinawa in March 1945, the 100 000 Japanese soldiers fought almost to the last person. Japanese pilots were flying suicide missions called kamikaze attacks. They deliberately crashed aircraft crammed with dynamite into U.S. warships, killing themselves as well as many U.S. sailors.

Some U.S. military leaders believed that Japan was too proud to surrender. To invade Japan, they argued,

THE LOST ART OF AUSCHWITZ

Auschwitz is perhaps the most infamous of the Nazi death camps. Here, between May 1940 and January 1945, nearly 2 million people were murdered, 90 percent of them Jews. As in all concentration camps, having a specialized skill was often the key to saving one's life or at least delaying death. Physicians, architects, engineers, mechanics, tailors, musicians, dentists, barbers, carpenters, shoemakers, and artists were all pressed into service by the Nazis. Artists in the concentration camps were forced to create propaganda art, such as posters celebrating Hitler's birthday, or to paint swastikas and eagles on captured tanks.

Many of the artists placed themselves at great risk by secretly painting images of their lives in the camps. Some of these paintings, hidden from the eyes of their Nazis captors, have been uncovered since the end of World War II. Included in the art that has been uncovered are murals depicting the work done in the penal company, prisoners in a rock quarry, washroom decorations, and slogans.

Ballerina Block 18, basement Main Camp

The Penal Company "Königsgraben" Birkenau, Block 1

The secret art of the inmates of Auschwitz served a dual function; it kept their spirits alive and became a record of life in the camps. The famous artist Pablo Picasso wrote, "Painting is an instrument of war to be waged against brutality and darkness." Such was the purpose of the "lost" art of Auschwitz.

The Pacific in 1941–1942

would mean huge military and civilian casualties. But the United States had a terrifying new instrument of war — the atomic bomb. The new U.S. president, Harry Truman, believed that the atomic bomb could force Japan to surrender without an invasion that might cost half a million American lives.

Making the Atomic Bomb

The American government had earlier decided to work on the invention of an atomic bomb by forming the top-secret **Manhattan Project**. Working under tight security, a group of scientists led by the brilliant physicist Robert Oppenheimer attempted to solve a wide range of theoretical and technical problems relating to the atomic bomb. Their aim was to have the bomb ready by mid-1945. It was a race against time, because Nazi Germany was thought to be working on the same problems.

Canada's Contribution to the Manhattan Project

In 1942, Canada was asked by Britain to help in the secret scientific project. The British wanted to create a laboratory out of reach of the Luftwaffe and close to the United States. The laboratory was built in Montreal in 1943, but by then it was too late to make a difference to the atomic weapons program. However, uranium was needed for the U.S. bomb. A uranium mine at Great Bear Lake in the Northwest Territories was secretly bought by the Canadian government to supply uranium for the U.S. project. Canada also had the only uranium refinery outside Nazi-occupied Europe, at Port Hope, Ontario.

Dropping the Atomic Bomb

By July 1945, word reached President Truman that the atomic bomb was ready. On July 26, he called for Japan to surrender or accept "prompt and utter destruction." He promised that if Japan surrendered, its economy, culture, and traditions would remain unchanged. The Japanese prime minister, Kantaro Suzuki, replied that his government would *mokusatsu*

Although the use of nuclear bombs brought a quick end to the war, it left the cities of Hiroshima and Nagasaki in ruins. Have nuclear weapons made the cost of war too high for us to allow another major conflict to erupt?

CANADIAN SOVEREIGNTY: A NATION COMES OF AGE

As with World War I, Canada's experience in World War II did a great deal to further strengthen Canadian sovereignty and build Canada's international reputation. When Britain declared war on September 3, 1939, it could no longer assume Canadian participation. Instead, Canadian Prime Minister Mackenzie King insisted that Parliament be allowed to decide on Canada's participation. Although the outcome of the debate in Parliament was never in doubt, the principle of allowing Canada's elected officials to decide what role the nation would play was critical to Canadian sovereignty.

By 1945, Canada's horizons had been broadened by the experiences of the war and its aftermath. Ralph Allen claimed, "No country in the world was more confident than Canada, or had better cause to be." The war had earned Canada respect in the world, as was reflected in its role in the creation of both the United Nations and the North Atlantic Treaty Organization. Canadian science had also come of age by 1945. Canada had played an important scientific role by helping to develop everything from synthetic rubber and penicillin to atomic power.

Canada's participation in World War II did much to establish its international reputation, a reputation it has maintained to this day.

---

the Allied demand — "kill it with silence." Truman and his military advisers decided against a demonstration of the bomb's awful powers to scare the Japanese into surrender. Instead, Truman decided to drop the bomb on a Japanese city.

On August 6, 1945, an American B-29 bomber, the *Enola Gay*, flew over **Hiroshima**, Japan's seventh-largest city. The *Enola Gay* carried an atomic bomb called "Little Boy." At 8:15 a.m., the United States dropped the "Little Boy" on Hiroshima. It was the first nuclear bomb ever used in war. More than 70 000 people were killed and 61 000 were injured; 20 000 of the dead and missing were schoolchildren. Only 10 percent of the Japanese who had been within 500 metres of the centre of the blast lived through the day. Some people in the streets were vaporized. Only their shadows remained, imprinted on walls. Others were scorched by radiation burns, killed by flying debris, or buried in the rubble of collapsed buildings. Many survivors of the first day later died of radiation sickness from deadly gamma rays. In later years, survivors had a higher risk of cancer and other diseases. The not-yet-born children and grandchildren of the atomic-bomb victims were also at risk from genetic mutations.

Three days later, a second nuclear bomb, called "Fat Man," was dropped on the Japanese city of **Nagasaki**. Another 40 000 people were killed. That night, Emperor Hirohito told the Japanese military that "the time has come when we must bear the unbearable." Japan agreed to unconditional surrender. The surrender was signed aboard the U.S. battleship *Missouri* in Tokyo Bay. World War II was over at last.

THE PRICE AND REWARDS OF PEACE

Peace returned in 1945, but at a terrible price. Nuclear weapons had forever changed human history. Now human beings had the power to destroy the human race. The threat of a new and horrible danger — nuclear war — darkened the future. Many people working on the bomb were deeply troubled by the morality of creating such a terrifying weapon. Robert Oppenheimer once said to Truman, "Mr. President, I have blood on my hands." But he also said later that he believed that developing atomic weapons made achieving peace "more hopeful...because it intensifies the urgency of our hopes — in frank words, because we are scared."

The coming of peace was a joy and relief for Canadians. World War II veterans returned to a nation more prosperous than the one they had left. They looked forward to settling down and rebuilding their lives in peacetime. Many Canadians were also proud of Canada's achievements in World War II. During the war years, Canada had built the world's third-largest navy and fourth-largest air force. It had become an important partner of Britain and the United States and had shared in major wartime projects. Canadians began to believe that their nation could play a bigger role on the world stage.

Across Canada, victory parades such as this one in Oshawa, Ontario, were held to celebrate the end of war. Why did the end of war bring a mixture of happiness and sadness to many Canadians?

KNOWING THE KEY PEOPLE, PLACES, AND EVENTS

In your notes, clearly identify and explain the historical significance of each of the following:

Operation Sea Lion	Battle of Britain
Operation Barbarossa	Pearl Harbor
Battle of Dieppe	Ortona
D-Day	Holocaust
Wannsee Conference	Manhattan Project
Hiroshima	Nagasaki

FOCUS YOUR KNOWLEDGE

1. Why did Japan launch a surprise attack on Pearl Harbor? How successful was this attack?
2. Why was the entry of the United States into World War II crucial in the defeat of Nazi Germany?
3. Why are many Canadian war veterans bitter about the government's decision to send Canadian troops to Hong Kong in 1941?
4. Why was the attack on Dieppe launched despite little expectation of success?
5. Why was the capture of Ortona significant to the Allied offensive in Italy?
6. How did the Allied forces prepare for the invasion of Normandy?
7. Describe the treatment of the Jews and other inmates of the Nazi concentration camps.
8. Describe the effect of the atomic bomb on the cities of Hiroshima and Nagasaki, both immediately and in the years following the war.

APPLY YOUR KNOWLEDGE

1. Describe the role played by Canadians in the air during World War II. How critical was this role to the eventual outcome of the war? Back up your answer with specific examples.
2. The bombing of civilian targets, such as the German bombing of London and the Allied bombing of Hamburg, was widespread during World War II. Were these bombings necessary evils in the course of war or unjustified atrocities? Explain your answer.

3. Hitler's attack on the Soviet Union proved to be a crucial factor in the defeat of Nazi Germany. Was Operation Barbarossa a miscalculated gamble, or could it have been a success? Explain your answer.

4. Select three events from the war that you consider to be crucial to its outcome. Rank the events in order of importance, and justify your ranking. Be prepared to defend your opinions in front of your classmates.

5. Research and debate the following issue in a group: Was the Battle of Dieppe a failure or a costly success?

6. How successful was the Canadian attack on Ortona, considering the number of casualties in comparison with the significance of the victory?

7. Could more have been done to prevent the atrocities against the Jews during the war? What can we do in the future to ensure that such persecutions never happen again? Have a classroom debate on which of the following options is the best choice. Can you think of others?

    (a) Educate people about prejudice and racism.

    (b) Put more power in the hands of the United Nations.

    (c) Guarantee all people, regardless of nationality, freedom from persecution.

    (d) Impose trade restrictions on countries guilty of persecuting any of their citizens.

8. Can the use of weapons of mass destruction, such as the atom bomb, ever be morally justified? Has the development of nuclear bombs made the prospect of world peace more or less likely? Why?

EXTEND YOUR KNOWLEDGE

1. Prepare an illustrated time-line of the major events of World War II. The time-line should incorporate events occurring from September 1939 to August 1945. Draw illustrations or use photographs from magazines to illustrate the important people, places, and events.

2. Write a short story or a poem describing the experiences of a victim of the Holocaust. You may want to read some literature on the Holocaust, such as *The Diary of Anne Frank* or Elie Wiesel's *Night*, to gain more insight into a victim's experiences.

3. Do further research on the long-term impact of the atomic bomb on the cities of Nagasaki and Hiroshima. In your research, try to find out how much was known about the effects of nuclear bombs in 1945 and what is known today. Then prepare a short presentation based on your research for your class.

4. Prepare a poster for one of the following purposes relating to World War II:

    (a) To encourage volunteers to enlist.

    (b) To encourage people to support the war effort.

    (c) To spread anti-Nazi feeling among Canadians.

    (d) To promote peace in the postwar period.

SKILLS FOCUS

UNIT REVIEW

1. In the years between 1939 and 1945, the darkest side of humanity showed itself in the forms of racism and the inhumane treatment of countless peoples. Show how this statement is true by discussing each of the following issues.

    The Holocaust
    Canadian Soldiers in Hong Kong
    Japanese Canadians

2. Prime Minister William Lyon Mackenzie King made Canadian independence a priority throughout his political career. Canada's participation in World War II was no exception. What examples in this unit illustrate Canadian autonomy during World War II?

3. Compare Canada's contributions in World Wars I and II in terms of their costs in lives and dollars. Use bar graphs to illustrate the comparison. You may need to do extra research to complete this exercise.

DEVELOPING EFFECTIVE PRESENTATION SKILLS

The ability to present information to an audience in an interesting and effective manner is a skill that requires practice. A good presentation should present a body of information while allowing the audience to become actively involved. To hold the attention of the audience requires creativity as well as a great deal of advance planning. Following are ten steps in making an effective presentation.

1. *Be the Expert:* Make sure you have done enough research so that you are an expert on the topic.

2. *Carefully Select the Information to be Presented:* Do not try to present too much information, and avoid boring your audience with unnecessary details.

3. *Be Creative:* Try to make your presentation distinct by including unique ideas and activities.

4. *Have a Purpose:* Clearly state what you intend to do in your introduction, and provide a summary of your presentation at the end.

5. *Be Organized:* Make sure your presentation has a logical flow.

6. *Provide Clear Notes:* Use overheads, handouts, or the blackboard to provide a summary of the key points.

7. *Enhance Your Presentation by Using a Variety of Resources:* Consider using films, slides, music, models, or other resources to assist you in your presentation.

8. *Involve the Class:* Plan your questions carefully in order to draw the class into discussions at various points in your presentation.

9. *Be Aware of Time Constraints:* Estimate the length of each part of your presentation to ensure that it runs neither significantly under nor over the time allowed.

10. *Speak Clearly and Confidently:* Avoid reading from a prepared text and be sure to project interest and enthusiasm. If you seem uninterested, your audience will lose interest too.

CAREER FOCUS

SALES

A career in sales is appealing to many people for a variety of reasons. Salespeople have a degree of independence that allows them to have flexible work hours and to earn an income based on how effectively they do their job. A career in sales can involve products and services ranging from homes to insurance and advertising.

In many professions, the ability to deliver effective presentations is a definite asset. Salespeople must convince clients of the merits of the product they are trying to market. To be successful in a career in sales, it is important for you to communicate effectively with potential clients. This may involve visually appealing displays, convincing sales pitches, or clear summaries of a product's main features.

The people most successful in sales careers are those who enjoy dealing with the public and who can convey information in an effective manner. They must also have extensive knowledge of the market in which they are dealing, including a knowledge of the products and services offered by their competitors.

The guide to effective presentations that is outlined on the previous page could be a valuable asset to someone pursuing a career in sales. No matter what career you choose, the skills you develop in this course will prove very useful in your life. The business world is only one place where the ability to deliver an effective presentation is a valued skill.

PRACTISING YOUR PRESENTATION SKILLS

Practise planning and carrying out an effective presentation by doing one of the following assignments.

1. Working in groups of three or four, prepare a presentation for the class. For this presentation, role-play one of the people who were hired by the government for a dollar a year to help with the war effort. Remember that your task is to convince the citizens (your classmates) to lend support to the war effort. Do sufficient research and planning for your presentation. Base the presentation on the following topics.

   Victory Bonds
   Enlistment
   Wage and Price Controls
   Saving Fat and Bones

2. In groups of three or four, prepare a presentation that explains to the class the important role that women played in the war. Focus on the WACs and the WRCNs. Structure your presentation so that it attempts to attract more women to join in the war effort.

3. Working in groups of three or four, select one of the following topics for a presentation. The focus of your presentation should be to shed more light on the events and to explore ways to ensure that such tragedies do not occur again.

   The Holocaust
   The Treatment of Prisoners of War
   The Internment of Japanese Canadians
   The Bombing of Hiroshima and Nagasaki

UNIT 6

THE DAWNING OF A NEW ERA:
THE COLD WAR AND BEYOND

THE WORLD IN 1945 WAS QUITE DIFFERENT from what it had been before the outbreak of war. The coming of the nuclear age altered the way people viewed war. The emergence of the Soviet Union and the United States as the dominant superpowers divided much of the world into two camps. Society was also changed by the postwar baby boom in North America, which, combined with an increase in general prosperity, created a consumer revolution. By the 1960s, the voice of youth was being heard throughout Europe and North America. Although none of the battles of World War II was fought on Canadian soil, the resulting changes that swept over Europe and North America transformed Canadian society. By 1970, a strong women's movement had developed in Canada, a violent separatist group had carried out terrorist attacks in Quebec, and American culture had spilled into Canada via television and radio.

Throughout this unit, the forces that have shaped Canada at home and abroad are examined to provide a clear understanding of how Canada's recent past has shaped the nation. Chapter 15 examines the role Canada has played on the international scene since 1945. The creation of the United Nations, NATO, and NORAD are discussed, as are Canada's involvement in conflicts in Korea, the Suez, and Vietnam. Chapter 16 focuses on

CHAPTER FIFTEEN
Canada's Role on the International Stage

CHAPTER SIXTEEN
French–English Relations

CHAPTER SEVENTEEN
Canadian–American Relations

the French–English relationship within Canada. Since the 1950s, a strong nationalist movement has arisen in Quebec. It has been a major factor in shaping French Canadian culture during the past four decades and has led to the rise of a separatist movement that at times has been violent. Chapter 17 explores the relationship between Canada and the United States since World War II. Americans have come to play an increasingly prominent role in the daily lives of Canadians. American television, radio, and fashions have all contributed to shaping contemporary Canadian society. This chapter examines Canada's relationship with the United States and its efforts to retain a clear cultural identity.

CHAPTER 15 CANADA'S ROLE ON THE INTERNATIONAL STAGE

GLOSSARY TERMS

Manchuria A region in northeastern China that had been occupied by Japan in World War II.
Aggressor A nation that engages in deliberate attacks on other countries.
Diplomats Officials employed to handle a nation's relations with other countries around the world.
Department of External Affairs The department within the federal government that is responsible for conducting the nation's relations with foreign countries.
Containment A post–World War II policy designed by the United States and supported by Canada and other western nations, that was aimed at limiting the spread of Soviet influence.
Espionage The use of spies to obtain military, political, or scientific secrets of other nations.
Fallout Shelters Underground chambers built for protection against radioactive materials released during a nuclear explosion.
Commonwealth A free association of Britain and other independent nations that had been former colonies of the British Empire.

FOCUS ON:

- Canada's middle-power status after World War II
- Canada's "golden age" of foreign policy
- the Gouzenko affair and the beginning of the Cold War
- the creation of NATO and NORAD
- the role of Canadian peacekeepers throughout the world
- how Canada's foreign policy has changed since 1945

Life had changed surprisingly little in Canada during the war years. Canada in 1945 still had the same Constitution, the same nine provinces, and the same prime minister that it had in 1939. The country had not suffered the ravages of war; in fact, it had prospered since 1939. Booming wartime industries had pulled Canada out of the Great Depression and set it on the road toward peacetime prosperity. Many soldiers returned home to take up their lives where they had left off. Canadians everywhere began settling into civilian jobs, starting families, and saving for their first cars, refrigerators, and radios. They were more than ready to enjoy the good life in peacetime North America.

While North America enjoyed its new prosperity, many other places still lay under the dark cloud of World War II. Europe was a wasteland of ruined cities and devastated countrysides. European governments were in disorder, and their economies were badly damaged. Food was in short supply, and millions of people teetered on the brink of starvation. France had been badly weakened by the German occupation during the war. Great Britain had been sapped of its economic strength by the enormous costs of the war.

Despite massive aid from Canada and the United States, Britain would take years to become part of the world economy again.

Defeated Germany had been carved up into four occupation zones by the major Allied powers — the United States, France, Great Britain, and the Soviet Union. The German capital of Berlin, now deep in the Soviet zone, was also divided into occupation zones. Although Germany remained a name on the map, all important decisions about its future were made by the occupying Allied nations. The Soviet zone would remain under communist control for decades. Japan had accepted defeat after the U.S. atomic bomb blasts and bowed to a U.S. occupation force. China was a huge but crippled giant. Not only had it suffered under wartime occupation by the Japanese, it was now in the grip of a civil war between the government and communist rebels led by Mao Zedong.

THE NEW SUPERPOWERS: THE SOVIET UNION AND THE UNITED STATES

Even though Great Britain and France had been badly weakened by the war, both nations were still considered major powers because they had been great world powers before the war. Although China was a poor and struggling nation after the war, it was also considered a major power because of its great size and its huge population. The two most important new superpowers, however, were the Soviet Union and the United States.

The devastation caused by World War II left much of Europe in rubble. Try to imagine the challenges cities must have faced as they tried to rebuild.

The Soviet Union had also been devastated in the war, but because of its large population, its massive sweep of land, and its wealth of natural resources, it was an undeniable world power. Most importantly, it led the world in military might. After the war, the Soviet Union still had armed forces of up to 6 million soldiers, 50 000 tanks, and 20 000 aircraft. Its army occupied central and eastern Europe as well as *Manchuria* and North Korea.

The only nation that could equal the Soviet Union in military strength was the United States. Like Canada, the United States had not suffered bombing or invasion during the war. It had been able to build up powerful armed forces, and it had created a terrifying new weapon, the atomic bomb. The threat of a nuclear attack alone was enough to keep its potential enemies in line. The United States had also taken over Britain's role as the world's greatest imperial power. American military bases and colonies were scattered across the Pacific Ocean, the Caribbean Sea, and Latin America. Above all, the United States was the richest country in the world. With a huge budget for both foreign aid and arms, its presence was felt in almost every corner of the globe in the postwar years.

This colourful poster was made for the United Nations by the famous American artist, Norman Rockwell. What do the picture and the statement tell you about the goals of the United Nations?

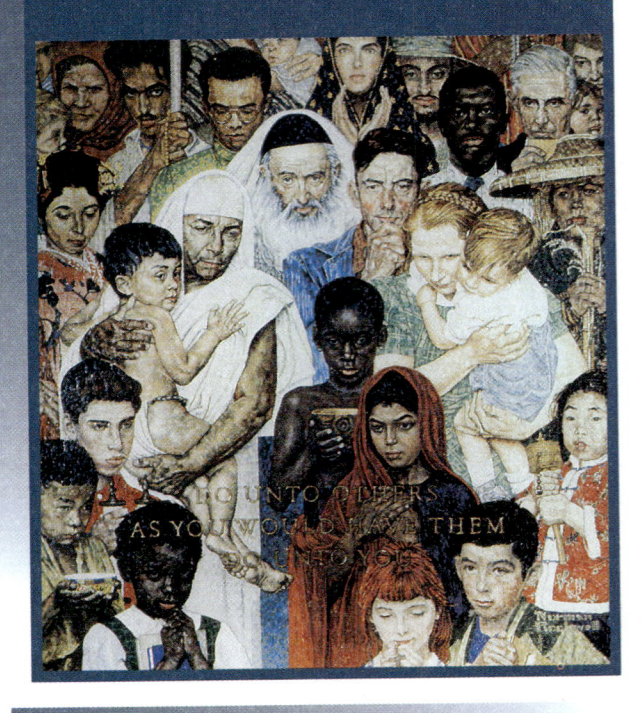

THE UNITED NATIONS

In 1945, the so-called "Big Five" nations — the Soviet Union, the United States, Great Britain, France, and China — took it upon themselves to attempt to shape a peaceful future. The major Allied powers had started preparing for peace even before the war ended. In the fall of 1944, officials from the United States, Britain, the Soviet Union, and China had gathered at Dumbarton Oaks, a mansion in Washington, D.C. There they laid plans for a new international organization called the **United Nations (U.N.)**. The United Nations was intended to provide a place where nations could meet to find peaceful solutions to world conflicts.

Although most details of the U.N. Charter were worked out at Dumbarton Oaks, the new organization was not born until after the war. In April 1945, delegates from 51 nations gathered in San Francisco to formally establish the United Nations. The opening words of the charter set out the U.N.'s most important goal. It reads, "We the peoples of the United Nations, determined to save succeeding generations from the scourge of war, which twice in our lifetime has brought untold sorrow to mankind...do hereby establish an international organization to be known as the United Nations." Some of the most important goals cited in the U.N. Charter are:

- to keep world peace and prevent the outbreak of new wars;
- to help advance justice and law throughout the world;
- to defend human rights and help promote equality among different individuals and groups around the globe; and
- to encourage friendly relations among nations.

The United Nations Today

The United Nations has grown and changed over the years. Dozens of former colonies of imperial powers such as Britain and France sought independence after the war. Many new nations sprang up from former colonies in Asia and Africa, and these new nations swelled the ranks of U.N. members. Today more than 150 nations belong to the United Nations and are represented in the General Assembly. Despite its growing membership, its aims and organization are still rooted in its original charter.

The General Assembly is an important body in the United Nations. Every member-nation has a seat — and a vote — in the General Assembly. It meets once a year at U.N. headquarters in New York City to discuss and debate important world issues. The General Assembly also makes recommendations to other U.N. bodies, approves U.N. budgets, and votes on accepting new members. The U.N. Charter also created an International Court of Justice to settle legal disputes between countries. It is headquartered in The Hague, capital city of the Netherlands.

The United Nations

[Organizational chart showing:
- Security Council
- Peacekeeping forces
- Trusteeship Council
- General Assembly
- International Court of Justice
- Secretariat
- Economic and Social Council

Under Economic and Social Council:
- United Nations International Children's Emergency Fund (UNICEF)
- Food and Agriculture Organization of the United Nations (FAO)
- Office of the United Nations Commissioner for Refugees (UNHCR)
- United Nations Educational, Scientific and Cultural Organization (UNESCO)
- United Nations Environment Programme (UNEP)
- World Health Organization (WHO)
- World Food Council (WFC)
- International Monetary Fund (IMF)
- International Labour Organization (ILO)
- International Civil Aviation Organization (ICAO)]

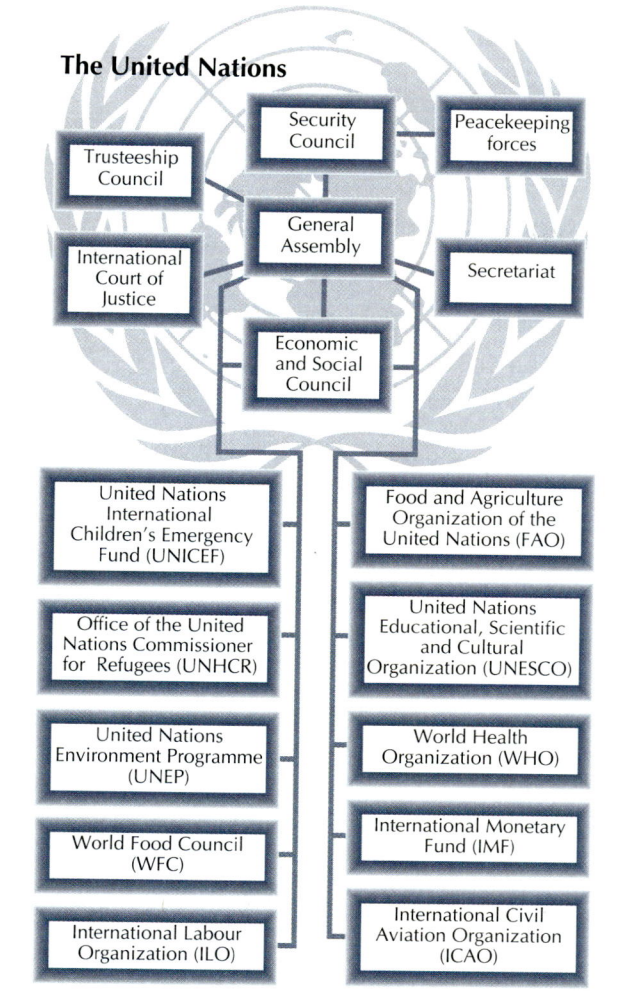

And the Secretariat, headed by the Secretary-General of the United Nations, looks after U.N. affairs.

The Security Council is one of the most important bodies in the United Nations. Its job is to maintain peace and security, investigate disputes, and recommend U.N. action against *aggressor* nations. Five countries now have permanent seats on the Security Council: the United States, Russia, The People's Republic of China, Britain, and France. Each of them has veto power over Security Council actions. As a result, every Security Council decision must be approved by all five permanent members. In addition, there are ten nonpermanent members of the Security Council who are elected for two-year terms by the General Assembly.

Many other councils and agencies are part of the United Nations. They include UNICEF (United Nations International Children's Emergency Fund), WHO (World Health Organization), UNESCO (United Nations Educational, Scientific, and Cultural Organization), FAO (Food and Agriculture Organization), GATT (General Agreement on Tariffs and Trade), and the World Bank. Their job is to preserve world peace and to promote the welfare of people around the world by helping to find solutions to major global problems such as poverty, health, human rights, education, and the environment.

When it was founded in 1945, many people pinned their hopes for world peace on the new United Nations organization. Over the years, the U.N. has provided a place where *diplomats* can meet, exchange views, and find points of common interest. But discussion and debate in the Security Council and the General Assembly have not always helped to end conflicts. Sometimes they have increased world tensions and heightened disagreements between member nations.

It was also hoped that the U.N. would have the "teeth" to enforce its decisions. But when conflicts break out between member countries, the U.N. is often powerless to take strong action. The Security

CANADA'S ROLE ON THE INTERNATIONAL STAGE

Member countries of the United Nations meet regularly at the United Nations assembly in New York City. Why is it important that nations of the world have the opportunity to meet on an ongoing basis?

Council veto power has been a major stumbling block. Time and again in the past, Security Council vetoes — usually by the Soviet Union or the United States — stopped the U.N. from taking a strong stand in times of international crisis. Despite its shortcomings, the U.N. continues to play a major international role. It is still an important forum for ending conflicts and for tackling pressing global problems like poverty, disease, overpopulation, and environmental destruction.

CANADA AS A MIDDLE POWER

Canada's prime minister, Mackenzie King, was among the world leaders who attended the United Nations conference in San Francisco in the spring of 1945. Although Canada was not one of the "Big Five," it was only one rung down on the international ladder and had become a major middle power. With its booming economy and undamaged industries, Canada was one of the most prosperous countries in the world in 1945. It had also put together a powerful and well-equipped army, including the third-largest navy and the fourth-largest air force in the world. By the end of the war, over 1 million Canadians were in uniform. Canada had also been an important wartime ally of Britain and the United States and had worked with the British and the Americans on the top-secret atomic bomb project.

For perhaps the first time, Canada was too important to be overlooked. Mackenzie King wanted to make sure that smaller nations like Canada would not be forced into future wars by the Big Five. His voice was heard at the U.N. conference. As a result of Canadian efforts, the U.N. Charter was changed so that any country asked to contribute troops or money to U.N. security operations had to be consulted about those operations first. King also wanted special powers for middle-power countries like Canada, Australia, New Zealand, and the Netherlands. But only the Security Council members received special powers. All other member-nations were treated equally and given one vote each in the General Assembly.

CANADA'S "GOLDEN AGE" OF FOREIGN POLICY

Canada's role as the voice of the middle powers at the U.N. conference in San Francisco marked the start of what some historians have called the "golden age" of Canadian foreign policy. A nation's **foreign policy** is its action plan for handling its relations with other countries of the world. Foreign policy is shaped to achieve a nation's goals in areas such as national sovereignty (independence), economic growth, peace and security, and the environment.

Lester Pearson, who would later become prime minister of Canada, addressed an international meeting in San Francisco in 1945. During this conference the formal charter of the United Nations was drafted.

SOLDIERS FOR PEACE

Since the end of World War II, Canadians have earned an international reputation for their efforts to mediate conflicts and maintain peace in the world. The first formal United Nations peacekeeping force was created by former Canadian prime minister and diplomat Lester B. Pearson. Pearson earned the Nobel Peace Prize in 1957 for his efforts to resolve the Suez Crisis. As a result of his work in that crisis, the United Nations began to send peacekeepers into various parts of the world. In November 1992, the magazine *Canadian Geographic* paid tribute to Canadian peacekeepers for their efforts around the world in a feature article entitled "Keeping the Peace." The letter that follows was written by Ian Darragh, editor of *Canadian Geographic*. As you read the letter, reflect on what role you feel Canadians should play in foreign conflicts. Also, consider what makes Canadians unique in the world. Do you agree that as Canadians we all belong to "the same family"?

It is one thing to put your life on the line defending your country. It is quite another to face death from a sniper's bullet or mutilation from a land mine while trying to mediate between combatants in a vicious civil war of the sort that has torn apart the former Yugoslav republic. Yet this is what we ask our soldiers to do when they serve with United Nations peacekeeping forces. We can take great pride in our soldiers for the contribution they are making to lessening tensions in the world's hot-spots and delivering aid to the innocent victims of war.

Canadians are currently involved in 12 peacekeeping operations around the world.... It was a Canadian, Lester B. Pearson, who helped invent the concept of neutral UN peacekeepers. When he was awarded the Nobel Peace Prize in 1957 for his role in sending a large UN force to defuse the Suez Crisis, he observed in his acceptance speech: "If there is to be peace, there must be compromise, tolerance, agreement." Since then Canadian peacekeepers have used their training and courage to advance the cause of peace, and they have won an international reputation for their professionalism and their ability to cool tempers and encourage compromises....

To truly appreciate what we have here in Canada and how much Canadians from different backgrounds have in common, I had to travel to the centre of Africa, to the tiny landlocked country of Rwanda. I had been invited to a wedding of a Belgian friend who was teaching there, so the purpose of my visit was ostensibly a happy occasion. But the country I visited in 1971 was ruled by a dictator and reeked of fear. Everywhere I travelled, there were roadblocks every few miles, where nervous soldiers with machine guns checked my identity papers before allowing me to proceed.

At the reception after the wedding, I was introduced to a Canadian who was teaching at the same school as my friend. He eagerly shook my hand and told me I was the first Canadian he had spoken to in months. His hometown, it turned out, was a village near Quebec City. Even though my French was halting and his English equally fractured, we discovered we spoke a common language. Soon we found ourselves talking like long-lost buddies about whitewater canoeing, cross-country skiing and the strangeness of celebrating Christmas in a land without snow.

Eventually another teacher joined us and introduced himself as a Belgian. He had read about Canada's constitutional debate, and asked with a mischievous smile if we were federalists or separatists. There was an awkward silence. Then my new friend put his arm around my shoulders and said, "That is a family matter we don't discuss in front of strangers." Seven thousand miles from home, in a strange country surrounded by foreigners, we both realized the things we had in common as Canadians far outweighed our differences. We belonged to the same family.

Source: Ian Darragh, "Soldiers for Peace," *Canadian Geographic*, November/December 1992, p. 6.

CANADIAN SOVEREIGNTY: FORMULATING FOREIGN POLICY

Governments usually develop a plan of action to deal with questions concerning international issues and relations. This plan is called "foreign policy." Foreign policy guides the government and its decision-makers when they make specific decisions. When making foreign policy, a state must decide what goals are important. Develop an organizer that lists each of the following goals. As you read through this unit, find examples of Canadian actions in foreign policy for each of the following categories.

1. Economic Growth — Canada's foreign policy should promote balanced and continuous growth in its economy.
2. Sovereignty — Canada must maintain its ability to control its own affairs without interference from other states.
3. Peace and Security — Canada seeks to minimize international violence. A less violent world improves the security of all nations, including Canada.
4. Social Justice — Canada should strive to improve the standard of living of people around the world and ensure that people are treated fairly and humanely.
5. Quality of Life — Canada's relations with other countries should enhance the lives of Canadians through such activities as cultural and scientific exchanges.
6. Safe Environment — The Canadian environment and its resources must be protected and managed well. Cooperation with other countries to solve global environmental problems is one way to achieve this goal.

A nation can use both military and nonmilitary "tools" to carry out its foreign policy. Military tools include forming military alliances like the Axis-power alliance of World War II; taking limited military actions, such as the U.S. bombing raids into Libya; and engaging in all-out warfare. World War II was a terrifying example of all-out war. Nonmilitary foreign-policy tools include diplomatic pressures, economic sanctions (penalties), international law, and foreign aid.

During and after the war, several senior diplomats with Canada's *Department of External Affairs* began crafting a new foreign policy for Canada. **Lester Pearson** and several other key Canadian diplomats wanted Canada to be a more important player on the world stage. They realized that with a population of only 10 million people, Canada would never be a great world power. But Canada had excelled in certain areas during the war. It had produced much of the Allies' food. It had also played a central role in pilot-training and aviation programs and contributed scientists and uranium for the atomic bomb project. In these areas and others, Canada did rank with the Big Five.

Canadian diplomats wanted Ottawa to have had a much larger say in areas where Canada's international contributions mattered.

But Canada's willingness to share in important international tasks after the war was also what one historian called a "declaration of responsibility." Canadians were ready to join other like-minded nations in the search for a permanent peace. Over the next two decades, Canadian diplomats were often at the front of the struggle to ease international tensions, to settle disputes, and to promote peace and security in the world. Led by Lester Pearson, Canadian diplomats came to be held in high regard both at home and abroad for their commitment to world peace.

CANADA AND THE BEGINNING OF EAST–WEST HOSTILITIES

The search for world peace was seriously threatened by growing tension between the two new superpowers. By the end of the war, relations between the United States and the Soviet Union were hostile. Over the next few years the hostility between the two nations deepened, and once again other nations began lining up with one side or the other. One of the early warning signals of growing postwar hostilities occurred on Canadian soil. On September 5, 1945, a young clerk with the Soviet Embassy in Ottawa, **Igor Gouzenko**, walked out of the embassy carrying 109 top-secret documents. He announced to authorities that he had evidence that the Soviet Union was running a spy ring of civil servants and military officers in Canada. Gouzenko claimed that the Soviets were trying to collect secret information about political activities, troop movements, and scientific secrets. He said that the Soviets were especially interested in getting information about the atomic bomb, which Canada had worked on with Britain and the United States. Gouzenko also claimed that the Soviets had set up spy rings in Britain and the United States.

At first, Gouzenko's claims were ignored. It was only when Soviet embassy officials broke down the door of the apartment where Gouzenko hid with his family that the government finally took notice. The Royal Canadian Mounted Police questioned Gouzenko for five hours and then placed him in protective custody. Soon, a shocked Mackenzie King was told the news of Gouzenko's defection and his claims about the Soviet Union's international spy ring. King immediately warned the new U.S. president, Harry Truman, and the British prime minister, Clement Attlee.

Growing East–West Conflict

The Gouzenko spy story made headlines around the world. Many Canadians were as shocked as Mackenzie King was to find out that the Soviet Union was trying to steal military secrets from its former wartime allies.

But many other Canadians had remained deeply suspicious of communism and communist intentions. The Soviet leader, **Joseph Stalin**, had risen to power not long after the Russian Revolution of 1917, when the

This is how Igor Gouzenko was known to the world after he exposed a Soviet spy ring operating in Canada. Why was it necessary that his identity be kept a secret?

Russian czar was toppled and replaced by a communist government. Stalin brutally repressed anyone in the Soviet Union who did not support his rule both before and after World War II. Stalin's secret police arrested Soviet citizens suspected of opposing him. Some were executed, and others were sent to horrifying labour camps called gulags.

The Soviet army came to occupy large areas of eastern Europe in 1944 and 1945. When World War II ended, Soviet troops stayed in Romania, Bulgaria, Hungary, Poland, East Germany, and Czechoslovakia. News was leaking out that in these countries, too, personal freedoms were being taken away and that one-party communist governments were being set up. The Soviet takeovers in eastern Europe peaked with the overthrow of a social-democratic government in Czechoslovakia in 1948. These countries were sometimes called Soviet "satellite states" because their communist governments were directly linked to Moscow.

Communism was also beginning to gain ground in western Europe. During the war, communists had often been at the heart of European resistance movements. They had worked underground to fight the Nazis in occupied countries, and many became national heroes. By the late 1940s, communist parties were firmly established in Italy, France, and elsewhere. Italian and French communist parties staged huge strikes and demonstrations. Many people in western Europe and elsewhere viewed the resulting economic and political turmoil as a communist attempt to shut down the western European economy and create social chaos. They began to fear a "red menace." They worried that Stalin would become another Hitler and try to extend the Soviet Union's power and influence across Europe and around the globe.

Canada's new prime minister, **Louis St. Laurent**, was one of the leaders of western nations who feared the Soviet Union. In 1948, St. Laurent made impassioned pleas to put a stop to the spread of communism. "For us there is no escape in isolation or indifference," he said. "Recent events have brought home to all of us the increasing threat to our democracy of the rising tide of communism." The only nation strong enough to oppose the Soviet Union was the United States. Canadian diplomats worried that the United States might retreat from its commitments in Europe now that the war was over. They wanted the Americans to stand fast against further Soviet expansion.

Many Americans shared St. Laurent's suspicions and fears. They were also prepared to take on a greatly expanded international role. U.S. officials were already crafting a new foreign policy aimed at opposing the Soviet Union. The new American foreign policy — sometimes called the Truman Doctrine — was built on a policy of "*containment*." It aimed at "containing," or halting, the spread of communism in Europe and around the world.

The North Atlantic Treaty Organization

Even though Canada encouraged the United States to oppose the Soviet Union, it still wanted to avoid being drawn into future U.S. wars without consultation. Canadian diplomats decided to propose an alliance of democratic nations in the North Atlantic region. They hoped that the new alliance would give Canada greater influence over American defence policy.

Although Canadian hopes for having major influence on American military policy were never realized, Canada did persuade the United States to join Canada, Britain, France, and eight other nations in signing a joint treaty in 1949. The treaty contained clauses about trade and cultural exchanges among member nations, but it was primarily a pact to create an organization for mutual defence, the **North Atlantic Treaty Organization (NATO)**. Each member-nation agreed to contribute army, navy, and air force units to a new NATO defence force. The combined strength of the NATO alliance membership was intended to discourage the Soviet Union from any attempted takeover of western Europe.

The Warsaw Pact

The Soviet Union was upset by the new western alliance. It argued that NATO was not needed because the Soviet Union was not a threat to western Europe. On the contrary, it claimed, the Soviet Union had twice been invaded by western European powers in the twentieth century. It was only interested in protecting itself from yet another invasion from the West. The Soviets also pointed to expanding U.S. power as an American attempt to extend its influence around the globe. The Soviet Union reacted by organizing its own defence alliance, the **Warsaw Pact**, in 1955. The Soviet satellite countries of eastern Europe agreed to defend each other and the Soviet Union if any Warsaw Pact member was attacked.

Now the two sides, East and West, had squared off across a line running from the Baltic Sea in the north to the Adriatic Sea in the south. On the eastern side stood the communist countries under the control of the Soviet Union. On the western side was the coalition of nations under the leadership of the United States. Winston Churchill had declared in 1946 that "an iron curtain had descended on Europe." The two new alliances — NATO and the Warsaw Pact nations — deepened the rift between East and West. The "Cold War" grew colder.

CANADA AND THE COLD WAR

The term **Cold War** was first used in 1947 to describe the power struggle between the Soviet Union and the United States that was being fought using every means short of all-out warfare. Both sides feared a nuclear war. So instead of waging a "hot" war with troops and weapons, the Cold War was fought with propaganda, *espionage*, economic

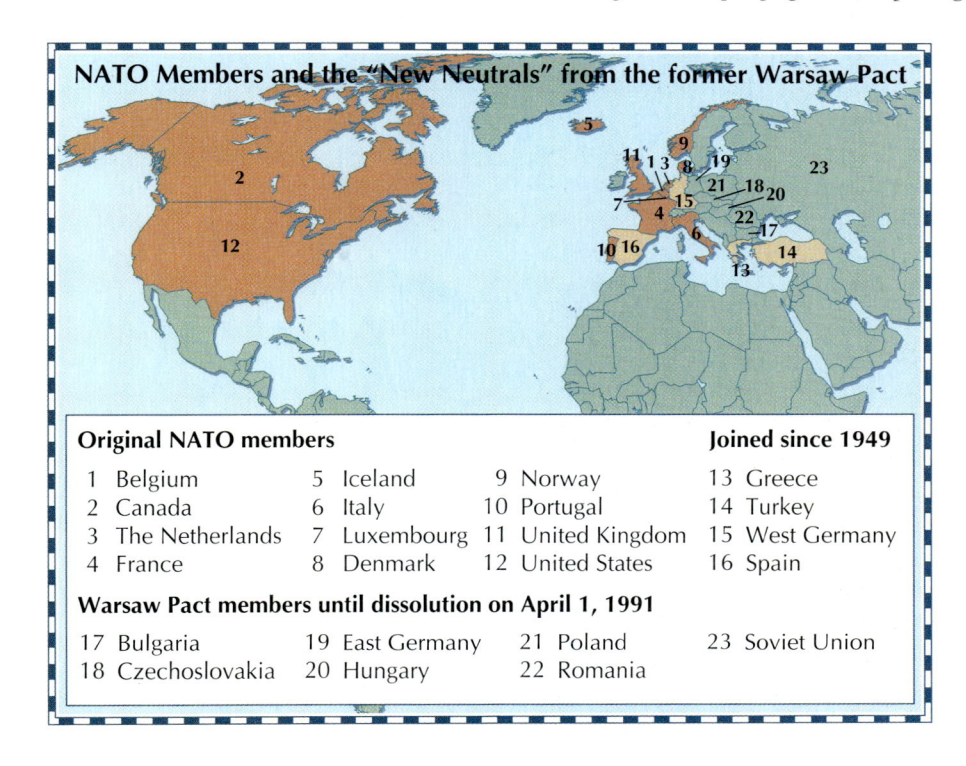

NATO Members and the "New Neutrals" from the former Warsaw Pact

Original NATO members

1. Belgium
2. Canada
3. The Netherlands
4. France
5. Iceland
6. Italy
7. Luxembourg
8. Denmark
9. Norway
10. Portugal
11. United Kingdom
12. United States

Joined since 1949

13. Greece
14. Turkey
15. West Germany
16. Spain

Warsaw Pact members until dissolution on April 1, 1991

17. Bulgaria
18. Czechoslovakia
19. East Germany
20. Hungary
21. Poland
22. Romania
23. Soviet Union

and political pressures, and limited military aggression. The Soviets and Americans used these tactics to win the support of uncommitted nations.

For example, the Soviet Union set up a communist government in Czechoslovakia in 1948 and put down revolts against communist rule in East Germany in 1953 and Hungary in 1956. The United States helped overthrow a pro-communist government in Guatemala in 1954 and landed troops in the Dominican Republic in 1965 to ward off a possible pro-communist victory there. Above all, the Cold War was fought with the scare tactics of an arms race. It became a war of nerves, as each side raced to stockpile larger, more destructive weapons to frighten its enemies into backing away from hostile acts.

Canada and the Marshall Plan

One of the first skirmishes of the Cold War was an economic fight over the recovery of western European nations. While the western nations wanted to see their war-torn allies back on their feet again, the Soviets wanted to prevent an economic recovery of the American allies in western Europe. In 1948, the U.S. secretary of state, George Marshall, proposed a European recovery plan that came to be known as the **Marshall Plan**. Canada had already loaned huge sums of money to Britain. Now it joined in the Marshall Plan and shipped $706 million in food, equipment, and raw materials to Europe. Between 1948 and 1953, Canada and the United States jointly contributed $13.5 billion in European economic aid — most of it from the United States.

Western Europe made an amazing recovery, far beyond the expectations of the people who had helped to engineer it.

The Korean War

The Cold War did not always stay cold. Sometimes, Cold War hostilities turned into armed conflict. After World War II, Japanese-held Korea had been divided into zones of occupation. North Korea was occupied by troops from the Soviet Union, and South Korea was occupied by U.S. troops. It was assumed that the country would finally be reunited as a single, independent nation. When the Cold War began, however, the situation in Korea froze into a permanent state of affairs. Korea remained divided into two hostile camps even after the Soviet and American occupation forces pulled out.

Without warning in June 1950, the communist North Koreans sent 100 000 troops armed with Soviet weapons across the border into South Korea. The United States demanded a response to what it saw as a new communist threat in Asia, and the U.N. Security Council met in a special session. The

These Canadian soldiers were part of the United Nations peacekeeping forces sent to Korea between 1950 and 1953.

Here, a Canadian soldier keeps a close eye on the Qatar air base as an American F-16 returns from a bombing mission during the Gulf War.

Soviets were boycotting the Security Council at the time and did not attend. The Security Council quickly voted to send U.N. forces, under American command, to defend South Korea.

Fourteen U.N. member-nations sent troops to take part, but the U.N. fighting forces were overwhelmingly American. At first, Canada sent three navy destroyers and an air-transport squadron to join the U.N. forces, but it later sent ground troops as well. In three long, bloody years of fighting, 22 000 Canadians fought in Korea. More than 1000 Canadians were wounded and more than 300 were killed before the war ended. Although the shooting stopped on the night of July 27, 1953, Korea has remained a divided country.

After the Cold War

Since the Korean War, Canadian troops have seen military action in other world conflicts. In January 1991, for example, Canadian troops joined combined attack forces under U.S. command in the Persian Gulf War. Five months before, Saddam Hussein's Iraq had invaded neighbouring Kuwait and taken over its vast oil reserves. The U.N. Security Council had imposed tough economic sanctions on Iraq to force it to withdraw its troops. But Iraq refused, and the United States asked Canada to join the American-led international military force launched against Iraq. Canadian Prime Minister Brian Mulroney agreed.

Canada's role in the Persian Gulf War was hotly debated in Parliament and the press. Some Canadians worried that taking part in U.S. military actions was not in keeping with Canada's U.N. role as a supporter of international peace. As one reporter put it, siding with the United States in the conflict was "an adventure that has nothing to do with respect for international law, but everything to do with U.S. interests and domestic politics." But when war broke out on the night of January 16, 1991, Canadian forces went into action. The short but destructive war ended with an Iraqi surrender on February 27. Canadian participation in the Persian Gulf War highlighted Canada's continuing problem of finding a balance between its sometimes conflicting roles as a U.N. member and a close ally of the United States.

CANADA AS A WORLD PEACEKEEPER

Since the 1940s, Canada has played a special role as a "peacekeeper" in helping to prevent the outbreak of war and bring an end to hostilities. Canadian diplomats and soldiers have often been called on to help ease world tensions in potentially explosive situations. Their aim has been to prevent small, isolated wars from breaking into major wars between the superpowers.

Lester Pearson and the Suez Crisis

Canada's finest hour as a peacekeeping nation came during the Suez Crisis. In 1956, Egyptian President Gamal Abdal Nasser seized the Suez Canal and removed it from British and French control. Britain and France saw Nasser's action as a threat to a vital water link to the East. A few months later, Britain and France joined Israel in an attack on Egypt. Their objective was to take back the Suez Canal.

MINES DON'T TAKE SIDES

Over the past half-century Canadians have made a major commitment to world peace and have earned a global reputation for their efforts. Since the end of World War II, over 87 000 men and women have served in over thirty operations worldwide. In fact, Canada has the unique distinction of being the only country to be involved in every United Nations sponsored peacekeeping initiative.

Working overseas in peacekeeping roles can pose several obstacles for Canadian soldiers. Being thrust into new environments where cultural differences are quite significant often challenges the ingenuity of Canadian peacekeepers. In the article that follows, Captain Jane Thelwell describes the challenges Canadians faced when attempting to teach mine awareness to Afghan women and children and mine clearance to Afghan men. Captain Thelwell taught mine safety to Afghan refugees in 1989 as part of a United Nations humanitarian assistance program.

I was with the first group of Canadians in Peshawar [Pakistan], teaching mine safety to Afghan refugees. There were actually two programs — mine awareness for the Afghan women and children, and mine clearance for the men.

We passed the word about the dangers of the mines in any way we could. Often we'd arrange to visit a refugee camp; once there, we'd be invited into one of the more liberal households. Soon neighbours would start showing up, along with twenty or thirty children, and it could get to be quite a zoo.

It was a very dynamic learning environment. You couldn't lecture at them. You had to tell stories, and let them tell you stories in return. For instance, I'd pick up a butterfly mine, and somebody would go into a long story about old Uncle Abdul who had picked one up, and how he had lost his fingers. "Oh, and by the way," they'd tell everyone, "Uncle Abdul's camels are dead now...." And so on. Twenty minutes later we'd get back to the class. At first it seemed very slow, coming from our structured learning environments. But that's the way it had to be done.

We'd take dummy mines with us, or mines with the explosives removed. We also had posters showing the various mines people might encounter. One day we held up one of the anti-tank mines and asked whether anyone knew what it was. One lady put up her hand and in genuine earnest said, "It's for cooking. It's a pot." Well, no wonder these people were dying when they went back to Afghanistan. Very few women would actually recognize a mine if they saw one.

Sometimes we would even set up little minefields inside one of their enclosed yards. We'd have them walk around to see if they could identify mines and ordnance. It was amazing; when you put trip wires on the mines, most of the women would walk right over them. They had to get attuned to looking for those things.

Another point we tried to make was that it didn't matter where the mines had come from. Mines left by Afghan rebels were as much a threat as those placed by the Soviets. If you stepped on one, it could still kill you. They had to keep their eyes open at all times. Mines don't take sides.

Source: Captain Jane Thelwell, "Mines Don't Take Sides," *Shadows of War, Faces of Peace: Canada's Peacekeepers* (Toronto: Key Porter Books Limited, 1992), p. 95

These Canadian soldiers are teaching mine safety.

The invasion caused an international uproar. The Soviet Union threatened to side with Egypt and attack Britain and France. Fighting around the Suez was stepped up, and the world edged closer to a major war. Lester Pearson, Canada's acting cabinet minister for external affairs, stepped forward to defuse the explosive situation. He went to the United Nations and suggested creating a United Nations Emergency Force (UNEF) in the Suez to "keep the borders at peace while a political settlement is being worked out."

Just a few days later, all battle forces were withdrawn from the combat zone and replaced by the blue-helmeted U.N. peacekeeping units. The fighting stopped, and peace was restored in the Suez. In 1957, Lester Pearson was awarded the Nobel Peace Prize for his efforts. Since the Suez Crisis, Canada has been a part of every U.N. peacekeeping mission. Canadians have been so active in U.N. peacekeeping efforts that when the 1988 Nobel Peace Prize was awarded to the "blue helmets," many Canadian veterans took it as a personal honour.

THE NEW ARMS RACE

The Cold War triggered a giant arms race between East and West. A year after the outbreak of the Korean War, the United States had almost doubled the size of its air force and navy and tripled its army. Canada also began recruiting new forces for Europe. In addition, it promised twelve squadrons of jet fighters and launched a crash program to build destroyer-escorts. In 1947, Canada spent $196 million on defence; by 1952, its defence spending had skyrocketed to $2 billion — two-fifths of all federal spending that year.

The Nuclear Arms Race

The arms build-up soon shifted from conventional (non-nuclear) weapons to nuclear arms. In 1945, only the United States had an atomic bomb, but by 1949 the Soviet Union had tested its first atomic bomb. Throughout the 1950s, the Americans and Soviets played a deadly game of "leapfrog," as each

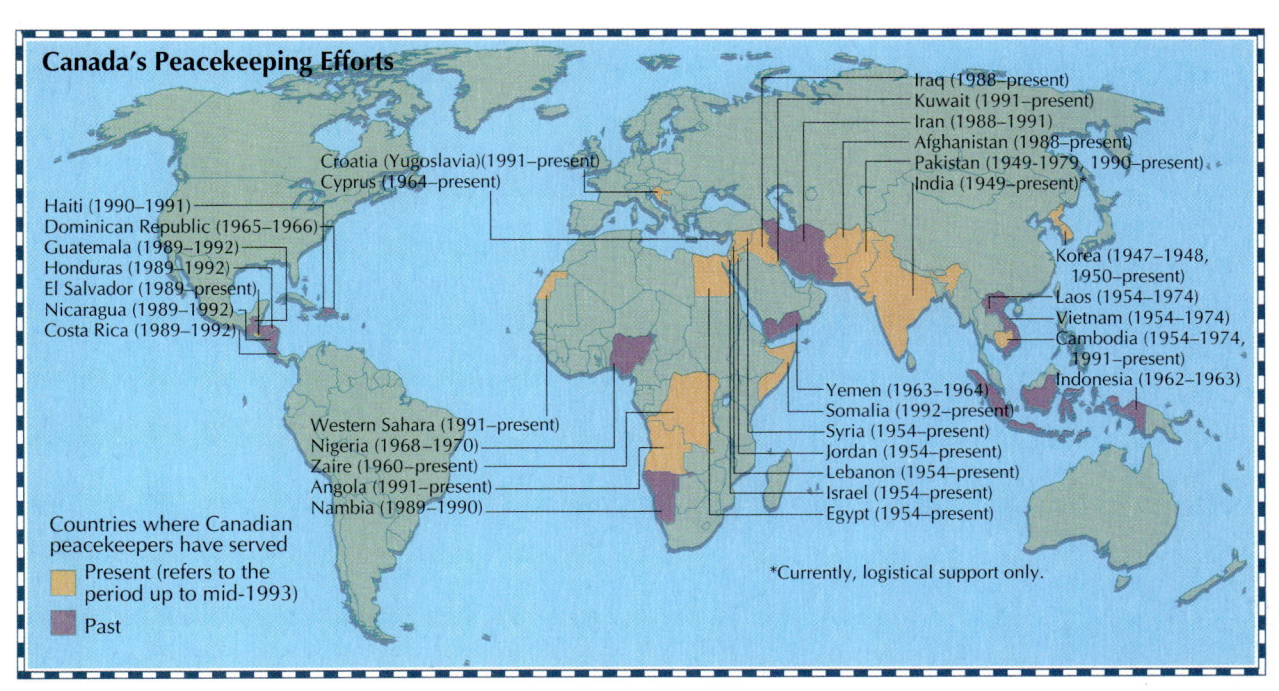

Canada's Peacekeeping Efforts

Haiti (1990–1991)
Dominican Republic (1965–1966)
Guatemala (1989–1992)
Honduras (1989–1992)
El Salvador (1989–present)
Nicaragua (1989–1992)
Costa Rica (1989–1992)
Croatia (Yugoslavia) (1991–present)
Cyprus (1964–present)
Iraq (1988–present)
Kuwait (1991–present)
Iran (1988–1991)
Afghanistan (1988–present)
Pakistan (1949-1979, 1990–present)
India (1949–present)*
Korea (1947–1948, 1950–present)
Laos (1954–1974)
Vietnam (1954–1974)
Cambodia (1954–1974, 1991–present)
Indonesia (1962–1963)
Western Sahara (1991–present)
Nigeria (1968–1970)
Zaire (1960–present)
Angola (1991–present)
Nambia (1989–1990)
Yemen (1963–1964)
Somalia (1992–present)
Syria (1954–present)
Jordan (1954–present)
Lebanon (1954–present)
Israel (1954–present)
Egypt (1954–present)

Countries where Canadian peacekeepers have served
- Present (refers to the period up to mid-1993)
- Past

*Currently, logistical support only.

Source: *Canadian Geographic,* November/December 1992.

tried to stay ahead in the race for dominance in nuclear arms. By 1957, both nations had developed the hydrogen bomb, which was 1000 times more powerful than the atomic bomb dropped on Hiroshima.

That same year, the Soviets launched the world's first space satellite, *Sputnik*. *Sputnik* demonstrated Soviet technological achievement and proved that the Soviets could use missiles to send nuclear warheads deep into the American heartland. The Americans scrambled to keep pace with the Soviets. By the late 1950s and early 1960s, both nations had developed long-range missiles called ICBMs — Intercontinental Ballistic Missiles. These huge rockets had hydrogen warheads attached to them. An ICBM launched from the Soviet Union could destroy targets in Canada and the United States within half an hour of firing.

Canada: Caught Between the Superpowers

Canadians realized that the next world war might be fought, not in Europe, but in North America. Canada was geographically in the middle of the superpower struggle. Soviet bombers carrying nuclear warheads could arc over the North Pole and streak across Canada toward targets inside the United States. American bombers carrying nuclear weapons could flash through Canadian airspace on their way toward the Soviet Union. Canada's vast northern territory suddenly became critically important to American — and Canadian — defence.

Canada and the United States drew closer together in an attempt to defend North America from a Soviet nuclear attack. In 1957, Canada's new prime minister, **John Diefenbaker**, made it one of his first acts to join the Americans in the **North American Air Defence System (NORAD)**. Three lines of radar were strung across Canada — the Pinetree, Mid-Canada, and Distant Early Warning (DEW) lines. The radar stations reported to a NORAD centre in North Bay, Ontario. From there, fighter planes could be sent over the Arctic to intercept attacking Soviet bombers. Diefenbaker's government also began buying American-made Bomarc missiles and Voodoo fighters, both of which could carry nuclear warheads. Meanwhile, a nervous Canadian government advised its citizens to build *fallout shelters* for protection during a nuclear attack. These moves tied Canada even more closely to American defence policies.

Nuclear Weapons and Deterrence

Canadians suddenly realized that they were living in a new and dangerous world. The new nuclear arms could utterly destroy a nation within hours. Any survivors would face a world lying in ruins and poisoned by nuclear radiation. In every previous war, nations could suffer terrible slaughter and still survive. But all that changed with the introduction of nuclear weapons.

Fighting a nuclear war was a no-win situation. The only use for these weapons of absolute destruction was deterrence, in which each side built up an arsenal of weapons so destructive that neither side dared to unleash them. Supporters of deterrence

Global Priorities
"To what extent do you think that CANADA should be involved in finding solutions to the following WORLD PROBLEMS?"

% Indicating "Highly Involved"

Environmental issues	73
Illiteracy	61
Human rights legislation	57
Arms control	48
Disaster relief	46
Third World development	40
Conflict within countries	32
Conflict between countries	30
Settlement of refugees	29
Overpopulation	26
Troubled national economies	24

Source: Reginald W. Bibby and Donald C. Posterski, *Teen Global Priorities* (Toronto: Stoddart, 1992), p. 163.

argued that building more and bigger nuclear weapons helped keep the peace. But many other people, including many Canadians, saw the nuclear arms race as threatening world peace. The new arms build-up, they said, was bringing the world closer and closer to nuclear devastation. Canada's growing involvement in U.S. defence activities set off waves of protest across Canada, as anti-nuclear activists crusaded to stop the arms race and keep nuclear weapons out of Canada.

The Cuban Missile Crisis

The fear of nuclear war grew as tensions between East and West continued to mount in the early 1960s. Tensions peaked with the **Cuban Missile Crisis** in October 1962. The Soviet Union had been shipping weapons to communist Cuba, including nuclear missiles targeted at the nearby United States mainland. U.S. President John F. Kennedy threatened military action if the Soviet leader, Nikita Khrushchev, did not remove all Soviet missiles from Cuba. Khrushchev refused. For five days, the world held its breath and waited for global destruction. But at last Khrushchev backed down, and the missiles were removed.

DETENTE AND THE END OF THE COLD WAR

After the Cuban Missile Crisis, the superpowers realized the dangers of a nuclear standoff. They had stepped to the brink of nuclear war once and did not want to risk it again. In the late 1960s and early 1970s, the Cold War began to thaw and a new era of **detente** — a relaxing of tensions — began. A direct "hotline" telephone was set up between Moscow and Washington, D.C., so that a nuclear war would not be sparked by a superpower misunderstanding.

The United States and the Soviet Union also signed a nuclear-test-ban treaty in 1963. This treaty was the first step in a new policy of cooperation and restraint. A series of arms-limitations talks began. These talks were aimed at disarmament — putting a stop to the arms race and reducing the stockpiles of Soviet and American nuclear weapons. As a result of these discussions, the United States and the Soviet Union had signed two strategic arms limitations treaties by 1979. These treaties set limits on specific types of nuclear arms.

But the treaties did not stop the Cold War from heating up again from time to time. In 1979, the Soviet Union placed 350 missiles in eastern Europe. In response, the United States announced plans to place Cruise missiles in western Europe. That same year, the Soviet Union invaded neighbouring Afghanistan. In protest, Canada, the United States, and other western nations boycotted the 1980 Moscow Olympic Games. The Soviet Union struck back by boycotting the 1984 Los Angeles Olympics. In 1981, U.S. President Ronald Reagan began loud verbal attacks on the Soviet Union, which he dubbed "the evil empire." He also began to talk about ways of "winning" a nuclear war and

What is the message this cartoonist is attempting to convey regarding an arms race? Do you think the cartoon is overly pessimistic or is it realistic?

THE 1972 SUMMIT SERIES: COLD WAR ON ICE?

Hockey has long been a favourite pastime of Canadians and a sport in which they have traditionally been world leaders. So, it was with some concern that Canadians watched the Soviet Union come to dominate international hockey in the 1950s and 1960s. Many people took consolation in the fact that Canada's best hockey players never competed in the international championships because they were committed to their NHL (National Hockey League) clubs. So, these people reasoned, Canada's best hockey players were still superior to the Soviet players, even if they no longer dominated world events such as the Olympics.

Increasingly, both communist and noncommunist countries came to see sports as an extension of the Cold War. So, when the Canada–USSR hockey series was announced in 1972, it quickly took on more importance than a battle between the world's two greatest hockey nations; it was the Cold War on ice, as capitalism and communism faced off.

The "Summit Series," as the event came to be called, was a series of eight games, four to be played in Canada and four in the Soviet Union. No one could have anticipated a more thrilling series. It came down to the last game; each team had three wins and one tie in seven games. Canadians gathered in front of televisions all across the nation to watch the final game. And what a game it was! End-to-end action and splendid goaltending left the teams deadlocked as the game neared the end. Then, suddenly, Paul Henderson broke in on the Soviet goaltender, Vladoslav Tretiak, and with a flick of his wrist scored one of the most memorable goals in hockey history.

Try to find someone who remembers this series and ask them how they felt when the winning goal was scored. How do you think this series reflects the importance of sports in defining a nation's identity?

Paul Henderson celebrates after scoring the winning goal in the 1972 Canada-Soviet hockey series.

Meetings such as this one between Soviet leader Mikail Gorbachev and American president Ronald Reagan were early indications that the Cold War was drawing to a close.

announced a $180 billion increase in defence spending. Later he proposed the expensive Strategic Defence Initiative (SDI), nicknamed **Star Wars**. It was a space-based technology intended to destroy Soviet missiles attacking the United States.

As Soviet–American relations worsened in the late 1970s and early 1980s, a new worldwide peace movement sprang up to push for nuclear disarmament, and more than 100 Canadian towns and cities voted to become "nuclear-free zones." Toward the middle of the 1980s, tensions began to ease again. Reagan and Soviet leader Mikhail Gorbachev held two summit conferences, renamed the **Strategic Arms Reduction Talks (START)**, to discuss arms reductions. The first summit ended with an agreement in 1987 to eliminate an entire class of nuclear weapons.

The Cold War Ends

Then, a completely unexpected series of events took place in eastern Europe. The Soviet Union was in turmoil in the late 1980s. Gorbachev attempted to make badly needed reforms under the slogans of perestroika — meaning "restructuring," or economic reform — and glasnost — meaning, in Gorbachev's words, "openness in public affairs, in every sector of life." The reforms were intended to shift the Soviet Union's economic and political systems toward those in the West.

As part of his reforms, Gorbachev loosened the Soviet hold over Warsaw Pact nations. In autumn of 1989, the "Iron Curtain" from the Balkans to the Baltic collapsed without any move by the Soviets to prevent it. To the surprise of a watching world, the Berlin Wall, which divided the German capital of Berlin, was torn down in 1989. Communist-controlled East Germany (known as the German Democratic Republic) melted away, and the territory was reunified with democratically governed West Germany (known as the German Federal Republic). Other Warsaw Pact countries also began to replace communist rule with democratic governments and to sever their ties with the Soviet Union.

By December 1991, the Soviet Union itself had broken into fifteen smaller states, including Russia, Ukraine, Georgia, Moldova, and Tajikistan. By far the largest state is Russia. It still stretches over eleven time zones and includes more than 75 percent of the area of the former Soviet Union. With the collapse of the Soviet Union, the Cold War came to an end.

The world is still grappling with the stunning economic, political, and social changes of the

In 1989 the Berlin Wall, which separated communist East Berlin from West Berlin, was torn down. Why do you think Berliners from both sides of the wall attacked it with such vigour?

post–Cold War period. Dramatic changes in the East brought a sense of hope to a world desperately weary with the Cold War. But a new era of world peace still seemed doubtful. Old hatreds between national, religious, and ethnic groups in eastern Europe rekindled old hostilities in places like Romania and Hungary. The former Yugoslavia collapsed into violent ethnic warfare. Other new eastern European states are still struggling for economic and political stability.

The Cold War is over, but the new order in eastern Europe is fragile. Canadians are now asking themselves questions about the new world order. With the collapse of the Warsaw Pact, what role should NATO play? How can Canada help smooth eastern Europe's path toward economic and political stability? What role should Canada play in a world no longer dominated by two superpowers?

CANADA AND THE WORLD: TRADE AND AID

In 1968, Prime Minister Pierre Trudeau called for a fresh look at Canada's foreign policy. He began by slashing Canada's defence spending and freezing Canada's contribution to NATO. Trudeau also wanted to loosen Canada's ties with the United States and forge new links with other nations. He signalled Canada's new direction in foreign policy in 1970 by breaking with official U.S. policy on the communist People's Republic of China. The communists, led by Mao Zedong, had taken over the government of mainland China in 1949. The United States was hostile toward the new communist government and continued to support the exiled government on Taiwan. But Canada broke rank with the Americans by officially recognizing the People's Republic of China. It also supported communist China's membership in the United Nations.

Trudeau began to build trading relationships with China, Japan, and other Asian countries along the Pacific Rim. He also made a "good will" tour to the Soviet Union to promote cultural exchanges and new trade partnerships with Warsaw Pact nations. In 1973, the Soviet Union agreed to buy $200 million worth of Canadian wheat. The Soviet–Canadian hockey games were also part of new ties between Canada and the communist countries of eastern Europe.

Trudeau also travelled to Europe to promote a closer trading partnership with the western European nations who belonged to the European Economic Community (EEC), now known as the European Community (EC). Canada and the EEC signed an agreement for commercial and economic cooperation in 1976. The agreement gave Canada a chance to trade technological information with Europe and to increase Canadian trade and investment activities in Europe.

Canadian prime minister Pierre Elliott Trudeau helped to promote Canada on the international stage. Here he is seen meeting with Chinese leader Chou En-Lai.

Canada and the Commonwealth

Canada also used its newly found strength as a middle-power nation to aid other nations. Under Pierre Trudeau, Canada extended support to the less developed nations, known as Third World nations. Canada had a special sympathy for former British colonies that had become newly independent nations after the war. Mackenzie King, and especially Louis St. Laurent, were important in extending membership in the formerly all-white British *Commonwealth* to these new, nonwhite nations. By 1987, the forty-seven member nations of the Commonwealth came from all parts of the globe and represented a quarter of the world's population.

Canada posted official representatives to several of these Commonwealth nations and supported independence movements in Asia and Africa in such former colonies as Angola, Mozambique, Rhodesia (now Zimbabwe), and Namibia. Canada also took a strong stand on South Africa. In 1961, Prime Minister John Diefenbaker helped to force South Africa out of the Commonwealth when it refused to change its racist policy of apartheid. Apartheid was the South African government policy of keeping the black majority population separate from the ruling white minority and denying them economic and political powers.

Canada is still one of the steadiest opponents of apartheid. It has continued to urge other nations to keep the pressure on the white South African government. One of the major policy tools has been the use of sanctions against South Africa. Sanctions are measures used to force a nation to change its policies by applying international pressure. The international sanctions used against South Africa have ranged from official sports boycotts that kept South African athletes from taking part in international competitions to embargoes on South African products that severely limited the sale of South African goods abroad. Recently, the South African government bowed to international pressure and changed its policy on apartheid. It also began talks with black African leaders about new power-sharing arrangements.

Canadian Aid to the Third World

Some of the new Third World nations are stable and self-sufficient, but many are desperately poor. They

Since 1931, when the British Empire was replaced by the British Commonwealth, meetings hosted by the ruling monarch with heads of state from former British colonies have taken place. How can countries such as Canada benefit from close relations with other Commonwealth countries?

As part of its continuing effort to help Third World nations, the Canadian government funds the Canadian Industrial Development Agency, which works abroad to learn from and assist developing countries.

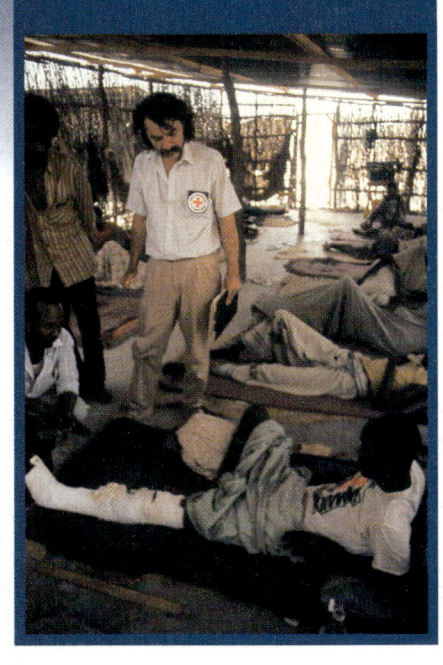

lack resources, their trade and industries are not fully developed, and they are experiencing huge population explosions. Their people are often poorly educated and lack job training. Some do not even have such basics as food, housing, clothing, clean water, and medical care.

Over the years, Canada has worked to reduce world poverty and help Third World nations onto the road to economic development. As early as the 1950s, thousands of young Canadians volunteered to work abroad in Third World development programs. Organizations like the Canadian University Service Overseas (CUSO) and World University Services of Canada (WUSC) helped bring money and technology to many less developed nations.

In the 1950s, Canada's spending on foreign aid was modest, however. In 1956–57, for example, Canada spent only $50 million on foreign aid. Its major contribution was $35 million for the Colombo Plan, an aid program for the Commonwealth countries of Asia. There, Canadian money helped pay for a cement factory in Pakistan, a nuclear-power generating plant in India, and several irrigation projects in other nations.

Canada's foreign aid increased in the 1960s after Lester Pearson became Canada's prime minister. It also expanded to include new areas. Canada began sending food to famine-stricken countries, making low-interest loans for economic development projects, and offering scholarships and technical assistance to people of the Third World. In 1968, Canada set up the Canadian International Development Agency (CIDA), which coordinates all Canadian aid projects from both government

Canadian Foreign-Aid Policy

The Canadian International Development Agency (CIDA) was created in 1968 to help the poorest countries and people in the world to help themselves. CIDA places special priority on decreasing poverty, improving economic management, promoting the increased participation of women in development programs, encouraging environmentally sound development, and ensuring secure food and energy supplies.

Canada's foreign-aid projects started with contributions to the United Nations during the 1940s. In 1950, Canada supported the Colombo Plan, assistance aimed at the newly independent Asian nations of India, Pakistan, and Ceylon (now Sri Lanka). During the next two decades, Canadian aid expanded to include the Caribbean (1958), Commonwealth Africa (1959), Francophone Africa (1961), and Latin America (1964). Below are the Canadian government foreign-aid statistics from 1980 to 1991.

Canadian Expenditure on Foreign Aid, 1980–1991

Year	Amount ($ million)
1980	1291
1981	1307
1982	1489
1983	1670
1984	1812
1985	2097
1986	2174
1987	2522
1988	2624
1989	2947
1990	2850
1991	3021

Source: Canadian International Development Agency

CUSO: LENDING A HELPING HAND FOR OVER 30 YEARS

Canadians live in a nation of prosperity, opportunity, education, and freedom. Not all nations are as fortunate. Since 1961, hundreds of Canadian volunteers working through Canadian Universities Service Overseas (CUSO) have been helping less fortunate people in nations around the world to learn important skills.

CUSO is a nongovernmental development organization founded by representatives of 21 universities and 22 organizations from across Canada. Although the majority of CUSO's budget comes from the Canadian government through the Canadian International Development Agency (CIDA), it remains an independent organization. Since 1961, over 9000 skilled Canadians have been placed in countries ranging from Bangladesh to Bolivia. Initially, the majority of the volunteers were recent university graduates who were placed in teaching positions in Third World countries. Today, however, there are far fewer requests for teachers because many nations can now fill these positions on their own. It is much more common for CUSO to receive requests for agriculturalists, foresters, mining experts, or tradespeople.

Today, CUSO workers are known as "co-operants" rather than volunteers because an emphasis has been placed on working cooperatively and in partnership with local communities. To help ensure equality, CUSO workers are paid the same wages as the local workers who are doing the same job. Although the work overseas may not be financially rewarding and the co-operants may experience some culture shock, most of them return to Canada enriched by their international experience.

Canadian environmentalist/broadcaster David Suzuki speaks to villagers in a rainforest in Papua, New Guinea, during his CUSO-sponsored tour of some of the world's last untouched tropical rainforests.

Many Canadians work overseas to help raise the standard of living in other parts of the world. Here, a Canadian nurse describes to a father in Somalia the importance of drinking plenty of liquids to avoid dehydration.

sources and nongovernmental sources. Nongovernmental organizations, sometimes called NGOs, are private groups that sponsor aid programs. NGOs receive some money from CIDA, but much of their funding comes from private citizens. Well-known NGOs include the Canadian Red Cross Society, CARE Canada, Oxfam Canada, the Unitarian Service Committee of Canada, and the Canadian Save the Children Fund.

Canada and the Global French-speaking Community

Before the 1970s, most Canadian aid still went to the English-speaking countries of the Commonwealth. But during Pierre Trudeau's years as prime minister, Canada widened the scope of its foreign aid to include former French colonies. Trudeau wanted to be sure that Canada's policy abroad matched its new commitment to the French language and culture at home. Between 1960 and 1968, the twenty-one French-speaking nations of Africa received only $300 000 in Canadian technical aid. But in 1973 they received $80 million, one-fifth of the total CIDA budget. Next to France, Canada became the biggest donor to French-speaking African nations. Canada is still an active member of the French-speaking world community, known as *la francophonie*.

CANADA'S FUTURE ROLE

Canada emerged from World War II as an important middle power. Today it still has an important role to play on the international stage. The Cold War has ended, but the world is not at peace. The future may be even more dangerous, as nations rush to stockpile massive arms supplies, ranging from highly sophisticated conventional weapons to fearsome chemical, biological, and nuclear weapons. Canada is still needed to help keep the peace and stop the spread of weapons of war.

Global poverty, hunger, and disease also threaten the future. Droughts and floods, exploding populations, and changing climates all add up to severe food shortages. It is estimated that 1 billion people do not have enough to eat and that 20 million people die every year from hunger and hunger-related diseases. Millions of people do not have the money, tools, and training to build themselves a brighter future. Canada has a history of friendship and generosity toward poorer nations, but it must continue to help relieve world poverty and help less developed nations stand on their own. Canadians recognize that they are citizens of the global village and have a share in shaping its future.

KNOWING THE KEY PEOPLE, PLACES, AND EVENTS

In your notes, clearly identify and explain the historical significance of each of the following:

United Nations (U.N.)	Foreign Policy
Lester Pearson	Igor Gouzenko
Joseph Stalin	Louis St. Laurent
North Atlantic Treaty Organization (NATO)	Warsaw Pact
Cold War	Marshall Plan
John Diefenbaker	North American Air Defence System (NORAD)
Detente	Cuban Missile Crisis
Star Wars	Strategic Arms Reduction Talks (START)

FOCUS YOUR KNOWLEDGE

1. Compare Canada's strength with that of the world's other leading nations following World War II. Explain what it means to be a "middle power."

2. Why is the "Gouzenko affair" considered to have signalled the beginning of the Cold War?

3. What actions on the part of the Soviet Union prompted western nations to fear communist expansion? How did they react?

4. How did NATO's formation ensure that both Canada's and the United States' foreign policy would be radically different from their policies before World War II?

5. Why did the Korean War occur? What role did Canadians play?

6. Describe the role Canadian peacekeepers play when they are sent to areas of conflict.

7. How did the nuclear arms race of the 1950s alter Canada's position in a potential war? How did Canada react to the new threat?

8. Why were three lines of radar strung across Canada's north? What were the names of these three lines?

9. Why were the events that occurred in eastern Europe in the late 1980s unexpected and considered by many to be revolutionary events?

APPLY YOUR KNOWLEDGE

1. Reflect on what you know about the presence of war in the world since 1945. How successful has the United Nations been in meeting the central goals of its charter?
2. If you had a role in shaping Canada's foreign policy, would you choose military or nonmilitary measures to meet your objectives? Why?
3. Explain why the two decades following World War II are regarded as Canada's "golden age" of foreign policy.
4. Explain how the Cold War between the United States and the Soviet Union was fought.
5. How did the development of nuclear weapons by both the Soviet Union and the United States alter the prospect for world peace?
6. Develop an organizer comparing Canada's foreign policy with that of the United States. In it, refer to the People's Republic of China, the Soviet Union, NATO, and NORAD.
7. Which of the following is the greatest danger facing the world in the next 50 years: war, poverty, hunger, disease, overpopulation, pollution, or climatic change? What contributions can Canada make toward achieving a solution?

EXTEND YOUR KNOWLEDGE

1. Working with one or two classmates, do some research into one of these United Nations agencies: UNICEF, WHO, UNESCO, FAO, GATT, or the World Bank. Write to the agency you are researching and ask for information about its activities. Prepare a bulletin-board display based on your research, and make a short presentation to your class.
2. Have your class put up a wall map of the world. On this map, place small Canadian flags to indicate where Canadian peacekeeping forces have been sent since 1945. In groups of three or four, research one of the areas on the map. Try to find out as much as you can about the country, the nature of the conflict, and the role Canadians played in keeping the peace. Add this information to the wall display along the borders of the map.

3. Working in groups, assume that you have been appointed as a committee by the federal government to prepare a report on Canada's foreign aid. The government has announced that it will spend an extra $100 million on foreign aid and needs to know where and how the money would be best spent. Your task is to:

   (a) do some research to find out what area(s) of the world most need Canada's aid;

   (b) decide how much to send to each of the areas researched;

   (c) suggest ways to ensure that the money is being used properly and effectively; and

   (d) suggest a creative campaign to encourage Canadians to contribute to Third World aid.

   You will find newspapers a valuable aid in this project.

4. Take a poll in your class to determine what your classmates feel is the most serious issue facing the world in the future. Write a letter on this issue, or on another issue of your choice, to the prime minister, the premier of your province, the United Nations, a major corporation, or a newspaper.

CHAPTER 16 FRENCH-ENGLISH RELATIONS

GLOSSARY TERMS

Armouries Government buildings where arms and ammunition are stored.
Referendum The process of putting a question of general importance to a direct vote of the citizens for approval or rejection.
Authority An individual, a group, or a government commanding power or respect in a community.
Urbanized A term describing a district that has developed the characteristics of cities or towns.
Jurisdiction The right or power of administering law or justice in a specific area.
Adhere To support with devotion.

FOCUS ON:

- the major social changes in Quebec since 1950
- the Quiet Revolution in Quebec
- the meaning behind Jean Lesage's election slogan, "Maîtres chez nous"
- the rise of the separatist parties, the Parti Québécois, and the FLQ
- Quebec's need for cultural and linguistic survival
- why the federal government imposed the War Measures Act in October 1970
- why Canadians rejected the Meech Lake and Charlottetown Accords

Expo 67 was the biggest birthday party in Canadian history. The day after the opening ceremonies, newspapers reported an event that marked the popular mood in Canada. A crowd of Canadian teenagers were standing in the chilly night air at the Île Ste-Hélène Expo Express subway station, waiting to leave the fairgrounds. They were from many ethnic backgrounds — English, Ukrainian, French, Italian, and more. And they were strangers to each other. Suddenly, they all joined hands and sang "O Canada." Canadians were proud of themselves and their 100-year-old nation.

But another event signalled future troubles between French and English Canada. The president of France, Charles de Gaulle, had been invited to take part in the festivities in Montreal. On July 24, 1967, de Gaulle stepped onto the balcony of Montreal's City Hall to say a few words to a jubilant Expo crowd gathered in the square. At the end of his speech, de Gaulle raised his hands into a "V" for "Victory." Then he spoke the words that jolted a nation: "Vive le Québec libre!" — "Long live free Quebec!" Many English

Canadians and some French Canadians in the crowd were outraged. Soon after, the Canadian prime minister, Lester Pearson, strongly rebuked the French president. "Canadians do not need to be liberated," he declared, and de Gaulle's visit to Ottawa was cancelled.

The four words spoken by the French president had a threatening meaning for many Canadians. "Vive le Québec libre!" had been scrawled on a wall near the Canadian National Railways building in Montreal, where a fire bomb had gone off in March 1963. It was the first attack by a group known as the **Front de Libération du Québec (FLQ)**. The FLQ were extreme separatists who wanted Quebec to be independent of English Canada, regardless of the cost. Small bands of FLQ members and other like-minded urban terrorists had been carrying out a violent campaign of sabotage against symbols of English power in Quebec. Under the slogan "Independence or death," the FLQ bombed mailboxes in Westmount, where most of the wealthy English-speaking Montrealers lived. They also firebombed *armouries* and placed dynamite in public buildings, such as the post office in Place Ville-Marie, in the name of "Québec libre." Fifteen young terrorists were eventually jailed for terrorist acts in the early 1960s, but outbreaks of violence continued until the end of the decade.

These were the actions of a small group of extremists. Most French Canadians disliked their violent tactics, but a growing number felt that Quebec had been badly treated by English Canada since Confederation. During Expo 67, some even put tags on their licence plates, saying "100 ans d'injustice" ("100 years of injustice"). Many wanted more independence for Quebec. In his Montreal speech, the French president had just given the Quebec independence movement France's support.

THE NATIONALIST MOVEMENT IN QUEBEC SINCE THE WAR

Only a small minority of French-speaking Quebeckers were separatist in 1967, but separatist feeling was growing. Less than ten years later, a political party called the **Parti Québécois (P.Q.)** would take power in Quebec. The P.Q. was a nonviolent separatist party dedicated to winning independence for the province through peaceful political means. By 1980, the people of Quebec would vote in a *referendum* on the question of independence for

When French president Charles de Gaulle spoke in Montreal in 1967, his words "Vive le Québec libre" excited many separatists. Should a foreign leader offer words of encouragement to separatists in Canada?

Quebec. Many English Canadians were confused by Quebec's demands. What had happened in Quebec? Why were French Canadians so unhappy in Confederation? What did they expect to get from separating from the rest of Canada?

French Canada had long been committed to **"la survivance,"** the survival of its own language and traditions. For two centuries, many Quebeckers had seen themselves as part of a distinctively French and Roman Catholic society. Their survival strategy was to retain the French language, the Roman Catholic faith, the traditional values of Quebec rural life, and obedience to *authority*, especially the authority of church leaders. Many wanted life to go on as it had in the past. To do so, Quebec tried to remain isolated from the rest of Canada and from the changes sweeping across postwar North America.

La Survivance After World War II

Maurice Duplessis was the premier of Quebec for all but a few years between 1936 and 1959. He, too, wanted to keep to the old ways by shutting out the outside world. He did not want English Canada to interfere in the social and cultural affairs of Quebec. But the federal government had become newly active in these areas after World War II. Duplessis believed that the province had to fight off outside influence by refusing to accept new federal programs that affected Quebec life. For example, he refused to take sizable federal grants for health care, education, and other programs because he saw them as a threat to the traditional ways of Quebec society and an intrusion of federal powers into provincial affairs. The cost of refusing federal money was a price he willingly paid for "la survivance."

But Duplessis saw no problem in encouraging the mostly English-speaking businesspeople to establish industries in Quebec. He offered businesses special privileges and tax breaks. American and English Canadian money built the factories that appeared alongside French Canadian churches on the St. Lawrence River. It paid for the new dams that were built across Quebec's rivers to harness the power for the new factories. Young French Canadians left family farms to work in the new peacetime industries. Half a million people left the Quebec countryside by 1961. They were mostly poorly paid, and they had to work hard to make ends meet.

Quebec workers soon became angry at their working conditions. The 1940s and 1950s were marked by bitter labour disputes. The Duplessis government had close links with Quebec's business community, and it sided with the mostly English-speaking owners against their mostly French Canadian workers. In the famous 1949 strike at Asbestos, Quebec, Duplessis ordered provincial police to break up the picket lines and arrest the strike leaders. What made the Asbestos strike stand out in memory was that some Roman Catholic clergy broke with the church and supported the strikers, as did some university students and young intellectuals — including the wealthy young lawyer and journalist, Pierre Trudeau. Trudeau, who would eventually become a prime minister of Canada, later

This traditional rural village in Quebec is dominated by the steeple of the Catholic church and surrounded by farms that still reflect a system of land division from centuries past.

edited a book about the Asbestos strike. The strike came to symbolize changing times in Quebec.

Support for the Asbestos workers was the beginning of the rejection of Duplessis's Quebec. "La survivance" had come to mean something different to many Quebeckers. They were tired of the old ways and the old authorities. The Roman Catholic Church was slowly losing its authority in public matters. Church attendance began to drop off, and Quebec moved toward a secular (nonreligious) society.

Quebec has undergone significant change since 1950. Modern-day Montreal is a busy cosmopolitan city dominated by skyscrapers.

The province had also become more urban and industrialized. By 1961, almost 75 percent of the people of Quebec lived in urban areas, making Quebec the second-most-*urbanized* province in Canada. Montreal was the fastest-growing city in Quebec; between 1941 and 1961, its population swelled by 1 million people. New neighbourhoods were patterned on the North American model, with single-family homes, smaller lots, and local shopping centres. French Canadians were generally poorer than other Canadians, but they were struggling to buy radios and televisions and get their share of the "good life" in North America. Many Quebeckers realized that the rural French Canada of farm and parish church was gone forever. They wanted to bring the economy, the government, and education into the twentieth century.

THE QUIET REVOLUTION

In 1959, Maurice Duplessis died suddenly. His Union Nationale government had been tainted by a scandal involving widespread bribes for government jobs and by corrupt election practices. "Il faut que ça change!" ("Things must change!") shouted the new Liberal leader, Jean Lesage. Lesage's Liberals won a narrow victory over the Union Nationale.

Reforms Under the Lesage Government

Quebec's new Liberal premier took office in 1960. Quebec had become an urban and industrial society. Lesage came to symbolize French Canadians' willingness to accept the new Quebec. His early years in power came to be called the **Quiet Revolution**. The Lesage government made sweeping changes. It created a professional civil service to replace the Union Nationale's habit of giving government jobs and money to political supporters. It breathed new life into an outdated educational system run by the Roman Catholic Church. Most French Canadians had no schooling after elementary school. Little preparation was provided in the high schools for careers in science, engineering, or business. By the end of the decade, the government-controlled school system had grown by more than 500 000 students. More than 40 000 students were attending new two-year colleges called CEGEPs. The Lesage government also began to build a large new social welfare system, gave broad powers to labour groups, and encouraged the growth of labour unions. The Quiet Revolution was modernizing Quebec and seemed to be making it more like the rest of Canada.

Nationalism and the Quiet Revolution

There was, however, a strong element of French Canadian nationalism in the Quiet Revolution. In 1962, Lesage had called an election on the slogan "**Maîtres chez nous**" — "Masters in our own house." He was not seeking independence for Quebec, but he did want more control for French Canadians inside their own province. English-speakers were a relatively small percentage of the population, but they controlled commercial life in Quebec. Of the fifty largest corporations in Quebec, only three were French Canadian. Only a handful of French Canadians occupied important management positions in major corporations in Quebec. On the other hand, most unskilled workers were French Canadian. They often made less money than workers doing the same jobs in English Canada, and the language in the workplace in Quebec was English. Many French Canadians bitterly resented their place at the bottom of the economic ladder.

The Lesage government wanted to break the dominance of English Canadians in the province and to encourage French Canadians to play a bigger role in Quebec's economic future. It wanted to take over foreign-owned power companies in Quebec and create a new government monopoly called Hydro-Québec. Only a huge government-owned company could build the power projects to supply Quebec's future needs for industrial power. This company would give the province more control over its economic future.

Quebec voters overwhelmingly agreed with Lesage's aims. His government won the provincial election with a large majority in 1962. Eleven private power companies were quickly taken over, and Hydro-Québec was born. The working language at Hydro-Québec was French, and the construction was planned and carried out by French Canadian managers and engineers. The success of Hydro-Québec gave French Canadians a new self-confidence.

Still, not all French Canadians were happy with Quebec's situation. When they looked at Canada, they did not see a nation made up of ten provinces. They saw a country founded on a partnership between "**deux nations**"—French and English. But they believed that Quebec had never been treated as an equal by English Canada. Lesage pressed the federal government for "special status" for Quebec. He felt that Quebec needed more powers than other provinces to protect the French "nation's" language and culture. Lesage warned that Canada had to find a way to "keep Quebec in," or Confederation would fail. He demanded that the federal government turn over money for federal programs affecting Quebec life to the province. Quebec would then use the money to pay for similar programs, but set up by the Quebec government — an arrangement called "opting out."

Lesage wanted Quebec to be able to opt out of a whole range of programs in health, education, and social security. Prime Minister Lester Pearson had promised that the Liberal Party would give greater recognition to French Canadians. His government also depended on support from Quebec, so it could not ignore Quebec's demands for special treatment. Pearson tried for compromise by allowing Quebec

Jean Lesage, premier of Quebec from 1960 to 1966, was famous for his slogan "Maîtres chez nous." What did this phrase mean to French Canadians? Does it still apply today?

to run its own pension plan. Not long after, Quebec was also allowed to use money from Ottawa to set up its own student loans, youth allowances, and medical insurance program. Quebec had won at least some special treatment.

French Canadians also wanted more recognition of their language and culture. They argued that under the British North America (BNA) Act, Canada was officially a country with two languages and two cultures. But many francophones were upset that English dominated everywhere, even in Montreal, and that English was the working language of the federal government in Ottawa. French-speaking communities outside Quebec had a hard time getting education in French for their children. In fact, many English Canadians did not think that the French language and culture had any place in Canada, despite constitutional guarantees for them. In 1966, a Liberal member of Parliament from Toronto told students in Quebec to give up their French heritage. "It's time you all accepted the English conquest of 1763," he said, "just as the English accepted conquest by William the Conqueror." He was sent a thousand letters of support from other English Canadians.

The Pearson government took Quebec's hopes and concerns more seriously, however. Pearson wanted French Canadians to feel more at home in Canada. Many French Canadians objected to Canada's flag because the Red Ensign was a British symbol. It seemed to be a slap in the face to French Canada. Pearson pushed for a distinctive new flag that represented all Canadians, hoping that a new flag would help to unite the country. But changing the Red Ensign seemed to many English Canadians to be a rejection of the English heritage in Canada. After a bitter debate, the Red Ensign was replaced by the red maple leaf flag in February 1965.

Pearson's government also set up a Royal Commission on Bilingualism and Biculturalism in 1963 to seek advice about working out "an equal partnership between the two founding races." As one historian put it, the commission did "as much teaching as listening." The commissioners told Canadians that French must be on an equal footing with English in Canada. They said that the federal government could no longer speak only English. They also warned Canadians that Quebeckers needed to be assured that all of Canada was their homeland. If they failed, then the country would break up.

FEDERALISM OR SEPARATISM?

Pierre Trudeau became the prime minister of Canada in 1968. He was widely seen as someone who could unite a badly divided country. Born in Montreal to a French Canadian father and English Canadian mother, Trudeau was fluent in

Did we make the right choice? The former Red Ensign (top right) and our present Canadian flag (top left), which was adopted in 1965, were among the choices for a new Canadian flag. Which do you think best represents Canada?

ROCH CARRIER'S *THE HOCKEY SWEATER*

Roch Carrier is one of Quebec's best-known writers. Many of his novels and short stories have been translated into English and have become widely known across Canada. *The Hockey Sweater* is a light-hearted story about a young French Canadian boy who faces a terrible dilemma when Eaton's mistakenly sends him a Toronto Maple Leafs sweater instead of a Montreal Canadiens sweater. As you read this story, consider how it reflects French–English relations and what aspects of French Canadian culture you can detect in it.

The winters of my childhood were long, long seasons. We lived in three places — the school, the church and the skating-rink — but our real life was on the skating-rink. Real battles were won on the skating-rink. Real strength appeared on the skating-rink. The real leaders showed themselves on the skating-rink. School was a sort of punishment. Parents always want to punish children and school is their most natural way of punishing us. However, school was also a quiet place where we could prepare for the next hockey game, lay out our next strategies. As for church, we found there the tranquillity of God: there we forgot school and dreamed about the next hockey game. Through our daydreams it might happen that we would recite a prayer: we would ask God to help us play as well as Maurice Richard.

We all wore the same uniform as he, the red, white and blue uniform of the Montreal Canadiens, the best hockey team in the world; we all combed our hair in the same style as Maurice Richard, and to keep it in place we used a sort of glue — a great deal of glue. We laced our skates like Maurice Richard, we taped our sticks like Maurice Richard. We cut all his pictures out of the papers. Truly, we knew everything about him.

On the ice, when the referee blew his whistle the two teams would rush at the puck; we were five Maurice Richards taking it away from five other Maurice Richards; we were ten players, all of us wearing with the same blazing enthusiasm the uniform of the Montreal Canadiens. On our backs, we all wore the famous number 9.

One day, my Montreal Canadiens sweater had become too small; then it got torn and had holes in it. My mother said: "If you wear that old sweater people are going to think we're poor!" Then she did what she did whenever we needed new clothes. She started to leaf through the catalogue the Eaton company sent us in the mail every year. My mother was proud. She didn't want to buy our clothes at the general store; the only things that were good enough for us were the latest styles from Eaton's catalogue. My mother didn't like the order forms included with the catalogue; they were written in English and she didn't understand a word of it. To order my hockey sweater, she did as she usually did; she took out her writing paper and wrote in her gentle schoolteacher's hand: "Cher Monsieur Eaton, Would you be kind enough to send me a Canadiens' sweater for my son who is ten years old and a little too tall for his age and Docteur Robitaille thinks he's a little too thin? I'm sending you three dollars and please send me what's left if there's anything left. I hope your wrapping will be better than last time."

Monsieur Eaton was quick to answer my mother's letter. Two weeks later we received the sweater. That day I had one of the greatest disappointments of my life! I would even say that on that day I experienced a very great sorrow. Instead of the red, white and blue Montreal Canadiens sweater, Monsieur Eaton had sent us a blue and white sweater with a maple leaf on the front — the sweater of the Toronto Maple Leafs. I'd always worn the red, white and blue Montreal Canadiens sweater; all my friends wore the red, white and blue sweater; never had anyone in my village ever worn the Toronto sweater, never had we even seen a Toronto Maple Leafs sweater. Besides, the Toronto team was regularly trounced by the triumphant Canadiens. With tears in my eyes, I found the strength to say:

"I'll never wear that uniform."

"My boy, first you're going to try it on! If you make up your mind about things before you try, my boy, you won't go very far in this life."

My mother had pulled the blue and white Toronto Maple Leafs sweater over my shoulders and already my arms were inside the sleeves. She pulled the sweater down and carefully smoothed the creases in the abominable maple leaf on which, right in the middle of my chest, were written the words "Toronto Maple Leafs." I wept.

"I'll never wear it."

"Why not? This sweater fits you... like a glove."

"Maurice Richard would never put it on his back."

"You aren't Maurice Richard. Anyway, it isn't what's on your back that counts, it's what you've got inside your head."

"You'll never put it in my head to wear a Toronto Maple Leafs sweater."

My mother sighed in despair and explained to me:

"If you don't keep this sweater which fits you perfectly I'll have to write to Monsieur Eaton and explain that you don't want to wear the Toronto sweater. Monsieur Eaton's an Anglais; he'll be insulted because he likes the Maple Leafs. And if he's insulted do you think he'll be in a hurry to answer us? Spring will be here and you won't have played a single game, just because you didn't want to wear that perfectly nice blue sweater."

So I was obliged to wear the Maple Leafs sweater. When I arrived on the rink, all the Maurice Richards in red, white and blue came up, one by one, to take a look. When the referee blew his whistle I went to take my usual position. The captain came and warned me I'd be better to stay on the forward line. A few minutes later the second line was called; I jumped onto the ice. The Maple Leafs sweater weighed on my shoulders like a mountain. That captain came and told me to wait; he'd need me later, on defense. By the third period I still hadn't played; one of the defensemen was hit in the nose with a stick and it was bleeding. I jumped on the ice: my moment had come! The referee blew his whistle; he gave me a penalty. He claimed I'd jumped on the ice when there were already five players. That was too much! It was unfair! It was persecution! It was because of my blue sweater! I struck my stick against the ice so hard it broke. Relieved, I bent down to pick up the debris. As I straightened up I saw the young vicar, on skates, before me.

"My child," he said, "just because you're wearing a new Toronto Maple Leafs sweater unlike the others, it doesn't mean you're going to make the laws around here. A proper young man doesn't lose his temper. Now take off your skates and go to the church and ask God to forgive you."

Wearing my Maple Leafs sweater I went to the church, where I prayed to God; I asked him to send, as quickly as possible, moths that would eat up my Toronto Maple Leafs sweater.

Source: Roch Carrier, *The Hockey Sweater and Other Stories* (Toronto: House of Anansi Press, 1979), pp. 77–81.

both French and English. Trudeau was also a committed federalist: he believed in a strong federal government. He opposed giving special status to Quebec, arguing that giving federal powers to a provincial government would weaken Canada. He believed that Quebec already had all the power it needed to protect the French language and culture. He urged Quebeckers to stop blaming English Canadians for their problems and to use their existing rights to help Quebec move forward.

The Federalist Answer for Quebec: Bilingualism

How was French Canada's demand for equal treatment to be met without giving the province of Quebec special status? Pierre Trudeau's answer was official bilingualism. Canada was to become a nation with two official languages, English and French. That way Canadians, whether their native tongue was French or English, would be at home anywhere in Canada. Trudeau believed that Canada's future as a unified nation depended on bilingualism and equal opportunities for Canadians who spoke either language. He wanted French-speakers to have education and other services in French wherever there were French-speaking communities in Canada. That meant that English Canadians had to treat French Canadians as full and equal partners in Confederation.

In 1969, Trudeau's government brought in the Official Languages Act. It gave all Canadians the legal right to deal with the federal government and courts in either French or English. Provinces also began offering more services in French, including French-language education — sometimes called "French immersion programs." By 1967, Ontario was offering education in French from kindergarten right through secondary school. Manitoba re-established the French school system that had been outlawed in 1916. British Columbia also began offering schooling in French. In the years ahead, hundreds of young English-speaking Canadians would be schooled in French. The packaging of all products was required to be labelled in both French and English, and a generation of youngsters were eating "cereal/céréales" for breakfast.

Canada's official bilingualism is evident on the products we buy. Can you read both the French and the English wording?

These people showed their support for bilingualism in 1968 by marching on Parliament Hill in Ottawa. How do you think Canada benefits from being officially bilingual?

Growing Quebec Nationalism

Despite government actions during the 1960s, Quebeckers continued to ask themselves if Canada was really their "home and native land." In the past, French Canadians had often faced hostility and prejudice in English Canada. Were they going to be better treated in English Canada now? Before 1960, people in Quebec had used the word "Canadiens" to describe themselves. During the 1960s, they began thinking of themselves instead as "Québécois," citizens of Quebec. The Quebec provincial government had become their "national" government.

The Growing Independence Movement in Quebec

More Québécois began wanting the "nation" of Quebec to have more power to run its own affairs. The leader of the Union Nationale Party in Quebec, Daniel Johnson, complained that Lesage had not been forceful enough with Ottawa. He ran against Lesage in Quebec's provincial election on the slogan "equality or independence." He used the threat of Quebec independence to press a vigorous fight for Quebec rights. After Johnson became premier of Quebec, he changed the name of the Quebec legislature to Assemblée Nationale du Québec. It was an unmistakable sign that nationalist feeling was on the rise in Quebec.

When Johnson took power in 1966, there were already two small separatist political parties in Quebec. These parties did not think that gaining more power from the federal government was enough. They wanted Quebec to separate from Canada and become an independent nation. But a few extreme separatist groups in Quebec, including the FLQ, were not willing to wait for democratic changes. They saw violence as the only way to achieve independence.

Premier Johnson suddenly died, and his Union Nationale Party began to flounder without his leadership. A Liberal government was elected in Quebec in 1970. The new Quebec Liberal premier, Robert Bourassa, was a strong federalist and shared Prime Minister Trudeau's belief that Quebec should stay in Canada. But Bourassa still faced rising separatist feelings in Quebec. The new official opposition in the Quebec National Assembly was the Parti Québécois (P.Q.), led by René Lévesque. The P.Q. had campaigned on a platform of independence for Quebec and won 23 percent of the popular vote, but only 7 of 109 seats.

The Parti Québécois leader, a former journalist and television celebrity, was widely known and respected in Quebec. René Lévesque had been a war correspondent and later hosted a popular

René Lévesque, in the centre of this 1968 photo, shows his support for students protesting the handing over of a school for French-speaking students to English-speaking students. Later, Lévesque would become the founder and leader of the separatist party, the Parti Québécois.

international-affairs program on CBC television. His television popularity had helped him launch his political career as a member of Jean Lesage's cabinet in 1960. But Lévesque had broken with the Liberal Party in 1967 to found a new political party dedicated to Quebec independence. He united the small and quarrelsome separatist political parties into a single and more powerful political party, the Parti Québécois.

The Parti Québécois had taken root in Quebec, and it was growing. The new separatist rumblings shook the province. What did Quebec's future hold? Should Quebec remain a province inside Canada or seek independence? Quebeckers were divided and increasingly anxious about the answer. Meanwhile, separatist extremists of the FLQ were fuelling the uneasiness in Quebec. FLQ members already claimed responsibility for more than 200 terrorist bombings. Where would the next FLQ attack occur?

The presence of a soldier standing by a Canadian Forces helicopter in October 1970 fascinates these young Montrealers.

The October Crisis of 1970

The answer came all too soon. On the morning of October 5, 1970, four men abducted the British trade commissioner, James Cross, at gunpoint from his Montreal home. The FLQ kidnappers demanded $500 000 in ransom money and transportation to Cuba in return for their hostage. They also demanded the release of so-called "political prisoners," FLQ members jailed for terrorist bombings. And they demanded that the FLQ manifesto (declaration of beliefs) be read over national television networks. Five days later, another FLQ group staged a second kidnapping. This time they seized Quebec cabinet minister Pierre Laporte in front of his house.

At first, many Quebeckers had some sympathy for the FLQ. Three thousand students rallied in Montreal's Paul Sauvé arena, chanting "FLQ, FLQ, FLQ." Some public figures urged the Bourassa government to negotiate with the FLQ. Among them were P.Q. leader René Lévesque and *Le Devoir* editor Claude Ryan. After consultations with the federal government, Robert Bourassa agreed to broadcast the FLQ manifesto and to give the kidnappers safe passage out of the country in return for Cross's release. But Bourassa refused to release the FLQ terrorists who were in prison.

As the crisis deepened, Bourassa turned to the federal government for troops to help police in a massive search for the kidnapped men. Prime Minister Trudeau took action. He sent in the federal troops and, for the first time in peacetime, brought in the **War Measures Act**, which took away the civil rights of Canadians. It made membership in the FLQ a criminal offence and banned political rallies. It also allowed the police to arrest, question, and detain suspects without charge for up to ninety days. Trudeau argued that invoking the War Measures Act was justified because the FLQ kidnappings were the beginning of widespread conspiracy to overthrow the government. Police swept across Quebec, conducted thousands of searches, and arrested more than 400 people. In the end, however, fewer than two dozen people were tried and convicted.

Polls showed that nine out of ten Canadians supported Trudeau's use of the War Measures Act. But for months afterward, newspapers and magazines carried on a debate about whether Trudeau had overreacted. Was there a major FLQ conspiracy against the government? Was the FLQ threat dangerous enough to justify taking away Canadians' civil liberties? Some Canadians are still asking these questions, but so far they have not been answered.

On October 17, Pierre Laporte's body was found in the trunk of a car on the St. Hubert air base. The mood in Quebec shifted after Laporte's death. Many people who had sympathized with the FLQ were horrified by the violent murder. Two months later, the RCMP and the Quebec police discovered that James Cross was being held hostage in a house in north Montreal. In return for his release, his captors and their families were allowed to go to Cuba. A month later, the last FLQ kidnappers remaining at large were found. A total of twenty-three people were brought to trial and sentenced to prison for terrorist acts during the October Crisis.

QUEBEC AND THE LANGUAGE CRISIS

The October Crisis put a stop to separatist terrorism. But trouble was brewing over the role of the French language and culture in Canada. Many Québécois were as unhappy as English Canadians with bilingualism. They did not want two languages across Canada. They wanted one language, French, in Quebec. "We are not asking to speak French in Vancouver," explained one French Canadian. "We don't want to feel at home in Winnipeg or be served in French in your post office. You write 'luggage' on your airport doors. We'll write 'bagage' and serve you in French in our post office."

The Quebec Liberals and Bill 22

Protecting the French language in Quebec was a growing concern for many Quebeckers. Before World War II, the birth rate among French Canadians had been the highest in Canada. But it began dropping slowly in the postwar years. In the 1960s it suddenly plunged, and by the end of the decade it was the lowest in Canada. In addition, immigration had skyrocketed in the postwar years, and many newcomers had settled in Montreal. Most of these new immigrants chose to send their children to English-language schools because English was the language of North America.

During the October Crisis of 1970, members of the Canadian Armed Forces could be seen on the streets of Montreal dressed in full battle fatigues. Why is this an unusual scene for Canada?

Under the double impact of dropping birth rates and climbing immigration, French-speakers began to fear for the survival of their language and culture in Quebec. One solution was to make French *the* language of Quebec and to make sure that newcomers became part of the French-speaking community.

The **Official Languages Act**, known as "Bill 22," was passed in 1974. It made French the official language of Quebec, brought in new measures to strengthen the use of French in the workplace, and sharply limited parents' right to choose the language in which their children would be educated. Only children who passed a test showing that they knew English could go to English-language schools. This meant that most children of recent immigrants had to attend French schools. Bill 22 sparked a bitter language battle, but the Quebec government defended the law as necessary for the survival of the French language. After all, it said, French Canada was merely an island in the wide sea of English North America. There were only 6 million French-speakers among 280 million English-speakers. Only strong measures would save the French language against those odds.

By 1976, the Bourassa government was faltering. The Quebec Liberals had been damaged by rumours of scandal and corruption. It was also a time of rising inflation and unemployment. A series of strikes by workers in the public service, including teachers, firefighters, and police, had caused chaos in the province. Quebeckers were deeply troubled by Quebec's economic woes, but the Bourassa government had no ready answers. Quebeckers began to look elsewhere for political leadership. Lévesque and the Parti Québécois seemed to be the best choice.

QUEBEC IN CRISIS, 1976–1980

On November 15, 1976, English Canada woke up with a shock. The Parti Québécois had swept in power in Quebec, partly on the promise of a referendum on Quebec independence. The P.Q. won 41 percent of the popular vote and 71 of the 110 seats in the Quebec National Assembly. "Now we have to build this country of Quebec," René Lévesque told a cheering crowd. The Parti Québécois had promised to win independence for Quebec; its election seemed to spell the end of Confederation.

Some P.Q. members were impatient for change and demanded immediate independence for Quebec. But the P.Q. government wanted to soothe the fears of people both inside and outside the province before it made a move. Many French Canadians were still afraid of sovereignty (independence) for Quebec. What would happen to Quebec if it left Confederation? Could it survive on its own? Lévesque did not want to rush down the road to independence. He chose a step-by-step approach called "étapisme."

French-Language Rulings Outside Quebec

1864 NOVA SCOTIA: French-speaking Catholic Acadians are forbidden to have French schools.

1871 NEW BRUNSWICK: Catholic schools are closed and teaching of French (and in French) is forbidden in public schools.

1877 PRINCE EDWARD ISLAND: Catholic and French schools become outlawed.

1890 MANITOBA: Separate (Catholic) schools are outlawed and teaching of French (and in French) is forbidden at the secondary level.

1892 NORTHWEST TERRITORIES (including what is now Alberta and Saskatchewan): Teaching in French is outlawed in public schools and Catholic schools are prohibited.

1905 ALBERTA AND SASKATCHEWAN: The regulations of 1892 (Northwest Territories) are confirmed.

1916 MANITOBA: Teaching of French is forbidden at all levels.

1930 SASKATCHEWAN: Teaching of French is prohibited even outside school hours.

Source: Bernard, *What Does Quebec Want?* p. 27, taken from Abbé Lionel Groulx, *L'Enseignement Francois au Canada* (Montreal: Granger Frères, 1935).

The Parti Québécois and Bill 101

The first step was to continue the French-language debate from where it had left off. The Parti Québécois had its own answer to the debate over Bill 22. After a furious battle in the National Assembly, the P.Q. passed a new and even stronger language law in 1977. The Charter of the French Language, known as **Bill 101**, placed strong restrictions on the use of English in Quebec. French was to be used by the government, the courts, and businesses in the province. Under Bill 101, commercial signs had to be in French only. The Supreme Court of Canada struck down this part of Bill 101, saying that the ban violated both the provincial and federal charters of rights.

In December 1988, however, a Quebec Liberal government under Robert Bourassa quickly used the "notwithstanding clause" in the Canadian Charter of Rights and Freedoms to sidestep the Supreme Court decision. The notwithstanding clause gave provincial legislatures the right to override the charter, but the override had to be confirmed by new legislation every five years. The Quebec override on Bill 101 was to expire in 1993. At the same time, the Bourassa government brought in Bill 178, which required all outside signs to be in French only.

Bill 101 also drastically limited access to English schools. Most children whose families came from outside Quebec were denied the right to education in English. Only children with at least one parent who had gone to an English school in Quebec (the "Quebec Clause") or who were already in English schools themselves could be taught in English. The 1982 Constitution Act contained a "Canada Clause" that superseded the Quebec Clause in Bill 101. The Canada Clause allowed children with at least one parent schooled in English anywhere in Canada to go to English schools. But children of recent immigrants now had no choice. They were forced to go to French schools. It seemed that the rights of newcomers to Quebec had been taken away to assure the survival of the French language. Even Lévesque regretted what he called "an unhealthy aspect" of Bill 101. But he believed it was necessary for Quebec's immigrants to be French-speakers if the French culture was to survive. Otherwise, he asked, what "can we do — just go down the drain?"

Bill 101 outraged many people in Quebec's English-speaking and immigrant communities. They formed a group called **Alliance Quebec** to challenge the new law in court. The head offices of many English-speaking corporations had already been relocating from Montreal to Toronto and Calgary. After Bill 101, even more English-speaking corporations shifted their head offices to English Canada. But other English-speaking Canadians stayed and began learning French. So did the children of newcomers who stayed in Quebec. With Bill 101, Quebec had achieved a major goal: it kept the French language — and therefore French culture — alive in North America.

Thousands of Quebeckers celebrated the Parti Québécois election victory in 1970. Do you think these people wanted a change in government or did they want out of Canada?

Many Canadians outside of Quebec felt that Bill 101, which made French the only official language in Quebec, violated the rights of non-francophones in Quebec. However, these protesters at the Quebec National Assembly show their support of Bill 101.

The Referendum on Sovereignty-Association

During the 1976 election campaign, Lévesque had promised voters a referendum on independence. Four years later, the P.Q. was ready to hold the long-promised referendum. Polls showed that most French Canadians wanted to change the federal system, but that only a minority wanted outright independence from Canada. So Lévesque proposed a vote on something less than full independence, called "**sovereignty-association**." Sovereignty-association meant that Quebec would be a "sovereign," or independent, state. In particular, Quebec would control its own taxes, its industrial and social policies, and its citizenship and immigration laws. But it would keep close economic ties with the rest of Canada. Lévesque was proposing an open economy with Canada, along the lines of the European common market. Money, goods, and people would flow freely between Quebec and the rest of Canada.

The referendum question was phrased to win the largest possible number of supporters: Did they authorize the Quebec government to negotiate for sovereignty-association with the government of Canada? If so, there would be a second referendum so that Quebeckers could vote on the results of the negotiations. The "Yes" side staged a rousing campaign, and so did the "No" side. Quebeckers were caught in an avalanche of campaign ads. The vote looked very close. Just six days before the Quebec referendum, Pierre Trudeau made a promise to Quebec. If Quebec voted "No" in the referendum, he would "set in motion the mechanism of constitutional renewal." Nothing, he promised, would stop him. Quebeckers could look forward to a new system of federal government.

May 20, 1980, was Referendum Day in Quebec. Almost 90 percent of the province's eligible voters went to the polls. Almost 60 percent of them voted "No." The referendum defeat was a major setback for the Parti Québécois. René Lévesque had predicted that the vote would "either open the door to the future or will close it for a long time." Quebec had shut the door on sovereignty-association, at least for a while.

THE CONSTITUTIONAL CRISIS

Now it was Pierre Trudeau's turn to make good on his promise of "constitutional renewal." Canada's Constitution, the British North America (BNA) Act, had served Canada for more than a century. But Canada was a different nation now, and Trudeau felt the old Constitution no longer fitted the times. Some Canadians believed that changing it might help keep Quebec in Canada. But to do so, the new Constitution would have to recognize that French Canada was an equal partner in Confederation. It would also have to recognize that Quebec was a distinct (unmistakably different) society.

The BNA Act had remained under the *jurisdiction* of the British Parliament at the request of the Canadian government. Attempts had been made to patriate, or bring home, the BNA Act, but they had all met with failure, in part because the provinces could not agree on an amending formula. After the Quebec referendum, Trudeau was more determined than ever to get constitutional change. In particular, he wanted a formula under which any amendment could be approved if the federal government and a certain number of provincial governments agreed to it. He also wanted to add a written charter of rights and freedoms to the Constitution. In particular, he wanted a charter guarantee of the right of all Canadians to be educated in English or French. These were measures that Quebec had opposed in the past.

Trudeau proposed his constitutional changes in a meeting of all the "first ministers" (provincial premiers and the prime minister) in September 1980. But only two provinces, Ontario and New Brunswick, supported him. Trudeau then announced that the federal government would carry out its plans for constitutional change with or without the support of the provinces. The Progressive Conservative opposition managed to block Trudeau's plans and forced him to agree to postpone further action until the Supreme Court of Canada ruled on the validity of his initiatives.

The court declared that the federal government's action was legal but unconstitutional. The judgment was so confusing that neither the federal nor the provincial governments knew whether the courts had ruled in their favour. But they did realize that the future would be very difficult unless they could hammer out a new agreement. The ten provincial premiers met with Prime Minister Trudeau for one last conference in Ottawa in early November 1981. After several exhausting days of negotiations, they had still had not reached an agreement. But after midnight on November 5, all the premiers except René Lévesque were awakened and called together to look at a last-minute compromise proposal.

Lévesque woke up the next morning to discover that the prime minister and the other nine premiers had reached an agreement. Trudeau announced to the press that a compromise — a new constitutional package, including an amending formula and a written charter of rights and freedoms — had been found. Quebec felt betrayed. Constitutional change had been promised as a way of meeting Quebec's needs; now the rest of Canada was forcing a Constitution on Quebec that it had not accepted. Other groups, such as women's groups who had lobbied hard for constitutional guarantees of equality and Native leaders who were pressing for guarantees of Native rights, also felt betrayed.

The rest of Canada went ahead in the face of Quebec's angry accusations. First the patriation package was revised to make some provisions for women, Native peoples, and other groups that had been left out of the November agreement. Then it was passed in the Parliament of Canada on December 2, 1981. Finally, Canada formally asked Britain to pass the requested legislation, and Canada's new Constitution was ready for patriation.

While the rest of Canada celebrated the signing of the new Constitution by Queen Elizabeth II and the prime minister, Pierre Trudeau, Quebeckers felt bitter about not having their needs addressed. Should Quebec be granted special status under the Canadian Constitution?

April 17, 1982, was patriation day. Queen Elizabeth II signed the Constitution on the steps of the Parliament buildings in Ottawa. Prime Minister Trudeau was at her side. At the stroke of a pen, Canada became a fully independent nation. Its Constitution had come home at last, complete with an amending formula and a new Charter of Rights and Freedoms. Only one province, Quebec, stayed away from the patriation ceremony. On that day in Quebec, flags were lowered to half-mast, and René Lévesque led a protest march through the streets of Montreal.

The Meech Lake Accord

Quebec would not agree to sign the Constitution until five years later. The P.Q. was out of power in Quebec, and the Liberals had returned to govern under the leadership of Robert Bourassa. When the Progressive Conservatives came to power, Canada's new prime minister, Brian Mulroney, promised "national reconciliation." He wanted to end the bitterness between Quebec and the rest of Canada over the Constitution. In April 1987, he invited the ten provincial premiers to a conference at a private retreat at Meech Lake, in the hills outside Ottawa. His aim was to find a new constitutional agreement that satisfied every province, including Quebec. To the amazement of most observers, the provinces managed to reach an agreement. It became known as the **Meech Lake Accord**. The five major points of the accord were:

- Quebec was recognized as a "distinct society."
- Three of the nine Supreme Court judges were to be from Quebec.
- Constitutional amendments about the structure or powers of the government (for example, changing the Senate or the Supreme Court, or creating new provinces) required the agreement of all ten provinces.
- Provinces could "opt out" of new federal programs and establish their own matching programs with federal money.
- Quebec had control of its own immigration policy in the province.

All ten premiers signed the Meech Lake Accord in 1987. Mulroney declared that the agreement was a way of welcoming "Quebec back into the Canadian family." The Meech Lake Accord gave all ten provinces more powers over federal–provincial relations, the Supreme Court, and the Senate. The House of Commons ratified (passed) the Meech Lake Accord with support from all three political parties. Quebec was the first provincial legislature to ratify it. This set in motion a three-year constitutional clock. All the other provincial legislatures also had to ratify the Meech Lake Accord by June 23, 1990, or the agreement was dead.

Between 1987 and 1990, however, conditions in Canada changed. There was a loud outcry against Meech Lake in many parts of the country. Some English Canadians were outraged by Bourassa's Bill 178, which had sharply restricted the right to English-language signs. Women's groups were concerned that the "distinct society" clause might take away Quebec women's constitutional rights under the Charter of Rights and Freedoms. Natives leaders were angry that their demands for Native rights had not been fully met by the Meech Lake Accord. Another problem for Native leaders was the amending formula. Could the Yukon and Northwest Territories, where Native peoples were in the majority, ever win enough support to become provinces? Under the Meech Lake Accord, they would need a "Yes" vote from all ten provinces. In addition, the three provinces of New Brunswick, Manitoba, and Newfoundland had elected new governments. Their premiers had not been at Meech Lake, and they were therefore not necessarily committed to the accord. Time was running out.

Mulroney and the ten provincial premiers met in Ottawa in June 1990 in a last, desperate effort to save the accord. After a week they emerged with a compromise, but the understanding quickly broke down. Time ran out on the Meech Lake Accord. It was not ratified, and the second attempt to give Quebec a place in the Canadian Constitution ended in failure. "This is a sad day for Canada," said Prime Minister Mulroney. The failure of Meech Lake was a sharp setback for Quebec and the Mulroney government.

The Charlottetown Proposal

The Meech Lake Accord came to be known as the "Quebec round." It had focused on meeting Quebec's needs and getting the province's signature on the Canadian Constitution. Part of the reason that Meech Lake died, however, was that other groups — including Native peoples, the smaller provinces, and people concerned with social and economic rights — had felt left out. They wanted their concerns taken into account in any new constitutional deal. The death of Meech Lake marked the birth of the "Canada round" a few months later. Quebec had decided to put together a new set of proposals for constitutional change. If the rest of Canada did not come up with acceptable counter-proposals, then Quebec would hold a referendum on independence for Quebec by October 1992.

The Canadian government sprang into action. It knew it had to get an acceptable constitutional package together or face another crisis over sovereignty for Quebec. Many people had objected to the way in which the Meech Lake Accord had been reached. It seemed to have been a political deal that was accomplished without public input.

The "Canada round" was a series of public forums and commissions at the federal and provincial levels. In addition, dozens of other conferences were organized by special-interest groups. The aim of all these conferences was to consult the public on the new constitutional package. Then Ottawa, the ten provinces, the two territories, and leaders of four major Native groups met in Charlottetown and reached an agreement on August 28, 1992. The outcome was a proposal called the **Charlottetown Accord**.

The Charlottetown Accord proposed sweeping changes to Canada's Constitution. Among its proposals were aboriginal self-government, Senate reform, a new division of federal–provincial powers, and a social and economic union that defined Canada's commitment to programs like universal health care, workers' rights, and environmental protection. It also included the "Canada Clause," which set out the principles and values on which the country was founded, including the statement that Quebec was a "distinct society."

Quebec had planned to hold a second provincial referendum on sovereignty. Then it switched to a referendum on the Charlottetown Accord. Ottawa then decided that all Canadians would vote on the Charlottetown proposal in a national referendum.

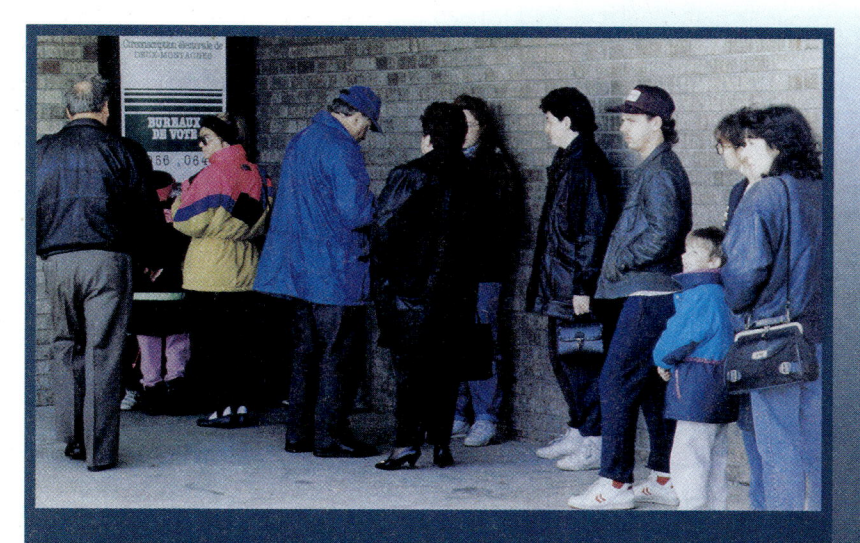

Since 1982 both the federal and provincial governments have worked to amend the Constitution to meet the needs of all Canadians, including French Canadians and Natives. These people are voting on the proposed changes in the Charlottetown Accord, which was defeated in the 1992 referendum.

"MY LANGUAGE IS FRENCH AND MY COUNTRY IS QUEBEC"

A common misconception held by many English Canadians is that French Canadians are no different except that they speak French. In fact, Quebec remains a distinct society, detached in significant ways from the rest of Canada. The former premier of Quebec, René Lévesque, once observed:

We are Québécois. What that means first and foremost — and if need be, all that it means — is that we are attached to this one corner of the earth where we can be completely ourselves; this Quebec, the only place where we have the unmistakable feeling that "here we can be really at home." Being ourselves is essentially a matter of keeping and developing a personality that has survived for three and a half centuries.

The distinctiveness of Québécois culture is reflected in the values and attitudes of Quebec teens. On topics ranging from sports to politics and entertainment, there is a significant difference between francophone Quebeckers and their English-speaking counterparts inside Quebec and throughout the rest of Canada.

The distinctiveness of Quebec teens is clearly reflected in their support for sports teams and whom they consider heroes. Unlike the rest of Canada, Quebec teens tend to adopt Canadiens, especially French Canadians, as their heroes. For sports franchises to be successful, point out authors Reginald Bibby and Donald Posterski: "The Québécois must be given the opportunity to create their own winners and superstars rather than have them parachuted in from English Canada or the United States. The Montreal Canadiens are widely supported in Quebec, not simply because they are a good hockey team but because historically they have been a team dominated by French Canadian talent."

Even the widespread increase in mass media and travel has done little to diminish Quebec's cultural isolation. Even though Quebec's teens watch more television than those in any other region of Canada do, they have a surprisingly low familiarity with national and international events. This can be explained by Quebeckers' preference for French-language television over

Hockey Favourites of Teens and Baseball Favourites of Adults
Top three in %'s

Quebec		BC		Prairies		Ontario		Atlantic	
Canadiens	78	Canucks	61	Oilers	28	Canadiens	30	Canadiens	47
Nordiques	12	Flames	9	Flames	24	Leafs	19	Bruins	12
Bruins	5	Canadiens	7	Kings	13	Kings	14	Oilers	11
Others	5	Others	23	Others	35	Others	37	Others	30
Expos	93	Jays	69	Jays	74	Jays	89	Jays	71
Tigers	1	Expos	10	Expos	8	Expos	5	Expos	24
Jays	<7	Indians	7	Reds	4	Red Sox	1	Pirates	2
Others	6	Others	14	Others	14	Others	5	Others	3

Adult source: *(Project Can90)*

programming from the United States. Furthermore, a 1992 survey found that 21 percent of Quebeckers aged 15 to 19 had never been outside of their province. This figure is far higher than that of any other province.

The next time you hear on the news or read in a newspaper that Quebec is struggling to preserve its distinct society, reflect on some of the cultural differences and remember that the differences between English and French Canada go much deeper than simply language.

Source: Adapted from Reginald W. Bibby and Donald C. Posterski, *Teen Trends: A Nation in Motion* (Toronto: Stoddart, 1992), pp. 115–136.

Teen Travel Experiences

In %'s

	Quebec Franco	Quebec Anglo	BC	PR	ON	ATL	ALL CDA
To Other Provinces							
Several times year or more	12	30	18	31	21	27	21
Yearly or less	46	61	64	64	54	63	57
Never have	42	9	18	5	25	10	22
To The United States							
Several times year or more	11	35	38	14	35	12	25
Yearly or less	47	55	51	66	52	55	54
Never have	42	10	11	20	13	33	21
Outside of N. America							
Several times year or more	2	6	5	1	4	1	3
Yearly or less	24	37	53	26	44	19	35
Never have	74	57	42	73	52	80	62
Never Outside Own Province	21	2	2	3	4	8	7

The question for voters was: "Do you agree that the Constitution of Canada should be renewed on the basis of the agreement reached on Aug. 28, 1992?"

All three major political parties supported the "Yes" vote. But in the last weeks before the October referendum, there was a groundswell of popular feeling against the accord. The "No" vote was led by a new western political party called the **Reform Party**, as well as other special-interest groups, including the National Action Committee on the Status of Women. The Assembly of First Nations (AFN) chiefs also refused to support the "Yes" campaign of AFN leader Ovide Mercredi. Mercredi had helped craft new constitutional guarantees concerning aboriginal self-government. But some Native leaders were suspicious of the guarantees and were unwilling to support them.

Other people stepped onto the "No" side because they felt that the Charlottetown proposals gave too much to Quebec or too little to their own regions. Almost every section of the agreement came under attack by some group. Many other Canadians were simply overwhelmed by the sheer size of the agreement. How could they possibly understand it all or make a reasonable choice? Should they vote for the whole package even if they did not agree with parts of it?

On October 26, 1992, the Charlottetown Accord went down to resounding defeat. It was approved by only four of the ten provinces: Newfoundland, New Brunswick, Prince Edward Island, and Ontario. Canadians were exhausted by the long constitutional battle. British Columbia Premier Michael Harcourt said, "We should put the Constitution on the back burner for a while and turn the burner off." He seems to have spoken for the whole nation. After the October referendum, most Canadians did not even want to hear the word

"Constitution." The first priority for most Canadians was surviving a deep recession that had sent the Canadian economy into a nosedive and put many Canadians out of work.

WHAT IS AHEAD FOR QUEBEC AND CANADA?

Quebec's future in Canada remained an open-ended question. In 1993, newly elected Prime Minister Jean Crétien, a French-speaking Quebecker, appealed to Canadians to "leave constitutional quarrels on the back burner." He feared that any future constitutional talks about Quebec's role in Confederation would tear the nation apart for good. But Quebeckers had also elected 54 Bloc Québécois members to Parliament — enough for the Bloc to become the official opposition party. The federal Bloc Québécois, like the provincial Parti Québécois, was a political party dedicated to creating a separate Quebec. The Bloc MPs seemed unlikely to back away from their demands for Quebec sovereignty. Indeed, their status as official opposition in Parliament gave them a new forum for making their demands heard across Canada.

Meanwhile, many English-speaking Canadians were losing sympathy with Quebec demands. In particular, the western-based Reform party — the other new political party to rise to national importance in the 1993 election — strongly opposed negotiating conditions for Quebec's independence. The political strength of the Bloc Québécois in Quebec and the reform party outside Quebec suggests that public opinion is deeply divided between French and English Canadians. At present, both sides appear unready for making major compromises to keep the country together. The question remains: What, if anything, can or should Canadians do to try to patch up the split between French and English Canada?

The independence movement remains very strong in Quebec. In fact, the defeat of the Charlottetown Accord fuelled the separatist movement. Why would the defeat of the accord have this effect?

In 1861, John A. Macdonald had said, "Whatever you do, *adhere* to the Union. We are a great country and shall become one of the greatest in the universe if we preserve it; we shall sink into insignificance and adversity if we suffer it to be broken." What will happen to Macdonald's dream of a single nation "from sea to sea"? Will Canada remain united, or is it destined to break apart? Only time will tell for certain.

KNOWING THE KEY PEOPLE, PLACES, AND EVENTS

In your notes, clearly identify and explain the historical significance of each of the following:

> Front de Libération du Québec (FLQ)
> La Survivance
> Maîtres Chez Nous
> War Measures Act
> Bill 101
> Sovereignty-Association
> Charlottetown Accord
> Parti Québécois (P.Q.)
> Quiet Revolution
> Deux Nations
> Official Languages Act
> Alliance Quebec
> Meech Lake Accord

FOCUS YOUR KNOWLEDGE

1. Why were the words spoken by Charles de Gaulle on his visit to Montreal so controversial?
2. Although the FLQ and the P.Q. had similar goals, their tactics were quite different. Briefly explain the similarities and differences between the two political organizations.
3. Why did Maurice Duplessis reject federal grants?
4. Why was the Asbestos strike in 1949 an important political event in Quebec?
5. Why did many French Canadians feel exploited in the 1960s? Use specific examples to support your answer.
6. Why was the creation of the new Canadian flag accompanied by so much controversy?
7. Why do many French Canadians feel their language is being threatened? What measures have been taken to help safeguard the French language in Canada?
8. Why was there a great need for constitutional reform in Canada by the 1980s?
9. Why was Quebec unhappy about both the constitutional changes and the process used to bring about these changes in 1982?
10. Explain how the Meech Lake Accord was eventually defeated.

APPLY YOUR KNOWLEDGE

1. How had Quebec society changed by 1961? Provide evidence to illustrate the nature and significance of the change.
2. Why were the years of the Jean Lesage government called the "Quiet Revolution"? Use concrete examples to support your answer.
3. Outline the measures taken by the Lesage government to enable French Canadians to gain greater control of Quebec's economy. How successful were these measures?
4. Describe the actions of the FLQ prior to October 1970. Did the plight of French Canadians justify such extreme actions? Explain your answer.
5. Explain Pierre Trudeau's views on French Canadians' status within Canada. Did Trudeau's views help to unite Canada, or did they widen the gulf between Quebec and the rest of Canada?
6. To many Canadians, the actions of the Parti Québécois government under René Lévesque seemed quite drastic. Are these actions defensible, considering the threats to French Canadian culture? Explain your answer by using specific examples.

EXTEND YOUR KNOWLEDGE

1. Working in groups, prepare a news story that examines how Canadians felt about the War Measures Act. First, prepare a list of questions to ask people who remember the October Crisis. Once you have prepared your questionnaire, survey three to five people about their reactions to Trudeau's handling of the crisis. Using the results of your survey, prepare a news report in the form of a newspaper article, or on cassette or videotape.
2. Conduct a poll in your school to see how other students feel about Quebec's role in Canada. Once you have your results, construct a series of bar graphs to illustrate your findings.
3. Recreate the debate about the Charlottetown Accord by dividing the class in half: one side represents the "Yes" forces, and the other side represents the "No" forces.
4. Write a poem or design a poster that reflects your feelings about Canada's future and the events that need to occur for Canada to enter the next century as a strong and united country.

CHAPTER 17 CANADIAN–AMERICAN RELATIONS

GLOSSARY TERMS

Nonconfidence Vote The result when a budget or another important government measure is defeated in a vote in the House of Commons. If a government loses a vote of confidence, it must resign.
White Paper An official report stating government policy or the result of a government investigation on an important matter.
Voodoos Supersonic F-101B jets that can carry nuclear and non-nuclear air-to-air missiles.
Cruise Missile An American-made missile that is launched from an aircraft and flies at an altitude of 61 metres to 183 metres.
Automotives Pertaining to cars, trucks, and other motor vehicles.

FOCUS ON:

- the role of the Canadian Broadcasting Corporation and the National Film Board in developing Canadian culture
- the American influence on Canadian culture
- Canada's close military ties with the United States
- the debate over foreign investment in the Canadian economy
- how free-trade agreements are reshaping the Canadian economy

The Canadian author Robertson Davies once described Canada as the "attic" of the North American continent: upstairs was the unimportant little nation of Canada and downstairs was the giant American superpower. Even though Canada occupies an enormous chunk of North America, Davies is not the only Canadian who sees this country as a small and unrecognized nation perched atop the huge and imposing United States of America. Many Canadians feel very uneasy about sharing a continental home with the Americans.

But in the late 1940s and early 1950s, Canadians were less worried about living so close to their downstairs neighbours. They were proud of their wartime achievements and looked forward to equally satisfying peacetime successes. They believed that they could do many things just as well as the Americans, and some things even better. Canada was at the forefront of science and technology. Canadians had discovered insulin and were pioneers in finding peacetime uses for nuclear energy, including nuclear radiation as cancer treatment. Canadians were also big winners in sports, especially winter sports. The **Canadian Broadcasting Corporation (CBC)** was recognized worldwide for its successful radio programming for people of all ages and tastes. The CBC Drama Department was alive with talent and produced memorable radio dramas. It was the golden age of Canadian radio. Canadians took pride in themselves and did not worry much about the problem of Canadian national identity.

THE AMERICANIZATION OF CANADIAN CULTURE

During the 1950s, however, the rising tide of American culture turned into a flood, and American radio, television, films, books, and magazines began pouring into Canada. American movies flickered across the screens of new drive-in theatres from Halifax to Vancouver. By 1956, the new transistor radios pulsed with the American blues/rock/country mix of Elvis Presley, "the king of rock and roll," and other popular American musicians. When Presley made an appearance at Toronto's Maple Leaf Gardens in 1956, he was mobbed by adoring fans.

Television swept across Canada in the 1950s. Another American "king" who became a Canadian favourite was the television character Davy Crockett, "king of the wild frontier." Hundreds of Canadian youngsters wearing fake raccoon-tailed hats and toting Davy Crockett rifles roamed their neighbourhoods, pretending to hunt bears on the American frontier. Canadians also loved American comedy and variety programs. Only "Hockey Night in Canada" could compete with shows like "I Love Lucy" and "The Ed Sullivan Show." Soon the CBC began televising American quiz shows and "sitcoms" (situation comedies) to get enough money from advertisers to air occasional Canadian dramas and news programs.

THE GOVERNMENT AND CANADIAN CULTURE

A whole generation of Canadians in the 1950s was growing up to the beat of American music, watching American television and movies, reading American books and magazines, and idolizing American stars. The trend toward Americanization had been noticed as early as 1949. The prominent Canadian Vincent Massey was asked to head the Royal Commission on National Development in the Arts, Letters, and Sciences to investigate the American influence on Canadian culture. It came to be known as the **Massey Commission**, and in 1951 it reported that Canadian culture was at risk. It recommended stronger support for Canadian cultural agencies like the CBC and the **National Film Board (NFB)**.

The CBC had been created in the 1930s to provide a Canada-wide radio network and later expanded to include television broadcasting, which began in Toronto in 1952. It operated in French and English, and produced drama, comedy, and news

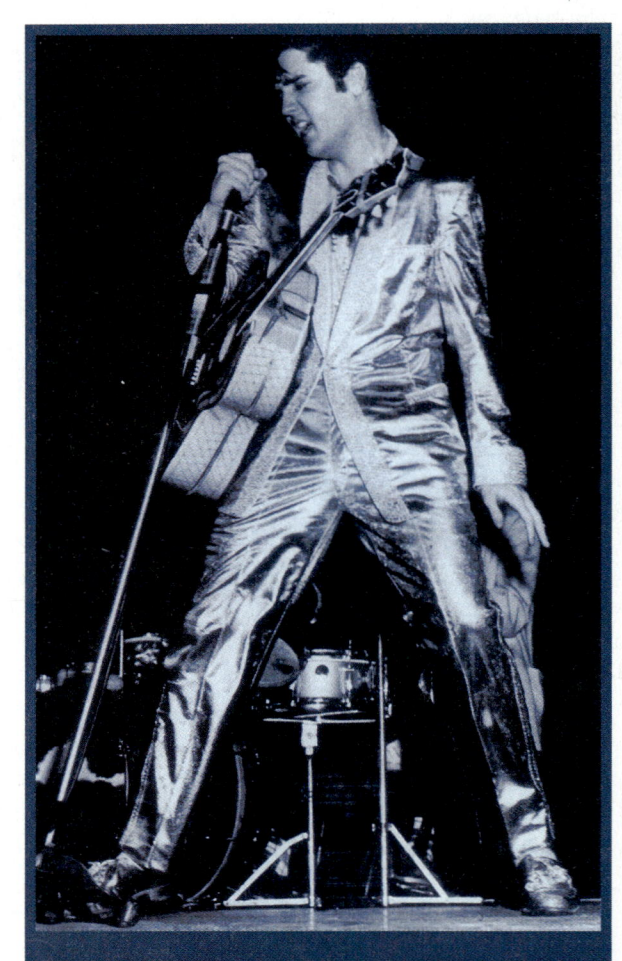

When Elvis Presley, the "King of Rock 'n' Roll," appeared at Maple Leaf Gardens in 1956, he was greeted by thousands of adoring fans. Are rock stars still worshipped by teenagers the way Elvis was?

In the early years of filmmaking, the National Film Board of Canada made films about Canada using Canadian talent. How important are institutions such as the NFB in preserving Canadian culture?

programs in both languages. The NFB had been set up in 1939 and produced hundreds of war propaganda films. After the war its aim was to make films about Canada by Canadians, including documentaries, feature films, and cartoons. Both CBC television and the NFB were intended to raise the quality of broadcasting and offer Canadian alternatives to the American mass media.

The Canada Council

The Massey Commission also recommended creating the **Canada Council**, which would use tax dollars to support the arts and culture in Canada. In 1956, the Canada Council was given government funding — thanks to two Canadian multimillionaires who died before they could protect their money from the Canadian tax authorities. The windfall taxes from the estates of Sir James Dunn and Isaac Walter Killam were used to give grants to Canadian writers, actors, painters, and other Canadian artists. Millions of dollars were also provided to ballet companies, theatre companies, and universities. The result was an enormous outburst of creativity beginning in the 1950s. The newly founded Shakespearean festival at Stratford, Ontario, and the Shaw Festival at Niagara-on-the-Lake won international acclaim. The Royal Winnipeg Ballet became one of the world's great ballet companies. The Toronto and Montreal symphony orchestras were models of musical professionalism. Writers like Margaret Laurence and Robertson Davies won loyal fans at home and abroad.

Although the Canadian arts community was thriving, American popular culture was still on the rise in Canada in the early 1960s. For example, in the first week of March 1963 seven of the top ten shows on CBC TV were made in the United States. American popular culture jammed the airwaves, filled TV screens, and leapt out of magazine and paperback book racks in every corner store in

Many Canadian actors began their careers on stage at the Stratford Festival Theatre performing in Shakespearean plays. Both Lorne Greene, left, and William Shatner, right, went on to become major Hollywood stars.

CANADIAN-AMERICAN RELATIONS

Bryan Adams has been one of the most successful recording artists in the history of Canadian music. He once created a great deal of controversy by claiming that government support for musicians promoted mediocrity. Do you agree with his statement?

Canada. The Canadian writer and editor Robert Fulford complained that some "large part of the furniture of my mind and imagination has always been clearly stamped 'Made in America'."

Government Action to Protect Canadian Culture

After the centennial celebrations of 1967, Canadians looked to the federal government to stem the tide of American culture flooding over Canada. In 1968 the government created the **Canadian Radio–Television Commission (CRTC)**, which was given the job of controlling radio and television licensing. The CRTC announced in 1970 that radio and TV stations would have to broadcast a certain percentage of Canadian content or risk losing their licences. Thirty percent of all music played on the radio had to be Canadian. Radio stations turned to Canadian singers like Anne Murray and Gordon Lightfoot and groups like Rush and Bachman–Turner Overdrive to meet the new "Canadian content" rules. Sixty percent of prime-time TV productions had to be made in Canada, and no more than 30 percent of programming could come from any other country. Soon television series like "The Beachcombers" and "King of Kensington," which featured Canadian actors, writers, and producers, turned up on Canadians' TV sets.

The government also spent millions of dollars to build a Canadian feature-film industry. In the 1970s, films like *Goin' Down the Road, Kamouraska, Mon Oncle Antoine,* and *Why Shoot the Teacher?* gave Canadians a chance to see their own country on the wide screen. Canadian book publishers were given special loans and grants to help them boost the sale of Canadian books. Tax laws about magazine advertising were changed to make it impossible for American magazines like *Time* to publish a Canadian edition. More Canadian history and literature courses were offered in public schools. Canadian-studies programs were established in universities, and the Department of Immigration

How much Canadian television do you watch? Some argue that the Canadian Broadcasting Corporation (CBC) should restrict itself to producing Canadian programs and should not import American shows. Do you agree?

severely restricted the hiring of foreign professors — mostly American — for Canadian university positions. It was hoped that these measures would help promote a distinctive Canadian culture.

The arts in Canada grew enormously in the 1970s. At the beginning of the decade, there were just five professional dance companies in Canada. Ten years later, there were twenty-three. The number of Canadian publishing companies almost doubled. There were 121 professional theatres in Canada — six times more than at the start of the decade. Half of the plays they produced were Canadian. In 1970, the Canadian author Pierre Berton had worried out loud that Canadians rarely discovered their own country in music and books. "We must sing our own songs, dream our own dreams," he told a Senate committee on the mass media. By 1982, however, the world-renowned literary critic Northrop Frye was able to say that "Canadian literature since 1960 has become a real literature and is recognized as such all over the world." The arts community thrived in the 1970s and early 1980s.

The distinctive brand of humour and music of the Canadian band, Barenaked Ladies, has made them very popular. Can you think of other Canadian bands who sing about unique Canadian experiences?

Government Funding Today

During the years when Brian Mulroney was Canada's prime minister, however, the federal government cut almost $500 million from the budgets of the CBC, the Canada Council, the NFB, and other cultural agencies. The Canada Council's funding, for example, was 20 percent less in 1992 than in 1986. Provincial-government and private funding for the arts was also drying up. Many Canadians were deeply concerned about the cutbacks. They worried that the future for the arts in Canada looked grim. Arthur Gelber, former chairman of the National Arts Centre in Ottawa, asked bitterly, "Why worry about U.S. takeovers when we have already scorched our own earth?" Should Canadians be concerned about funding to support Canadian culture? Do we need Canadian artists and performers to help us "sing our own songs, dream our own dreams"?

DEFENCE AND FOREIGN POLICY: CANADA–U.S. RELATIONS

Culture was not the only area in which American dominance posed problems. Political relationships between Canada and the United States were troubled as well. John Diefenbaker, who became prime minister in 1957, was a strong Canadian nationalist, and he was uneasy about American attitudes toward Canada. Diefenbaker's mixed feelings about Americans were shared by many Canadians in the late 1950s and early 1960s. The Cold War had brought the United States and Canada closer together than ever before: Canada had joined the United States in opposing communism in Europe and Asia; both nations were NATO (North Atlantic Treaty Organization) members, and both had fought in the Korean War. From time to time there had been disagreements, but relations in general were close and friendly. Still, some Canadians felt that Americans

SHAPING AMERICAN CULTURE: CANADA'S INFLUENCE ON THE UNITED STATES' ENTERTAINMENT

Everyone is aware of the tremendous influence of American culture on Canada, but have you ever stopped to think about how much Canada has influenced American culture? Over the past three decades, American television has highlighted the talents of many Canadians, from Lorne Greene on "Bonanza" to William Shatner on "Star Trek," and recently Jason Priestley, the heart-throb on "Beverly Hills 90210." Other Canadians enjoying considerable success south of the border include Mike Myers of "Wayne's World," Michael J. Fox, and k.d. lang. Canadians are so prevalent in American entertainment that someone once stated in a skit on "Saturday Night Live" (a Canadian creation), "I remember a time when America wasn't Canadian." Below is a list of Canadians past and present who have become famous in the United States and often have been mistaken for Americans. How many can you identify? Try to add other names to this list.

Stage and Screen
Genevieve Bujold
Raymond Burr
Len Cariou
Brent Carver
Hume Cronyn
Colleen Dewhurst
Marie Dressler
Glenn Ford
Lorne Greene
Margot Kidder
Raymond Massey
Kate Nelligan
Leslie Nielsen
Mary Pickford
Christopher Plummer
Jason Priestley
Ivan Reitman
William Shatner
Helen Shaver
Jay Silverheels
Donald Sutherland
Kiefer Sutherland

Broadcast News
Peter Jennings
Arthur Kent
Robert MacNeil
Morley Safer

Magicians and Psychics
Doug Henning
The Amazing Kreskin

Comedy
Dan Aykroyd
John Candy
Jim Carrey
Tommy Chong
Phil Hartman
Rich Little
Howie Mandel
Lorne Michaels
Rick Moranis
Mike Myers
Martin Short
David Steinberg
Alan Thicke
The Kids in the Hall

Cartoon Heroes
Superman (created by a Canadian, Joe Shuster)
Ren and Stimpy (created by a Canadian, John Kricfalusi)

Music
Bryan Adams
Paul Anka
Bachman-Turner Overdrive
The Band (except for Levon Helm)
Leonard Cohen
Celine Dion
Jeff Healey
k.d. lang
Gordon Lightfoot
Joni Mitchell
Anne Murray
Oscar Peterson
Rush
Paul Shaffer
Neil Young

Game Show Hosts
Monty Hall
Alex Trebec

k.d. lang

Source: Adapted from *The New York Times*

took Canada for granted and ignored Canadian concerns. Diefenbaker was not alone in complaining that the United States treated Canada like a "forty-ninth state composed of Mounted Police, Eskimos, and summer vacationers."

The Battle Over the Bomarc Missiles

The defence of North America became a top military priority for the United States after World War II, and Canada played a big part in American defence planning. By the mid-1950s, Canadians felt they could safeguard themselves from a Soviet nuclear bomber attack only by a policy of joint air defence with the more powerful United States. America's military might was Canada's defence against a Soviet nuclear attack on North America.

It was John Diefenbaker who reluctantly put Canada under the American defence umbrella. Shortly after taking office in 1957, Prime Minister Diefenbaker agreed to join the North American Air Defence Command (NORAD) and to share in building a network of radar defences across the Canadian North. He accepted U.S. Bomarc-B missiles for Canada and a battery of American-made Honest John missiles for the Canadian army in Europe. These weapons were effective only when armed with nuclear warheads. Diefenbaker also agreed to supply Canada's air force squadrons in NATO with CF-104 airplanes. To meet NATO military objectives in Europe, these airplanes were also intended to carry nuclear weapons. Diefenbaker also signed the Defence Production Sharing Agreement, which tied the defence industries of the two countries more closely together. His decisions seemed to commit Canada to a strong role in North American and NATO defence and to the use of nuclear weapons.

But defence relations between the two nations were not smooth. Diefenbaker met the newly elected American president, John F. Kennedy, face to face for the first time in 1961. The two men took an instant dislike to each other. The World War I veteran from Saskatchewan had little in common with the wealthy young president from New England. When the subject of Canada's defence commitments came up, the Canadian prime minister backed away from accepting American nuclear weapons for Canadian armed forces. There had been a recent upsurge of protest against nuclear weapons in Canada. The Co-operative Commonwealth Federation (CCF), the Liberal Party, women's groups, and many intellectuals raised a storm of protest against "nukes." The prime minister told Kennedy that "in view of public opinion in Canada it would be impossible politically at [the] moment...to accept nuclear weapons."

It was not the last time Diefenbaker turned a cold shoulder to the American president. During the 1962 Cuban Missile Crisis, Kennedy insisted that the Soviets remove nuclear missiles from Cuba, but the Soviet leader Nikita Khruschchev refused.

By the 1960s Canadians had become very aware of the dangers of the nuclear arms race. Would you have joined an anti-nuclear rally such as this one?

THE AVRO ARROW

As the Cold War intensified in the 1950s, Canada became increasingly concerned with the possibility of a Soviet attack. To guard against an attack, Canada required modern supersonic aircraft. The CF-100 Canucks, which had been in use since 1953, were slow and outdated despite their reliability. As early as 1949, the Canadian government had backed the A.V. Roe Company in the ambitious project of developing one of the world's fastest supersonic jets: the Avro Arrow.

The jet developed by the A.V. Roe company was a twin-engine, all-weather interceptor jet and was reputed to be the fastest and most advanced interceptor of its time. Reports from test pilots praised the speed and handling of the Arrow. Despite this acclaim, the Avro Arrow project was cancelled on February 20, 1959, and led to a loss of 14 000 jobs. Many of those who lost their jobs were top scientists and engineers who fled Canada to find employment in the American space program.

Why would the government give up on a jet with so much potential? The answer to this perplexing question could have been the high costs of the project. When the Arrow was proposed, it was estimated that each aircraft would cost $2 million to produce. At this cost, Canada could expect international sales and planned to make about 600 planes. However, during the development of the Avro Arrow, costs skyrocketed by over 600% to $12.5 million per plane. Therefore, the government was not successful at selling the Arrows to foreign buyers because the price had become too high. It decided to scrap the Avro Arrow and opted to buy F-101 Voodoo fighters from the United States.

The government, led by Prime Minister John Diefenbaker, received a great deal of criticism for this decision. The loss of jobs, as well as the renewed reliance on American military technology and the blow to Canada's aerospace industry, did not sit well with Canadians. What advice would you have given Prime Minister Diefenbaker? Should the project have been shelved or continued?

The sleek-looking Avro Arrow was a technological marvel for its time. Unfortunately, the development project was plagued with problems, leading to a quick demise for this Canadian fighter plane.

American NORAD aircraft were put on immediate alert for a possible Soviet nuclear attack over the Canadian Arctic. Kennedy had counted on Canadian military support in the looming conflict, even though Canada was told about the U.S. plans for a naval blockade of Cuba just two hours before Kennedy made a televised announcement to the American people. Diefenbaker, however, delayed putting Canada's NORAD aircraft on the alert until just before the crisis ended.

The Americans were enraged at Diefenbaker's lack of enthusiasm, and so were many Canadians who supported Kennedy's action. However, after the nuclear showdown over Cuba, many other Canadians were even more strongly opposed to nuclear weapons. By the end of 1962, it was time for a debate over Canada's defence commitments and nuclear weapons. The newly founded New Democratic Party (formerly the CCF) was firmly against nuclear weapons for Canada. But Liberal leader Lester Pearson, who had also opposed nuclear weapons, changed his mind. He declared that Canada had made defence promises about nuclear arms to its American and European allies and should keep them. Diefenbaker was still undecided, torn by bitter debate among his cabinet ministers on the question of nuclear weapons. In a speech to the House of Commons he waffled, making statements that could be taken as either for nuclear weapons or against them. As a result, the Diefenbaker government was brought down by a *nonconfidence vote* in Parliament in February 1963 on the question of nuclear weapons.

Diefenbaker ran for re-election in 1963 on an anti-U.S. appeal. "It's me against the Americans, fighting for the little guy," he declared. It was the first time since 1911 that Canadian–American relations were a major issue in an election. The Liberals and Progressive Conservatives were in a "dead heat" in the final days of the campaign. Lester Pearson's Liberals won a narrow victory but failed to win a majority of seats in Parliament. Pearson had to settle for a minority government.

Pearson had promised to accept nuclear weapons and to smooth relations with the United States, and he kept his word. The new prime minister told Kennedy that Canada was ready to arm its Bomarcs, Honest Johns, and CF-104s with nuclear warheads. He also used his famous diplomatic skills to try to protect Canadian interests without irritating the Americans too much. For the next few years, relations between Ottawa and Washington were mostly friendly.

Pearson encountered occasional rough spots in Canadian–American relations, especially during a head-to-head conflict with U.S. President Lyndon Johnson over American policy in the increasingly bloody and unpopular war in Vietnam. In a speech at Temple University in Philadelphia in April 1965, Pearson gently prompted the Americans to "rethink their position" on bombing raids over North Vietnam. During a lunch meeting with Lyndon Johnson the next day, the American president grabbed Pearson by the lapels and harangued him for making a speech critical of American policy in Johnson's own back yard. The matter was quickly smoothed over by both sides, but the incident shows how difficult it sometimes was for Canada to keep an independent stance in foreign policy and still maintain friendly relations with the United States.

Canada's Defence Policy Under Trudeau

In 1968, Pearson retired as prime minister. Pierre Trudeau, the new Liberal leader, had very different ideas about Canadian–American relations. In Pearson's 1964 *"white paper"* on defence, Canada and the United States were called "partners" in the defence of North America. But the Cold War had started to thaw in the 1960s, and Trudeau was less concerned about the Soviet threat. Trudeau decided to reduce Canada's defence commitments, especially in Europe. He also wanted to set Canada on a more independent foreign policy. Trudeau stepped away from official U.S. foreign policy by building new political, cultural, and economic relations with the

In the late 1970s, the testing of cruise missiles in Canadian air space became a controversial issue. Many Canadians such as these joined in demonstrations, determined to keep cruise missiles out of Canada.

communist world and with other nations in Europe, Asia, and Africa.

Trudeau was also determined to change Canada's nuclear policy. During the Trudeau years, Canada slowly backed out of its nuclear commitments to NATO and NORAD. Between 1970 and 1972, the Honest John nuclear missiles were taken away from Canadian NATO forces in Europe. The CF-104 airplanes in Germany were stripped of nuclear missiles and rearmed with conventional (non-nuclear) rockets. At about the same time, the NORAD Bomarc missile sites in Canada were removed. In 1984, the aging *Voodoos* bought by the Diefenbaker government were finally replaced with CF-18 Hornets armed with conventional (non-nuclear) weapons. By July 1984, the last nuclear warheads had been removed from Canadian soil.

Canada was still indirectly linked to nuclear arms through its membership in NATO and NORAD. The Canadian government still allowed U.S. ships with nuclear-arms capacity to sail into Canadian ports, and the Canadian defence industry was still closely tied to the United States. Canadian companies continued to accept million-dollar defence contracts for developing, building, and testing nuclear parts from missile launchers to guidance systems.

Ronald Reagan, who became the U.S. president in January 1981, pledged to "make America strong again" by rebuilding U.S. military power. The Reagan government pressed Canada to take a more active defence role because Americans felt that Canadians were taking a "free ride" on the American defence system. It insisted that Canada should give something in return. Reagan asked Trudeau for permission to test the new nuclear *Cruise missile* in the Canadian Arctic.

Canadians raised a storm of protest, and "Refuse the Cruise" signs sprang up all across the nation. Despite the massive anti-nuclear protest and his own personal dislike of nuclear arms, Trudeau felt he could not say no. He signed a five-year agreement in 1983 that allowed the United States to make up to six tests a year of unarmed Cruise missiles in Canadian air space. The first Cruise missile test took place at the Primrose Lake test range near Cold Lake, Alberta, in March 1984.

Canadian prime minister Brian Mulroney developed a close friendship with American president Ronald Reagan. What are the potential benefits and dangers that could result from close ties between the Canadian and American governments?

Mulroney and Canadian–American Defence

Pierre Trudeau's defence alliance with the United States was reluctant, and personal relations between Trudeau and Reagan were chilly. But when the new Progressive Conservative leader swept into office not long after Trudeau retired, it was another story. Brian Mulroney's first order of business as prime minister was closer friendship with the United States. On September 24, 1984, he told an American journalist, "Good relations, super relations, with the United States will be the cornerstone of our foreign policy."

On Saint Patrick's Day, 1985, President Reagan flew to Quebec City for talks with Prime Minister Mulroney. Both leaders were of Irish descent, and they ended their first day at a gala concert, singing together "When Irish Eyes Are Smiling." Their talks were quickly nicknamed the "**Shamrock Summit.**" They announced a number of agreements, including new defence arrangements and more joint ventures in space like the very successful Canadarm for the American space-shuttle program. However, Mulroney later wavered about accepting Reagan's invitation to take part in the Strategic Defence Initiative (SDI) space-weapons system known as "Star Wars." Many Canadian nationalists and peace groups did not want Canada to become involved in a new and dangerous U.S. nuclear-defence effort. Although Mulroney turned down official Canadian participation, he left the door open for Canadian companies to accept SDI defence contracts.

Canadian Sovereignty in the Arctic: The *Polar Sea*

At about the same time, another event stirred up trouble between the United States and Canada. The U.S. Coast Guard ship the **Polar Sea** planned to sail from Greenland to Alaska in August 1985. As a courtesy, the U.S. Coast Guard had told Canadian officials about its plans, but the Americans did not feel they needed Canada's permission to make the voyage. They viewed the Northwest Passage through the Arctic as an international waterway. On the other hand, the Canadian government claimed that the Northwest Passage belonged to Canada and that foreign ships needed permission to sail through Canadian waters.

When the *Polar Sea* voyage became public knowledge, there was an unexpected public outcry in Canada. Opposition leader Jean Chrétien accused Mulroney of selling out Canadian interests. Mulroney's first action was to give the U.S. Coast Guard permission for the *Polar Sea* voyage, even though they had not asked for it. Then he turned around and warned the Americans that failing to recognize the Arctic as Canadian territory was "an unfriendly act." "It is ours," he declared. "We assert sovereignty over it." He promised angry Canadians that Canada would build a large icebreaker, upgrade the Canadian military in the Arctic, and buy nuclear-powered submarines for Arctic patrol duty. (Neither the icebreaker nor the submarines were ever built.) The Mulroney government also began talks with the United States on the Arctic. These talks resulted in the Agreement on Arctic Co-operation in 1988. The

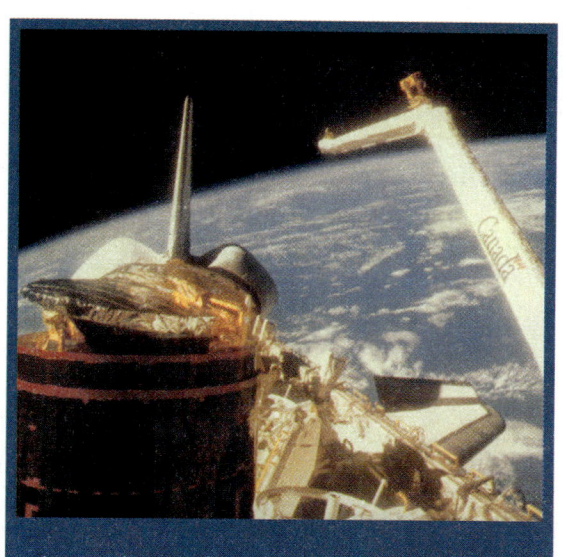

Innovations such as the Canadarm showcase the talent of Canadian scientists. Can you think of other examples that have shown Canada to be among the world leaders in technolgical developments?

ROBERTA BONDAR: CANADIAN IN SPACE

Few people will ever have the opportunity to view the world the way Roberta Bondar has. In 1992, Bondar became the second Canadian astronaut and the first Canadian woman to travel in space. She was selected as one of six Canadian astronauts to be involved in the U.S. space program. In 1984, at the age of thirty-seven, Bondar started to prepare for her adventure. The wait proved to be far longer than anticipated. Canada plays only a small part in the U.S. space program, so placing Canadians aboard space shuttles was not a high priority. This factor, combined with rocket fuel leaks and cancelled launch dates, made Bondar's wait frustrating. Finally, in January 1992, Roberta Bondar lifted-off in the space shuttle *Discovery*.

Bondar worked a gruelling sixteen to eighteen hours a day while in space. Her role was to conduct life-sciences research, including dozens of experiments concerning motion sickness, the effects of weightlessness, the ways in which the human body adapts to space flight, and the amounts of energy astronauts use in space.

Bondar brought several mementoes along on her trip to remind her of home, including tapes made especially for her by Canadian singers Tommy Hunter, Anne Murray, and Ginette Reno. Her thoughts and feelings about Canada were reinforced by seeing her country and the planet from space. She observed, "When you see Earth from space, it is small. It is a planet to explore. I thought it's time to come back to a strong country and be talking about the real issues of unity, not division. I feel we've got to pull together. People need to understand what the whole country is about. We shouldn't be bound by the rivalries between provinces. I'm proud to be Canadian."

Roberta Bondar's experience aboard the *Discovery* brought much pride to Canada and will continue to benefit the Earth. She believes the shuttle voyages provide an opportunity to renew our love for the planet. Bondar believes that seeing Earth from space will inspire her and others to help save the planet.

Roberta Bondar, the second Canadian astronaut in space, carries out experiments aboard the space shuttle *Discovery*.

United States agreed to get prior permission every time a U.S. government-owned or -operated ship wanted to cross the Arctic.

The United States had used the *Polar Sea* voyage to test Canadian sovereignty in the Arctic and, after some hesitation, the Mulroney government decided to stand firm against the Americans. Nevertheless, Mulroney still believed that friendship with the United States produced direct benefits for Canada. When George Bush took over the American presidency, Prime Minister Mulroney quickly established what the American president described as the "warmest" relationship between the two leaders in the history of Canada–U.S. relations.

Acid Rain: Canada–U.S. Negotiations

Mulroney's close ties with the United States were not always viewed with favour in Canada. But in March 1991, U.S. President George Bush conceded that pressure from Mulroney played a key role in the passage of a U.S. law limiting **acid rain** emissions in the United States.

Canadian lakes and forests were being poisoned by acid rain, a deadly shower of sulphuric and nitrous oxides from industries and automobiles across North America. Fish were dying and trees were withering away. Winds often carried the pollutants hundreds of kilometres from their source before they fell to earth in dust, rain, or snow. Because of wind patterns, more than half the acid rain in Canada came from the United States — much of it from the steel mills of Pennsylvania and Ohio.

Canadian sources were also responsible for acid rain, however. In fact, four of the five largest sulphur dioxide polluters in North America were in Canada, and the Inco smelter at Sudbury was at the top of the list. But the Mulroney government offered a $150 million program to help Canadian industries clean up their operations, and Inco was the first to apply. Canada also followed the United States in bringing in automobile pollution-control standards, beginning with 1988-model cars.

But acid rain was not just a Canadian problem, and Canada needed the United States' help to solve it. Mulroney had told President Ronald Reagan at their first meeting in 1984 that acid rain was his "number one priority." However, the Reagan government strongly resisted efforts to promote U.S. action on acid rain. Although hardworking Canadian environmental lobbyists and the Canadian government continued to urge the United States to take action, not until George Bush became president did the U.S. government finally decide to act. In 1990, the U.S. Congress passed a new law to control acid rain.

CANADA–U.S. ECONOMIC RELATIONS

Great Britain had always been an important trading partner for Canada. But its economy had faltered after World War II, and trade relations between Canada and Britain dropped off. Meanwhile the American economy was booming.

Acid rain, which is killing Canadian lakes and forests, is a problem that must be jointly addressed by Canadians and Americans. Why can we not solve the problem without the cooperation of the United States?

Canada was right next door, and many Canadian industries found it easy to sell their products on the American market. Canadian consumers and Canadian industries were also eager to buy American goods. The two countries became each other's most important trading partners.

The St. Lawrence Seaway

The construction of the **St. Lawrence Seaway** symbolized the expanding economic relations between the two countries. The seaway was a massive construction project that would enable large, ocean-going freighters to sail past the dangerous rapids of the St. Lawrence River and into the Great Lakes. The United States and Canada had been discussing the building of a seaway for decades but without any result. In 1949, however, the Canadian government decided to build the seaway, with or without American help. In 1954, the United States agreed to take part in the project. Each country agreed to pay for the portions of the seaway inside its own territory.

The St. Lawrence Seaway was planned, designed, and largely built by Canadians. The size of the project was staggering. Huge rapids were dynamited out of the river. Whole towns and villages were flooded, and 6500 people were relocated in new homes elsewhere. Railways and highways were rerouted around the new flood zones. Seven new locks were built, five of them by Canada. The seaway was officially opened in a joint ceremony in June 1959, with Queen Elizabeth II representing Canada and President Dwight Eisenhower representing the United States. One Canadian observer commented that the new St. Lawrence Seaway "was like a huge economic zipper knitting these [two] countries together."

The Auto Pact

Another agreement signed in 1965 — the **Auto Pact** — also tied the Canadian and United States economies more closely together. To this day, historians wonder why the United States gave Canada what seemed like such a favourable trade deal. One possibility is that Prime Minister Pearson had sent Canadian troops to Cyprus to prevent a war between Greece and Turkey even before a U.N. peacekeeping force was ready to go. Canada's quick response helped to avert a war. The American president, Lyndon Johnson, was so grateful that he telephoned Pearson personally. "You'll never know what this has meant," he told the Canadian prime minister. "Now, what can I do for you?"

By the mid-1960s, Canadians had become upset by a growing trade imbalance with the United States: Canada was spending more to buy American goods than it was making by selling Canadian goods to the United States. The biggest trade deficit was in automobiles and automobile parts. For example, in 1962, while Canada exported $62 million worth of *automotives* to the United States, it imported $642 million worth from the United States. The Canadian government argued that Canadians needed a new deal in the cross-border automotive industry. Although Canadians bought more than 7 percent of the cars produced by America's "Big Three" automobile manufacturers — Ford, Chrysler, and General Motors — the Big Three plants in Oshawa, Oakville, and Windsor, Ontario, produced only 4 percent of these manufacturers' cars. The Canadian government wanted the number of cars bought and produced in Canada to be equalized. Talks began in July 1964, and by January 1965, Pearson was on his way to President Johnson's ranch in Texas to sign the Auto Pact.

The Auto Pact was so complicated that both Johnson and Pearson admitted they did not understand it all. But it essentially guaranteed free trade in automobiles between the two countries. The automobile manufacturers could locate their plants wherever they wanted and sell their cars duty-free in either country. The only major qualification was that the Big Three manufacturers had to build one car in Canada for every car sold in Canada. The Auto Pact brought real benefits to

The auto industry is a vital part of the Canadian economy, especially in Ontario and Quebec. Plants such as this one employ thousands of workers.

Canada, but it also tied the Canadian economy even more closely to the U.S. economy.

American Investment in Canada

After World War II, Canada found that it had many of the natural resources that the United States needed to keep its economy in high gear. The Americans needed oil, and Alberta's newly discovered Leduc oil field gave them what they needed. They bought aluminum from Kitimat, British Columbia, and uranium from northern Saskatchewan and Elliot Lake, Ontario. They also bought nickel, natural gas, and a host of new chemical products.

Resource development has always been risky. For instance, Imperial Oil spent $23 million and drilled 133 dry wells before it struck "black gold" at Leduc in 1947. Most often, it was American rather than Canadian investors who were willing to take risks. Because American companies put money into Canadian resources, they also collected most of the profits. Still, the growth of American-backed industries did help Canada to prosper. New industries meant more jobs and a higher standard of living for many Canadians.

Many Canadians welcomed the flow of American money into Canada in the 1950s. But by 1967, 81 percent of the $34.7 billion worth of foreign investment in Canada was from American sources. Public opinion shifted: a 1967 poll showed that two-thirds of Canadians wanted the government to control American investment in Canada. Several government reports, including the Watkins Report of 1968 and the Grey Report of 1971, raised concerns about the extent of the foreign ownership of Canadian firms.

The Foreign Investment Review Agency and Investment Canada

In 1971, the Trudeau government set up the **Foreign Investment Review Agency (FIRA)**. Its job was to ensure that any foreign investment in or foreign takeover of Canadian companies had important benefits in Canada. Did the investment or

Petro-Canada was established in the 1970s by the Liberal government of Pierre Trudeau. It was intended to ensure a strong Canadian presence in the oil and gas industry. Do you think the government should be involved in the effort to ensure Canadian ownership of essential resources?

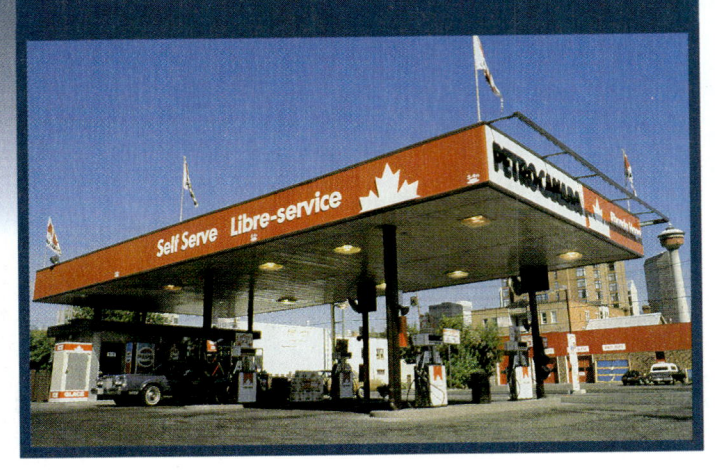

takeover create jobs? Did it increase exports or expand research and development in Canada? FIRA could block any foreign investment that was not in the best interests of Canada, especially in cultural industries such as magazines and newspapers. But FIRA had little effect on the flow of foreign investment, and some of its critics called it a "paper tiger." Americans owned a little more than 25 percent of all shares of Canadian corporations (except financial institutions) when FIRA was set up. Ten years later, Americans owned the same proportion. By 1982, FIRA was approving nine out of ten applications for foreign takeovers of Canadian companies.

FIRA was scrapped by the Mulroney government in 1984 and replaced by **Investment Canada**. Investment Canada's role was more limited; it reviewed takeovers of Canadian companies only if the selling price exceeded $5 million — about two-thirds of the takeovers that FIRA would have reviewed. It kept the power to review all takeovers in cultural industries, but its main goal was to welcome back American investment. During his first major speech in the United States, Mulroney told the Economic Club in New York that "Canada is open for business again."

Petro-Canada and the National Energy Program

In the 1970s, the Canadian oil and gas industry was mostly foreign-owned. Canadians worried that they might not control future supplies of gasoline for their cars and natural gas or oil for their homes. As a result, the Trudeau government in 1975 set up a government-owned petroleum company called Petro-Canada. With taxpayers' dollars, Petro-Canada grew quickly and competed with foreign-owned oil companies like Imperial Oil, Shell, and Gulf.

The **National Energy Program (NEP)** was created in 1980 to ensure Canada's future oil supply, control oil prices, and achieve a 50 percent Canadian ownership of the oil industry by 1990. It gave Canadian oil and gas companies special grants and special terms for northern exploration. It also gave the federal government a bigger share of oil and gas revenues. American oil companies were shocked and angry. Oil-producing provinces in western Canada were also outraged and bitterly fought against the NEP, but "Canadianizing" the petroleum industry was popular in Canada. An opinion poll in 1981 showed that 84 percent of Canadians supported the goals of the NEP.

However, the NEP had been built on the assumption that oil prices would keep going up. Instead, the combination of an increase in world oil production and a recession caused a drop in oil prices. The NEP did not work well when oil prices dropped: the tax schedules and oil pricing systems had to be continually changed. The economic recession that began in 1982 was also making some Canadians lose interest in Canadian economic nationalism if they thought it threatened their own economic survival. A poll showed that the number of Canadians "who would like to see more" foreign investment increased from 21 percent in 1981 to 36 percent in 1982. When the Mulroney government took power in 1984, it abandoned the NEP. Because of changes in the ownership of the oil industry in the 1980s,

COMMON CONTINENT — DIFFERENT CULTURE?

When Canadians travel abroad, few things irritate them more than being mistaken for Americans. Outwardly, it is understandable why this occurs. We look much the same and speak the same language; we listen to similar music and watch similar television shows; we even eat the same kinds of food. But take a closer look and you'll find substantial differences between Canadian and American perspectives and attitudes.

In May 1990, *Maclean's* magazine conducted "The Two Nations Poll" to see where Canadians and Americans stood on several issues. Following are six of the poll questions and responses on topics ranging from pollution to immigration. Conduct your own poll, using these six questions as well as four of your own. Ask at least twenty people to complete your survey. Graph the information from both the *Maclean's* poll and your own poll to compare results.

1. *In your opinion, what is the most important problem facing the United States/Canada today, the one that concerns you the most?*

	Americans	Canadians
Pollution/environment	17	20
National unity/bilingualism	—	19
Economy/jobs/inflation	8	19
Govt./deficit/debt	9	10
Drugs/alcohol problems	21	1
Other social/moral issues	24	6
Taxation (Canada GST)	3	15
World issues/war/peace	5	1
Foreign trade/investment	2	2
No problem/DK/NA	10	6

2. *Who do you feel best serves your personal economic interests — business, government or unions?*

	Americans	Canadians
Business	48	56
Government	22	20
Unions	19	20
DK/NA	12	5

3. *Would you oppose or favor shutting down a major company that provided many jobs in your community if it was polluting the environment?*

	Americans	Canadians
Oppose	34	36
Favor	58	60
DK/NA	9	4

4. *Would you strongly oppose, oppose, favor or strongly favor Canada and the United States becoming one country?*

	Americans	Canadians
Total oppose	43	81
Total favor	47	18

5. *Do you think we should encourage more immigration, keep immigration at existing levels or reduce the number of immigrants allowed into the United States/Canada?*

	Americans	Canadians
Encourage more	6	18
Existing levels	33	42
Reduce immigration	58	39

6. *Many people have told us that they have had contact either through work or socially with Canadians/Americans. As a result of your own experience, would you rather deal with someone from Canada or the United States, or have you really not had enough contact to tell?*

	Americans	Canadians
Canada	8	39
United States	18	11
Not enough contact	69	44

Source: Adapted from "The Two Nations Poll: Where North Americans Stand on 32 Questions," *Maclean's Magazine*, Maclean Hunter Ltd., June 25, 1990, pp. 50–53.

the Canadian share of the industry had increased to 46 percent by August 1985. As a result, the fury over the NEP faded away.

FROM THE "THIRD OPTION" TO FREE TRADE

Making investments in Canada was not the only way in which the United States played a major role in the Canadian economy. Seventy percent of all Canada's exports went to the United States. Canada was also the biggest customer for American goods. Any change in American economic policy sent major shock waves through the Canadian economy. In a famous comment, Pierre Trudeau described Canada's uncomfortable dependence on the U.S. economy: "Living next to you is in some ways like sleeping with an elephant: no matter how friendly and even-tempered the beast, one is affected by every twitch and grunt."

Just a few months after Trudeau's comment, the elephant twitched and Canadian businesspeople trembled. In 1971, U.S. President Richard Nixon ordered a 10 percent tariff on goods imported into the United States. As a result, Canadian-made goods cost more in the United States, and Canadian businesses faced the prospect of losing $300 million in exports. Because of its close links to the United States, Canada had always been exempted from such tariffs in the past. Although worldwide pressure forced the United States to cancel the 10 percent tariff a few months later, Canadians were shocked to discover how economically dependent they were on the United States and how badly they could be hurt by changes in American economic policy.

The "Third Option"

After the "Nixon shock," Trudeau began actively pursuing the **Third Option Policy**. As one of Trudeau's advisers explained the situation, Canada had three choices: it could maintain its present relationship with the United States, move toward even closer relations, or try to create a more independent Canadian economy. Trudeau's government opted for the third choice. Canada began to look for new trading partners around the world as a way of lessening its dependence on the United States.

During the 1970s, Canada tried to forge new trade links in Europe, Asia, and Africa. These efforts met with only a few successes. Japan bought more raw materials, especially lumber and coal, but it did not want Canadian manufactured goods. Britain and the rest of Europe bought Canada's uranium and timber, but not its manufactured goods. China bought Canadian wheat, but few Canadian-made goods. By the mid-1980s, it looked as if the only important market willing to take Canadian goods was the United States. The United States, however, was thinking about creating its own trade barriers to keep out goods from other nations.

Ottawa began to worry that Canada would be locked out of global markets, including the American market. Trudeau seriously considered closer trade ties with the United States. The mood in Canada was swinging toward closer economic relations with its southern neighbour; in June 1984, opinion polls showed that 78 percent of Canadians favoured free trade with the United States. In September 1985, the Royal Commission on the Economic Union and Development Prospects for Canada made its report. It called for a "leap of faith" into free trade with the United States.

Mulroney and the Free Trade Agreement

By the time the royal commission's report was ready in 1985, Trudeau had retired and the Progressive Conservatives were in power. Before becoming prime minister, Mulroney had attacked free trade. "Free trade is terrific until the elephant twitches, and if it ever rolls over, you're a dead man," he had said. But once in office, he changed his mind and

Carefully examine this cartoon. What impact is the cartoon suggesting the 1988 Free Trade Agreement will have on Canada? Is there any evidence so far that these fears are justified?

proposed a full-fledged free-trade deal between Canada and the United States. Because of GATT (General Agreement on Tariffs and Trade) negotiations since World War II, about 80 percent of the tariff barriers that had existed between the United States and Canada in 1935 had been removed. The free-trade deal would remove trade barriers from most, but not all, goods that still remained under trade restrictions.

A team of Canadian free-trade negotiators held a series of talks with U.S. negotiators. The new Free Trade Agreement (FTA), signed in January 1988, committed the two countries to dropping cross-border tariffs by the end of 1998. It also dealt with other trade concerns, including energy, the movement of people for business purposes, investment, and financial services.

Free trade became *the* issue in the 1988 federal election, just has it had been in the 1911 election. This time around, however, the Conservatives were battling for free trade and the Liberals were fighting against it. The New Democratic Party (NDP) also opposed free trade. Arguments for and against free trade raged across the country in the weeks before election day. The debate forced Canadians to think hard about their economic future. Were their fears about job loss justified? Did they want closer economic ties with the United States or not? Would the FTA have a major effect on Canada's political and economic future? In the election, the combined votes for the anti–free-trade parties represented a majority of the popular vote, but the Progressive Conservatives won a majority of the seats in Parliament. As a result, the FTA became law on January 1, 1989.

The North American Free Trade Agreement

In North America, the FTA gave Canada and the United States open access to each other's markets for most goods. Soon, Mexico wanted to become a close trading partner of Canada and the United States. In 1992, after another round of trade talks,

Brian Mulroney turns away from a hostile crowd protesting against the proposed Free Trade Agreement during the 1988 election campaign.

the leaders of Mexico, the United States, and Canada signed the North American Free Trade Agreement (NAFTA), which included Mexico in the free-trade region created by the FTA. By 1993, however, NAFTA still had to be voted into law by the legislatures of the three countries. If approved, NAFTA would create the world's largest free-trade bloc by linking 370 million people in three countries, with 31 percent of the world's wealth, into a single trade region.

The Global Economy and the 1990s

In the 1980s and 1990s, trade has become increasingly globalized: countries are seeking markets for their goods all over the world. The value of world trade in 1993 was an astonishing $8 trillion — more than twenty times the figure in 1950. At the same time, nations are finding it harder to secure new world markets. Many of them have formed free-trade areas to ensure access to markets in neighbouring countries. The European Community (EC) created a single market out of twelve European countries: 350 million Europeans can now trade among themselves without as much as a wave at their border guards. The European Economic Area is also underway; it will bring another seven countries into the EC trade net. Several South American countries are now trying to piece together a South American free-trade region called the Southern Cone Economic Market. The globalization of the economy poses new challenges for Canada. The nation's future success lies in its ability to carve out a place in the new global economy.

KNOWING THE KEY PEOPLE, PLACES, AND EVENTS

In your notes, clearly identify and explain the historical significance of each of the following:

> Canadian Broadcasting Corporation (CBC)
> National Film Board (NFB)
> Canadian Radio–Television Commission (CRTC)
> *Polar Sea*
> St. Lawrence Seaway
> Foreign Investment Review Agency (FIRA)
> National Energy Program (NEP)
> Massey Commission
> Canada Council
> Shamrock Summit
> Acid Rain
> Auto Pact
> Investment Canada
> Third Option Policy

FOCUS YOUR KNOWLEDGE

1. What developments in the mass media led to an influx of American culture into Canada in the 1950s? To what degree was the Americanization of Canadian culture a valid concern for Canadians?

2. What actions did the federal government take in the 1970s to promote Canadian culture? How successful were these measures? Use concrete examples to support your answer.

3. How many current Canadian musicians, actors, and television programs can you name? Which of them reflect something distinctly Canadian?

4. Why did the Cold War lead to closer military ties between Canada and the United States?

5. What was the major issue of the 1963 election campaign in Canada? Contrast the platforms of the Liberal and Progressive Conservative parties. Which party would you have supported?

6. How did Pierre Trudeau's foreign policy differ from Lester Pearson's?

7. How did the Shamrock Summit reflect the state of Canadian–American relations in the 1980s?

8. Why was there a public outcry in Canada when the United States sent its Coast Guard ship through the Northwest Passage?

9. Why is a joint Canada–United States agreement essential to limit acid-rain emissions?

10. How did the Auto Pact help to ensure a healthy auto industry in Canada?

APPLY YOUR KNOWLEDGE

1. Should government play an active role in promoting Canadian culture? Explain your answer.
2. Do the CRTC's Canadian-content rules help to ensure the development of high-quality Canadian music, or do they allow mediocre musicians to enjoy undeserved success? Explain your answer.
3. What aspects of Canadian culture distinguish it from American culture? Canadians seem far more preoccupied with preserving a unique culture than are many other nations. Should this be a primary concern for Canadians?
4. How important is government funding to the preservation of a uniquely Canadian culture?
5. Have Canadians been successful in their efforts to limit acid-rain emissions? Provide specific examples to support your answer.
6. Has foreign investment been good or bad for Canada? Does it help to foster long-term economic growth and stability? Can you think of an example of foreign investment in your community?
7. Should the government interfere in the economy to regulate key resources such as oil?
8. In chart form, record the nature of the relationships between the following prime ministers and the United States. Use brief examples to support your conclusions.

    John Diefenbaker   Lester Pearson
    Pierre Trudeau   Brian Mulroney

EXTEND YOUR KNOWLEDGE

1. Working in groups, prepare two collages that reflect Canadian and American culture. Make sure that both collages are similar in their design and layout so that they will complement each other. Describe in a caption what the collages attempted to capture.
2. Research the automobile industry in Canada and prepare a set of bar and pie graphs on the following topics:

    (a) the number of automobiles sold in Canada in the past year;
    (b) the percentage of sales for each automobile company in Canada;
    (c) the number of automobiles imported versus the number exported; and
    (d) the total number of automobiles built in Canada in the past year.

Considering the evidence presented by your graphs, do you think Canada continues to benefit from the Auto Pact?

3. Take on the role of a reporter at the time of the Cuban Missile Crisis. Before filing your story, do some additional research to make sure you clearly understand the events and the positions adopted by John F. Kennedy and John Diefenbaker. File your news story before the end of the crisis. (This means that you must speculate about the outcome on the basis of the evidence you gathered.)

SKILLS FOCUS

UNIT REVIEW

1. Since 1945, Canada has earned an international reputation for being a fair and just society. What evidence in this unit supports or disputes this reputation? Refer to events that occurred both within Canada and abroad.
2. The second half of the twentieth century has seen rapid changes in science and technology. How have the advances in science and technology altered both the lives of Canadians and their relationships with other nations?
3. For much of Canada's history, its citizens have grappled with the question of the Canadian identity. What does it mean to be Canadian? What distinguishes Canadians from the British and Americans? In answering these questions, consider the events discussed in this unit's chapters.

FORMULATING AND DEFENDING A THESIS

An important skill to develop is the ability to adopt a position on an issue and to defend your point of view. In history courses you will often be asked to write a research essay. This will require you to use a variety of sources of information to gather facts on a specific topic and to develop a carefully considered argument based on the evidence you have found. All research essays must have a clear thesis. A thesis is a statement of intent that clearly defines the argument presented in the essay. A good thesis does not merely identify the topic or state the obvious; it sets out the essay's argument in one or two sentences. To be effective, a thesis must not only be clearly stated in the introduction but should also be the central focus of the entire essay. The purpose of the evidence presented throughout the essay is to support the thesis. An effective thesis is always formulated after the research is completed and is based on the evidence gathered, not on the writer's biases.

Following are five thesis statements. For each thesis, state whether or not it is a strong thesis and explain why.

1. The Roaring Twenties were followed by the ten hard years called the Great Depression.
2. Belonging to a military alliance is contrary to Canada's foreign-policy objectives, and therefore Canada should withdraw from NATO.
3. Throughout the twentieth century, many people have fought to win political, social, and economic equality for Canadian women.
4. The 1960s were years of radical social change led by militant and vocal youth.
5. In recent years, the separatist movement in Quebec has gained strength because of English Canada's indifference to the needs of French Canadians and their desire to protect French Canada's unique culture.

Select an issue from one of the chapters in this unit on which you would like to do further research. After doing some additional reading, reflect on what you know about this issue and formulate a clear thesis. Also, prepare a list of five arguments that you could use to support your thesis.

CAREER FOCUS

TRAVEL AND TOURISM

An industry that has experienced considerable growth over the past decade is that of travel and tourism. Many Canadians are travelling long distances to explore various regions of Canada and the rest of the world. Meanwhile, Canada has become a popular destination for many travellers from other countries. As a result, many career opportunities have opened up in the travel and tourism industry. Job opportunities range from travel agents and tour guides to government workers promoting tourism. A career in travel and tourism can be quite rewarding, especially if you enjoy learning about various places, customs, and cultures and if you like to work with people.

Studying history is a great asset for those pursuing careers in travel and tourism. Knowing about the history of a region provides insights into its culture and major attractions, which would help in planning exciting and marketable trips for clients. Also, the skills that have been developed throughout this book would be helpful in a career related to tourism. Being able to think creatively would help you to plan unique vacations, while the ability to do an effective presentation would be crucial in helping to sell vacation ideas to the travelling public. The research skills you developed earlier could be very helpful in researching various destinations. Thus, the many skills and the knowledge gained from the study of history could be an important tool for anyone choosing a career in travel and tourism.

Select a region of Canada that you find interesting and would like to learn more about. Prepare a travel brochure for this region. Your brochure should include a description of the following aspects of the region:

- geographical features
- cultural composition
- customs and festivals unique to the region
- a brief review of the history of the region
- foods
- major sources of revenue

Be sure to contact travel agencies when doing your research. They will be able to help you find information and may be able to supply you with pictures to include in your brochure.

When you have completed your research, prepare a visually appealing and informative brochure. Once you have finished your brochure, share it with the class as a way of learning more about the various regions of Canada.

UNIT 7

THE CHANGING FACE OF CANADA

CANADIAN SOCIETY HAS UNDERGONE SIGNIFICANT CHANGES during the second half of the twentieth century. In 1950, there was no medicare or assistance for students who wished to attend postsecondary schools, the workforce was predominantly male, and even the largest cities had no expressways. During the past forty years, Canada has emerged as a leading nation in many respects. Its cities are vibrant cosmopolitan centres, and many have diverse populations representing cultures from around the world. Canada can also boast leading experts in many fields, including science, medicine, sports, entertainment, and business. For the average Canadian, an increase in wealth and an explosion in consumer products have led to a lifestyle far different from the previous generation's. Microwave ovens, cable television, home computers, and high-quality stereos are luxuries that Canadians did not enjoy thirty years ago.

The three chapters in this unit provide an overview of the major changes that have occurred in Canada since the end of World War II. They help to put into perspective many of the issues now facing Canadians — Native demands for self-government, the women's movement, regionalism, and multiculturalism. Chapter 18 explores the major

CHAPTER EIGHTEEN

Life in Canada after World War II

CHAPTER NINETEEN

Canada from the 1960s to the 1980s

CHAPTER TWENTY

Canada as a Multicultural Nation

changes and issues facing Canadians in the years between 1945 and the mid-1960s. The Diefenbaker and Pearson years are examined with a focus on issues such as regional development, French–English relations, and Natives in Canadian society. Chapter 19 covers the Trudeau and Mulroney years, examining the events and issues in Canada from the mid-1960s through the 1980s. Issues such as the changing role of women in society, the youth revolution of the 1960s, and the terrorist activities of the FLQ are addressed. Chapter 20 brings the study of Canadian history up to the mid-1990s. This chapter examines issues relating to contemporary Canada, such as constitutional change and regional and ethnic diversity in Canada.

CHAPTER 18 LIFE IN CANADA AFTER WORLD WAR II

GLOSSARY TERMS

Mass Marketing The use of a marketing program to sell goods that appeal to the average consumer to a large number of people.

Consumerism The theory that a continued increase in the consumption of goods is economically sound.

DEW Line Distant Early Warning Line. A system of radar stations near the Arctic Circle for detecting and signalling the approach of enemy aircraft.

Cosmopolitanism The quality of being composed of many different languages and nationalities.

FOCUS ON:

- how the new wealth enjoyed by Canadians changed their daily lives
- the impact of television and automobiles on the lives of Canadians
- how suburbs transformed the urban landscape
- attempts to develop the North and the resulting impact on the lives of the Native peoples
- John Diefenbaker's attempts to deal with regional imbalances
- the arrival of new kinds of immigrants to Canada and the emergence of a multicultural nation

"My, how you've grown!" Anyone looking at Canada in the 1950s would have been astonished to see how fast the country was growing up. Canada's economy was expanding by leaps and bounds, and so was its population. Ordinary Canadians were earning more money, and the middle class was swelling. More money meant more buying power, and Canadians went on a national shopping spree. They began buying more consumer goods than their parents had ever dreamed of owning. Consumer spending helped fuel the expansion of Canadian industries. One writer called it the decade when Canadians "learned to lived with bigness."

THE CONSUMER REVOLUTION

North American industries had switched from wartime to peacetime production with ease. Thanks to techniques of mass production, consumer goods were suddenly available in North America at affordable prices. Refrigerators, radios, and even automobiles were now within the reach of ordinary income earners. Wartime savings and fatter peacetime paycheques meant that people had more money to spend. An American historian described American affluence (wealth) in the 1950s: "If few [people] can cite the figures, everyone knows that we have, per capita, more automobiles, more telephones, more radios, more vacuum cleaners, more electric lights, more bathtubs...than any other nation."

Americans may have been the front-runners in the race for consumer goods, but Canadians were right on their heels. The average take-home pay of Canadians grew rapidly after the war. Canadians enjoyed the second-highest living standard in the world. For example, only three other cities in the world bought more Cadillacs per capita than did Toronto. Canadian shoppers earned their 1950s label as "consumers" by rushing to buy the new mass-produced goods that tumbled off the production lines.

New Products and Mass Marketing

Wartime technology also helped to set off an explosive increase in peacetime technological inventions. These included the long-playing record, the digital computer, nylon, cellophane, jet airplanes, antihistamines, aerosol spray cans, and electric typewriters. All kinds of specialized products, new gadgets, and games were also finding their way onto store shelves. Canadian consumers had a dazzling array of products to tempt them, including ballpoint pens, frozen TV dinners, "home permanents" for hair, hula hoops, electric can openers, and Scrabble games. But the most important product was television. Millions of the little boxes found their way into Canadian living rooms in the 1950s, and family life was revolutionized. Family conversations, eating habits, humour, political attitudes, personal styles, and social values were all influenced by television.

The 1950s also saw the introduction of *mass marketing*. Manufacturers began spending huge sums on advertising campaigns to convince Canadian consumers to pick their products over rival brands — often called "Brand X" in television commercials. Canadians were blitzed with media advertisements for brand-name products ranging from Kleenex Facial Tissues to Kellogg's Corn Flakes. Vance Packard, author of the 1957 bestseller *Hidden Persuaders*, argued that advertisers were unfairly manipulating consumers. He claimed that

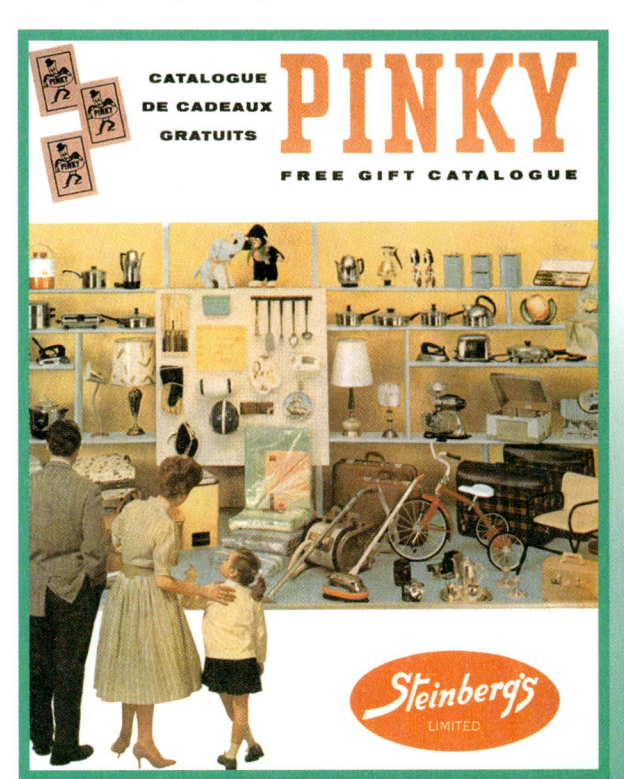

New wealth and a wide range of products led to new methods of marketing. Stamps, received when purchasing goods, could be cashed in for a number of gifts, such as those shown on the cover of the Pinky Gift Catalogue. Can you think of instances in which this kind of marketing is still used?

TELEVISION AND CANADIAN SOCIETY

Few technological innovations have affected society as television has. Many people claimed that the introduction of television sets into Canadian homes weakened community organizations, reduced significantly the amount of conversation between family members, and distracted children from reading and their homework. Yet, despite the dire warnings of some, the "idiot box," as the television was called by its critics, did not ruin Canadian society. In fact, in many ways the television age contributed to a cultural boom in North America and placed information at everyone's fingertips.

Although television was first pioneered in Britain in 1926, the Depression and World War II delayed its development. By the early 1950s, television was beginning to make its way into North America. In 1952 the Canadian Broadcasting Corporation (CBC), which had been established during the 1930s to ensure quality Canadian radio programming, began broadcasting television programs. Its goal was to provide Canadian programs that would serve the interests of national unity. A year earlier, the Massey Commission had argued in favour of government controlling television rather than following the American approach, which placed broadcasting in the hands of business.

Despite the best efforts of the CBC and the Massey Commission, Canadians fell in love with American television programs. A generation of Canadians and Americans grew up sharing a fascination with programs such as "I Love Lucy," "Howdy Doody," and "Your Hit Parade." Television introduced many new American stars and heroes — including Davy Crockett, Ed Sullivan, and Elvis Presley — to Canadians. Although Canadian broadcasters did not have the money to compete with American programs, several successful programs hit the airwaves in the 1950s, including "Front Page Challenge," "Tugboat Annie," and "Hockey Night in Canada."

Many Canadians had grave reservations about what the coming of the television age would mean to Canadian society. They feared that American-dominated television would undermine the Canadian identity by blurring the distinctions between Canadians and Americans. There was also a fear that Canada's youth would cease to excel in school and would spend too much time in front of the television, becoming passive receivers of information. Today the number of channels available to many Canadians is virtually limitless.

To what degree have the fears of television's early critics been realized? How do you balance your television viewing with other activities in your life? What, if anything, should be done to ensure that quality Canadian programs continue to be available to Canadians?

The introduction of television drew thousands away from the movie theatres and into their living rooms. In an attempt to win back the crowds, 3-D movies were introduced. Using a tinted pair of cardboard and celluloid glasses, viewers were given an experience billed as "more sensational than real life."

advertisers used new psychological techniques to trigger consumers' unconscious fears and wishes in order to persuade them to buy advertised products. But mass advertising continued to grow in the 1950s, and so did consumer sales.

Cars, Houses, and the Baby Boom

Polls showed that at the very top of Canadians' shopping lists were cars and houses. During the 1950s, Canadians bought 3.5 million new cars, and double-car garages became status symbols. The garages were often attached to the thousands of new houses built in the 1950s. Many Canadians had also put off getting married and starting families until after the war. The huge increase in the number of babies born in Canada from about 1945 to about 1965 was known as the "**baby boom**." The baby boom peaked in 1959, when 20 percent of all women in their twenties had babies. Canadians wanted homes where they could raise their new families. To meet the demand, more than 1.1 million new housing units were built in the 1950s. Home-building and car-making became two of the most important industries in Canada.

The Growth of the Suburbs

With the development of streetcar systems before World War II, suburbs had begun to appear in Canada. But the 1950s were the first decade of "urban sprawl." Many of the new houses were built in the subdivisions that were springing up almost overnight on the outskirts of Canadian cities. Farms and pastures disappeared beneath dozens of new "planned communities" that were designed to provide affordable single-family houses for the stampede of first-time home-buyers. Suburban streets were lined with look-alike split-level bungalows, complete with picture window, carport, newly seeded front lawns, and a scrawny maple tree or two. Schools and shopping centres were built nearby and became the centre of suburban life. The opening of a new shopping mall was a major social event in suburbia. Opening day was often heralded by brass bands, balloons, clowns, and the offer of "freebies" to attract shoppers.

The first postwar suburb in North America was Levittown, New York, which was built in 1947. Houston and Los Angeles were the first American cities to experience suburban sprawl. But suburbs were quickly becoming a fact of life in Canadian towns and cities from Halifax to Vancouver. At least 50 000 Canadians a year took out mortgages for their first homes, often with the help of the Canadian government under the 1944 **National Housing Act** (NHA). In the Toronto suburb of Agincourt, for example, a three-bedroom bungalow cost about $11 500 with an NHA mortgage of 5.5 percent. By

By the early 1950s, the first wave of baby boomers and children of immigrant families was entering Canadian schools. How would the increasing diversity of students enrich Canadian schools? What additional burdens would it create?

mid-decade, about a quarter of a million Canadians had bought their share in the "suburban dream."

Life in Suburbia

Living in a suburb was a whole new way of life. Many suburbanites enjoyed being able to buy larger homes with green lawns, indoor plumbing, and new electrical appliances. Their children played on safe streets in front of their homes and went to new neighbourhood schools. In the summertime, suburbanites barbecued on backyard grills and washed their new cars in their driveways. They prided themselves on their friendliness. When a moving van arrived in the community, neighbours carrying sandwiches and coffee, and Kool-Aid for the kids, often came out to greet the newcomers. Although many critics were writing about the negative side of suburban life — its blandness, conformity, and materialism — for many Canadians in the 1950s, a home in the suburbs was a dream come true.

The Automobile

Life in the suburbs was made possible by the automobile. In 1949, Canada had only 16 000 kilometres of paved roads. But car owners were demanding more roads like the impressive new four-lane Queen Elizabeth Way that linked Toronto and Hamilton, which became the model for highways across Canada. Soon, tentacles of new highways curled out from city cores to the new suburbs around major Canadian cities. The Canadian government had also started work on the Trans-Canada Highway in 1949. The new cross-Canada link symbolized the importance of the automobile.

But a car was much more than a mode of transport to school, work, and the shopping mall. Canadians had fallen in love with the automobile. They were mad about the new "chrome boats" — the Chryslers, Fords, and Chevrolets being churned out by autoworkers in Windsor, Oakville, and Oshawa. The bigger and faster and fancier these cars were, the better. Power steering, V-8 engines, two-tone finishes, metre-long rear-winged fins, whitewall tires, and vast chrome strips were all viewed with awe and admiration. Kids argued passionately about which were better — Chevies or Fords. Teenagers could hardly wait until they turned sixteen and could start driving. Many teenagers spent months customizing old cars and turning them into fantastic

An unmistakable sign of the prosperity of the 1950s was the subdivisions that began to appear. Don Mills, Ontario, was Canada's first planned subdivision.

Canadians' love affair with the automobile reached a new high during the 1950s. Each year new models of cars, many with white-washed tires and plenty of chrome trim, were put on the market.

368

"road machines." High-powered, chrome-shiny cars were the ultimate status symbols in the 1950s. No one thought much about the problems that *consumerism*, urban sprawl, and the automobile were creating. Environmental awareness lay two decades into the future.

NATURAL RESOURCES AND THE "LAST FRONTIER"

Much of Canada's economic growth was powered by the booming sales of natural resources. One late afternoon in the winter of 1947, a jet of oil, gas, and mud spewed fifteen metres up into the Alberta sky. Oil — "black gold" — had been discovered near Leduc, Alberta. Imperial Oil's fabulous strike at Leduc set off an oil and natural gas boom in Alberta. Fort St. John, British Columbia, became another centre for a spree of oil and gas exploration. These and other new oil fields created a demand for drilling rigs, refining plants, and pipelines and sparked growth in other industries as well.

Potash was discovered in Saskatchewan, nickel in Manitoba, iron in the Ungava Peninsula of northern Quebec, and aluminum in British Columbia. The Aluminum Company of Canada built the first planned suburban-style community in the wilderness up the coast from Vancouver, complete with schools, a shopping mall, and a sports centre. The new town of Kitimat housed workers for the company's huge hydro-electric and aluminum smelting project.

In mineral-rich Ontario, an explosion of mining ventures saw the discoveries of zinc, nickel, copper, and other valuable minerals. The wartime development of atomic energy had sparked a new peacetime demand for the uranium needed to produce atomic energy. One of the biggest uranium discoveries was first signalled by a coded message from a prospecting geologist in northern Saskatchewan to his boss. "Come quick," read the telegram, "I've shot an elephant." He had just discovered a huge uranium deposit, and the rush for uranium was on in the North.

An even bigger uranium strike was made at Elliot Lake, Ontario, in 1954, and eleven mines went into production. The Consolidated Denison mine near Elliot Lake turned out to be the world's biggest uranium mine. By 1960, Ontario was producing almost 60 percent of Canada's metal output, and Canada was becoming one of the world's leading exporters of raw materials. Because of this rush of exploration and mining, the Canadian North was sometimes called the "last great frontier."

Oil, discovered in Alberta in 1947, brought billions of dollars into the Canadian economy. Wells such as this one at Leduc were responsible for making Alberta one of Canada's wealthiest provinces.

THE DIEFENBAKER YEARS

By the mid-1950s, the Liberal Party had been in power for more than twenty consecutive years. Prime Minister **Louis St. Laurent** had presided over Canada during its boom years. St. Laurent had entered politics during World War II out of a sense of duty. His dignity, personal decency, and courage had made him popular with Canadians. He was nicknamed "Uncle Louis" in the press because he was "like everyone's favourite uncle." St. Laurent had been handpicked by the old and ailing Mackenzie King to replace him as the Liberal leader. In 1949, St. Laurent's Liberals had won the biggest majority in any Parliament since Confederation. Most Canadians expected him to stay in office for a good while.

But a debate in 1956 over a new natural gas pipeline marked the end of the Liberals' long political reign. The pipeline was to carry Alberta's oil and gas to eastern Canada. When the St. Laurent government announced that the pipeline contract — and a loan of $80 million — had been awarded to a company that was 83 percent American-owned, many Canadian nationalists were outraged. Why, they asked, should the contract and government money go to an American company and not a Canadian one? Was Canada handing over control of its resources to outsiders? There was a storm of controversy over the pipeline bill in Parliament. The Liberals managed to push the bill through by cutting off debate and forcing a vote. But the Liberal government's reputation was shattered by what many Canadians saw as its arrogant tactics in Parliament.

In the election campaign of 1957, the new Progressive Conservative leader, **John Diefenbaker**, made rousing speeches against the "American pipeline buccaneers." He promised to free Canada from American influence. The small-town Saskatchewan lawyer was a passionate and gifted speaker. Diefenbaker seemed to bring a new spark and energy to dreary Canadian politics. By contrast, St. Laurent was elderly and tired, worn down by years in public life. The 1957 election was the first time that a national campaign was televised, and many Canadians noticed striking differences between the two leaders in their TV appearances. Despite Diefenbaker's impressive showing on the new medium of television, however, most Canadians expected a Liberal win. *Maclean's* magazine even published an election editorial handing victory to St. Laurent's Liberals.

After the ballots were counted, however, the Conservatives had won 112 seats and the Liberals 105. St. Laurent admitted defeat, and Diefenbaker formed a minority government. A year later, Lester Pearson became the new Liberal leader. Canadians went to the polls again in 1958. Once again Diefenbaker was a spell-binding campaigner, and Canadians flocked to hear his stirring speeches. They were moved by his passionate promises of a "new vision" for Canada. On election day, Diefenbaker's Conservatives won a landslide victory over Pearson's Liberals.

Diefenbaker and Regional Concerns

When Diefenbaker became prime minister, Ontario, British Columbia, Alberta, and Quebec were booming. So were many Canadian cities, but not all regions had a slice of the "good life" of the 1950s. The Atlantic provinces did not share in the general prosperity; neither did most rural areas. Prairie farmers were having trouble selling their wheat. Many older people could barely get by on their pensions. Some people in seasonal work such as construction or fishing found it hard to make ends meet in the long off-season months.

The new Conservative prime minister promised to smooth out inequalities across Canada. Because of his boyhood experiences, John Diefenbaker was a "populist": he cared about the struggles of ordinary people and was known as a champion of the underdog. He had grown up on a prairie homestead 125 kilometres north of Saskatoon. Money was tight, and Diefenbaker worked hard to become a successful lawyer. He wanted to help other Canadians get the chance to enjoy prosperity and success. "All Canadians should share in the nation's general economic advance," he told Canadian voters. "There should be no permanent 'haves or have nots' in Canada."

Diefenbaker's government raised old-age pensions and set up a winter-works program to create construction jobs in the slack winter season and to encourage a year-round construction industry. It also brought in government crop subsidies, set up a government farm-loan program, and negotiated a huge sale of wheat to China in 1960. Canada sold off a 19.9-million-tonne backlog of wheat. The Diefenbaker government also helped to pay for provincial job-creation projects in the Atlantic provinces, for example, the establishment of small fish-packing, textile, and hardboard plants in Nova Scotia.

But Diefenbaker's policies failed to work economic miracles. Federal and provincial governments offered shared-cost programs to increase rural incomes under the **Agricultural and Rural Development Act**, but the government aid did not end rural poverty. Only the large mechanized farms were successful in the postwar era. As a result, Canadians continued to leave their small family farms and to seek a living in urban centres.

The people of the Atlantic provinces also continued to struggle against poverty. When Newfoundland joined Confederation in 1949, many Newfoundlanders were poor because they were not able to make a living from traditional jobs in farming, fishing, and logging. Newfoundland had few natural resources to develop besides fish, pulpwood, and some minerals. New industries were launched with government support, and a few — such as the cement plant at Corner Brook — succeeded. But many of the new industries — including the huge oil refinery at Come by Chance — failed, and unemployment remained a major problem.

Under several government resettlement programs between the 1950s and 1970s, Newfoundlanders were encouraged to leave their small outport communities and settle in larger communities on the island where social and economic opportunities were thought to be better. Many other Newfoundlanders left for central or western Canada or the United States in search of jobs. Other Atlantic provinces were facing similar problems as fishing, farming, and coal mining declined. In 1958, seventy-four miners died in a mining disaster in Springhill, Nova Scotia. The tragedy seemed to symbolize the hard lives of many Atlantic workers and their families.

Diefenbaker had promised to bring equality to Canada and to draw together the bickering "have" and "have not" regions into a single unified nation. But, if anything, the country was more divided along regional lines than it had been before Diefenbaker became prime minister. In the 1962 election, the Progressive Conservatives hung onto power — but just barely.

"A Canada of the North"

In the 1958 election campaign, Diefenbaker had talked about a new era of economic development in the North. He wanted to unlock the resource riches of the Canadian Shield and the Arctic. "I see a new Canada," Diefenbaker declared, "*a Canada of the North!*" Diefenbaker's "vision" for the Canadian North included massive oil and mineral exploration, a huge program of building "roads to resources," new townsites for the North, and increased government services for the Yukon and Northwest Territories.

Under Diefenbaker, more was achieved in the Canadian North than ever before in the nation's history. But the achievements were far short of

Diefenbaker's campaign promises. Bridges, dams, roads, and railways were built, often with the help of the provinces. The 6500 kilometres of new roads completed by 1963 helped open up the North. Government money guaranteed that there was plenty of exploration for oil and minerals. But only one new gold mine and one new tungsten mine came into operation, while two uranium mines shut down. The markets for resources were smaller than expected, and the costs of development were higher than expected. Northern development did not change Canada's economy in any important way or fulfil Canada's great economic "destiny."

Changes in Inuit Life

Still, northern development, especially the construction of the *DEW (Distant Early Warning) Line*, resulted in huge changes in the lives of the Inuit. Government money poured into the North, bringing dozens of airports and regular air service, as well as better harbours and water transport. These changes meant the arrival of fresh food, mail, and personnel from the South. The federal government also began to take full responsibility for the education, health, and welfare of the Inuit. Teachers, doctors, traders, and government administrators could now travel more easily across the vast and sparsely populated northern spaces, and badly needed services began to be provided. Health care slowly improved for the Inuit, but nurses, doctors, and medical facilities remained in short supply. The average life expectancy of a Canadian Inuit was only 29 years, while for most other Canadians it was 67.6 years. It was estimated that half of all Inuit babies died in their first year.

Education also improved in the Far North. The Diefenbaker government spent $20 million on new classrooms, and the number of Inuit children with access to schooling shot up. In 1957, only 18 percent of Inuit children had access to education, but by 1963 the figure stood at 66 percent. Still, their education was in English, their textbooks were "Dick and Jane" books written for city schoolchildren in the South, and their teachers knew little or nothing about the language and culture of their Inuit students. Education was meant to give students better employment opportunities, but there were few good jobs in the Canadian North. Despite the climbing enrolment in the lower grades, only a handful of Inuit students went on to high school. The result was a generation of partly educated

Despite the introduction of motorized vehicles, electricity, and other modern conveniences, many Dene continue to follow the customs and traditions of the past. How does this photograph reflect traditional Dene culture?

Trapping remains an important staple in the economy of the North. How does this Inuit trapper reflect the blending of traditional culture with modern technology?

young people who no longer fit easily into either Inuit or white culture.

Traditional patterns of Inuit life were also severely disrupted. The Inuit people had lived a nomadic lifestyle, moving from place to place while hunting, fishing, and trapping. But the federal government encouraged the Inuit to move into permanent settlements, where it could more conveniently provide government services. Many Inuit gave up their traditional practices for a completely foreign way of life in the new permanent communities. Some Inuit found jobs there as unskilled labourers, but they usually earned less money than many of the white workers doing more highly skilled work. Others did not find work at all and began living on government assistance money. The Inuit lived in much poorer housing than their white neighbours from the South and were often treated as social inferiors by the white community. Relations between whites and nonwhites were strained in many Arctic settlements.

Major changes were coming to the Far North, but Inuit people had little say in all of the planning and building going on in their homeland. As the Inuit journalist Alootook Ipellie described it, the new permanent settlements seemed to be run from the outside:

> *It seemed the government ran everything in [Inuit] communities. It owned the schools, gave them welfare, and employed them. When new buildings or houses were built, the government was behind them. When a new car or truck came in on the annual sea-lift, it was for the government.... It was government this, and government that, year in and year out.*

Some Inuit groups were relocated to remote Arctic areas by the federal government despite protests by the people themselves. For example, Inuit from Port Harrison in northern Quebec were relocated to Grise Fiord on Ellesmere Island, where, they were told, game was much more plentiful. But government documents later revealed that the Arctic had become vital for strategic defence purposes in the 1950s. The Canadian government wanted to have Canadian Inuit living on Ellesmere Island as proof of Canadian sovereignty in the Arctic. Because many Inuit did not understand how government worked and spoke little English, they had little control over government decision-making.

The Far North after 1960

The Inuit people were caught between the old ways of their ancestors and those of the newly developing Far North. They did not seem to belong completely

This cartoon depicts the Inuit claim that they were used as human flagpoles by the federal government in order to assert Canadian sovereignty in the Arctic.

ME, A CANADIAN?

Canada is a nation like few others in the world — a vast land touching three oceans and comprising an incredible diversity of people. In the short essay below, Inuit author Alootook Ipellie describes why he is proud to call himself Canadian. As you read this essay, consider whether Canada's multicultural heritage hampers our national identity or helps to build a stronger nation. Reflect on your own feelings about being Canadian.

Where I grew up there was no such place as Canada. I knew no Canada. I had never heard of it. My elders never mentioned Canada because they did not know Canada existed either. Later in life, I found out that I had been born in Canada, raised in Canada, and lived in Canada. Why did I not know about this place? Had the existence of Canada been censored in our land? I found the answers to these questions soon enough.

I was born in a small hunting camp on Baffin Island where my elders lived off the land. They had never heard anything about the outside world. Survival was a daily preoccupation when food was scarce, and they travelled from one hunting camp to the next in search of game. The Arctic was a hard land to live on but it was part of their lives and the only place they knew how to exist in. The land and the animals were sacred to them. Even if someone had told them they could lead easier lives in the cities and towns south of their land, they simply could not have survived there, or for a very short time only. Their upbringing had taught them to follow the traditions of their ancestors, and that was the only real life they knew. In earlier times, Canada did not exist for their ancestors although they walked on it every day.

I was brought up in the tradition of our ancestors. I suffered the hard days along with my elders when the hunters from our camp did not bring back any animals after being away for days at a time. And when food became plentiful, I rejoiced with my elders. We suffered when there was a lack of food and rejoiced when there was plenty of food. Life

This series of stamps, issued by Canada Post, celebrates aspects of traditions and community life among the Inuit. Try to identify each of the activities depicted.

sent to our land to teach and tell us about a whole new world we didn't know about. She taught us the language she spoke, and soon after that first year of school I heard her say the word "Canada" for the very first time. She then explained to us the history of Canada and how it began.

One thing I didn't understand at first was when she told me I was a resident of Canada and that I was a Canadian. Me, a Canadian? As long as I could remember I had been brought up as an Inuk first and foremost, and here was this teacher telling me otherwise. When she explained that I was an Inuk as well as a Canadian, I relaxed.

As I grew up and learned more about Canada and what it stood for, I became proud to be called a Canadian. Canada, I found out, respected my freedom to express myself through speech and civil liberties. This was important to me then and is today.

Canada is one of the few countries in the world that can say it has living in it a group of people who, through sheer determination and will to live, have survived for thousands of years on a land that tried to starve them out during its many fierce winters and brought them face to face with death and the possibility of extinction almost every day. Their survival speaks of hearts of steel.

The history of the Inuit is so long it surpasses human memory, although we do have some idea of where they came from. As the original people of Canada, they are in one sense "hosts" to all the nationalities who have settled in Canada and become Canadian citizens. Since Canada respects the cultural heritage of the Inuit and the freedom they enjoy, to live as they please, the Inuit have accepted the invitation to be called Canadians. By choosing to accept one another and live side by side, both benefit. Brother to brother, sister to sister, they are stronger today.

Without this sense of belonging to one another, we cannot hope to have a strong Canada.

Source: Alootook Ipellie is editor of *Inuit Today* and an author and artist from Baffin Island and Ottawa.

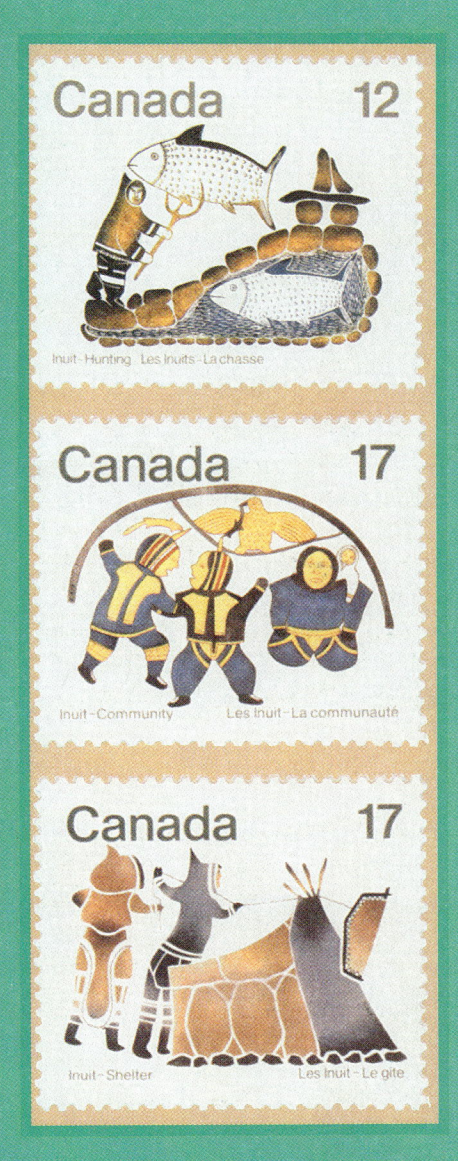

went on like this in our part of the world from day to day, week to week, month to month, and year to year. Food meant survival. The land provided the food and this land happened to be Canada.

When I was about eight years old, I went to school for the first time. I did not know a word of English then. Our teacher was a Qallunaaq (White) who spoke no Inuktitut, my mother tongue. She was more alien to me than I was to her. She had been in either the old or the new world. Many found the clash of cultures too difficult to cope with and sank into poverty and despair. Alcoholism, suicide, crime, and violence became a tragic part of life for many Inuit families. Many Inuit people worried that their people and way of life might not survive the overwhelming cultural changes. "Will the Inuit disappear from the face of this earth?" asked Inuit spokesperson John Amagoalik. "Will our culture, our language and our attachment to nature be remembered only in history books?... Is our culture like a wounded polar bear that has gone out to sea to die alone? What can be done?"

Questions such as these began a movement toward political activism among the Inuit people. One answer was the creation of a new political organization. The **Inuit Tapirisat of Canada** was set up in the early 1970s to protect Inuit culture and the Inuktitut language, and to work on Inuit land claims. Since then, the Inuit have had some successes. Today, Inuktitut is being taught in schools. Newspapers and radio and television programs are also available in Inuktitut. A campaign for Inuit control of government climaxed for eastern Inuit in a recent agreement with the federal government to create a new territory, Nunavut, by 1999. **Nunavut** — meaning "Our Land" in Inuktitut — will cover more than 5 million square kilometres in what has been the eastern portion of the Northwest Territories. It will have its own territorial legislature, elected from a population in which the majority of voters are Inuit. Nunavut will be the most dramatic change to the map of Canada since Newfoundland joined Confederation in 1949.

Immigration and the New Face of Canada

The North was not the only part of Canada to experience major cultural changes. Immigration boomed after World War II, and almost 1.5 million people came to Canada between 1945 and 1957. The earliest

Following World War II thousands of immigrants, such as this Jewish family, arrived in Canada from Europe. How did the influx of these immigrants change Canada?

arrivals were the "enemy aliens" who had been sent to Canadian internment camps from Britain during the war. Large numbers of them, in fact, were German Jews who had fled Nazi Germany. On their release in 1945, many stayed on to become some of the nation's most respected scientists, artists, professors, and writers. One of them, Gerhard Herzberg, won Canada's first Nobel Prize in chemistry in 1971.

About a fifth of the new arrivals came from Great Britain. Many were war brides who were brought to Canada by their soldier husbands. Most other immigrants came from the Netherlands, Germany, Poland, Hungary, southern Italy, and Ukraine. Many others were "displaced persons," European refugees who could not return to their homelands because they had no homes or because it was dangerous to go back. Four thousand anti-communist Polish soldiers left Europe for Canada after the Soviet Union seized Poland. After a failed anti-communist revolution in Hungary in 1956, 35 000 Hungarians also fled to Canada. The newcomers were not always welcomed. One Ontario government minister protested about the cost of supporting new immigrants. "These people are arriving with absolutely nothing, not even an extra suit of underwear," he complained. "Who is going to pay for the underwear?" The federal minister

IMMIGRANTS: THE SECOND GENERATION

Canada is a nation of immigrants. For decades people have arrived here from all over the world, and for decades immigrants and their children have faced the challenges of learning a new language and adapting to a new culture. The poem "Immigrants: The Second Generation" by Kevin Irie captures some of the challenges faced by those who arrive in Canada from non–English-speaking countries.

The streets are
always crowded on
weekends, wide enough
to hold the world —
Asians, Indians,
Europeans as well.

One boy grows
from his mother's grip —
held that tightly.
Together they travel
in search of cheap pants,

the mother cursing
the high price of denim,
leaving it to the boy
to translate her ire
into English tact
for the smiling salesman
who politely informs them that, no,
there is nothing else.

English is standard currency here;
the boy knows that,
he hoards his small allotment
of words like
a miser his pennies,

the one allowance no one can confiscate.

Out here, he is
the word and the way; his first
language fell away like milk teeth.
Only his mother,
stranded by his side,
still speaks in the old tongue alone.

A few English phrases
glint in her mouth
like fillings placed there
by other hands: a foreign substance
given for her own good:
hard, and impacted for life.

Source: Reprinted with permission by Mosaic Press from *Relations: Family Portraits*, edited by Kenneth Sherman, ©1986. "Immigrants: The Second Generation" by Kevin Irie.

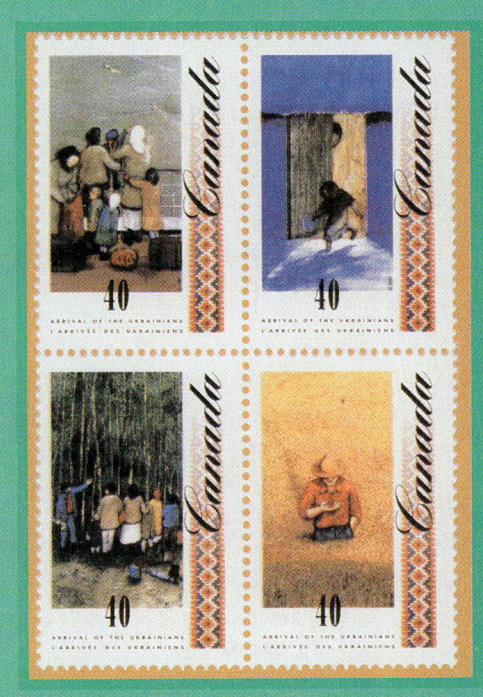

Throughout our history, immigration has played a critical role in Canada's development. This series of stamps recalls the arrival of Ukrainians to the Canadian prairies.

of citizenship and immigration shot back, "We will." In addition to government support, many Canadians took European refugees into their homes, found clothing and shelter for them, and helped them learn English and get jobs.

Most of the newcomers settled in Canadian cities, especially Toronto, Montreal, and Vancouver. The Italian community in Toronto had 140 000 people by the end of the 1950s, and displays of Italian pasta, imported cheeses, and other Mediterranean delicacies became familiar sights in Toronto stores. German immigrants set up shops along Robson Street in Vancouver, and Viennese pastries, Bavarian sausages, and German-language newspapers attracted the eye of passing shoppers. In cities across the country, Canadians became accustomed to pronouncing a whole host of unfamiliar European names. Although some hostility toward immigrants remained, many Canadians were proud of their new *cosmopolitanism*.

Diefenbaker was a representative of the new face of Canada. Unlike all former prime ministers, who were of either French or British heritage, Diefenbaker was of German stock. As a boy he had been taunted because of his strange-sounding last name, and as an adult he made a reputation as a battler against discrimination toward minorities. Diefenbaker called for a new national unity based on equality for all Canadians, regardless of race or creed. He called it a policy of "unhyphenated Canadianism."

Once in office, Diefenbaker appointed a Native to the Senate and named a member of Parliament of Ukrainian descent as his minister of labour. He also brought the first woman into the cabinet: Ellen Fairclough was appointed secretary of state. Diefenbaker's proudest achievement, however, was passing the **Canadian Bill of Rights** in 1960.

Former prime minister John Diefenbaker considered the passing of the Canadian Bill of Rights in 1958 one of his proudest moments in office. Why is a bill of rights an important piece of legislation?

The Canadian Bill of Rights

The full title of the Canadian Bill of Rights was "An Act for the Recognition and Protection of Human Rights and Fundamental Freedoms." It provided certain legal protections, including rights to free speech, religious freedom, freedom of the press, freedom of assembly and association, and the right to equal protection before the law. But the new bill was limited. It was a federal statute — not a constitutional guarantee of human rights — and it could be changed or abandoned at will by Parliament. It did not apply to areas under provincial authority, and it could be ignored at will by the provinces. The Canadian Bill of Rights did prompt some provinces to pass similar human-rights acts, however, and it clearly committed Canada to certain fundamental human principles. It set a precedent for the later constitutional guarantees in the Canadian Charter of Rights and Freedoms of 1982.

The End of the Diefenbaker Years

By 1962, the Progressive Conservatives were losing popular support, and the Liberals would soon be back in the political saddle. Diefenbaker's government was seen by many Canadians as floundering over issues such as nuclear weapons and relations with the United States. In 1963, the Diefenbaker government was brought down by a nonconfidence

THE EMERGENCE OF THE NORTH AMERICAN TEENAGER

After the end of World War II, Canada enjoyed a new level of prosperity and families had more money to spend on luxuries such as television sets, vacations, and long-playing records. One of the results of the affluence enjoyed by Canadians was the emergence of the teenager as an independent consumer. Wealth in the hands of teenagers gave them economic power and forced the business world to pay attention to their likes and desires. As a result, the affluence of the 1950s allowed for the development of teen culture in North America.

The clearest expression of the explosion in youth culture in the 1950s could be seen in music. By the late 1950s, popular music was clearly divided between the older generation, who listened to singers such as Patti Page and Frank Sinatra, and the younger generation, who jived with Elvis Presley, Chuck Berry, and Jerry Lee Lewis. Teenagers flocked to record stores to buy the latest hits by their favourite singers, who included Canadians such as Paul Anka, the Crewcuts, and the Diamonds.

The music of Elvis Presley was a radical departure from that of earlier white performers. His songs, a mixture of country, bluegrass, and rock, were performed with an electrifying amount of energy and hip gyrations that were highly controversial. Led by the music of Elvis Presley, rock and roll became a subculture for the youth of North America.

Youth culture has continued to thrive in North America. Each year, hundreds of new products designed for teens hit the marketplace and millions of dollars of advertising are spent to attract the teen consumer. The movie, music, fashion, and food industries are specifically geared to attract the teens of North America.

---

vote in Parliament. Lester Pearson's Liberals then won the 1963 federal election and formed a minority government. Diefenbaker remained in office as leader of the opposition, however, and Pearson's years as Canada's prime minister were often marked by bitter wrangling between the two political leaders. Both men gave up the leadership of their political parties in 1967 — one hundred years after Canada became a nation.

Canada was quickly becoming younger, more urban, and more American in its tastes. Because of the baby boom and the flood of new immigrants, almost half of all Canadians were under twenty-five years of age. There was a new word to describe the younger generation: "teenagers." The younger generation of Canadians looked to the United States for the latest styles in dance, music, fashion, and even politics. Many young Canadians admired the handsome young American president, John Kennedy. President Kennedy became a Canadian celebrity—the ideal of what a national leader should be. Many young Canadians were ready for a Canadian leader with youthfulness, wit, and personal style to match that of the American president. In 1967, many of them believed they had found it in the new Liberal leader, Pierre Trudeau.

KNOWING THE KEY PEOPLE, PLACES, AND EVENTS

In your notes, clearly identify and explain the historical significance of each of the following:

> Baby Boom
> Louis St. Laurent
> Agricultural and Rural Development Act
> Nunavut
> National Housing Act
> John Diefenbaker
> Inuit Tapirisat of Canada
> Canadian Bill of Rights

FOCUS YOUR KNOWLEDGE

1. Describe the economic changes that occurred in Canada in the 1950s.
2. Why was life in the suburbs attractive to Canadians in the 1950s? Do you think the suburbs hold the same attractions for people today?
3. Describe the role that automobiles came to play in the lives of Canadians during the 1950s.
4. Why was the Canadian North referred to as the "last great frontier"?
5. How did Diefenbaker's childhood help to shape the style of his politics and the policies he pursued?
6. Why did urban Canadians eventually withdraw their support from the Diefenbaker government?
7. Describe the events that strained relations between the Canadian government and the Native peoples of the North.
8. What steps have been taken since 1970 to help ensure the survival of Inuit culture?
9. How did the origins of the people immigrating to Canada change after 1945?
10. Why was the Canadian Bill of Rights an important document, despite its limitations?

APPLY YOUR KNOWLEDGE

1. Define consumerism, and describe the changes that occurred in Canada as a result of the increased wealth of Canadians after World War II.
2. Create a chart that contrasts the political styles of Louis St. Laurent and John Diefenbaker.
3. How did the 1950s heighten regional differences in Canada? Are the wealthy regions of Canada obligated to help the less fortunate areas?
4. Organize a chart that compares the Atlantic and Prairie provinces' responses to the policies of the Diefenbaker government with those of the urban areas of central Canada.
5. How successful was the government in developing Canada's North? What major obstacles were faced by the government?
6. How did the development of the North affect the lives of the Native peoples living there? In your answer, assess both the positive and negative changes.
7. Working in groups, research life among the Inuit during the 1950s. How did their lifestyles reflect a clash between traditional customs and the new influences that accompanied development?

EXTEND YOUR KNOWLEDGE

1. Try to imagine what it would have been like to have been a teenager before the age of television. To do this, spend an evening at home without watching any television. Before going to bed, summarize how you spent your evening. Compare your experience with that of someone who grew up during the 1950s by interviewing a relative or neighbour. Try to find out what forms of entertainment they enjoyed and how they spent their spare time. When you have finished your interview, write a one-page description of "A Day in the Life of a 1950s Teenager."
2. Prepare a bulletin-board display of entertainment during the 1950s. Your display should include movies, television, music, sports figures, and popular leisure activities. In preparing your display, give some thought to its organization, so that those who see it will find it visually appealing as well as informative.
3. Prepare a natural-resources map of Canada. This project will require you to consult a geographical atlas. Select two or three natural resources that you consider the most important for each province. On your map, label each province and use a symbol to illustrate the natural resources you have selected. Include a key in your finished map

CHAPTER 19 CANADA FROM THE 1960s TO THE 1980s

GLOSSARY TERMS

Counterculture The standards and values of a mostly younger generation who have rejected the cultural norms of established society.

Generation Gap Differences between the personal attitudes and social values of a generation of teenagers and young adults, and the attitudes and values of their parents' generation.

Progressive Education The philosophy of American educator John Dewey and others, based on the idea that teachers should focus on developing students' ability to think rather than on teaching a specific body of information.

Emission standards Government-set maximum limits on the amount of pollution permitted from a source.

CFCs An abbreviation for chlorofluorocarbons, a family of chemicals used for decades as coolants in refrigerators and air conditioners and as propellants in aerosol spray cans. Once released into the atmosphere, they drift upward and destroy the ozone layer that protects the earth from harmful ultraviolet (UV) rays from the sun.

Global Village A term coined by Canadian communications specialist Marshall McLuhan to describe the modern world, where the electronic communications media have reduced the distances between the peoples of the world and given them a sense of belonging to the same group or village.

Deficit The amount by which a sum of money falls short of the expected or required amount.

FOCUS ON:

- how Pierre Trudeau captured the imagination of a nation
- the youth generation of the 1960s
- educational reform in the 1960s
- the new Canadian environmental awareness
- the debate over Canada's social programs and the growing deficit
- the creation of Canada's medicare system

"The year 1967 changed us all profoundly," said Judy LaMarsh, secretary of state during the planning for Canada's centennial celebrations, "and we will never look back." The overwhelming success of **Expo 67** gave Canadians a new pride in themselves. According to many, Montreal's world's fair was the best ever staged. Fifty million visitors swarmed the fairgrounds on artificial islands in the St. Lawrence River and went away raving about Canadian style. "What's got into our good, gray neighbors?" asked one American magazine after Expo 67 was in full swing. Canada was no longer dull, placid, and a bit bashful. It was bright and lively and completely self-assured.

All the catchy and even zany centennial events held across Canada to celebrate the nation's one-hundredth birthday added to the new Canadian self-confidence. Dozens of centennial races were held in cars, on foot, in canoes, on snowmobiles, and even in hot-air balloons. Canadians suddenly became flag-wavers in 1967, and the new Canadian maple leaf flag turned up everywhere. The official centennial train rattled across the country, tooting the first bars of "O Canada" on its whistle, while Canadians cheered it on. The centennial year brought Canadians together in a new spirit of optimism and pride. When they looked ahead, the future seemed promising.

The year 1967 also marked the end of an era, as the Diefenbaker–Pearson years came to a close. John Diefenbaker was still head of the Progressive Conservatives, but he was in disfavour even in his own party. At a Conservative Party convention in September 1967, he was forced to step down as party leader. Just three months later, Lester Pearson resigned as prime minister and Pierre Trudeau became the new Liberal leader. When Trudeau stepped into the national spotlight, a new era in Canadian politics began.

TRUDEAUMANIA

Pierre Trudeau was a different kind of Canadian politician. One political commentator called him "our permanent Expo." Trudeau seemed to have the same mix of wit, style, and surprise that had made Expo 67 a winner. Trudeau was nearly fifty years old, but he did not look and act like a middle-aged politician. The bachelor millionaire dressed casually, drove fast sports cars, and charmed women. He clowned for the press and tossed off quotable comments that made instant headlines. He slid down banisters and pirouetted for the cameras. As a member of Parliament (MP), he had scandalized John Diefenbaker by walking into the House of Commons wearing sandals and a bright yellow scarf around his neck.

Trudeau was something of a newcomer to politics in 1968. He won a seat as an MP in 1965 and became the justice minister in Pearson's cabinet in 1967. As justice minister, he made a reputation as a social reformer. With the remark that the "state has no place in the bedrooms of the nation," Trudeau eased federal laws about divorce, homosexuality, and abortion. His reforms found favour with many young people who were protesting against old social conventions. As a French Canadian strongly opposed to Quebec separatism, Trudeau also won the admiration of many English Canadians. Many remembered the televised images of Trudeau coolly facing jeering, bottle-hurling Quebec demonstrators at a 1968 St. Jean Baptiste Day parade.

In the election campaign of 1968, Trudeau became an instant celebrity across Canada. Everywhere Trudeau went, he was mobbed. His enormous popular appeal reminded people of "Beatlemania," and was quickly called "**Trudeaumania**." Trudeau seemed to capture the new centennial spirit of adventure. He shook up Canadians and challenged them to welcome experiment and change. The Toronto *Globe and Mail*

From 1968 to his retirement in 1984, Pierre Trudeau dominated Canadian politics. Shown here playing baseball, Trudeau brought a flair to the prime minister's office, making him popular with many Canadians.

speculated that "what Canadians see in Mr. Trudeau is this new side of themselves, a readiness to gamble on the unknown, to move into areas not explored before." Trudeau seemed to be the right politician for the 1960s, and he won the 1968 election with ease.

LIFE IN THE 1960s AND 1970s

The period called "the Sixties" actually extended from the 1960s into the early 1970s. It was the time of the "**Youth Generation**." For the first time, young people — the two million baby boomers born between the late 1940s and mid-1960s — took centre stage in Canada. Many young Canadians of the Sixties led their lives in ways that were little different from those of their parents. But some young people became known as "hippies" and "revolutionaries." They rejected whatever they saw as part of "the Establishment" — especially the police (known as "The Man" or "pigs"), the government, and big business. They wanted "liberation" — personal freedom — and social change. It was a time of hope, restlessness, and rebellion. The American singer Bob Dylan's popular song, "The Times They Are a'Changing," captured the sense of a new social revolution.

The phrase "*counterculture*" came into the language. There were new cultural standards among the young that ran counter to (against) the values of their parents' generation. Sixties hippies were contemptuous of middle-class tastes, so they wore tie-dyed T-shirts in psychedelic colours, jackets from the Salvation Army, old jeans, and sandals or bare feet. Long, flowing hair — sometimes held back by leather thongs or a bandana tied around the forehead — became *the* unisex style in the Sixties. Hippies drove broken-down Volkswagen vans across the country and hitchhiked through Europe or Asia or Africa. They went by the thousands to rock festivals like Woodstock and folk festivals like Mariposa.

Many young people gathered in the hippie districts such as Haight–Ashbury in San Francisco, Fourth Avenue in Vancouver, and Yorkville in Toronto. They published underground newspapers filled with stories about drug raids and protest marches, revolutionary activities in Latin America, and the war in Vietnam, as well as giving information on local movies and rock concerts. They danced to the driving music of Jimi Hendrix, Janice Joplin, the Doors, the Rolling Stones, and the Beatles. They also listened to Canadian musicians who became famous in the 1960s, including the Band, Neil Young, the Guess Who, Ian and Sylvia, Buffy Sainte-Marie, Bruce Cockburn, and Joni Mitchell.

Some pop music celebrated the new drug culture ("Turn on, tune in, drop out") and the new morality ("Make love, not war"). Young people "turned on" to drugs and "dropped out" of society. Marijuana, LSD, amphetamines, and barbiturates were part of the hippie "scene," and mobile clinics were set up in major Canadian cities to rescue young people on "bad trips" from drug-taking. The birth-control pill opened the door to a new sexual permissiveness. People were also talking and writing more openly about sex, and censorship was challenged.

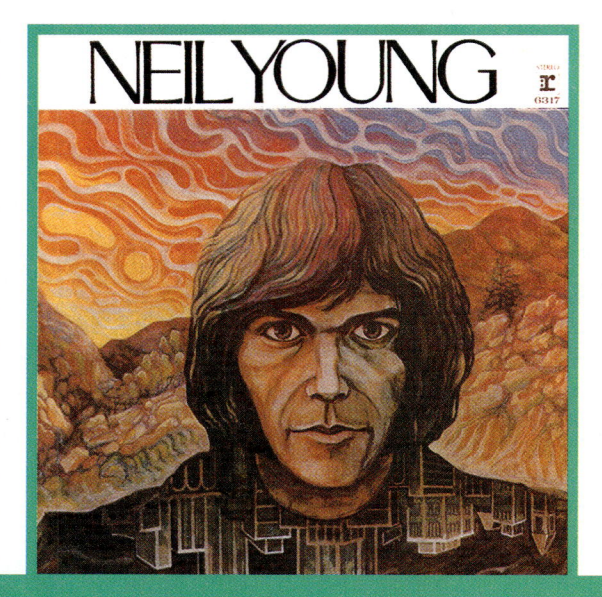

The 1960s saw an explosion in the Canadian music industry. Performers such as the Guess Who, Gordon Lightfoot, Buffy Saint-Marie, and Neil Young recorded albums that enjoyed tremendous success inside and outside of Canada. Try to name other Canadian musicians who began their careers in the 1960s or 1970s.

John Meredith, *Ulysses*, 1968. Canvas, 182.9 x 243.8. VAG.

PAINTING REBORN: ART OF THE 1960s AND 1970s

The 1960s ushered in a new wave of cultural activity in Canada. Buoyed by prosperous times and the approaching centennial celebration in 1967, all aspects of Canadian culture enjoyed unprecedented support. Bob Dylan's astute comment, "The times they are a'changing," was as applicable to the world of art as to any other aspect of society. For centuries painting had been the predominant art form, but in the midst of the cultural boom of the 1960s, artists and critics agreed that painting was dead.

Changing technology had much to do with the apparent death of painting. Many artists felt that painting was too confining and insufficient, so they turned to alternative art forms, including sculpture, photography, film, video, and performance art. But not all artists were willing to give up on painting. Across Canada, many important painters continued to adapt their art and managed to keep painting exciting and relevant. By the end of the 1970s, painting had been reborn in artistic centres throughout Canada and the western world. It is a tribute to those who persevered that painting remains one of the most important and adaptable visual art forms.

Do some research on a Canadian painter of the 1960s, 1970s, 1980s, or 1990s. Present your favourite painting to the class, and provide a brief explanation of why it appeals to you. The art department in your school may be helpful in your research.

There was a negative side to "liberation." Drugs and alcohol ruined many young lives. Sexual permissiveness meant less stable personal relationships and growing problems with sexually transmitted diseases. The "free speech" championed by the underground press lifted old-fashioned censorship but also paved the way for graphic and sometimes brutal pornography. The unconventionality and excess of the counterculture offended so many older Canadians that the term "*generation gap*" came into the language.

Only a fraction of young Canadians were Sixties-style hippies and aspiring revolutionaries. For many in their teens and twenties, life went on much as before. But few young people were completely untouched by what one writer called the "youthquake." There would be no return to earlier times. The Sixties made deep and lasting changes in Canadian values.

REVOLUTION IN THE SCHOOLS

In the 1960s, many Canadian students were still expected to obey strict dress codes, to walk through the halls without making noise, and to sit in neat rows in the classroom, facing the teacher. With the changing attitudes of the Sixties, however, students and many teachers began demanding a different kind of education. Many wanted school to be a relaxed place, where students could learn at their own pace and in their own way without the threat of failure or competition for grades. Teachers were supposed to become "resource people" who helped students in their own "discovery" of knowledge. In some schools, formal teaching methods, dress and discipline codes, compulsory courses, strict timetables, and sometimes grades, tests, and examinations became things of the past.

Educational reform came out of what is sometimes called "progressive" or "child-centred" educational philosophy. Battles between people who favoured and opposed progressive reforms had broken out even before the Sixties. In 1953, Hilda Neatby, a history professor at the University of Saskatchewan, wrote a book called *So Little For The Mind*. She argued that *progressive education* neglected traditional content and intellectual discipline in favour of "self-development." More recent critics have also argued that many students struggle in progressive schools because they need more order, guidance, and structure to help them learn effectively. Today education is still under fire from governments, educators, parents, and students. All agree that change is still needed, but they strongly disagree about how to reform the education system. Supporters and opponents of child-centred educational philosophy continue their public disputes across the nation.

A NEW ENVIRONMENTAL AWARENESS

Another issue that came to centre stage in the mid-1960s was the state of the environment. Canadians gradually opened their eyes to the problems of polluted air and water, the destruction of forests and farmlands, threats to wildlife, and toxins seeping from industrial sites. Cars and factories were emitting dangerous gases into the air, producing acid rain. The Great Lakes were dying: fish and other marine life could not survive in the badly polluted waters. Many Canadian cities still poured raw sewage into rivers, lakes, and ocean waters, and Canadian citizens were throwing out millions of tonnes of garbage each year. Even in the Arctic, massive doses of mercury and other contaminants were found in whales, seals, and polar bears, threatening the health of the animals and of the Inuit who hunted them for meat. It was a recipe for environmental disaster.

Young people across Canada have become very aware of environmental issues. This student participated in Earth Day activities at her school. What are you doing in your community, school, and home to help the environment?

Saving the environment became a focus for activists in the late 1960s and 1970s. Dozens of environmental groups formed from coast to coast — including the Vancouver-born Greenpeace, the Society for Pollution and Environmental Control, and Pollution Probe. These environmental activists were successful in capturing public attention. In a 1969 poll, more than two-thirds of Canadians said that pollution was so serious that they were willing to pay more taxes to help control it.

In the 1970s, governments began taking steps to clean up the environment. They gave money to support environmental groups and passed laws to reduce environmental damage. For example, cars and industries were forced to reduce their harmful emissions. Efforts were also made to control the use and disposal of poisonous chemicals and to clean up polluted rivers, lakes, and landfill sites. Governments began setting *emission standards*, and courts began fining polluters. There were also attempts to save valuable forests and farmlands and to review the environmental impact of major public projects before approving their construction.

In the 1980s, many Canadians also looked at their own lifestyles and became "**green activists.**" They began composting garbage and recycling cans, bottles, and paper. They bought products made of recycled materials. They stopped buying aerosol cans with *CFCs* (chlorofluorocarbons) and boycotted the products of known polluters. They used unleaded gasoline and bought pesticide-free fruits and vegetables. They continued to press governments at all levels to take stronger stands on important environmental issues. As a result, governments began to respond. For example, CFCs and leaded gasoline were banned, and curbside "blue box" recycling programs were started in many communities.

But environmental awareness soon deepened into extreme concern. Newspapers in the 1980s were filled with headline stories of environmental tragedies — huge gaps in the world's ozone layer, acid rain, the greenhouse effect, vanishing rainforests, a release of deadly gas in the Indian city of Bhopal, a nuclear disaster in the Ukrainian city of Chernobyl, and the *Exxon Valdez* oil spill off the coast of Alaska. These were matters of international concern. An estimated half-billion people around the world showed their commitment to saving the planet by celebrating Earth Day in 1990. Many people and nations around the world are trying desperately to make the necessary changes and avert global environmental disaster.

JUST HOW COMMITTED ARE WE?

What a Waste

We, in the industrialized world, have never paid the true cost of our resource exploitation. One of the costs we've ignored is that of cleaning up the environmental messes our industries produce. Even now, many industries approach the problem of hazardous wastes by "sweeping them under the carpet." They do this by sending millions of tonnes of untreated toxic goo to the Third World.

Altogether, 81 countries now ban the importation of wastes; in Nigeria, the penalty for being caught doing so is death. However, that still leaves 90 or so countries that aren't too fussy about what comes ashore in unlabelled barrels.

It's estimated that Western businesses dumped 24 million tonnes of hazardous waste in West Africa alone in 1988. East Germany is thought to have earned between 10 and 20% of its hard currency from importing toxic waste. This was in the days before the communist government collapsed, and it's reasonable to assume most of that waste was just dumped untreated. It's said that Poland and Hungary also have active waste importing businesses. A waste importing scandal in Romania in 1989 saw some government officials jailed for up to 18 years.

Guinea-Bissau in West Africa was offered $600 million over five years to store 15 million tonnes of pharmaceutical and tanning waste. The $600 million is equal to four times the country's Gross Domestic Product. The deal was turned down after strong local protests.

And it's not just wastes that have been dumped. The United States exports 270 million kilos of pesticides each year, a quarter of which are either banned or severely restricted at home. A not unrelated statistic is that of the roughly one million pesticide poisonings a year around the globe, the vast majority occur in the Third World. Between 5000 and 20 000 of these poisonings are fatal.

Just How Committed Are We?

A public opinion poll in the spring of 1990 suggests that Canadians have mixed feelings about protecting the environment. Yes, we want a clean world, but, no, we don't want to give up any goodies to get it. The Angus Reid poll found that:

- About 60% of Canadians oppose banning private cars from cities during certain hours, or applying tax on parking.
- Nearly 75% oppose adding a special fuel tax on all cars in cities.
- More than 50% oppose charging for garbage pickup based on how much individuals throw out.
- More than 50% oppose a tax on packaging to reduce the amount used.
- More than 50% oppose increases in downtown residential density as a way to limit urban sprawl.

Source: Reprinted with the permission of *Canada and the World* magazine, Oakville, Ontario.

Harvey Jahen, of Edmonton, came up with a creative way to help reduce waste. His company, Superwood Western Ltd., turns plastic bottles and jugs into plastic wood which, like real wood, can be nailed, sawed, or drilled. Try to think of other ways to reduce waste.

Buttons were the "in" thing in the 1960s. Many teenagers and young adults wore a variety of buttons that made social and political statements. Which of these buttons would you have worn?

SOCIAL AND POLITICAL CHANGES

The 1960s were also a decade of social and political protest, and hundreds of young Canadians waved banners and wore buttons with the new slogans of the Sixties, such as "Flower Power," "Power to the People," and "Peace." The war in **Vietnam** was a major issue. Troops from communist North Vietnam were helping South Vietnamese guerilla fighters to overthrow the American-backed government of South Vietnam. The war in Southeast Asia had escalated sharply in the mid-1960s; by 1967, there were almost 500 000 American troops in Vietnam. It was a brutal and destructive war, and for the first time television brought the full horror of war home to the watching world.

Some Canadians supported U.S. military actions in Vietnam, and some young Canadians even volunteered for the American army. Some Canadian industries also produced weapons for use in Vietnam. But many other Canadians opposed the Vietnam war. They staged protests against the war and against the sale of Canadian weapons to the United States. Canada became a refuge for young American draft resisters who refused to fight in Vietnam.

Television also brought other global events instantly to Canadian viewers. The famous Canadian communications expert Marshall McLuhan declared that the world had become "a *global village*." Canadians became newly aware of the struggles of people all over the world for civil rights and social justice. They also became more alert to injustices in Canada — especially among the Native peoples, women, racial and ethnic minorities, and the poor. In 1964, the Pearson government funded the **Company of Young Canadians** to enable idealistic young activists to work for social change in local programs across the nation. Other youth projects followed in the 1970s, including Opportunities for Youth, the Local Initiatives Program, and Katimavik.

During the 1960s, protests such as this one were highly critical of the United States' participation in the Vietnam War. Are protests an effective way to achieve goals? What issues would you be willing to join a protest over?

Canada's Postwar Social Programs

A continuing problem was poverty in the midst of plenty. Many Canadians did not have a share in the affluence of the 1950s and 1960s. Social programs had been growing since World War II, and many were aimed at helping Canadians who were suffering because of low incomes or job loss. Canadian economic growth after 1963 gave the federal government more money to expand existing welfare programs and add new ones.

Under the BNA Act of 1867, providing social welfare programs was the responsibility of municipalities and provinces. But some needy Canadians had suffered because they lived in poor regions that could not afford many social welfare programs. Gradually, the federal and provincial governments began sharing responsibility for social welfare programs such as old-age pensions and hospital insurance. In the 1950s, they agreed on a policy of equalization, in which the federal government made payments to poorer provinces to help them provide their residents with social services and a standard of living comparable to that of the richer provinces. Ottawa also paid money to poorer regions to develop new industries and to help out-of-work people relocate in other parts of Canada.

The Pearson government broadened the range of Canadian social welfare programs. Pearson brought in the nation-wide Canada Pension Plan in 1966 and the **Canada Assistance Plan** in 1965. Under the Canada Assistance Plan, the federal government agreed to share with the provinces the costs of a whole range of programs, including child care, health care for the needy, employment projects, and aid for disadvantaged groups such as widows and disabled Canadians.

Medicare

Medicare was perhaps the most important new federal social program proposed by the Pearson government. The proposed new medicare program was patterned on a bold new plan pioneered by the NDP government in Saskatchewan in 1962. The Pearson government offered to share with any province the costs of a medical plan that paid for all necessary medical services for the people of that province. After some disagreements with Ontario and British Columbia, the Canadian government finally introduced the medicare scheme in 1968. Medical fees were now paid, not by the patient, but by the government. It freed Canadians from the nightmare of huge and unexpected medical bills.

Social Welfare Programs in the 1970s and 1980s

Canada's generous social welfare safety net protected Canadians from the insecurities of the modern industrial world. When Pierre Trudeau campaigned in 1968, however, he told Canadians that "Ottawa is not Santa Claus." His government was not going to give out any more "free stuff." But his popularity slipped badly over the next four years. Canadians saw a new side of Trudeau; he seemed arrogant and uncaring. Many people in regions outside central Canada — especially those in the West — felt that their problems were ignored by the Trudeau government. Trudeau's Liberals barely won the 1972 election and had to settle for a minority government.

To win back political support in Parliament and across the country, Trudeau committed his government to spending freely and passing popular legislation. There were no big changes in the social welfare net, but government spending went up. Unemployment insurance benefits were expanded, and so were pensions and family allowances. Schemes for rural and regional economic development were also heavily funded. By the end of the 1970s, the government was spending half a billion dollars a year under its regional economic expansion program.

At the same time, however, inflation was soaring, and the costs of social and economic programs were spiralling upwards. In 1978, the federal government debt was growing so quickly that the auditor general warned Canadians that the government "has lost or is close to losing effective control of the public purse." Trudeau argued that the only way to cut the huge federal *deficit* was to slash government spending.

But Canadians were unhappy about cutting funds for families, old-age pensioners, and the unemployed — especially in a time of high unemployment. Joe Clark's Conservative Party defeated the Trudeau government in 1979. In its first budget, however, the Conservatives imposed an unpopular gasoline tax. The opposition parties combined to defeat the budget and force an unexpected election in 1980. To the astonishment of many Canadians, Trudeau was returned to power. "Welcome to the 1980s," a beaming Trudeau greeted his political supporters on election night. But between 1980 and 1984, the federal deficit continued to climb.

Brian Mulroney's government came to power in 1984. It had promised to safeguard Canada's social safety net as a "sacred trust." But Mulroney inherited a huge national debt. The Conservatives argued that because of the size of the national debt, Canada could not afford to pay well-off Canadians benefits such as family allowances and old-age pensions. In 1989, the Mulroney government "taxed back" some social welfare payments from wealthier recipients. In 1992, it did away with family allowances and replaced them with an income supplement for working families. It looked to some observers as if Canada's social welfare system was being taken apart bit by bit.

Changes in federal social welfare programs triggered a debate in Canada over questions such as these: Are social programs the right of all Canadians? Should some programs, such as old-age pensions and family allowances, be available only to less well-to-do Canadians? Should unemployment insurance (UIC) benefits or medicare benefits be changed? These and other social welfare questions await answers in the 1990s.

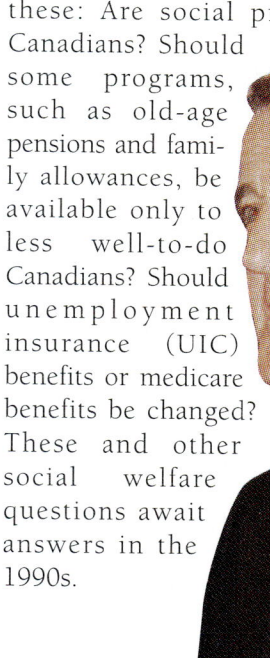

Brian Mulroney's Progressive Conservative government (1984–1993) brought many changes to Canada, including a Free Trade Agreement with the United States and the controversial goods and services tax (GST). His two attempts to amend the Constitution to meet Quebec's desires both ended in failure.

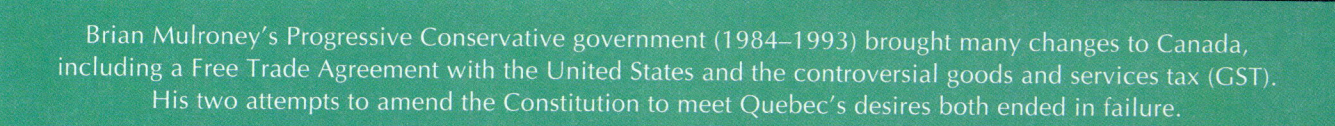

KNOWING THE KEY PEOPLE, PLACES, AND EVENTS

In your notes, clearly identify and explain the historical significance of each of the following:

> Expo 67
> Youth Generation
> Generation Gap
> Vietnam
> Canada Assistance Plan
> Trudeaumania
> Counterculture
> Green Activists
> Company of Young Canadians
> Medicare

FOCUS YOUR KNOWLEDGE

1. Describe the Canadians of 1967.
2. What aspects of his character made Pierre Trudeau a refreshing change in Canadian politics?
3. How did the youth of the 1960s differ from earlier generations?
4. What problems accompanied the very liberal attitudes of the 1960s?
5. What measures have been taken in the past two decades to clean up the environment?
6. Why did the war in Vietnam become a central issue in North America during the 1960s and 1970s?
7. What actions have been taken by the government in the past decade to reduce the deficit?

APPLY YOUR KNOWLEDGE

1. In groups of two or three, prepare a bulletin-board display that captures some of the attitudes of the youth in the 1960s. Share your display with the class, and discuss that generation's similarities to and differences from today's youth.
2. How was education affected by the attitudes of the 1960s? Write an editorial report expressing the direction that you think education should now be taking.

3. Make a list of the environmental problems that Canadians became aware of in the 1960s. What actions have since been taken to deal with these problems? What further actions should be taken by: (a) individuals; (b) corporations; (c) governments?

4. Should Canada's social programs be preserved and protected, or should they be reduced to save the government money? If you were given the task of reducing the deficit, which social programs would you cut? Discuss your choices in groups of three or four.

5. Should wealthy Canadians be equally entitled to government benefits such as family-allowance payments and old-age security? Defend your answer.

EXTEND YOUR KNOWLEDGE

1. Prepare a medley of three to five songs from the 1960s, and provide a written explanation of how these songs reflect the attitudes of youth in the 1960s. Include at least one Canadian artist and song in your medley.

2. Prepare a poster that could be used to encourage individuals, corporations, or government to be more active in protecting the environment.

3. Write a letter to a local, provincial, or federal politician outlining your concerns about an injustice you see occurring in Canada. Explain why you are concerned, and make some constructive suggestions about how the situation could be improved.

CHAPTER 20
CANADA AS A MULTICULTURAL NATION

GLOSSARY TERMS

Melting Pot A term for a city, region, or country in which immigrants coming from various cultural or racial backgrounds lose touch with their own culture and take on the behaviour and values of the place where they have settled.

Mosaic A term for a city, region, or country in which immigrants coming from various cultural or racial backgrounds maintain their own culture.

Persecution Causing harm or suffering to a person or group of people, especially for religious or political reasons.

Deportation Expelling individuals who are considered undesirable (and are noncitizens) from a country.

Ancestral Lands Territory that has been occupied by the ancestors of a particular group for many generations.

Activism Working energetically in support of a social or political cause.

FOCUS ON:

- Trudeau's desire for a "Just Society"
- changing patterns of immigration in Canada
- racism in Canada
- the women's movement and the changing roles of men and women
- the struggle of Native peoples to preserve their cultural heritage

The face of Canadian society has changed quickly in the last decades of the twentieth century. At the beginning of the century, just over 95 percent of Canadians were of French or British descent. By the mid-1980s, the figure had dropped to just under 70 percent. People from many different places have come to Canada, and it is now a genuinely multicultural nation.

CANADA AS A MULTICULTURAL NATION

In the centennial year, 1967, the **Royal Commission on Bilingualism and Biculturalism** described a new vision of Canadian society. Its report recommended that Canada have two official languages — French and English. It also said, however, that Canada should be officially a nation of many cultures. A "multicultural nation" meant that the heritage of all Canada's ethnic groups would be respected and valued. As a multicultural liaison officer later described it, multiculturalism was accepting "all the goodness and all the values people have brought here."

Trudeau and the "Just Society"

In 1971, Pierre Trudeau accepted the royal commission's recommendations. He proclaimed a policy of "multiculturalism within a bilingual framework." Trudeau's announcement was in keeping with his 1968 election pledge to make Canada a "Just Society" — a place where all Canadians were equals. His policy pleased many non-British, non-French groups who had felt like second-class citizens in the formerly "bicultural" Canada. It was a formal recognition that Canada was not an American-style "*melting pot*," in which people were expected to give up their ethnic identities in favour of the dominant culture. Instead Canada was a "*mosaic*," where pride in one's ethnic heritage could go hand in hand with pride in Canada.

Important new laws supporting multiculturalism were passed over the next decade. The Citizenship Act of 1977 did away with special treatment for British subjects seeking Canadian citizenship. The **Canadian Human Rights Act** of 1977 outlawed discrimination against members of racial or ethnic groups. Most important of all, the Constitution Act of 1982 contained two new clauses enshrining individual and group rights in the Canadian Charter of Rights and Freedoms. One clause protected individuals from discrimination. Another stated that the charter should be interpreted so as to preserve and enhance "the multicultural heritage of Canadians."

Changing Patterns of Immigration

As the Canadian economy expanded in the 1960s, more skilled workers with technical and professional training were needed. Before, Canada's major source of skilled workers had been Europe, but Europe's economy had also recovered after the war. As a result, fewer Europeans were asking to immigrate to Canada. To fill the gap, Canada began accepting more immigrants from countries of the Third World. The largest number came from Asia,

These children, from a variety of ethnic backgrounds, are holding a Canadian flag made of numerous flags from other countries. How does this photograph capture the true essence of Canada?

CANADIAN SOVEREIGNTY: CARVING OUT A UNIQUE IDENTITY

Throughout the late twentieth century the world has increasingly become a global village. Advanced telecommunications allow television and radio programs to be beamed into Canada from the United States. With the development of affordable and powerful satellite dishes, more and more Canadians are tuning in to American programs and listening to American music. Also, the increasingly multicultural nature of Canada has led some people to question Canada's national identity. Although sovereignty usually refers specifically to legal issues, in recent years it has also come to be used in relation to a country's ability to control its economy and cultural development.

Canadian Music Industry: The enormous American market allows for millions of dollars to be poured into the American music industry. With a limited market, Canadian musicians must struggle to establish a name for themselves. In 1971 the Canadian government set up CanCon, which is a body of regulations that requires that radio stations play a minimum of 30 percent Canadian music. Some feel that Canadian musicians should have to achieve success solely on their merit and should not be supported by regulations that force Canadians to listen to Canadian music. How important do you think content regulations are in promoting the Canadian music industry? Does the support for Canadian musicians help to preserve Canadian sovereignty?

Canadian Broadcasting Corporation: The Canadian Broadcasting Corporation (CBC) was set up in 1936 with its mandate being to develop and promote Canadian culture on radio and later television. In 1993, the federal government helped finance CBC production of programs such as "Street Legal" as well as documentaries, and variety programs such as "Friday Night with Ralph Benmergui" that highlight Canadian acts. Aside from producing Canadian-made programs, the CBC imports a large number of hit programs from the United States. Some feel the CBC should receive much less funding and should generate more revenue by showing the programs the public wants to see regardless of whether they are Canadian or American. Costs could be lowered by importing American programs, since it is far more expensive to produce episodes of Canadian programs than it is to buy existing American shows. Others feel that the CBC should be given more funding and show exclusively Canadian programs. Should the CBC's mandate be to earn a profit or to develop Canadian programs and promote Canadian culture? How does support for the CBC help to ensure Canadian sovereignty?

followed by the Caribbean, Latin America, and Africa. Many of these immigrants came in under a new "point system" that ranked applicants according to their education, skills, and resources. They were mostly professionals, technicians, and managers who had been picked to fill Canada's need for highly trained workers.

The Immigration Act of 1978

Changing needs in Canada and a shifting pattern of immigration led to a complete redrafting of the nation's immigration laws. After much public discussion and sometimes heated debate, the new **Immigration Act** was passed by Parliament. The 1978 Immigration Act recognized three classes of immigrants: Independent Class, Family Class, and Refugee Class. The Independent Class included potential immigrants (1) who satisfied the point system, (2) who were willing to be self-employed or set up businesses in Canada, or (3) who had family members willing to "sponsor" them and help them get established. The Family Class included close relatives of people who were citizens or permanent residents of Canada — husbands or wives, parents, grandparents, and unmarried children under the age of twenty-one. The Refugee Class applied to people who feared harm or had already suffered *persecution* in their own countries because of their religion, race, nationality, social identity, or political ideas.

Since the late 1970s, 60 percent of Canada's immigrants have come from countries other than the United States or the European nations. Many recent immigrants are nonwhites, sometimes called "visible minorities." Many are well educated and highly skilled. For example, 9.9 percent of Canadian males and 6.2 percent of Canadian females have university degrees. But 20.8 percent of recent nonwhite male immigrants and 12.7 percent of recent nonwhite female immigrants have degrees. Canada has gained by attracting high-quality immigrants. Unfortunately, many Third World countries have lost people with badly needed skills.

Racism in Canada

Today, most Canadians still support multiculturalism. In a recent poll, 74 percent of the respondents said that Canada's tradition of welcoming people of diverse backgrounds was one of the best things about the nation. But the first wave of visible minorities in Canadian history was met with racism, and thousands of nonwhite newcomers had to struggle for acceptance in their new country. Some people feared and hated Canada's new visible minorities.

In postwar Canada, the problem was at its worst in the cities, where most new immigrants

Immigrants from all over the world have arrived in Canada during the past half-century. In many Canadian cities, ethnic neighbourhoods have developed. Here, an Asian women strolls through "Chinatown" in Vancouver.

How does this Canadian family reflect its pride in its ethnic heritage?

were settling. In the 1970s, attacks on Southeast Asians in Toronto and Calgary and on Sikh families in Vancouver cast a shadow over Canada. Troubles continued in the 1980s and early 1990s, as Canadians faced racial tensions that they had once thought were other people's problems. In cities such as Toronto and Montreal, many black and Asian Canadians face job discrimination and racism. For example, in 1984 a Montreal taxi company dismissed twenty-four Haitians because, it claimed, many customers did not want to be driven by black taxi drivers.

Racism was also increasing in other parts of the country. On the basis of radio callers' negative comments about nonwhite immigrants, Winnipeg radio host Peter Warren said, "Amongst us, I fear, there are many Archie Bunkers and Ku Klux Klanners. I'm hearing people say they want to keep Canada white." Calls to other Canadian talk-radio shows were much the same. A study done for Employment and Immigration Canada found a disturbing level of racism in Canada, mostly based on the fear that Canada's dominant British and European culture would be swallowed up by immigration from the Third World. Yet, less than 7 percent of Canada's total population in 1986 was nonwhite. Even if 70 percent of all immigrants between 1990 and 2001 were nonwhite, Canada's total nonwhite population would not exceed 10 percent in 2001.

The government has established a race-relations unit to combat racism in Canada. Schools now give courses to change racist attitudes. The courts offer legal weapons to victims of discrimination. Many other people are working to combat racism and create social harmony in Canada. As one black Canadian put it, "If we can solve the problems of making it possible for people of every kind to live together in reasonable harmony, we have a message for the world. The problems of this shrinking planet are problems we're solving in Canada."

The Refugee Issue

Another immigration problem surfaced in the late 1980s. A boatload of Tamils arrived in Newfoundland without visas in August 1986. They asked to be admitted to Canada as refugees. But were they genuine refugees — people fleeing danger, persecution, or death in their own country? Or were they "queue jumpers"? Queue jumpers are

Don't be a wall... be a window

What could you change within your own school community to create better racial relations among all peoples?

would-be immigrants who come to Canada and falsely claim to be refugees in order to by-pass thousands of other potential immigrants who are making legal applications from outside Canada.

The arrival of the Tamils triggered a huge public debate about Canada's refugee policy. Under the Immigration Act of 1978, Canada set out two major objectives. One was to promote the "domestic and international interests of Canada." The other was to meet Canada's humanitarian commitment to the United Nations to aid "the displaced and persecuted." The Canadian government has allowed many groups of refugees into Canada over the last few decades. Canada took in 7000 Ugandans in 1972. It has also accepted 17 000 Chileans since 1973, 72 000 Vietnamese since 1975, and more than 10 000 Lebanese from 1976 to 1978. From 1980 to 1986, Canada accepted a total more than 130 000 refugees — more per capita than any other country in the world.

But Canadian immigration officials were completely unprepared for the flood of refugees coming to Canadian shores and asking for asylum. Some were genuine refugees, some were not. The system was swamped; by 1986, the backlog of refugee claims was over 23 000. Changes were made to immigration regulations in the late 1980s and early 1990s to try to deal with the growing number of refugee claims. Changes included trying to make faster decisions on refugee cases, increasing penalties for "people smugglers" who brought in questionable refugees, and making *deportation* easier for people whose refugee claims were rejected. An unfortunate result of the refugee crisis has been a hardening of attitudes toward all refugees — even people who are genuinely fleeing repression in their own countries.

Immigration and the Future of Canada

In the midst of the refugee crisis, former immigration minister Flora MacDonald reminded Canadians that "this country is composed of people who are very compassionate and who have always seen immigration as being a major factor in the development of the country." Immigrants have traditionally brought their talent, skills, and hard work to Canada and helped a sparsely populated country to flourish. Canada's future economic well-being may well depend on immigration. As the baby boomers move into retirement, there will be fewer workers than nonworkers in Canada. The nation's economic future might be in jeopardy without additional workers from abroad. Many individuals and groups who favour immigration are pressing the Canadian government to broaden its immigration policies and take in more immigrants. However, many other Canadians want more restricted policies and a reduction in the number of future immigrants.

Canada faces important decisions about future immigration. The Mulroney government took steps toward restricting immigration under the Family Class and emphasizing job skills needed in Canada under the Independent Class. Should Canada look for immigrants who are young, well educated, and skilled to replace retiring workers? What are the costs and benefits of immigration? What steps should be taken to make sure that immigrants settle easily into Canada and become productive members of their communities? How can racial tensions be eased and tolerance promoted? These are just some of the questions for the 1990s and beyond.

"THE SECOND WAVE": THE NEW WOMEN'S MOVEMENT

Like students in the 1960s, many Canadian women were ready to push hard for social change. With some exceptions, women had won the right to vote after World War I. But as one suffragist rightly predicted in 1897, the vote was just the beginning — not the end — of women's struggle for

NOVA SCOTIA REALITY SONG

Among the earliest black Canadians were those who arrived in Nova Scotia following the American Revolution. Hundreds of former plantation slaves fought with the British army during the revolution and fled north to Nova Scotia at the end of the war. Despite black Canadians' long history in Canada, they continue to feel the anger and pain of racism. David Woods, a Nova Scotia writer and artist, celebrates the Afro-Canadian identity while struggling with despair. His poems "speak the dreams of a new freedom while contemplating the hardship of the past." As you read the poem "Nova Scotia Reality Song," consider how racism has scarred the past and what can be done to ensure a better future for Canadians of all races.

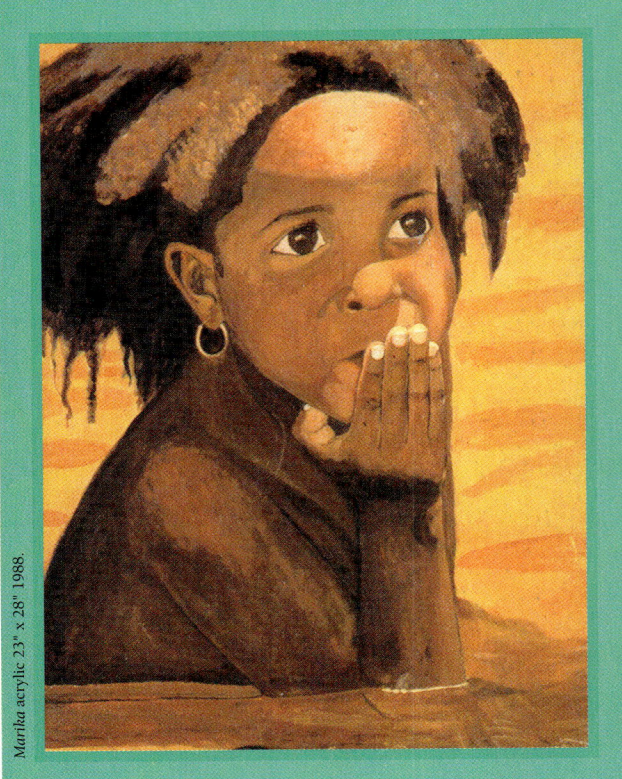

Marika acrylic 23" x 28" 1988.

Nova Scotia Reality Song

In North Preston today
Ingram Byard married Marion Downey,
Ingram is called "Butch," Marion — "Mainey,"
(After the tradition of nicknaming that
exists in that community),
The reception was held in Dartmouth,
With the women resplendent in white and green

But some white men passing
Flicked ugliness into the scene:
"Look at them niggers!" they shouted,
And made my soul scream.

I CRY —
Feeling the depth of black pain.

In 1832,
An African Baptist Church was organized in Halifax,
The African Baptist Church is a church for black people,
A black church was needed because the white church closed its doors,
"Negroes smell and sing too loud,"
Whites complained,
And set off a petition to the Bishop and the King.

I CRY —
Feeling the depth of black pain.

In 1947
Viola Desmond was arrested
At the Roseland Theatre in New Glasgow,
Viola had gone that evening to see her favourite show,
In New Glasgow a law forbid blacks from sitting in the downstairs section,
It was reserved for whites only.
They wanted her to go upstairs

Because it was the balcony —
They called it "A Nigger's Heaven."

I CRY —
Feeling the depth of black pain.

In 1962 —
The city of Halifax approved the destruction
of Africville,
Africville was a black community on the rim
of the Bedford Basin,
It was founded in the 1800s and ignored by
the city.
There was no sewage,
— no lights,
— no sidewalks
— no water
In Africville,
The people did the best they could —
Building from their dreams and industry
They built a church — houses for their families.
Starting in 1960 they listened as their homes
were called "shacks,"
Their community, "Canada's worst slum,"
By 1969 houses, church, people were all gone.

I CRY —
Feeling the depth of black pain.

Mary Desmond
Looked out of the squalor of her country
room,
Room that was cold, dark and lonely,
Heard the shouts of her crying child.
Felt the sharp movements inside her swollen
belly,
Reaching out from the pain,
She suddenly grabs for an area of peace,
Pounds against the swell
And kills the substance of her unborn child
I heard her cry out from pain.

And I CRY —
Feeling the depth of black pain.

Where is my way in Nova Scotia?
In whose words will I find my comfort?
I cry out for dignity.
Must it always be to go and so
continually hear
Words of insult tossed cruelly
into the air?
Must it always be to go and so
continually see
The destruction of things
dear to me?
I beat inside a black skin
Stare out from inside a black brain,
I was there at the moment of
Butch's marriage to Mainey,
I was there when the white church closed its
doors,
I was there when Viola Desmond was arrested,
I was there when Africville was taken,
I was there when Mary Desmond killed her
child,
I was there at those moments,
And I am there now,
Feeling their weight press against me —
Feeling their substance pulse through my
veins.

I attempt to defeat them —
I attempt to keep them in place,
But with each new turn
That brings another cruel voice
Or hate-filled face,
I feel these scenes awake
again and again,

And I am forced to cry —
Feeling the depth of black pain.

Source: David Woods, *Native Song: Poetry and Paintings* (Lawrencetown Beach, N.S.: Pottersfield Press, 1990), pp. 37–39.

equality. During the 1930s, the women's movement lost momentum, perhaps because of the Great Depression. It was reborn in the late 1960s, when the so-called "second wave" of the women's movement swept across Canada. Women once again took up the struggle for political, social, and economic equality.

Women in the 1960s still had little say in politics. There were only a handful of women in Parliament and a scattering of women in local and provincial governments. As the **Royal Commission on the Status of Women** reported in 1970, "The voice of the government is still a man's voice." The old adage "A woman's place is in the home" still expressed a popular belief about women's roles. In TV sitcoms and grade-school textbooks, women were pictured as cheerful wives, mothers, and housekeepers in homes where "father knows best." Betty Friedan's bestselling book, *The Feminine Mystique*, was important in speaking out about women's discontent with their limited public roles and unequal partnerships in marriage.

More women were beginning to work outside the home in the 1960s. The trend has continued right into the 1990s. By 1971, more than a third of all married women were in the labour force. In 1981, the figure had risen to just under 50 percent; and in 1991, it had jumped to 69 percent.

There were many reasons for women entering the outside workforce. In earlier days, marriage had been the great dividing line. Many women worked until they married. Then they were expected to quit in order to raise families. But many families were finding that they needed a second income to keep up their standard of living. As a farmer's wife in Saskatchewan explained, "Grain sales were so low that we couldn't make ends meet, and I had to get a job." Her story has been repeated all over the country right into the 1990s. "The inescapable fact is that many families would be well and truly hard-pressed to maintain anything remotely like their standard of living without two incomes," commented one Canadian labour specialist in 1993.

Women also wanted the choice of combining work and a family — or choosing a career over having a family. The new birth-control pill and other forms of contraception in the 1960s meant that women could postpone pregnancy and have fewer children. The 1960s saw the beginning of new patterns of family life. Since then, women have been marrying later or not at all. They have also been having children later in life, and having fewer children. More women return to work shortly after giving birth and combine work at home and on the job.

But Canadian women did not meet equal treatment in the workforce. They were in jobs that were lower paid and had less prestige. More than 96 percent of all secretaries in the early 1960s were female, for example, but fewer than 7 percent of women were doctors and fewer than 3 percent were lawyers. Women seemed to have no place in positions of power. John Porter's 1965 book, *The Vertical Mosaic*, was a massive study of

Women's increasing role in Canadian society is reflected in the large number of women attending university. Here, several women participate in the graduation ceremonies at the University of Toronto.

the power structure in business and society. Women were not mentioned.

Women's Liberation

Many young women activists in the 1960s and 1970s began to push for "**women's liberation**" in a society dominated by men. Some used the counter-culture ideas, slogans, and tactics of radical peace activists to press for changes in women's roles. The so-called "women's libbers" called for a revolution everywhere in society, from the boardroom to the bedroom. As Gloria Steinem — founder of *Ms.* magazine and a media star of North American feminism — told an audience in Winnipeg, "The term politics refers not only to what happens in our electoral systems, but is any power relationship in our daily lives."

By 1969, women's liberation groups had sprung up all over Canada. The media was fascinated with their deliberately outrageous street demonstrations and the "new" issues of sexism and male domination. Women's liberationists used "zap actions" to take political concerns onto the streets. One of the best-known demonstrations was a picket of the 1969 Toronto Miss Winter Bikini Contest. Female protesters paraded a mannequin marked off like a butcher's meat chart to protest the "sale" of women's bodies.

Women's liberationists wanted equal treatment with men and refused to be defined by their sex or marital status. Many rejected the symbols of "feminized" women, such as dresses, nylons, and high heels. Instead, many chose to wear unisex jeans and T-shirts and refused to use make-up. They called themselves Ms. instead of Miss or Mrs., and many kept their own last names when they married. At first, many Canadians dismissed talk of "sexism" and "male chauvinism" and the need for "women's liberation." But the feminist movement forced people to take a fresh look at women's roles in society and to change their thinking about men and women. Many ideas considered extreme in the 1960s — such as using the title "Ms." — are accepted without comment today.

The Royal Commission on the Status of Women in Canada

Other women's groups approached the need for change in a different way. Thirty women's groups, led by Laura Sabia, formed the Committee on Equality for Women. They pressed the government for a royal commission on the status of women. At first, Prime Minister Lester Pearson tried to sidestep their demands. But loud and continuous pressure won the day.

In 1967, the Royal Commission on the Status of Women, headed by journalist and broadcaster Florence Bird, began touring the country. Its job was to look into the status of women and to recommend "what steps might

"Take Back the Night" marches began in the late 1980s in many Canadian cities as a way for women to protest against increasing violence against women. Do you think this is an effective means to raise awareness among Canadians?

be taken by the federal government to ensure for women equal opportunities with men in all aspects of Canadian society."

The commission's report came out in 1970. It included 167 recommendations to ensure equality of opportunity between men and women. They included major reforms in education, family law, and the workplace, as well as changes in maternity leave, day-care, and the Indian Act. The recommended reforms were so sweeping that a *Toronto Star* columnist called the report a "bomb already primed and ticking...a call to revolution." The problems facing women in Canada were now in the national spotlight. Thanks to the report, women's concerns could no longer be ignored. Some of the recommendations were acted on fairly quickly. Other changes were slower in coming, and some are still awaiting action.

In 1971, Pierre Trudeau appointed a first minister responsible for the status of women. Two years later, the Federal Advisory Council on the Status of Women was created. Its job was to educate the public and advise the government on important women's issues. At the same time, a federal women's program began giving grants, resource materials, and advice to women's groups across Canada. The Trudeau government also began appointing more women to key government jobs to set an example. Jeanne Sauvé became speaker of the House of Commons in 1978 and Canada's governor general in 1984. Other women became cabinet ministers and superior court judges.

The creation of the **Canadian Human Rights Commission** in 1977 was a major breakthrough for women. It prohibited discrimination on the basis of sex. It also provided for "equal pay for work of equal value." Men and women doing jobs that demanded similar skills, effort, responsibility, and working conditions were to be paid the same wage. Another major breakthrough came in 1982, when equality clauses were included in the Canadian Constitution. And in 1985, publicly owned corporations were told to establish plans to end discrimination against women, visible minorities, and people with disabilities in their companies.

In the same year, the **Indian Act** was changed to end discrimination against Native women. Before, Native men who married non-Native women were still considered Status Indians. Status Indians are officially registered as band members. They have rights to use lands on the band's reserve and access to federal programs providing housing, education, and other benefits. But Native women who married non-Native men and their children lost their Indian status. The act was changed so that, in future, status would no longer be gained or lost through marriage.

The Struggle Goes On

In the 1990s, many women look back on the changes since the 1960s with a mixture of satisfaction and frustration. Many gains have been made. Political leaders talk more about major women's issues, and more women are entering politics. Audrey McLaughlin of the NDP became the first woman to be the national leader of a major political party. Kim Campbell became Canada's first female prime minister

Attitudes Toward Bilingualism, The Mosaic, Women, and Minorities
In %'s

	Teens 1984	Teens 1992	Adults 1990
Favour			
Bilingualism	71	66	53
Mosaic model	74	59	54
Too Little Power			
Natives	53	52	50
Women	48	53	55
Blacks	42	54	43
Very Serious			
Racial Discrimination	22	59	16
Unequal treatment of women	15	41	21

Source: *Teen Trends* by R. Bibby and D.C. Posterski, Stoddart Publishing Co. Limited, 1992, p. 104.

Why do you think teens have become more concerned about racial discrimination and the unequal treatment of women, while adults have not? What else does this chart tell you about teen attitudes?

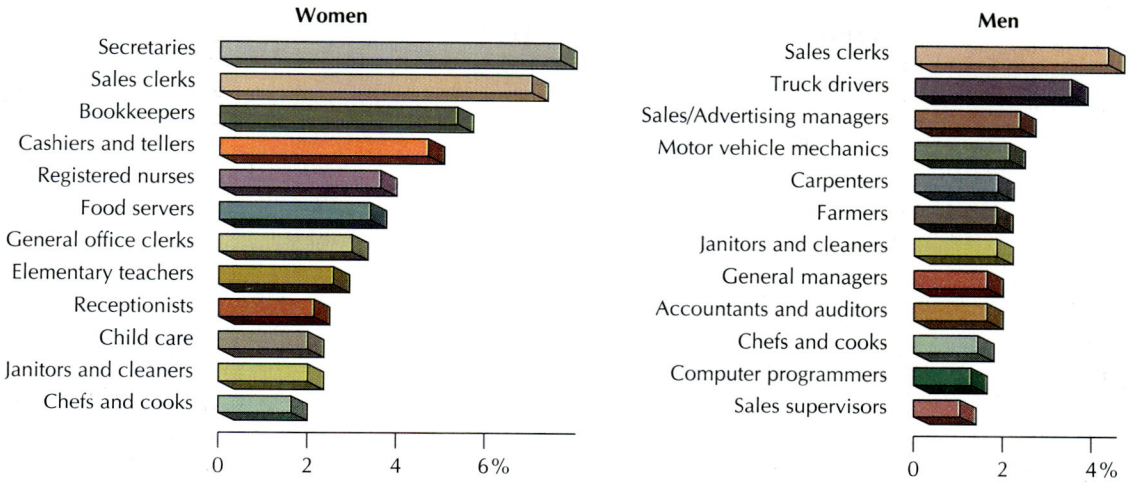

Twelve Most Common Occupations of Canadian Women and Men, 1991

Women		Men	
Secretaries	~7%	Sales clerks	~4%
Sales clerks		Truck drivers	
Bookkeepers		Sales/Advertising managers	
Cashiers and tellers		Motor vehicle mechanics	
Registered nurses		Carpenters	
Food servers		Farmers	
General office clerks		Janitors and cleaners	
Elementary teachers		General managers	
Receptionists		Accountants and auditors	
Child care		Chefs and cooks	
Janitors and cleaners		Computer programmers	
Chefs and cooks		Sales supervisors	

Percentages of experienced female/male labour force

Source: Census, 1991

when Brian Mulroney resigned and she was elected by her party as national leader of the Progressive Conservatives. More women are taking office as members of provincial legislatures, mayors, and city councillors. Although women are still not fully represented in politics, their numbers are growing.

Public attitudes toward men's and women's roles are also changing. The old notion that men and women had different jobs, family duties, and even recreational activities is dying. Between 1986 and 1991, the number of female lawyers jumped by 71 percent and of female economists by 65 percent. The number of female architects, engineers, and community planners doubled. It is no longer odd to see men doing the grocery shopping, working in parent groups in schools, and taking paternity leave to spend time with newborn babies. Sports barriers to women are dropping. Women's sports are again starting to make headlines, and women sportscasters are reporting sports highlights on radio and TV. Not everyone supports the new directions in women's public and private roles. In a recent public opinion poll, however, almost three out of four people agreed that the women's movement had a positive effect on Canadian society.

But much remains to be done. In almost 70 percent of Canadian households, both parents work outside the home, and it is difficult for them to find good-quality, affordable day-care. The number of households headed by women is growing fast, but 60 percent of these households live below the poverty line. Older women are also much more likely to be poor than are older men. Women represented 45 percent of all workers in Canada in 1991, but almost a third were still working in low-paid, low-status jobs. Women accounted for two-thirds of workers earning minimum wage. Job discrimination is still a fact of life for Canadian women; many women are still not welcomed in jobs formerly considered "men's work." Even at home, working women still do more of the housework than men do. Real equality for women still lies in the future.

Canada's first woman prime minister, Kim Campbell, was elected by the Progressive Conservatives to lead their party following Brian Mulroney's resignation. Do you think gender should be an issue during an election campaign?

THE "JUST SOCIETY" AND CANADA'S NATIVE PEOPLES

Many people wondered if Trudeau's promise of the "Just Society" would bring relief to Canada's Native peoples, who had suffered decades of discrimination and hardship. In the 1960s, many Natives lived either on small, scattered reserves or in large cities such as Vancouver, Edmonton, Winnipeg, and Toronto, where unskilled work was easier to find. Grim statistics on lifespan, income, unemployment, family breakdown, law-breaking, and suicide showed how difficult and painful life was for many Native people. In a speech at a centennial birthday party in Vancouver in 1967, Chief Dan George spoke of his sadness:

> Oh Canada, how can I celebrate with you this Centenary, this hundred years? Shall I thank you for the reserves that are left to me of my beautiful forests? For the canned fish of my rivers? For the loss of my pride and authority, even among my own people? For the lack of my will to fight back?

But he still looked to the future with hope. He called for the rebuilding of the Native peoples into "the proudest segment of our society" over the next century.

Trudeau's Proposals

In the 1960s, Natives' lives were still regulated by the Department of Indian Affairs under the Indian Act. Many Natives felt badly treated by the department. A territorial court judge in the Northwest Territories agreed. He described the department as so "swollen with its own authority that [it] has attempted to ride roughshod over the rights and liberties of its subjects." The Trudeau government said that it was time for fairer treatment of Canada's Native peoples. In 1969, Trudeau proposed to do away with the Indian Act. The idea was to slowly reduce Native peoples' special legal status under the act until Native Canadians had exactly the same rights as all other Canadians. Trudeau suggested that Native peoples set out on "a road that would lead gradually away from different status to full social, economic, and political participation in Canadian life."

But Trudeau found himself caught up in a whirlwind of controversy. Many Natives were deeply angered by a policy based on assimilating (absorbing) them into white culture. It seemed to them that Ottawa wanted Natives to disappear into the Canadian mainstream and to let their cultures fade away. In a book called *The Unjust Society* (1969), Native leader Harold Cardinal accused Trudeau of attempting to destroy the Native cultures. As Cardinal angrily put it, Ottawa seemed to think that the "only good Indian is a non-Indian."

In addition, the Trudeau government was against recognizing Native claims over disputed *ancestral lands*. He also challenged Native rights under treaties signed in the past. "We can't recognize aboriginal rights," Trudeau announced, "because no society can be built on historical 'might-have-beens.'"

Vancouver Art Gallery Aquisition Fund "Elegy for an Island" by Jack Shadbolt.

Jack Shadbolt's painting, "Elegy for an Island," makes a strong statement against the logging of the unique wilderness environments of Lyell and Moresby Islands. In the painting, a mythological bird of the Southern Kwakiutl band is flying over a wasteland of stumps.

Native groups angrily rejected his ideas. The National Indian Brotherhood declared, "If we accept this policy, and in the process lose our rights and our lands, we become willing partners in cultural genocide [the deliberate killing of a particular group]. This we cannot do." Native protests over the proposed cancellation of the Indian Act and treaty rights were so fierce that the measures were finally dropped.

The battle over the Indian Act marked a major turning point. Native groups across the country became aware of their common concerns. They saw that strong and unified political action had worked. Native leaders began building up new organizations to protect and increase special status for Natives. It was the beginning of a new *activism*. During the next decades, Native communities began taking control of their own schools, health clinics, and child welfare agencies. Some communities even brought back traditional forms of self-government.

In many places, Native groups have also tried to tackle social problems such as alcohol abuse and family violence. One of the most successful efforts was at Alkali Lake, British Columbia, where band leaders began a campaign against drunkenness. After a time, almost everyone on the reserve had given up drinking. The band also began to revive its language and culture through new school programs. The "Shuswap success story" had attracted nation-wide attention by the mid-1980s. Other Native groups began to make a similar effort on their reserves.

Land Claims

A major focus of the new activism in the 1970s was Native land claims. There were no formal treaties signed between Native bands and the British or Canadian governments in most of northern Quebec, the Northwest Territories, and all but the northeast corner of British Columbia. Native groups in these regions claimed that they had never surrendered their aboriginal rights over their land. The term **"aboriginal rights"** means that the Native people have certain land rights because they occupied Canada before the coming of the Europeans. The Nisga'a of northern British Columbia, for example, had been seeking title to lands as early as the 1890s. But Native demands were put aside time after time. A parliamentary committee even amended the Indian Act in 1927, making it a crime to raise money to pursue land claims. The amendment was not repealed until 1951.

THE NATIVE EXPERIENCE IN CANADA

These two poems written by Native women provide us with two very different perspectives of what it means to be a Native Canadian. If you could meet each of these poets, what would you say to them?

Poems
by Rita Joe

I

They say that I must live
a white man's way.
This day and age
Still being bent to what they say,
My heart remains
Tuned to native time.

I must dress conservative in style
And have factory shoes upon my feet.
Leave the ways they say
Are wild.
Forfeit a heritage
That is conquered.

I must accept what this century
Has destroyed and left behind —
The innocence of my ancestry.

I must forget father sky
And mother earth,
And hurt this land we love
With towering concrete.

II

If I must fight
Their war as well
Or share in conquests
And slip away in drink or drugs,
All wished for wealth
Is mockery to me.

My body yields, wanting luxuries,
But my heart reverts
To so-called savagery.

If we are slow
Embracing today's thoughts,
Be patient with us awhile.
Seeing
What wrongs have been wrought,
Native ways seem not so wild.

Source: *Poetry of Rita Joe.*

I Grew Up
by Lenore Keeshig-Tobias

i grew up on the reserve
thinking it was the most
beautiful place in the world

i grew up thinking
i'm never going
to leave this place

i was a child
a child who would
lie under the trees

watching wind's rhythms
sway leafy boughs
back and forth

back and forth
sweeping it seemed
the clouds into great piles

and rocking me as
i snuggled in the grass
like a bug basking in the sun

i grew up on the reserve
thinking it was the most
beautiful place in the world

i grew up thinking
i'm never going
to leave this place

i was a child
a child who ran
wild rhythms

through the fields
the streams
the bush

eating berries
cupping cool water
to my wild stained mouth

and hiding in the
treetops with
my friends

we used to laugh at teachers and
tourists who referred to
our bush as forests or woods

forests and woods
were places of
fairytale text

were places where people
especially children, got lost
where wild beasts roamed

our bush was where we played
and where the rabbits squirrels
foxes deer and the bear lived

i grew up thinking
i'm never going
to leave this place

i grew up on the reserve
thinking it was the most
beautiful place in the world

Source: Lenore Keeshig-Tobias is an Ojibway storyteller, writer, and culture worker from Neyaashiinigmiing (Cape Croker) on the Bruce Peninsula.

What do the images accompanying these two poems represent? How do you think the two authors would feel about these images?

Key Land Claim Negotiation Areas, 1993

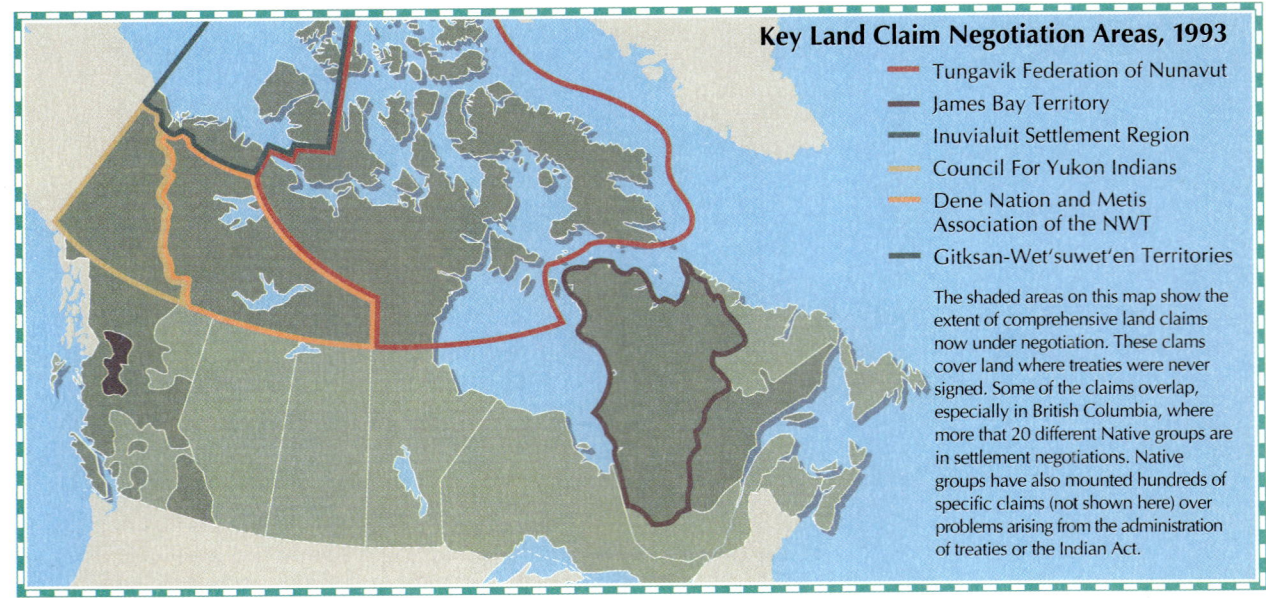

- Tungavik Federation of Nunavut
- James Bay Territory
- Inuvialuit Settlement Region
- Council For Yukon Indians
- Dene Nation and Metis Association of the NWT
- Gitksan-Wet'suwet'en Territories

The shaded areas on this map show the extent of comprehensive land claims now under negotiation. These claims cover land where treaties were never signed. Some of the claims overlap, especially in British Columbia, where more that 20 different Native groups are in settlement negotiations. Native groups have also mounted hundreds of specific claims (not shown here) over problems arising from the administration of treaties or the Indian Act.

By the 1970s, the federal government realized that it had to consult with Native groups. It began funding Native organizations to defend their land claims. In 1973, the Supreme Court of Canada agreed that aboriginal rights did exist, and the governments began a long, slow process of negotiating land-claim settlements. At stake were millions of dollars of government money in exchange for Native land given up to the government. In addition, Native bands were seeking rights over resources such as timber and minerals, as well as hunting, trapping, and fishing rights. Claims based on aboriginal title in regions where no treaties were signed are known as "comprehensive claims."

The Quebec government was the first to reach a comprehensive land-claims settlement. It wanted to open the way for the huge new James Bay hydroelectric project. In return for giving up their claim to 60 percent of northern Quebec, the Cree and Inuit residents were given complete control of almost 14 000 square kilometres of land and the exclusive rights to hunt, trap, and fish in more than 155 000 square kilometres. Although many other Native bands spoke out against the settlement, it was a major milestone. It meant that in regions not covered by treaties, land-rights claims could be pursued by Native groups.

Other comprehensive land claims soon followed. The Inuit of the western Arctic won a settlement package that included about 90 000 square kilometres of land, $45 million, and other benefits. The Inuit Tapirisat made a much larger claim in the eastern Arctic. The Council of Yukon Indians also claimed 70 percent of the Yukon, and more than twenty Native groups made land claims covering most of the province of British Columbia.

This photo shows a man dressed for the Native Chicken Dance ceremony in Alberta. How does this photo represent the re-emergence of tradition and history in Native culture?

Land claims are slowly being settled. In 1992, for example, the eastern Arctic's Inuit voted to accept a $580 million federal land-claim settlement in the area called Nunavut. In the same year, Prime Minister Brian Mulroney and British Columbia Premier Michael Harcourt signed a treaty with the province's Native chiefs, agreeing to settle the province's land claims by the end of the 1990s. Draped in a brightly patterned ceremonial blanket, Mulroney held the historic treaty up before a cheering audience of Native leaders.

Specific Claims

Before the twentieth century, about half of Canada's Native bands had signed treaties that surrendered their rights to certain lands or traditional activities such as hunting or fishing. In return they were promised land on reserves, money, and other guarantees. Since the 1970s, Native groups have also launched hundreds of so-called "specific claims" over treaties. These specific claims are about promises they believe were made but not kept by the government. They include grievances such as promised treaty rights that they claim were never fulfilled or lands that were taken out of reserves after treaties were signed.

Several hundred specific claims are still being fought, and more claims may be launched in the future. The government has been slow to reach settlements. In the 1980s and 1990s, Native groups have become more militant about their demands. In recent years, dozens of protest marches and road and rail blockades on Native reserves have thrown a spotlight on the many Native claims about treaty promises and land title. The most dramatic confrontation over a land dispute was near the town of Oka, Quebec, in 1990, when heavily armed Mohawks entrenched behind a highway barricade stood off Canadian soldiers for eleven weeks.

Native Self-Government

Since the 1970s, another major concern for Native peoples has been **Native self-government**. Native groups have grown dissatisfied with government control over the years; many argue that they never gave up their right to self-government to the European newcomers. As a result, they have pressed for the right to run their own affairs. But Native individuals and bands have disagreed about just what "self-government" means and how to achieve it. In the 1970s, many Native leaders wanted to rewrite the Indian Act, which had not undergone a major revision since 1951. Getting agreement among the many individuals and Native groups, however, was a very hard task. Some changes were made to the act in 1985, but even these changes caused major clashes in the Native community.

The model for Native self-government already exists in the political and social framework of some of Canada's First Nations. This photograph, for example, shows a meeting of the Dene Nation Assembly. Can you think of some problems that may be encountered when Native people are granted self-government?

NATIVE RESISTANCE: THE OKA STANDOFF

These two Mohawk warriors are taking down their flag from the barricade to prevent it from being seized by the Canadian army.

For centuries, Canada's Native peoples have been moved off their ancestral lands. In recent years, they have become increasingly militant in order to assert their rights. During the summer of 1990, a land dispute between town officials and Mohawks from nearby Kanesatake turned into a seventy-eight-day armed standoff. The conflict arose over a proposed golf course that would have been built on land considered sacred by the Mohawks.

The standoff began after about one hundred provincial police attempted to break through a barricade erected on the highway by Mohawk warriors. A gun battle ensued, and one police officer was killed by a stray bullet. In the following weeks, negotiations failed to convince the heavily armed warriors to take down the barricade. Finally, on September 26, 1990, the Mohawk warriors surrendered to police, calling it an "honourable disengagement." The Natives considered the eleven-week standoff a success because they were able to raise the profile of Native issues throughout Canada.

In the early 1980s, the Canadian Constitution was being rewritten. Some leaders wanted Native self-government and aboriginal rights included in the new Constitution. But the prairie premiers strongly opposed the move. When the Canadian Charter of Rights and Freedoms was drafted by nine provincial premiers and Prime Minister Trudeau in a late-night agreement of November 1981, it did not mention Native rights. Like women, whose rights had also been left out of the original draft, Native people raised a storm of protest. After weeks of energetic lobbying by Native groups, Native rights were written into the new Constitution. The revised charter said that "existing aboriginal and treaty rights" of Canada's Native peoples were "recognized and affirmed."

The Charlottetown Accord

But what exactly did "existing aboriginal and treaty rights" mean? Nobody knew for certain. During the 1980s, the government and Native leaders met for a series of talks to settle the question. By the time of the Charlottetown Accord, a somewhat clearer understanding had been hammered out. The Charlottetown Accord proposed a series of constitutional amendments on Native self-government. These amendments recognized the inherent right to aboriginal self-government. They also recognized aboriginal government as one of three orders of government in Canada. (The other two orders of government are the federal and provincial governments.)

Although the Charlottetown Accord was rejected in a national referendum, its defeat is not the end of the push for Native self-government. As Native leader Georges Erasmus declared,

> We are the dominant force in the northern part of most provinces. We're going to create political institutions that will reflect our beliefs and our thinking.... Native people will have much to contribute over the next century. It's our turn.

Questions of Native land claims and self-government will no doubt continue to capture national headlines throughout the 1990s. The **Royal Commission on Aboriginal People** was created in 1992 to help in finding answers to these and many other questions. The search for answers is a task for everyone in Canada. As one commissioner commented, all Canadians need to try to see Canada through the eyes of its Native peoples "because all Canadians will have to help us devise solutions."

In June 1990, Elijah Harper, a Native MLA in the Manitoba legislature, became Canada's top newsmaker by blocking the passage of the Meech Lake Accord. Driven by a concern that Native rights were being ignored, Harper became a symbol of aboriginal power and activism.

KNOWING THE KEY PEOPLE, PLACES, AND EVENTS

In your notes, clearly identify and explain the historical significance of each of the following:

> Royal Commission on Bilingualism and Biculturalism
> Immigration Act
> Women's Liberation
>
> Indian Act
> Native Self-Government
>
> Canadian Human Rights Act
> Royal Commission on the Status of Women
> Canadian Human Rights Commission
> Aboriginal Rights
> Royal Commission on Aboriginal People

FOCUS YOUR KNOWLEDGE

1. How has the ethnic make-up of Canada changed since the turn of the century?
2. Why did the arrival of Tamil refugees in Newfoundland create a problem for Canada?
3. Why does Canada's economic well-being depend, in part, on continued immigration?
4. What has happened to the number of women in the workplace since the 1960s? How can you explain this change?
5. What efforts were made during the Trudeau years to promote women's equality with men?
6. How did the introduction of the birth-control pill and other effective means of contraception change the pattern of family life in Canada?
7. What actions have been taken to ensure greater equality for women since the Royal Commission on the Status of Women issued its report in 1970?
8. How did the battle over the Indian Act help to unify Native groups across Canada?

APPLY YOUR KNOWLEDGE

1. What was meant by Trudeau's promise to make Canada a "Just Society"? What measures were taken to move Canada toward the "Just Society"? How successful have Canadians been in creating the kind of society promised by Trudeau?

2. In groups of two or three, discuss the degree of racism in Canada today. Support your views with specific examples, either from the news media or from your personal experience.

3. How was the "second wave" of the women's movement different from the "first wave"? How successful has the women's movement been in achieving its objectives?

4. To what degree are women able to participate fully (on an equal basis with men) in Canadian society? What still needs to happen for full equality to be realized?

5. Discuss the following questions in groups of three or four. What was the significance of the Supreme Court of Canada's decision that aboriginal rights do exist? Why is granting Native self-government a far more complex issue than it at first appears to be?

6. Why did Chief Dan George speak of sadness for Native people during the centennial celebrations? Do you think Canada has since begun the process of enabling Natives to become "the proudest segment" of society?

EXTEND YOUR KNOWLEDGE

1. Work with a group of two or three students to prepare a collage that reflects the richness of Canada's multicultural population. Select a phrase (for example, "Peace and Harmony") and try to write it in as many languages as possible on your collage.

2. In Chapter 11 there is a collage showing the many faces of women in the 1920s. Prepare a similar collage that reflects the many faces of women in the 1990s. Explain your collage to your classmates. Be sure to include as many facets of life as possible.

3. Select and research one major Native land claim. Present your findings to the class by using maps and other visual aids. After you have finished your presentation, lead a discussion in class about how this particular land claim should be settled.

SKILLS FOCUS

UNIT REVIEW

1. If you could be transported back in time, in which decade would you like to have been a teenager in Canada: the 1950s, the 1960s, the 1970s, or the 1980s? Explain your answer.

2. What is meant by the phrase "quality of life"? Have the consumer revolution since 1945 and the increase in wealth enjoyed by the average Canadian family enhanced the quality of life? Defend your answer.

3. Which political figure since 1950 did the most to shape modern-day Canada? Explain your choice. Select one nonpolitical person who made an important contribution to Canada in the past four decades. Explain his or her contribution.

4. What will be the most pressing concern for Canadians in the next two decades? Explain why this issue is or should be a major concern for Canadians.

EFFECTIVE PROBLEM SOLVING

Developing the skills necessary to be an effective problem solver can help to make you more successful in both your career and your personal life. People often encounter situations that require them to solve a problem and to be effective decision-makers. Whether they are deciding what to do on a Saturday night or selecting the college or university they wish to attend, students encounter problems that force them to make decisions almost daily. When making a decision, it is important to think through the issues clearly and not to allow one's emotions to dominate. A sound, logical decision can best be made by using a decision-making model. In making a decision, use the following five steps.

1. *Define the Problem:* Be sure that you clearly understand the issue or situation that is being dealt with.

2. *State the Alternatives:* Prepare a list of all possible solutions to the problem. Do not disregard any ideas at this point.

3. *Choose the Criteria:* Determine what your major objectives are in solving this problem. You may want to prioritize your criteria.

4. *Apply the Criteria to the Alternatives:* Go through each of the alternatives to determine which ones meet the chosen criteria.

5. *Choose the Alternative that Best Suits the Criteria:* Which alternative best satisfies the largest number of criteria? You have now made an effective decision.

Apply this decision-making model to one of the following historical situations:

1. The FLQ have kidnapped a British diplomat and a Quebec cabinet minister. How should the federal government react to this situation?

2. The A.V. Roe Company, in conjunction with the federal government, has developed a fighter jet called the Avro Arrow, considered one of the best in the world. Production costs have skyrocketed to six times the original estimates, making American-made jets less costly and foreign buyers reluctant to place orders. What should the government do about the production of the Avro Arrow?

3. As head of the National Action Committee on the Status of Women, you read a report stating that women earn 65 percent of the income of men for doing work of equal value. You want to raise this as an issue in the upcoming election. What can you do?

CAREER FOCUS

ECONOMICS

In the decades since the end of World War II, statistics have come to be an important tool for governments and business. Statistics are used for two main purposes: to assist us in seeing trends and to help in forecasting future events. The extensive use of statistics is a fairly recent occurrence. Although census-taking was first begun in North America during the nineteenth century, it is only in the past four decades that statistics have been gathered on a wide variety of topics. Statistics were first used by governments when they began to be heavily involved in the economy and needed to be able to forecast future events in order to plan effectively. Since the 1960s, large corporations have also begun to make extensive use of statistics. The use of statistics allows businesses to plan product development and advertising campaigns and helps them to predict with some accuracy changes in the marketplace.

Would you like to have a career in which statistics were used to assist you in advising a government on policy decisions? If this appeals to you, then a career in economics may be in your future. Economics is the study of how people choose to make use of a limited amount of resources to satisfy the maximum amount of their desires. Because economics is based on human behaviour, which is unpredictable in some circumstances, it is not considered a pure science. Economists draw on a variety of disciplines, including mathematics, history, sociology, and psychology, in formulating government policy and predicting future trends.

Economists are often employed by governments and government agencies as policy analysts. By analyzing the various factors that may affect a government decision and by studying a wide range of statistics, economists make recommendations to the government. For example, they are consulted by governments before a new tax is put into place. Economists attempt to predict, on the basis of careful study, the impact of the new tax on consumer spending and ultimately on the economy in general. Economists are also employed by financial institutions such as banks. By forecasting future economic trends, economists help financial institutions to make effective decisions for the future. The study of history can be a valuable asset for people pursuing a career in economics. By understanding the past, economists are better able to predict human reactions to events such as depressions or declines in interest rates. The skills learned in history can also be helpful to economists. The ability to think effectively, to present ideas in an appealing way, and to be an effective decision-maker are all important skills for an economist.

Select one of the following topics on which to gather statistics. Using the statistics you gather, prepare either a bar graph or a functional graph to illustrate your findings. Place your graph on a bulletin board in the classroom for other students to see. Also, write a brief explanation of what these statistics seem to tell us about trends in Canada. You may wish to seek assistance from your math or economics teacher in finding statistics or creating the graph(s).

Topics: Inflation, Immigration, Population Growth, Violent Crimes, Unemployment, Birth Rates, Interest Rates.

EPILOGUE

ENTERING THE TWENTY-FIRST CENTURY

At the end of this decade, Canada and the rest of the world will enter the twenty-first century. Several challenges will face Canada in the next hundred years, and the understanding of our past that you have gained from reading this book will help you to respond to the present and prepare for the future. In the prologue to this book, Wilfrid Laurier proclaimed the twentieth century as Canada's century. Now that you have completed this study of modern Canada, you probably will agree that Canada is now one of the world's leading nations. But what does the next century hold in store for us? By reflecting on recent cultural, social, and political issues, you should be able to speculate about what Canada will be like in the next few decades.

CANADA'S FUTURE

Although most Canadians would agree that many challenges face their country in the next century, it would be very difficult to get them to agree on the issues that are the most pressing. The issues *you* perceive as the most important will depend on factors such as your age, where you live, and perhaps your ethnic background.

Like all other nations, Canada has a limited amount of resources with which to meet an endless list of challenges. Choosing to clean up Canada's environment could cost substantial amounts of money — which would mean either higher taxes, a larger deficit, or less money to spend on health care and education. Consequently, choosing how to make use of our country's limited resources is the first challenge we face.

Tackling the National Debt

Several politicians and economists have argued that Canada's growing national debt is the most crucial problem facing this country and that it should take precedence over other concerns. Some people maintain that a large national debt inhibits Canada's international competitiveness and will become a burden to future generations. Others feel that, although the national debt is large, it should not affect spending in essential areas such as health, education, and the environment. They argue that by putting money into Canada's "infrastructure" — transportation, education, research, and development — Canada will have a stronger economy and will therefore be better able to reduce the deficit.

Social Programs: Expensive Luxury or Canadian Birthright?

With a soaring national debt and a crippling recession in the late 1980s and early 1990s, Canada's social programs have come under close scrutiny. It has been suggested that Canada's social programs may have to be reduced because they cost too much. Not everyone agrees with this view. Many people feel that good education, health care, and a welfare system that ensures a minimum standard of living for all Canadians is an important part of Canada's national fabric. But can we afford the luxury of such programs? Should we raise taxes or let the deficit increase in order to maintain our social programs? This is a critical issue as we attempt to use our limited resources to address a seemingly endless list of wants.

Dealing with Regional Diversity

A flight across Canada like the one we imagined in the prologue reveals the vastness and diversity of this land. Each region of Canada is unique in its landforms and natural resources. As a result, the people who live in each region have their own special interests and concerns. What matters most to a prairie farmer is likely to be quite different from what most concerns an urban industrial worker in central Canada.

This diversity leads to a number of crucial questions. What kind of government best suits this country? Should greater power lie in the hands of the provinces, which represent the regions, or with the federal government, which looks after the nation as a whole? Should we use protective tariffs to encourage east–west trade, or should we trade more freely with the United States, allowing goods to flow north and south? How should we deal with regional disparity? Should the wealthier provinces be expected to help ensure that all Canadians enjoy a decent standard of living and receive good health care and a good education? These are only a few of the critical questions that Canadians have dealt with in the past century and will continue to address in the coming century.

A Divided Canada?

The differences that divide this country are in many ways rooted in our history. For over three centuries, a unique French Canadian culture has flourished in Quebec. Feeling increasingly threatened by the English-speaking majority in Canada, French Canadians in the late twentieth century have become very politicized and at times militant in defence of their language and culture. The rejections of both the Meech Lake Accord and the Charlottetown Accord have left many French Canadians feeling that English Canada is indifferent, if not hostile, to their desire for cultural survival. Some English Canadians, however, feel that Quebec is demanding too many special rights and that addressing Quebec's demands might further erode the ties that bind Canada together as a nation. The question of how to deal fairly with Quebec without creating different laws for English and French Canada must be faced if we are to keep Quebec in Canada.

Recognizing the Rights of Native Peoples

One of the major stumbling blocks the government of Canada has faced in its recent attempts at constitutional reform has been recognizing in very real terms the inherent rights of Native peoples. To do so, the federal government must settle many land claims, which could cost Canadian taxpayers billions of dollars in the next few decades. Natives are also demanding the right to self-government. Although the government and a majority of Canadians support the demand, the details of implementing a system of Native self-government still need to be worked out. Issues such as a Native justice system and the rights of Native women need to be addressed before Native self-government can become a reality in Canada.

The Canadian Mosaic

Aside from including Canada's three founding nations — Native peoples, the French, and the English — Canada is made up of people from all over the world who speak a variety of languages, practise many religions, and celebrate customs from a wide range of cultures. Canada's major cities, such as Vancouver, Edmonton, Toronto, and Montreal, have become increasingly cosmopolitan. Towns and cities across Canada have been enriched by the vitality of new Canadians. Whether they are from Europe, Asia, Africa, or the Caribbean, the flood of immigrants to Canada since the end of World War II has transformed this nation.

Unfortunately, not all Canadians have been willing to open their arms to immigrants. Often, people arriving in Canada bring customs, foods, fashions, and, of course, languages that are unfamiliar to us. Some people, ignorant of cultures other than their own, become "xenophobic" — fearful of other cultures. To help rid Canada of racism and prejudice, we must continue to pass and enforce laws that protect minority rights and educate Canadians about cultures other than our own. This education can happen through schools, through the media, or through festivals such as Toronto's Caribana.

Equality for All: The Women's Rights Movement in Canada

At the beginning of the twentieth century, Canadian women had few economic or political rights. But the women's movement has been successful in gaining political and legal equality for women. The struggle for social and economic equality continues, however. On average, women are still paid less than men, even for work of equal value and requiring a similar level of skill. Addressing inequities in the workplace is difficult because raising women's wages to equal those of men can make a business less competitive or cost a government millions of dollars. In difficult economic times, this poses a dilemma for both the public and private sectors. But pay equity is only one of the issues facing women today. Violence against women, the portrayal of women in the media, adequate day-care facilities, and sexual harassment in the workplace are all crucial issues facing Canadians in the coming decades. Will the full equality of men and women be achieved in the next century? This depends on changing attitudes about women's roles in society.

Canadian Identity

Perhaps as a result of their varied cultural backgrounds, Canadians have some trouble in defining who they are. When asked to define what it means to be Canadian, we often respond by explaining what we are not! "We're not violent like the Americans" is a common response to the question of our national identity. Having completed a study of Canada in the twentieth century, how would you define a Canadian? What distinguishes us from other nations?

Because our small population is spread over an enormous land mass, fostering a sense of national unity is a daunting task. How can Canadians in Estevan, Saskatchewan, identify with those in Truro, Nova Scotia? One of the ways to build a sense of national unity is to support Canadian radio and television programs, publishers, and musicians. Some people argue that we cannot afford to continue funding Canadian cultural programs, while others see the survival of Canadian cultural institutions as vital if we are to remain a truly independent nation.

The United States: The Elephant Next Door

The United States is our largest trading partner, our closest military ally, and the greatest influence on our national culture. What kind of relationship with the United States will yield the greatest benefits? The 1988 Free Trade Agreement with the United States and the proposed 1993 North American Free Trade Agreement between Mexico, the United States, and Canada may have economic benefits, but these gains may carry a high price. With tariff barriers coming down, will Canada be able to sustain its steel, textile, or auto industries? Can Canada remain competitive with the United States and still maintain the social programs important to so many Canadians? Can we maintain a unique Canadian culture while forging closer ties with a nation ten times our size?

Canada in the World

Over the past century, Canadians have developed a reputation for a commitment to world issues. Our peacekeepers have served on every United Nations peacekeeping mission, and our foreign aid has assisted many countries in their efforts to modernize and develop into healthy economies. Will we be able to continue to play such a positive role in the future? What are our obligations to other countries?

In the past, many countries were able to adopt an isolationist approach to foreign policy by ignoring much of the world. This will be virtually impossible in the next century. Pollution and the depletion of the world's forests pose a threat to the world's environment, while the potential for nuclear war is still a world threat.

On a positive note, global media and extensive trading between nations have brought the world to our doorstep. As Canada enters the twenty-first century, we must look beyond our borders to a future in the global marketplace.

The world is becoming an increasingly competitive place. If we are to maintain the high standard of living to which we have become accustomed, we will have to continue to provide a sound education for young people, retrain workers whose skills are no longer relevant, and support research and development programs.

What does the future hold for Canadians? Will Quebec remain a part of Canada? How can Native self-government be achieved in a fair and just manner? Will our cultural institutions survive the coming decades to help us establish a clear Canadian identity? What does being Canadian mean to you? The issues raised in this book show that being Canadian means different things to different people. We hope that this study of Canada's history and heritage has educated you for your future.

RESPONDING TO THE ISSUES

1. Reflect once again on the words of Wilfrid Laurier that appear in this book's prologue. Write a response to his claim. Has this been Canada's century? Write a one-page defence of or attack on Laurier's prophecy by using factual support from this text to support your answer. Compare your answer now with the one you wrote when you began reading this text.
2. Canada's regions differ greatly from one another. What problems can this create in attempting to govern the nation fairly? Can Canadians be united despite the country's vast regional differences?
3. Attempt to define Canadian culture. What makes Canadian culture distinct? Does the presence of the United States pose a significant threat to Canadian culture? What should be done to help preserve and promote Canadian culture?
4. List the four issues that you feel will be the greatest challenges that Canada will face in the next few decades. For each issue, provide a brief explanation and explain what should be done by the government or people of Canada to ensure that we meet the challenge.

In the following poem, poet Duke Redbird captures the diversity of Canada and Canadians by showing that we are not lacking in identity; rather, we are fortunate in our differences. What does it mean to you to be Canadian?

I Am a Canadian

I'm a lobster fisherman in Newfoundland
I'm a clambake in P.E.I.
I'm a picnic, I'm a banquet
I'm mother's homemade pie
I'm a few drafts in a Legion hall in Fredericton
I'm a kite-flyer in a field in Moncton
I'm a nap on the porch after a hard day's work is
　　done.
I'm a snowball fight in Truro, Nova Scotia
I'm small kids playing jacks and skipping rope
I'm a mother who lost a son in the last great war
And I'm a bride with a brand new ring
And a chest of hope
I'm an Easterner
I'm a Westerner
I'm from the North
And I'm from the South
I've swam in two big oceans
And I've loved them both
I'm a clown in Quebec during carnival
I'm a mass in the Cathedral of St. Paul
I'm a hockey game in the Forum
I'm Rocket Richard and Jean Beliveau
I'm a coach for little league Expos
I'm a baby-sitter for sleep-defying rascals
I'm a canoe trip down the Ottawa
I'm a holiday on the Trent
I'm a mortgage, I'm a loan
I'm last week's unpaid rent
I'm Yorkville after dark
I'm a walk in the park
I'm a Winnipeg gold-eye
I'm a hand-made trout fly
I'm a wheat-field and a sunset
Under a prairie-sky
I'm Sir John A. Macdonald
I'm Alexander Graham Bell
I'm a pow-wow dancer
And I'm Louis Riel
I'm the Calgary Stampede
I'm a feathered Sarcee
I'm Edmonton at night
I'm a bar-room fight
I'm a rigger, I'm a cat
I'm a ten-gallon hat
And an unnamed mountain in the interior of B.C.
I'm a maple tree and a totem pole
I'm sunshine showers
And fresh-cut flowers
I'm a ferry boat ride to the Island
I'm the Yukon
I'm the Northwest Territories
I'm the Arctic Ocean and the Beaufort Sea
I'm the prairies, I'm the Great Lakes,
I'm the Rockies, I'm the Laurentians,
I am French
I am English
And I am Métis
But more than this
Above all this
I am a Canadian and proud to be free.

Source: Reprinted by permission of Duke Redbird.

Photo and Illustration Credits

NAC National Archives of Canada; **DND** Department of National Defence

page 11 Canapress/Ron Poling; **page 13** F.M Denison Papers, Thomas Fisher Rare Book Library, University of Toronto; **page 14** Victor Pilon for the Department of the Secretary of State for Canada; **page 16** UPI/Bettmann Newsphotos; **page 17** NAC/C7125; **page 20** Canapress/Blaise Edwards; **page 24** Canapress; **page 27** Canapress/Blaise Edwards; **page 33** (left) Archives of Ontario/ACC2218, S1244; **page 33** (right) Skydome, Toronto, Canada; **page 35** Canapress; **page 36** Reproduced by permission of Adrian Raeside; **page 37** Canapress; **page 38** (top) Canapress/Bill Becker; **page 40** (bottom) Canapress/Ron Poling; **page 40** (top) Canapress; **page 41** Courtesy of Canada Post Corporation; **page 44** Canapress; **page 45** Government of the NWT; **page 47** Canapress; **page 48** Canapress; **page 54** (top and bottom) Metropolitan Toronto Police Video Production Unit; **page 55** (bottom) Metropolitan Toronto Police; **page 57** By permission of the Globe & Mail; **page 59** (top) Sacha Warunkiw; **page 59** (bottom) Michael I. Bedford Photography; **page 61** Courtesy of the Ontario Ministry of Correctional Services; **page 62** Toronto Star/Ron Bull; **page 63** Metropolitan Toronto Police Video Production Unit; **page 65** By permission of the British Library, Harley 4375; **page 67** Photo by Paul J. Lawrence; **page 69** Courtesy of the Correctional Service of Canada; **page 79** NAC/C-733 G.P. Roberts; **page 80** W.J. Topley/NAC/C-3207; **page 83** British Columbia Archives and Records Service, 67609; **page 84** NAC/C-1875; **page 86** NAC/C-16748; **page 87** O.B. Buell/National Archives/C-1875; **page 89** NAC; **page 90** Painting by Ken Marshall from the *The Discovery of the Titanic* by Dr. Robert Ballard published by Penguin/Madison Press Books and is protected by copyright as provided therein; **page 91** NAC/PA-61772; **page 93** Glenbow Archives, Calgary, NC-6-1746; **page 95** Courtesy of Multi Media Techniques, Hamilton; **page 96** "The Stone Road" by Homer Watson, National Gallery of Canada, Ottawa; **page 101** Courtesy of Astral Film Enterprises Inc.; **page 102** "The Habitant Farm" by Cornelius Krieghoff, National Gallery of Canada, Ottawa. Gift of Gordon C. Edwards, Ottawa, 1923, in memory of Senator and Mrs. W.C. Edwards; **page 103** NAC/C-30936; **page 105** Courtesy of Garfield Newman; **page 107** M927.1.8.2 Dog Blanket, Indian, Subarctic, Athapaskan, fibre, bead, metal, skin, 45.0 x 42.0. Collection: McCord Museum of Canadian History, Montreal; **page 108** (top) G.M. Dawson/National Archives/C-81787; **page 108** (bottom) NAC/C-16408; **page 110** NAC/C-3844; **page 111** NAC/C-27360; **page 112** NAC/PA-016388; **page 116** NAC/C-8449; **page 117** (top) Prints & Photographs Division, Library of Congress; **page 117** (bottom) Armed Forces History Division, Smithsonian Institute; **page 119** Courtesy of the Ontario Black History Society; **page 120** NAC/C-4988; **page 121** NAC/C-6536; **page 122** NAC/PA-34099; **page 123** Courtesy of Canada Post Corporation; **page 125** NAC/PA-93160; **page 134** Imperial War Museum; **page 135** NAC/PA-4909; **page 137** DND/NAC/PA-2195; **page 139** (top) NAC/C-36116; **page 139** (bottom) Courtesy of the City of Toronto Archives SC244-824; **page 140** NAC/PA-568; **page 142** NAC/C-118612; **page 144** DND/NAC/PA-832; **page 145** NAC/C-80027; **page 150** NAC/C-097752; **page 151** National War Museum (72-2125); **page 152** Imperial War Museum; **page 153** (top) NAC/C-095730; **page 153** (left) NAC/C-095269; **page 153** (right) NAC/C-097748; **page 154** Courtesy of the City of Toronto Archives SC244-981; **page 155** Imperial War Museum; **page 156** NAC/PA-2279; **page 160** NAC/PA-002318; **page 161** NAC/C-019945; **page 165** (top) NAC/C-28029; **page 165** (bottom) NAC/PA-122515; **page 166** (top) National Archives of Canada/PA-118281; **page 166** (bottom) Courtesy of the Library of Congress; **page 167** Imperial War Museum; **page 168** NAC/PA-1215; **page 169** Collection: François Baby House, Windsor's Community Museum, P6110; **page 170** NAC/PA-622; **page 171** DND., William Rider-Rider/NAC/PA-2156; **page 172** (bottom) "Returning to the Reconquered Land" by Sir George Clausen, Canadian War Museum 8135, photos for CWM by William Kent; **page 172** (top) "The First German Gas Attack at Ypres" by William Roberts, National Gallery of Canada, Ottawa, Transfer from the Canadian War Memorials, 1921; **page 173** NAC/PA-5686; **page 175** "A War Record" by Stanley F. Turner, Canadian War Museum, 8907; **page 185** (top) Metro Toronto Reference Library; **page 185** (bottom) NAC/C-009064; **page 187** (top) F.M. Gee/NAC/C-26782; **page 187** (bottom) Manitoba Archives, Foote Collection (N2736); **page 188** Manitoba Archives, Foote Collection 288 (N1888); **page 189** (top) "Big Raven" by Emily Carr, 1931 oil on canvas, 87.3 x 114.4 cm, Collection Vancouver Art Gallery, Emily Carr Trust; **page 189** (bottom) "Petroushka," 1939 by Paraskeva Clark, 1898–1986,

Collection of the National Gallery of Canada. Reproduced with permission of the Estate of Paraskeva Clark; **page 191** Glenbow Archives, Calgary ND-3-6742; **page 192** NAC/C-30811; **page 194** National Archives of Canada/C-13236; **page 195** NAC/C-3869; **page 196** Glenbow Archives, Calgary NA-2496-1; **page 197** NAC/C-29397; **page 200** (top) Courtesy of Eaton's of Canada Archives; **page 200** (bottom) DND NAC/PA-35132; **page 201** NAC/C-24840; **page 202** Glenbow Archives, Calgary NA-2434-1; **page 203** J.A. Castongway/NAC/C-34443; **page 209** (top) Tom Thomson 1877–1917, "Afternoon, Algonquin Park," 1914, oil on canvas 63.2 x 81.1 cm., McMichael Canadian Art Collection, In memory of Norman & Evelyn McMichael, 966.16.76; **page 209** (bottom) Courtesy of the Craven Foundation; **page 211** Toronto City Archives, James Collection #8054; **page 213** Archives of Ontario/14154-6; **page 214**; (bottom) NAC/C20918; **page 215** (top) Bombardier Inc.; (middle) The Hockey Hall of Fame; (bottom) Courtesy of the Craven Foundation; **page 216** Photo courtesy of The Windsor Star; **page 217** Archives of Ontario/S15000; **page 218** (top) Canada Post Corporation; **page 218** (bottom) Provincial Archives of Alberta/A11413; **page 219** (top) National Archives -74583; (middle) Courtesy of the City of Toronto Archives SC 244-1028; (bottom) Courtesy of the City of Toronto Archives SC 244-1902; **page 220** City of Toronto Archives, James Collection/SC244-2534; **page 222** NAC/C-19533; **page 223** Canadian National Exhibition Archives, Poster Collection, 1939; **page 231** NAC/PA-110921; **page 232** (top) Imperial War Museum, London; **page 234** (bottom) Archiv für Kunst und Geschichte, Berlin; **page 233** (bottom) NAC/C-11452; **page 233** (top) NAC/C-016791; **page 235** Canadian Jewish Congress National Archives; **page 236** Canadian Jewish Congress National Archives; **page 237** Heinrich Hoffman NAC/PA-164759; **page 239** NAC/PA 119013; **page 241** NAC/C-16812; **page 243** NAC/C-87518; **page 247** (top) Glenbow Archives, Calgary, NA-4777-23; **page 247** (bottom) NAC/C-87131; **page 248** (top) NAC/C-87431; **page 248** (bottom) NAC/PA-137847; **page 249** Tak Toyota/NAC/C-046356; **page 252** Jack Long/NAC/C-049271; **page 253** NAC/C-000467; **page 255** Courtesy of the Library of Congress; **page 256** (bottom) NAC/C-29458; **page 256** (top) NAC/C-033442; **page 258** H.G. Aikman/DND/NAC/PA-108174; **page 259** Ken Bell/DND/NAC/PA-132838; **page 261** Arthur L. Cole/DND/NAC/PA-175788; **page 266** The Trustees of the Imperial War Museum; **page 267** Courtesy of the Canadian Forces; **page 268** NAU.S./War and Conflict #1135; **page 270** DND/NAC/PA151738; **page 273** "Dieppe Raid" by Charles Comfort, C.N. #12276, Copyright Canadian War Museum, Canadian Museum of Civilization, photo from CWM by William Kent; **page 272** Jack H. Smith/DND/NAC /PA170290; **page 273** G. Milne NAC/PA122765; **page 276** The Trustees of the Imperial War Museum, London; **page 278** Reprinted with the permission of Atheneum Publishers, an imprint of Macmillan Publishing Company from *Last Traces: The Lost Art of Auschwitz* by Joseph P. Czarnecki, introduction by Chaim Potok. Copyright ©1989 by Joseph P. Czarnecki. Introduction copyright ©1989 Chaim Potok; **page 279** NAC/C373264; **page 281** Courtesy of the City of Toronto Archives/SC266-100525; **page 290** United Nations photo 169325/M. Grant; **page 291** United Nations photo 38998; **page 292** United Nations photo 2131; **page 295** Montreal Star NAC/PA-129625; **page 298** Bill Olsen NAC/PA-115564; **page 299** Canapress; **page 300** UN photo 159289/J. Isaac; **page 303** Reprinted with permission — The Toronto Star Syndicate; **page 304** The Toronto Star/F. Lennon; **page 305** (top) Canapress; **page 305** (bottom) Wide World Photos Inc.; **page 306** Canapress; **page 307** NAC/C-00012/Lester B. Pearson Collection; **page 308** CIDA photo by Robert Semeniuk; **page 309** Photo Nick Fog, CUSO; **page 310** Canapress Photo/Andrew Vaughan; **page 315** NAC/C-5306; **page 316** NAC/C-022859; **page 318** Quebec Ministry of Tourism; **page 317** Photographie-Ville de Montréal; **page 319** Canapress; **page 321** Craig Abel Photography; **page 322** (bottom) NAC/PA-11237-1; **page 322** (top) Reprinted with permission of Kellogg Canada Inc. ©1993; **page 323** Canapress; **page 324** Canapress; **page 325** Canapress; **page 327** Canapress/Tim Clark; **page 328** Hrair Hawk Khatcherian-Ponopresse /Quebec; **page 329** Canapress; **page 331** Canapress Photo/R. Remiorz; **page 334** Canapress/Paul Chiasson; **page 338** NAC/C-035680; **page 339** (top) From a National Film Board of Canada production; **page 339** (bottom) Stratford Shakespearean Festival, Ontario, Canada. Scene from "Julius Ceasar," 1955; **page 340** (top) Canapress/F. Thornhill; **page 340** (bottom) Merle Tingley/London Free Press; **page 341** Courtesy of the Barenaked Ladies; **page 342** Albert Sanchez ©Visages 1993; **page 344** Canapress; **page 345** NAC/C-039893; **page 347** (top) Canapress/R. Taylor; **page 347** (bottom) Canapress; **page 348** NASA; **page 349** NASA-National Aeronautics and Space Administration; **page 350** Cuyler Black; **page 351** General Motors of Canada Ltd.; **page 352** Petro-Canada Library; **page 353** Reprinted with permission — The Toronto Star Syndicate;

PHOTO AND ILLUSTRATION CREDITS

page 355 (top) Dennis Pritchard/Star-Phoenix; (bottom) Canapress/Ron Poling; **page 365** Steinberg's Limited; **page 366** United Artists; **page 367** F. Tyrell NAC/PA111378; **page 368** (top) York University Archives: Toronto Telegram Collection B117/F844/#1123; **page 368** (bottom) Courtesy of General Motors of Canada Ltd.; **page 369** Courtesy of Petro-Canada; **page 372** Courtesy Government of the NWT; **page 373** Globe & Mail/Anthony Jenkins; **page 374** Courtesy of the Canada Post Corporation; **page 376** Canadian Jewish Congress National Archives; **page 377** Courtesy of the Canada Post Corporation; **page 378** Duncan Cameron/NAC/PA112659; **page 383** NAC/PA115163; **page 384** © 1968 Reprise Records.; **page 385** By permission of John Meredith, slide courtesy of the Isaacs/Innuit Gallery, Toronto; **page 387** Canapress; **page 388** Canapress; **page 389** (top) Natural Science of Canada; **page 389** (bottom) NAC/PA93759; **page 391** NAC; **page 395** Courtesy of the Ministry of Culture, Tourism & Recreation; **page 397** Canapress/Andy Clark; **page 398** (top) Edmonton Journal; **page 398** (bottom) Reproduced with the permission of the Government of Canada; **page 400** "Marika," Courtesy of David Woods; **page 402** By permission of Jewel Randolph; **page 403** Glenbow Archives, Calgary Herald collection; **page 406** Canapress; **page 407** Courtesy of Vancouver Art Gallery, "Elegy for an Island" by Jack Shadbolt; **page 408** Courtesy Canada Post Corporation; **page 409** Courtesy Canada Post Corporation; **page 410** NAC; **page 411** Courtesy Government of the NWT; **page 412** Canapress/Tom Hanson; **page 413** Canapress/Hans Deryk.

Text Credits

page 6 ©Jeanette Armstrong, from *The Seventh Generation* published by Theytus Books; **page 22** Permission granted by IPI Publishing; **page 25** Permission granted by IPI Publishing; **page 27** From *Teen Trends: A Nation in Motion* by R. Bibby and D.C. Posterski, 1992. Reprinted with the permission of Stoddart Publishing Co. Limited, Don Mills, Ont.; **page 41** Courtesy of The Canadian Press; **pages 42 and 43** *Maclean's Magazine,* Maclean Hunter Ltd. Sept 13, 1993, pp. 20–21; **page 46** Adapted with permission from Prentice-Hall Canada, *Canadian Scrapbook: Government and Law* by Donald Santor, 1992; **page 62** From *Teen Trends: A Nation in Motion* by R.W. Bibby and D.C. Posterski, 1992. Reprinted with the permission of Stoddart Publishing Co. Limited, Don Mills, Ontario; **page 64** R. v. JMG (1986) Dominion Law Reports (4th) 277. From *Applying the Law* by M. Leipner and B. Griffith, 1990. Used by permission of McGraw-Hill Ryerson; **page 68** Toronto Marlboros v. Tonelli, 23 Ontario Reports (2d) 193. From *Canadian Law* by Zuber, Zuber, Zuber and Jennings, 1991. Both case studies used by permission of McGraw-Hill Ryerson; **page 138** From *Letters Home* by John Macfie, ©1990. Reprinted by permission of the author; **page 198** Excerpts from "A home where buffalo ought to roam" and "The dance" from *Why Shoot the Teacher?* by Max Braithwaite. Used by permission of the Canadian Publishers, McClelland & Stewart, Toronto. Reprinted by permission of Curtis Brown Ltd. Copyright © 1965 by Max Braithwaite. **page 238** Used by permission of the National Archives of Canada; **page 252** From *Inventing the Future: Reflections on Science, Technology and Nature* by David Suzuki. Copyright ©1989 by David Suzuki. The articles first appeared in *The Toronto Star* and *The Globe & Mail*. Reprinted by permission of Stoddart Publishing Co. Limited, Don Mills, Ontario; **page 259** Reprinted with permission from *Greatcoats and Glamour Boots: Canadian Women at War (1939–1945)* by Carolyn Gossage, Dundurn Press, Toronto, 1991, p. 171; **page 261** Excerpts from *Promise You'll Take Care of My Daughter* by Ben Wicks. Reprinted with the permission of Stoddart Publishing Company Limited of Don Mills, Ontario; **page 274** Excerpts from *And No Birds Sang*. Reprinted with permission of Farley Mowat Limited; **page 293** Reprinted by permission of Ian Darragh, *Canadian Geographic;* **page 300** Reprinted with permission from *Shadows of War: Faces of Peace* by J.L. Granatstein and Douglas Lavender, published by Key Porter Books Ltd. Toronto, Ontario, ©1992 John Muller; **page 301** Used by permission of *Canadian Geographic* magazine; **page 302** *Teen Trends: A Nation in Motion* by R. Bibby and D. Posterski; Stoddart Publishing Co. Limited; **page 320** Permission granted by Roch Carrier, The House of Anansi Press. Reprinted with the permission of Stoddart Publishing Co. Limited, Don Mills, Ontario. **page 332** From *Teen Trends: A Nation in Motion* by R. Bibby and D.C. Posterski, ©1992. Permission granted by Stoddart Publishing Co. Limited, Don Mills, Ontario; **page 333** From *Teen Trends: A Nation in Motion* by R. Bibby and D.C. Posterski, ©1992. Permission granted by Stoddart Publishing Co. Limited, Don Mills, Ontario; **page 353** From *Maclean's Magazine*, Maclean Hunter Ltd., June 25, 1990, pp. 50–53; **pages 374** From *My Canada* by Glenn Keith Cowan, ©1984. Reprinted by permission of Stoddart Publishing Co. Limited, Don Mills, Ontario; **page 377** From *Relations: Family Portraits* edited by Kenneth Sherman, ©1986. Reprinted by permission of Mosaic Press; **page 388** Reprinted with the permission of *Canada and the World* magazine, Oakville, Ontario; **pages 400** From *Native Song* published by Pottersfield Press, ©1990. Reprinted by permission of the author; **page 404** From *Teen Trends: A Nation in Motion* by R. Bibby and D.C. Posterski, ©1992. Used by permission of Stoddart Publishing Co. Limited, Don Mills, Ontario; **page 408** *Poetry by Rita Joe*. Reprinted by permission of the author; **page 409** Reprinted by permission of Lenore Keeshig-Tobias who is an Ojibway storyteller, writer and culture worker from Neyaashiinigmiing (Cape Croker) on the Bruce Peninsula; **page 423** Duke Redbird.

Care has been taken to trace ownership of copyright material contained in this text. The publishers will gladly accept any information that will enable them to rectify any reference or credit in subsequent editions.

INDEX

Aberhart, William, 202–203
Aboriginal rights, 406, 407, 410
Acadians, 106
Acid rain, 349
Activism, 208, 394
Afghanistan, 303
Agricultural and Rural Development Act, 371
Air war, 266–267
Airplanes, 210
    bush planes, 188, 210
    in World War I, 164–166
Alabama (ship), 117
Alaska Boundary Dispute, 85, 122–123, 124
Alliance Quebec, 327
Alliances (1914), 132, 133, 134
Alternative Measures Program, 51, 65
Ambassadors, 30
Amending formula, 10
American Civil War, 115, 116–117
American Revolution, 116
Anglais, les, 104
Annexation by United States, 115, 117, 118
Anschluss, 233, 240
Anti-Semitism, 276–277
Apartheid, 307
Appeasement, 237
Arctic sovereignty, 18
Aristocracy, 12
Armistice, 164
Armouries, 314
Arms race, 298, 301–302
Arms-limitations talks, 303
Arrest, 55, 56
Art, 94–95, 96, 102, 208
    of 1960s and 1970s, 385
    of Auschwitz inmates, 278
    in World War I, 172
Asbestos strike (1949), 316–317
Atlantic provinces, 3, 371
    and Confederation, 79–80
Atomic bomb, 279–281, 289
Auschwitz, 278
Austria, invasion of, 240
Auto Pact, 351–352
Automobiles, 209–210, 367, 368–369
Autonomy, 10, 184, 185–186, 204
Avro Arrow, 345

"Baby bonus", 256
Baby boom, 286, 367
Backbenchers, 47
Bail hearing, 56
Barnstorming, 208
Battle of Britain, 266
Beer Hall Putsch, 233
"Bennett buggies", 201, 202
Bennett, R.B., 195, 197, 199, 200, 203
Berlin Wall torn down, 305
Bias, 128
Bilingualism, 322
    and Biculturalism, 319, 395
"Bill 101", 327
Bills, 37, 45, 46
    becoming laws, 46, 47
Bishop, Billy, 164, 165
Black Canadians, 400–401
Blackout, 246
Blitzkrieg, 241–242, 268
Bloc Québécois, 43, 44
Boer War, 111

Bondar, Roberta, 349
Bootlegging, 208, 216, 217
Borden, Robert, 123, 132, 154, 156, 159, 177
    and Canadian sovereignty, 173–176
Bourassa, Henri, 110, 111, 112, 158, 160
Bourassa, Robert, 24, 323, 324, 327, 330, 334
Britain, political system, 15
British Columbia, 2
    and Confederation, 80, 82
British Commonwealth Air Training Plan, 251
British heritage in Canada's Parliament, 16
British North America (BNA) Act (1867), 17, 19, 31, 80, 328
Bush, George, 349
Bush planes, 188, 210

Cabinet, 34–35, 39, 45–47
Campbell, Kim, 41, 44, 404–405
Canada Act (1982), 16, 20, 26
Canada Assistance Plan, 390
Canada Council, 339
Canada East, 101
Canada West, 101
Canada–U.S. relations, 3–4, 122–124, 354–356, 421
    acid rain, 349
    culture, 338, 339–340, 342, 353, 366, 379
    defence and foreign policy, 341, 344–348, 349
    economic relations, 349–352
    opinions on issues, 353

429

Canada's Hundred Days, 171, 173
Canadian Bill of Rights, 378
Canadian Broadcasting Corporation (CBC), 212, 337, 338–339, 366, 396
Canadian Charter of Rights and Freedoms, 2, 20–23, 378, 395, 413
   legal rights under, 53, 54, 59, 64
   notwithstanding clause, 327
Canadian Human Rights Act (1977), 395
Canadian Human Rights Commission, 404
Canadian identity, 421
Canadian International Development Agency (CIDA), 308
Canadian Pacific Railway (CPR), 82–83
Canadian Radio-Television Commission (CRTC), 340
Canadian Shield, 3, 103, 188, 208
Capone, Al, 213
Carrier, Roch, 320–321
Cartier, George-Étienne, 110
Cartier, Jacques, 100
Caucus, 30, 47
Census, 30
CFCs, 382, 387
Chamberlain, Neville, 237, 240
Champlain, Samuel de, 100
Chanak Affair, 204
Charlottetown Accord (1992), 26, 27, 331, 333, 413
Charlottetown Conference (1864), 78–79
Chinese railway workers, 83
Chlorine gas, 133, 143
Chrétien, Jean, 348

Churchill, Winston, 242, 266, 297
Cities, growth of, 91–92
Citizenship Act (1977), 395
Civil law, 51–52, 67–69, 71
Civil lawsuits, 69
Civil servants, 30, 35, 184
Cold War, 297–298
   ending of, 305–306
Colonies, 134, 135
Commonwealth, 288, 307
Communist Party of Canada, 201
Company of Young Canadians, 389
Concentration camps, 276–277
Confederacy, 115, 117
Confederation, 79, 80, 85, 115
Conscription, 100
   in World War I, 158–160
   in World War II, 260, 262
Constitution Act (1982), 20, 327, 395
Consumer Price Index (CPI), 88
Consumerism, 364, 365–369
Containment, 288, 296
Continentalism, 115, 121, 124
Contracts and youth, 68
Convoy ships, 246, 247
Co-operative Commonwealth Federation (CCF), 40, 202
Cosmopolitanism, 364
Costs of war (World War I), 157
Counterculture, 382, 384
Court appearance, 56
Court system, 35, 55, 58–61
   Youth Court, 65, 66
Crime syndicates, 208, 213
Criminal Code of Canada, 52
Criminal Harassment Bill, 70
Criminal law, 51, 52, 54
   youth and, 61–67

Criminal procedure, 56
Cross, James, 324, 325
Cruise missiles, 337, 347
Cuban Missile Crisis, 303, 344, 346
Culture, Canadian, 4, 421
   Americanization of, 338, 339–340
   government and, 338–341
   mosaic, *see* Mosaic
Currie, Arthur, 169–170
CUSO, 309
Czechoslovakia, taken over by Hitler, 240

D-Day (June 1944), 273, 275
De Gaulle, Charles, 314
Decision-making, 416
Defence of Canada regulations, 246
Deficit, 382, 391
Demilitarized zone, 230
Democracy, 11
   advantages and disadvantages, 12
Deportation, 394
Depression, the Great, 184, 191–203, 205
   causes, 192, 194
   memories of, 222–223
Detente, 303
Deterrence, 302–303
Deux nations, 318
DEW Line, 364, 372
Dictatorship, 12
Diefenbaker, John, 302, 307, 341, 344, 346, 370–372, 378, 383
Dieppe, Battle of, 271
Diplomats, 288, 295
Direct democracy, 11
Discrimination, 22–23

Disposition, 51, 66
"Dollar-a-year-men", 254
Dominion Lands Act (1872), 84
Dreadnoughts, 134
Drought, 184, 195–196
Dunkirk, 242–243
Duplessis, Maurice, 316, 317

Economists, 417
Edmonton Grads, 218
Education:
    for the Inuit, 372–373
    progressive, 382, 386
Election to Commons, 37, 38, 44–45
    parties in 1993, 42–43
Electoral district, 30
Elizabeth II, Queen, 14, 16
Emigration to United States, 119
Emission standards, 382, 387
"Enemy aliens", 150–151
Enfranchisement, 149.
    See also Voting rights
Entrepreneurs, 75
Environmental concerns, 386–388, 421
Espionage, 288
European Community (EC), 356
European Economic Community (now European Community), 306
Executive branch, 34–35
Expansionism, 115, 118
"Expo 67", 314, 382
External Affairs, Department of, 288, 294. See also Foreign policy

Fallout shelters, 288, 302
Fascism, 230, 234
    in Canada, 234–235
Fathers of Confederation, 78

Federal government.
    See also Parliament
    functions, 34–35
    powers, 31, 33
    responsibilities, 33
    structure, 34
    systems, 14, 15, 19
Federation, 116
Fessenden, Reginald, 125, 211
Flag of Canada, 14, 319
Flak, 265, 266
FLQ, 315, 323, 324–325
Food from Canada in World War I, 151
Food shortages, global, 310
Ford, Henry, 209
Foreign aid, 308, 421
Foreign Investment Review Agency (FIRA), 352
Foreign policy, 292–295, 341, 344–348, 349, 421
    and Canadian sovereignty, 18, 294, 348
Francophonie, La, 310
Free Trade Agreement (FTA), 40, 354–356, 421.
    See also Reciprocity
French Canada.
    See also Metis; Quebec
    in the 1850s, 101
    Confederation and, 104, 106
    conflicts in World War I, 158–160
    conscription in World War II, 260, 262
    cultural traditions, 101, 102, 105
    future, 419–420
    migration to cities, 103–104
    migration to United States, 103
    schools in the West, 109–110
    tensions in Montreal, 104

Generation gap, 382, 386
Geography of Canada, 2–3
German rearmament, 235
Global village, 382, 389, 396
Globalization of economy, 356
Golden Horseshoe, 3
Gorbachev, Mikhail, 305
Gouzenko, Igor, 295
Government:
    division of powers, 31–33
    federal, see Federal government
    powers of, 10–11
    purpose of, 10
    types of, 12
Governor-General, 14, 37
Green activists, 387
Grievance, 51
Group of Seven, 95, 208

Habitants, 100
Haig, Douglas, 145, 170
Halifax, 247
    Explosion (1917), 160, 161
Hewitt, Foster, 212
Hippies, 384
Hiroshima, 280
History, importance of, 4
Hitler, Adolf, 232–234, 235, 237, 240–242, 243, 266, 275
    Mackenzie King meets, 238–239
Holocaust, 276–277
Hong Kong, invaded, 269, 270, 271
House of Commons, 15, 19, 35, 37, 39
Howe, C.D., 254
Hudson's Bay Company, 80–81
Hughes, Sam, 139, 140, 142, 152
Hyde Park Declaration, 254–255
Hydrogen bomb, 302

431

ICBMs, 302
Ilsley, James, 255
I'm Alone (ship), 217
Immigration, 82, 86, 92, 120, 420
    1960s–present, 395, 397
    after World War II, 376–378
    "open door" policy, 84
Immigration Act (1978), 397, 399
Imperial Conferences, 186
Imperial Federation League, 121–122
Imperial Munitions Board, 152
Imperial War Cabinet, 174
Imperialism, 115, 121–122, 132, 134–135
Indian Act, 89, 404, 406, 407, 411
Indian Affairs Branch, 208
Indictable offences, 52, 54, 58
Inflation, 88
    in 1920s Germany, 231–232
    in World War II, 255, 256
Inuit, 410
    changes in lives, 372–376
Inuit Tapirisat of Canada, 376
Inventions, 92, 119, 125, 209
Investment Canada, 352
Isolationism, 230, 235
Italian Campaign, 272–273

Japan, 248, 249
Japanese Canadians, internment, 249–250, 252–253
Jazz Age, 208
Jewish immigrants, 236
Jews, persecution by Nazis, 233–234, 235
Johnson, Daniel, 323
Johnson, Lyndon, 346, 350
Journalism, 129

Judiciary, 35, 55, 58–61
Jury trials, 59–60
"Just Society", 395
Jutland, Battle of, 167
Juvenile Delinquency Act (1908), 63

Kennedy, John F., 303, 344, 379
Khrushchev, Nikita, 303
King, Mackenzie, 243, 246–247, 250, 254–255, 295
    autonomy for Canada, 185–186, 204, 280, 292
    conscription issue, 260, 262
    economic views, 203, 205
    mistakes, 194–195, 237–239
    skills, 185
King–Byng Affair, 204
Klondike Gold Rush, 85, 87
Korean War, 298–299
Krieghoff, Cornelius, 102

Labour unrest, 92, 94, 186–187
Laissez-faire economic policies, 184, 201, 203, 205
Language crisis in Quebec, 325–326
Laporte, Pierre, 324, 325
Laurier, Wilfrid, 1, 109–110, 111, 112, 160, 418
    problems, 84, 86, 94, 96–97, 119, 123–124
    successes, 86–87, 96, 97, 122
Laurier Years, 86–97
Law as a career, 181
Laws, 30–31, 35, 46, 47, 51–52, 54
League of Indians, 221
League of Nations, 175–176
Lebensraum, 233
Legislative branch, 34, 35

Legislature, defined, 10
Legislatures, provincial, 17, 35
Lesage, Jean, 317–318
Lévesque, Rene, 323–324, 326–328, 329, 330, 332
Liberal Party, 38, 40, 42
"Liberation", 384, 386
Literature, 95, 96, 97, 101
Lobby groups, 48, 70
Local governments:
    organization, 32, 35
    responsibilities, 32–33
Luftwaffe, 266, 267
Lusitania (ship), 166, 167

McClung, Nellie, 93, 94, 218
McCoy, Elijah J., 119
Macdonald, John A., 36, 37, 82, 84, 89, 108, 109, 119
    and Confederation, 78, 79, 80, 117, 334
Mackenzie, Alexander, 82
Macphail, Agnes, 218
Magna Carta, 16
"Maitres chez nous", 318
Majority government, 45
Malnutrition, 184
Manchuria, 288
Manhattan Project, 279
Manifest Destiny, 118
Manitoba Act (1870), 82, 106
Manitoba schools, 109–110
Mao Zedong, 306
Marconi, Guglielmo, 211
Maritime provinces, 78
    in the 1920s, 190–191
    (by 1900), 91
Marshall Plan, 298
Mass marketing, 364, 365, 367
Massey Commission (1951), 338
Media, and elections, 44
Medicare, 30, 33, 390

Meech Lake Accord, 24, 26, 330–331
Meighen, Arthur, 260
Mein Kampf, 233
Melting pot, 394, 395
Members of Parliament (MPs), 37, 48
Mercier, Honoré, 110, 119
Metis, 81–82, 106–108
   culture and society, 107
Militarism, 132, 134
Militarization of the Rhineland, 235
Military Service Act (1917), 159, 160
Militia, 149, 150
Mineral resources, 188, 190, 369
Minority government, 45
Minority groups, rights, 2
Minority parties, 40
"Mobocracy", 116
Mockup, 164
Monarchy, 12, 14
   constitutional, 14, 15, 16, 17, 19
Montgomery, Bernard, 271, 272
Montreal, 91, 103–104, 317
Mosaic, 78, 86, 394, 395, 420
Motion pictures, 212–213
   "talkies", 223
Mowat, Farley, 274
Mulroney, Brian, 24, 40, 411
   efforts at constitutional agreement, 330–331
   foreign policy, 348, 349, 354–355
Multiculturalism, 2, 395
Munich Agreement (1938), 240
Municipalities, 32–33
Munitions industry in World War I, 152, 154
Munitions and Supplies, Department of, 254

Murphy, Judge Emily, 220–221
Music, 338, 379, 396
Mussolini, Benito, 234, 275

Nagasaki, 280
National debt, 391, 418–419
National Energy Program, 352
National Film Board (NFB), 213, 338, 339
National Housing Act, 367
National Policy, 82, 119, 120
National Resources Mobilization Act, 260
National Selective Service, 251, 257
National unity, 421
Nationalism, 115, 124, 132, 135
   economic, 349–352, 354–356
   in Quebec, 110–112, 287, 315, 318–319, 323
Nationhood. *See* Sovereignty, Canadian
Native peoples, 2, 87, 89, 151, 156
   in the 1920s and 1930s, 221–222
   and the Just Society, 406–413
   land claims, 407, 410–411
   self-government, 411, 413, 420
   treaties, 81
   women, 404
   in World War I, 142
Natural resources, 369
Naval Service Bill, 112
Naval warfare (World War I), 166–168
Nazi–Soviet Pact (1939), 241
Nazis, 233–234, 235
"New Deal", 203
New Democratic Party (NDP), 40, 43, 346
Newfoundland, 80, 371
   in World War II, 248

No-man's land, 132, 137
Nonconfidence vote, 37, 337
NORAD, 302, 344
Normandy invasion, 273, 275
North American Free Trade Agreement (NAFTA), 355–356, 421
North Atlantic Treaty Organization (NATO), 296, 297
North-West Rebellion (1885), 108
North-West (Northwest) Territories, 2, 81–82, 371–376
Nuclear war, 302
Nunavut, 376, 411

October Crisis, 324–325
Official Languages Act, 322, 326
Oil in Alberta, 369
Oka dispute, 411, 412
Oligarchy, 12
Oliver, Frank, 86
On-to-Ottawa Trek, 200
Operation Barbarossa, 267, 268
Operation Sea Lion, 265, 266
Opposition, 39, 45, 47
Ortona, 272–273

Pacific scandal, 82
Pacifists, 149
Panhandlers, 184
Parliament:
   Canadian, 11, 14, 35, 37–40
   defined, 10
   powers, 17
Parole officers, 51
Parti Québécois (P.Q.), 315, 323–324, 326–328
Party whip, 47
Passchendaele, Battle of, 170–171

Patriation of Canada's Constitution, 10, 19–20, 329–330
Patronage, 37
Peacekeeping, 293, 299–301, 421
Pearl Harbor, 250, 268–269
Pearson, Lester B., 294, 308, 315, 318, 319, 346, 370, 379
  peacekeeping efforts, 293, 295, 301, 350
Perri, Rocco, 213, 216
Persecution, 394
Persian Gulf War, 299
"Persons Case", 220–221
Petro-Canada, 352
"Phoney War", 242
Pickford, Mary, 213
Pipeline debate, 370
"Pogey", 196–197
Poland, invasion by Germany, 240, 241–242
Polar Sea (ship), 348, 349–350
Police, 54–55, 57
Political parties, 30, 38, 40, 44
  new parties in 1930s, 201–203
  platforms in 1993 election, 42–43
Posters and propaganda in World War I, 153
Poverty, 92
Prairie provinces:
  and Confederation, 80–82
  during the Depression, 195–196, 198–199
  geography, 2–3
  in the 1920s, 190
Preliminary hearing, 56
Presentation skills, 284, 285
Presumption of innocence, 59
Prime minister, 39, 45

Prince Edward Island, 80
Prisoners of war in Japan, 270
Private enterprise, 149
Private law, 52
Privy Council, 184
Profiteering, 149, 154
Progressive Conservative Party, 38, 40, 42
Progressive education, 382, 386
Prohibition, 78, 216–218
Protectionism, 194
Province of Canada, 78
Provincial governments:
  powers, 31–32
  responsibilities, 33
Provisional government, 78
Public law, 52
Putsch, 230, 233

Quebec. *See also* FLQ; French Canada; Parti Québécois
  future in Canada, 334, 419–420
  nationalism, 110–112, 287, 318–319, 323
  refuses new constitution, 20, 24. *See also* Charlottetown Accord; Meech Lake Accord
Quebec Civil Code, 67, 69
Quebec Resolutions (1864), 79
Question period, 47
"Queue jumpers", 398–399
Quiet Revolution, 317–319

Racism, 2, 397–398, 400–401, 420
Radio, 210–212, 337
Railways, 92, 119
  transcontinental, 82–83, 85
Rationing, 255–256
Reagan, Ronald, 303, 305, 347, 348, 349

Reciprocity, 115
  agreement of 1911, 123–124
  earlier agreement ended, 118
Reconnaissance, 164
Red River settlement, 81, 106
Referendum, 1980 (Quebec), 314, 315–316, 328
Reform movement, 94
Reform Party, 43, 44, 333
Reforming the political system, 419
Refugees, 376, 378, 398–399
Regina Manifesto, 202
Regional concerns, 370, 371
Regional diversity, 419
Regulation 17 (1913), 158
Rehabilitation, 51
Reichstag, 230
Relief, 196–197
Relief camps, 200, 205
Reparations for World War I, 176–177, 230, 231
Representation by population, 37
Representative democracy, 11
Republic, 15
Research skills, 180–181
Responsible government, 15, 37
Riel, Louis, 81, 83, 106, 108, 109, 118
Rights, 20–23. *See also* Canadian Charter of Rights and Freedoms
"Roaring Twenties", 184, 188–190
Roblin, Rodmond, 93, 94
Rome–Berlin Axis, 234
Rommel, Erwin, 271–272
Roosevelt, Franklin Delano, 243, 254–255
Rosenfeld, "Bobbie", 220
Ross rifle, 132, 139

INDEX

Royal Canadian Air Force (RCAF), 210
Royal Canadian Mounted Police (RCMP), 54
Royal Commission on Aboriginal People, 413
Royal Commission on Bilingualism and Biculturalism, 319, 395
Royal Commission on the Status of Women, 402, 403–404
Royal visit (1939), 246, 247
Ruhr, 265
Rum-running, 216, 217
Rupert's Land, 80–81
Russian Revolution, 168

St. Laurent, Louis, 262, 296, 370
St. Lawrence Seaway, 351
St. Louis (ship), 236
Salesperson, 285
Sanctions, 307
Sarajevo, 135–136
Schlieffen, Alfred von, 136–137
Secondary manufacturing, 184
Seigneurial land ownership, 100
Self-evaluation, 226
Senate, 15, 19, 35, 37, 116
    need for reform, 36, 419
Sentencing, 60–61
Separatism. *See* Nationalism in Quebec
Seven Years War, 100
Shadow cabinet, 39
Shell Committee, 152, 154
Shrapnel, 132, 133
Sifton, Clifford, 84
Small Claims Court, 69, 71
Smith, Goldwin, 121
Smuggling, 208
Social Credit Party, 202–203

Social programs, 205, 256, 390–391, 419
Social reform, and women, 155–156
"Soldiers of the soil", 150
Somme, Battle of, 144, 145–146
South Africa, 307
Sovereignty, Canadian, 18, 85, 173–176, 185–186, 204, 294, 330, 396
    in the Arctic, 18, 348, 349
    effects of World War I, 176
    and World War II experience, 280
Sovereignty-association, referendum on, 314, 315–316, 328
Soviet Union
    after World War II, 289
    breakup of, 305
    in World War II, 267–268, 271
Speaker in House of Commons, 39
Special-interest groups, 48, 70
Sputnik, 302
Stalin, Joseph, 237, 241, 295–296
Standard of living in 1900, 88
Standing Committees, 46
Status symbol, 208
Statute of Westminster (1931), 19, 186
Stevens, Harry H., 201
Stock market, 184
    crash (1929), 191–192
Strategic Arms Reduction Talks (START), 305
Strategic Defence Initiative (SDI), 305, 348
Strikes, 92
    Winnipeg General Strike, 186–187

Suburbs, 367–368
Sudetenland, 240
Suez Crisis, 299, 301
Suffragists, 149, 156
Summary conviction offences, 52, 54, 58
"Summit Series" (hockey), 304
Superpowers after World War II, 289
Survivance, La, 110, 316–317
Suzuki, David, 252–253

Tariffs, 78, 118, 119, 121, 354, 355
Taxation, 35, 156
Technology. *See also* Inventions
    in World War I, 133
Teenagers, 379. *See also* Youth
    confidence in institutions, 27
    values and attitudes, 332–333
Television, 365, 366
Tenement, 78
Thesis, 360
Thinking skills, 74, 75
Third Option Policy, 354
Third World, 307–310, 395, 397
Three founding nations, 2
Titanic (ship), 90
Toronto, 33, 91
Trade agreements. *See also* Free Trade Agreement; Reciprocity; North American Free Trade Agreement
    and Canadian sovereignty, 18
Trades, 227
Trans-Canada Air Lines, 210
Travel and tourism, 361
Treason, 246
Treaty of Versailles (1919), 174, 175, 176–177, 231

435

Trench warfare, 137, 138, 140–141, 143
Trial, 56, 59–60
Triple Alliance, 134
Triple Entente, 134
Trudeau, Pierre, 37, 316–317, 319, 324, 325, 379, 383–384, 390
   and constitutional change, 328–330
   economic nationalism, 351–352, 354
   federalist views, 322
   foreign policy, 306, 310, 346–348
   and the "Just Society", 322, 395
   on Native peoples, 406–407
Trudeaumania, 383
Truman Doctrine, 296
Truman, Harry, 279

U-boats, 166–168, 247, 248
Unemployment during Depression, 195, 196–197, 199, 200
Unemployment insurance, 205, 246, 256
Union government (1917), 160
Union movement, 186, 187
Union Nationale Party, 201
Unitary system, 14, 15
United Empire Loyalists, 3
United Nations (U.N.), 290–292
   Emergency Force, 301
   Human Development Report, 1

United States of America:
   after World War II, 289
   political system, 15
   relations with Canada, see Canada–U.S. relations
   in World War II, 268–269
Urbanization, 314
   in Quebec, 317

Valcartier Camp, 139–140
Van Horne, Cornelius, 82, 83
Vancouver, 33, 91
Veterans' benefits, 256
Victim impact statements, 61
Victory Bonds, 158
Vietnam War, 389
Vimy Ridge (battle), 169–170, 176
Voting rights, 13
   for women, see Women

Wage and price controls, 255
Wannsee Conference (1942), 277
War brides, 261, 376
War Measures Act, 246, 324–325
War in the Pacific, 248–249
Warsaw Pact, 297
Wartime economy (World War II), 251, 254–256
Wartime Elections Act (1917), 156
Wartime Prices and Trade Board, 255

Western settlement, 83–84
Wheat farming, 87, 89, 188, 190, 192, 194, 195, 196
Winnipeg, 91
Winnipeg General Strike (1919), 186–187
Women:
   after World War II, 258, 260
   in Canadian politics, 41
   and changes in civil law, 71
   as persons, 220–221
   social reform, 94, 155-156, 160
   in sport, 218, 220
   voting rights for, 13, 93, 156, 160, 218
   in World War I, 154–155
   in World War II, 256–258, 259
Women's movement:
   1960s–present, 399, 402–405, 420
   turn of the century, 94
Woodsworth, J.S., 94, 149, 188, 202, 203, 231

Young Offenders Act (1984), 63, 64, 65–67
Youth. See also Teenagers
   and contracts, 68
   and criminal law, 61–67
Youth Court, 65, 66
Youth Generation, 384
Ypres, Battle of, 143, 145